KT-173-218

THE BLUE GUIDES

BLUE GUIDE

PARIS
AND ENVIRONS

Ian Robertson

With maps and plans by John Flower

A. & C. Black
London

W. W. Norton
New York

Sixth Edition 1985

Second impression 1985

Published by A. & C. Black (Publishers) Limited
35 Bedford Row, London WC1R 4JH

Published in the United States of America by
W. W. Norton & Company Inc.
500 Fifth Avenue, New York, N.Y. 10110

Paris and environs.—6th ed.—(The Blue guides)
  1. Paris (France)—Description—
Guide-books
  I. Robertson, Ian, *1928–*   II. Series
  914.4'3604838   DC708
  ISBN 0-7136-2614-3

ISBN 0-7136-2614-3

ISBN 0-393-30073-0 (U.S.A.)

PREFACE

'To visit Paris at random is a most foolish and dangerous thing' wrote Thomas Cook in *The Excursionist*, and the same warning advice still applies. This SIXTH EDITION of the *Blue Guide Paris and Environs* incorporates several revisions, for a number of important changes have taken place in the French capital and its surroundings since the publication in 1983 of the previous edition, although the basic structure of the latter remains unchanged. The section on Practical Information and amenities has been up-dated; it retains a summary Historical Introduction to Paris in relation to French history in general, which will, it is hoped, provide the chronological framework necessary for a better understanding of her past.

Since 1984 travellers have been able to acquire an entirely new Blue Guide covering the whole of France (including a very condensed section only on Paris and its environs), providing them with a wide-ranging yet compact description of its landscapes and monuments, the very diversity of which should satisfy the demands of the most energetic and enthusiastic tourist.

In this guide to Paris and Environs two routes may be combined with ease by those wishing to return to the centre by a different road. The twenty urban routes are described for sightseeing on foot, almost always the most convenient and enjoyable way of getting about, while some of the nearest *métro* stations are also indicated along each route. Visitors to Paris are warned that, because of the sheer scale of many of her monuments, and the extensive sweep of many of her vistas, it is only too easy to underestimate distances, and one should not attempt too much sightseeing in a day. Indeed, the *Musée du Louvre* itself deserves and physically demands several visits.

The publication of this edition coincides with an era of continuing uncertainty in which a number of the major museums of Paris are still undergoing radical reorganisation, as with the *Musée des Arts Decoratifs*, or the *Musée du Louvre* itself, where whole departments are being moved around, and certain sections are likely to be closed entirely for long periods of time, while others may well be shut temporarily for partial re-arrangement. All will attempt to keep a proportion of their collections on view during this period of upheaval, but in certain cases the Editor has little alternative but to list a selection of important works which may be seen *somewhere* in the building rather than specify their precise whereabouts, an unsatisfactory situation it is hoped will be put right by the time the next edition of this Guide is called for. Among the more drastic changes which will take place during the next few years will be the removal of the collections still in the *Jeu de Paume* to the projected *Musée d'Orsay*, in the reconstructed *Gare d'Orsay*, which will likewise house a number of subsidiary collections temporarily accommodated in the *Palais de Tokyo* and elsewhere. Among other museums awaiting inauguration as this edition goes to press is that devoted to the work of Picasso in the restored *Hôtel Salé*; the *Musée Carnavalet* will be extended eventually into an adjacent edifice, and the scientific collections of the '*Palais de la Découverte*', among others, will be transferred from the *Grand Palais* to a spacious site at *La*

Villette, where new buildings are in the course of erection.

Successive Présidents, ambitious to leave their mark on French culture, continue to inaugurate prestigious monuments, some of which may redound to their credit. Among recent projects, which *may* be completed within the decade, are the redevelopment of *Bercy*, the construction of the new opera-house at the Pl. de la Bastille, and the restoration and reorganization of the *Grand Louvre*, with its controversial pyramidal entrance.

Although endeavouring to keep abreast of all the most recent changes and rearrangements, inevitably the latest facts are not always forthcoming, and getting advance information accurate enough to print is virtually impossible.

Travellers returning to Paris after a period of years will find many changes, not all for the good. Certainly the cleaning of façades (even if *only* the façades in some cases) has improved its general appearance, and indeed, in spite of aggressive traffic flowing along the *quais* of the Seine (unobtrusively underground at some stretches), much of the centre still retains its immense charm. One continues to be diverted by the gushing runnels of water cleansing the gutters, although the more fastidious will continue to complain, not unreasonably, of the unedifying state in which the canine population of Paris chooses to leave the adjacent *trottoirs*. One still awaits the completion of the latest project to transform the area occupied by the old *Halles*: many have suffered from agoraphobia after visiting the commercial *Forum* now filling the immense 'trou', but at least one now has a better view of both *St-Eustache* and the nearby *Bourse du Commerce*, a structure one may have previously overlooked, which is some compensation. Meanwhile many familiar horizons have been broken by the erection of vast blocks of buildings, perhaps the most injudiciously placed—apart from the *Centre Beaubourg*—being the *Tour Montparnasse*, which, dominating the surrounding area, has also irreparably affected the townscape. Nevertheless, much of the modern architecture of Paris is of a high standard (although there are many much-vaunted exceptions), and while certain squalid outlying districts are being transformed out of all recognition, others of considerable architectural interest—such as the *Marais*—continue to be tastefully restored when not too derelict. Unfortunately the view of many monuments is spoiled by shoals of coaches blatantly parked in their immediate vicinity, but not every site is surrounded by such swarms of tourists: there is still a great deal to see not far off the track beaten by the lemmings.

A wide range of accommodation is available in the area covered, lists of which, together with those of inexpensive restaurants, are readily obtainable free of charge from the French Government Tourist Offices.

The practice of 'starring' the highlights has been continued, even if the system is subjective and inconsistent, for such asterisks do help the hurried traveller to pick out those things which the general consensus of opinion (modified occasionally by the Editor's personal prejudice, admittedly) considers he should not miss. (It has been suggested that he might also include 'daggers' to indicate what would be better avoided, if possible.) In certain cases a museum has been starred, rather than individual objects among those described, when the standard of its contents is remarkably high.

Selection remains the touchstone by which guide-books are

judged, and it is hoped that this edition will provide a balanced account of most aspects of a great city and its surroundings without intentionally neglecting any that might appeal to the intelligent resident or visitor, and without being so exhaustive as to leave him no opportunity of discovering additional pleasures for himself; and yet, in the words of Richard Ford (author of the famous *Hand-Book for Spain* of 1845): '... how often does the wearied traveller rejoice when no more is to be "done"; and how does he thank the faithful pioneer, who, by having himself toiled to see some "local lion", has saved others the tiresome task, by his assurance that it is not worth the time or trouble'.

Most of the revisions—the amount of alteration varying from very minor correction to the addition of considerable new matter—have been made from personal observation on the spot during recent walks and tours made in the service of this edition, but not every locality in Paris, nor every château and Gothic church in its environs can be visited in person for each edition of so comprehensive a guide. Its preparation has depended largely on the Editor alone, and certain omissions are inevitable, since Paris offers an 'embarras de richesses' that can never be encompassed in a single volume. The readers' co-operation is therefore solicited. Any constructive suggestions for the improvement of future editions will be welcomed and acknowledged by the Editor, who alone is responsible for all inexactitudes, shortcomings, inconsistencies, and solecisms.

Its street-atlas, maps, and plans have been corrected; the cartography again being undertaken by **John Flower**.

In addition to those providing facilities and material assistance, or offering information and advice, who were listed at this point in the previous edition, the following must be mentioned: *Jean-Jacques Poulet-Allamagny*, Chef du Service Photographique, Caisse Nationale des Monuments et des Sites, and the French National Tourist Office in London, for providing several illustrations; *Léone Nora, Michèle Richet*, and *Dominique Gambier*, who have outlined what is projected at the Musée d'Orsay, Musée Picasso, and the Grand Louvre, respectively; *Claudie Ressort, Geneviève Pierrat*, and *François Barrat* (Musée du Louvre); *Pascale de Vleeschouwer* (Union Centrale des Arts Décoratifs); *Marianne Delafond* (Musée Marmottan); *Aggy Lerolle*, and *Veronique Alemany-Dessaint* (Direction des Musée de France); and *Edith Carves*, at the Office de Tourisme de Paris.

The Editor must again record his appreciation of the generous hospitality he has continued to enjoy both Chez Boyars in London, and Chez Scott de Martinville in Paris; while Paul Langridge and Tom Neville have given all essential support and practical assistance in producing the Guide during the period of transition to Bedford Row, Chez Adam & Charles Black.

Blue Guides: their History

Although over half a century has now elapsed since there was any direct collaboration, there are many who assume that there is still a close connection between the English **Blue Guides**, published by *A & C Black (Publishers) Ltd*, and the French **Guides Bleus**, published by *Librairie Hachette*, and it may be convenient therefore to include here an explanatory note. Further confusion has been caused by the translation into English of some of Hachette's editions under the title *World Guides*. Prior to the outbreak of the First World War, the English editors of the German *Baedeker Guides*, marketed from 1908 by T. Fisher Unwin, were *Findlay* and *James Muirhead*. During 1915, with influential backing, the editors acquired the copyright of the majority of the famous 'Red' *Hand-Books* published by *John Murray*, at standby of English travellers to the Continent and elsewhere for the previous three-quarters of a century; they also bought the copyright of a series published by *Macmillan*, who were to market the new series, the first of which was announced for publication by *Muirhead Guide-Books Limited* by early 1916. In the following year an agreement for mutual co-operation with *Hachette et Cie* of Paris was entered into: the French house, who had previously published the blue cloth-bound *Guides-Joanne*—named after their first editor *Adolphe Joanne* (1813–81)—were to handle a translation of a guide to 'London', which was in fact the first '*Guide Bleu*'; this, and other volumes originating with Muirhead, were entitled *The Blue Guides* (further distinguishing them from *red* Baedekers and Murrays). In 1921 an adaptation—not a direct translation—of Hachette's Guide Bleu to 'Paris et ses Environs' (edited by Marcel Monmarché) was published in London, another example of the collaboration between the two firms, who made a new agreement in 1927, which lasted for six years, when it lapsed. *Litellus R. Muirhead* acted as assistant editor at this period. Meanwhile, in 1931, editorial control of the Blue Guides was transferred from Macmillan to *Benn Brothers*, who in 1926 had bought T. Fisher Unwin (who were again handling Baedekers after the war, but Baedekers then transferred to Allen and Unwin). In 1934 *L. Russell Muirhead* (1896–1976), Findlay Muirhead's son, became Benn's Blue Guide editor, and from 1954 he was assisted by *Stuart Rossiter* (1923–82), who succeeded him in 1963.

Paul Langridge assumed the general editorship in 1975, since when the series has grown spectacularly. In April 1984, a year after Benn Brothers had itself been taken over by Extel, their book-publishing side, *Ernest Benn Ltd*, which included the Blue Guides, was bought by *A & C Black (Publishers) Ltd*.

A & C Black itself has a long history of guide-book publishing, beginning in 1826 with 'Black's Economical Tourist of Scotland' and including several written by Charles Bertram Black, eldest son of the firm's founder. The hey-day of Black's guide-book publishing was perhaps the 1890s, when more than 55 titles were in print.

CONTENTS

MAPS AND PLANS

EXPLANATIONS

Type. The main routes are described in large type. Smaller type is used for sub-routes, excursions, or deviations, for historical and preliminary paragraphs, and (generally speaking) for descriptions of greater detail or less importance.

Asterisks indicate points of special interest or excellence: two 'stars' are used sparingly.

Distances, total and intermediate (in Rtes 21–38), are measured in kilometres, and total route distances are also given in miles. Road distances along the routes themselves record the distance between the towns and villages, etc., described, but with the realignment of roads, one-way systems, and by-passes, it is almost certain that these will vary from those measured by motorists on their milometers, and are at best approximate. **Altitudes**, and the measurements of buildings, etc., are expressed in metres. It should also be noted that some road numbers are still in the process of being changed.

Street Numbering. In Paris, in streets parallel to the river, the houses are numbered from E. to W.; in those at right-angles to the Seine, from the end nearest the river.

The **Population** figures given (in round figures) are based on those of the census of 1982, or revisions of them. Figures are not given for places with fewer than 5000 inhabitants.

Anglicisation. For the sake of consistency, place-names and the names of kings, etc. have retained their French form.

Abbreviations. In addition to generally accepted and self-explanatory forms, the following occur in this guide:

Av. = Avenue	N.-D. = Notre-Dame, Our Lady
C = Century	Pl. = Place, or Plan
Blvd = Boulevard	R = Room
IGN = Institut Géographique National	r. = right
	Rte = Route
l. = left	St- or Ste- = Saint; SS = Saints
M = Michelin	S.I. = *Syndicat d'Initiative* or
m = metres	Tourist Office

The initials (CN) immediately after certain monuments and buildings indicates that the *Caisse Nationale des Monuments Historiques et des Sites* is responsible for them; see p172.

HISTORICAL INTRODUCTION

The foundations of modern France may be said to date from the passage of the Alps by the ROMANS in 121 B.C. and the establishment of the province (Latin *provincia*; modern *Provènce*) of *Gallia Narbonensis*, where important remains such as the Pont du Gard, and the theatres and amphitheatres at Nîmes, Arles, and Orange, etc. are still extant. But the whole of France as we now know it did not become subject to Rome until after *Julius Caesar's* decisive defeat of *Vercingetorix* at *Alésia* in 52 B.C. In the previous year Caesar had first mentioned—under the name of *Lutetia*—the fortified capital of the *Parisii*, an insignificant Gallic tribe, confined on islands in the Seine, which he nominated as the rendezvous of deputies from conquered GAUL.

The speech, culture, and the roads of Rome slowly spread over this territory, in spite of occasional local revolts; and by c. A.D. 250 the country had become partially Christianised, *St Dionysius* (Denis) being its first bishop, but within a few decades the first Barbarian invasions commenced. In 292 Paris became a base of the emperor *Constantius Chlorus*, although it was not until 360 that the name was applied to the river-port. Barbarian mercenaries (among them Visigoths and Burgundians) were employed to defend the frontiers of the Empire in its decline, but they wearied of their alliance with the degenerate Gallo-Romans, and after the repulse of *Attila* and his Huns at the *Catalaunian Fields* (451) became virtually masters of the land, the most powerful tribe being the Salian FRANKS under their leader *Merovius*.

His grandson *Clovis I* (481-511) defeated *Syagrius* (the Roman governor of Soissons) in 486, and the ALEMANNI at *Tolbiac* in 496, after which he adopted the Christian religion, and in the following year Paris opened her gates to him (traditionally on the advice of *St Geneviève*), although he did not make it his official capital until 508. On his death in 511 the kingdom, according to Frankish custom, was divided between his three sons into AUSTRASIA (between the Meuse and the Rhine), NEUSTRIA (the territory to the N.W., from the Meuse to the Loire), and BURGUNDY (to the S.), and although the **Merovingians** remained in control, the dynasty was weakened by internecine warfare during the next 200 years.

Eminent among the Merovingians was *Chilperic I* (king of Neustria from 561–84) and *Dagobert* (king of Austrasia from 622 and of all France from 628 until his death in 638). Paris remained the political centre of conflicting Frankish interests, its growing population overflowing to form suburbs around monasteries situated on both banks of the river; but after the death of Dagobert, who refounded the abbey of St-Denis, most of the power past into the hands of the 'maires du Palais', one of whom, *Charles Martel* (714–41), an Austrasian, was to check at *Poitiers* in 732 the invading Moors, who had overrun Spain during the previous two decades. His son, *Pepin 'le Bref'* (the Short; 751–68) deposed *Childéric III*, the last of the Merovingians, and founded a new dynasty.

Carolingians
Pepin (le Bref; 751–68)
Charlemagne (768–814)
Louis I (le Débonnaire; 814–40)
Charles (le Chauve; 840–77)
Louis II (Le Bègue; 877–79)
Louis III, and Carloman (879–82)
Carloman (882–84)
Charles (le Gros; 884–87)
Count Eudes (887–98)
Charles (le Simple; 898–922)
Louis IV (d'Outremer; 936–54)
Lothaire (954–86)
Louis V (le Fainéant; 986–87)

Although Pepin resided occasionally at Paris, his son *Charlemagne* (768–814), in alliance with the Pope, extended his dominion over Germany and Italy, and crowned 'Emperor of the West', moved the seat of government from France to Aix-la-Chapelle. The system of dividing territories on the death of kings was to cause the eventual disintegration of Charlemagne's empire, and in 843, by the *Treaty of Verdun*, those areas which were to form modern France were transferred to his grandson *Charles 'le Chauve'*. Further division ensued, and France became little more than a collection of independent feudal states.

The situation was further disturbed by the invasion of Scandinavian or Norse pirates, who by 912 had settled in Rouen and had carved out the duchy of NORMANDY for themselves, having meanwhile (in 885) besieged and pillaged Paris itself from their encampment possibly on the present site of the Louvre. The Cité had been successfully defended by *Eudes*, duc de France and comte de Paris, who in 888 deposed *Charles 'le Gros'*. What remained of the Carolingian monarchy (the Île de France) was taken over in 987 by *Hugues Capet*, first of the Capetian dynasty, elected by the nobles in preference to other Carolingians. At *Cluny*, in Burgundy, the influential Benedictine abbey had been founded in 910, but the great period of the building of Romanesque abbeys was in the 11–12Cs.

Capetians
Hugues Capet (987–96)
Robert (le Pieux; 996–1031)
Henri I (1031–60)
Philippe I (1060–1108)
Louis VI (le Gros; 1108–37)
Louis VII (le Jeune; 1137–80)
Philippe Auguste (1180–1223)
Louis VIII (le Lion; 1223–26)
Louis IX (St Louis; 1226–70)
Philippe III (le Hardi; 1270–85)
Philippe IV (le Bel; 1285–1314)
Louis X (le Hutin; 1314–16)
Jean I (1316; died 4 days old)
Philippe V (le Long; 1316–22)
Charles IV (le Bel; 1322–28)

Hugues Capet was elected by the nobles at *Senlis* in preference to any more incapable Carolingians, and he and his successors proceeded to make Paris the base of a centralising policy by which they might control the disunited country. It grew steadily in size and importance, particularly on the North Bank, and during the reign of *Louis VI*, if not earlier, a second town wall was thrown up. The 'Hanse Parisienne', a league of merchants, was established, marking the foundation of the municipality. Paris has remained very much at the centre of a centralising process which developed in France from this period.

The next 50 years were occupied by conflict between the central government and subordinate feudal lordships. A further complication was the marriage in 1152 of the future *Henry II* of England to *Eleanor of Aquitaine* (the divorced wife of *Louis VII*), who brought him about one-third of France as her dowry, which precipitated a long struggle between the two countries. In 1163 the foundation-stone of Notre-Dame—one of many similar Gothic cathedrals erected during the 12–13Cs—was laid, while some years later *Philippe II (Philippe Auguste)* built the fortress of the Louvre. During his energetic reign he promulgated the expulsion of the Jews (in 1182); and later the cathedral schools of Paris (at which Guillaume de Champeaux and Abélard had taught) were united to form one University, which was granted its first statutes by Pope Innocent III in 1208. This was established on the Left Bank of the Seine, where the growing student population settled; the Right Bank became the centre of commerce, industry, and administration. Some streets were paved; the two ancient wooden bridges were replaced by ones of stone; and the city was enclosed by an extensive line of fortifications. In the political field Philippe Auguste won back a large part of the lost provinces (Normandy and Anjou), having inflicted a heavy defeat on the allies of *John* of England at *Bouvines* in 1214; and the sanguinary Albigensian Crusade of 1209–13 eventually restored LANGUEDOC to French rule.

During the long reign of *Louis IX*, the Hospice des Quinze-Vingts and the theological college of the Sorbonne were founded, the latter to become a dominant influence in the University. The Palais de la Cité was rebuilt (parts of which, notably the Ste-Chapelle, still exist), and the office of Provost was reformed; statutes were drawn up for the many guilds, which were to remain in force until the Revolution. Louis, canonised in 1297, was a great crusader, and eventually lost his life at Tunis. He was succeeded by *Philippe III, Philippe IV*, and *Louis X*, respectively. With the death of *Charles IV* in 1328 the direct branch of the Capetian dynasty became extinct.

House of Valois
Philippe VI (1328–50)
Jean II (le Bon; 1350–64)
Charles V (le Sage; 1364–80)
Charles VI (le Bien-Aimé; 1380–1422)
Charles VII (le Victorieux; 1422–61)
Louis XI (1461–83)
Charles VIII (l'Affable; 1483–98)
Louis XII (le Père du Peuple; 1498–1515)
François I (1515–47)
Henri II (1547–59)
François II (1559–60)
Charles IX (1560–74)
Henri III (1574–89)

The claim of *Philippe de Valois* to the throne was disputed by *Edward III* of England, who invaded France, precipitating the 'Hundred Years War' (1337–1453). He routed the French army at *Crécy* (1346) and inflicted a further defeat on *Jean II* at *Poitiers* in 1356. The ravages and depredations of both French and English soldiery roused the peasants (the *Jacquerie*) and the burgesses to revolt. In Paris, *Étienne Marcel* (Maire du Palais and provost of the merchants) took advantage of the situation to increase the influence of the municipality, but he offended public opinion by attempting to hand over the city to *Charles of Navarre*, and was assassinated in 1358. Two years later, by the *Treaty of Brétigny*, England abandoned her claims, but before long desultory warfare between the two countries was to break out again, and continued until 1369, successfully for France, largely due to the tactics of *Du Guesclin* (c.1320–80).

Charles V was able to bring back some order to the kingdom, and raised the fortress of the Bastille, but anarchy returned during the following reign, when his weak-minded son *Charles VI* provoked the citizens of Paris—at that time numbering some 280,000—by excessive taxation. Although the resulting revolt of the 'Maillotins' was bloodily suppressed, the king became the pawn of rival regents, and for the next 40 years France suffered from dissensions between the aristocratic party, the Armagnacs, and the Burgundians, the popular party (Jean II had made his fourth son—*Jean sans Peur*—Duc de Bourgogne).

Seizing the opportunity, *Henry V* of England invaded France, and supported by the Burgundians, defeated a French force at *Agincourt* (1415). By the *Treaty of Troyes* (1420) he received the hand of *Catherine*, Charles VI's daughter, together with the right of succession to the throne. Indeed, from 1420, when Henry entered Paris, until 1436, the English controlled the city, *John, Duke of Bedford* having repelled in 1429 an assault led by *Jeanne d'Arc* (Joan of Arc; 1412–31), the champion of *Charles VII*. After a brilliant campaign Joan defeated the English at *Orléans* in 1429, but captured at Compiègne by the Burgundians in the following year, she was handed over to the English, and condemned as a heretic by a court of ecclesiastics, was burned at the stake in Rouen. But the successful revolt she had inspired, continued, and by 1453 only Calais remained of the once extensive English possessions in France. A vivid account of conditions prevailing in Paris during the years 1405–49 is given in the anonymously compiled 'Journal d'un Bourgeois de Paris'. The poet *Villon* was born here in 1431.

With the reign of *Louis XI* the change from a medieval social system to the modern state was accelerated. A brilliant and unscrupulous politician (and relieved of the menace of England), he proceeded to crush the great feudal lordships which encroached on his territory, the most threatening being that of *Charles the Bold* ('le Téméraire') of Burgundy. The *Peace of Péronne* (1468) gave Charles a momentary advantage, but Louis managed to alienate his English allies by the *Treaty of Picquigny* (1475), and after Charles's death before the walls of Nancy, soon overwhelmed his lesser adversaries, and brought ARRAS, the FRANCHE-COMTÉ, ANJOU, and MAINE into direct allegiance to the crown. In 1469/70 the first printing-press in France was set up in the Sorbonne; and in 1484 the first meeting of the Estates-General was convened at Tours, near which, in the Loire valley, a number of châteaux were being rebuilt as royal residences.

The following three reigns—of *Charles VIII, Louis XII,* whose principal residence was Blois, and *François I*—were largely occupied with indecisive campaigns in Italy, the only tangible results of which—particularly during the latter reign—was the establishment in France of the cultural concepts of the Italian Renaissance. Among the more important literary figures of the period were *Marot, Rabelais, Du Bellay,* and *Ronsard*—the last two being members of the circle known as La Pléïade. Charles VIII and Louis XII were successive husbands of *Anne de Bretagne,* whose dowry, the important duchy of Brittany, was formally united to France in 1532 on the death of her daughter, wife of François I. The reign of *Henri II* saw the acquisition by France of the Three Bishoprics (Metz, Toul, and Verdun), while Calais fell to the *Duc de Guise* in 1558. In 1564 an edict fixed the beginning of the year as 1 January, inaugurating the 'new style' of dating.

The short reign of *François II* (who while still dauphin had married *Mary Stuart,* Queen of Scots) was followed by that of *Charles IX,* who, instigated by his domineering mother, *Catherine de Médicis* (1519–89; consort of Henri II, and mother also of François II, Henri III, and of *Marguerite de Valois,* who married Henri of Navarre), signed the order for the massacre of Protestant Huguenots on the *Eve of St Bartholomew* (23 August 1572), and until the promulgation of the *Edict of Nantes* in 1598 the country was ravaged by the Religious Wars of the *League* (La Ligue), although there had been sporadic politico-religious skirmishing since 1560. The ultra-Catholic Henri, Duc de Guise, was assassinated at Blois by Henri III, against whom he was an overt rebel, who himself was assassinated at St-Cloud the following year.

Henri IV (king of Navarre; of the Bourbon branch of the Capetian dynasty, descending from Robert of Clermont, sixth son of Louis IX), a Protestant, eventually defeated the Catholics at *Ivry* (near Évreux) in 1590, but was unable to enter the besieged capital until 1594, when as a condition he abjured his faith with (it is said) the cynical remark that 'Paris vaut bien une messe'. Nevertheless, although accepting conversion, by the Edict of Nantes he granted Protestants freedom of worship. Among the many who joined in the general recognition of Henri as the legitimate heir to the throne was *Montaigne,* whose 'Essays' were published in part in 1580.

House of Bourbon
Henri IV (le Grand; 1589–1610)
Louis XIII (le Juste; 1610–43)
Louis XIV ('le Roi Soleil'; 1643–1715)
Louis XV (le Bien-Aimé; 1715–74)
Louis XVI (1774–92)
Louis XVII (never reigned)
Louis XVIII (1814–24)
Charles X (1824–30)

Peace established, Henri set about enlarging the palaces of the Louvre and the Tuileries, planned several squares including the Place Royale, and completed the Pont Neuf, but in 1610 he was assassinated by *Ravaillac*. During the minority of *Louis XIII,* until 1617, his mother *Marie de Médicis* (1573–1642; whom Henri had married in 1600 after his divorce from Marguerite de Valois) was regent. Regrettably, the admirable reforms and economies instituted by Henri IV and his able minister *Sully* (1559–1641) were brought to naught by the extravagant favourites of young Louis, at least until 1624, when *Card. Richelieu* (1585–1642) took over the reins of government. His main aim was the establishment of absolute royal power in France, and of French supremacy in Europe, and the suppression of Protestant influence in politics. La Rochelle, the Protestant stronghold, was captured in 1628, and the insurrections of nobles were repressed with heavy penalties. Richelieu next turned his attention to the House of Habsburg, which under the Emperor *Charles V* had been encroaching on the frontiers of France, and in alliance with *Gustavus Adolphus* of Sweden (with the ostensible object of aiding the German Protestants) France involved herself in the *Thirty Years' War*, in which the campaigns of the *Grand Condé* (1621–86; a member of a collateral branch of the Bourbons) resulted in the temporary acquisition of PICARDY, ALSACE, and ROUSSILLON.

Meanwhile, in 1635 and 1640 respectively, the 'Académie Française' and the 'Imprimerie Royal' were founded; a fifth wall was erected around Paris, where several new quarters arose, such as the Pré-aux-Clercs (Faubourg St-Germain), the Île-St-Louis, and the Marais, which became a favourite residence of the nobility. Marie de Médicis built the Palais du Luxembourg; *Anne of Austria*, consort of the king since 1614, founded the church of Vâl-de-Grace in thanksgiving for the birth of a son (later Louis XIV) in 1638; and Richelieu built for himself the Palais-Cardinal, later the Palais-Royal.

In 1643—the year of young Condé's victory over the Spanish at *Rocroi*—*Louis XIV* succeeded as a minor. *Card. Mazarin* (1602–61), Richelieu's successor—for he had died in the previous year—carried on his predecessor's policy, although the expenses of campaigning were later to cause trouble. After the *Treaty of Westphalia* (1648), which assured to France the possession of Alsace and the Three Bishoprics, the civil war known as the *Fronde* broke out, in which Condé, having quarrelled with the court party, allied himself with Spain (who had not subscribed to the Westphalian treaty), but the victory of *Turenne* (1611–75; the royalist commander) at the *Battle of the Dunes* forced the Spaniards to accept the *Treaty of the Pyrenees* (1659), formally ceding Artois and Roussillon.

On Mazarin's death Louis decided to govern alone, duped by the conviction that 'L'État c'est moi'; the nobility were reduced to ineffectual courtiers. The king selected his ministers from the *haute bourgeoisie*, some, such as *Colbert* (1619–83), being very able. He then started a series of costly wars of self-aggrandisement, which although they eventually increased the territory of France—its frontiers fortified by *Vauban* (1633–1707)—were to bring his long reign to a disastrous close, while his indulgence in such extravagant projects as the building of a palace fit for the 'Roi Soleil' at Versailles (extended by *Hardouin-Mansart*, with gardens laid out by *Le Nôtre*, and its lavish decoration supervised by *Le Brun*), where Louis had chosen to transfer his court in 1672, further beggared the country. At Versailles were gathered most of the great artists of this and succeeding epochs, while among composers both *Lully* (from 1652 until his death in 1687), *Couperin*, and *Rameau* in the following reign, provided music to entertain the court.

In Paris, now grown to a metropolis containing some 500,000 inhabitants and 25,000 houses, boulevards were laid out on the lines of Étienne Marcel's wall. The Invalides were founded in 1671. The

University quarters were incorporated within the city, which had become one of the cultural centres of Europe—*Corneille, Racine, Molière, La Fontaine, Boileau,* and *Pascal* (the latter associated with the activities of the reforming Jansenists of *Port-Royal)* making their home there—while the salons of *Mme de Rambouillet* and *Mme de Sablé,* among others, had become the influential intellectual rendezvous of such figures as *La Rochefoucauld,* the *Scudérys,* and *Bossuet.* Meanwhile, in 1685, Louis had revoked the Edict of Nantes, again imposing Catholicism on the country.

The king's preoccupation with 'La Gloire' involved him first in the rapid campaign of 1667–68, which secured the possession of many towns in Flanders; while the *Dutch War* of 1672–78 ended in the *Peace of Nijmegen* and the absorption of the Franche-Ćomté. Less successful were the campaigns against the *League of Augsburg* (or the *Grand Alliance;* 1686–97), and of the *Spanish Succession* (1701–13), in which French forces suffered repeatedly at the hands of *Marlborough* and *Prince Eugène* (at *Blenheim* in 1704; *Ramillies* in 1706; *Oudenarde* in 1708; and *Malplaquet* in 1709), although *Marshal Villars* won a victory at *Denain* (1712) after the withdrawal of the English from the war. 'If greatness of soul consists in a love of pageantry, an ostentation of fastidious pomp, a prodigality of expense, an affectation of munificence, an insolence of ambition, and a haughty reserve of deportment; Lewis certainly deserved the appellation of Great. Qualities which are really heroic, we shall not find in the composition of his character'. Such was Smollett's condemnation. Life at court during the latter part of the reign and subsequent regency (under *Philippe, duc d'Orléans;* 1715–23) is brilliantly recorded in the 'Memoires' of the *Duc de Saint-Simon.* A number of bad harvests decimated the peasantry—forming four-fifths of the population of twenty million in 1700—but colonial trade improved, and merchants thrived in such provincial centres as Bordeaux, Nantes, and Marseille.

The marriage in 1725 of *Louis XV* to *Maria,* daughter of *Stanislas Leczinski* (the deposed king of Poland) drew France into the *War of the Polish Succession* (1733). But further ruinous wars followed, including that of the *Austrian Succession* (in which Louis was allied with *Frederick the Great* of Prussia in opposition to England and Holland, who supported the cause of *Maria Theresia,* Empress of Austria). In spite of *Saxe's* brilliant victory at *Fontenoy* (1745) the French gained little, while the English improved their position as a maritime power, and Prussia likewise gained in strength. The *Seven Years' War* (1756–63), in which France was allied to Austria, was disastrous to her arms, and saw the loss of flourishing colonies in India, North America, and the West Indies. By 1788 the cost of these wars had created a situation whereby three-quarters of the State expenditure was being spent on reducing the national debt and on defence.

Nevertheless, grandiose buildings continued to be erected in Paris, such as the Panthéon, and the Palais-Bourbon; but a sixth wall, raised as a simple customs-barrier at the instigation of the powerful and rapacious farmers-general of taxes, only fostered further discontent ('Le mur murant Paris rend Paris murmurant'). In spite of the general degradation of his court, and the corruption and negligence rife among his administrators, the reign of Louis XV was made illustrious by some of the great names in French literature: *Voltaire, Rousseau, Montesquieu, Marivaux,* the Encyclopédistes (*Diderot,* and *d'Alembert*, etc.), who were among the many who frequented such salons as those of the *Marquise de Lambert*, *Mme de Tencin*, *Mme du Deffand*, *Mlle Lespinasse*, *Mme Geoffrin*, or *Baron d'Holbach*, and others of lesser influence.

Louis XVI on his succession found the populace critical of his predecessor's extravagance and lack of military success, but was too weak to cope with the interminable financial crises (in spite of the reforms initiated by *Turgot* from 1774, and of *Necker* from 1777), and the economic problems precipitated by bad harvests in the neighbouring provinces, particularly in the years 1787–88, provoked grain riots in Paris. These crises, although they inspired reforms, inspired those which, if accepted, would have adversely affected the privileged estates ('Les Privilégiés'): the upper ranks of the clergy (the First Estate), and the majority of the nobility (the Second Estate), who therefore rejected them. His foreign policy, which gave support to the American colonies in their struggle for independence from England, was not only financially disastrous, but indirectly did much to disseminate democratic ideals.

In an attempt to reform methods of taxation—for Les Privilégiés held innumerable hereditary rights by which they avoided paying taxes yet levied taxes to their own advantage—the king convoked an assembly of the *États généraux* or States General, and the 1165 deputies elected met at Versailles on 5 May 1789, and for the first time since 1614. As a result, the first political act of the Third Estate, the Non-Privilégiés (which numbered almost 600) was the creation of a *National Assembly* (17 June), which meeting separately in the Salle de Jeu de Paume on the 20th, swore not to disband until a constitution had been given to the country which would limit royal autocracy, and guarantee liberty, equality, and fraternity. Three days later *Mirabeau* defied the king: 'Nous sommes ici par la volonté du peuple et . . . on ne nous arrachera que par la force des baïonnettes'; and on the 9 July, reinforced by many of the clergy and a minority of the nobility, the renamed *Assemblée constituante* set to work to frame such a constitution. Two days later Necker, who had promised further financial reforms, was dismissed by the king, and it was feared that this gratuitous act would be followed by the dissolution of the Assembly.

The **Revolution**. The citizens of Paris—and also in the provinces (at Dijon, Rennes, Lyon, Nantes, and Le Havre)—were provoked into a more open rebellion, culminating in the storming of the Bastille on 14 July, but while the next few months saw numerous reforms, there was little political or economic stability, and tensions heightened. In an attempt to avoid bankruptcy, Church lands were nationalised, which produced some opposition. Many of the nobility—a class shortly, but temporarily, to be abolished—sought asylum abroad. The king and his unpopular consort *Marie-Antoinette* were virtually prisoners in the Tuileries, whence they attempted to flee the country, but were arrested (at Varennes in June 1791) and brought back to Paris. On 1 October 1791 a new Legislative Assembly was formed, which in the following April declared war on Austria to forestall foreign intervention. They were at first swayed by the moderate *Girondins*, but the following year the extreme *Jacobins* seized power under *Danton, Robespierre*, and *Marat*, and as the *National Convention*, meeting on 20 September (the day on which the victory of *Valmy* turned the tide of war in France's favour), established the *Republic*.

On 21 January 1793 Louis XVI was executed in the Place de la Révolution, an act soon followed by the setting-up in March of the dictatorial *Committee of Public Safety*, which, suspicious of the moderate party, ruthlessly suppressed all suspected of royalist sympathies, and the guillotine was in constant action. In July Marat was assassinated, and even the Dantonists found themselves to be a moderating force opposed to the sanguinary *Hébertists*, even more extreme in their rigorous Reign of Terror. But Robespierre brooked no rivals, and early in 1794 both *Hébert* and Danton were guillotined. However, after some months of ferocious intimidation of the people, the reaction came, and on 27 July (9 Thermidor; see below), his own head fell.

A **Republican Calendar**, the object of which was to make a break with Christian tradition, the mathematician Romme being responsible for its chronology, was instituted during the autumn of 1793, which was to remain in force until January, 1806, when it officially reverted to the Gregorian Calendar (introduced in 1582). It was antedated, as it was considered that the first year (An I) had begun at the autumnal equinox (22 September) of 1792, the day of the proclamation of the Republic. The year was divided into 12 months of 30 days each; each month being sub-divided into three periods of ten days or *décades*; and 5 days ('*sansculottides*') were added at the end of each year (6 in leap years) to be observed as national festivals.

The days were named in numerical order: *primidi, duodi, tridi, quartidi, quintidi, sextidi, septidi, octidi, nonidi, and décadi* (the day of rest). More poetic names, devised by Fabre d'Églantine, were given to the months: *Vendémaire, Brumaire,* and *Frimaire* being the autumn months of vintage fog, and frost; *Nivôse, Pluviôse,* and *Ventôse* the winter months of snow, rain, and wind; *Germinal, Floréal,* and *Prairial,* the spring months of seed-time, flowers, and meadows; while *Messidor, Thermidor,* and *Fructidor* were the summer months of harvest, heat, and fruit.

By the following year the Girondins were again in control, although the Royalists continued to make determined efforts to change the course of events, particularly in the *Vendée*, where they were eventually suppressed by *Hoche*. On the 28 October 1795 a *Directory* of five members assumed power. During the next four years French republican armies were more successful abroad under their young commander, *Napoleon Bonaparte* (1769–1821), who had come into prominence in campaigns against the Austrians in Italy, whom he was to crush at *Marengo* (14 June, 1800). But Bonaparte, on returning to Paris after the less effectual attempt to destroy the British fleet at the *Battle of the Nile*, finding the tyrannical Directory generally detested, with the help of the army, and with the support of *Siéyès*, established the *Consulate* by a coup d'état on 9–10 November 1799. Bonaparte became First Consul, assisted by Siéyès and *Roger Ducos*. A new constitution awarded him the consulate for life, but such was his personal ambition that he caused himself to be declared 'Emperor of the French', and as Napoleon I was crowned in Notre-Dame by Pope Pius VII (18 May 1804). A Civil Code, largely retaining the liberal laws of the Revolution, was laid down. Paris itself was suitably embellished with monuments and bridges, as befitted the capital of an expanding empire, and was further enriched by the spoils of conquest.

First Empire. Faced by a new coalition of England, Austria, and Russia, Napoleon crushed the last two at *Austerlitz* in 1805, and imposed on them the humiliating *Peace of Pressburg*, but his fleet had been virtually destroyed at *Trafalgar* only six weeks earlier. In the following year Prussian armies were cowed at *Jena* and *Auerstadt*, and a further campaign against Russia was ended by the *Treaty of Tilsit*, which brought temporary peace to the Czar. Austria attempted to renew the struggle, but suffered disastrous defeats at *Essling* and *Wagram*. The subsequent *Peace of Vienna* (1809) marked perhaps the apogee of the Emperor's power.

Meanwhile, his brother *Joseph* had been imposed on the Spaniards, whose guerrilla methods of carrying on the war in the Peninsula were to cause a continual drain on Napoleon's reserves of manpower. England sent out two expeditionary forces to assist the Spaniards, and under *Wellington* they inflicted a series of defeats on the French, among them *Salamanca*, and culminating in the battles of *Vitoria* (1813), and—on French territory itself—*Toulouse*. Napoleon himself had just returned from the suicidal invasion of Russia, where the 'Grande Armée' although successful at *Borodino*, was virtually annihilated at the crossing of the Beresina by 'Generals January and February'. The Prussians, having recovered from their previous defeats, were able to retaliate at *Leipzig* (October 1813), and also entered France. Paris itself surrendered to the Allies (31 March 1814) after skirmishing on the heights of Montmartre. The emperor abdicated at Fontainebleau, and retired to the island of Elba. The Bourbons were restored, but the *Treaty of Paris* (30 May 1814) cut down the empire to size. During the Hundred Days' (26 March–24 June 1815), Napoleon made a desperate attempt to regain absolute power, having claimed at Grenoble (en route to Paris from Elba) that he had come to deliver France from 'the insolence of the nobility, the pretensions of the priests, and the yoke of foreign powers'. His defeat at *Waterloo* (18 June), and subsequent banishment to St Helena, where he died in 1821, enabled the king—Louis XVIII—to resume his precarious throne, which he was only able to retain by repressive measures: the University was supervised by the clergy. The reign of his successor, *Charles X*, under whom were passed the reactionary *Ordinances of St-Cloud*, suppressing the liberty of the press, and reducing the electorate to the landed classes, only proved that the bigoted Bourbons could 'learn nothing and forget nothing', and led to the '*July Revolution*' of 1830, and the loss of his throne.

House of Orléans. *Louis-Philippe* (1830–48; son of 'Philipe-Égalité d'Orléans of the Revolution) was chosen as head of the 'July Monarchy', and the upper-middle class, who had striven for power since 1789, now achieved it, although the urban populace in general still lived in pestilential conditions: some 19,000 Parisians of a total of c.900,000 had died in an outbreak of cholera in 1832. The total population of France was about 32,500,000. The only other towns of any size were Lyon and Marseille, with c.115,000 each, and Bordeaux and Rouen with about 90,000 each. France was still essentially a country dominated by agriculture and by a rural population.

The king devoted himself, with perhaps more energy than taste, to the further embellishment of the capital, and many pretentious buildings date from this period. Gas lighting had been first installed there in 1829. In 1840 the body of Napoleon was transferred with much pomp to its last resting-place under the Dôme des Invalides. The city was surrounded by fortifications during the years 1841–45, but these could not defend the 'citizen-king' against the mass of his people, among whom socialist ideas were spreading, nor did the conservative policy of *Guizot* suit their temper, and by the '*February Revolution*' of 1848, Louis-Philippe was overthrown. In the elections which followed, which introduced universal male suffrage, the electorate leapt from 250,000 to 9,000,000. Among famous literary figures during the first half of the century were *Balzac, Chateaubriand, Hugo, George Sand, Stendhal, Flaubert, Gautier,* and *Sainte-Beuve.*

A *Second Republic* was set up by the provisional government, and *Louis Napoleon* (the undistinguished and indolent, but shrewd and cynical nephew of Bonaparte, who as pretender had already made two abortive attempts to regain the throne), was elected Prince-President by almost 75 per cent of those who voted; but such was the sentimental prevalence of the idea of Empire, that in December 1851 a coup d'état (involving the temporary imprisonment of some 30,000 in opposition) placed him in a position to be almost unanimously accepted by a plebiscite as the Emperor *Napoleon III* some months later, inaugurating the *Second Empire.*

Having adopted the clever but misleading motto of 'L'Empire c'est la paix', he proceded to embroil the country in a succession of wars, notably in the *Crimea* (1854–56), and by undertaking the deliverance of Italy from Austrian oppression, afterwards unchivalrously demanding Savoy and Nice in recompense. Meanwhile he continued the expedient policy of his predecessor, by clearing the mass of congested, evil-smelling, and tortuous lanes of old Paris, which had so favoured the erection of barricades in 1830 and 1848, and in their place *Baron Haussmann* laid out a number of broad boulevards which are still characteristic of much of the centre, while from 1861 Garnier's Opera-house, representative of the expansive taste of the time, was being built, and the Bois de Boulogne and the Bois de Vincennes were transformed into public parks.

But these peaceful projects were halted abruptly by the outbreak, in 1870, of the *Franco-Prussian War.* An inglorious campaign ended with the capitulation of *Sedan*, where Napoleon III was himself taken prisoner and deposed (dying in exile at Chislehurst, near London, in 1873).

Third Republic
Presidents in office:
1871–73 Adolphe Thiers
1873–79 Maréchal MacMahon
1879–87 Jules Grévy
1887–94 Sadi Carnot
1894–95 Jean Casimir-Périer
1895–99 Félix Faure
1899–1906 Émile Loubet
1906–13 Armand Fallières
1913–20 Raymond Poincaré
1920 Paul Deschanel
1920–24 Alexandre Millerand
1924–31 Gaston Doumergue
1931–32 Paul Doumer
1932–40 Albert Lebrun

Gambetta and *Thiers* were largely instrumental in forming the *Third*

Republic, which had been proclaimed (4 September, 1870) while German troops advanced on Paris, which, invested on 19 September, its defenders commanded by Trochu, capitulated four months later, on 28 January 1871, after much suffering and famine. At this time the fortified enceinte of Paris, which formed the municipal boundary, was rather more than 21 miles (almost 34km) long , and had 67 entrances or gates. The Louvre had been turned into an armament workshop, the Gare d'Orléans into a balloon factory, and the Gare de Lyon into a cannon-foundry; but the army was ill-prepared. Order was not re-established until after the *Communard Insurrection*, which then broke out (18 March–29 May, 1871), had been overthrown at the cost of pitched battles in the streets, in which some 3–4000 Communards were killed, and the destruction of parts of the Tuileries and other public buildings such as the Hôtel de Ville. Retaliatory measures included the summary execution of 20,000–25,000 Parisians, mostly of the working classes; and in addition some 4–5000 were deported. Thiers, who was ultimately responsible for these mass killings, was then declared Président. An amnesty bill, introduced by Gambetta, was not adopted until 1880.

By September, 1873 the last German occupation troops had gone, but France was left to pay a heavy war indemnity, and lost the provinces of Alsace and Lorraine. Various political crises, embittered by the reprehensible 'Dreyfus affair' (1894–1906), coloured much of the period up to the outbreak of the First World War. An 'Entente Cordiale' between Britain and France was established in 1904, putting an end to colonial rivalry, and paved the way to future co-operation. During these decades building continued apace, even if much of it was of a meretricious nature. The 'Grand Palais' and 'Petit Palais', a new Hôtel de Ville, the Gare d'Orsay, the Eiffel Tower, and the basilica of Sacré-Coeur are representative examples of the taste of an age, differing facets of which were well described by *Zola*, and later by *Proust*. In 1910 extensive areas of Paris were inundated by the flooding of the Seine.

Soon after the start of the *First World War* (3 August, 1914) French troops were dramatically reinforced at the *Marne* by some 11,000 men rushed to the front in taxis from Paris, whose citizens had the satisfaction of hearing the din of battle gradually recede, and little damage was done to the capital by air raids or long-range bombardment. But ten departments were occupied, and the attrition of three long years of trench warfare followed. On 11 November, 1918 an armistice was signed. Although the provinces lost in 1871 were restored, the loss in manpower to France and her allies during these years had been staggering. For every ten Frenchmen between 20 and 45, two had been killed–a total of over 1,300,000. Slowly the country recruited her strength, even if, politically, she showed little initiative. In Paris, Thiers's fortifications were demolished in 1919–24, affording an opportunity to lay out a new ring of boulevards. A number of new edifices were erected for the Exhibition of 1937, including the Musées d'Art Moderne and the Palais de Chaillot. Meanwhile her defensive policies were concretely expressed in the construction of a costly and supposedly impregnable barrier along the German frontier–the Maginot Line (named after a minister of war)–which was immediately side-stepped by invading armoured divisions at the start of the *Second World War* (Sept. 1939), underlining the sagacity of the French high command.

Demoralised French forces, in no state to resist, and not capable of mounting a successful counter-attack, ostensibly capitulated to the triumphant Reich, while a high proportion of the British army was able to re-cross the Channel from Dunkerque (27 May–4 June, 1940) in a fleet of open boats sent to its rescue. The Germans proceeded to occupy the northern half of the country and the Atlantic coast. For the rest of the war, the underground Resistance Movement did what it could to thwart the collaborating policies of the 'Vichy Government' presided over by the octogenarian *Marshal Pétain*, hero of Verdun, among others.

Meanwhile, a provisional government had been set up in London by *Gén. Charles de Gaulle* (1890–1970), and Free French forces co-operated in the liberation of France. Allied troops disembarking in Normandy and in the South of France (on 6 June and 15 August, 1944, respectively) converged on Paris, which was free by late August, but an armistice with Germany was not signed until 8 May, 1945. The occupying troops were, after a fierce campaign, driven from French soil, and France was able to participate in the victory celebrations.

In Oct. 1946 the *Fourth Republic* was proclaimed, of which *Vincent Auriol* (1947–54), and *René Coty* (1954–58) were presidents. Women now had the vote, and proportional representation was adopted. Slowly, despite many changes in government and despite defeat in Indo-China and revolt in Algeria, the country was restored to economic prosperity after the physical and moral devastation of war. In 1957 a *Common Market* (EEC) was established, in which France, West Germany, Italy, and the Benelux countries were founder members.

Fifth Republic

1958–69 Charles de Gaulle
1969–74 Georges Pompidou
1974–81 Valéry Giscard d'Estaing
1981–   François Mitterrand

In 1958 de Gaulle prepared a new constitution, which was approved by a referendum, and the general was elected the first president of the new republic by universal direct suffrage, for a period of seven years. The powers of the head of state were considerably—some would say inordinately—increased: he nominates the prime minister, who in turn recommends the members of the government; he can make laws and refer decisions of major importance to popular vote by referendum; in extreme cases he has the power to dismiss the National Assembly.

In 1962 Algerian independence was proclaimed, since when a remarkable number of Algerians can be seen in the industrial towns of France. In 1965 de Gaulle was returned to power with enthusiasm, but with a reduced majority. In May 1968 a serious 'Student Revolution' took place in Paris, which precipitated overdue educational reforms. The following year de Gaulle was succeeded by *Pompidou*, who died in office in 1974. His successor was *Giscard d'Estaing*, whose somewhat cavalier attitude to the mass of his countrymen produced a reaction, and a swing to the Left, with *Mitterrand* moving into the Élysée. But, like the Bourbons, the Socialist regime appears also to have 'learnt nothing and forgotten nothing'. Mitterrand immediately alienated many of his supporters by the inclusion of Communist ministers in the government, a devious manoeuvre which in turn provoked reaction.

Jacques Chirac remained *maire* of Paris, a position he has occupied since March 1977, when the title was changed from that of Préfet de la Seine.

Bibliography and Maps

The list of books in English on French topography, History, and Culture, is extensive, and the brief list appended (containing also one or two titles in French) does not pretend to be more than a very general compilation of titles which may be found useful for reference, or of interest in providing background, for the visitor to Paris and its environs, and most of them contain comprehensive biographies for further or more specialized reading. The library of the French Institute at S. Kensington, London, should not be overlooked.

Topographical and General: *Pierre Couperie*, Paris through the Ages (an illustrated historical atlas of urbanism and architecture); *Jacques Hillairet*, Connaissance du Vieux Paris; *Henri Bidou*, Paris (1939); *John Russell*, Paris; *Klaus Bussmann*, *Theodore Zeldin*, The French.

Historical: *Alain Decaux* and *André Castelot*, Dictionnaire d'Histoire de France PERRIN; *Alfred Cobban*, A History of Modern France, 1715–1962; *Saint-Simon*, Historical Memoires (trans. and ed. Lucy Norton); *Theodore Zeldin*, France, 1848–1945; *D.W. Brogan*, The Development of Modern France (1870–1939); *J. Ardagh*, The New France; *R.D. Anderson*, France 1870–1914; *Alistair Horne*, The Fall of Paris; *J. Huizinga*, The Waning of the Middle Ages; *Richard Cobb*, Paris and its Provinces, 1792–1802, and several other studies by the same author.

Literary: *Paul Harvey* and *J.E. Heseltine*, The Oxford Companion to French Literature; *D.G. Charlton* (Ed.), France: a Companion to French Studies; *J.M.H. Reid*, The Concise Dictionary of French Literature; *L. Cazamian*, A History of French Literature; *A. Ewert*, The French Language; *P.E. Charvet* (Ed.), A Literary History of France (6 Vols.).

Art and Architecture: *Anthony Blunt*, Art and Architecture in France, 1500–1700; *Kalnein* and *Levey*, Art and Architecture of the 18C in France; *Vivian Rowe*, Royal Châteaux of Paris; *Ian Dunlop*, Versailles, and The Cathedral's Crusade; *Allan Braham*, The Architecture of the French Enlightenment; *Joan Evans*, Art in Medieval France; *Pierre Lavedan*, French Architecture; *Otto von Simson*, The Gothic Cathedral; *Michel Gallet*, Paris Domestic Architecture of the 18C; *David Thomson*, Renaissance Paris.

Maps

For Paris itself, and its immediate surroundings, the following are recommended to supplement the Atlas section at the end of this Guide.

Michelin, *Plan de Paris* (No.196, at 1:10,000), also available with street references as No.12, and—perhaps more convenient when walking, and now containing métro and bus maps—their *Paris Atlas* (No.11). These show the position of underground car-parks, and

24-hour petrol stations, etc., while the Atlas also includes a list of names, addresses, and telephone numbers of organisations likely to interest visitors. Other maps published annually by *Michelin* are *Outskirts of Paris* (No.*101, at 1:50,000), *Environs of Paris* (No.196, at 1:100,000), *Paris Region* (No.237, at 1:200,000), the latter apparently superseding No.97, while No.236 covers the area between the Channel ports and Paris. The same company have recently produced map No.170, covering the same area as No.96, but concentrating on Sports and open-air recreations.

The **Institut Géographique National** (IGN) map of the *Environs de Paris* (No.*90, at 1:100,000) may well be preferred by some to the Michelin map of the same area as it gives a better indication of contour and the general lie of the land. It may be supplemented by four sheets of their *Série Verte* at 1:100,000, Maps Nos 8, 9, 20, and 21 covering slightly more than the area described in this guide. Also of use are the IGN map of *Région d'Île de France: patrimoine artistique* at 1:150,000, which will help with the pin-pointing of monuments, and, covering a more extensive area, No.103 in their *Série Rouge* (Carte de l'Environnement Culturel et Touristique) at 1:250,000. IGN also produce an excellent series of *Forest Maps* at 1:25,000, Nos 401–407, 413, 418 and 419 covering the wooded areas in the environs of the capital. IGN No.101 (Série Rouge) covers the Pays du Nord.

For planning one's route to Paris, or on from Paris, either Michelin's *France-Grandes Routes* (No.989) or the IGN *France-Routes: autoroutes* (No.901), both at 1:1,000,000, are recommended, perhaps supplemented by the IGN map No.902 (richesses artistiques).

It is always advisable to have the *latest* editions of all such maps, which should be found at Messrs Stanfords, 12–14 Long Acre, London WC2, and at all good booksellers in the U.K. or France. In case of difficulty, one may apply to the offices of the Michelin Tyre Co. Ltd, 81 Fulham Road, London SW3 6RD, or McCarta Ltd, 122 King's Cross Road, London WC1X 9DS, for the IGN series. A visit to the saleroom of IGN at 107 Rue La Boétie, 75008 Paris (the Champs-Élysées end of the street; Métro Franklin Roosevelt), will be found rewarding, particularly for maps of a more specialised nature: the offices of Pneu Michelin are at 46 Av. de Breteuil, S. of the Invalides.

Glossary of Architectural and Allied Terms

ACAJOU, mahogany
ARC-BOUTANT, flying buttress
ARCHIVOLT, the series of mouldings which form the ensemble of an arch
ARDOISES, slates
AUTEL, altar
BOISERIES, decorative woodwork
CARREFOUR, crossroads
CARRELAGES, floor tiles

CASERNE, barracks

CHEMIN DE RONDE, battlement walk

CHEVET, exterior of an apse; also ABSIDE

COLOMBIER, dovecote

COLONNETTE, little column for a vaulting shaft

CONTREFORTS, buttresses

CORBELS, wooden or stone projections supporting a beam or parapet, and often elaborately carved.

CORPS DE LOGIS, main residential part of a château

DESSUS DE PORTE, a painting above a door

DOUVES, moat; wet or dry

EBÉNISTE, cabinet-maker

ÉCHAUGUETTE, fortified corner turret, or bartizan turret

ÉGLISE, church

ÉMAIL, enamel

FLÉCHE, spire

GRENIER, granary or attic

HÔTEL, mansion

HÔTEL-DIEU, principal hospital in many towns

JEU DE PAUME, a real tennis-court

JUBÉ, rood-screen

MAIRIE, town hall or municipal building; also HÔTEL DE VILLE

MANDORLA, pointed oval-shaped frame used as an aureole in medieval sculpture and painting; also a VESICA

MANSARD ROOF, roof of which each face has two slopes, the lower steeper than the upper, named after the architect François Mansard (1598–1666)

NACRE, mother of pearl

NEF, nave

OEIL-DE-BOEUF, small circular, sometimes oval, window (bull's eye)

POIVRETTES, pepper-pot turrets

PORTE-COCHÈRE, carriage gateway

POUTRES, beams or joists·

REZ DE CHAUSSÉE, ground floor

TIERCERON, curved rib in Gothic vaults springing from the same point as the intersecting diagonal rib, and rising to the end of the ridge-rib

TYMPANUM, space, often decorated, between door lintel and arch

VERMEIL, silver-gilt

VITRAIL, stained-glass window

VOUSSOIRES, wedge-shaped stones used in constructing arches or vaults

PRACTICAL INFORMATION

Formalities and Currency

Passports are necessary for all British and American travellers entering France. British passports, valid for ten years, are issued at the Passport Office, Clive House, Petty France, London SW1, and from certain provincial offices, or may be obtained for an additional fee through any tourist agency. *British Visitors' Passports* (valid one year), available from Post Offices in the UK, are also accepted. No visa is required for British or American visitors, but should any foreigner intend to remain in France for more than three months, he should apply in advance to the nearest French Consultate, or if already in France, to the Préfecture de Police (Service des Étrangers) in Paris (7 Blvd due Palais, 4e). Procedures are at present in the process of revision.

British subjects seeking employment in France should write to the *Consular Section* of the Embassy, at 109 Rue du Faubourg-St-Honoré, 8e (4th floor), but it should be emphasized that they are not an employment agency, nor can they help to find accommodation. They will advise on the procedure to be followed, according to the status of the person concerned under the E.E.C. regulations.

Custom House. Except for travellers by air, who have to pass customs at the airport of arrival, or those travelling on international expresses, where their luggage is examined in the train, luggage is still liable to be scrutinized at the frontier, or ports of departure and disembarkation. Provided that dutiable articles are delcared, bona-fide travellers will find the French customs authorities (*douaniers*) courteous and reasonable.

It is well to check in advance with French Consultates or Tourist Offices before starting out as to the latest regulations with regard to the importation of firearms, whether sporting or otherwise.

Embassies and Consulates, etc. *British Embassy*, 35 Rue du Faubourg St-Honoré, 8e; the *Consulate* is at 105–109, some 5 minutes' walk to the W.; *British Chamber of Commerce*, 6 Rue Halévy, 9e (with branches at Marseille, Lyon, le Havre,Lille, and Bordeaux): at the same address is the *British Colony Committee for Paris and District*, who produce a useful 'Digest of British and Franco-British Clubs, Societies, and Institutions in France'; *British Council*, 9 Rue De Constantine, 7e.
   American Embassy, 2 Av. Gabriel, 8e (just N. of the Pl. de la Concorde) with consulates at Lyon, Marseille, Bordeaux, Strasbourg, and Nice; *Canadian Embassy*, 35 Av. Montaigne, 8e, with consulates at Bordeaux, Marseille, and Strasbourg; *South African Embassy*, 59 Quai d'Orsay, 7e; *Australian Embassy*, 4 Rue Jean Rey, 15e; *New Zealand Embassy*, 7ter Rue Léonard-de-Vinci, 16e; *Irish Embassy*, 4 Rue Rude, 16e.

Security. No objects of any value should be left visible in the interiors of cars parked overnight near hotels, for example, which is merely tempting providence. Women should beware of bag-snatchers. In general, it is advisable to deposit any valuables with the manager of one's hotel, against receipt. Normally, however, with a reasonably amount of circumspection the tourist will find his property respected.

The police should be applied to in case of any trouble.

Currency Regulations. In Oct. 1979 the British Government announced the suspension of exchange controls. There is now no restriction on the amount of sterling the traveller may take out of Great Britain, but it is advisable to enquire in advance at one's bank as to the latest regulations with regard to the export or re-export of money from France, for proof in the form of a 'declaration of entry' may be required if the sum involved is in excess of 5000 francs.

Money. The monetary unit is the *franc*, subdivided into 100 *centimes*. Bank notes of 10, 20, 50, 100, 200, and 500 francs are in circulation, and there are also coins of 5, 10, 20, and 50 centimes (½fr.), 1 franc, 2 francs, 5 francs, and 10 francs.

Branches of most French Banks are open from 9.00 to 16.30 from Mon. to Fri.; most branches close on Sat. morning, but some central branches of the principal banks may have a 'bureau de change' open from 9.00 to 12.00. At some main-line stations, the 'bureaux de change' are open daily from 6.30 to 7.30 to 22.00 or 23.00. Those at the international airports operate a daily service from 6.00 to 23.00, while the C.C.F. bank at 115 Champs Elysées is likewise open from Mon. to Sat. from 9.00 to 20.00, and U.B.P. at 125 Champs Elysées from 8.45 to 5.15 on weekdays, and on Sat. and Sun. from 10.30–13.00, and 14.00–16.00.

Larger hotels will also accept travellers' cheques, but they will give a lower rate of exchange. It is advisable to obtain a sufficient supply of French change for incidental expenses before leaving home, particularly if arriving in France during a week-end. It is also often worth while to 'shop around', for different banks give different rates of exchange—some good; other not so good.

Among British banks in Paris are the following: *Barclays*, 33 Rue de Quatre-Septembre, 2e, with a number of branches; *National Westminster*, 18 Pl. Vendóme, 1 er; *Lloyds*, 43 Blvd des Capucines, 2e; and *Midland*, 5 Rue Royale, 8e. Many American and Canadian banks also have branches near the centre.

Approaches to Paris and Transport in Paris

Paris may be reached directly from Great Britain by a variety of ways, and although a car taken across the Channel will render the tourist independent of other forms of transport in the Île de France, it is not essential if only Paris and its immediate surroundings are intended to be visited. Most important towns, railway termini, and airports, now provide **Car-hire** facilities.

There are a number of rapid *rail* services from London to Paris, while the quickest, but least interesting, means of transit is by *air*: see below.

Travel Agents. General information may be obtained gratis from the *French Government Tourist Office*, 178 Piccadilly, London W1.

They have offices in the United States at 610 Fifth Av., New York, with branches at 645 N. Michigan Av. Chicago; 9401 Wilshire Blvd, Beverly Hills;

360 Post Street, San Francisco, 2050 Stemmons Freeway, Dallas: their Canadian office is at 1840 Ouest, Rue Sherbrooke, Montreal, with a branch at 372 Bay Street, Toronto.

Any accredited member of the *Association of British Travel Agents* will sell tickets and book accommodation. As some once-reliable firms appear to concentrate on 'groups' rather on the individual private traveller, the latter is advised to contact one of the many good but smaller organisations offering a personal service. They are warned that some agents have chosen to impose an additional charge when booking open-dated return air tickets not originally issued by themselves, and it is preferable to visit the individual airline's offices in such cases.

Rail and Ferry Services. Numerous and frequent Passenger, Car, and Coach Ferry services are operated by British and French Railways, Townsend Thoresen, Southern Ferries, Normandy Ferries, etc. from British to northern French ports. For the latest information about services available, inquiries should be made to the *Sealink Car Ferry Centre*, 53 Grosvenor Gardens, London SW1. Those wishing to make use of the various *Hovercraft* services should be warned that the quality of service may be erratic in adverse weather conditions.

The *British Railway Travel Centre*, Rex House, Lower Regent Street, London SW1, provides travel tickets, sleeping-berth tickets, seat reservations, etc. on Continental as well as British Transport services. The offices of *French Railways*, (SNCF, or Société des Chemins de Fer Française) adjacent to the French Tourist Office in Piccadilly, are equally helpful, but do not actually sell tickets. Both can provide the prospective traveller with full details of the variety of services available, together with their cost.

The Paris office of British Railways is at 12 Blvd de la Madeleine, 9e.

For railway stations in Paris, see pp35-6.

To avoid considerable inconvenience and irritation on train journeys, travellers are advised to check their tickets closely at the point of issue, particularly as to their validity (including the return trip), and should make sure that the 'global' charge has been made, including all possible supplements, etc.

Service *on board* some passenger **Ferries** has deteriorated, more attention being given to the selling of 'bingo' tickets than to the comfort of passengers, who are frequently treated like cattle. Often required to queue during the crossing for 'Passport control' (a procedure which could be simplified with ease if some administrator gave it his attention), travellers are then left to disembark with their luggage without the least form of organisation or even an attempt to control their movement to the gangways. Those finding conditions unacceptable should complain without compunction to the purser while on board, and on their return by writing to higher authorities (such as the European Rail Traffic Manager, Eversholt House, London NW1): otherwise no improvement can be expected.

Motorists driving to Paris will save much trouble by joining the *Automobile Association* (Fanum House, Basingstoke, Hants RG21 2EA), the *Royal Automobile Club* (83 Pall Mall, London SW1), the *Royal Scottish Automobile Club* (17 Rutland Sq., Edinburgh), or the *American Automobile Association* (8111 Gatehouse Road, Falls Church, Virginia 22042). These organisations will provide any necessary documents, as well as information about rules of the road abroad, restrictions regarding caravans and trailers, advice on routes, and arrangements regarding delivery of spare parts, insurance, etc. Motorists who are not the owners of their vehicle should possess the owner's permit for its use abroad. The use of safety-belts is now compulsory in France. Both the A.A. and R.A.C. have offices in Paris, the former c/o the *Touring Club de France*, 6–8 Rue Firmin Gillot, 15e; the latter at 8 Pl. Vendôme. The insurance facilities offered by *Europ Assistance* should be taken advantage of. It is advisable to buy maps in advance of the tour: see p26.

By Road, the most rapid approach to Paris from *Calais* or *Boulogne* is the A1 *autoroute* (on which there are tolls—*péages*—to pay, unlike in England), which is reached just N.E. of *Arras* (of interest in itself) by a new approach motorway (A26) running S. of and approx. parallel to *St-Omer, Lillers*, and *Béthune*. This area is described in detail in *Blue Guide France*. The A1 may also be joined at *Lille* by those disembarking at **Dunkerque**, by following the A25, but it may be preferable to join the A26 just S. of St-Omer, reached by taking the D928 not far S. of Dunkerque.

There are of course a variety of alternative roads, the most frequented being the N1 from **Calais**, passing through **Boulogne**, *Montreuil*, and *Abbeville*, thence following the D901 to *Beauvais*, there regaining the N1 for Paris. Alternative routes from Abbeville are the continuation of the N1 via *Amiens* and *Breteuil* to *Beauvais*; from Amiens on the D934 to meet the A1 motorway 108km N. of Paris; or bearing S.E. from Breteuil via *Clermont* to either *Chantilly* or *Senlis* for Paris.

Travellers disembarking at **Dieppe** may follow either the D915 via *Gournay-en-Bray* and the N31 to *Beauvais*, or continue on the D915 via *Gisors* and *Pontoise*. Another route from Dieppe is the N27 driving S. to *Rouen*, thence following the N14 S.E. via *Magny-en-Vexin* to Paris (or the slower N15 S. of the Seine via *Vernon* and *Mantes*), or alternatively, we can join the A13 autoroute S. of Rouen for Paris. This may also be approached from **Le Havre** via the *Pont de Tancarville*, or via *Rouen*. *Évreux* may also be visited with ease by travellers approaching Paris from the N.W.

The roads converging on the capital from the N. and N.W. are described in reverse in this Guide in the following routes: from Senlis, Rte 25; from Clermont, Rte 24; from Beauvais, Rte 38; from Gisors, Rte 37; from Magny, Rte 36C; from Vernon, Rte 36A; and from Évreux, Rte 35.

Motorways radiating out from Paris are listed at the beginning of each route they approx. follow.

It is as well to have a good idea of exactly where in Paris one is making for, and to familiarise oneself in advance as to which exit (*sortie*) to aim for prior to entering the *Ceinture* or *Blvd Périphérique*. These are usually well indicated some distance in advance, but care must be taken to be in position to make one's exit well before bearing off the motorway.

Parking is restricted in central Paris, and use should be made of its underground parks. A meter system is in operation, the meters being either along the pavement's edge, or tickets may be obtained in machines in the street concerned, which must be then placed in the interior of the windscreen. Certain areas in which one may see a number of cars parked may not necessarily be permissible sites, and the police, if feeling officious, may either fine one of have the car towed away. Ill-parked foreign cars are removed as ruthlessly as native ones, and may take hours to recover from the *'fourrière'* or pound, and at a considerable charge; there will be a heavy fine to pay in addition. Alternatively, a clamp or *sabot* may be attached to a wheel. In either case, the owner should apply to the nearest gendarme or *Commissariat de Police.*

Beware the light-blue uniformed wardens (familiarly known as periwinkles—*pervenches*), who have superseded those previously known as 'aubergines' from their plum-coloured uniforms: they do not attempt to camouflage their presence.

Regular **Air Services** between England and France are maintained by *Air France* working in conjuction with *British Airways.* Full information regarding flights from London and other cities in the U.K. may be obtained from British Airways, Dorland House, Lower Regent Street, London SW1, and from Air France, 158 New Bond Street, W1. There are also daily flights from Gatwick with British Caledonian (215 Piccadilly, W1, and 29A Royal Exchange, Threadneedle Street EC 3).

There are regular international flights from most European capitals and larger cities to Paris, and direct services from New York, and Montreal, etc., and from many other non-European countries, apart from those provided by Charter companies.

British Airways have Paris offices at 91 Av. des Champs-Elysées and 34 Av. de l'Opéra; Air France offices are at 119 Av. des Champs-Elysées; and British Caledonian at 5 Rue de la Paix, 2e.

Internal or domestic services are maintained by *Air Inter*, 232 Rue de Rivoli, Paris 1er, and branches.

Paris is served by two international airports: *Roissy-Charles de Gaulle* (near the village of Roissy-en-France, 23km N.E. of the capital), recently extended and now comprising two separate termini; and *Orly (South* and *West)*, 14km S. of the city.

The former is linked by a train shuttle-service with the Gare du Nord; the latter with the Gare d'Austerlitz, etc., and in due course there will probably be a direct service between the two. They are also connected by an Air France bus service leaving each terminus every 20 mins. between 6.00 and 23.00.

A frequent and regular bus service is also provided between Charles de Gaulle and Porte Maillot (W. of the Arc de Triomphe), and between Orly and the town terminal of Les Invalides. They run during the same period, and also operate later at night to meet scheduled flights, even if delayed.

Taxis will also meet planes, and car-hire firms have offices at the airports.

Railway termini in Paris. The main stations, all on Métro lines, have most of the facilities required by the traveller, including left-luggage offices (*consigne*) or lockers, trolleys, information bureaux, etc. Some, such as Gare d'Austerlitz and Gare du Nord, are also connected by regular bus services.

The Main stations of the SNCF, providing an unusually efficient service, are:

Gare d'Austerlitz (Pl. 15;6–8), serving the Région Sud-Ouest (Tours, Bordeaux, Toulouse, Bayonne, the Pyrenees, Madrid, etc.).

Gare de l'Est (Pl. 9;3) for the Région Est (Reims, Metz, Strasbourg, Frankfurt, Bâle, Zurich, etc.).

Gare de Lyon (Pl. 15;6) for the Région Sud-Est (Lyon, Dijon, Provence, Côte d'Azur, Italy, etc.), including the new *Trains à Grande Vitesse* or TGV.

Gare Montparnasse (Pl. 12;8), terminus for the Région Ouest (Brittany, La Rochelle, etc.).

Gare du Nord (Pl. 9;3) for the Région Nord (Lille, Brussels, Amsterdam, Cologne, Hamburg, etc., and also for boat-trains to Boulogne, Calais, and Dunkerque).

Gare St-Lazare (Pl. 7;4), another terminus of the Région Ouest (Normandy lines, Rouen, and boat-trains to Dieppe, Le Havre, Cherbourg, etc.).

Note. French Railways have abolished ticket control at platform barriers. Passengers purchasing a ticket *in France* must themselves punch-and-date-stamp (or '*composter*') their ticket in an orange red-coloured machine at the platform entrance *before* boarding the train. Those inadvertently failing to do so are liable to pay a supplementary fee/fine to the inspector. This procedure does not apply to tickets purchased outside France.

Public Transport in Paris. Buses (*autobus*) and the underground railway (*Métro*) in Paris are controlled by the RATP (Régie Autonome des Transports Parisiens), with offices at 53bis Quai des Grands-Augustins (just S. of the *Pont Neuf*), with a branch in the Pl. de la Madeleine (on the E. side of the church). They issue useful maps of the Métro and bus systems (including lines of the RER: see below), and also a leaflet giving details of various Summer Excursions.

They also sell a 2, 4, or 7-day *billet de tourisme* (also available at the main Métro stations and from the Tourist Office at 127 Av. des Champs-Elysées; also from French Railways in London), allowing unlimited travel on the RATP system for the period concerned, which can be useful and comparatively cheap if used constantly. The yellow weekly ticket is known as a *coupon hebdomadaire jaune*. Visitors staying any length of time should consider purchasing a *Carte Orange* (available at any Métro station), for which a passport-size photograph is required. Normally, the most convenient method is to buy a '*carnet*' of ten tickets at any booking office of the Métro. First and Second-class tickets are available, but the latter compartments are usually perfectly satisfactory, although occasionally more crowded. Tickets, which operate a turnstile, should be retained until the end of one's journey, as they are occasionally inspected and may be required for making one's exit or change.

The **Métro** (*Métropolitan*) provides a rapid means of transport throughout Paris, and its modernisation continues. The most convenient Métro stations are listed at the commencement of each urban route described in this Guide. Trains glide silently on rubber wheels through impressively clean stations, for the most part, which lie approx. 500 metres apart. Some platforms—such as those at the *Louvre* station—are lavishly decorated with casts from the collections of the museum, while at *Varenne* are casts from the adjacent Musée Rodin. The service, from 5.30 in the morning until approx. 12.30 at night, is normally frequent and regular. Women should avoid travelling alone late at night, and travellers in general should beware of bag-snatchers and pickpockets. Holders of Second class tickets may use First class carriages between 5.30–9.00 and 17.00–1.15. The fare is the same for any distance on the main inner network, including all necessary changes, making long journeys reasonably inexpensive in comparison to the shorter distances covered—and certainly cheaper than the London 'Underground'.

The various lines of the Métro (the first of which was opened in 1900, and certain stations, notably the Bois de Boulogne entrance of *Porte Dauphine*, retain their 'art nouveau' decoration) are called by the names of their terminal stations: e.g. Ligne 1, *Vincennes–Neuilly*. The direction in which the train is running, and they keep to the right, is indicated by a sign naming the terminal station. At interchange stations, the passages leading to the line concerned are clearly indicated by an orange-lighted sign marked *'Correspondance'*, followed by the name of the terminal stations of the connecting line. Certain interchanges necessitate an inordinately long walk.

The fast exterior lines of the **RER** (*Réseau Express Régional*) have been recently extended, and line **A** now runs W. to E. across Paris from *St-Germain-en-Laye* to *Boissy St-Léger* or *Torcy* (connected to the Métro at *Étoile*, *Auber*, *Châtelet-Les Halles*, *Gare de Lyon*, and *Nation*). The transverse line **B** leads S. from *Châtelet-Les Halles* to *Sceaux* and *Robinson*, and to *St-Rémy-lès-Chevreuse* (the latter connected to the Métro at *Châtelet* and *Denfert-Rochereau*). It leads N. from *Châtelet-Les Halles* via the *Gare du Nord*, to the airport of *Roissy-Charles de Gaulle*, or *Mitry-Claye*.

A third line (**C**), running S. of the Seine, now connects *St-Quentin-en-Yvelines* and *Versailles-Rive-Gauche* with *Orly*, on the line to *Massy-Palaiseau*, and to other suburban lines, and is connected to the Métro at *Javel*, *Champ-de-Mars*, *Invalides*, *Quai d'Orsay (Solférino)*, *Saint-Michel*, and *Gare d'Austerlitz*. Those making the excursion to *Versailles* will find this latter a convenient means of transport thence, but should make sure that they are on the correct branch line. Line **B** is likewise useful when visiting *Sceaux*.

These three lines are *not* covered by the otherwise inclusive Métro ticket, and a separate one must be bought at the interchange stations, which have elaborate automatic ticket machines.

Buses. Bus-stops, which are now all 'request stops' (*arrêt facultatif*), are indicated by small placards showing the numbers of the routes and their destinations. Depending on the length of the journey, either one or two tickets of the *carnet* will be required, the tickets for buses and the Métro being interchangeable. Buses therefore are generally more expensive than the Métro; ask the driver-conductor if in doubt as to the fare. It will be noticed that buses, owing to the large number of one-way streets, do not necessarily return along the same route that they follow to their destination, and this can lead to confusion until the visitor finds the position of the stops concerned.

Smoking is forbidden on both buses and the Métro. Where possible, avoid the use of public transport during 8.00–9.00, and during 17.30–19.30, when the 'rush-hour' is at its height. In some areas traffic is also heavy between 12.00 and 14.00.

Excursions. Apart from those excursions organized by the RATP, many tourist agencies run daily coach tours to sites outside Paris, and, during the summer, to view the floodlighting in Paris. Tourist Offices will be able to advise on the termini of the various regular coach routes into the outer environs of Paris, and into the provinces.

River Trips. *'Les Bateaux-Mouches' (Pont de l'Alma)* and *'Les Bateaux-Parisiennes' (Pont d'Iéna* or *Pont Neuf)* run trips along the

Seine both during the day and after dark, which can offer some unusual and attractive low-level' vistas as the launch emerges from beneath the numerous bridges spanning it, but perhaps a better idea of the importance of the river in the growth and planning of Paris is made more apparent by taking a leisurely walk, between the *Pont d'Iéna* and the *Pont de Sully*, along the embankment or the Quais. Unfortunately these are less attractive than they once were since traffic has been diverted along the water's edge.

Taxis. The number of taxis in Paris now approaches 15,000, and many will be found cruising or waiting at a rank, marked 'Tête de Station', and with a telephone. Visitors making regular use of a taxi from their place of residence should make a note of the telephone number of the nearest rank.

Some taxi-drivers still optimistically expect a tip of 10 per cent in addition to the charge on the meter. Rates are displayed inside the vehicle. Note that the night tariff (between 22.00 and 6.00) is considerably higher than the day. There is an additional charge for luggage placed in the boot, and—unaccountably—taxis waiting (or merely arriving at a queue) at a railway terminus, are also allowed to charge extra.

No one need be intimidated by the fact that Parisian taxi-drivers have gained for themselves an unenviable reputation over the years for truculence and rapacity. Usually their bark is worse than their bite, even if the many female taxi-drivers are escorted by their protective Alsatians, etc.; but in case of real trouble, make for the nearest *gendarme*, or complain (having taken their number) to the *Service des Taxis de la Préfecture de Police*, 36 Rue des Morillons, 15e.

Topography of Paris

Paris, the capital of France, lies on both banks of the *Seine*, near the centre of the so-called Paris Basin. Its height above sea-level varies from 25 to 130m, and its distance from the sea is 150km (or over 320km by the windings of the river). The Seine, the third in length of the four great rivers of France, enters the capital some 500km. from its source, and describes a curved course through the city, at the same time forming two islands, the *Île St-Louis* and the larger *Île de la Cité*. Much of the attraction of Paris stems from the way the river, with its numerous bridges, has been used to unite rather than divide the northern or Right Bank (*Rive Droite*) and the southern or Left Bank (*Rive Gauche*); indeed, the two are much more nearly of equal importance than the N. and S. banks of the Thames. Unlike London, Paris was always (until comparatively recently) bounded by a definite line of ramparts, which although they have long been demolished and their sites built upon, served to contain its population, denser than in any other European city (recently over 21,800 inhab. per km^2), and enclosed an area of 7800 hectares. The line of the 19C defensive walls can be imagined by following the exterior Blvd Périphérique, and certain forts still remain some distance beyond, although largely engulfed by suburbs (*banlieues*).

The total municipal population of *Paris*, according to the census of 1982, was—in round figures—2,189,000, some 20 per cent of which was made up of foreigners, many from the poorer nations of Europe, but also including large numbers of

Algerians, Tunisians, Moroccans, and others from Black Africa, as confirmed by recent demographic surveys, which this edition of the Guide will not attempt to detail, but those interested in such figures are advised to contact that useful and helpful organisation, the *Institut National de la Statistique et des Études Économiques* (INSEE), its head offices at 18 Blvd Adolphe Pinard, 14e, and with its centre for the Île-de-France in Tour Gamma A, 195 Rue de Bercy, Paris 12e (easily approached from the level of the Gare de Lyon).

With the growth of Paris, the old department of the Seine was by a decree which took effect in 1968, subdivided into four new departments: *Ville-de-Paris* (75; again with a *Maire*); *Hauts-de-Seine* (92; préfecture *Nanterre*); *Seine-St-Denis* (93; préfecture *Bobigny*); and *Val-de-Marne* (94; préfecture *Créteil*). The old department of Seine-et-Oise was similarly divided into three: *Val-d'Oise* (95; préfecture *Cergy-Pontoise*); *Yvelines* (78; préfecture *Versailles*); and *Essonne* (91; préfecture *Évry*). At the same time the department of *Seine-et-Marne* (77; préfecture *Melun*) was incorporated to make up the District de la Région Parisienne, now known as *La Région d'Île-de-France*.

This *Blue Guide* takes in a somewhat wider area, to include parts of the departments of OISE (60; préfecture *Beauvais*); to the N.W.; AISNE (02) to the N.E.; YONNE (89) to the S.E.; EURE-ET-LOIR (28; préfecture *Chartres*), and EURE (27; préfecture *Évreux*) to the S.W. and W. respectively.

The population in 1982 of this whole area totalled approx. 10,056,000 (of which 2,189,000 comprised that of the Ville-de-Paris), and the total population of France was approx. 54,257,000. It is of some interest to note that a century earlier (1881) the figures were 3,726,000 (of which 2,269,000 lived in Paris), and the total population for France was 39,238,000.

The topography of Paris can perhaps be best understood by taking PL. DE LA CONCORDE (Pl. 7;7) as a focal point, although historically the *Pl. du Parvis-Notre-Dame* (from which kilometric distances are measured) might be more appropriate. Hence (and elsewhere) we can appreciate the artistic town-planning of the past, which deliberately allowed vistas from one bank of the river to extend to the far bank in further impressive perspectives. Indeed it is these great perspectives that are particularly memorable about Paris.

Turning to the N.W., we can discern the *Arc de Triomphe* (and *La Défense* beyond), at the far end of the *Av. des Champs-Élysées*: in the opposite direction, the immense bulk of the *Louvre* beyond the gardens of the *Tuileries*. This is flanked, to the N., by the *Rue de Rivoli*, which with its continuation, the *Rue St-Antoine*, leads to the *Pl. de la Bastille*; and further E., by the *Rue du Faubourg St-Antoine*, to the *Pl. de la Nation*, and *Vincennes* beyond. It is perhaps this diagonal road axis, which, more than the river, cuts Paris into two almost equal parts.

The **Arrondissements**. These municipal districts, of which there are twenty in central Paris, each with its Maire and *Mairie*, or town hall, are important administrative and topographical entities, and their names and numbers convey far more than that of a municipal borough or mere postal district in London, and the visitor should make himself familiar with the situation of some of them: see plan on pp2–3 of Atlas.

As in London, certain areas are known more familiarly by their unofficial titles. Their numeration follows a spiral working out clockwise from the centre. When addressing correspondence to Paris the arrondissements should be written as 75001, 75002, etc. rather than 1er, 2e., etc., the prefix 75 indicating the department.

1er;   Louvre; the W. half of the Cité, the *Louvre*, Pl. Vendôme, *Palais-Royal* and *St-Eustache*.

2e;   Bourse: containing also the *Bibliothèque Nationale*.

3e;   Temple: comprising the N. half of the Marais, the Temple, and *Archives*.

4e;   Hôtel de Ville: includes the E. half of the Cité, with *Notre-Dame*, the Île St-Louis, and the *Centre Pompidou*, and the S. part of the Marais, with the Pl. des Vosges, and is bounded by the Pl. de la Bastille to the E.

5e;   Panthéon: the 'Quartier Latin', with the *Sorbonne*, *Panthéon*, *Val-de-Grâce*, and *Jardin des Plantes*.

6e;   Luxembourg: with *St-Germain-des-Prés*, *St-Sulpice*, and the *Palais du Luxembourg*.

7e;   Palais-Bourbon: comprising the Faubourg St-Germain, *Les Invalides*, the *École Militaire*, and bounded to the W. by the *Eiffel Tower*.

8e;   Élysée: with the Pl. de la Concorde, the *Madeleine*, the Champs-Élysées, and Faubourg St-Honoré, and including the Parc Monceau to the N., and containing the Av. George-V to the W.

9e;   Opéra: reaching up to the Blvd de Clichy and Pl. Pigalle.

10e;   Enclos St-Laurent: with the *Gares du Nord*, and *de l'Est*, and *Hôpital St-Louis*.

11e;   Popincourt: the area N.E. of the Pl. de la Bastille, and reaching to Pl. de la Nation.

12e;   Reuilly: the area S.E. of the Pl. de la Bastille, including the *Gare de Lyon* and Bercy.

13e;   Gobelins: the area S. of the *Gare d'Austerlitz*, including the *Gobelins*, and Pl. d'Italie.

14e;   Observatoire: including the *Cimetière de Montparnasse*, Parc de Montsouris, and *Cité Universitaire*.

15e;   Vaugirard: the area S.W. of the *Tour Montparnasse* and Av. de Suffren.

16e;   Passy: between the *Seine* and Bois de Boulogne, its N. half crossed by the Avenues Foch, Victor-Hugo, and Kléber, radiating from the *Étoile*, and containing the districts of Chaillot, Passy, and Auteuil.

17e;   Batignolles Monceau: the area N.W. of the *Étoile*.

18e;   Butte Montmartre: the area N.E. of the Pl. de Clichy, and reaching as far E. as the Rue d'Aubervilliers.

19e;   Buttes-Chaumont: and including the district of La Villette.

20e;   Ménilmontant: including *Père Lachaise*.

It must be admitted that few of the *banlieues* of Paris merit the attention of the visitor, unless he is interested in the cult of 'Urbanisme', but whatever one may feel about the usual vast schemes of 'aménagement' and 'rénovation' taking place in all areas, proceeding on a scale resulting too often in huge windswept spaces between ugly horizontal and/or vertical boxes, the efforts of the road engineers have been conspicuously successful.

Employment of Time

A good deal of Paris *itself* may be seen in a week by the energetic traveller, but this will allow only a superficial glance at some few treasures of its museums. With the information given on pp45–9, the visitor will be able to plan his campaign, and should have no difficulty, using the index and Atlas section, in choosing and following his own itinerary. The arrangement of routes has been designed to assist the less experienced traveller to explore the city systematically.

A list of convenient *Métro stations* is given at the beginning of most routes: see also Atlas, pp4–5.

For those with the time and curiosity, an interesting general view of parts of Paris may be had, for the price of a single ticket, by taking the Métro at the *Étoile* (for example, or indeed anywhere on Ligne 6), direction *Nation*; there changing onto Ligne 2, direction *Porte Dauphine* (two stops beyond *Étoile*). In this way, because much of the journey is made *over*ground rather than under, one can get a glimpse of certain areas which one would not otherwise have any particular reason for visiting. The journey can of course be made in the reverse direction.

For those spending only a short time in Paris it is perhaps advisable to visit first the *Cité* (Rte 1), before crossing to the Left Bank, where one might concentrate on the 'Quartier Latin' (including the *Musée de Cluny*) and the Faubourg St-Germain (Rtes 2 and 5); nor should the *Invalides* be overlooked (Rte 7).

Crossing to the Right Bank, one may follow Rte 8 (including the *Musée des Arts Décoratifs*) to the *Louvre*, the contents of which are described in Rte 9. One may combine Rte 10 with a view of the *Madeleine* and the *Opéra*, but of more interest is the *Marais* (Rte 12; including the *Pl. des Vosges* and the *Musée Carnavalet*), while at least the *Musée d'Art Moderne* at the *Centre Pompidou* should be seen (Rte 11). It must be emphasised, however, that this recommended itinerary will only provide an imperfect view of the capital, and each visitor will have his own priorities and preferences.

As far as the *environs* are concerned, perhaps the most important routes are those concentrating on *Versailles* itself (Rte 21); on *Écouen* and *Chantilly* (Rte 24), which might—time permitting—be combined with a visit to *Senlis* (Rte 25); *Fontainebleau* (Rte 31), which may include an excursion to *Provins* (Rte 29); *Chartres* (Rte 33C); and *Beauvais* (Rte 38). In most cases they may be approached directly and rapidly by motorways.

Hotels and Restaurants

Hotels of every class, size, and price abound in Paris, but it is prudent to book rooms in advance either directly or through a travel agency, for they are often full during the tourist season, particularly at Easter and during the course of Exhibitions, Trade Fairs, etc. Branches of the *Office de Tourisme de Paris* (see p43) will, endeavour to make on-the-spot bookings, which are automatically cancelled if not taken up within 1½ hours. They can also provide an up-to-date *Guide des Hôtels* for Paris and region. Among other useful lists is that published by *Michelin*, entitled *Paris et sa banlieue: Hôtels et Restaurants*, which includes the better-known and well-equipped hotels by arrondissements.

Those visiting the environs are recommended to acquire the *latest* edition of any of the annual publications of *Michelin, Kléber, Gault-Millau*, the *Logis de France*, or the *Guide des Relais Routiers*, among others, which will be found useful in the selection of accommodation and restaurants to suite the individual's taste and purse. Local S.I.s can also provide a brochure listing hotels in their area. It is wise, during certain seasons, to book in advance if a weekend excursion is planned.

The availability of accommodation is *not* indicated in this Guide, there being a wide range of every category in the area described. For hotels for the disabled, see p43.

All **Hotels** are officially classified by the *Direction de Tourisme*, and their grading is shown by stars, depending on their amenities and the type of hotel, from 4-stars 'L' (Luxury) to 1-star (plain but comfortable). Hot and cold running water will be found in all bedrooms, but only a proportion of hotels in the 1-, 2-, and even 3-star categories have rooms with a private bath and W.C. en suite, although many more will provide a shower and bidet. Similarly, many hotels have no restaurant, although almost all will provide a continental breakfast: but see below.

Charges vary, of course, according to the grade of hotel and the time of year, being at their highest from mid-June to mid-Sept. In most hotels (especially when quoting 'en pension' terms) 15 per cent is now added to the bill for 'service'—whether provided or not—and certainly when the bill is marked 'service et taxes compris' (s.t.c.) no additional gratuity is expected.

Most of the more expensive hotels in Paris are situated in the 1st, 6–10th, and 16–17th arrondissements, although a number of large establishments have been built at some considerable distance from the centre (which may be all very well for groups and those attending Trade Fairs, etc.), but inconvenient for the tourist, and it is advisable to make certain in advance as to the exact situation of the hotel in question before booking; and likewise, in his own interest, the traveller should have a very precise understanding as to the charge before taking possession of his room, particularly in view of the fact that too many appear to be geared to the 'expense-account' visitor. Valuables should be deposited with the management in exchange for a receipt.

Restaurants of every kind and category are plentiful in Paris, and have likewise been officially graded to indicate that they adhere to certain criteria. Although the prices tend to be comparatively high, very often (but by no means always) one will obtain better value for money than in some other countries who do not take the ritual and etiquette of eating so seriously, and who are prepared to accept lower standards.

At most restaurants the day's set menu, 'à prix fixe', is available, with a certain choice of dishes, and at a much lower price than 'à la carte', even if somewhat unimaginative in the more modest establishments; and this is displayed, with prices, at the entrance, and should be perused in advance. Frequently there is more than one selected menu to choose from, apart from the recommended 'plat du jour', even if the cheapest is so uninspired that the client is thus obliged to take one at a higher price.

The **wine**, either *rouge*, *blanc*, or *rosé*, in bottles or carafes, is usually very fair at most restaurants, while many can provide a liberal choice of superior wines at relatively high prices. When dining à la carte, the traveller should not allow the suggestions of the waiter, however plausible, to add more dishes to the menu than he really wants, for the slightest additions (of vegetables, for example) can easily swell the bill by a disproportionate amount. The bill (*l'addition*), which should be carefully scrutinised, should be in writing; the normal 15 per cent gratuity is now usually included in the price of a set menu; this is not so if one has chosen à la carte, but any misunderstanding can be avoided by asking 'Le service est-il compris?'. If no gratuity has been included, the waiter may be rewarded with some 10–12 per cent of the bill, according to the quality of service: less where a considerable proportion of the total is for a single bottle; but see also *Tipping*, p53.

There are, of course, a number of French gastronomic guides (see above) listing a great range of eating-places in Paris and elsewhere in France, among them the better-known 'de luxe' restaurants where French cookery *should* reach its perfection—at a price which few can afford—but it must be admitted that the traveller without inside knowledge will often have better value for his money at the less pretentious establishments.

Unfortunately there is a tendency, particularly in areas frequented by tourists rather than by a regular clientele, to serve stereotyped meals of a mediocre quality for the prices charged. Some restaurants, which can easily be avoided, also assume that piped music is conducive to a better appetite. It will be noticed that many restaurants are closed on Sundays, and (in Paris) during August. It is advisable to book a table in advance at the better-known or more fashionable restaurants.

The many **Cafés** of Paris—there were said to be as many as 300 as early as 1715 (although the custom of drinking coffee had only been introduced by the Turkish ambassador, Soliman-Aga, in 1667)—are more numerous in the larger streets and squares of Paris (and usually in or near the main 'Place' of most towns in the environs). In many cases tables and chairs are set out on the adjacent pavement (known as the 'terrasse')—or behind a glazed conservatory/observatory—where the customer may spend an entertaining hour watching the passers-by. The *café* or *café crème* is usually very good, but tea-making is still a perfunctory performance. A 'Continental breakfast' or 'petit déjeuner' may be obtained in the mornings at many cafés, with fresh rolls, croissants, or brioches, and butter, with coffee—less frequently—chocolate.

The usual order for a small beer is a *demi*; draught beer is à la pression. It is cheaper to stand at the bar; prices are automatically raised if one subsequently takes a seat. The waiter should not be paid after each drink, but just prior to the time one wishes to leave. Travellers are warned that the prices charged at some pretentious cafés or patisseries for a mere coffee, beer, vin ordinaire, or other beverage, are quite exorbitant, and it is always as well to check before ordering, to avoid an unpleasant shock.

The standard of toilet facilities in restaurants, brasseries, bistros, bars, and cafés, is improving; they are not all the Stygian bogs they once were, but towels (paper or otherwise) are often hard to come by. However, when there is reason for complaint—likewise in hotels—

travellers should not hesitate to do so, both to the proprietor and the next S.I. they pass.

Postal and Other Services

Most **Post Offices**, indicated by the sign **P.T.T.**, are open from 8.00 to 19.00 on weekdays, and until 12.00 on Sat. The main Post Office in Paris is at the Hôtel des Postes, 52 Rue du Louvre, 1er, which provides a 24-hour service in some departments, while that at 71 Av. des Champs-Elysées, 8e, is open from 8.00 until 23.00. At both branches are English-speaking hostesses who can help with postal queries. The former is the destination of all letters, etc. marked merely 'Poste Restante, Paris', without any arrondissement number being given. When this has been added, the head post office in the appropriate district should be visited. Correspondence marked 'poste restante' may be addressed to any post office, and is handed to the addressee on proof of identity (passport preferable). Letters may be sent registered ('recommandé') for a small fee, and are likewise not delivered without proof of identity.

Telegrams in English may be telephoned to 2332111. There are *Telex* offices at 7 Rue Feydeau and 9 Pl. de la Bourse, both 2e. Telex messages may be telephoned to 2471212.

Letter-boxes are painted yellow. Postage-stamps (*timbres*) are on sale at all post offices and most tobacconists.

Among other services, that of the *pneumatiques* (peculiar to Paris) may be mentioned as a much cheaper way of sending messages within Paris and suburbs, which is almost as rapid as a telegram. Both letters and 'cartes télégrammes' may be transmitted by these pneumatic tubes, and should be posted in special letter-boxes so marked.

Telephones. The telephone service in France has been much improved. Public call-boxes may be found at most post offices, métro stations, cafés, restaurants, and at some bus stops (taxiphones). With patience and sufficient small change, one should have little difficulty in making the right connection. Paris is in S.T.D. communication with the British Isles, and most of Europe, etc. Reversed-charge calls ('P.V.C.') are accepted. Some call-box instruments are constructed to take 'jetons' only, which have to be bought at the counter near which the telephone is installed. Note that the charge for calls made from hotels may be as much as 40 per cent higher than for those made from public telephone boxes. When calling abroad, one must wait after dialling the prefix 19 (international) for a change in the dialling tone before continuing. When calling the Provinces from Paris, the prefix 16 is first dialled.

The normal tariff applies from 8.00–18.00 on weekdays, and until 14.00 on Sat. It is 30 per cent less between 18.00–21.30 Mon.–Fri.; 50 per cent less between 6.00–8.00, and 21.30–23.00 Mon.–Fri., 6.00–8.00, and 14.00–23.00 on Sat., and 6.00–23.00 on Sun. The charge is 50 per cent less between 23.00–8.00 daily (or rather, nightly); these reductions only apply within France.

Information Bureaux. The *Office de Tourisme de Paris*, with its headquarters at 127 Av. des Champs-Elysées, open daily from 9.00 to 22.00 (until 20.00 in Winter, and until 18.00 or 20.00 on Sun.), has a patient and helpful English-speaking staff. These long-suffering blue-uniformed 'hostesses' endeavour to answer most general queries concerning Paris and the environs (apart from giving information on the rest of France). Otherwise known as *Le Bureau Central d'Accueil* ('Welcome' reception office), it has subsidiary branches at the Gare d'Austerlitz, Gare de l'Est, Gare du Nord, Gare de Lyon, and in summer at the *Tour Eiffel*.

A more central office near the Louvre may be opened in the not too distant future, which should supercede the *municipal* office in the N. vestibule of the *Hôtel de Ville*, 29 Rue de Rivoli, 4e.

For a comparatively small charge, depending on the category of hotel, they will book accommodation in Paris, and from the head office, by telex, in the provinces. They will supply visitors with leaflets giving information about temporary exhibitions, entertainment, inexpensive restaurants, swimming pools, etc., etc. They are *not* set up to give detailed information concerning train timetables, etc., and regrettably the Travel Agency sharing accommodation with them at 127 Av. des Champs-Elysées are reluctant to help the prospective traveller requiring such information, a situation which it is hoped will be put right.

Students and young people generally may also find the following organisations of assistance: *Service d'Accueil aux Étudiants Étrangers*, 13 Rue de Vaugirard, 6e; the *Centre d'Information et de Documentation Jeunesse*, 101 Quai Branly, 15e; the *Office du Tourisme Universitaire*, 137 Blvd St-Michel, 5e; the *Accueil des Jeunes en France* (A.J.F.) at 12 Rue des Barres, 4e, with branches at the Plateau Beaubourg, 119 Rue St-Martin, 4e, at the Gare du Nord (opposite quai 19), and at the Hôtel de Ville, 16 Rue du Pont Louis Philippe, 4e; *Union des Centres de Rencontrers Internationales de France* (UCRIF), 21 Rue Béranger, 3e, and at the Gare du Nord. They will also find 'The Young Traveller's Guide to France' (Duo Publishing) full of useful information.

Most of the towns in the environs of Paris have a local *Syndicat d'Initiative* (indicated in this Guide by the initials S.I.). They often provide useful information with regard to accommodation (without actually recommending specific hotels), local events, etc.

Medical Services. Hospitals with English-speaking staff: the *British Hospital (Hertford)*, 48 Rue de Villiers, N.W. of the Porte de Champerret, with an entirely new wing; and the *American Hospital*, 63 Blvd Victor-Hugo, Neuilly. In an emergency, dial 17 for the *Police*, and 15 for SAMU (Service Aide Médicale d'Urgence).

The *Pharmacie Anglaise* is at 62 Av. des Champs-Élysées, 8e; other chemists (indicated by a *green* cross) open daily are the *Pharmacie des Arts*, 106 Blvd du Montparnasse, 14e; *Pharmacie Mozart*, 14 Av. Mozart, 16e; and the *Pharmacie du Départ*, 3 Rue du Départ, 14e.

The Disabled. The French are to be highly commended for their consideration for the disabled, and those who have difficulties in coping with hotels might find the solution to their problem at a hostel run by the *Association des Paralysés de France*, 17 Blvd Auguste-Blanqui, 13e. The disabled person can have a single room or, sharing with an able-bodied helper, a studio equipped with cooking facilities, refrigerator, shower, and wash-basin. The warden and his wife are available at all times (and will even supply meals if due notice is given); and there is an underground lock-up garage. Lifts and special lavatories are provided for those in wheelchairs.

Disabled people will find 'Access in Paris' useful. It is available from 'The Paris Survey Project', 68b Castlebar Road, Ealing, London W5. Helpful advice can also be given by the Central Council for the Disabled, 34 Eccleston Sq., SW1.

Lost Property Office. Articles lost on the Métro or in buses (in which case they are held for claiming for the first 48 hours at the terminus of the route concerned), in the street, theatres or cinemas, etc., should be enquired for at the *Bureau des Objets Trouvés*, 36 Rue des Morillons, 15e (open Mon.–Fri., 8.30–17.00 and on Thurs. until 20.00 except July–Aug.); the nearest Métro is *Convention*. Property lost on trains, at stations, on planes and airports should be reclaimed at the Lost Property office of the terminus or airport in question.

Museums, Collections, and Monuments

A table giving hours of admission, etc. is printed below, but it should be noted that the times shown are liable to be changed without warning, or the collection may be closed owing to a strike of guardians, for instance. As a general rule, the *National Museums are closed on Tuesdays*, and the *Municipal Museums are closed on Mondays*. Some museums are closed on public holidays (jours fériès), and on such days it is wise to check in advance to avoid disappointment. The convenience of guardians rather than of the interested visitor being the governing factor, most museums—with some enlightened exceptions—still open late and close early, and in addition, particularly in the environs, but also in Paris, may be shut between the sacred hours of 12.00–14.00 (sometimes 15.00). This also applies in the case of some churches, and other monuments. In many cases the admission fee is reduced on Sundays, when in a few cases entry may be free (but the museum may also be uncomfortably crowded, as the Centre Pompidou is most of the time).

Lecture tours are organised by several bodies; those promoted by the *Caisse Nationale des Monuments Historiques* (who also publish a number of informative guides, and edit a bi-monthly magazine entitled 'Musées et monuments historiques') are listed in a bi-monthly leaflet entitled 'Musées, Expositions, Monuments de Paris et de l'Île de France', obtainable from the Hôtel de Sully, 62 Rue St-Antoine, 3e; the Bureau d'Action Culturelle de la Direction des Musées de France, Palais du Louvre, 34 Quai du Louvre, 1er; and Tourist Offices, etc. A list of such visits will also be found in some newspapers.

No advance application is normally necessary: the visitor merely goes to the place indicated at the time stated, and pays a fee. The group is conducted by a competent official French-speaking guide-lecturer; Guided tours by English-speaking lecturers may be arranged. See also under *Versailles*, etc.

It may be remarked that visitors coming from countries where they are used to entering museums free of charge may sometimes baulk at paying the fee imposed. In fact, in many cases, the charge is in no way disproportionate to the size and quality of the collections to be seen, an increasing number of which are being reformed and displayed with imagination and taste. Unfortunately this is not always so, and the same charge can apply to museums and monuments whose conservateurs appear to remain unconcerned as to whether they are giving value for money, and who are insensitive to the comparative excellence of other collections.

It may also be mentioned that although considerable work seems to have gone into the preparation and production of lavishly illustrated catalogues, selling at high prices, of *temporary* exhibitions, few of the important museums—perhaps because so many of them are undergoing drastic change—publish good general catalogues or inventories of their *permanent* collections of use to the discriminating visitor, for whom the few 'Publications scientifiques' available are both too detailed and highly priced, and who find the slighter booklets too superficial, a situation which it is hoped will be improved before too long. Indeed, there are signs of this, with the recent publication by the *Editions de la Réunion des musées nationaux* of a 'catalogue sommaire illustré des peintures du musée du Louvre', which is issued in three volumes. A list of catalogues in print by this organisation is available from the bookstalls of any of the national museums. The catalogue of the Musée Cognacq-Jay (Peintures et Dessins), published by the Ville de Paris, is likewise exemplary.

Hours of Admission to the Principal Museums, Collections, and Monuments

With the exception of the *Musée Rodin*, this list does not include collections devoted to individual artists or sculptors, for which see Index. The more important are indicated by bold type. Some museums will not allow entry some 45 minutes before closing time—even in mid-morning, prior to their lunchtime closure! Sections of some museums may be closed at times other than those indicated; some will remain open later during Summer months. Many are closed on Bank Holidays (*jours fériés*).

NAME, AND ADDRESS	OPEN	CLOSED	DESCRIBED ON PAGE
Art Moderne de la Ville de Paris 11 Av. Prés.-Wilson, 16e	10.00-17.30 10.00-20.30 on Wed.	Mon.	215
Arts Africains 293 Av. Daumesnil, 12e	9.45-12.00; 13.30-17.15	Tues.	235
Arts Décoratifs 107 Rue de Rivoli, 1er	rebuilding in progress, but open for temporary exhibitions	Tues.	120
Arts et Traditions Populaires 6 Rte du Mahatma-Gandhi (Bois de Boulogne)	10.00-17.15	Tues.	224
Beaubourg: *see* **Pompidou**			
Cabinet des Médailles, Bibliothèque Nationale 58 Rue de Richelieu, 2e	12.00-17.00	—	157

Carnavalet 23 Rue de Sévigné, 3e	10.00-17.40	Mon.	183
Cernuschi 7 Av. Velasquez, 8e	10.00-17.40	Mon.	212
Chasse 60 Rue des Archives, 3e	10.00-17.30	Tues.	187
Cinema Palais de Chaillot, 16e	10.00-17.30	—	219
Cluny 6 Pl. Paul-Painlevé, 5e	9.45-12.30;14.00-17.15	Tues.	74
Cognac-Jay 23 Blvd des Capucines, 2e	10.00-17.40	Mon.	193
Conciergerie 1 Quai de l'Horloge, 4e	10.00-18.00	—	56
Ennery 59 Av. Foch, 16e	14.00–17.00 Sun. & Thurs.	—	224
Guimet 6 Pl. d'Iéna, 16e	9.45-12.00; 13.30-17.15	Tues.	216
Hôtel de Soubise (Archives Nationales) 60 Rue des Francs- Bourgeois, 3e	14.00-17.00	Tues.	186
Homme, Musée de l' Palais de Chaillot, 16e	9.45–17.15	Tues.	220
Instrumental 14 Rue de Madrid, 8e	14.00-16.00 Sun.–Tues.	—	201
Invalides, Les (Musée de l'Armée) Esplanade des Invalides, 7e	10.00-17.00/18.00	—	105
Jacquemart-André 158 Blvd Haussmann, 8e	13.30-17.30	Mon. & Tues.	210
Jardin des Plantes 57 Rue Cuvier, 5e	(see text)	Tues. but zoo open daily	77
Jeu de Paume (Impressionnisme) Pl. de la Concorde, 1er	9.45-17.15	Tues.	114
Louvre, Musée du Palais du Louvre, 1er	9.45-17.15 / 18.30	Tues.	124
Marine Palais de Chaillot, 16e	10.00-18.00	Tues.	219
Marmottan 2 Rue Louis-Boilly, 16e	10.00-18.00	Mon.	221
Mode et du Costume, La Palais Galliéra, 16e	10.00-17.40	Mon.	214
Monuments Français Palais de Chaillot, 16e	9.45-12.30; 14.00-17.15	Tues.	218
Nissim de Camondo 63 Rue de Monceau, 8e	10.00-12.00; 14.00- 17.00	Mon. & Tues.	211

Notre-Dame, Crypte Archéologique	10.00-18.00	—	60
Orsay, Musée d'	(see text)		97
Palais de Tokyo 13 Av. Prés.-Wilson, 16e	9.45-17.15	Tues.	215
Panthéon Pl. du Panthéon, 5e	10.00-12.30; 14.00–18.00	—	69
Petit-Palais Av. Winston Churchill, 8e	10.00-17.40	Mon.	206
Picasso			188
Pompidou, Centre (CNAC),	12.00-22.00 10.00-22.00 Sat. & Sun.	Tues.	165 4e
Postal museum 34 Blvd Vaugirard, 15e	10.00-17.00	Sun.	84
Rodin, Musée 77 Rue de Varenne, 7e	10.00-17.45	Tues.	100-1
Sainte-Chapelle Blvd du Palais, 4e	10.00-17.00	—	59
Serrure, La (locksmiths) 1 Rue de la Perle, 3e	10.00-12.00; 14.00-17.00	Mon. & Tues.	188
Techniques (Science museum) 270 Rue St-Martin, 3e	13.00–17.30 10.00-17.15 on Sun.	Mon.	190
Vincennes, Château de	10.00-18.00	—	233

Environs of Paris

Champs, Château de	10.00-12.00; 13.30-17.30/18.00	Tues. & Wed.	287
Chantilly (Musée Condé)	10.00-18.00	Tues.	267
Compiègne, Château de	9.30-12.00; 13.30-17.00	Tues.	276
Écouen, Château de (Musée de la Renaissance)	9.45-12.30; 14.00-17.15	Tues.	265
Fontainebleau, Château de	9.30-12.30; 14.00-17.00 Petits Appartements open Sat. & Sun. only.	Tues.	298
Maisons, Château de	9.00–12.00; 14.00–18.00	Tues. & Sun. morn.	261
Malmaison and *Bois-Préau*	10.00-12.30; 13.30-17.30	Tues.	258
Nemours, Prehistory of the Île-de-France	10.00–12.00; 14.00–17.00	Tues.	305

St-Denis, Basilique de	10.00-17.30	—	262
St-Denis, Musée d'Art	10.00-18.00 14.00-18.30 on Sun.	Tues.	264
St-Germain-en-Laye (Musée des Antiquités Nationales)	9.45-12.00; 13.30-17.15	Tues.	260
Sceaux, Château de (Musée de l'Île de France) (see text)		Tues.	306
Sèvres, Céramique de	9.30-12.00; 13.30-17.15	Tues.	238
Vaux-le-Vicomte, Château de	10.00-18.00 from April-Oct. 14.00-17.00 on Sat. & Sun. at other times		293
Versailles, Château de	9.45-17.30	Mon.	243
Grand Trianon	9.45-17.30	Mon.	254
Petit Trianon	14.00-17.30	Sat. & Sun.	256

Note. Readers are recommended to check in advance with an S.I. or Tourist Office with regard to the days and hours of admission to other monuments, museums, and châteaux in the environs, many of which will be closed on Tues., and some also on Wed., or in Winter months, etc., otherwise they may be disappointed.

Although this table includes many of the principal attractions of Paris and environs, it by no means exhausts the list of things to see or the heights to which one can ascend (such as the terrace of the *Arc de Triomphe*, the *Tour Montparnasse*, or *Tour Eiffel*, etc.). The visitor is reminded of the following additional points of interest, to mention a few only which deserve a visit, details of which will be found in the text. In **Paris**: the *Arènes de Lutèce*; the *Palais-Royal; Palais Luxembourg; Palais de Justice*; the *Hôpital St-Louis*, and *Hôpital de la Salpêtrière*; *École Militaire*; and the churches of *La Madeleine*, *Val-de-Grâce*, *St-Eustache*, *St-Étienne-du-Mont*, *St-Germain-l'Auxerrois*, *St-Germain-des-Près*, *St-Roch*, *St-Médard*, *St-Séverin*, *St-Sulpice*, *Ste-Ursule de la Sorbonne*; the cemeteries of *Père Lachaise*, *Montmartre*, *Montparnasse*, and *Picpus*; the *Pl. Vendôme* and *Pl. des Vosges*, without listing individually the numerous hôtels of the Marais and the Faubourg St-Germain.

The cemeteries are normally open from 7.30 to 18.00 in summer, and from 8.00 to 17.00 in winter; that of *Picpus* is open during the afternoon only.

Among the outstanding buildings of interest in the **environs** of Paris which should be visited, one may mention: the churches of *Morienval*, *St-Leu-d'Esserent*, or *St-Loup-de-Noud*; the châteaux at *Dampierre*, *Maintenon*, or *Rosny-sur-Seine*; but throughout the whole region of the Île de France those that merit a detour are legion.

An up-to-date brochure giving **times of admission** to some châteaux and gardens open to the public may be obtained from *La*

Demeure Historique, 55 Quai de la Tournelle, 5e; *Vieilles Maisons Françaises*, 93 Rue de l'Universite, 7e, can likewise provide similar information, and the *Caisse Nationale des Monuments Historiques*, 62 Rue St Antoine, 4e, publishes 'Ouvert au Public'.

Examples of medieval architecture range from the Merovingian crypt at *Jouarre* to the cathedrals of *Sens* and *Évreux*, and to the even greater churches at *Chartres* and *Beauvais*; the impressive ruins of *Royaumont, Longpont*, or *St-Jean-des-Vignes* (Soissons); the imperious ramparts of *Gisors*, or *Château-Gaillard*; the agreeable towns of *Senlis, Montfort-l'Amaury*, or *Provins*, are among the more obvious. the area is rich indeed, and the historical associations are endless.

Unfortunately, as in every country, certain sites are spoiled by the sheer density of tourists congregating in their vicinity, but once beyond the suburbs of Paris and the other towns in its neighbourhood, the attractions of the landscape of the Île de France offer a welcome relief, and forest tracts, wooded valleys, and fertile agricultural land extend in every direction.

A torch, and a pair of binoculars, will be found useful equipment when exploring the recesses of churches and cathedrals, and perusing the details of capitals and stained-glass windows, etc.

Entertainment

Topical information about theatres, cinemas, cabarets, night clubs, 'manifestations', 'sporting' events, fairs, exhibitions, etc., are advertised in the Press, or may be found in any of the magazines and guides' devoted to What's On, among them *'Pariscope', 'L'Officiel des Spectacles', 'Paris selection'* (with an English text), etc., available from most tourist offices, agents, and kiosks.

Theatres. The National, or State-subsidised, theatres are the *Comédie-Française*, Pl. André-Malraux, 1er; the *Théâtre de France* (de l'Odéon), Pl. Paul-Claudel, 6e; *Théâtre National Populaire* (TNP), Palais de Chaillot, 16e; *Théâtre de l'Est Parisien* (TEP), 17 Rue Malte-Brun, 20e; *Théâtre de la Ville* and *Théâtre Musical de Paris* (TMP), the latter devoted to ballet, and concerts (see below), both in the Pl. du Châtelet, 4e; and the 'Théâtre Lyrique', better known as the *Opéra*, Pl. de l'Opéra, 9e (see Rte 13). The once-famous *Opéra-Comique* is now used as an experimental theatre.

Some smaller establishments, *Music Halls, Chansonniers*, etc., also survive, often devoted to revues of no very refined nature. Many specialise in political satire, for there are targets in plenty (comp. 'Le Canard Enchaîné', a periodical wittier than most), but these can only be appreciated by those with a fairly thorough knowledge of the language and the latest *argot*.

Few **Cabarets** leave much to the imagination, although some purport to offer 'artistic performances', and attempt to provide something to suit all tastes in their entertainment, from the exotic (or simply *érotique*) to the grossly vulgar; but the curious visitor is warned that the announcement of *entrée libre* (free admission) to any of these *boîtes*, night-clubs, and other 'tourist traps' simply means that the price of admission is added to the already exorbitant charge for *'consommations'* which he is expected to order. The obscure world of *'dancings'*, *Cafés-théâtres*, *discothéques*, and what not, lies outside the scope of this Guide.

Cinemas of all types, many of the larger converted to show various films in the same building, abound—Paris claims to contain 500—and most of them run continuously from 12.00. Many of them are devoted to 'porno', in a variety of shades of 'bleu'. Programmes normally change on Wednesdays. Prices charged in the better-known cinemas are high, and yet ushers still expect a tip, although the practice is frequently ignored. The same applies in theatres.

Many theatres close for some weeks in the summer, and on one evening a week, usually Mon. or Tues. *Smoking is forbidden.* Note that tickets bought through an agency will cost as much as 25 per cent more than at the box-office of the theatre concerned, usually open between 11.00 and 18.30 or 19.00.

Concerts take place at the *Théâtre des Champs-Elysées*, 15 Av. Montaigne; the restored *Théâtre Musical de Paris*, Pl. du Châtelet; *Salle Gaveau*, 45 Rue La Boétie; *Salle Pleyel*, 252 Rue du Faubourg-St-Honoré; *Salle Cortot*, 78 Rue Cardinet; the *Palais de Chaillot*, Pl. du Trocadero; the *Maison de l'ORTF* (or 'de la Radio'), 116 Av. du Président-Kennedy; and at the *Palais des Congrès*, Porte Maillot, and elsewhere.

Church Music and *Organ Recitals* can be heard to advantage at Notre-Dame, St-Eustache, St-Germain-des-Prés, St-Louis des Invalides, St-Séverin, St-Sulpice, St-Roch, St-Clotilde, St-Étienne-du-Mont, and the Madeleine, among other churches, and any special concerts are usually well advertised.

Art Exhibitions. Although smaller shows devoted to individual artists can be seen at any number of galleries and art-dealers' shops, many of them in the 6e arrondissement, the more important temporary exhibitions are held in the *Grand Palais, Petit-Palais, Palais de Tokyo, Musée des Arts Décoratifs*, etc., while the *Centre National d'Art et de Culture Georges Pompidou* (CNAC, or *Centre Beaubourg*) is now an important focus of exhibitions of modern art, 'pop' and otherwise, etc.

General Information

Directories. Almost any address may be turned up in 'Le Bottin' (the *Annuaire-Almanach du Commerce et de l'Industrie Didot-Bottin*, to give its full title), which may be consulted at post offices, hotels, restaurants, shops, etc., where a notice may be displayed: 'Ici on consulte le Bottin'. Residential and official addresses may be found also in the 'Bottin Mondain'. *Le Bottin* was initiated in 1819 by Sébastien Bottin (1764–1853), who took over an earlier *Almanach du Commerce* founded in 1798. At Bottin's death it merged with the *Annuaire général du commerce* published by Didot. Although a somewhat ponderous example of Gallic methodology, it can be found useful on occasions.

Season. The main characteristic of the weather in Paris is changeability, particularly in the winter and spring, although long periods of fine weather occur each year. Perhaps because of its long wide boulevards, which sometimes act as wind tunnels, the wind is more noticeable than in London, and bitterly cold blasts can be experienced in some quarters during certain seasons, and it can remain cold until well after Easter. Its mean temperature is 11·6°C; only for a few days a year does it become oppressively hot (30°C). The average number of days a year on which the temperature falls below freezing-point is about 35; the number of days of snowfall has averaged 15 in recent decades. In spring and autumn, although the days are shorter, the weather is better adapted for the active sightseer, for in summer (June–Aug.) Paris is packed with tourists, although in Aug. the city is deserted by a high proportion of its regular residents, and many of the theatres, libraries, etc., and even restaurants, are closed.

Language. The visitor who knows no language but English can usually get along without too much trouble in Paris, although he will probably pay in cash for his ignorance. Any *attempt* to speak some French is always appreciated.

Manners. Forms of politeness in France are still less casual than in some other countries, and there is more handshaking at meeting and parting. It is also polite to use 'Monsieur', 'Madame', or 'Mademoiselle' as a form of address (without the surname) even after some acquaintance, but such standing on ceremony is becoming progressively relaxed in most circles.

Public Holidays. 1 Jan. (*Jour de l'An*; gifts—*étrennes* —exchanged); Easter Monday; Whit Monday (*Pentecôte*); Ascension Day; 1 May (with Lily of the Valley sold in the streets); 8 May (commemorating the end of the war in Europe); 14 July (Fête Nationale); 15 Aug. (*Assomption*); 1 Nov. (*Toussaint*; All Saints' Day); 11 Nov. (Armistice Day); and 25 Dec. (*Noël*; Christmas). Banks are likely to shut at noon on days preceding public holidays.

Shopping, and **Markets**. Many of the smartest and most expensive shops are to be found in the 1er, 6e, 8e, and 16e arrondissements, particularly in the area of the Rue du Faubourg-St-Honoré, but in fact good shops and departmental stores (among which are *Les Galeries Lafayette* and *Au Printemps*, at 40 and 69 Blvd Haussmann respectively) can be found in most districts of central Paris, and their prices are usually less extravagant. Many of the Antique shops and *brocanteurs* (second-hand dealers) are to be found in the 6e, while the so-called *Village Suisse* (shut Tues.–Wed.; W. of the École

Militaire), and the extensive *Marché aux Puces* (open Sat.–Mon.; a few minutes walk N. of the Porte de Clignancourt Métro), attract crowds in search of the rare bargain among the bric-à-brac. A recent attraction is the *Louvre des Antiquaires* (see Rte 11), between the Palais du Louvre and Palais-Royal.

Auctions are held regularly at the rebuilt *Salle Drouot*, 6 Rue Rossini, 9e. Nearby, in the Rue Drouot and further S. in the arcades of the Palais-Royal, are the haunts of philatelists; while an open-air *Stamp Market* is held at weekends and Thurs. mornings at the junction of the Av. de Marigny and Av. Gabriel. Other colourful markets are devoted to *flowers*: in the Pl. Louis-Lépine (not far E. of the Conciergerie), on the E. side of the Madeleine, and at the Pl. des Ternes, and Pl. de la République. On Sundays the flowers of the Pl. Louis-Lépine give way to a *Bird* Market, while opposite, on the Quai de la Mégisserie, is a *Pet* Market (not Sun.).

On the N. side of the Pl. de la Madeleine some superbly displayed food shops may be seen, although less sumptuous establishments will tempt the eye and palate throughout Paris; indeed, one of the great pleasures of wandering about the city is the quality and display of the merchandise seen in many of the smaller shops selling cheese, *patisserie*, or *charcuterie*.

Food markets not too far from the centre may be visited in the Rue de Montorgueil (leading N. from Les Halles Métro); the Rue Mouffetard, 5e; Rue des Martyrs, 9e; Rue de Lévis (N.E. of the Parc de Monceau); Rue Cler, 7e; and Rue Buci (just N. of the Odéon Métro); and there are of course many others. Food shopping on a Sunday morning at one of the street markets of Paris is almost always an agreeable occupation.

Bookshops and Libraries. The former continue to proliferate throughout central Paris, but differ widely in the range of books stocked, and in the quality of their service. English newspapers and magazines can be found at a price at many kiosks near the centre. A selection of books in English is provided by *Brentano* (37 Av. de l'Opéra), *Galignani* (224 Rue de Rivoli: near the Tuileries Métro), *W.H.Smith* (248 Rue de Rivoli; also with a teashop), among others.

The Library of the *British Institute* is at 9 Rue du Constantine, on the E. side of the Esplanade des Invalides. There is an *American Library* at 10 Rue de Gén. Camou, 7e.

Working Hours, etc. It will be found that in France work starts earlier than in the U.K., and generally meals are also begun at an earlier hour. Although there is a movement towards the 'English' week-end, most food shops are open on Sunday mornings, and remain open later on weekday evenings; but they are likely to be shut on Mondays.

Sports. General information about a variety of sporting events, sporting facilities, addresses of tennis-clubs, squash-courts, golf-courses, swimming-pools, etc. in Paris and environs, may be obtained from the *Office de Tourisme de Paris*, 127 Av. des Champs-Élysées, and its branches, and from the *Direction de la Jeunesse et des Sports*, 17 Blvd Morland, 4e.

They can also advise on the capacities of the French sporting federations to assist the visitor, who is recommended to apply well in advance to the offices of his *own* home club or sporting organisation (whether it be hunting, shooting, fishing, mountaineering, winter-sporting, fencing, rugger, sailing, polo, or hang-gliding, etc., which may be his interest): they may well be able to give more practical information.

Metric System. The decimal system of weights, measures, and coins, was legalized in France in 1801, and became obligatory in 1840. The *mètre* is the unit of length, the *gramme* of weight, the *are* of land-measurement, and the *litre* of capacity. Greek prefixes (*déca-, hecto-, kilo-, myria-*) are used with these names to express multiples; Latin prefixes (*déci-, centi-, milli-*) to express fractions: kilomètre = 1000 mètres; millimètres = 1000th part of a mètre.

For approximate calculations the mètre may be taken as 39 inches; the litre as 0·22 gallons or $1^3/_4$ pints; the hectare as $2^1/_2$ acres; 150 grammes as 5 oz.; and 5 kilomètres as 3 miles (or 8km as 5 miles).

Tipping. However anachronistic may be this stultifying system of rewarding waiters, taxi-drivers, cloakroom attendants, et al., who now invariably expect more than they merit for the quality of service often grudgingly given, it still persists. However, many restaurants and hotels have replaced it by adding 15 per cent (no less) to the bill, leaving little room for discussion, even when the 'service' has been indifferent or merely perfunctory.

Any serious irregularity should be reported, without compunction, to Tourist Offices, or to the director of the local S.I.

ILE DE LA CITE

0 yards 300
0 metres 300

Centre Beaubourg

Louvre

Faculté des Sciences

ILE ST LOUIS

ILE DE LA CITÉ

St-Germain-l'Auxerrois

Tour St-Jacques

St-Gervais St-Protais

Hôtel de Sens

St Paul — RUE ST-ANTOINE

Hôtel de Ville

Tourist Off

Hôtel de Ville

Chatelet — PLACE DU CHATELET

RIVOLI

RUE DE

Pont Neuf

Pont Neuf

St Michel

Hôtel des Monnaies

Pont au Change

Conciergerie

Palais de Justice

Sainte Chapelle

Tribunal de Commerce

Préfecture de Police

Pont Notre-Dame

Pont d'Arcole

Hôtel Dieu

Crypt
PL DU PARVIS
NOTRE-DAME

Notre-Dame

RUE DE LA CITÉ

Cité

RUE DE LUTÈCE

BOULEVARD DU PALAIS

QUAI DE L'HORLOGE

PLACE DAUPHINE

QUAI DES ORFÈVRES

Petit Pont

Pont St-Michel

BLVD. ST-MICHEL

St Severin

St Julien le Pauvre

Pont au Double

Pont de l'Archevêché

Pont de la Tournelle

Pont St-Louis

QUAI D'ORLÉANS

QUAI DE BÉTHUNE

QUAI DE LA TOURNELLE

BOULEVARD ST-GERMAIN

St Louis en l'Île

Pont Marie

Pont Louis-Philippe

Pont Marie

QUAI D'ANJOU

QUAI DE BOURBON

R. DES DEUX-PONTS

QUAI DE L'HÔTEL DE VILLE

QUAI DES CÉLESTINS

SQUARE H. GALLI

SQUARE BARYE

Pont Sully

RUE ST-LOUIS-EN-L'ÎLE

SQ. DE L'ÎLE DE FRANCE

Seine

QUAI DU LOUVRE

SQ. DU VERT-GALANT

PL. DU PONT NEUF

THE CITÉ AND THE ÎLE-ST-LOUIS

1 The Île de la Cité and the Île-St-Louis

MÉTROS: *Cité, St-Michel, Pont-Neuf, Châtelet, Pont-Marie, Sully-Morland.*

The **Île de la Cité** (Pl. 14; 2-4 and opposite), the earliest inhabited part of Paris, lies in the river like a ship, the 'Pointe' as its prow and *Notre-Dame* as its poop, moored to the banks by numerous bridges; and the freighted vessel on a sea argent, which has always figured in the arms of Paris, with the device 'fluctuat nec mergitur' (tossed but not engulfed), is indeed appropriate. The Cité was the site of the original Gallic settlement of Lutèce or Lutetia Parisiorum, and after the destruction of the later Roman city on the Left Bank, became the site of Frankish Paris.

It remained the royal, legal, and ecclesiastical centre long after the town had extended onto both river-banks, and for the visitor with but little time even a brief tour of the Cité will give a good idea of its importance in the historical development of Paris.

The Cité derives its importance from its situation at the crossroads of two natural routes across northern France. The Capetian kings were the great builders of the Cité, and it remained little changed from 1300 to the Second Empire, when Haussmann, after massive demolition, left it more or less with its present appearance.

From the QUAI DU LOUVRE the picturesque **Pont-Neuf** crosses the W. extremity of the island. It is, in spite of its name, the oldest existing bridge in Paris, begun by *Baptiste du Cerceau*, completed in 1607, and several times repaired since. It was also the first to be built without houses lining each side, and with pavements. This 'Pointe de la Cité' is occupied by the SQ. DU VERT-GALANT, so-called in allusion to the amorous adventures of Henri IV, a statue of whom, by *Lemot* (1818), stands adjacent, replacing another, by Giambologna and Tacca, which stood here from 1635 to 1792.

E. of the Pont-Neuf, entered by the Rue Henri-Robert, is the ***Pl. Dauphine**, retaining two rows of houses, some dating from the reign of Louis XIII, but many have been altered since. Unfortunately the E. wing of the triangle was demolished in 1874 to provide an unmerited view of *Louis Duc's* W. façade of the *Palais de Justice* (1857–68; see below).

During the 17th and 18C the PL. DU PONT-NEUF and the bridge swarmed with pedlars and mountebanks. Tabarin set up his 'théâtre' in the Pl. Dauphine. Here, too, was the original site of the *Samaritaine*, one of the earliest hydraulic pumps, constructed by a Fleming for Henri IV to supply water for the royal palaces of the Louvre and Tuileries. It derived its name from a figure of the Good Samaritan on the fountain.

Other bridges connecting the Cité to the Right Bank of the Seine are the *Pont au Change* (1858–59), replacing a stone bridge dating from 1639 lined with moneylenders' shops; the *Pont Notre-Dame* rebuilt in 1913 on the site of the main Roman Bridge; and beyond is the *Pont d'Arcole* (1855), named after a youth killed in 1830 leading insurgents against the Hôtel de Ville.

To the S., the Cité is connected to the Left Bank by the *Pont St-Michel*, rebuilt several times since the late 14C (last in 1857), affording a fine view of the façade of *Notre-Dame*. Beyond is the *Petit-Pont* (1853), on the site of another Roman bridge. Until 1782 it was defended at the S. end by the *Petit Châtelet*, the successor of the Tour de Bois, which in 886 held Norman marauders at bay. From the W. front of *Notre-Dame*, the *Pont-au-Double* (1882) replaced a mid 17C bridge, for crossing which the toll of a diminutive coin known as a 'double' was charged; while from the E. extremity of the Cité after skirting the cathedral, on the site of the archbishop's palace (pulled down in 1831), is the *Pont de l'Archevêché* (1828), providing a good view of the apse, with its profusion of flying buttresses.

Following the QUAI DE L'HORLOGE (N. of the *Palais de Justice*), and entered just beyond twin towers (see below), is the *CONCIER-GERIE(CN), oneof theworld's famous prisons, occupying part of the lower floor of the Palais, and originally the residence of the 'Concierge', chief executive of the Parlement.

Its historical associations are numerous. In 1418 the Comte d'Armagnac was massacred here with many of his partisans by the hired assassins of the Duc de Bourgogne. The Marquise de Brinvilliers, the poisoner, was held here. During the Revolution, Marie-Antoinette, Bailly, Malesherbes, Mme Élisabeth, Mme Roland, Mme du Barry, Camille Desmoulins, Charlotte Corday, Danton, André Chénier, and Robespierre passed their last days in the Conciergerie. 288 prisoners perished here in the massacres of Sept. 1792. Later prisoners were Georges Cadoudal (d. 1804) the Chouan leader, Marshal Ney, and the Duc d'Orléans (1890).

The *Salle des Gardes*, a handsome vaulted room of the 14C (restored 1877), where visitors await the guide, contains two stairs (no adm.) ascending (r.) to the *Tour de César*, where Ravaillac, the murderer of Henri IV, was imprisoned (1610); the other leads to the *Tour d'Argent*, which served as a prison for Damiens, who attempted to kill Louis XV (1757). The spiral staircase in the r.-hand corner as we leave the room was climbed by Marie-Antoinette and some 2275 other prisoners on their way from their cells to the Tribunal (see below).

The impressive four-aisled Gothic *Salle des Gens-d'Armes* (restored in 1868–80), was the original 'Salle des Pas-Perdus', said to be so called because the victims of the Revolution walked through it on their way to the Cour du Mai and execution; the name has since been transferred to the hall above (and to the waiting-rooms of other public buildings accommodating French functionaries).

Near the far end, to the l. a curious open spiral stair leads to the so-called *Cuisines de St-Louis* (14C), also vaulted, and with four huge fireplaces. Returning to the first bay, we turn l. past a grille flanking the Rue de Paris, reserved for the *'pailleux'* (prisoners who slept on straw, being unable to bribe their gaolers). We next enter the diminutive *Galerie des Prisonniers*, the windows of which look out onto the *Cour des Femmes* where the female prisoners took exercise, and also the scene of the massacres of Sept. 1792. A railing which still exists divided off a section for men. To the l. in the Gal. des Prisonniers was the cell where the condemned had their hair shorn and awaited the departure of the tumbril for the guillotine. At the end is the iron wicket which was the only entrance to the prison in Revolutionary times.

At the opposite end of this gallery is the original door (but in a different position) of Marie-Antoinette's cell, where the queen remained from 2 Aug. to 16 Oct. 1793. Adjacent, and now communicating with it, is Robespierre's cell.

Staircase in the interior of the Conciergerie

Next comes the *Chapel* (with a gallery for the prisoners) where the Girondins were incarcerated. It now displays a collection of souvenirs, including a blade of the guillotine, a crucifix said to have been found in Marie-Antoinette's cell, orders for arrest, etc.

On making our exit, we turn r. into the BLVD DU PALAIS passing the *Cour du Mai*, on the E. side of the Palais de Justice, named after the maypole set up here annually by the 'Basoche' or society of law clerks.

The **Palais de Justice**, a huge block of buildings occupying the whole width of the island, also includes within its precincts the *Sainte Chapelle* (see below), which, with the four towers on the N. side, are the oldest surviving portions.

The Sainte Chapelle

The site of the *Palais de Justice* was occupied as early as the Roman period by a palace, which was a residence of Julian the Apostate, proclaimed emperor here in 360. The Merovingian kings divided their time between the Thermes and this Palais de la Cité, which was inside the walls, when not in the country. Louis VI died in the palace in 1137; Louis VII in 1180; and in 1200 or 1201 Philippe Auguste was married here to Ingeborg of Denmark. Louis IX altered the palace and built the *Sainte Chapelle*. From 1431 it was occupied entirely by the *Parlement*, who had previously only shared it with the king, but it was not until the Revolution that it acquired its present function.

The main buildings, of the 18C, were greatly enlarged in 1857–68 and 1911–14. The 14C *Tour de l'Horloge*, at the N.E. corner, with a clock copied from the original dial designed c.1585 by *Germain Pilon*, was virtually rebuilt in 1852. The upper part of the N. façade was also rebuilt in the style of the original work (14C) by *Enguerrand de Marigny*. The domed *Galerie Marchande*, dominating the *Cour du Mai*, is adorned with sculptures by *Pajou*.

The most interesting part of these law courts may be entered directly from the Boulevard just N. of the Cour du Mai, by stairs ascending to the ***Salle de Pas-Perdus**. This magnificent hall, which replaced the great hall of the medieval palace (where in 1431 the coronation banquet of Henry VI of England was celebrated), was rebuilt in 1622 by *Salomon de Brosse*, and restored in 1878 after being burned by the Communards. At the far end of the room, divided in two by a row of arches, and to the r., is the entrance to the *Première Chambre Civile*, formerly the *Grand'Chambre* or *Chambre Dorée* (restored in the style of Louis XII), perhaps originally the bedroom of Louis IX. Later it was used by the *Parlement*, in contempt of which Louis XIV here coined his famous epigram 'L'État, c'est moi'. The Revolutionary Tribunal, with Fouquier-Tinville as public prosecutor, sat here in 1793 (see *Conciergerie*, above).

A vaulted gateway leads from the *Cour du Mai* to the *Cour de la Sainte-Chapelle*.

The ***SAINTE CHAPELLE** (CN) was built in 1243–48 by St Louis as a shrine for miscellaneous relics, among them those purporting to be the Crown of Thorns and fragments of the True Cross, etc. The building is ascribed to *Pierre de Montreuil* (comp. St-Denis, and St-Germain-en-Laye), and is remarkable for the impression of lightness it conveys. It was often the scene of royal marriages, and Richard II of England was betrothed here in 1396 to Isabelle of France. It was 'restored' in 1837-57 by *Duban, Lassus* (who reconstructed a leaden flèche in the 15C style; the 5th on this site), and the ubiquitous *Viollet-le-Duc*.

36m long, 17m wide, and 42·50m high, the building gives an impression of great height in proportion to its length and breadth. It consists in fact of two superimposed chapels, the lower for servants and retainers, the upper reserved for the royal family and court. The lofty windows of the upper chapel, an innovation, are surmounted by delicately sculptured gables and a graceful balustrade. The leaden roof is modern. The portal consists of two porches, one above the other; the statues are 19C restorations.

The interior of the *Chapelle Basse*, with carved oak bosses, and forty columns sustaining the upper chapel, is darkened by the repellent decoration of *Emile Boeswillwald* (1815–96). There are a number of 14–15C tombstones in the pavement.

A spiral staircase leads to the *Chapelle Haute* (20·50m high), certainly one of the outstanding achievements of the Middle Ages; but sadly in need of cleaning. With the walls stripped of its 19C painting and gilding, the simple lines of its architecture would be seen to better advantage; its *Stained-Glass* (restored 1845) would glow more luminously.

The eighty-six panels from the Apocalypse in the large rose-window were a gift of Charles VIII. The 1st window on the r. represents the Legend of the Cross and the removal of the relics. The other windows in the nave and apse depict scenes from the Old and New Testaments. Beneath the windows on either side runs a blind arcade; of the apostles against the pillars, the 4th, 5th, and 6th on the l., and the 3rd, 4th, and 5th on the r., are original.

The two deep recesses under the windows of the 3rd bay were the seats reserved for the royal family. In the centre of the restored arcade across the apse is a wooden canopy beneath which the relics used to be exhibited on Good Friday; those few surviving the Revolution are in the treasury of Notre-Dame.

We make our exit by a second spiral stair.

To the S., at 36 QUAI DES ORFÈVRES is a *Museum of Police History*, with a room devoted to the part they played in the Resistance, and Liberation of Paris.

Opposite the Cour du Mai, the Rue de Lutèce leads between (r.) the *Préfecture de Police* and (l.) the domed *Tribunal de Commerce* (by Bailly; 1860–65), behind which the *Marché aux Fleurs* offers a colourful contrast. A Bird Market is held here on Sundays.

Crossing the Rue de la Cité, we turn r. and then l. into the PL. DU PARVIS NOTRE-DAME, the area of which Haussmann increased sixfold by his demolitions. To the l. is the *Hôtel-Dieu*, rebuilt here in 1868–78 to the N. of its original site. The first hospital was founded here by St Landry, Bp of Paris, c. 660.

On the *Parvis* the archbishops of Paris tried heretics, and here the condemned knelt before execution to acknowledge their sin and beg absolution. In 1314 Jacques de Molay, grand master of the Templars, summoned to repeat his confession publicly and accept sentence of imprisonment, unexpectedly protested the innocence of his Order, and was hustled off to the stake.

Near the W. end of the Parvis is the entrance to the *Crypte Archéologique* (CN), displaying architectural remains of all ages of the Cité's past uncovered in 1965 when the area was being excavated for the construction of the adjacent underground car-park. The site is exceptionally well exhibited, and dioramas and models explain the growth of the district prior to the ravaging fire of 1772. Sections are illuminated by press-button lighting, and explanatory notes are printed both in French and English.

The path we first follow leads above the foundations of the *Gallo-Roman rampart* (late 3C), a section of which is later seen. Further to the E., beyond the excavated area, lie the foundations of the W. end of the Merovingian cathedral of St-Étienne (6C). After passing cases displaying artefacts here uncovered, we follow the foundations of the demolished Hospice des Enfants-Trouvés and other medieval buildings once flanking the Rue Neuve Notre-Dame, some (to the r. as we approach the exit) as early as the 2C, and (l.) relics of hypocausts, etc.

To the E. rises *NOTRE-DAME* (Pl.14;4), the exterior of which has been cleaned. Although ranking after some others in beauty, archaeologically and historically it is one of the most interesting of the Gothic cathedrals of France. Commenced at the time when Gothic art was beginning to throw off the traditions of the Romanesque style, Notre-Dame was completed in the 13C, so that it is possible to follow the gradual progress of the new style until its decadence in the 14C.

Road distances in France are calculated from its W. door.

A photograph of Notre-Dame from the South, taken in 1842, before its restoration

The idea of replacing by a single building, on a much larger scale, the cathedral of St-Étienne (founded by Childebert in 528: see above) and that of Notre-Dame, further E., was due to Maurice de Sully, Bp of Paris (d. 1196). The old Notre-Dame replaced a Roman temple of Jupiter more or less on the site of the present cathedral, the foundation stone of which was laid by Pope Alexander III in 1163. The choir was finished by 1182, except for the roof; the nave was added in 1208; and the W. front and its towers c. 1225–50. A girdle of chapels was added: in the nave (1235–50) and apse (by *Pierre de Chelles* and *Jean Ravy*; 1296–1330). The side porches were begun in 1258; the crossings of the transept were built by *Jean de Chelles* and *Pierre de Montreuil* (1250–67).

Henry VI of England was crowned king of France in the cathedral choir in 1430, at the age of ten; and here were celebrated the marriages of François II to Mary Stuart (1558), Henry of Navarre to Marguerite de Valois (1572), and Charles I of England (by proxy) to Henrietta Maria (1625).

Until the end of the 17C Notre-Dame had preserved intact its appearance of the 14C, but the reigns of Louis XIV and Louis XV brought deplorable alterations, particularly in the destruction of tombs and stained glass. Many sculptures and treasures were destroyed during the Revolution, when an opera-singer, Mlle Maillard, was enthroned here as the Goddess of Reason. In 1804, Napoleon I and Joséphine were crowned here by Pius VII; Napoleon III and Eugénie de Montijo were married here in 1853. In 1845 a thorough 'restoration' was begun under the direction of Lassus (d.1857) and Viollet-le-Duc.

On 26 Aug. 1944 the thanksgiving service, following Gén. de Gaulle's entry into liberated Paris, was interrupted by sniping from internal and external galleries. It continues to be the scene of ceremonial functions, state funerals, etc.

EXTERIOR, The •W. front in three distinct storeys, forms one harmonious whole. The central *Porte du Jugement*, ruined by *Soufflot* in 1771, has a 19C Christ on the pier, and in the tympanum, the Last Judgment, restored by Viollet-le-Duc; only the upper tier of sculptures is ancient.

The *Porte de la Vierge* (l.) contains a restored Virgin on the pier; three kings and three prophets, and the Resurrection of the Virgin, in the lower part of the tympanum; above is the Coronation of the Virgin.

The sculptures of the *Porte de Ste-Anne* (r.) are mostly of 1165–75, designed for a narrower portal, with additions of c. 1240. On the pier is St Marcellus (19C); above, scenes from the life of St Anne and the Virgin, and the Virgin in Majesty, with Louis VII (r.) and Maurice de Sully (l.). The two side doors retain their medieval wrought-iron hinges.

Above the portals is the *Gallery of the Tree of Jesse* (reconstructed by Viollet-le-Duc), destroyed in 1793 because the Parisians assumed that they were kings of France. The magnificent rose-window, 9.6m in diameter, is flanked by double windows within arches. Higher still is an open arcade.

The *Towers*, originally intended to be crowned with spires, may be ascended for the view; entrance in the N. tower. In the S. tower hangs the great bell, recast in 1686 and weighing 13 tonnes; Hugo's bell-ringer, Quasimodo, may be remembered. The Chimières (gargoyles), grotesque figures of devils, birds, and beasts, were designed by *Viollet-le-Duc*.

The side façades and apse likewise consist of three distinct and receding storeys; the bold flying buttresses of the latter, by *Jean Ravy*, are also admired for their elegance. The S. porch, according to a Latin inscription at the base, was begun in 1257 (1258 n.s.) under the direction of *Jean de Chelles*. The story of St Stephen, as depicted in the tympanum, and the medallions of student life, are original. The N. porch, of the same period, retains an original statue of the Virgin, and in the tympanum, the story of Theophilius. Just to the E. of this porch is the graceful *Porte Rouge*, probably by *Pierre de Montreuil*. To the l., below the windows of the choir chapels, are seven 14C bas-reliefs. The Flèche (90m above the ground), a lead-covered oak structure, was rebuilt by Viollet-le-Duc in 1859–60, the original having been destroyed in the 18C.

The best view of the **Interior** is obtained from beneath the *Organ* (1733, by *Cliquot*, rebuilt in 1868 by *Cavaillé-Coll* and electrified in the 1960s), at the W. end. The cathedral (130m long, 48m wide, and 35m high) consists of a nave of ten bays of great purity of design, flanked by double aisles continued round the choir (of five bays). 37 chapels surround the whole. A vaulted gallery overlooks the nave; the windows above were altered in the 13C. The vaulting is supported by 75 piers, surmounted by bold yet graceful capitals. New glass, with an abstract design, was placed in the nave in 1963–64. Of the three *Rose-windows*, retaining their original 13C glass, the N. is the best preserved and finest.

At the crossing, 'Notre-Dame de Paris', a 14C figure, stands against the S.E. pillar; against the N.E. pillar is St Denis, by *N. Coustou*. On the S.W. pillar a tablet commemorates the million subjects of the British Empire who died in the *First* World War, the greater part of whom rest in French soil. Seven paintings (by *Ch. Le*

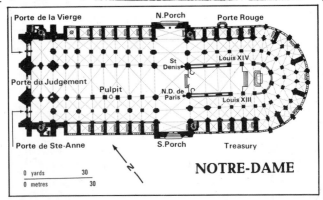

Detail of the West front of Notre-Dame

1963–64. Of the three *Rose-windows*, retaining their original 13C glass, the N. is the best preserved and finest.

At the crossing, 'Notre-Dame de Paris', a 14C figure, stands against the S.E. pillar; against the N.E. pillar is St Denis, by *N. Coustou*. On the S.W. pillar a tablet commemorates the million subjects of the British Empire who died in the *First* World War, the greater part of whom rest in French soil. Seven paintings (by *Ch. Le Brun, Seb. Bourdon*, and others∫, presented by the Goldsmiths' Guild of Paris in 1634-51, hang in the side-chapels of the nave.

The *Choir*, modified in 1708-25 by Louis XIV in fulfilment of his father's vow of 1638, attracted Viollet-le-Duc's 'restoring' hand. 78 of the original 114 *Stalls* remain, adorned with bas-reliefs from the designs of *Jules Degoullons* (1711–15). Canopied archiepiscopal stalls stand at either end. The bronze angels (1712–13) against the apse-pillars escaped the Revolutionary melting-pot.

In front of the high-altar Geoffrey Plantagenet, son of Henry II of England, was buried in 1186. Behind Viollet-le-Duc's altar is a Pietà by *N. Coustou* with a base sculptured by *Girardon*, part of the 'Voeu de Louis XIII'. The statue of Louis XIII (S.) is also by *Coustou*; that of Louis XIV (N.) is by *Coysevox*.

In the first four bays of the choir may be seen the remains of the screen which, until the 18C, extended round the whole apse; the expressive bas-reliefs on the exterior, finished in 1351, were unfortunately restored and repainted by Viollet-le-Duc. In the blind arches below are listed some of the eminent people buried in the church.

The *Ambulatory* contains the tombs of 18–19C prelates. Behind the high altar is the tomb-statue of Bp Matiffas de Bucy (d. 1304). In the 2nd chap. S. of the central chapel is the theatrical tomb, by *Pigalle*, of the Comte d'Harcourt (d. 1769); here are also the restored tomb-statues of Jean Jouvenel des Ursins and his wife (d. 1431, 1451).

On the S. side of the ambulatory is the entrance to the *Sacristy*, now containing the *Treasury*, a somewhat indifferent collection of ecclesiastical plate, reliquaries, etc.

In the Rue du Cloître Notre-Dame, adjacent to the N. tower of the cathedral, stood (until 1748) the chapel of *St-Jean-le-Rond*, on the steps of which was found exposed the natural son of Mme de Tencin (1682–1749). Baptised Jean-le-Rond, he grew up to become famous under the name d'Alembert (1717–83). At No.10 is the *Musée Notre-Dame de Paris*, preserving collections relative to the history of the cathedral.

The Rue Massillon turns N. into the Rue Chanoinessé, where on the site of a house at their junction, the poet Joachim du Bellay died in 1560; opposite died the famous anatomist M.-F.-X. Bichat (1711–1802). Parallel to the N. (at No.19 Rue des Ursins; but no adm.) part of the nave is preserved of the *Chap. St-Aignan* (1115–18), where mass was said in secret in 1789–91. Nicolas Boileau (1636–1711) died nearby in a house destroyed when the SQ. DE L'ARCHEVÊCHÉ was laid out.

In the SQ. DE L'ÎLE-DE-FRANCE, at the extreme E. end of the Cité is a *Memorial* to some 200,000 Frenchmen deported to German concentration camps during the 1939–45 war.

The **Île St-Louis** island is reached by crossing the *Pont St-Louis* (dating from 1614, but replaced in 1969). Still a comparatively quiet backwater, although in danger of exploitation, it was formerly two islets, and was not built over until the 17C, when as an annexe of the Marais to the N., it became the site of a number of imposing mansions. It is connected to the N. bank by the *Pont Louis-Philippe* (rebuilt 1862); beyond stands the *Pont Marie* (1635; named after its builder), crossing to the QUAI DES CÉLESTINS. Further E., the island is crossed obliquely by the *Pont de Sully* (1876), at the N. end of which, beyond the SQ. H.-GALLI, stands the striking *Hôtel Fieubet* (see Rte 11).

On the S. side of the island the *Pont de la Tournelle* (built of wood in 1369; rebuilt in 1654, and again in 1928) crosses from the Rue des Deux-Ponts (in which Restif de la Bretonne once lodged) to the QUAI DE LA TOURNELLE.

To the S.E. is the new *Science Faculty Building*, with its tower, replacing the old *Halles aux Vins*.

In the transverse Rue St-Louis-en-l'Île is the *Hôtel Chenizot* (No.51, with a balcony), of 1730, residence of Teresa Cabarrus (later Mme Tallien) in 1788–93. No.21, the richly decorated church of **St-Louis-en-l'Île**, was begun by *Le Vau* in 1664 and finished in 1726 by *Jacques Doucet*. The tower and curious openwork spire were added in 1765. The ornamental stone-carving in the interior was executed under the direction of *J.-B. de Champaigne* (died 1681; buried in the church). It contains six Nottingham alabasters from the same series as those in St-Leu-St-Gilles.

At No.12 in this street lived Philippe Lebon (1769–1804), who first introduced the principle of lighting by gas in France (1799). Between Nos 7 and 9 is an arch of the *Hôtel de Bretonvilliers*, finished by *Jean I du Cerceau* in 1640. Fénelon (1651–1715) lived at No.3. No.2 is the **Hôtel Lambert** by *Le Vau* (c. 1650), once the residence of Voltaire and Mme du Châtelet, and from 1842 the home of the Czartoryski family and a centre of Polish life in Paris.

On the N.E. side of the island, in the QUAI D'ANJOU, No.3 belonged to Le Vau; No.9 was the home of Honoré Daumier (1808–79) from 1846. The **Hôtel de Lauzun** or *de Pimodan* (No.17; 1657), by *Le Vau*, was the residence in 1682–84 of the Duc de Lauzun, commander of the French contingent at the Battle of the Boyne, who resided here with 'la Grande Mademoiselle'.

Baudelaire lived on the third floor in 1845, and Gautier had apartments here in 1848, where meetings of the Club des Haschichins took place. The artists responsible for its splendid decoration were *Le Brun*, *Le Sueur*, *Patel*, and *Sébastien Bourdon*. Adm. Sat. and Sun. 10.00–17.40; at other times apply to the Municipal Tourist Office, Hôtel de Ville.

Further W., Nos 13 and 15 QUAI DE BOURBON were the *Hôtel Le Charron* (17C), with a delightful courtyard; while No.11 was owned by Philippe de Champaigne. No.1 was the *Franc-Pinot*, an inn kept during the Revolution by the father of Cécile Renault, who had attempted to murder Robespierre.

Turning S., in the QUAI D'ORLÉANS, No.6 is the *Musée Adam Mickiewicz*, with an important Polish library, and souvenirs of the poet (1798–1855), and also of Chopin.—Further E., in the QUAI DE BÉTHUNE, is the mansion of Armand, Duc de Richelieu, grand-nephew of the cardinal (Nos 16–18).

At the eastern extremity of the island is the triangular SQ. BARYE.

THE SOUTH OR LEFT BANK: LA RIVE GAUCHE

2 The 'Quartier Latin'

MÉTROS: *St-Michel, Maubert-Mutualité, Card. Lemoine, Luxembourg.*

The area deriving its present name (conferred by Rabelais) from the language spoken by the early students, is a district S. of the *Île de la Cité*, which grew up with Abélard's removal in c. 1200 to the Montagne Ste-Geneviève from the school attached to Notre-Dame. Orginally known as the *Université*, it has remained to a large extent the learned quarter of Paris, and still contains the main educational and scientific institutions. Not the least interest of the district is that it occupies the site of Roman *Lutetia*.

With the growth of the University, the student population overflowed, and occupied a much more extensive area than the originally confined and swarming alleys on either side of the Rue St-Jacques. In the mid-19C the BLVD ST-GERMAIN was driven E. through the old streets, and many ancient buildings were swept away. In 1968 its paving-blocks were found to be useful missiles during the 'student revolution'. Cafés and bookshops abound, and the students appear to spend more time in the former than in the various faculty buildings. In 1922 a 'Cité Universitaire' was founded in the 14th Arrondissement, to the S. (see Rte 4).

From the PL. ST-MICHEL (Pl. 14;4), linked to the Cité by the *Pont St-Michel*, and with the *Fontaine St-Michel* at its S. end, erected by *Davioud* in 1860, and incorporating a memorial of the Resistance of 1944, the busy BLVD ST-MICHEL (popularly known as the 'Boul Mich') leads S. to the *Carrefour de l'Observatoire*, in part following the Roman Via Inferior (see pp73 and 83).

It was laid out by Haussmann as a direct continuation of the *Blvd de Strasbourg* and the *Blvd de Sébastopol*, and shortly crosses the *Blvd St-Germain*, running roughly parallel to the Seine. Almost the only interest of these main thoroughfares lies in their animation; the architectural and historical character of the Quartier is found in the side-streets.

Immediately to the E. of the Pl. St-Michel, in a still decrepit corner of Old Paris, diverges the Rue de la Huchette (the 'Narrow Street' of Elliot Paul), off which run the Rue Xavier-Privas and Rue du Chat-qui-Pêche, an alley named after an old shop-sign. Théophile de Viau composed his 'Parnasse Satirique' at No. 1 Rue de la Huchette, and at No.8 (or 10) Napoleon lodged in 1795; here also is the diminutive *Théâtre de la Huchette*.

Diverging r. along the Rue de la Harpe, and taking the first turning l., brings us to *St-Séverin*, rebuilt in the 13–16C on the site of an oratory of the time of Childebert I, where Foulque of Neuilly-sur-Marne preached the Fourth Crusade.

The lower part of the W. front and the W. bays of the nave date from the early 13C; the outer S. aisle was added c. 1350, the outer N. aisle and the E. part of the church were in construction in 1450–96, the chapels in 1500–20. The main W. portal, of the early 13C, was brought piecemeal from St-Pierre-aux-Boeufs in the Cité in 1837. The upper two storeys date from the 15C. On the l. is a tower of the 13C, completed in 1487, with a door which was once the main entrance; the tympanum dates from 1853, but in the frame is a 15C inscription; 'Bonnes gens qui par cy passés, Priez Dieu pour les trespassés'. To the l. of the tower, a niche holds a statue of St Séverin.

The INTERIOR impresses by the breadth of its double ambulatory. The most striking details are the ribs of the vaulting and the choir triforium, which approach English Perpendicular in style. The apse was partially classicized in the 17C at the expense of Mlle de Montpensier. In the nave, the first three bays contain late-14C glass from St-Germain-des-Prés, but much restored; from the fourth bay on the glass is mid-15C. One of the subjects on the S. side of the nave is the murder of Thomas Becket, while the W. rose-window contains a Tree of Jesse (c. 1500) masked by an organ of 1745.

To the S. of the choir are the 15C galleries of the graveyard, beneath which the first operation for the stone was successfully carried out in 1474.

On the far side of the Rue St-Jacques diverges the Rue Galande. one of the oldest existing streets in Paris (14C), with, on No.42, a carved representation of the life of St Julian.

The church of **St-Julien-le-Pauvre** (r.) rebuilt c. 1170–1230 and used in the 13–16C as a university church and in 1655–1877 by the old Hôtel-Dieu for various secular purposes, has since 1889 been occupied by Melchites (Greek Catholics subject to papal authority). The present W. front was built in 1651. Note the foliated capitals within; an iconostasis obscures the E. end.

A good *View of the *Cathedral of Notre-Dame* may be had from the SQ. RENE-VIVIANI, just to the N.

From the N.E. side of this square runs the Rue de la Bûcherie, where No.13 was occupied by the École de Médecine from 1483 to 1775, with a rotunda built in 1745 by the Danish doctor Jacques-Bénigne Winslow. Restif de la Bretonne (1734–1806) died at No.16 (prev. No.27).

S. of the Sq. René-Viviani is the Rue du Fouarre (named after the 'straw' on which the students sat), the centre of four 14C schools of the University, and referred to by Dante, who is supposed to have attended lectures here.—The Rue Lagrange leads S.E. to meet the Blvd St-Germain at the PL. MAUBERT ('la Maub'), where Étienne Dolet (1509–46) was burnt as a heretic. Crébillon fils (1707–77) was born in a house here.

The ancient Rue de Bièvre runs N.E., just E. of the Pl. Maubert, in which Dante is said to have written part of the 'Divina Commedia'.—To the W. is the Rue des Anglais, infested by English students in medieval times.

A short distance along the Rue Monge, leading S.E., is (l.) **St-Nicolas-du-Chardonnet** ('of the thistle-field'), a Renaissance church built mostly in 1656–1709; the clumsy tower (1625) is a relic of an earlier edifice. Some of the statues and stucco work are by *Nicolas Legendre*.

In the dark interior, in the 1st chapel on the r., is *Corot's* study for the Baptism of Christ; the 2nd chapel on the r. of the choir, beyond the transept, contains a monument by *Girardon* of Bignon, the jurist (d. 1656). In the 8th chapel (round the apse) is the tomb of Le Brun's mother, by *Tuby* and *Collignon*, designed by *Le Brun* in the theatrical style of Bernini; against the window is a monument of Le Brun (d. 1690) and his widow, by *Coysevox*. Note the 18C

The West front of St-Étienne-du-Mont

organ-case. A Crucifixion by *Brueghel the Younger* is preserved in the Sacristy.

Diverging l. along the Rue St-Victor, we pass (l.) the Rue de Poissy, where at No. 24 are the remains of the 14C refectory of the ancient *Collège des Bernardines*; it was occupied by firemen between the years 1844–1970.

At the far end of this street, where it meets the QUAI DE LA TOURNELLE, stands the 17C *Hôtel de Nesmond* (Nos 55–57), restored, and now accommodating the offices of *La Demeure Historique*.

This association of proprietors of privately-owned historic residences throughout France, founded in 1924, is devoted to promoting a public interest in this aspect of their architectural and cultural patrimony. They publish a map showing the situation of c.330 châteaux, etc. also indicating hours of admission, etc.

At No.47 in the quai is a small *Museum* devoted to Hospitals of Paris, accommodated in what was once the convent of the 'Miramiones' or Filles Ste-Geneviève, founded by Mme de Miramion (d. 1696). No.15 is *La Tour d'Argent*, a famous restaurant built on the site of an earlier tavern dating from 1582, which gained its gastronomic reputation in the Second Empire.

On the r. is the interesting church of *ST-ÉTIENNE-DU-MONT (Pl. 14;6), showing the transition from the Gothic to the Renaissance style.

It was almost continuously in construction from 1492 to 1586. Marguerite de Valois laid the foundation stone of the portal in 1610 and even this preserves certain Gothic motifs. The tower, begun in 1492, was completed in 1628. The N. side, with its picturesque porch, dates from 1630–32.

It replaced an earlier parish church dependent upon and entered through the abbey church of *Ste-Geneviève* (comp. above). During the Revolution, it became the 'Temple of Filial Piety'.

The INTERIOR has lofty columns, a wide ambulatory, and ribbed vaulting with pendent keystones. Its originality lies in the balustrade which runs along the supporting pillars of the nave and choir. The beautiful fretted *Rood Screen*, built in 1525–35, is a masterpiece of design and carving; the date 1605 on the side refers only to the door admitting to the spiral staircases by which it is ascended. The organ-case by *Jean Buron* dates from 1631–32; the pulpit of 1651 is the work of *Germain Pilon*, with sculptures designed by *Laurent de la Hire*. The *Stained-glass* ranges in date from c.1550 to c.1600; the oldest windows are those in the apse.

Between the 6th and 7th chapels in the S. aisle a tablet commemorates the Jacobins, an order of preaching friars established in the Rue St-Jacques in 1218. Above the 1st chapel in the choir is an ex-voto to St Geneviève, with the provost and merchants of Paris, by *F. de Troy* (1726), while higher, to the r., is a similar painting by *Largillière*, of 1696. On either side of the chapel are the epitaphs of Pascal and Racine (by Boileau), whose graves are at the entrance to the *Lady Chapel*. Also buried in the church are Rollin, and the artist Eustache Le Sueur (1616–55). The next chapel S. of the choir contains the copper-gilt shrine of St Geneviève (1853). Within is a fragment of her tomb; her remains were burned by the mob in the Pl. de Grève in 1801.

From the next bay runs a corridor, at the end of which (r.) is the Presbytery, built in 1742 for Louis d'Orléans (son of the Regent), who died here in 1752. On the l. is the *Charnier*, or gallery of the graveyard, with twelve superb *Windows* of 1605–09; note one depicting the Mystic Wine-press. Most of them are after the designs of *Léonard Gautier*.

To the W. of the PL.-STE-GENEVIÈVE (Pl.14;6) rises the grandiose bulk of the **PANTHÉON** (CN) , situated on the 'Mont de Paris', the highest point on the Left Bank (60m) and the legendary burial-place of Geneviève, a young woman of Nanterre, later regarded as the patron saint of Paris (fl.5C).

In 1744, lying ill at Metz, Louis XV vowed that if he recovered, he would replace

The Panthéon, designed by Soufflot, its portico embellished by a pediment representing France, between Liberty and History, distributing laurels to her more eminent sons, an ambitious work by David d'Angers.

the former church, and the present building was begun some twenty years later, although not completed until 1789. Its architect *Soufflot* died, of anxiety it is said, owing to criticism that subsidence of the walls (noticeable near the choir) would occur because the foundations had Panthéon been laid on clay pits dug by Roman potters.

In 1791, after the death of Mirabeau, the Constituent Assembly decided that the church should be used as a Panthéon or burial-place for distinguished citizens, and the pediment was inscribed with the words 'Aux Grands Hommes la Patrie reconnaissante'. From the Restoration to 1831 and from 1851 to 1885 it was again used as a church, but on the occasion of Victor Hugo's interment it reverted to the name and purpose decreed in 1791.

Exteriorly imposing, the *Panthéon* is built in the shape of a Greek cross, 110m long, 82m wide, and 83m high to the top of the majestic *•Dome*. The pediment above the portico of 22 Corinthian columns is a masterpiece of *David d'Angers*, representing France between Liberty and History, distributing laurels to famous men. Forty-two windows were walled in during the Revolution.

The INTERIOR is of slight interest. Coldly Classical, it is adorned with paintings, among which are some pallid works by *Puvis de Chavannes*, while in the transepts are monuments by *Landowski*. The colossal group of the Convention, at the E. end, is by *Sicard*.

The *Dome*, supported by four piers united by arches, contains three distinct cupolas, of which the first is open in the centre to reveal the second, with a fresco by *Gros*. By the first pillar (r.) is a monument to Rousseau by *Bartholomé*: on the l. another to Diderot and the Encyclopaedists by *Terroir*. Other tablets commemorate Saint-Exupéry and Bergson. Within the dome, in 1852, the physicist Léon Foucault gave the first public demonstration of his pendulum experiment proving the rotation of the Earth.

Conducted tours of the **Crypt** (entrance in the N.E. corner) may be made, first passing a shrine containing the heart of *Gambetta* (d. 1882). Among the tombs are those of *Rousseau* (d. 1778; and transferred here in 1794); *Voltaire* (d. 1778; trans. 1791), with a statue attr. to *Houdon*; and *Jacques-Germain Soufflot* (1714–80), the architect. Of men whose remains have been reinterred in the vaults, the most famous are *Victor Hugo* (d. 1885); *Émile Zola* (d. 1902); *Marcelin Berthelot* (1827–1907), the chemist; *Jean Jaurès* (1859-assassinated 1914), the socialist politician; *Louis Braille* (1809–52), benefactor of the blind; and the explorer *Bougainville* (1729–1811; from St-Pierre-de-Montmartre), and *Jean Moulin* (1899–1944), the Resistance hero. *Mirabeau* and *Marat* were interred here with great state, but their remains were soon cast out with ignominy: the former now rests in the cemetery of Ste-Catherine, the latter in the graveyard of St-Étienne-du-Mont.

At No.32 in the Rue du Card.-Lemoine, the next main street running S., stood the *Collège des Bons-Enfants*, where Vincent de Paul founded his congregation of mission-priests.—Further S., No.49 is the *Hôtel Le Brun*, built by *Boffrand* for the artist in 1700, and later occupied by Watteau and Buffon.

Ascending S.W. at the junction of the Rue du Card.-Lemoine with the Rue Monge, we approach the Rue Clovis, where a section of Philippe Auguste's perimeter *Wall* may be seen.

No. 65 Rue du Card.-Lemoine, the *Institution Ste-Geneviève*, was the **Scots College** (*Collège des Écossais*; apply to the concierge), re-founded in 1662 by Robert Barclay. The earlier Scots College had been founded in 1326.

The *Chapel*, on the first floor, contains the tomb of Frances Jennings, Duchess of Tyrconnel (d. 1731), the spirited elder sister of Sarah, Duchess of Marlborough; a memorial erected to James II (who bequeathed his brain to the college) by James Drummond, Duke of Perth, with a long Latin epigraph; the tomb of Sir Patrick Menteith, who died in 1675 in the service of Louis XIV, etc.

Blaise Pascal (1623–62) died on the site of No.67.

No.5 Rue Descartes, crossing the Rue Clovis, is the entrance to the influential *École Polytechnique*, founded by Monge in 1794 for the training of artillery and engineer officers, and transferred in 1805 to the buildings of the *Collège de Navarre*, greatly extended in 1929–35.

Founded in 1304 by Jeanne de Navarre, queen of Philippe le Bel, the Collège de Navarre numbered among its pupils Gerson, Ramus, Henri III, Henri IV, Henri de Guise, Richelieu, Bossuet, Condorcet, and André Chénier. The *Collège de Boncourt* (No.21), taken over by the Collège de Navarre in the 17C. had earlier contained perhaps the first theatre in Paris. In 1792 G.-B. Piranesi's sons established their engraving works in the college.

At No.34 Rue Montagne-Ste-Geneviève, further down the hill, are remains of the *Collège des Trente-Trois*, founded in 1633 by Claude Bernard, friend and follower of Vincent de Paul, and named after its 33 scholarships (one for each year of Christ's life).

At No.23 Rue Clovis is the entrance to the *Lycée Henri-IV*. The *Tower* (restored) has a Romanesque base and two Gothic upper storeys (14–15C) and is a relic of the church (demolished 1802) of the *Abbaye Ste-Geneviève*.

Practically the whole of the conventual buildings were rebuilt in the 18C, but the former refectory (now the chapel), is an over-restored 13C building; the kitchens are likewise medieval. The fact that the abbey came under papal jurisdiction, not that of the Bp of Paris, influenced Abélard's choice of this area (comp. above). Bernardin de Saint-Pierre lived at No.4 Rue Rollin from 1781 to 1786, where he wrote 'Paul et Virginie'. The street is named after Charles Rollin (1661–1741; the uncritical historian), who died at No.8; Descartes lived at No.14 in 1644–48. Mérimée (1803–70) was born at No.7 Carré de Ste-Geneviève, which was adjacent.

In the N.W. corner of the PL. DU PANTHÉON was the *École de Droit*, begun by *Soufflot* in 1771 and subsequently enlarged and now known as Universities I and II, see below.—Opposite is the *Mairie of the 5th Arrondissement* (1844–50), built in the same style.

The **Bibliothèque Ste-Geneviève**, on the N. side of the Place, originated in the library of the famous Abbey of Ste-Geneviève. The present building, also of 1844–50, by *Labrouste*, is on the site of the *Collège de Montaigu*, founded in 1314, where Loyola, Erasmus, and Calvin were students. It was also known as the *Hôtel des Haricots*, as it was presumed that beans were the staple fare of its inmates. It was in later years a prison.

The library contains c. 700,000 vols (nearly 4000 MSS.) and over 30,000 prints and engravings (including 10,000 portraits). Rooms are devoted to Scandinavian literature (c. 90,000 vols) and the *Bibliothèque Jacques Doucet* comprising c. 8000 vols of late 19th and 20C French authors, including MSS. of Rimbaud, Verlaine, Baudelaire, Gide, and Valéry. Among the illuminated MSS. which are occasionally exhibited, are an English Bible, copied by Manerius in the 12C; the Chronicles of St-Denis (late 13C); several MSS. of the Carolingian period; the 'De Proprietatibus Rerum' of Barthélemy l'Anglais (Catalan translation of the 15C); and 'La Cité de Dieu' of St Augustine (late 15C). The building also contains a number of busts by *Coysevox, J.-J. Caffieri, Lemoyne,* and *Houdon.*

On the r. of the Library, in the Rue Valette, are the remains of the *Collège Fortet* (No.21), dating from 1397, where Calvin was a student in 1531.

Further downhill to the r., in the Rue des Carmes, is *St-Ephrem*, a Syrian Catholic church, formerly the chapel (1760) of a community of Irish priests, who established themselves in the 17C buildings of the *Collège des Lombards*.

To the l. of the Library, on the r. in Rue Cujas, is the *Collège Ste-Barbe*, founded in 1460, the oldest existing public educational establishment in France, at which Francis Xavier was a scholar. The *Law Faculty Library* has been built on part of the grounds.

Descending W. from the Panthéon towards the *Luxembourg Gardens* is the wide Rue Soufflot, where (r.) at No. 14 a tablet commemorates the site of the Dominican or Jacobin convent (1217–1790) where Albertus Magnus and Thomas Aquinas taught.

The Rue St-Jacques, which we first cross, an important thoroughfare in medieval times, following the course of the Roman road—the Via Superior—from Lutetia to Orléans, also formed part of the pilgrim route to St James of Compostela (Santiago; whence its name), and so attracted many convents. The S. section is described in Rte 4.

Turning r. along the Rue St-Jacques, we pass (r.) the *Lycée Louis-le-Grand*, formerly the Jesuit *Collège de Clermont*, founded in 1560 and rebuilt in 1887–96. Molière, Voltaire, Robespierre, Desmoulins, Delacroix, and Hugo studied here.

We next pass the **Collège de France**, with its entrance in the Pl. Marcelin-Berthelot (Pl. 14; 4–6). In the courtyard, with its graceful portico, is a statue of Guillaume Budé (Budaeus; 1468–1540). It was founded by François I in 1530 under Budé's influence, to spread humanism and counteract the narrow scholasticism of the Sorbonne. It was independent of the University, and its teaching was free and public. The present building was begun in 1610, completed by *Chalgrin* c.1778, and since enlarged. During work in 1894 traces were found of Gallo-Roman baths.

In a garden on the N.E. side of the college is a monument to the 'Pléïade', the 16C poetical coterie (notably Du Bellay and Ronsard) which originated in a vanished college near this site (the Collège Coqueret; founded in 1418, but surviving only until 1643). Other members of the group, formed in 1549, were Antoine de Baïf, Rémy Belleau, Jodelle, Pontus de Tyard, and Jean Dorat (who took the place of Jacques Peletier).

To the W. of the *Collège de France* stands the **SORBONNE**, founded as a modest theological college in 1253 by Robert de Sorbon, chaplain to Louis IX. It was rebuilt at Richelieu's expense by *Jacques Lemercier* in 1629 but, with the exception of the church, the present buildings date from 1885–1901.

The *University of Paris*, which disputes with Bologna the title of the oldest university in Europe, arose in the first decade of the 12C out of the schools of dialectic attached to *Notre-Dame*. Transferred by Abélard to the Montagne Ste-Geneviève, it obtained its first statutes in 1208, and these served as the model for Oxford and Cambridge and other universities of northern Europe. By the 16C it comprised no fewer than forty separate colleges.

Before the end of the 13C the *Sorbonne* had become synonymous with the faculty of theology, overshadowing the rest of the University and possessing the power of conferring degrees, and was distinguished for its religious rancour, supporting the condemnation of Joan of Arc (Pierre Cauchon came from the Sorbonne), justifying the massacre of St Bartholomew, and refusing its recognition of Henri IV. Nevertheless in 1469 it was responsible for the introduction of printing into France, by allowing Ulrich Gering and his companions to set up their presses within its precincts.

In the 18C it attacked the 'philosophes', and in 1792 was itself suppressed. It was refounded by Napoleon, and in 1821 became the official headquarters of the University of Paris. The student 'revolution' of May 1968 eventually had the effect of instigating overdue reforms in the university system, and in 1970 the University of Paris was replaced by the formation of thirteen autonomous universities in the region. The Sorbonne accommodates Universities III and IV.

The ponderous buildings, which still house the University Library of 700,000 volumes, the *Académie de Paris*, and minor learned institutions, include the *Grand Amphithéâtre* (the main lecture hall, containing *Puvis de Chavannes'* mural, 'Le Bois sacré'), which may be visited on application at the main entrance in the Rue des Écoles.

Apply here also to visit the Church of ***Ste-Ursule de la Sorbonne**, facing the PL. DE LA SORBONNE, founded in the 13C and rebuilt by *Lemercier* in 1635–59 at the expense of Richelieu. The dramatic

Tomb of the great cardinal (1585–1642) was designed by *Le Brun* and sculptured by *Girardon* (1694). The *Dome* was the first example of a true dome in Paris.

Opposite the entrance to the Sorbonne is the SQUARE PAUL-PAINLEVÉ (Pl. 14;3–4; with a statue of Montaigne by *Landowski*), to the N. of which is the *Hôtel de Cluny, built at the end of the 15C on the site of Roman ruins and one of the finest extant examples of medieval French domestic architecture. It houses the **MUSÉE DE CLUNY, devoted to the arts and crafts of the Middle Ages, and one of the most rewarding to visit of the museums of Paris. The entrance is in the r.-hand corner of the courtyard, beyond an archway surmounted by the Amboise arms.

The property was bought in 1340 by Pierre de Chalus, Abbot of Cluny in Burgundy, and the mansion was built c. 1490 by Abbot Jacques d'Amboise as the town house of the abbots, although rarely occupied by them. In 1515 it became the residence of Mary Tudor (1496–1533), daughter of Henry VII and later widow of Louis XII. She was known as 'La Reine Blanche' from the white mourning worn by her as queen-dowager of France. James V of Scotland was lodged here before his wedding with Madeleine, daughter of François I, in 1537. Later occupants were the Card. de Lorraine, Claude de Guise, Mazarin, and the papal nuncios (1600–81).

In the 18C the tower was used as an observatory by the astronomer Messier. At the Revolution the mansion became national property, but in 1833 it was bought by *Alexandre Du Sommerard* (1771–1842) and filled with the treasures which he spent his lifetime in collecting. These were bought by the State and supplemented by many new acquisitions, during the long curatorship of Edmond Du Sommerard (d.1889; son of Alexandre), and since. The number of items in the inventory now approaches 23,000, but only a proportion are on display. Certain sections are still closed for restoration and reorganisation.

GROUND FLOOR. **R1** is devoted to the accessories of medieval costume, such as buckles, clasps, ornamental trinkets, etc.; shoes—one 'à la poulaine', with a pointed toe (late 14C); and metal and leather caskets, etc. Outstanding in this and the next four rooms are the collection of *Tapestries*, mostly 15C, although that of The Resurrection is early 14C. Among them are The Concert; The Miracle of St Quentin; Vintage Scenes; and the set of six scenes illustrating the activities of a noble household of c.1500, entitled 'La Vie seigneuriale' in **RR4** and **6**. Also remarkable are the carved Head of Jeanne of Toulouse (c.1280) in **R2**; the textiles and embroidery in **R3**, some Coptic or Byzantine, others of French, Italian, English, and Spanish origin, including examples of Hispano-Moresque fabrics. **RR5** and **6** are devoted to carpentry and woodwork, and display an interesting series of misericords (from St-Lucien, Beauvais: see also Rte 38) and a chest-front on which jousting scenes are depicted.

In the corridor (**R7**) adjoining R5 are a number of Nottingham alabasters, and a charming statue of St Ursula sheltering some of her eleven thousand companions.—A room to the r. will accommodate sculptural fragments from the central portal of Notre-Dame, and mutilated heads from the Tree of Jesse gallery of the cathedral, recently discovered, and at present in the adjacent Thermae.—The fine collection of medieval sculpture in **R8** (l.) will probably be moved elsewhere in the building.

Among outstanding works are statues of the Magdalen from Brussels, said to be a portrait of Mary of Burgundy, daughter of Charles the Bold; the seated Virgin reading to the Child, from the lower Rhine; the group with the Virgin swooning, carved at Burgos in the Dutch style; a marble Virgin, from Le Breuil (Marne); and the

One of six late 15C 'millefleurs' tapestries depicting 'La Dame à la Licorne', and said to represent the non-submission of the five Senses shown in the other tapestries.

painted Pietà from Tarascon (mid 15C), among other remarkable examples of the period, apart from a number of carved altar-pieces.—**R9** contains four mutilated statues of the Apostles from the Sainte Chapelle (1243–48); carved capitals, some of Catalan workmanship; carved altar-pieces, and further examples of wood and stone statuary; and ivory oliphants.—Earlier capitals, some of the 7C from St-Denis, and from St-Germain-des-Prés (mid 11C) are displayed in **R10**, together with a number of tombstones and a fine 7C Sarcophagus.—Hence we descend into the *Frigidarium* of the Gallo-Roman baths, remarkable in that it still preserves its vault, unique in France. The room, the *Piscina* of which was probably on the N. side, measuring 20m by 11·5m, and 14m in height, is all that remains in its entirety of the baths of the building (almost certainly not a 'palace'), probably erected during the ·reign of Caracalla (212–17): slight ruins are extant of its *Tepidarium* and *Caldarium*. Here are displayed the Gallo-Roman sculpture of the museum's collection.

Returning through R10, we ascend to the FIRST FLOOR and enter **R11**, circular in shape, in which are displayed the series of six exquisite *'millefleurs'* tapestries known as '****La Dame à la Licorne**' (or Unicorn), probably woven in the southern Netherlands for Jean Le Viste between 1484 and 1500: the arms of the family—gules, a band azur with three crescents argent—being frequently seen. They had long hung in the Château of Boussac, and were first brought to public notice by both Mérimée (when Inspector of Historical Monuments) and George Sand, and were eventually acquired by the museum in 1883.

They illustrate the Senses, and their disposition is the same as when originally hung: to the r., *Sight*, in which the unicorn gazes into the mirror held before him by the Lady; and *Hearing*, in which the Lady plays a portative organ: to the l., *Touch*, in which the Lady gently grasps the horn of the unicorn; and *Smell*, in which a monkey sniffs a flower, while the Lady weaves a garland: beyond the latter is *Taste*, with the Lady feeding both the monkey and a parakeet from a bowl of sweetmeats; while further to the r. the Lady stands before a tent-like pavilion, while returning jewels to a casket held by her maid, a gesture said to indicate 'Free Choice', and the *non*-submission to the senses; the top of the pavilion is embroidered with the motto 'A mon seul désir'.

Hence we turn into **R12**, containing a collection of Enamels, including late Roman and Byzantine examples; others from the Rhineland and Meuse region, including a mid 12C altarpiece from Stavelot; remarkable *Collections of Limoges enamel-ware from the late 12C to 14C, among them a number of reliquaries, chalices, pyxes, shrines, plaques, croziers, and crucifixes of outstanding workmanship; and a Brussels tapestry of the legend of Augustus and the Sibyl (early 16C).—**R13–14** are devoted to jewellery, including gold torques, bracelets, buckles, and fibulas; ornamented belts; two rock-crystal lion-heads (5C; probably once decorating a Consular chair), found on the banks of the Rhine; part of the Treasure of Gurrazar (Toledo), Visigothic votive crowns with their pendant crosses, dating from the late 7C, and discovered in 1858; the Treasure of Colmar—early 14C coins and jewellery found in a wall of the Rue des Juifs, Colmar, in 1853; the Golden Rose given by Pope Clement V to the prince-Bishop of Basle (early 14C); a silver-gilt and coral statue of Daphne (by Wenzel Jamnitzer, Nüremburg; mid 16C); the Reliquary of St Anne (1472; by Hans Greiff); a collection of cameos, intaglios and glyptics; Merovingian and Gallo-Roman jewellery; Processional Crosses, including one from Barcelona (14C) and another from Siena (mid 15C); the Reliquary of the Sainte-Chapelle, made to the order of St Louis; and the Tapestry of the Prodigal Son (early 16C).

We next traverse a corridor (**R15**) in which are displayed a variety of medieval artefacts, among them domestic utensils; mirrors; riding accessories; games-boards; stamps, dies, and seals; and writing equipment, etc.—An adjacent room will later display more Goldsmiths' and Silversmiths' work.—To the r. are **RR16** and **17**, the former containing examples of stained glass, including panels from St-Denis (1144), Troyes (c. 1200), and medallions from the Sainte Chapelle (mid 13C); the latter is devoted to ceramics, including a fine collection of Hispano-Moresque ware, and other examples of lustreware from Manises (Valencia); and a 17C German Organ.

Returning through R16 we turn r. into **R18**, containing the reassembled *Choir-stalls from the abbey of St-Lucien at Beauvais (1492–1500), some misericords from which are shown in R5.—**R19** displays the gold *Altar-frontal from Basle cathedral (c. 1015), made for the Emperor Henry II ; a collection of Byzantine and Consular Ivories, including a large figure of *Ariadne (c.500); a richly mounted reliquary-casket; a 15C Italian Bust-reliquary, etc.

Adjacent is the *Chapel (**R20**), a masterpiece of Flamboyant vaulting from a central pillar, with a filigree of delicate moulding between the main ribs. Above the Oriel window are 15C sculptures, with the Father blessing His dying Son, and angels with the instruments of the Passion, etc. Also notable is the recumbent funeral effigy of copper on wood of Blanche of Champagne (d. 1283), from the abbey of La Joie, near Hennebont (Morbihan); and the first part of a set of tapestries depicting the Life of St Stephen, woven for Jean Baillet, Bp of Auxerre c. 1490: the series is continued in the adjoining rooms.

From R18, we turn l. into **R21**, devoted to metalwork, largely of copper and bronze, including an eagle-lectern (1383); measures and weights; 'aquamaniles'; cauldrons, candlesticks, and other implements.—**R22** Ironwork, with fine examples of grilles (12C); a metal-plated chest; bolts, locks and keys; a small selection of arms and armour, spurs, and knives; shields and targes or bucklers; coffers, etc.—**R23** contains articles of pewter, tin, and lead, including a collection of medallions, pilgrims' badges (and their moulds); guild counters, toys, etc.—**R24**, with an imposing Jewish Tabernacle of the Law (1471), and other items of medieval furniture, etc., which brings us to the head of a staircase, descending which we make our exit.

Most of the later objects, from the era of the Renaissance, but part of the collections of this museum, are now to be seen to advantage at **Écouen**: see Rte 24.

3   Jardin Des Plantes; Gobelins; St-Médard

MÉTROS: *Monge, Gare d'Austerlitz, St-Marcel, Gobelins, Censier-Daubenton.*

At the E. end of the Rue des Écoles (conveniently approached from Métros. Maubert Mutualité or Cardinal Lemoine) rises the extensive new utilitarian block of buildings, and obtrusive tower, housing departments of the *Faculty of Science* (Universities V and VI; see p72), to the N. of which the Rue des Fossés-St-Bernard descends towards the Seine at the *Pont Sully* (see Rte 1). At No. 5 in this street are displayed the mineralogical collections of the university.

Here, until their transfer to Bercy, stood the huge bonded warehouses of the Halles aux Vins, itself on the site of the *Abbaye de St-Victor*. This had been dispersed in 1790: here Thomas Becket and Abélard resided, and in its library, Rabelais studied.

Between the Quai St-Bernard and the Seine, among riverside gardens, extends the *Musée de Sculpture en Plein Air* (Pl.15;5), set up in 1980, in which some 40 characteristic examples of contemporary 'sculpture', fabrications, etc., are exhibited. Few are notable; the most noticeable is *Nicolas Schöffer's* gyrating metallic tower, with its struts and discs, while among earlier works are some by *Brancusi*, and *Zadkine*.

Bearing S. from the Rue Jussieu, we ascend the Rue Linné, off which the Rue des Arènes climbs r. to the relics of the 2–3C amphitheatre of Roman Paris, only discovered in 1869 and fully excavated since 1883. The **Arènes de Lutèce** are now surrounded by the gardens of the SQ. CAPITAN, named after Dr Capitan, who restored the ruins in 1917–18.

At the junction of the Rue Linné with its continuation, the Rue Geoffroy-St-Hilaire, stands the *Fontaine Cuvier* (1840), and the N.W. entrance to the **Jardin des Plantes** (previously known, until 1793, as the *Jardin du Roi*), officially the *Muséum National d'Histoire Naturelle* (Pl. 15;7), 28 hectares in area, and combining the attractions of a menagerie, botanical gardens, and natural history galleries. Its collections of wild and herbaceous plants are unrivalled, and in May and June the peonies make a magnificent show. The *Library* contains a remarkable collection of botanical MSS., including the *Vélins du Roi*, illustrated by *Nicolas Robert* (1614–85) and others; also works by *Redouté*, etc.

Adm. The *Gardens* are open daily 7.00–20.30, and until dusk in winter; likewise the *Menagerie, Aquarium*, and *Vivarium*. The *Jardin d'Hiver* is open from 13.30 to 17.00 except Tues.; the *Jardin Alpin* is closed from Oct. to April; and the *Zoological Galleries* are open from 13.30 to 17.00 daily, except Tues.

There are other entrances in the Rue Geoffroy-St-Hilaire, and in the semicircular PL. VALHUBERT to the E. opposite the *Gare d'Austerlitz*. The nearest MÉTRO stations are *Jussieu, Monge, Censier Daubenton*, and *Austerlitz*.

Founded in 1626 under Louis XIII as a 'physic garden' for medicinal herbs by the royal physician Guy de la Brosse, the garden was first opened to the public in 1650. Its present importance is mainly due to the great naturalist *Buffon* (1707–88), who was superintendent from 1739, and greatly enlarged the grounds. In 1793 it was reorganized by the Convention under its present official title, and provided with twelve professorships. The animals from the royal collection at Versailles were brought to form the nucleus of a menagerie during Bernadin de Saint-Pierre's brief directorship. In 1792, Richard Twiss was told by the director that the names of some plants had been changed: 'We will not have any aristocratic plants!' Many distinguished French naturalists have taught and studied here, and are commemorated by monuments in the garden or nearby. A statue of Lamarck (1744–1829) faces the E. entrance. Among other scientists associated with the Jardin des Plantes are Geoffroy Saint-Hilaire (1772–1844), Louis Daubenton (1706–99), Joseph de Tournefort (1656–1708) and Bernard de Jussieu (1690–1777).

Entering from the N.W. we pass (l.) the *Maison de Chevreul* (named after the centenarian chemist) and the *Maison de Cuvier*, where Georges Cuvier (1769–1832), zoologist and palaeontologist, gave Saturday evening receptions during the 1820s and 30s, attended by Mérimée, Stendhal, and Delacroix, among others. Here also are the *Administrative Building*, in a mansion of 1785, and the *Amphithéâtre* or lecture hall, of 1788 (restored). The *Menagerie* occupies most of the N. side of the gardens. It is said that many of its earlier occupants were killed in 1870–71 to feed besieged Parisians during the Franco-Prussian War.

On the r. as we enter is the *Butte*, a hillock with a maze, the first cedar of Lebanon (from Kew Gardens) to be planted in France (by Jussieu, in 1734), and on the summit, a *belvedere*. The sundial here bears the inscription 'Horas non numero nisi serenas': I only count the sunny hours. In the centre are the *Jardin d'Hiver* and *Jardin Alpin*, while along the S. side of the gardens are ranged the *Zoological Galleries*, in the N. vestibule of which is the tomb of Guy de la Brosse (died 1641); the *Mineralogical Galleries*, with the *Library* (c.500,000 vols and 2500 MSS.) and *Buffon's House*, occupied by him from 1773 to his death; the *Botanical Gallery*; and *Palaeontological Gallery*. To the S., on the far side of the Rue Buffon, is an Annexe to the museum.

The *Association des Parcs Botaniques de France*, 15 bis Rue de Marignan, 8e, may be applied to with regard to other botanical establishments in France.

To the W. of the Rue Geoffroy-St-Hilaire stands the *Institut franco-musulman*, with a green-tiled *Mosque*, complete with minaret, opened in 1925.

Slightly further W. (in the Rue Puits-de-l'Ermite) stood the *Prison de*

Ste-Pélagie, where Joséphine, the future empress, and Mme du Barry, were confined under the Revolution, and where Mme Roland (1754–93) wrote her memoirs.

Not far to the S., we reach the BLVD ST-MARCEL, near which point was the *Cimetière Ste-Catherine*, where the bodies of Mirabeau and other revolutionaries were reburied after being ejected from the *Panthéon*. This thoroughfare leads N.E. to meet the BLVD DE L'HÔPITAL.

To the r. of this latter junction stands the huge ***Hôpital de la Salpêtrière** (Pl. 15;8), founded in 1656 as a home for aged or insane women, on the site of a gunpowder factory.

In 1684 a criminal wing was built, in which 'Manon Lescaut' and Mme de la Motte were gaoled, and which was notorious for its filth and vice, to which a house of correction for wayward wives and young girls was added, and in 1790 there were said to be 8000 females living there. Part of the building contained political prisoners during the Revolution, and here took place some of the worst massacres of Sept. 1792.

The main building, by *Le Vau* and *Le Muet*, dates from 1657–63; the domed *Church of St-Louis*, built in 1670–77, is by *Libéral Bruant*. Statues by *Étex* were added after 1832. As a whole, it is a notable example of the austere magnificence of the architecture of the period, and may be compared in many ways to the Invalides.

Dr Charcot (1825–93), the hypnotist, is commemorated by a monument to the l. of the gateway; his consulting-room, laboratory, and library have been preserved intact.

Adjacent to the S. is the *Hôpital de la Pitié*, transferred in 1911 from the Rue Lacépède, where it had been founded by Marie de Médicis in 1612.

To the N.E. is the **Gare d'Austerlitz**, the main railway terminus for Bordeaux, Bayonne, Toulouse, etc.; see Pl.15;6.

The BLVD ST-MARCEL diverges S.W. to meet the Av. des Gobelins, beyond which it divides to be continued by the BLVD ARAGO (leading due W. to the *Pl. Denfert-Rochereau*), and the BLVD DE PORT-ROYAL (eventually meeting the *Blvd du Montparnasse*).

A short distance S. of this junction stands (r.) **La Manufacture Nationale des Gobelins** (CN) (Pl.14; 8; adm. Wed.–Fri. afternoons only; guided tour), the famous tapestry factory which has been a state institution for over three hundred years, and still retains some of its 17C buildings.

The original manufactory at Fontainebleau was moved to Paris by Henri II. Suspended during the 16C Religious Wars, the industry was revived by Henri IV and installed in 1601 in the buildings of the Gobelins, named after *Jean Gobelin* (died 1476), head of a family of dyers, who made their reputation with the discovery of a scarlet dye, and who had set up their dye-works here on the banks of the Bièvre in 1443. In 1662, under Colbert, the royal carpet factory of the *Savonnerie*, started in 1604 in the galleries of the Louvre, and subsequently moved to a 'savonnerie' (soap-factory) at Chaillot, was placed under the same management (it transferred its workshops to the Gobelins' factory in 1826). In 1667 Louis XIV added the royal furniture factory, and Charles Le Brun and then Pierre Mignard (in 1690) were appointed as directors. The workshops of the Beauvais tapestry, destroyed in 1940, have also been transferred here (but see Beauvais itself, Rte 38).

On the l. are two workshops, separated by a staircase. The tapestry is woven on high-warp looms,.several of which date from the time of Louis XIV. The weaver works on the reverse side of the tapestry, having the painting which he is copying behind him and reflected in mirrors. The average amount of tapestry that a weaver can produce in a day is 15cm^2.

We are conducted to the former *Chapel*, where hang two tapestries made for it, and cross the Rue Berbier-du-Mets, behind the factory, which now covers the non-calcareous waters of the Bièvre, which used to flow between the dye-works and workshops. A new building has been erected here, containing workshops for the weaving of carpets, where the original methods are still followed.

Adjacent are the buildings of the *Mobilier National*, and beyond them, where stood the allotments of tapestry workers, is the SQ. RENÉ-LE-GALL (with the hunting lodge of M. de Julienne, the patron of Watteau).

The Av. des Gobelins ends to the S. at the PL. D'ITALIE, the hub of seven important thoroughfares, on the N. side of which is the *Mairie of the 13th Arrondissement*.

Turning N. down the Av. des Gobelins, we shortly reach the picturesque church of **St-Médard** (Pl. 14;8), dedicated to the 'St Swithin' of France. The nave and W. front are of the late 15C; the choir, in construction from 1550 to 1632, was 'classicized' in 1784, when the *Lady Chapel* was added. Sacked by the Huguenots in 1561, not much of the 16C glass survives. The churchyard, now a garden, was notorious for the hysterical orgies of the Jansenist fanatics, or 'convulsionnaires', at the tomb of the Abbé Pâris (died 1727).

The narrow, shabby, and populous Rue Mouffetard (an ancient thoroughfare now closed to traffic at its lower end) climbs N. from the front of the church through a squalid district (but with a good street market) past (l.) the Rue de l'Arbalète, where at No.3 Auguste Rodin was born in 1840. Eventually we pass (r.) the PL. DE LA CONTRESCARPE, where No.1 has a tablet commemorating the 'Cabaret de la Pomme-de-Pin', immortalized by Rabelais and the 'Pléïade'. There was another cabaret of the same name in the Rue de la Cité.

We shortly enter the Rue Descartes, at No.39 in which Paul Verlaine (1844–96) died, before reaching the Rue Clovis, see Rte 2.

Also in this district, but slightly to the W., and best approached by the Rue d'Ulm (leading S. from the *Panthéon*), is the Maronite church of *N.-D. du Liban* (No.17). The *Collége des Irlandais*, founded in 1578 by John Lee, and re-founded in 1687 by English Catholics as a seminary, stands at the corner of the adjacent Rue des Irlandais.—At No.29 Rue Lhomond, leading S.E., with an 18C façade seen from the Rue Amyot, Mme du Barry and Juliette Drouet were educated in the *Couvent de Ste-Aure*.— A short distance beyond, at the *École de Physique et de Chimie industrielles*, in the Rue Pierre-Brossolette, Pierre and Marie Curie did their experimental work in 1883–1905.

At No.45 Rue d'Ulm is the *École Normale Supérieure*, established in 1794 for the training of teachers, and sited here since 1843. Pasteur worked in laboratories here between 1864 and 1888. Among its pupils were Taine, Bergson, Péguy, Romain Rolland, Giraudoux, Jules Romains, Jean Jaurès, and Édouard Herriot.

4   Val-de-Grâce; Observatoire; Montparnasse

MÉTROS: *Luxembourg, Port-Royal, Denfert-Rochereau, Cité-Universitaire, Vavin, Montparnasse-Bienvenue.*

Turning S. from the Rue Soufflot along the Rue St-Jacques (Pl. 13;8;

see p72) we pass at No.195 the *Institut Océanographique* (adm. 10.00–17.30 except Mon. and August), and No.218, which occupies the site of the house of Jean de Meung, part-author of the 'Roman de la Rose' (c. 1300). On the r. is **St-Jacques-du-Haut-Pas**, a plain classical building (1630–88), replacing an earlier chapel, and the favourite church of the Jansenists, completed with the help of the Duchesse de Longueville (1619–79; who is buried here), together with Jean Duvergier de Hauranne (1581–1643), the prominent Jansenist; and Jean-Dominique Cassini, the astronomer, in 1712.

No.254, at the corner of the Rue de l'Abbé-de-l'Épée, is the *Institut National des Sourds-Muets*, a Deaf and Dumb Asylum founded by the Abbé de l'Épée about 1700 and taken over by the State in 1790; the building, once the Oratorian seminary of St-Magloire, was reconstructed in 1823. In the courtyard is a statue of the Abbé by *Félix Martin*, a deaf and dumb sculptor (1789).

Further on, at No.269 (l.) is the **Schola Cantorum** (visitors admitted), a free conservatoire of singing and music established in 1894 by three pupils of César Franck, including Vincent d'Indy. Among composers who studied there were Albéniz, de Falla, Granados, Roussel, and Turina. Among directors in recent years has been the distinguished composer and musicologist Daniel Lesur.

The buildings (1674) are those of the English Benedictine monastery of St Edmund, founded in France in 1615, and established on this site from 1640 to 1818. The salon and staircase are good examples of the Louis-XIV style; the lower part of the chapel is now a concert hall; the 'chapelle ardente', where James II's body lay in state, may also be seen.

James II (d. 1701), his daughter Louise Maria-Theresa (1692–1712), and the Duke of Berwick (1670–1734), his son by Arabella Churchill were buried here; their bodies, hidden at the Revolution, are probably in the catacombs, which were once accessible from the house. The last burial here was that of Berwick's second son Charles (died 1787). Dr Johnson (1775) and Benjamin Franklin were guests of the English monks here.

At No.284 (l.), the door between columns at the end of the courtyard was once the entrance to the distinguished Carmelite convent to which Louise de la Vallière, mistress of Louis XIV, retired in 1674. Another relic of the convent is a *crypt* beneath No.25 Rue Henri-Barbusse, to the W.

The street widens (at Nos 277–279) opposite the impressive front of the ***VAL-DE-GRÂCE** (Pl. 13;8), since 1790 a military hospital, and from 1624 the house of the Benedictine nuns of Val-Profond, whose patroness was N.-D. du Val-de-Grâce. The present more extensive buildings were erected by Anne of Austria in thanksgiving for the birth of Louis XIV in 1638 (she had been married 22 years without issue), and the first stone of the new works was laid by the young king in 1645. In the courtyard is a bronze statue of Napoleon's surgeon, Baron Larrey (1766–1842), by *David d'Angers*.

François Mansart was succeeded as architect before 1649 by *Jacques Lemercier*, and after 1654 the buildings were finished by *Le Muet* and *Le Duc*, the church being completed in 1667. The remains (often only their hearts) of royal personages interred here, including Anne of Austria, Henrietta Maria of England, Marie-Thérèse (wife of Louis XIV), La Grande Mademoiselle, and the Regent Philippe II d'Orléans, were dispersed at the Revolution. The Army Medical School was added in 1850.

The façade of the church (by *Mansart*) is a good example of the Jesuit style, and the lead and gilt **Dome* (by *Le Duc*) is one of the finest in France. The sculptures within are by *François* and *Michel Anguier*, *Pierre Sarazin*, and others. The high-altar, with its six huge twisted marble columns, is inspired by Bernini's in St Peter's at Rome; but the sculptured Nativity on it is a copy of Anguier's original (now at *St-Roch*). The painting in the dome is by *Pierre Mignard*; in the chapel on the r. of the choir is a portrait of Anne of Austria borne by an angel; and in the *Chapel of the Sacrament* (shown by the sacristan), is the Communion of the Angels, by *J.-B. de Champaigne*. The imposing Cloisters may be visited, and also, in the former *Refectory*, a *Museum of Military Hygiene*.

The *Val-de-Grâce* was only one of the many religious houses which, until the Revolution, were established in this district. To the N. are the Rue des Ursulines and Rue des Feuillantines (in which the youthful Victor Hugo spent the years 1808–13), whose names recall vanished convents; almost opposite were the Carmelites (see above); to the S. stood *Port-Royal* (see below), beyond which, in the BLVD ARAGO, stood a 13C Franciscan nunnery.

To the r. on the far side of the BLVD DE PORT-ROYAL, a maternity hospital has, since 1814, occupied the buildings of *Port-Royal de Paris*, a branch of the Jansenist abbey of *Port-Royal-des-Champs*, destroyed at the instigation of the Jesuits and its site ploughed over in 1709 (see Rte 33B). In the chapel, completed by *Le Pautre* in 1647, is the tomb of Angélique Arnauld (1591–1661), the famous reforming abbess.

The extensive buildings of the *Hôpital Cochin* lie to the l. of the Rue Faubourg-St-Jacques, where No.38 (r.), the *Hôtel de Massa* (1784), transferred here from the Champs-Élysées in 1927, and re-erected, has since been occupied by the Société des Gens de Lettres.

We turn up the Rue Cassini, where at No.2 lived Alain-Fournier in 1910–14, and wrote 'Le Grand Meaulnes'; Balzac lived in 1829–34 at a house on the site of No.1, where he wrote 'La Peau de Chagrin'.

We pass (l.) the entrance of the **Observatoire** (Pl. 14;7), founded by Louis XIV in 1667 and completed by *Claude Perrault* in 1672. It was visited in 1698 by Dr Martin Lister, who here met Jean Cassini, the first of the family of cartographers.

The four sides of the building face the cardinal points of the compass, and the latitude of the S. side is the recognized latitude of Paris (48°50′ 11″ N.). A line bisecting the building from N. to S. is the meridian of Paris (2°20′ 14″ E. of Greenwich), which until 1912 was the basis for the calculation of longtitude on French maps. The Observatoire is also the headquarters of the *Bureau International de l'Heure*, and a 'speaking' clock (tel. 699 84 00) is installed in its cellars.

Application to attend a guided tour (on the 1st Sat. of each month, at 14.30) should be made in advance to the Secrétariat at 61 Av. de l'Observatoire.

On the first floor of the main building is a *Museum of Instruments*, and the contents of the Rotunda in the W. tower illustrate the history of astronomy. The room on the second floor, on the pavement of which is traced the Paris meridian, contains older instruments. A shaft descending from the roof of the main building into the catacombs has been used for the study of falling bodies. In the E. cupola is an equatorial telescope of 38cm aperture.

Turning N. from the *Observatoire*, we shortly cross the Av. Denfert-

Rochereau to reach the CARREFOUR DE L'OBSERVATOIRE.

To the N.W. is *Rude's* statute of Ney (1769–1815), who was shot close by, for ('traitorously') espousing Napoleon's cause on his return from Elba. Among those 'Royalists' who voted for his death were marshals Marmont and Victor. Behind it is the *Closerie des Lilas*, long a literary resort, and frequented by Baudelaire, Verlaine, Gide, Jarry, Apollinaire, etc. To the N. is the *Fontaine de l'Observatoire* (1875) by *Davioud, Frémiet,* and *Carpeaux.*

The Av. Denfert-Rochereau leads S.W. to the PL. DENFERT-ROCHEREAU, passing (r.) the *Hôpital St-Vincent-de-Paul,* with a chapel of 1650–55. Chateaubriand lived in 1826–38 in the grounds of the Infirmerie Marie-Thérèse, which occupied an adjacent site, and which was directed by his wife.

This focus of traffic was known as the *'Pl. d'Enfer'* until 1879, when it received its present name in honour of the defender of Belfort during the Franco-Prussian War. In the centre is a reduced copy of Bartholdi's sculpture of the 'Lion of Belfort'. The earlier name originated as *Via Inferior,* the Roman road (now the Blvd St-Michel) leading S. to it from the Île de la Cité, parallel to and W. of the *Via Superior* (now the Rue St-Jacques).

On the S.W. side of the Place, in one of the octroi pavilions of the old Barrière d'Enfer (1784), is the main entrance to **Les Catacombes**, a labyrinthine series of underground quarries dating from the time of the Romans and extending from the *Jardin des Plantes* to the *Porte de Versailles* and into the suburbs of Montrouge, Montsouris, and Gentilly. In the 1780s they were converted into a charnel-house for bones removed from disused graveyards, and most of the victims of the massacres of the Terror were later transferred here. In 1944 they were a headquarters of the Resistance Movement.

Escorted tours take place Tues.–Fri. between 14.00–16.00, and Sat.–Sun. 9.00–11.00, 14.00–16.00. It is advisable to take a torch. The perambulation lasts over an hour, through a macabre series of galleries lined with bones and skulls, to a huge ossuary containing the debris of over 6 million skeletons, but tends to be monotonous.

Leading S. from the Pl. Denfert-Rochereau, the Av. René-Coty approaches the **Parc de Montsouris**, some 16 hectares in area and laid out in 1875–78. Near its N.E. corner is a lake (which suddenly dried up on the day of inauguration, and the engineer responsible committed suicide); near the centre of the S. side is a reproduction of the *Bey's Palace* at Tunis (erected for the Exhibition of 1867), to be restored.

Among artists who lived in this quarter was Braque (1882–1963), with a studio in the Rue du Douanier (Rousseau), to the W. Lenin lived at No.4 Rue Marie-Rose, some minutes walk further N.W., in 1909–12.
    Facing the S. side of the park, flanked by the BLVD JOURDAN, is the **Cité Universitaire**, founded in 1922, accommodating c. 7,000 students in some 37 halls of residence, the individual style of each reflecting the characteristic architecture of their own country. The U.S. foundation dates from 1928; the British hostel from 1937; and the huge *Maison Internationale* (with a swimming-pool, theatre, etc.) from 1936. Few of these heterogeneous buildings are of any great interest, although *'Le Corbusier'* (the designer of the Swiss and Brazilian halls) will have his admirers.
    The church of *Sacré-Coeur,* reached by a footbridge over the BLVD PERIPHERIQUE to the S., is a landmark to traffic approaching Paris by the A6 autoroute and Orly.

Montparnasse

From the CARREFOUR DE L'OBSERVATOIRE the long BLVD DU MONTPARNASSE leads N. W. across the BLVD RASPAIL, where to the N. stands *Rodin's* statue of Balzac. This junction may be regarded as the centre of a quarter which replaced Montmartre ·as the principal artistic and bohemian rendezvous, when they no longer found inspiration on the N. heights of Paris. Gauguin had a studio at No.8 Rue de la Grande-Chaumière, leading N.E. Then, inexorably, the smaller intimate cafés were replaced by *Le Dôme, La Coupole, La Rotonde*, etc., and the district was invaded by a horde of hangers-on and parasitic pseudo-bohemians; the 'boîtes' in the Rue de la Gaité and elsewhere still attract this polyglot crowd.

Nevertheless, the neighbouring streets are replete with (fast fading) associations with late-19C and early 20C artists and intellectuals. Trotsky and his fellow-revolutionaries frequented the *Rotonde* prior to 1917. Rilke and Modigliani lived in the Rue Campagne-Première, to the S. E., as did Whistler, who, with Rodin, had studios at 132 Blvd du Montparnasse (demolished). In earlier decades, Sainte-Beuve, the critic (1804–69), lived at No.19 Rue N.-D.-des Champs, to the N.E., and died at No.11 Rue du Montparnasse. Romain Rolland lived at No.162 Blvd du Montparnasse in 1901–14.

Both Henry Miller and Hemingway have described the café life, disreputable and otherwise, of the district in its heyday, which was largely blighted by the mid-1930s, and which may disappear for ever with the present transformation and development of the area, already dominated by the obtrusive **Tour Montparnasse** (1973; 200m high), which has little to recommend it except for the impressive panoramic views (fee) from the 56th floor. An open-air terrace forms its 58th floor.

To the S. W. and parallel to the Blvd de Montparnasse, is the BLVD EDGAR-QUINET, with the main entrance of the **Cimetière Montparnasse** (Pl. 13;7), an 18-hectare site laid out in 1824. Maupassant, Louÿs, Baudelaire, J.-K. Huysmans, and Sainte-Beuve, among writers; César Franck, D'Indy, Saint-Saëns, Chabrier, and Clara Haskil, among composers and musicians; Fantin-Latour, Gérard, Houdon, Rude, Soutine, Zadkine, Bourdelle, and Brancusi, among artists and sculptors; Proudhon, the socialist reformer and Arago, and Alfred Dreyfus, are all buried here; as was André Citroën, the manufacturer of automobiles, and Pierre Laval, prime minister in the wartime Vichy régime.

From near the S. W. corner of the cemetery the Rue Raymond-Losserand leads S. W. Just S. of its junction with the Rue du Château stood, until the turn of the century, the *Château du Maine*, a hunting-lodge of the Duc de Maine, on the road to Sceaux: see Rte 32.

Adjacent to the *Tour*, and forming part of the glass and concrete complex, is the **Gare Montparnasse** (Pl.13;7), 18 storeys high, surrounding, on three sides, the station platforms.

At No.34 in the BLVD DE VAUGIRARD, flanking the station to the N. W., is the impressive new *Musée de la Poste**, not only of interest to the philatelist, a well-displayed collection vividly explaining the history of the postal system from its earliest days, laid out in some 15 rooms, descending in stages from the Fifth Floor (lift). Sections are devoted to methods of communication and transport; to postmen themselves, illustrated by old costumes and prints, etc; to letter-boxes; to stamps and their printing; to telecommunication and the mechanisation of the service, etc. The Catalogue is well-produced and informative.

Further to the W. is the BLVD PASTEUR, off which runs the Rue du Docteur-Roux, with (l.) the *Institut Pasteur*, founded by Louis Pasteur in 1887–89 and built by private subscription. Pasteur (1822–95) is buried in the crypt; the tomb of Dr Émile Roux (1853–1933), inventor of the treatment of diphtheria by serum-injection, lies in the garden.

At No.16 Rue Antoine-Bourdelle, N. of and parallel to the Blvd de Vaugirard, is a *Museum* devoted to the sculptor *Bourdelle* (1861–1929).

The Métro at Montparnasse-Bienvenue is well-connected with lines returning to the centre.

5 The Faubourg St-Germain: Eastern Sector

MÉTROS: *Pont-Neuf, Odéon, Luxembourg, St-Sulpice, St-Germain-des-Prés, Mabillon.*

The district still known as the Faubourg St-Germain stretches S. from the Seine opposite the *Louvre*, from the *Institut* on the E. to the *Pont de la Concorde* to the W. Until the end of the 16C, much of this area, the property of the *Abbaye St-Germain-des-Prés*, was open country. In the following century, with the religious revival, several convents were built here, and in 1670, the *Hôtel des Invalides* was constructed on the outskirts to the W. By 1685 the new *Pont Royal* provided easy access to the *Château des Tuileries*, which became the home of the court during the Regency, and this, together with the creation of the *École Militaire*, were the main reasons for the building of this new aristocratic quarter, which gradually took the place of the *Marais*. About half the houses were built between 1690 and 1725, a quarter between 1725 and 1750, and most of the rest between 1750 and 1790. In style they are very similar; often the most handsome façade faces the garden, and the gateway or 'Porte-cochère' from the street leads to the 'Cour d'Honneur'.

Today, the main thoroughfares are the Blvd St-Germain and the Blvd Raspail, which have done much to alter the character of the quarter. The most characteristic streets of the once 'noble faubourg' are the Rue de Lille, Rue de l'Université, Rue St-Dominique, and Rue de Grenelle. About a hundred old mansions remain, many of them converted to house embassies or government offices, but the whole area still retains numerous characteristic streets, and the 6th and E. half of the 7th Arrondissements remain two of the most pleasant districts of Paris in which to linger.

It is convenient to divide the large area into two sections: **Rte 5** describing the Luxembourg and St-Germain-des-Prés (from the Blvd St-Michel to the Rue des Saints-Pères and Blvd Raspail): **Rte 6** describing the rest of the 7th Arrondissement.

Facing the Louvre is the PL. DE L'INSTITUT, flanked by the curved wings of the ***INSTITUT DE FRANCE** (Pl. 14;1), surmounted by a dome, which, since its recent cleaning and restoration, is one of the more attractive features of this reach of the quays.

The building may be visited on Sat. afternoons by prior arrangement with the Secrétariat, 23 Quai de Conti.

The E. wing of the *Institut* and the adjacent *Hôtel des Monnaies* (see below) cover the site of the *Hôtel de Nesle* (13C), in which was incorporated the 12C *Tour de Nesle* or *Tour Hamelin*, the river bastion of Philippe Auguste's Wall (which ran S. E. parallel to the Rue Mazarine). The tower was notorious in legend as the scene of the amours of Marguerite (c. 1290–1315) and Jeanne of Burgundy, wives of Louis X and Philippe V respectively, who are said to have had their lovers thrown into the river. Later occupants were Isabeau de Bavière, Charles the Bold, and Henry V of England.

The W. part, known as the *Petit-Nesle*, and the workshop of Benvenuto Cellini in 1540–45, was demolished in 1663. The E. part, or *Grand-Nesle*, rebuilt in 1648 by Fr. Mansart, became the *Hôtel de Conti*, and in 1770, the *Mint*.

The present building was erected in accordance with the will of Card. Mazarin, who bequeathed 2 million *livres* in silver and 45,000 *livres* a year for the establishment of a college for sixty gentlemen of the four provinces acquired by the Treaties of Münster and the Pyrenees: Flanders, Alsace, Roussillon, and Piedmont (Pinerolo). The building, designed by *Louis Le Vau*, was erected in 1662–74. The official name of the new college was the *Collège Mazarin*, but its popular name was the *Collège des Quatre-Nations*. The Institut, founded in 1795, and installed first in the Louvre, acquired the former Collège Mazarin in 1806.

The *Institut de France* comprises five academies: the exclusive *Académie Française*, founded by Richelieu in 1635 and restricted to forty members (and already satirized by Saint-Évremond in 1643), whose particular task was the editing of the dictionary of the French language; the *Académie des Beaux-Arts* (1816), founded by Mazarin in 1648 as the *Académie Royale de Peinture et de Sculpture*; the *Académie des Inscriptions et Belles-Lettres*, founded by Colbert in 1663; the *Académie des Sciences*, founded by Colbert in 1666; and the *Académie des Sciences Morales et Politiques*, founded in 1795 and reconstituted in 1832.

The *Académie Française* holds special receptions for newly elected members, tickets of admission to which are much sought after (apply to the general secretary). An annual general meeting of all five academies is held on 25 Oct. (adm. by ticket only).

Members are known, satirically, as 'Les Immortels' (comp. Daudet's novel of that title), but it may be remarked that among the considerable list of great figures of French literature who were *not* members were Pascal, Descartes, Molière, La Rochefoucauld, Diderot, Rousseau, Beaumarchais, Balzac, Flaubert, Maupassant, Zola, and Proust.

It was not until 1980 that the first *non-male* member—Marguerite Yourcenar (an anagram of her real name, Crayencour)—was elected.

Passing into the first octagonal courtyard (beyond which are two others, the third being the *Kitchen Court* of the old Collège Mazarin), the door on the l. leads to the *Bibliothèque Mazarine*, containing c. 350,000 vols, 5800 MSS., and 1900 incunabula. Originally the cardinal's personal library, which, opened to scholars in 1643, became the first public library in France, it was considerably augmented by other collections during the Revolutionary period.

The *Institute Library* is also in this wing, together with a number of rooms decorated with academic statues and busts of distinguished academicians. Among many of little merit, *Pigalle's* Voltaire is striking.

In the W. wing is the *Salle des Séances Solennelles*, in the former chapel. Recent restoration has undone the damage caused by Vaudoyer, and Mazarin's tomb by *Coysevox* has been returned from the Louvre. His niece, the Duchesse de Mazarin (d. 1699), the famous beauty of the court of Charles II, was also buried here. The room contains about 400 seats (green for members of the Académie Française; red for the others), and here take place receptions and general meetings.

At No.13 QUAI DE CONTI (the riverside embankment here, as elsewhere in this central reach of the Seine, lined with the bookstalls of the *bouquinistes*) is the *Hôtel Guénégaud* or *de Sillery-Genlis*, by *Fr. Mansart* (1659), often visited by Napoleon when on leave from the École Militaire. Larrey lived here from 1805 to 1832.

No.11, the ***Hôtel des Monnaies**, the *Mint*, is a dignified building by

J.-D. Antoine (1771–75). The handsome doorway is ornamented with Louis XVI's monogram and elegant bronze knockers; above is the fleur-de-lys escutcheon with Mercury and Ceres as supporters. From the vestibule, a notable example of 18C architecture, a double staircase on the r. ascends to the second landing, from which we enter the *Musée de la Monnaie* (Mon. to Fri., 11.00–17.00), containing an impressive collection of stamping presses, punches, medals, and coins. Medals are for sale in the far wing.

The *Salle Guillaume Dupré*, in the centre of the building is (apart from the modern ceiling) representative of the best period of the Louis XVI style; showcases display medals from the Renaissance to the present. The *Salle Sage* contains new acquisitions; the *Salle Jean Warin*, portraits of the Walloon medallist Warin (1604–72) and directors of the Mint; the *Salle Denon* is devoted to medals of the Consulate and Empire period and the *Salle Duvivier* displays examples of coins illustrating the evolution of French currency from Merovingian times.

On the r. of the second courtyard is the entrance to the *Ateliers* or workshops, where, under escort (no gratuity) one may see processes in the production of coins and medals (adm. only Mon. and Wed. from 14.15–15.00; closed during summer vacation). In 1973 the minting of French coins was transferred to a new establishment at *Pessac*, near Bordeaux.

At No.5, on the corner of the Rue Guénégaud, Col de Marguerittes, of the Resistance, set up his headquarters while conducting operations for the liberation of Paris 19–28 Aug. 1944.

At the end of the adjacent Rue de Nevers (entered below an arch), one may see part of Philippe Auguste's *Wall*.

From the S. end of the Pont Neuf, the Rue Dauphine leads S., passing (l.), at No.9 Rue Mazet, the site of *chez Magny*, a famous restaurant and literary rendezvous in the 1860s, to the CARREFOUR DE BUCI, with its busy street market.

No.5 Rue Mazet was until 1906 the site of the 'Cheval Blanc' inn, terminus in the 17–18Cs of the diligence to Bourges, Bordeaux, and La Rochelle, etc.

The parallel Rue des Grands-Augustins (with the restaurant *Lapérouse* on the corner), contains the *Hôtel d'Hercule*, dating from the 17C (Nos 3–7); No.21 was the birthplace of the lexicographer Émile Littré (1801–81), and Heine lived at No.25 in 1841, as had La Bruyére in 1676–91, and Augustin Thierry, the historian, in 1820–30.

At No.35 QUAI DES GRANDS-AUGUSTINS (where stood the famous convent of that name from 1293 until its demolition in 1797) is another 17C mansion, at the corner of the Rue Séguier, home of the printer François Didot in 1740, and of Laplace during the Directory. This street, lined with old houses, leads S. to meet the Rue St-André-des-Arts, also containing several notable 17–18C buildings (Nos 27, 28, and 52).

From the PL. ST-ANDRÉ-DES-ARTS, to the E., where at No.11 Gounod was born in 1818, the Rue Hautefeuille leads S., with (No.5) the *Hôtel des Abbés de Fécamp*, with a pretty turret. Among its occupiers was Godin de Sainte-Croix, an accomplice of the Marquise de Brinvilliers. Baudelaire (1821–67) was born at No.15 (demolished).—J.-K. Huysmans (1848–1907) was born at No.9 Rue Suger, leading W. from the Pl. St-André-des-Arts.

Leading S. from the Rue St-André-des-Arts, the Rue de l'Éperon shortly meets (r.) the Rue du Jardinet, in which Saint-Saëns

(1835–1921) was born. Continuing along the latter alley, we enter the *Cour de Rohan* (16–17C), originally part of the palace of the Abp of Rouen. Turning l. on passing through an archway, No.4 in the ancient *Cour de Commerce-St-André* is the basement of one of Philippe Auguste's towers. At No.8, Marat's journal 'L'Ami du Peuple' was printed.

At No.9, opposite, popular myth has it that Dr Joseph-Ignace Guillotin perfected his 'philanthropic beheading machine', although in fact he merely proposed to the *Assemblée constituante* that beheading should be the only method of capital punishment, preferably by a machine. A mechanic built one to the specifications of the secretary of the College of Surgeons, a certain Dr Louis, and it was first put into operation on 25 April 1792.

The Rue de l'Ancienne Comédie (the next street to the W.) takes its name from the Comédie Française of 1689–1770, which occupied No.14, while opposite, the *Café Procope* (after its founder, a Sicilian named Francesco Procopio dei Coltelli), which originated before 1700, was a favourite haunt of Voltaire and the Encyclopaedists, Musset, George Sand, Balzac, Gautier, Gambetta, Verlaine, Huysmans, and Wilde, et al.

To the N. the Rue Mazarine (in which Smollett stayed—at the Hôtel de Montmorency—in 1763) leads back to the *Institut*, passing the sites (at No.42) of the *jeu de paume 'de la Bouteille'*, where the Abbé Perrin established the Opéra in 1669–72; occupied by Molière's company in 1673–80, after his death in 1673; and by the Comédie-Française in 1680–89, and (at No.12), another *jeu de paume*, where the 'Illustre Théâtre' was opened in Dec. 1643 by Molière's company. No.30, known as the *Hôtel des Pompes*, was the headquarters of the *pompiers* or fire brigade of Paris until 1760, where in 1723 died François Dumouriez du Périer, *père*, who had founded them the previous year. He was an actor, and also the father of 32 children (by two marriages, admittedly).

In the mid-19C the BLVD ST-GERMAIN was cut through this picturesque area of narrow lanes leading S. from the river. Opposite the Rue de l'Ancienne Comédie is the CARREFOUR DE L'ODÉON (Pl.14;3), beyond the PL. HENRI-MONDOR, both busy crossroads, where the *Benjamin Franklin Library* has replaced the Café Voltaire (No.1), where a banquet was held in honour of Gauguin before he left for Tahiti in 1891. At No.2 Camille Desmoulins was arrested in 1794; the statue of Danton (1759–94) marks the site of his house, where he was likewise apprehended.

   To the E. is a building of the **Faculty of Medicine** (University V) erected by *Gondouin* in 1769–76 on the site of the *Collège de Bourgogne* and *Collège des Prémontrés*, and since enlarged. The older part, facing the Rue de l'École-de-Médecine, is considered one of the most Classical works of the 18C. The façade facing the Blvd St-Germain was added in 1878.

In the courtyard is a statue of the anatomist Bichat (1771–1802) by *David d'Angers*. The *Library* contains c. 600,000 vols, and commentaries of the heads of the faculty from 1395 onwards. Also of interest are the *Lecture Hall*, the *Musée d'Histoire de la Médecine*, and the *Salle du Conseil*, hung with four Gobelins tapestries of the Louis-XIV period, *after Le Brun*.

Opposite is the entrance to the former *Refectory* of the *Couvent des Cordeliers*, a 15C Franciscan convent, which during the Revolution was a meeting-place of the extremist Club des Cordeliers, the leaders of which were Marat (a doctor by profession, and partly educated at Edinburgh), Camille Desmoulins, and Danton. The former was stabbed in his bath by Charlotte Corday in 1793 at No.20 (demolished).

At No.5, the *Institut des Langues Modernes* occupies the old *Amphithéâtre de Jardin du Luxembourg St-Côme* (1691–94), with a beautiful portal. This was originally the lecture-hall of the College of Surgery. A plaque here commemorates the birth of the actress Sarah Bernhardt (1844–1923).

Further E. (l.) at the corner of the S. section of the Rue de Hautefeuille (No.32), Gustave Courbet (1819–77) had his studio in the former chapel of the *Collège des Prémontrés*.

The Rue de l'École-de-Médecine narrows before meeting the BLVD ST-MICHEL.

From its W. end, we may ascend steps before turning l. along the Rue Monsieur-le-Prince (de Condé). At No.10, Auguste Comte (1798–1857), the positivist philosopher, lived from 1841; Saint-Saëns at No.14 in 1877–89, and Longfellow had lodgings at No.49 in 1826 (and in a subsequent winter, at No.5 in the adjacent Rue Racine). At No.54 (altered) Pascal lived in 1654–62 and wrote his 'Pensées'.—To the l., on meeting the Rue de Vaugirard, is the *Lycée St-Louis*, built by *Bailly* on the site of the *Collège d'Harcourt*, the greatest of the University colleges (1280), its entrance facing the Pl. de la Sorbonne. Racine and Boileau studied here.

Adjacent to the S. end of the Rue Monsieur-le-Prince is the PL. EDMOND-ROS-TAND, with a good view of the *Panthéon* (see Rte 2).—George Sand's last Paris home, in the 1870s, was at No.5 Rue Gay-Lussac, to the S.E.—To the S., on the r. of the BLVD ST-MICHEL, the *École Supérieure des Mines* occupies the *Hôtel de Vendôme*, an 18C building enlarged after 1840, and having its principal façade towards the Luxembourg Gardens. It contains a *Museum of Mineralogy and Geology*. At No.95 in the Boulevard died César Franck (1890). Leconte de Lisle, leader of the 'Parnassiens', a poetic coterie, lived at No.64 in 1872–94.

One of many entrances to the *Jardin du Luxembourg* (Pl.14;5) is a few paces S. of the Pl. Edmond-Rostand. These extensive gardens (23 hectares), embellished by numerous statues, form one of the pleasanter and more colourful open spaces in central Paris. Laid out in the 17C, they were deplorably mutilated in 1782 and 1867, and little remains of the original garden as known by Marie de Médicis.

Steps descend from the E. Terrace to lawns surrounding an octagonal pond with its fountain. Beyond the formal W. Terrace is the Jardin Anglais; while to the S., beyond the PL. ANDRÉ-HONNORAT, gardens are continued between the two branches of the Av. de l'Observatoire, which were laid out under the First Empire on the site of a Carthusian monastery demolished at the Revolution.

Turning N. from the central octagonal pond, we pass on our r., at the end of an oblong pool, the **Fontaine Médicis**, attrib. to *Salomon de Brosse* (c. 1627), moved here in 1861.

In the central niche is Polyphemus about to crush Acis and Galatea; on either side are Pan and Diana, and at the back a bas-relief, the Fontaine de Léda, brought from the Rue du Regard in 1855.

At No.19 Rue de Médicis, flanking the gardens to the N.E., was born André Gide.

The *Palais du Luxembourg*, once a royal residence, with its heavily rusticated masonry, is more visually attractive externally than internally, although the S. façade, facing the gardens, is a 19C copy,

Detail of the Fontaine Médicis, Jardin du Luxembourg

by *Gisors*. The N. façade is the original, where the main entrance is surmounted by an eight-sided dome. The two wings, terminating in steep-roofed pavilions, with three orders of columns superimposed, are connected by a single-storeyed gallery.

The Luxembourg was built by *Salomon de Brosse* in 1615–27 for Marie de Médicis, widow of Henri IV, who, it is said, wished to have a palace which reminded her of the Pitti Palace in Florence, her birthplace. She also acquired the adjacent mansion of the Duc de Tingry-Luxembourg (the *Petit-Luxembourg*; 1570–1612), hence its name. The building was altered in 1808 and enlarged in 1831–44.

After Louis XIII's death, the palace passed to her second son Gaston, Duc d'Orléans, and the 'Palais Médicis' became known as the 'Palais d'Orléans'. Subsequently, it belonged in succession to Mlle de Montpensier, the Duchesse de Guise (1672), Louis XIV (1694), and the Orléans family. Among prisoners confined here during the Revolution were Marshal de Noailles (executed at the age of 79 with his wife, daughter, and granddaughter); Hébert, Danton, Desmoulins, Fabre d'Églantine, the painter David, and Tom Paine (imprisoned here in 1793 for voting in the Assembly against the king's execution, and who escaped the guillotine only by an accident).

In 1794 the Directory transferred the seat of government from the Tuileries to the Luxembourg, and here Gén. Bonaparte presented the Treaty of Campo

Formio. In 1800 the 'Palais Directorial' became the 'Palais du Consulat'; under the Empire it was the 'Palais du Sénat', and later, the 'Palais de la Pairie'. Marshal Ney was confined and tried here in 1815. The ministers of Charles X were tried here under Louis-Philippe in 1830, and Louis-Napoléon Bonaparte after landing at Boulogne in 1840. From 1852 to 1940 the Palais was the meeting-place of the Senate, the upper chamber of the French Republic, except in 1871–79, when it was the seat of the Préfecture de la Seine.

In 1940–44 it was occupied by Sperrle, commander-in-chief of the Luftwaffe on the Western Front. In 1946 it was the seat of the Conseil de la République, but in 1958 it reverted to the Senate. Here also was held the ineffectual Peace Conference of 1946.

Adm. at 10.00–11.00; 14.30–15.30 on Sun., when small groups are conducted round parts of the building.

The INTERIOR, drastically remodelled by *Chalgrin* under Napoleon I, is decorated in the sumptuous but decadent 19C manner, replete with statues, and paintings, historical and allegorical, few of which are of any merit. The series of paintings devoted to the Life of Marie de Médicis, by *Rubens*, which once hung in the palace, are now in the Louvre.

By far the most interesting room is the luxuriously gilt **Cabinet Doré**, Marie de Médicis's audience chamber. Other rooms (on the First Floor) through which parties are conducted are the *Salles des Conférences*; the hemicycle of the *Salle de Séances*; the *Library*, overlooking the gardens, and containing some mediocre paintings by *Delacroix*, that in the cupola being the Limbo of Dante's Inferno.

The adjoining **Petit-Luxembourg** (now the residence of the President of the Senate; no adm.) was presented to Richelieu by Marie de Médicis in 1626. It includes the cloisters and chapel of the Filles du Calvaire, for whom the queen built a convent; the chapel is a charming example of the Renaissance style; the cloister forms a winter-garden. To the W. is the *Orangery*, once occupied by a museum.

A few paces to the N.E. of the Palais stands the ***Théâtre de l'Odéon**, built in the form of a classical temple by *Wailly* and *Peyre* in the garden of the Hôtel de Condé, which was demolished by Louis XV to this end.

This town house of the family from 1612–1764 stood on the site of Nos 5–9 in the Rue du Condé, parallel to the W. Here was born the Marquis de Sade (1740–1814), his mother being a lady-in-waiting to the Princess.

Inaugurated in 1782, the Théâtre-Française was rebuilt by Chalgrin after a fire in 1799, and re-opened in 1808. Its auditorium, with an interesting ceiling, is one of the finest in Paris.

From its N. entrance, the Rue de l'Odéon, bordered by 18C houses, slopes downhill towards the Carrefour de l'Odéon. At no.12 once stood the *Librairie Shakespeare*, founded by Sylvia Beach, where in 1922 the first edition of James Joyce's 'Ulysses' was published, in an edition of 1000 numbered copies. At No.22 in this street lived Lucile Duplessis before her marriage to Desmoulins; No.26 was the home of Beaumarchais in 1763–76, the period of 'Le Barbier de Séville'.

From the main entrance of the *Palais de Luxembourg*, in the Rue de Vaugirard (the longest street in Paris, stretching from the Blvd St-Michel to the Porte de Versailles), the wide and stately ***Rue de Tournon** leads gently down to the Blvd St-Germain, N. of which it is extended by the Rue de Seine, also containing a number of attractive houses, to the *Institut*.

Balzac lived at No.2 in the Rue de Tournon in 1827–30; Marie Lenormand, the fortune-teller consulted by Revolutionary celebrities, lived at No.5 for over fifty years and died there in 1843; Hébert ('Père Duchesne'; 1755–94), the journalist, lived here in 1793, and

Charles Cros, one of the pioneers of the phonograph, died here in 1888. No.6, the *Hôtel de Brancas*, was reconstructed during the Regency by *Bullet*; Gambetta lived on the top storey of No.7, the *Hôtel du Sénat*, where Alphonse Daudet also resided when he first came to Paris. No.10 (now barracks of the Garde Républicaine) was the *Hôtel de Concini*. Paul Jones, the first admiral of the U.S. navy, died at No.19 in 1792; the actor Gérard Philipe (1922–59) died at No.17.

Parallel, to the W., is the Rue Garancière, with the *Hôtel de Sourdéac* (No. 8; 1640).

At No.20 Rue de Vaugirard stood the *Café Tabourey*, a famous literary rendezvous; while at No.48 the composer Massenet (1842–1912) long resided, and died.—In the picturesque Rue Férou, diverging r., died Mme de La Fayette (1634–93), fifteen years after writing 'La Princesse de Clèves'; No.50, at the corner, her birthplace, later became the *Hôtel de la Trémoille*. Fantin-Latour lived at No.15.

Turning r. down the next street, the Rue Bonaparte (which narrows as it approaches the Seine), containing numerous antique shops and galleries, one of the most pleasant and characteristic in the commercial part of the Faubourg, we shortly enter the PL. ST-SULPICE (Pl. 13;6) dominated to the E. by the church. In the centre is the *Fontaine des Quatre-Évêques*, by *Visconti*, with statues of four famous preaching bishops: Bossuet, Fénelon, Massillon, and Fléchier.

In 1843–44 Renan was a scholar at the seminary which stood on the S. side; opposite, No.6 is a dignified mansion by *Servandoni* (1754), the first of a range which never materialized. Many of the neighbouring shops display cloying modern ecclesiastical art and furniture.

ST-SULPICE, the wealthiest church on the Left Bank, and noted for its music (frequent organ recitals; enquire at the church for details), is a somewhat ponderous classical building, imposing mainly for its size, although described by Gibbon as 'one of the noblest structures in Paris'. The W. front consists of an Ionic colonnade over a Doric. The N. tower, 73m high, has seated figures of the Evangelists; the S. tower is 5m lower. Hugo compared them to clarionets.

It was begun in 1646 by *Gamard* on the site of an older church, and continued on a larger scale by *Le Vau* in 1655 and *Gittard* in 1670. After an interval from 1675 to 1719 the work was resumed by *Oppenordt*. The building of the W. front was entrusted to *Servandoni*, who, however, failed to give satisfaction, and was replaced in 1745 by *Maclaurin*. His successor, *Chalgrin*, rebuilt the N. tower in 1777, since Maclaurin's design had also failed to please, but the S. tower was left incomplete.

Camille Desmoulins was married here to Lucile Duplessis in 1790. Under the Convention St-Sulpice became the 'Temple de la Victoire', and in 1799 a public banquet was given here by Gén. Bonaparte. Saint-Simon, writing earlier, was contemptuous of its clergy, with their 'barbes sales'.

The stately INTERIOR, a representative example of the 'Jesuit' style, is 110m long, 56m wide, and 33m high.

In the nave are two huge tridacna gigas shells serving as holy-water stoups, presented to François I by the Venetian Republic; the marble 'rocks' supporting them were sculpted by *Pigalle*. The late-18C pulpit, by *Wailly*, bears gilded figures of Faith and Hope by *Guesdon*, and Charity by *Dumont*.

The famous *Organ*, one of the largest in existence (6588 pipes), was built in

1781 and remodelled in 1860–62; the case was designed by *Chalgrin*, and is adorned by statues by *Clodion*, and decoration by *Duret*.

In the paving of the S. transept is a bronze table connected by a meridian line with a marble obelisk in the N. transept; at noon the sun's rays, passing through an aperture in a blind window in the S. transept, strike the meridian at different points according to the time of year.

The CHAPELS encircling the church are decorated with frescoes: in the first (r.) are late works by *Delacroix* (1853–63). In the 5th chapel, the tomb, by *Slodtz*, of the curé Languet de Gergy (1674–1750), founder of the *Enfants Malades*, and responsible for the completion of the church. In the *Choir*, works by *Bouchardon*. The *Lady Chapel* was designed by *Servandoni*. In a niche behind the altar is a marble Virgin by *Pigalle*, with angels by *Mouchy*. The wall-paintings are by *Carle Van Loo*; those in the dome, by *Lemoyne*. Remains of the 16C church may be seen in the crypt.

The next cross street to the N. is the Rue du Four.—Chardin lived from 1720–44 at No.1 Rue Princesse, leading S. from the Rue du Four, and at No.13 from 1744–57.

We shortly reach the busy intersection of the PL. ST-GERMAIN-DES-PRÉS (Pl. 13;4). Diagonally opposite, at Nos 170 and 172 respectively, are the *Café des Deux Magots* (grotesque Chinese figures), and the *Café de Flore*; while at No.151 in the boulevard is the *Brasserie Lipp*. All were once known for the artistic and literary set which frequented them; perhaps poseurs are now predominant.

*ST-GERMAIN-DES-PRES, the oldest church in Paris, and also the only one retaining any considerable remains of Romanesque work, dominates the N.E. of the square. It has been cleaned and restored recently.

The church, a relic of the great Benedictine abbey founded in 558 by Childebert I, who was buried there, as was St Germanus, Bp of Paris (d. 576), was rebuilt at the beginning of the 11C (body of the W. tower), in the late 11C (nave), and in the mid-12C (choir), and was consecrated by Pope Alexander III in 1163. It was the chief house of the reformed Congregation de Saint-Maur in the 17C, and numbered the scholar Jean Mabillon (1632–1707) and Bernard de Montfaucon (1655–1741) among its distinguished members.

The massive flying buttresses of the choir are among the earliest in France. The W. porch dates from 1607, but preserves the jambs of a 12C door and a battered lintel depicting the Last Supper. The transepts were remodelled c. 1644. The bell-chamber of the tower was added in the 17C. Flanking the choir are the bases of two towers pulled down in 1822, when the church was drastically restored, after its partial destruction following an explosion and fire in 1794, just prior to which its refectory had been used as a saltpetre store.

The INTERIOR (65m by 21m, and 19m high) would be more imposing if stripped of its 19C decoration; but is nevertheless interesting architecturally for the combination of the Romanesque style in the nave with the first attempts at the Gothic style in the choir. The vault of the nave and aisles dates from 1644–46. The pillars are flanked by four columns, the sculptured capitals of which in 1848–53 were either re-cut or removed to the Musée de Cluny and replaced by copies, with the exception of one remaining in the N. W. corner. Both nave and choir are daubed with murals by *Hippolyte Flandrin* (1842–64), among others.

S. Aisle. To the r. is a marble statue of N.-D. de Consolation, presented to the Abbey of St Denis by Queen Jeanne d'Évreux in

1340. In the S. transept is the tomb of Olivier and Louis de Castellan, killed in the king's service in 1644 and 1669, by *Girardon*. In the *first ambulatory-chapel* is the tomb of Lord James Douglas (d. 1645; son of the first Marquess of Douglas), a Scottish gentleman in the service of Louis XIII. *2nd chapel*: tombstones of Descartes (1596–1650), removed from Ste-Geneviève (1819), and of Mabillon (see above). *4th chapel*: fragments of stained glass of 1245–55.

Choir. The small marble columns in the triforium are re-used material from the 6C abbey of St Vincent; their bases and capitals are of the 12C. The *Lady Chapel* was rebuilt at the beginning of the 19C.

N. Aisle (as we return). *3rd chapel*: tombstones of Nicolas Boileau (1636–1711) removed from the Sainte Chapelle. *4th*: the tomb of William Douglas, 10th Earl of Angus (d. 1611), who died in the service of Henri IV. In the N. transept are a statue of St Francis Xavier, by *G. Coustou*; and the theatrical tomb, by *G.* and *B. Marsy*, of John Casimir V, King of Poland, who became abbot of St-Germain in 1669 and died in 1672.

In the garden to the N. of the church are fragments of sculptures from the great lady-chapel built in 1212–55 by Pierre de Montreuil within the precincts of the abbey.—In the Rue de l'Abbaye, but further E., are the buildings of the old *Abbot's Palace*, erected c. 1586 by Card. de Bourbon, behind which was the *Prison de l'Abbaye* (its site crossed by the present boulevard), where Brissot wrote his memoirs, and Charlotte Corday spent her last days.

In 1857, six years before he died at 6 Rue de Furstenberg (or Fürstemberg) Delacroix built a studio in the adjoining PL. DE FÜRSTEM- BERG, which with its four Paulownias, is now less of a back-water than it once was. This was later shared by Monet and Bazille, and now contains a small *Delacroix Museum* (open 9.45–17.15 except Tues.).

No.1 Rue Bourbon-le-Château, a few paces E., was Whistler's first home in Paris (1855–56), while the *Pré-aux-Clercs*, which lay to the N. (now crossed by the Rue Jacob), was a favourite promenade, and the scene of medieval student brawls.

For streets radiating S.W. and W. of the Pl. St-Germain-des-Prés, see below.
The Rue Bonaparte continues N., crossing the Rue Jacob. At No.18 in the former street the Czech government was formed in 1916; No.14 is the main entrance to the *École des Beaux-Arts* (see below), while the *Hôtel du Marquis de Persan* (Nos 7–9) was the home of Monge in 1803, and the birthplace of Manet (1832–83).

Both the Rue Jacob, and two streets diverging r. off the Rue Bonaparte, have interesting associations. Laurence Sterne put up in the Rue Jacob on his arrival in Paris in 1762 (at the 'Hôtel de Modène'), and was later a guest of Mme de Rambouillet at No.46. Wagner lodged at No.14 in 1841–42, working on 'The Flying Dutchman'; the social reformer Pierre-Joseph Proudhon later resided at the same address. In 1848 Mérimée lived at No.18 (rebuilt); No.32 belonged to du Cerceau, architect of the Pont Neuf; Stendhal stayed at both Nos 28 and 52 in 1808–10. At No.56 was signed a provisional treaty recognizing the independence of the United States (3 Sept. 1783); since 1810 it has been the offices of the printer Didot. Gen. Sikorski, head of the free Polish government, lived at No.58 in 1939–40.

To the N. in the parallel Rue Visconti (then the Rue des Marais) Racine

(1639–99) lived from 1693 until his death (house demolished); at No.16 Adrienne Lecouvreur (1692–1730) died in the arms of Marshal Saxe; at No.17 Balzac had a printing business, liquidated in 1828, and on the 2nd floor is a studio once occupied by Delaroche (1827–34) and Delacroix (1838–43).

In the next street to the r., the Rue des Beaux-arts, Mérimée and later Corot lived at No.10; Fantin-Latour lived at No.8 in 1868. At No.13 Oscar Wilde died in debt in 1900; his drama *Salomé* had been produced in Paris in 1896, while he was in Reading Gaol.

The **École des Beaux-Arts** (Pl. 13;4), begun in 1820 by *Debret* and finished in 1862 by *Duban*, replaced the convent of the Petits-Augustins, founded in 1608, of which certain relics remain. It was here that Alexandre Lenoir collected together numerous pieces of sculpture, saving them from destruction during the Revolutionary period (comp. St-Denis). The recently cleaned buildings, the main entrance of which is No.14 Rue Bonaparte, further enlarged in 1885 on the acquisition of the *Hôtel de Chimay* (see below) may now be visited; occasionally exhibitions are held here. The *Library*, containing c. 80,000 volumes and c. one million engravings and drawings, may be visited by scholars and artists on application to the director.

The main points of interest are the former convent *Chapel* (c. 1600), against the S. wall of which is the central part of the façade of the Château d'Anet, by *Philibert Delorme* (see Rte 34); in the adjoining *Chapel of Marguerite de Valois*, the small domed hexagon has claims to be the first dome built in Paris. Part of a Renaissance façade from the Château de Gaillon (1500–10) in Normandy separates the first courtyard from the second. An arcade from the *Hôtel de Torpane* (c. 1570) and the façade from the *Hôtel de Chimay* are also preserved. Both in the courtyards and inside the buildings are many sculptured fragments, antique marbles, etc., while the *Salle de Melpomène* is used for the display of students' work when competing for the Grands Prix de Rome.

Leading S.W. from the Pl. St-Germain-des-Prés is the Rue de Rennes, at the far end of which obtrudes the *Tour Montparnasse* (see Rte 4).—A short distance down the street we reach the Rue Cassette, diverging l., in which Alfred Jarry (1873–1907) died at No.20, and the de Musset family lived from 1818–32 at No.27; Rainer Maria Rilke lived at No.29 in 1906.

Turning r. at the end of this street into the Rue de Vaugirard, we pass the domed church of *St-Joseph-des-Carmes*, once the chapel of a Carmelite convent dating from 1613–20 and containing a number of interesting 17C canvases, etc. The crypt contains the bones of some 120 priests massacred in the convent garden in Sept. 1792. Prisoners held here and later released included Gén. Hoche, Joséphine de Beauharnais, and Mme Tallien. Adjacent are the buildings of the *Institut Catholique*, where, in 1890, radio waves were discovered by Édouard Branly (1844–1940).

Some distance S. in the next crossroad, the Rue d'Assas, is No.62, where Strindberg lived in 1895–96, while Auguste Bartholdi (1834–1904), sculptor of the Statue of Liberty (New York), died at No.82. At 100 bis is the former *Studio*—from 1928–67—of Ossip Zadkine, with a small museum devoted to his work.

Turning r. into the Rue d'Assas, and recrossing the Rue de Rennes, we shortly reach the Rue du Cherche-Midi (deriving its name from an 18C sign on No.19 representing an astronomer tracing a sundial), containing a number of attractive 17–18C houses. For its W. section, beyond the *Blvd Raspail*, see p102.

From the animated CARREFOUR DE LA CROIX-ROUGE (Pl. 13;5) the Rue de Sèvres leads S.W. At No.11 lived J.-K. Huysmans from 1872 to 1898.—Off the N. side of the street, the Rue Récamier recalls the *Abbaye aux Bois*, the home of Mme Récamier in 1819–49, where the most frequent visitor to her famous salon was Chateaubriand. Here also, from 1831–38 lived Mary Clarke, who had resided in Paris since c.1814 (see p101).

For the W. section of the Rue de Sèvres, see Rte 6; likewise for the Rue de Grenelle, which also commences at the *Carrefour de la Croix-Rouge*. Crossing this junction, we enter the Rue du Dragon, the possible site of the pottery workshop of Bernard Palissy (1510–89). Hugo lived at No.30 in 1821; No.3 is an American Cultural Centre.

At No.71 in the parallel Rue des Saints-Pères, to the W., died Rémy de Gourmont (1858–1915).

At the junction of the Rue des Saints-Pères and the Blvd St-Germain stood the *Hôtel de Selvois*, where the Duc de Saint-Simon (1675–1755) was born and lived until 1714.—At No.184 in the Boulevard is the *Hôtel de la Société de Géographie*, founded in 1821.

On the E. side of the Rue des Saints-Pères, after crossing the Boulevard, is the *Chap. St-Pierre*, rebuilt in 1611, the sole relic of the Hôpital de la Charité, which stood on this site from 1605 to 1937. It is now the church of the Ukrainian Catholic community in Paris (St-Vladimir-le-Grand). Adjacent are buildings of the *Faculty of Medicine* (1936–53), while opposite, in the 18C *Hôtel de Fleury*, by *Antoine*, is the *École des Ponts et Chaussées*, a civil engineering school founded in 1747.

Further N., at the corner of the Rue de Lille is the *École des Langues Orientales*, founded by the Convention in 1795. Manet died at No.5 Rue des Saints-Pères, and the organist Widor (1844–1937) lived at No.7, the *Hôtel de Falconet* (c. 1650). From the *Hôtel Tessé*, on the corner of the Quai Voltaire, the Marquis de Becqueville attempted to glide with wings, Icarus-like, across the Seine in 1742.

In the QUAI MALAQUAIS, leading E. to the *Institut*, are some charming 17–18C mansions. Anatole France (1844–1924) was born at No.19 (the home of George Sand in 1832–36), but until 1853 he lived at No.15. At No.17, part of the *Hôtel de Chimay*, built by *Fr. Mansart* c. 1640, and altered in the 18C for the Duchesse de Bouillon (d. 1714), the friend of La Fontaine, lived Henrietta Maria of France (the widow of Charles I of England; in 1662).

No.9, at the corner of the Rue Bonaparte, the *Hôtel de Transylvanie*, is a good example of Louis-XIII architecture (1622–28). No.5 was occupied by Marshal Saxe from 1744 until his death in 1750; and No.3 was the residence of the naturalist Alexander Humboldt during the Restoration.

6 The Faubourg St-Germain: Western Sector

MÉTROS. *Solferino, Chambre des députés, Invalides, Varenne, Sèvres-Babylone, Rue du Bac;* also *Gare d'Orsay* (RER)

From the *Louvre*, the *Pont du Carousel* crosses the Seine to the QUAI VOLTAIRE (Pl. 13;3), which continues the *Quai Malaquais* to the W, (see above), and was formerly the *Quai des Théatins*. Voltaire died in 1778 at the house of the Marquis de Villette (No.27); *St-Sulpice* refused to accept his corpse, which was rushed to the *Abbaye de Sellières* near Troyes by his nephew to save it from a common grave.

Louise de Kéroualle, Duchess of Portsmouth, occupied Nos 3–5 in 1695–1701. Ingres died at No.11 in 1867. At No.13 was installed the 'Moniteur Universel', an influential newspaper during the Revolution. Here as a tenant in 1829–36, Delacroix was preceded by Horace Vernet and followed by Corot. At No.19 Baudelaire lived in 1856–58, working on 'Les Fleurs du Mal', while Wagner completed the libretto of 'Die Meistersinger' there in 1861–62; both Sibelius and Oscar Wilde were later tenants. De Musset lived at No.25 in 1841–49.

To the W. extends the QUAI ANATOLE-FRANCE and the QUAI D'ORSAY (the latter, beyond the Pont de la Concorde, being a focus of 'foreign affairs'). The former is dominated by the huge and ornate bulk of the old *'Gare' d'Orsay*, erected in 1898–1900 by *Victor Laloux* on the site of the ancient *Cours des Comptes*, set ablaze in 1871 during the Commune.

By 1939 the station, with its comparatively short platforms, had virtually outlived its usefulness, and during the war became a depot for parcels destined for prisoners of war, and was later used as a reception centre for those liberated. It then served in part to house a theatre, and as a temporary home for the Hôtel Drouot, but the edifice progressively deteriorated, and its demolition was planned—after all, Baltard's pavilions at Les Halles had gone—but with the belated revival of interest in the conservation of 19C industrial architecture it was decided to transform the building into a *Museum* rather than attempt to destroy the all-too-solid structure.

The projected **MUSÉE D'ORSAY** will accommodate the dispersed collections of art from the Romantic period to the 'Art Nouveau', or more specifically, from c. 1848 to c. 1914, indeed following on from the collections of the neighbouring Louvre, and yet out of place among the modern and contemporary works hanging in the Centre Pompidou. Numerous selected canvases long relegated to the 'Réserves' of museums will again see the light—and another fluctuation of fashion is forecast—for there is more than sufficient space to fill: the vault alone is 138m long, 40m wide, and 32m high, and some 16,000 sq m have been reserved for the permanent collection, and another 1,200 sq m for temporary exhibitions.

So far, the plan is to make the main entrance at its W. end. Its vestibule will also give access to a café, the library, and some of the rooms reserved for temporary exhibitions (also with independent entrances), while stairs will ascend to a long central hall containing a display of *Sculpture*. Off this will open several galleries exhibiting *Paintings* from c. 1848 to c. 1870, together with a section devoted to the *Decorative Art* of the epoch, to the town-planning projects of Haussmann, and early photography, etc.; also separate rooms containing the Chauchard, Mollard, Moreau-Nélaton collections.

Lifts will ascend from the *Lower* or *Ground Level* to the *Fourth Level*, comprising a series of rooms housing the Impressionists, and (in the Bellechasse Gallery) Post-Impressionists, the Pont-Aven School, and the Nabis, adjacent to which will be a display of *Graphic Arts* and *Photography* from c. 1880 to 1914. To the N., the Seine will be overlooked by a terrace-café.

Hence one may descend to the *First Level*, with terraces above the central court, displaying examples of sculpture from the period

1870–1914, and several sections containing the more academic art of the era, together with rooms devoted to the Art Nouveau movement, apart from other transitional forms of the early 20C. A room at the N.E. corner will accommodate material relating to the early history of the *Cinema*, while the W. end of the building retains the restaurant of the fin-de-siècle hotel.

The *Second* and *Third Levels*, flanking the central coffered vault, will contain several sections concerned with the *Press and Typography*, with *Illustrated Books*, with the *Architecture* of the period, the Universal Exhibitions, and other facets of the second half of the 19C and the first decade of the 20th. The *Basement* will accommodate a lecture-hall, etc.

Among the collections that are to be translated there are the *Impressionists* now in the *Jeu de Paume* and those works at present in the *Palais de Tokyo* (see Rtes 8 and 17 respectively). Whether works of art of the period displayed in the autonomous museums of the Ville de Paris will be merged with them remains to be seen. A number of important donations have already been made, and an active policy of acquisition is filling certain lacunae in the wide field to be covered, which will also include sculpture, objets d'art, and other decorative features.

The completion of the ambitious programme is awaited with interest, and it is hoped that the new museum will be inaugurated by the time the next edition of this Guide is called for.

We now reach the **Palais de la Légion d'Honneur*, flanked by a colonnade with bas-reliefs by *Roland* on the attic storey. The Corinthian portico in the courtyard is adorned with a frieze of arabesques with the motto 'Honneur et Patrie'. Facing the quay is a rotunda with Corinthian columns and symbolic busts, etc.

Built by *Rousseau* in 1782–86 for the Prince de Salm-Kyrbourg, at the Revolution it was raffled and won by a former wig-maker's apprentice who had made a fortune. He was later imprisoned for forgery, and the house became the Swedish Embassy in 1797. Mme de Staël, the ambassador's wife, gave her famous receptions here under the Directory, but in 1804 it was bought by the government for the grand chancellory of the Legion of Honour. It was restored in 1878, having been severely damaged by fire during the Commune.

The entrance to the *Musée National de la Légion d'Honneur et des Ordres de Chevalerie*, exhibiting medals, decorations, etc., relating to the history of the Order, together with foreign heraldic trappings, is to be found at No.2 Rue de Bellechasse, adjoining (adm. 14.00–17.00, except Mon.).

This non-hereditary Order, instituted in May 1802, comprises five classes (in ascending order): Chevalier, Officier, Commandeur, Grand-Officier, and Grand-Croix.

At No.80 Rue de Lille (to the S.) is the *Hôtel de Seignelay* by *Boffrand*, architect also of the adjacent *Hôtel de Beauharnais* (1714), once the home of Queen Hortense, and later the German Embassy (now the ambassador's residence) with a curious neo-Egyptian peristyle.

A few minutes' walk to the W. brings one to the W. end of the BLVD ST-GERMAIN and the **Palais-Bourbon**, seat of the *Assemblée Nationale* (Pl. 12; 7), facing the *Pont de la Concorde* (see Rte 8).

In 1722 a mansion was erected on this site for the Dowager Duchess of Bourbon (legitimized daughter of Louis XIV and the Marquise de Montespan), of which only the inner courtyard and main entrance (at 128 Rue de l'Université) have survived. The Prince de Condé, forced to leave his home because of the construction of the *Théâtre de l'Odéon* (see p91), bought the palace from Louis XV and enlarged it from 1764 until the Revolution. He incorporated the *Hôtel de Lassay*, in which he lived after the Revolution. The Palais became national property under the name of Maison de la Révolution, the meeting-place of the Council of Five Hundred, and was later occupied by the Archives (1799–1808). Since 1815 it has been used by the *Chambre des Députés*, the French equivalent to the House of Commons, its name being changed to the *Assemblée Nationale* in 1946.

In 1940–44 the *Palais-Bourbon* was the headquarters of the German military administration of the Paris region, and at the time of the Liberation considerable fighting took place in the neighbourhood, causing some damage to the building, and the destruction of over 30,000 volumes in the Library.

Adm. Those wishing to visit the interior, or to attend a session of the Assembly, must first apply in writing to the Questor's Office. The main entrance is in the Pl. du Palais-Bourbon (see below).

The N. façade (1804–07), a neo-Hellenistic piece of imperial bombast designed principally to balance the *Madeleine* when seen from the *Pl. de la Concorde*, is entirely decorative, and consists of a portico of twelve Corinthian columns, with statues of statesmen, allegorical bas-reliefs, etc. by *Poyet*.

The decoration of the interior is of slight artistic merit; certain rooms contain historical paintings by Horace Vernet and Ary Scheffer, and by Delacroix (in the *Salon du Roi* and Library); the *Salle des Séances* retains bas-reliefs by Lemot (1798).

The *Galerie des Fêtes* (1848) connects the building to the *Hôtel de Lassay* (1724), the official residence of the President of the Assembly.

Further along the QUAI D'ORSAY (with which it is synonymous) stands the *Ministère des Affaires Étrangères* (Foreign Office), built by *Lacornée* in 1845.

Adjacent, on the ESPLANADE DES INVALIDES, is the *Gare des Invalides* and *Aérogare* (or Air Terminus).

For the *Hôtel des Invalides* and *Musée de l'Armée*, see Rte 7.

Turning E. along the Rue de l'Université, we shortly reach the PL. DU PALAIS-BOURBON, an elegant ensemble of Louis XVI mansions all built to the same pattern after 1776.

At No.108 Rue de l'Université (but with its entrance at No.121 in the Rue de Lille, parallel to the N.) is the *Institut Néerlandais*, with a good collection of Dutch and German paintings (adm. 13.00–19.00, except Mon.). Jacques Turgot (1727–81), the economist, died here; La Fayette lived at No.123, adjacent, in 1799.

Further E. (on the far side of the Blvd St-Germain), at No.51 Rue de l'Université, is the *Hôtel de Soyécourt*, of 1707 by *Lassurance*; No.24, the *Hôtel de Senneterre*, has a notable façade perhaps by *Servandoni* in the courtyard (1700). Franklin's first lodging on his arrival in Paris in 1776 was at the Hôtel de Hambourg in this street. Alphonse Daudet (1840–97) died at No.41; and from 1885 he had lived in the neighbouring Rue de Bellechasse, which leads S. to regain the BLVD ST-GERMAIN, flanked to the W., at this point, by the extensive buildings of the *Ministère de la Défense* (by *Bouchot*; 1867–77), with a clock-tower at the corner of the Rue de Solferino.

Nos 1, 3, and 5 Rue St-Dominique, running W. from the BLVD ST-GERMAIN, date from c. 1710. No.5 was the home of Gustave Doré (1832–83) from 1849 until his death. Nos 10–12 (since 1804 part of the *Ministère de la Défense*) occupy the former *Couvent des Filles de St-Joseph* (1641), established for orphaned girls, and generously supported by Mme de Montespan (1640–1707), who retired here in

1687 after being supplanted c.1674 by Mme de Maintenon in royal favour. Mme du Deffand (1697–1780) in 1755 likewise supported it, and here, until 1764, held her literary salons, being later much neglected, except by a few such as Horace Walpole (1717–97; 4th Earl of Orford), who visited Paris in 1765, '67, and '75.

Nos 14–16, in the same block of buildings, the _Hôtel de Brienne_ (1714 and 1730), was once the home of Lucien Bonaparte, and later of Laetitia Bonaparte. No.28 was the _Hôtel Rochefoucauld-d'Estissac_ (1710), while further W., the _Hôtel de Sagan_ (No.57), built by _Brongniart_ in 1784 for the Princess of Monaco, now the Polish Embassy, was the British Embassy prior to the purchase of the Hôtel de Charost: see Rte 16B.

S. of the Rue St-Dominique rises the uninspired Gothic-revival church of Ste-Clotilde, built in 1846–56 by _Gau_ and _Ballu_, where César Franck was organist from 1858 until his death in 1890; a commemorative monument, by _Lenoir_, stands opposite.

The Rue de Grenelle, flanked by a number of Embassies and Ministries, may be conveniently approached by following the Rue de Bellechasse S., in which, at No.41, the _Conseil de la Résistance_ and the _Comité Parisien de la Libération_ organized operations for the rising of 19 Aug. 1944.

Turning l. at their junction, we pass, at No.106, the _Temple de Panthemont_ (by _Constant d'Ivry_; 1747–56), once the chapel of a convent where Joséphine de Beauharnais lived for several years. Its main buildings (now Nos 37–39 in the Rue de Bellechasse) housed an aristocratic school for girls, where Jefferson's daughter was a pupil during her father's embassy.

No.102, the _Hôtel de Maillebois_, built early in the 18C by _Deslisle-Mansart_, was the home of the Duc de Saint-Simon from 1738, when he was working on his 'Mémoires', until his death in 1755. Robert Browning and his wife were later tenants. No.87 is the _Hôtel de Bauffremont_ (1721–36), with a curved façade; No.85, the _Hotel d'Avaray_ (1718; by _Leroux_), where Horace Walpole (1678–1757) stayed in 1727 during his Paris embassy, is now the _Netherlands Embassy_. No.79, the _Hôtel d'Estrées_, the _Soviet Embassy_, was built by Robert de Cotte in 1713.

Retracing our steps towards the W., we pass No.110, the _Hôtel de Courteilles_ (1778; now the _Min. de l'Éducation Nationale_); No.116, the old _Hôtel de Brissac_, rebuilt for Marshal de Villars by _Boffrand_ and _Leroux_ (1731), is now the _Mairie of the 7th Arrondissement_. No.101, opposite, the former _Hôtel Rothelin_ (or _de Charolais_), built by _Lassurance_ in 1700, is now the _Min. du Développement Industriel et Scientifique_. Nos 138 and 140 were built by _Jean Courtonne_ in 1724 and decorated by _Lassurance_ in 1734 for Mlle de Sens. Marshal Foch (1851–1929) died in the former; the latter is occupied by the _Institut Géographique National_ (whose maps are available from 107 Rue La Boétie). No.127, the _Min. du Travail_, was the _Hôtel du Châtelet_, one of the finest examples of the Louis-XV style; it was at one time used as the Archbishop's Palace. The _Hôtel de Chanac_, at No.142, opposite (by _Delamair_; 1750), is now the _Swiss Embassy_.

We turn l. along the BLVD DES INVALIDES, passing the N.E. corner of the _Hôtel des Invalides_ (see Rte 7), and back into the Rue de Varenne. At No.77, at the corner, the *Hôtel Biron (Pl. 12;4), is installed the *MUSÉE RODIN (METRO: _Varenne_), containing an important and impressive collection of sculpture by *Auguste Rodin* (1840–1917), which he left to the State, many being the originals of works executed in marble or bronze, and a fine selection of drawings.

The mansion, built in 1728–30 by *Aubert* and *Gabriel*, was occupied by the Duc de Biron in 1753, after the death there of Louise de Bourbon, widow of the Duc de Maine, and in 1820 by the aristocratic convent of the Sacré-Coeur. The State bought the house in 1901. In 1910 two ground-floor rooms were used as a studio by Rodin, who lived here from 1907 until his death in 1917, while Rilke, at one time his secretary, also had lodgings there (1908–11). Much of the painted and gilt panelling, which had been removed by the Philistine superior of the convent as being mere ostentation, has been recovered, and replaced.

Of the many outstanding examples of Rodin's work displayed here, a few only are listed. *Grand Salon*: St John the Baptist; 'L'Homme qui marche'; the Kiss; the Hand of God; Iris; and two studies of hands.—In a room to the l.: 'L'Age d'Airain'; busts of Carrier-Belleuse, Mahler, and Puvis de Chavannes. In rooms to the r. of the Grand Salon: the Thinker; Orpheus; Eve; bust of Lady Sackville-West; of Eve Fairfax, the suffragette; Rodin's father, etc.—On the *Staircase*: Three Shades (from the Gate of Hell).

FIRST FLOOR. Case of models for the Gate of Hell; two busts of Hugo; four nude studies of Balzac; Man with a broken nose; the Good Genius; Eternal Spring; Triton and Nereid on a dolphin; Water-fairy; Young Mother. Also shown are dance studies by *Renoir*, and paintings by *Renoir, Monet*, and *Van Gogh*, including the latter's Le Père Tanguy.

The *Gardens* are embellished by numerous bronzes and marbles, including: the Thinker; Hugo at Guernsey, formerly in the gardens of the Palais-Royal; Balzac; and the Gate of Hell; also, near the entrance, and seen from the street, the Burghers of Calais.

There is an Annexe to the Museum at *Meudon*, see Rte 21.

No.72 in the Rue de Varenne is the *Hôtel de Castries* (1700), sacked by the mob in 1790 after the duel between the reactionary Duc de Castries and the radical Comte Charles de Lameth. No.69, the *Hôtel de Clermont* by *Leblond* (1708), is now offices of the *Haut Commissariat à l'Energie atomique*.—At 1bis in Rue Vaneau (r.) André Gide (1869–1951) died.

Just beyond is the ***Hôtel de Matignon** (No.57), built by *Courtonne* in 1721 and altered in the 19C; having served as the Austro-Hungarian Embassy (1888–1914), since 1935 it has been the residence of the *Présidence du Conseil*. One of the most beautiful mansions in the Faubourg, it has an unusually large garden. Talleyrand lived here in 1808–11.

No.50, the handsome *Hôtel de Gallifet*, with an Ionic peristyle built by *Legrand* in 1775–96, is now the *Italian Institute*; their *Embassy* is at No.47.—We shortly reach the Rue du Bac. See p102 for the continuation of the route N.

To the S., No.98 Rue de Bac, with gilt angels above the door, and good iron balconies, was the *Café des Deux-Anges*, the secret rendezvous of the Chouans (c.1800), and here Cadoudal hatched the conspiracy of 1804. At No.108bis died Laplace (1749–1827), the astronomer and mathematician. At No.110 Whistler (from 1892) was visited by Beardsley and Mallarmé, and scandalised his landlord by letting his child-models run naked in the garden. Nos 118–120, with doors designed by *Toro*, are the *Hôtel de Clermont-Tonnerre*, where Chateaubriand (1768–1848) lived from 1838 until his death. On the third and fourth floors Mary Anne Clarke (1776–1852), once mistress of Federick, Duke of York, and her daughter Mary (1793–1883; Mme Mohl after 1847) had their salon, and were visited by Dean Stanley, Thackeray, Mrs Gaskell, and Florence Nightingale. No.128 is the *Séminaire des Missions Étrangères*, founded in 1663, with mementoes and relics of martyred missionaries. Nos 136–140 are the *Hôtel de la Vallière*, with handsome portals, occupied by the Soeurs de Charité.

To the l. is the *Grands Magasins du Bon Marché*, built on the site of an earlier asylum, the *Petites Maisons*, to the E. of which is the SQ. BOUCICAUT (Pl. 13;5; named after the foundress of the *Bon Marché*).

A short distance to the S.W., in the Rue de Sèvres (No.42) is the *Hôpital Laënnec*, formerly a home for incurable women, founded by Card. de la Rochefoucauld c.1635, which retains its original courtyard and chapel. At No.95 is the *Église des Lazaristes*, with a silver shrine preserving the body of Vincent de Paul (1576–1660) canonised in 1737. Barbey d'Aurevilly (1808–89) lived for thirty years and died at No.25 in the adjacent Rue Rousselet.

At No.31 Rue St-Placide, the S. extension of the Rue du Bac, J.-K. Huysmans (1848–1907) died; David d'Angers and Michelet lived in the same street, while Parmentier resided in the parallel Rue de l'Abbé-Grégoire.

No.40 in the Rue du Cherche-Midi, near the BLVD RASPAIL, belonged to Rochambeau (1725–1807), who fought for the Americans in the War of Independence, notably at Yorktown. At No.38, the *Maison des Sciences de l'Homme* has been built on the site of the *Prison Militaire du Cherche-Midi*, where many French patriots were imprisoned between 1940 and 1944.

The Rue du Bac leads N. from the Rue de Varenne, shortly crossing the Rue de Grenelle, where to the r. (Nos 57 and 59) is the ***Fontaine des Quatre-Saisons**, designed by *Bouchardon* in 1739, with sculptures of the City of Paris with the Seine and Marne at her feet, and with bas-reliefs of the Seasons. Alfred de Musset lived at No.59 from 1824 to 1840.

Half-l. across the BLVD ST-GERMAIN, government offices occupy Nos 244-248, two early-18C houses. No.246, the *Hôtel de Roquelaure* (1722), by *Lassurance* and *Leroux*, has a fine courtyard. Cambacérès, Second Consul in 1799, lived here in 1808.

Guillaume Apollinaire (1880–1918) lived and died at No.202 BLVD ST-GERMAIN; off which, to the r., leads the Rue St-Guillaume, where the 16C *Hôtel de Mesmes* (No.27), enlarged in 1933, is the *Institut National des Sciences Politiques*; No.16, the *Hôtel de Créqui*, built in 1660–64, and extended in 1772, was for a time the home of Lamartine, and later of Renan.

Crossing the Boulevard, the Rue du Bac leads N. to the Seine, and is named after the ferry operating there before the construction of the Pont Royal.

No.46 Rue du Bac, the former *Hôtel de Boulogne*, with its courtyard, was built in 1744 by *Boffrand* for Jacques Bernard, who died after a scandalous bankruptcy in 1753; it was the lodging of Chateaubriand in 1815–18.

To the E. is the church of **St-Thomas-d'Aquin**, begun in 1682 by *Pierre Bullet* in the Jesuit style, and completed, with the construction of the façade, in 1787. The ceiling-painting in the Lady Chapel is by *Lemoyne*.

7 The Invalides and Musée de L'Armée; École Militaire; Eiffel Tower

MÉTROS: *Invalides, Varenne, La Tour-Maubourg, St-François-Xavier, École-Militaire, Cambronne, Bir Hakeim-Grenelle.*

The districts to the W. of the Faubourg St-Germain are overshadowed by the *Dôme* of the *Invalides*, the *Tour Eiffel* to the W., and the *Tour Montparnasse* rears up not far to the S.E. (see Rte 4).

From the Right Bank, the best approach is by the *Pont Alexandre-III* (see p206), which affords an impressive vista of the *Invalides* at the end of its esplanade. This walk can be conveniently combined with a return via the Palais de Chaillot.

The ESPLANADE DES INVALIDES, 487m by 250m, was laid out in 1704–20 by *Robert de Cotte*, and planted with trees along the sides. At its N.E. corner is the *Aérogare* (see p33).

To the W., the QUAI D'ORSAY extends as far as the *Pont de l'Alma*. At No.63 on the Quai is the *American Church*, built in a Gothic style in 1927–31; the playwright Jean Giraudoux (1882–1944) died at No.89.—For the adjacent public entry to the *Sewers* of Paris, see p214— At No.7 Rue Edmond-Valentin, a short distance S.W., off the Av. Bosquet, lived James Joyce from 1935 to 1939.

From the PL. DES INVALIDES S. of the Esplanade, the Av. de la Motte-Picquet leads S.W. past the front of the *École Militaire* (see below); the BLVD DES INVALIDES skirts the E. side of the *Hôtel des Invalides*, the formal façade of which contrasts with the domestic architecture opposite. To the l. diverges the Rue de Grenelle and the Rue de Varenne, and near the corner of the latter is the *Musée Rodin* (see Rte 6).

The ****HÔTEL DES INVALIDES** (Pl. 12;4; headquarters of the military governor of Paris) was founded by Louis XIV in 1671 as a home for disabled soldiers, the first enduring institution of its kind; at one time it housed between 4000 and 6000 pensioners or *invalides*. At present about 70 wounded live there. The buildings, which form a majestic ensemble, were erected from the designs of *Libéral Bruant* (d. 1697), and *J. Hardouin-Mansart* continued the work. It was known both as the 'Temple de l'humanite', and 'Temple de Mars' during the Revolution. It was restored under Napoleon I, who was later buried beneath its Dôme. Part of the building now houses the *Musée de l'Armée; see below.*

Tickets, which may be used on two *consecutive* days, cover both the museums and entry to Napoleon's Tomb (the main entrance to which is in the Pl. Vauban). Adm. daily 10.00–17.00 or 18.00.
    Facing the Esplanade are two artillery batteries: St-Louis the unmounted *Batterie Trophée*, and the *Batterie Triomphale*, whose salvos announcing victory were last heard at the end of the First World War; the latter were removed by the Germans in 1940. Made for Frederick the Great in 1708, these eight pieces were captured by Napoleon at Vienna in 1805.

From the entrance gate we approach the dignified façade, over 200m long. The dormer windows take the form of trophies, each different. Flanking the main entrance are copies of the original statues of Mars and Minerva, by *Guillaume Coustou* (1735). The equestrian bas-reliefs above the central door, of Louis XIV accompanied by Justice and Prudence, by *Pierre Cartellier*, replaced (in 1815) an earlier design by Coustou.

Opposite the entrance to the *Cour d'Honneur* (102m by 63m) is the door of the church of St-Louis, above which are *Seurre's* original bronze statue of Napoleon, formerly surmounting the *Vendôme Column* (see Rte 10), and an astronomical clock (1781).

On the E. side of the courtyard is the main entrance to the *Musée de l'Armée*. At the foot of the staircase to the r. of the entrance to the church, is one of the Renault cars (the Marne taxis), which, commandeered by Gén. Gallieni, carried troops to the Front in Sept. 1914.

The *Church of St-Louis (the chapel of the *Invalides*) was built by *Bruant* and *Mansart*. The plain but imposing interior, decorated with captured colours, has a gallery built at the same level as that of the dormitories of the disabled. In 1837 it resounded to the first performance of Berlioz's 'Grande Messe des Morts', the orchestra being reinforced by a battery of artillery on the esplanade. The *Organ* (1679–87), by Alexander Thierry, was restored in the 1950s. Concerts still take place here.—Behind the high-altar a sheet of plain glass separates the chapel from the *Dôme des Invalides*.

In vaults below (no adm.) are the graves of many French marshals (and génerals), among them Jourdan, Bertrand, Grouchy, and Oudinot, and, more recently, Leclerc de Hautecloque, and Juin.

On leaving the chapel, we turn l. along the Corridor de Nimes to reach the entrance of the *Dôme*. Visitors approaching from the Pl. Vauban, to the S., will find the ticket-office just W. of its main entrance (Pl. 12;4).

The *Dôme des Invalides*, begun by *J. Hardouin-Mansart* in 1675, and finished in 1706, was added to the church of St-Louis as a chapel royal. In the niches on either side of the entrance are statues of Charlemagne and St Louis by *Coysevox* and *Nic. Coustou*. The ribbed dome is roofed with lead, adorned with gilded trophies, and crowned with a flèche 107m above the ground.

The admirably proportioned interior, 56m square, is in the form of a Greek cross.

The focus of attention is the sumptuous *Tomb of Napoleon*, designed by *Visconti*, in which the Emperor was placed in April 1861, forty years after his death at St Helena, whence his remains were brought to the Invalides in Dec. 1840: see *Arc de Triomphe*.

They lay in the Chap. St-Jérome while this sarcophagus of dark red porphyry (from Finland), resting on a pedestal of green Vosges granite, was being prepared.

The tomb, its dimensions 4m by 2m, and 4·5m high, is surrounded by a gallery with ten bas-reliefs *after Simart* representing the benefits conferred on France by the emperor, and facing the sarcophagus are twelve figures by *Pradier* symbolizing his greater victories, between which are six trophies of 54 colours taken at Austerlitz. The statue of Napoleon in his coronation robes is also by *Simart*.

The error of placing the tomb in an inappropriately inferior position as seen from the circular gallery is now generally recognized. An imposing view is gained by descending to the *Crypt*, the inscription on the impost of the entrance to which may be translated: 'I desire that my ashes rest on the banks of the Seine, in the midst of the French people whom I have loved so dearly'.

On re-ascending we may visit the surrounding chapels, passing (in an anti-clockwise direction from the S.E.) the tombs (some enshrining only hearts) of Joseph Bonaparte (d.1844), Vauban (d.1707), Foch (d.1929; tomb by

The Dôme des Invalides seen from the South

Landowski), Lyautey (d.1934; tomb by *Albert Laprade*); La Tour d'Auvergne (d.1800; 'the first grenadier of the Republic'); and Turenne (d.1675), to reach the Chap. St-Jérome, standing anticipatively empty. Relics of the Roi de Rome (1811–32), Bonaparte's only son, who died prematurely of phthisis and was originally buried in Vienna, were brought here by the Germans in 1940 (on the centenary of the burial of his father), and since 1969 have lain in the vaults of the crypt (see above).

The ****MUSÉE DE L'ARMÉE** comprises one of the world's most interesting, extensive, and well-displayed collections of arms and armour, weapons, uniforms, military souvenirs, etc., and without an excessive display of chauvinism. The building also houses a library, and a small cinema.

The Musée des Plans Reliefs (see below) is open from 10.00–12.30; 14.00–17.30 daily.

From the main entrance (E. side of the *Cour d'Honneur*), we may visit first the restored *Salle Turenne* (r.), in which colours of French regiments from the First Republic to the present have been re-hung, and the fine frescoes, variously attributed to *Martin des Batailles* (1659–1735) or pupils of *Van de Meulen*, are now seen to advantage. The maquette of the Invalides (made prior to 1757) is also of interest.—To the l. is the *Salle Vauban*, containing cavalry uniforms and equipment, and similar frescoes.

From the Vestibule, stairs ascend to the SECOND FLOOR. To the r. is the entrance to a series of rooms devoted to the military exploits of the Ancienne Monarchie (1618–1792), set out in chronological order. It should be emphasized that most figures are displayed in such a way that the visitor may see them in the round: this applies likewise to the suits of armour to be seen in the W. wings. Among the numerous plans, engravings, prints, and portraits, those individual objects which may be pointed out are the cannon-ball that killed Turenne, and the perforated back plate of his cuirass, his marshal's baton, and his portrait attr. to *Le Brun*. Note also the colours of the Irish Clancarty regiment (1642).

Another room contains souvenirs of Gén. La Fayette (1757–1834). We next enter recently opened compartments concentrating on the Revolutionary, Directory, and Consulate periods, with many Napoleonic souvenirs, including one of Bonaparte's grey coats; his tent and furniture; and the stuffed skin of his white horse, 'Vizier', which outlived the emperor by eight years. Among portraits of his marshals, that of Ney, by *Gérard*, is notable. A further series of cabinets devoted to Napoleon at St Helena, and the period 1830–52, bring us back to the stairs.

On the THIRD FLOOR are sections devoted to the Second Empire, Crimean War, and Franco-German War of 1870, additionally illustrated by early photographs, and paintings by *Alphonse de Neuville* and *Edouard Detaille*.

On the ATTIC FLOOR above are housed the important collections of the autonomous ***Musée des Plans-Reliefs**, which, once work on the restoration of the roof has been completed, will—one is assured—be displayed in a way they deserve. It consists of some 80 models (apart from those dismounted or in *réserve*), the majority built to the scale 1:600, together with maquettes, maps and plans, representing the form of fortresses—both in France and near her frontiers—since the time of Vauban, and are of considerable historical, architectural, and topographical interest. The idea of their construction is attributed to Louvois. Until 1776 they remained secreted in the Louvre, and were only shown to such important visitors as Peter the Great (1717), who could be trusted. They were then moved to the Invalides where—although evacuated to Chambord during the last war—they have remained since. The models were made over the period 1668–1870, although many have been since restored. Among the more interesting are such strongholds as *Antibes, Bayonne, Belfort, Besançon, Briançon, Grenoble, Neuf-Brisach, Laon, Mont St-Michel, Perpignan, St-Martin-de-Ré, St-Tropez, Metz*, and *Strasbourg*, among many others.

On the W. side of the *Cour d'Honneur* are the **Collections of Arms and Armour**, extraordinarily rich in weapons of all periods, many exhibits being of great artistic interest, and masterpieces of damascening and chasing. To the r., the *Salle François I*, retaining the original frescoes (restored) of the dining-rooms and a painting of the Founding of the Invalides by *Pierre Dulin*, contains suits of armour (including parade armour) and the horse armour of François I, his sword, and plaques from his tomb. Note the heavy armour of the

Elector Palatine Otto Henry.

A small room near the entrance, containing arms *before the 9C*, may be visited on request.

To the l. of the entrance to this wing is the Salle Henri IV, with frescoes by 'Martin des Batailles', concentrating on jousting armour. Note the diminutive 'sample' suits made by the armourer to obtain orders for complete suits.—From the Vestibule we may enter, straight ahead, galleries containing the important **Collection Pauil-hac**. Among the numerous medieval and Renaissance pieces are suits belonging to Louis XIII, Henri III, Henri IV, and Louis XIV. The extensive *Collection of Firearms*, showing the evolution of such weapons, is outstanding.

A recently opened section is devoted to collections of **'Oriental' arms and armour** from the Balkans, Turkey, Persia, India, and China, etc. Among individual helmets of interest are those of Voivode (Russia; 16C) and of the Ottoman sultan Bajazet II (1447–1512).—On the far side of the adjacent courtyard is a wing containing some thousands of *figurines*.

One may obtain a view from these galleries into adjacent courtyards, in which stand a number of artillery pieces, while the walls of the *Cour d'Angoulême* (N.) are embellished by the 'Danube Chain', with which the Turks held their vessels in position during the Siege of Vienna in 1683. Other pieces, usually unmounted, are arranged around the main courtyard.

On the SECOND FLOOR are galleries devoted to the 1914–18 War and France's participation in the 1939–45 War: and 'animated' maps describe graphically the movements of troops during the various campaigns: *Occupied* France, France *Liberated*, and the sad history of deportations are likewise covered, as are the *Normandy Landings*.

Further rooms on the THIRD FLOOR are also devoted to France's Allies during the last war, while in the *Gribeauval Hall* are displayed an extensive collection of scale models of French and foreign artillery of all periods.

From the PL. VAUBAN (Pl. 12;4), to the S. of the *Hôtel des Invalides*, the Av. de Tourville leads W. towards the *École Militaire*, and the Av. de Villars leads S.E., shortly meeting the S. section of the BLVD DES INVALIDES (by the church of *St-François-Xavier*; 1875), which continues as far as the Rue de Sèvres, beyond which it is extended by the BLVD DE MONTPARNASSE.

At this latter junction are the buildings of the *Institut National des Jeunes Aveugles*, founded in 1793 by Valentin Haüy.—Vincent d'Indy (1851–1931) lived for 70 years and died at No.7 Av. de Villars.
S. of the Rue de Sèvres are the *Hôpital des Enfants-Malades* (founded 1724) and *Hôpital Necker*, once a Benedictine nunnery, founded in 1779 by Louis XVI, directed at one time by Mme Necker, and rebuilt in 1840.

Also radiating from the PL. VAUBAN are the wide tree-lined Av. de Breteuil,; and to the S.W., the Av. de Ségur passing (r.) the *Min. des Postes et Télécommunications*, and the controversial buildings of the UNESCO headquarters, perhaps best approached by the Av. de Lowendal.

The main **UNESCO Building** (by *Breuer, Zehrfuss*, and *Nervi*; 1958), flanking the semicircular Pl. de Fontenoy, consists in fact of three buildings: one for the permanent delegation; a *Conference Building*, with its accordion-pleated concrete roof covered in copper, and containing murals by *Picasso* and *Rufino Tamayo*; and the dominating Y-shaped *Secretariat* of seven floors supported by 72 pylons. In the *Piazza* are 'decorative works' by *Henry Moore*, *Alexander Calder*, *Jean Arp*, and *Miro*, et al., and a Japanese Garden has been designed by *Noguchi*. An annexe, to house even more functionaries, lies a short distance due S. The main building was the object of arson in March 1984.

To the N. lies the ***École Militaire** (Pl. 12;3-5), a handsome structure covering part of the former 'ferme' and 'château' of Grenelle, built by *J.-A. Gabriel*, and enlarged in 1856.

The school was founded in 1751 by Louis XV (influenced by Mme de Pompadour) for the training of noblemen as army officers. It was opened in 1756 and completed in 1770. In 1777 its rigid rules for entry were modified so that it could take in the élite of provincial military academies; thus in 1784 Bonaparte (who was confirmed in the chapel during his training) was chosen from the Collège de Brienne. It was closed in 1787 and used as a depot and barracks. It is now occupied by the *École Supérieure de Guerre*, or staff college.

18C railings separate the *Cour d'Honneur* from the PL. DE FONTENOY, which has lost its 18C character. On the entablature of the entrance façade, the figure representing Victory is in fact Louis XV, and is probably the only likeness that escaped destruction during the Revolution.

On written application to the Commandant, 1 Pl. Joffre, a guided tour of the interior can be arranged. The most impressive room is the *Salon des Maréchaux*, with its fine woodwork. The *Chapel* is open to the public daily.

A short distance S.W. is the PL. CAMBRONNE. It was Gén. Cambronne (1770–1842) who made the famous and defiant expletive—'*Merde!*'—when the Imperial Guard was summoned to surrender at Waterloo, since known as 'le mot de Cambronne'. Hence the Rue Frémicourt and its extension the Av. Émile-Zola lead due W. to the *Pont Mirabeau*: see below.

Between the *École Militaire* and the Seine lies the **Champ-de-Mars**, almost 1km long, laid out in 1765-67 as a parade ground on the old Plaine de Grenelle, with its market-gardens; it was used as a racecourse after the Restoration, and converted into a park after 1913.

The ground was the scene of several early aeronautical experiments by the Montgolfiers, by Charles and Robert, and by Blanchard (1783–84). Numerous revolutionary festivals were held here, the most famous of which was the Fête de la Fédération on 14 July 1790, when the king, the Assembly, and the delegates from the provinces, and the army, took the oath at the Autel de la Patrie to observe the new Constitution; the 'Champ de Mai', held by Napoleon on his return from Elba; and many international exhibitions.
  Bailly, president of the Constituent Assembly, was brutally executed here in 1793; and Capt. Alfred Dreyfus was publicly degraded here in Dec. 1894.

The **Eiffel Tower** (Pl. 11;7), with its base at the river end of the Champ-de-Mars, still one of the tallest structures in the world (300m high, or 320m including the television installation), an inseparable part of the Paris landscape, continues to dominate this quarter, although the equally obtrusive *Tour Montparnasse* threatens to divide one's attention.

Built in 1889 on the occasion of the important Paris Exhibition of that year, the *Tour Eiffel* was originally granted only twenty years of life, but its use in radio-telegraphy in 1904 saved it from the demolition it deserved. Constructed by the engineer *Gustave Eiffel* (1832–1923), the tapering lattice-work tower

A plunging view of the Eiffel Tower

weighs over 7000 tonnes, and is composed of 15,000 pieces of metal, fastened by 2,500,000 rivets, while its four feet are supported by masonry piers sunk 9–14m into the ground.

The first, second, and third platforms, the latter 274m from the ground, are reached by lift. The ascent is not recommended in misty, windy, or cold weather, but on a clear day, particularly about one hour before sunset, the extensive *Views* are remarkable.

It may be of interest that among the far-reaching influences of the 1889 Exhibition was the sound of a *gamelan* orchestra from Jakarta, which here introduced oriental music to Debussy, Ravel (aged 14), Satie, and Rimsky-Korsakov, among other composers.

Hence the *Pont d'Iéna* (see p218) crosses the Seine to the *Palais de Chaillot*: see Rte 17.

Further S. W. is the *Pont de Bir Hakeim* (see p218), from which the BLVD DE GRENELLE leads S.E., on No.8 of which a plaque records the round-up of some thousands of Parisian Jews in the *Vélodrome* (or cycling-track) here in July 1942 prior to their deportation.

The QUAI DE GRENELLE leads S.W., with a view across the *Allée des Cygnes* (an island used as a charnel-house for dead horses in the 18C) to the *Maison de la Radio* (see Rte 17), passing (l.) a concrete-jungle area of tower blocks now flanking the Seine, joined to the far bank by the *Pont de Grenelle* and *Pont Mirabeau* (1895–97), leading to *Auteuil.*

To the S.E., facing the Rue de la Convention, in this not very interesting 15th arrondissement, are the buildings of the *Imprimerie Nationale* (founded 1640), moved here in 1925 from the *Hôtel de Rohan.*

The riverside beyond the latter bridge, until recently the site of a large Citroën factory, is now described as a 'Secteur en travaux', the result of which is unlikely to be inspiring.—Beyond the BLVD VICTOR, and the *Pont du Garigliano*, is the BLVD PÉRIPHÉRIQUE (*Quai d'Issy*; with the *Porte de Sévres* further E.), on the far side of which is the *Héliport de Paris*, while adjacent to the E. are various buildings of the *Armée de l'Air* and other Service departments, exhibition areas, Palais des Sports, and what not.

THE NORTH OR RIGHT BANK:
LA RIVE DROITE

8 From the Pl. de la Concorde to the Pl. du Louvre

MÉTROS: *Concorde, Tuileries, Palais-Royal, Louvre.*

The *PL. DE LA CONCORDE (Pl. 7;7), occupying a central position by the Seine, and midway between the *Étoile* and the *Île de la Cité*, is still—in spite of the traffic swirling round it—one of the world's most impressive squares. Although its perspectives were evidently a design of the First Empire, the present appearance of the square dates from 1852, when the surrounding ditch was filled in.

The site, then a vacant space to the W. of the main built-up area of the city (but within the enceinte of the Fermiers-Généraux raised some thirty years later), was chosen in 1757 to receive a bronze statue of Louis XV commissioned by the 'échevins' (or magistrates, see p169), and unveiled in 1763. The surrounding square was named after the king, but already in 1770 panic during a firework display celebrating the marriage of the dauphin Louis and Marie-Antoinette had provided its first holocaust (133 dead).
    Young was impressed by the Place in 1787: 'a very noble entrance to a great city . . . here one can be clean and breathe freely'. In 1792 the statue was replaced by a huge figure of Liberty, designed by *Lemot* (the object of Mme Roland's famous apostrophe: 'O liberté, que de crimes on commet en ton nom'), and the square was called Pl. de la Révolution. In the same year a guillotine was erected here for the appropriate execution of the robbers of the crown jewels (comp. below).
    Louis XVI was guillotined on 21 Jan. 1793 on the site now occupied by the fountain nearest the river, and between May 1793 and May 1795 the blade claimed among its 1119 victims Charlotte Corday (17 July 1793), Marie-Antoinette (16 Oct.), the Girondins (31 Oct.), Philippe-Égalité (6 Nov.), Mme Roland (10 Nov.), Hébert (24 Mar. 1794), Danton (5 Apr.), Mme Élisabeth (9 May), and Robespierre (28 July). The square first received its present name in 1795 at the end of the Reign of Terror.

On the N. side of the square are two handsome mansions designed by *Gabriel* in 1763–72 (with pediment sculptures by *M.-A. Slodtz* and *G. Coustou* the younger) and originally intended as official residences. That to the r., from which the crown jewels were stolen in 1792, has been since 1789 the *Ministère de la Marine*; that to the l. has long been shared between the *Automobile Club* and the *Hôtel Crillon*.
    Between these buildings leads the Rue Royale, at the end of which rears the *Madeleine* (see Rte 13), while in the opposite direction the southern perspective is designedly completed by the assertive Classical façade of the *Palais-Bourbon*, see Rte 6.
    To the W. of the *Pl. de la Concorde*, the *Av. des Champs-Élysées* (see Rte 16A) rises gently towards the *Arc de Triomphe*, the vista framed by the *Marly Horses*, two groups by *G. Coustou*—'ces marbres hennissants' as Hugo called them—which were brought from the Château de Marly in 1794 and now form pendants to the winged horses at the W. entrances of the *Tuileries*.

In the opposite direction the view extends to the Louvre. On the S. side of the Place, the *Pont de la Concorde*, offering magnificent perspectives, was built by *Perronet* in 1788–90, and widened in 1932. Stone from the Bastille was used in the construction of the upper part; one reason for this is said to be that the Parisians would be able to tread under foot the symbol of royal despotism.

In the centre of the Place rises the **Obelisk of Luxor**, a monolith of pink syenite, almost 23m high and c.230 tonnes in weight. It originally stood before a temple at Thebes in Upper Egypt, and commemorates in its hieroglyphics the deeds of Rameses II (13C B.C.).

The obelisk was presented to Louis-Philippe in 1831 by Mohammed Ali (the donor of Cleopatra's Needle in London). The pedestal, of Breton granite, bears representations of the apparatus used in its erection in 1836 (see also *Musée de Marine*, Rte 17). The two fountains, by *Hittorf*, copies of those in the piazza of St Peter's at Rome, are embellished with figures emblematic of Inland (N.) and Marine Navigation.

The eight stone pavilions round the Square, built by *Gabriel* in the 18C, support statues personifying the great provincial capitals. Strasbourg (as capital of Alsace, lost to France in 1871) was hung with crape and wreaths until 1918. *Pradier's* model for Strasbourg was Juliette Drouet.

The public entrance to the *Sewers* of Paris, which used to be near the statue of Lille, has been moved to the S. end of the *Pont de l'Alma*: see Rte 17.

The **Jardin des Tuileries**, the tree-lined formal garden of 25·5 hectares adorned with a wealth of statues, extends eastwards to the *Pl. du Carrousel*, and is crossed by the Av. du Gén.-Lemonnier. The W. section was the private garden of the Tuileries, and has been little altered since it was laid out anew by *Le Nôtre* in 1664.

The earlier gardens, in the Italian style, had been designed by his grandfather. It became the favourite promenade of the fashionable nobility until superseded by the Palais-Royal just before the Revolution.
    Here, on 1 Dec. 1783, took place the ascent, in a gas-filled balloon, of the scientists Charles and Robert, watched by a vast crowd. The first such ascent had been made some 40 days previously: see *La Muette*.

The gateway opening from the *Pl. de la Concorde* has pillars crowned by equestrian statues of Fame and Mercury, by *Coysevox* (brought from Marly in 1719).

The large octagonal pond is surrounded by statuary of the 17–18C by *N.* and *G. Coustou* and *Van Cleve*; on the steps to the S. is 'Hommage à Cézanne' by *Maillol*; to the N., a copy of Coysevox's bust of Le Nôtre (original in *St-Roch*).

Terraces extend along both sides of the gardens. On the S., overlooking the QUAI DES TUILERIES (from which the *Pont Solferino*, demolished in 1963 and replaced by a footbridge, crosses to the *Quai Anatole-France*), is the *Terrasse du Bord-de-l'Eau*. Beneath this, a passage led from the palace cellars to the *Pl. de la Concorde*, providing Louis-Philippe with an escape route in 1848. At the W. end of the terrace is the *Orangerie* (1853), see below.

On the N. side, the *Terrasse des Feuillants*, skirting the Rue de Rivoli, is named after a Benedictine monastery which in 1791 was the meeting-place of the 'Club des Feuillants' (moderate republicans, among whom were Lavoisier and André Chénier).
    Below the E. side of the terrace are fragments of the *Palais des Tuileries, not*

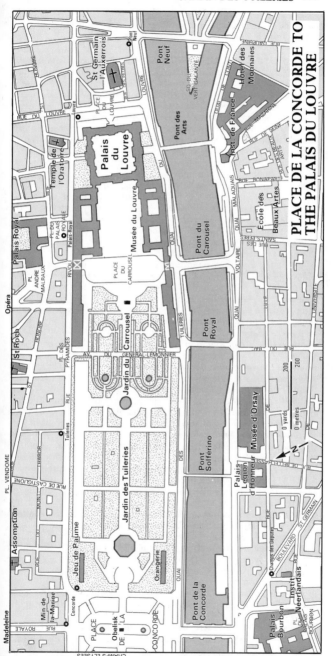

PLACE DE LA CONCORDE TO
THE PALAIS DU LOUVRE

in situ. Further E., nearly opposite the Rue de Castiglione, was the site of the *Manège*, the riding-school of the palace, where the National Assembly met from 1789 to 1793, and where Louis XVI was condemned to death.

Here, the ****MUSÉE DU JEU-DE-PAUME**, or *'de l'Impressionnisme'* (Pl. 7;8; METRO; *Concorde*), is accommodated in a real tennis-court built in 1851. On the terrace on its S. side is a monument to Charles Perrault (1628–1703), the writer of fairy tales, at whose suggestion the gardens were thrown open to the public by Colbert.

The collection, which will be transferred to the new *Musée d'Orsay* (see Rte 6), entered at the W. end of the building, contains paintings by the Impressionist School, and several rooms are named after the donors of bequests to the collection.

From the Vestibule, displaying panels by *Toulouse-Lautrec*, we enter **R1** (to the r., but unnumbered); containing: *Degas* (1834–1917), Self-portrait and other early portraits including H.-R. de Gas, his grandfather (painted on his visit to Italy in 1857), and of the Bellelli family; 'Danseuse sur la Scène'; Orchestra (with portraits of the musicians); A young woman; The absinthe drinker; The pedicure; Horse-racing scenes (and bronzes of horses).

R2 *Degas*, studies of dancers, including 'Répétition', and bronzes; 'Les repasseuses'; 'Le tub'; and other bath scenes.

R3 Four large portrait groups, of historical interest, by *Fantin-Latour* (1836–1904), including Hommage to Delacroix (with portraits of Baudelaire, Manet, and Whistler), The corner of the table, and Studio in the Batignolles; Portrait of Renoir by *F. Bazille* (1841–70), and Portrait of Monet, by *Renoir* (1841–1919). Near the stairs, illustrations of Impressionist techniques, etc.

R4 Landscapes by *Camille Pissarro* (1830–1903), *Boudin* (1824–98), *Corot* (1796–1875), *Jongkind* (1819–91), *Lépine* (1836–92), and *Sisley* (1839–99).—There are more landscapes in **R5**, including *Sisley's* Snow at Louveciennes; Portrait of Bazille, by *Renoir*; La Charrette (a snow scene), and Women in a garden, by *Monet* (1840–1926); and Family Reunion, and The pink dress, by *Bazille*.

R6 Works by *Manet* (1832–83), including 'Déjeuner sur l'herbe', which caused much scandal in 1863, as did 'Olympia', which met with the usual shower of abuse at the Salon of 1865. Portraits of Zola and Mallarmé; The balcony (portrait of Berthe Morisot); The fife-player, Mme Manet on a blue couch; 'Angelina'; 'Lola de Valence'; 'La serveuse de bocks'. Also The cradle, by *Berthe Morisot* (1841–95); and *Eva Gonzalès* (1849–83), Box at the theatre.

R7 *Manet*, Lady with a fan (Berthe Morisot); Still-lifes, and flower paintings; 'La Blonde aux seins nus'; and 'Déjeuner sur l'herbe' by *Monet*.

R8 Mainly landscapes by *Pissarro* and *Sisley*, including the latter's The Saint-Martin canal; and 'Les coquelicots' (poppies) and 'Le repos sous les lilas', by *Monet*.

R9 *Monet*, The church at Vetheuil; The hospital of St-Paul at St-Rémy, *van Gogh* (1853–90); Breton peasants, *Gauguin* (1848–1903); Auvers, *Cézanne*; landscapes by *Sisley*, *Seurat*, and *Pissarro*.

At the foot of the stairs: *G. Caillebotte* (1848–94), The floor. Ascending, we pass a Judgement of Paris (original plaster), by *Renoir*.

Turning r., we enter **R10**, with five studies of Rouen Cathedral; The Gare St-Lazare; and landscapes by *Monet*; also further examples of the art of *Sisley* and *Pissarro* (Red roofs).

R11 *Monet*, Two studies of water-lilies; The Houses of Parliament; Turkeys, 'Le déjeuner'; *Renoir*, various voluptuous nudes, and portraits of Mme Georges Charpentier, Mme Alphonse Daudet, and Richard Wagner, among others; also 'Le moulin de la Galette'; The swing; and The path through long grass. Some studies by *Toulouse-Lautrec* (1864–1901) are displayed in the centre of the room.

R12 *Degas*, 'La repasseuse'; *Toulouse-Lautrec*, 'Le lit'; Woman dressing her hair; *Mary Cassatt* (1845–1927), Woman sewing; *Monet*, The bridge at Argenteuil; landscapes by *Pissarro* (The vegetable garden), and *Guillaumin* (1841–1927).

We return to **R13** (at the head of the stair), displaying *Cézanne* (1839–1906), Still-lifes; Self-portrait (c. 1880); 'La douleur'; Card-players; 'L'Estaque'; Poplars; Dr Gachet's house at Auvers; 'La femme à la cafétière'; Dahlias in a Delft vase (and the original vase).

R14 *Pissarro*, Route de Louveciennes; *Sisley*, Canal Saint-Martin; *Guillaumin*, Self-portrait; *van Gogh*, Cottages at Cordeville, Portrait of Dr Gachet, Auvers church, and Self-portrait.

R15 *Gauguin*, The Seine, 'La belle Angéle', 'Les Alyscamps', The white horse, Vairumati, Breton scenes, Haystacks, Arearea, Tahitian women, and others. Carvings by Gauguin and other souvenirs from Tahiti are displayed in the centre case. Also *van Gogh*, Restaurant de la Sirène, His bedroom at Arles, 'La Guinguette', 'L'Arlésienne'; *Odilon Redon* (1840–1916), Portrait of his wife; *Rousseau*, 'le douanier' (1844–1910), War, and Portrait of a woman; *Seurat* (1859–91), Nude studies; and *Signac* (1863–1935), The river bank.

In the **Orangerie**, 3 min. walk to the S. across the Tuileries gardens, are displayed *Monet*'s series of mural paintings, 'Les Nymphéas' (see also *Musée Marmottan*, Rte 17.

Since the summer of 1984 the upper gallery has been the permanent home of the works of art acquired by *Jean Walter and Paul Guillaume*, and donated to the State on the condition that they remained a separate collection. It comprises 144 works, not many of which are of the first quality, including 28 examples of the work of *Derain*, 24 by *Renoir*, 22 by *Soutine*, 14 by *Cézanne*, 12 by *Picasso*, 11 by *Matisse*, 10 by *Utrillo*, and 9 by *Henri Rousseau, le Douanier*, apart from representative works by *Sisley, Monet, Modigliani, Marie Laurencin*, and *Van Dongen*. Among the more notable canvases are: *Cézanne*, Portrait of his wife, c. 1885; *Renoir*, Gabrielle and Jean, Young girls at the piano, Claude playing, and Dressed as a clown, and Snowscape, apart from several lush nudes; *Derain*, The artist's niece, and Portrait of Mme Guillaume; *Picasso*, The embrace, and Nude on a red background; *Henri Rousseau*, The wedding, and Père Junier's cart; and *Modigliani*, The young apprentice, and Portrait of Paul Guillaume.

The central avenue of the **Jardin des Tuileries**, of chestnuts and plane trees, leads to the Round Pond, between which and the Av. du Gén.-Lemonnier survive the railings put up by Louis-Philippe to isolate the 'private garden'. *Galignani's* 'New Paris Guide' (1841 ed.) stated that Great care is taken in keeping the garden clean; persons in working habits or carrying any parcels, except books, are not allowed to enter it'! Among the flower-beds are groups of sculpture, notably by *G.* and *N. Coustou, Coysevox*, and *Le Pautre*.

The main W. wing of the famous **Palais des Tuileries**, which used

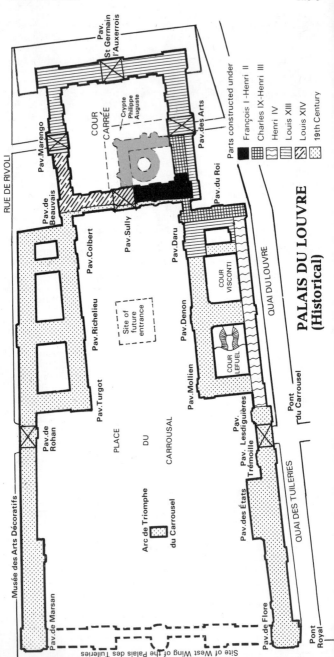

PALAIS DU LOUVRE (Historical)

Parts constructed under

- François I – Henri II
- Charles IX – Henri III
- Henri IV
- Louis XIII
- Louis XIV
- 19th Century

RUE DE RIVOLI

Pav. St Germain l'Auxerrois

COUR CARRÉE

Crypte Philippe Auguste

Pav. des Arts

Pav. Marengo

Pav. de Beauvais

Pav. Colbert

Pav. Sully

Pav. Daru

Pav. du Roi

Pav. Richelieu

Site of future entrance

QUAI DU LOUVRE

COUR VISCONTI

Pav. Denon

COUR LEFUEL

Pav. Turgot

Pav. de Rohan

PLACE DU CARROUSAL

Pav. Mollien

Pont du Carrousel

Musée des Arts Décoratifs

Arc de Triomphe du Carrousel

Pav. Lesdiguières

Pav. Trémoille

Pav. des États

QUAI DES TUILERIES

Pav. de Marsan

Site of West Wing of the Palais des Tuileries

Pav. de Flore

Pont Royal

to flank the E. side of the Av. du Gén.-Lemonnier, no longer exists, except for the *Pavillons de Flore* and *de Marsan* (to the S. and N. respectively), both of which have been restored or rebuilt, and which now form the W. extremities of the wings of the Louvre. The *Pavillon de Marsan* accommodates the *Musée des Arts Décoratifs* (see below).

The palace was begun in 1564 by *Philibert Delorme* (c. 1515–70) for Catherine de Médicis, who left the *Hôtel des Tournelles* after Henri II's lingering death. The site beyond the city walls was known as the 'Sablonnière' and occupied by tile-kilns (tuileries). Delorme was succeeded by *Jean Bullant* and then, in 1595, by *Jacques du Cerceau*, who built the *Pavillon de Flore*. The *Pavillon de Marsan* was built in 1660–65 by *Louis Le Vau* and his son-in-law *François d'Orbay*.

Louis XVI was confined here after being brought from Versailles (except during his ineffectual attempt to escape in 1791) until the riot of 10 Aug. 1792, when his Swiss Guards were massacred. In 1793–96 it was the headquarters of the Convention. Pius VII was lodged in the *Pavillon de Flore* for four months in 1804–05.

The Tuileries became the permanent residence of Napoleon I, Louis XVIII (who died here), Charles X, Louis-Philippe, and Napoleon III. Hence Eugénie escaped in Sept. 1870 via a garden gate near the Pl. de la Concorde, where stood the coach of Dr Thomas Evans, her American dentist, who cleverly extracted her from Paris. Sir John Burgoyne's yacht awaited the Empress at Deauville. In May 1871 the Communards set fire to the building, which, like the Hôtel de Ville, was completely gutted. Its charred remains stood until 1884, and the site was converted into a garden in 1889, which is embellished by nineteen heavy female statues in bronze, by *Aristide Maillol* (1861–1944).

The **Arc de Triomphe du Carrousel**, a copy on a reduced scale of the Arch of Septimius Severus at Rome (14·60m high instead of 23m), was begun in 1806 from the designs of *Fontaine* and *Percier* to commemorate the victories of Napoleon I in 1805. It then constituted the main entrance to the courtyard of the Tuileries from the Cour du Carrousel.

On the top are figures of Soldiers of the Empire and a bronze chariot-group by *Bosio* (1828) representing the Restoration of the Bourbons. The original group incorporated the antique horses looted from St. Mark's, Venice, and replaced there in 1815. The four sides are decorated with marble bas-reliefs: the Battle of Austerlitz; the Capitulation of Ulm; the Meeting between Napoleon and Alexander at Tilsit; the Entry into Munich; the Entry into Vienna; and the Peace of Pressburg.

The PL. DU CARROUSEL, lying to the E. of the Arch, was until the middle of the 19C a small square amidst a labyrinth of narrow and noisome alleys, which for centuries had remained almost encircled by the royal palaces. It derives its name from an equestrian fête given here in 1662 by Louis XIV.

The archways to the N. lead to the Rue de Rivoli and beyond to the S. end of the Av. de l'Opéra; those on the S. give onto the QUAI DES TUILERIES opposite the *Pont du Carrousel* (see below).

To the E. lies the *Square du Carrousel*; westwards the Square commands an impressive view towards the *Arc de Triomphe* (see Rte 16A).

The ***PALAIS DU LOUVRE** (Pl. 13;2), surrounding three sides of the square, and occupying an extensive site between the Rue de Rivoli and the Seine, and with a complex history, is one of the most magnificent of the world's great palaces, and the most important public building in Paris.

The interior of the edifice is described together with the *Musée du Louvre* in Rte 9. For the *Musée des Arts Décoratifs*, see Palais du Louvre below.

The Arc de Triomphe du Carrousel

The name is derived either from an early wolf-hunter's rendezvous known as 'Lupara' or 'Louverie', or from a 'Louver', a blockhouse. It first appears in history as one of Philippe Auguste's fortresses (1190–1202), fragments of which survive in the basement store-rooms (perhaps from the time of Dagobert I, 628–38). Charles V made it an official residence, and surrounded it by a moat. The W. and S. sides were rebuilt under François I (1515–47) and extended by his successor Henri II. Catherine de Médicis, Henri II's widow, began the LONG GALLERY, flanking the river, to connect the Louvre with her new palace at the *Tuileries*. The building was further extended during the reigns of Henri IV and Louis XIII, and the quadrangle was completed, on Colbert's orders, during the minority of Louis XIV. The king soon lost interest in the new buildings, and they were left in a state of disrepair, and were occupied by squatters until 1754, when Louis XV commissioned *Gabriel* to renovate and restore the palace. Under Napoleon I the W. part of the northern gallery was erected, and under Napoleon III the main wings which enclose the Square du Carrousel on the N. and S. were completed.

Catherine de Médicis lived in the palace after the death of her husband in 1559. Here she extorted from Charles IX (whose sister Marguerite de Valois had married Henri de Navarre—later Henri IV—five days earlier) the order for the Massacre of St Bartholomew (24 Aug. 1572). In 1591, during the Wars of the League, the Duc de Mayenne hanged three members of the 'Council of Sixteen' in the *Salle des Gardes* (now the *Salle des Cariatides*). Henrietta Maria, the widowed queen of Charles I of England, found refuge in the Louvre. In 1658 Corneille's 'Nicomède' was performed in the Salle des Gardes. In 1793 the *Musée de la République* was opened in the Louvre, which has remained the national art gallery and museum ever since. During 1830 the Louvre was stormed by the revolutionaries; and it was set on fire by the Communards, but serious damage was limited to the library: but see *Palais des Tuileries*, above.

Few 19C travellers did *not* visit it. One, according to Crabb Robinson, was Southey, who cared 'for nothing else at Paris but the old book-shops'!

The Louvre consists of two main divisions: the OLD LOUVRE, comprising the buildings surrounding the *Cour du Louvre* (or Cour Carrée); and the NEW LOUVRE, the 19C buildings N. and S. of the *Square du Carrousel*, together with their extensions to the W. It is proposed to call the whole, once renovated, THE GRAND LOUVRE. An ambitious project, the basic idea of which makes some sense, has been under way since Feb. 1983, when M. Mitterrand approved the plan proposed by *Ieoh Ming Pei* (a Chinese-born American architect). It will comprise the following transformations, apart from continuing restoration of the fabric and façades of the Palais du Louvre itself, and the redesigning of the Jardin des Tuileries in due course.

Firstly, the *Cour Carrée* is to be excavated, to lay bare the foundations of the medieval fortress and the palace of Charles V: this will be then known as the 'Crypte Philippe Auguste', and in archaeological interest it may vie with the recent excavation of the Pl. du Parvis de Notre-Dame.

The *Cour-Napoléon*, further W., will also be dug up, and in a central position between the Pavillon Denon and the Pavillon Richelieu will rise a *glass* 'Pyramid' (an idea which might have well be championed by Champollion, and which is admittedly less ostentatious than the monument projected there a century ago by Louis-Ernest Lheureux). It will nevertheless break the architectural lines of the palace, and will in part be surrounded by fountains.

From its W. side steps will descend into a large well or Entrance Vestibule, with an Information Bureau. Passages hence will lead to the basements of the Cour Carrée (and Crypte; see above), to the S. Wing of the Louvre, and similarly to the N. Wing, into which the museum will eventually expand. It is also expected that direct communication will be provided between the adjacent métro stations and the Louvre. From the W. side of the vestibule a passage will lead to extensive subterranean car and coach parks beyond the foundations of the Arc de Triomphe du Carrousel, entered from the Av. du Gén. Lemonnier. Below the Pl. du Carrousel and Cour Napoléon will be a complex providing space for the 'rèserves' of the Louvre, studios for the restoration of works of art, service areas, bookstalls, and other facilities, etc. Further information on work in progress, or completed, will be given in the next edition of this Guide.

On the W. side of the *Cour du Louvre*, to the S. of the *Pavillon Sully*, is the oldest visible part of the early 16C Palace, by *Lescot*, with sculptural decorations by *Jean Goujon* and *Paul Ponce*. The N. half of the W. façade, and part of the N. façade, were designed by *Lemercier* in imitation of Lescot; the caryatids on the *Pavillon Sully* are after *Sarazin*. The remainder of the court was built by *Le Vau* after 1660.

The top storeys on the N., E., and S. sides, out of keeping with *Lescot*'s attic, were added in the 17–18C, to bring them up to the

height of the great *Colonnade* of 52 Corinthian columns and pilasters that now forms the exterior E. façade. The work of *Claude Perrault* (1667–70), it was designed without due regard to dimensions, and a new outer façade was added to the S. side of the *Old Louvre* to meet the projecting S. end. To give this E. façade its correct proportions, as intended by Perrault, a moat was excavated and *terreplein* added (1966–67), during which works the base was discovered of an earlier façade begun by *Le Vau* and abandoned when Colbert became superintendent of the building.

The *Galerie du Bord de l'Eau*, the long S. façade flanking the Seine, was the work of *Pierre Chambiges*, architect to Catherine de Médicis, and *Thibaut Métezeau*, as far as the *Pavillon de Les-diguières*. *Jacques du Cerceau* was responsible for the prolongation of this wing, largely rebuilt in 1863–68. The building of the *New Louvre* (N. and S. of the *Square du Carrousel*) was undertaken by *Visconti* in 1852 and completed in 1871 by *Lefuel*; the N. side has since been occupied by the intrusive *Ministère des Finance*.

In previous editions of this Guide the Editor remarked that it was hoped that the functionaries of this ministry might be moved elsewhere. It is now planned that they will be transferred by 1987 to a new building at Bercy, thus enabling the Musée du Louvre to spread its wings again, necessitating further drastic reorganisation.

The autonomous ****MUSÉE DES ARTS DÉCORATIFS** (MÉTRO *Tuileries* or *Palais-Royal*), with its main entrance at No.107 Rue de Rivoli, is housed in the *Pavillon de Marsan*, the N.W. wing of the *Palais du Louvre*.

It contains an outstanding collection of French *decorative and ornamental art*—as its name implies—from medieval times to the

*The Pont Royal, and (l.) the former West wing of the Tuileries, in
1860, by* Thomas Shotter Boys

present, and is one of the most interesting and rewarding museums
to visit in Paris. As with the Musée du Louvre, it is in the throes of a
thorough reorganisation of its extensive collections, which the
quality of the objects it contains deserves, and the completion of the
work—planned for 1985—is eagerly awaited. Until then many
sections will be closed, and the provisional description given below is
only a rough indication of the future rearrangement and display, and
lists only a number of representative objects in order to give some
idea of their value and range.

Its history is bound up with the 'Union Centrale des Beaux-Arts appliqués à
l'Industrie' and the 'Société du Musée des Arts Décoratifs' (founded in 1864 and
1877 respectively), which in 1882 merged to become the *Union Centrale des
Arts Décoratifs.* In 1901 work commenced on the rehabilitation of the interior of
the Pavillon de Marsan, then ceiling-high with archives and dossiers from the
Cours des Comptes, and the Musée des Arts Décoratifs was inaugurated in May
1905. Today, its inventory lists some 80,000 items.
   It is affiliated with the *Musée Nissim de Camondo,* 63 Rue de Monceau, 8e,
and the *Musée de l'Affiche* (posters), 18 Rue de Paradis, 10e: see Rtes 16B and
14 respectively.

It also accommodates the *Centre National d'Information et de
Documentation sur les Métiers d'Art,* and an important specialised
Library (over 100,000 volumes, and 1,500 periodicals) with a
Photographic Service. A new and enterprising departure is the
department selling replicas of choice objects from the collections
themselves, or of contemporary design, their reproduction being
undertaken in collaboration with Tiffany, and in co-operation with
French manufacturers and craftsmen of quality. For the most part

they will be porcelain or faïence objects, silver, glass, and jewellery.

Temporary exhibitions, usually in the fields of design and decoration, are held here throughout the year.

Among sections which may be visited by appointment are the *Cabinet des Dessins* (containing some 15,000 drawings), and the *Departments of Textiles*, and of *Wall-papers* (among the latter are the series depicting Views of Naples, and the 'Inca' series of wall-papers manufactured by Dufour, Leroy, and Zuber, among others, in the 1820s).

The six main floors of the building will be arranged as follows: GROUND FLOOR—entrance hall, Information bureau, Shop, and Library, etc.; FIRST FLOOR—Late 19C, 20C and Contemporary collections. Notable is the *Salle 1900*, with art nouveau woodwork by *Georges Hoentschell* (1855–1915), and furniture by *Hector Guimard*.

The SECOND FLOOR is devoted to collections of the Gothic and Renaissance periods, with 13–16C tapestries—among them the 'Woodcutters' (Tournai; 15C)—among other hangings, and furniture; also representative examples of German woodcarving; medieval metal work; and Renaissance bronzes; a richly carved retable (Brussels; early 16C); an *anon.* Portrait of a young girl (Bruges; c.1550), and a Portrait of Madeleine de France, Queen of Scotland, by the *'Maître de Marie Tudor'*.

Another section is devoted to the arts of Spain, including Catalan paintings by *Jaume* and *Pere Serra*, and the Retable of the Baptist (c.1415–20) by *Luis Borrassa*; also stalls from Rueda (Valladolid; early 16C); and stamped leather panels or *guadameciles*.

The THIRD and FOURTH FLOORS are mainly devoted to collections from the time of Louis XIII to the Second Empire period (17–early 19C), among which will be found examples of panelling of c.1707 from No.7 Pl. Vendôme, and oak-panelling of c.1735; a ceiling of c.1710 by *Claude Audran* (1658–1734) from the Hôtel Bertier de Flesselles, Rue de Sévigné, and another of c.1715 from the Hôtel de la Comtesse de Verrie in the Rue du Cherche-Midi; also decorative panels by *N. Coypel*, and by *Hubert Robert*; painted panels in the Etruscan style (c.1780), and a number of carved wood brackets, panels, picture-frames, and mirrors, etc.

Among furniture are a collection of 17–18C chairs arranged to show their evolution in style; a fine marquetry cabinet of c.1670; a marquetry armoire attrib. to *Boulle* of c.1680, and another by *Charles Cressent* (c.1725); and examples in the Chinese taste, together with other Chinoiserie objects. Also chairs by members of the *Jacob family*; and a boat-shaped bed by *F. Baudry* (1827).

Among paintings are a Portrait of the Chancellor d'Anguesseau by *Robert Tournières*; a pastel of Molière; five garden scenes by *Pillement*; three flower studies (1614–15) by *G. Pini*; watercolours by *Lavreince*, *J.-B. Huet*, *Debucourt*, and *Mallet*; an early work (c.1806) by *Ingres* of 'The Casino de Raphael at Rome'; and 'Houdon's Studio', by *Boilly*. Note also a series of wax-portrait moulds, some by *G.-B. Nini* (c.1717–80).

Among the extensive ceramic collections are examples from St-Cloud, Moustiers, Strasbourg, Rouen (some exhibiting strong Chinese influence—Oriental works of art at that time entering France at Dieppe), Sceaux, Sinceny, Marseille; faïences 'en trompe-l'oeil', and 'fine blanches'; ware from Vincennes, Sèvres, Mennecy, and Chantilly; biscuit figures, and a curious terracotta of a girl playing with her pet dog, by *Clodion* (1738–1814); an important collection of Chinese cloisonné; and Delft, and Meissen porcelain, etc.

Complementary collections, which may be shown with other displays of their period, or 'thematically' and separately, are such diverse objects—usually of very fine quality—as door furniture; bronze appliqués, and ornaments (and also a 'coiffeuse' used by Joséphine at the Tuileries); silverware; mathematical instruments; pewter; clocks and watches; ivory boxes; snuff grinders; rings; cutlery; 'nécessaires'; embroidered purses; shuttles; walking-sticks; paperweights; pipes; plaster plaques; portrait miniatures; statuettes; glass ornaments; decorative embossed leather cases; toys; and book-bindings, etc.

The third floor also contains space for temporary exhibitions, and the *Jean Dubuffet Donation*; the fourth floor will display furniture and furnishings in the Louis-Philippe taste, and in the style of the Second Empire (Napoleon III). The important *Islamic Collection*, and Charles Le Brun's projects for tapestries of The Months, and certain other sections, are not at present on display.

Three bridges cross the Seine from the Louvre to the *Quai Voltaire*. To the W. is the *Pont Royal*, a five-arched bridge by *Père F. Romain* and *Gabriel* (1685–89); the last pillar on either bank has a hydrographic scale indicating the low-water mark (zero; only 24m above sea-level), besides various flood-marks.

The *Pont du Carrousel* (1834, but rebuilt in 1939) retains four seated figures by *Petitot* and *Pradier*, from the original structure.

The pedestrian *Pont des Arts* was built of cast iron by Cessart and Dillon in 1801–03, deriving its name from the 'Palais des Arts' as the Louvre was then called. It was rebuilt in a similar style to the original in 1983–84, having been dismantled for several years.

Immediately E. of the Louvre is the PL. DU LOUVRE which claims to be the area where Caesar's legions encamped in 52 B.C. Opposite stands the *Mairie of the 1st Arrondissement* (1859), which, according to Viollet-le-Duc, seems to have been intended as a caricature of the adjoining church, to which the conspicuous N. tower was added in the following year.

*ST-GERMAIN-L'AUXERROIS (Pl. 14;1), a Gothic church of the 13–16C, was itself drastically restored in the 18–19C. The most striking exterior feature is the porch, by *Jean Gaussel* (1435–39), with a rose-window, and a balustrade above, which encircles the whole church. The transeptal doorways (15C) and Renaissance doorway (1570), N. of the choir, are noteworthy. Nothing remains of the cloister.

In 885, the Norman invaders turned the church dedicated to the 5C St Germanus, Bp of Auxerre, into a fortress. A second church was built on the site in the 11C, which, in the following century, being the parish church of the adjacent palace, was found to be too small, and was replaced by the present building in the 13C. In 1572 it was involved unwittingly in the massacre of St Bartholomew (24 Aug.), for the ringing of its bells for matins that day was to be the signal for the slaughter of Huguenots to commence.

Molière was married and his first son baptized here, and Danton was also married here. During the Revolution, having first served as a granary and then as a printing-works, it became the 'Temple of Gratitude'. It was sacked in 1831, and poorly restored after 1838.

Among those buried in St-Germain are the poet Jodelle, and Malherbe; the architects Lemercier, de Cotte, Gabriel, and Le Vau; the artists Coypel, Boucher, and Chardin; the sculptors Coysevox, N. and G. Coustou; and the engraver Israël Silvestre.

The INTERIOR (78 by 39m) is double-aisled. The 'restoration' of 1745, mingling the classicism of the 18C with 14–15C architecture, mangled the choir-arches, converted the piers into fluted columns, and heightened their capitals. Fragments of the destroyed rood-screen are preserved in the Louvre. The pulpit and royal pew are fine examples of late 17C woodwork by *Fr. Mercier* (designed by *Le Brun*). Behind the latter is a sculptured triptych with painted wings (16C; Flemish), and in the aisle-chapel opposite is another altarpiece (1519; from Antwerp) in carved wood. The wrought-iron choir-railings date from 1767. On the l., at the choir entrance is a wooden statue of St Germanus, on the r. a stone figure of St Vincent (both 15C).

The outer S. aisle is occupied by the *Chap. de la Vierge* (late 13C), containing a 14C Virgin of the Champagne School, a 15C St Mary of Egypt, a 13C St Germanus (of the Paris School), and a 13C wooden Crucifixion. The transepts alone have preserved their 15–16C stained-glass. Above a small door in the *Ambulatory* (S. side) is a late-15C polychrome Virgin. The first inner bay is the base of the 12C belfry. In the 4th chapel are marble statues of Étienne d'Aligre and his son, both Chancellors of France (d.1635; 1677); 6th chapel, a relic of a Pietà by *Jean Soulas* (1505); and in the 7th chapel, effigies from the tomb of the Rostaing family (1582 and 1645).

Gabrielle d'Estrées (1573–99) died at the *Hôtel de Sourdis*, No.21 Rue de l'Arbre-Sec, behind the church, a few days before she was to have married Henri IV. The candle-manufactory at No.54 was founded in 1643.—No.17 Rue des Prêtres, to the S., was the site of the *Café Momus* from 1841 to 1861.

9 The Musée du Louvre

The exterior of the Palais du Louvre and its architectural History is described on pp117–20.

Convenient MÉTROS are *Tuileries, Palais-Royal, Louvre,* and *Pont-Neuf.*

The principal Entrances—for the time being—are the *Porte Denon*, S.E. of the Sq. du Carrousel, and the *Porte Barbet-de-Jouy*, on the Quai du Louvre.

Other entrances are by the *Porte Barbet-de-Jouy*, on the Quai du Louvre; the *Porte de La Trémoille*, opposite the Pont du Carrousel; the *Porte Jaujard*, on the N. side of the Pavillon de Flore (the S.W. wing); the *Porte Champollion*, on the S. side of the Cour Carrée, opposite the Pont des Arts.

Admission. The galleries of the Louvre are *closed on Tuesdays*, but are otherwise normally open every day from 9.45 to 17.15 or 18.30. Certain rooms may be closed in rotation between 11.30 and 14.00: see notice board at the entrance. Tickets may be obtained at each subsidiary entrance, and in the *Salle du Manège*, inside the Porte Denon. Adm. is free on Sundays.

Hand cameras are admitted without charge, but a special ticket is required for those with tripods: the use of 'flash' is prohibited.

In the *Salle du Manège* (or Salle des Ventes) is an *Information Bureau*, who can advise on the times of lectures, guided tours (in English), etc. Here also are a *bureau de change*, Cloakrooms (no charge), where umbrellas, parcels, capacious bags, etc. *must* be deposited prior to entering the museum. Adjacent, and elsewhere, lavatories may be found. Lifts are at the disposal of the elderly or disabled. Refreshments are available in the Gal. Mollien (first floor).

In the Salle du Manège are ranges of stalls selling catalogues, photographs, postcards, and books (not necessarily concerned with the collections of the Louvre), etc.

A catalogue listing some 10,000 colour diapositives available of objects in the Musées Nationaux is also produced, and may be obtained at the *Service Commercial de la Réunion des Musées Nationaux*, 10 Rue de l'Abbaye (just N. of St-Germain-des-Prés), and at the *Service Photographique des Musées Nationaux*, 89 Av. Victor-Hugo, 16e (Métro *Victor-Hugo*).

Also displayed in the Salle de Manège are numerous casts (*moulages*) of objects in the Musées Nationaux, and copies of jewellery (of very fine quality, and priced accordingly), which may be bought here.

The **Chalcographie du Musée du Louvre**, often overlooked by the visitor, and of particular interest, is to be found to the S., on the first floor, where engravings from a range of some 14,000, many of them from the original plates, may be purchased.

Selective lists of casts, jewellery, and prints are available gratis.

The collections of the ****MUSÉE DU LOUVRE** are divided into seven sections (although Paintings and Drawings are considered as one in this Guide): these and the pages on which each department is described, are listed below.

A. Paintings (pp129-35) and Drawings (p135-6); **B**. Greek and Roman Antiquities (pp136-8); **C**. Egyptian Antiquities (pp138-41); **D**. Oriental Antiquities (pp144-6); **E**. Objets d'Art (pp146-9); and **F**. Sculpture (pp149-51).

The approx. position of each department is indicated on the Plan of the Louvre (pp142-3) by the letters A, B, C, etc., but see *Note* on p126-7.

History of the Collections. The nucleus of the royal art collection was formed by François I (d. 1547). At his request Leonardo da Vinci spent the last few years of his life in France, dying there in 1519. Henri II and Catherine de Médicis carried on the tradition; Louis XIV made some notable additions to his collection of Old Masters, and Louis XVI acquired some important paintings of the Spanish and Dutch Schools.

In 1793, the *Musée de la République* was opened to the public, and during the next few years a large number of the most famous paintings of Europe—spoils of conquest by the victorious Republican and Napoleonic armies—were exhibited here; although after 1815 the French government was obliged to restore some 5000 of them to their former owners. Under Louis XVIII, the Vénus de Milo and over a hundred pictures were acquired.

In 1848 the Museum became the property of the State, and an annual grant was made for the purchase of works of art, and these have been supplemented subsequently by private bequests. During the years 1939–45 the collections were dispersed throughout the country, for the sake of security. There have been a number of changes in the disposition of departments, or parts of collections, and individual items during post-war decades, and the long-drawn-out process of change continues: see below.

It is very easy to underestimate the size of the *Louvre*, and while each Department is described in sequence, this is not in any way a suggestion that the perambulation of all their galleries should be attempted at one visit. It is recommended that the visitor plans his campaign carefully: most will have their priorities.

The picture galleries themselves are enough for one day, for, in the

words of that experienced 19C connoisseur and traveller Richard Ford, 'picture-seeing is more fatiguing than people think, for one is standing all the while, and with the body the mind is also at exercise in judging, and is exhausted by admiration'.

It is perhaps worth mentioning here the more important analogous or supplementary collections *in Paris*, which will interest the visitor to the Departments of the Louvre itself: the *Jeu-de-Paume*; *Petit-Palais*; and *Palais de Tokyo*; the *Cabinet des Médailles* of the Bibliothèque Nationale; *Musée des Arts Décoratifs*; the *Musées Guimet, Cernuschi*, and *d'Ennery* (for Oriental Antiquities); the *Musée de Cluny*; and the *Musées Carnavalet, Cognacq-Jay, Nissim de Camondo*, and *Jacquemart-André*. And also, in due course, the *Musée d'Orsay*.

The more important collections in the *environs of Paris* are those at *Versailles, St-Germain-en-Laye, Écouen, Chantilly, Compiègne*, and *Fontainebleau*.

Note. Work has started on perhaps the most drastic reorganisation the Musée du Louvre has yet experienced. With what speed it will be carried out, how it will be implemented, and how long it will take, it would be foolish to predict. What is certain is that during the life of this edition of the Guide, a proportion of the objects displayed will not be in the position previously assigned to them in any one room or even gallery: indeed many departments, or large sections of them, are likely to be closed entirely for months at a time.

In view of this general upheaval, it has been decided, reluctantly, not even to attempt to describe the contents of each room, but rather to give some idea of the range of works which *may* be seen *somewhere* in the building by listing representative items of outstanding quality or interest in each Department, and in the section devoted to Paintings, to sub-divide them into their various Schools. However unsatisfactory this may be, there appears to be little alternative at present, but it is hoped that by the time the seventh edition of this Blue Guide is called for, the dust might have cleared to a large extent, permanent positions will have been

Detail of the Grande Galerie du Louvre, painted by Hubert Robert in 1796, showing an artist copying Raphael's Holy Family. A companion painting is a view of the same gallery in ruins, a remarkable 'imaginary scene' in his usual manner.

provided, and a more detailed description can again be given. It is quite possible that some of the later French canvases listed below will be translated to the transpontine *Musée d'Orsay* and replaced by others at present out 'on loan' in other museums, by new acquisitions, or by those in 'rèserve'. Meanwhile, the visitor will no doubt be directed to those Departments, or parts of them, open to the public, and will bear with us.

The plan is to separate the various disparate departments, which at present too often impinge on each other, and in the case of the paintings, to distribute them in a more sensible chronological order, divided into Schools, which may then be studied without the intrusion of works of other Schools or periods, an enlightened policy on the part of the curators, and which they will no doubt implement with their customary thoroughness and taste.

A brief description of the **Interior** of the edifice itself may be helpful, the exterior having been described on pp119–20. Some of the main rooms are shown on the *Plan*, pp142–3.

At the E. end are the four wings surrounding the *Cour Carrée*, entered by an archway in the centre of each wing. Below each archway is a *Crypt*, enabling one to walk round the rooms of the Ground Floor while remaining within the building.

Some distance further W. is the main entrance to the museum, the *Porte Denon*. Between this entrance vestibule and the *Escalier Daru*, a hub of communication within the palace, is the *Galerie Daru*. A passage below the stair leads to a rotunda (decorated by *Michel Anguier* in 1635, and with a ceiling painted by *Mauzaisse*), which communicates with the buildings surrounding the above-mentioned Cour Carrée.

Here, to the l., is the *Salle des Cariatides*, the oldest surviving room in the palace, built by *Pierre Lescot* for Henri II, who commissioned *Jean Goujon* to execute the caryatids supporting the gallery at the far end. Other decoration, and the chimney-piece at the near end, are by *Percier* and *Fontaine* (c.1806). Mary Stuart married François II in this room in 1558, and here Louis XIV washed the feet of thirteen poor men on Maundy Thursday.

The monumental staircase (Escalier Daru) is—still—dominated by the **'Nike of Samothrace** or 'Winged Victory'.

This imposing statue of Parian marble, the centrepiece of a fountain, was found in the Sanctuary of the Great Gods, on the island of Samothrace, in 1863. Further excavations in 1950 led to the discovery of the mutilated right hand (in a case to the r.), and established the probable date of the statue as c. 200 B.C. The breast and left wing are of plaster.

On the FIRST FLOOR, the passage to the r. of the Nike of Samothrace leads through an upper rotunda, off which is the *Galerie d'Apollon* entered through impressive wrought-iron gates of c. 1650, brought from the Château de Maisons (see Rte 22). The gallery, built originally during the reign of Henri IV, burned down in 1661, and rebuilt by *Le Brun*, is admirably decorated. The central ceiling painting is of Apollo's Victory over the Python, by *Delacroix*.

Further E. is the *Salle des Sept Cheminées*, beyond which two galleries (the southernmost being the *Galerie Campana*) extend E. to the top of the *Escalier Champollion*. The *Salles de la Colonnade*, at r.-angles, face E. Here the small *Escalier du Chien* ascends to the Second Floor of galleries surrounding the Cour Carrée.

At the head of the staircase ascending from the Nike of Samothrace we turn l. into the *Salle des Sept Metres*, beyond which, to the l. is the *Salon Carrée*, in which the wedding feast of Napoleon and Marie-Louis was celebrated in 1810, with a richly decorated ceiling. To the r. extends the fine perspective of the *Grande Galerie*, (which span the arches leading from the Quai du Louvre to the Pl. du Carrousel) to the *Pavillon des Etats*, beyond which, in the *Aile de Flore*, is the *Cabinet des Dessins*, and at the end of this long wing, the *Pavillon de Flore*, above which is a Second Floor, in which Drawings and Engravings are displayed.

Off the Grande Galerie lead the *Salle des États* and the *Aile Mollien*. At the end of the latter are stairs descending to the *Galerie Mollien*, above which the *Salle Mollien, Salle Denon* (with a notable ceiling), and the *Salle Daru*, extend E. to regain the Escalier Daru opposite the Nike of Samothrace.

Certain rooms, such as the *Chambre à Alcôve*, and *Chambre de Parade*, retain restored panelling originally in Henri II's apartments in the Louvre; the vestibule adjacent to the former contains 17C boiseries from the Queen's Pavilion of the Château de Vincennes.

Among the more important recent **donations**, or **acquisitions** by the Musée du Louvre in recent years are the following, some of which are already on display; they are listed according to departments.

A. *Piero della Francesca*, Portrait of Sigismond Malatesta; *Corneille de Lyon*, Portrait of Pierre Aymeric (1534); *Rubens*, Hélène Fourment descending to her coach; *Sébastian Bourdon* (1616–71), The meeting of Anthony and Cleopatra; *Georges de la Tour*, St Irene weeping over St Sebastian; *Pieter de Hooch*, La buveuse; *Chardin*, Still life with hare and powder-flask; *Fragonard*, Portrait of Marie-Madeleine Guimard; *Hubert Robert*, Two imaginary views of the Louvre, one in ruins; *Goya*, Portrait of Mariana Waldstein, Marquesa de Santa Cruz; *Turner*, watercolour View of St-Germain-en-Laye; *Manet*, Portrait of his parents; *Renoir*, Nude, Dancing in town, and in the country; *Van Gogh*, Night scene. More recent acquisitions include: *Sébastien Stoskopff*, Still Lives; *John Linnell*, Hampstead Heath; *Goya*, Christ in the Garden of Olives; *Greuze*, Portrait of Claude Henri Watelet; *Vestier*, Portrait of Marguerite Lachapelle; *Joachim Wtewael*, Perseus and Andromeda; *Louis Bréa*, Pietà; *Zoppo*, Virgin and Child with angels; *Batoni*, Portrait of Charles John Crowle; *G.B. Lampi*, Count Stanislas Félix Potocki and his sons; *Lorenzo Lotto*, Christ carrying the Cross; and *Pierre Subleyras*, Portrait presumed to be of Joseph Baretti.

B. two red-figure stamnoi (c.300 B.C.).

C. Group of Seny-Nefer and his wife, painted sandstone (18th Dyn.).

D. Bronze quiver from Luristan (7C B.C.).

E. *Mathieu Criaerd* (1689–1776), Commode in the Chinese taste; *Cressent*, Pair of cupboards; Red-lacquered commode (c. 1755–60); *J.-J. de St-Germain*, Clock supported by rhinoceros (c.1750); *Jacques Roettiers* (1707–84), Silver surtout of the Duc de Bourbon; the 'Sancy' diamond (54 carats).

F. Virgin and Child (Lorraine; early 14C); *Ponce Jacquiot* (c.1515–72), terracotta Nude extracting thorn from her foot; *Jacques Prou* (1655–1706), Amphitrite; *Pigalle*, Mme de Pompadour, as Friendship; *Clodion* (1738–1814), Satyrs and nymphs dancing.

A. Paintings

French School

14–16Cs: *Girard d'Orléans* or *Jean Coste*, Portrait of Jean II (le Bon; 1319–64); *Henri de Vulcop*, The raising of Lazarus; *Jean Fouquet* (c.1420–c.1480), Portraits of Charles VII of France, and of Guillaume Juvénal des Ursins; *Jean Hey*, the 'Master of Moulins' (fl. 1480–1500), two panels from a triptych of Pierre II, Duc de Bourbon, and Anne of Beaujeau, and a small portrait of their daughter Suzanne de Bourbon; *Enguerrand Quarton* (attrib.; fl. 1444–66), The Pietà of Villeneuve-lès-Avignon; *School of Avignon*, Three Prophets; *anon.* (Flemish; mid 15C) panel of the Parlement of Paris (note background); *Master of the Annunciation of Aix*, Books in a niche; *Nicolas Froment* (fl. 1461–83), The Matheron Diptych, with portraits of King René of Anjou and his wife Jeanne de Laval; *Josse Lieferinxe* (fl. 1493–1505), Calvary, and Adoration of the Child; *Jean Cousin the Elder* (c.1490–c.1560), Eva Prima Pandora; *Pseudo Félix Chretien*, Portrait of a Man 'à l'antique'; *School of Fontainebleau* (mid 16C), Diana the huntress; *Jean Clouet* (c.1485–c.1540), Portrait of François I; *Toussaint Dubreuil* (c.1561–1602), The toilette; *anon.* Double portrait, possibly by *Daniel Dumonstier* (1574–1646); *anon.* One-eyed flautist (1566); *François Quesnel* (attrib.; c.1543–1616), Portrait of Henri III; *School of Fontainebleau* (late 16C), a titillating Portrait of Gabrielle d'Estrées and her sister the Duchesse de Villars; Portraits, mostly from the collection of Roger de Gaignières (1642–1715), which included 1096 items, from the workshops of *Corneille de Lyon* (fl. 1540–74), *Pourbus the Younger* (1569/70–1622)—note his portrait of Henri IV—and *François Clouet* (c. 1505–72): note the latter's portrait of Elisabeth of Austria, wife of Charles IX, painted in 1571.

17–18Cs: *Valentin de Boullogne* (1591–1634), Tavern scene; *Nicolas Poussin* (1594–1665), Echo and Narcissus, and The poet's inspiration. Among other Arcadian scenes by Poussin are Orpheus and Eurydice, Diogenes throwing his bowl, and the Four Seasons are notable; also a self-portrait; *Philippe de Champaigne* (1602–74), Portrait of Robert Arnauld d'Andilly, The artist's daughter with Mère Catherine-Agnès Arnauld, and The magistrates of Paris; *Georges de la Tour* (1593–1652), The cardsharper, Adoration of the shepherds, Joseph the carpenter, and Magdalen watching the candle; *Louis le Nain* (1593–1648), The guard house, The peasants' meal, and Peasant family, among others; *Lubin Baugin* (1612–63), Still-life; *Claude Gellée*, better known as *Claude Lorrain* (1600–82), View of the Campo Vaccino, Rome, Ulysses and Chryseis, and three luminous Port scenes; *Charles le Brun* (1619–90), Chancellor Séguier; *Joseph Parrocel* (1646–1704), Louis XIV's army crossing the Rhine; *François de Troy* (1645–1730), Charles Mouton, the musician; *Hyacinthe Rigaud* (1659–1743), The sculptor Martin Desjardins, Portrait of the artist's mother; *Nicolas de Largillière* (1656–1746), Self-portrait, with his wife and daughter, Portrait of Président De Laage; *François Desportes* (1661–1743), Self-portrait 'en chasseur'; *Jean-Baptiste-Siméon Chardin* (1699–1779), The skate, and 'Le souffleur'; Boy with a teetotum, and Man with a violin, still-lifes, and genre scenes; *Antoine Watteau* (1684–1721), Gilles, the clown; *Jean Honoré Fragonard* (1732–1806), Two figures: Inspiration and Study; *Jean-Baptiste Oudry* (1686–1755), Bittern and partridge watched by a white dog; *Louis Tocqué* (1696–1772), The painter Louis Galloche; *Joseph Silfrein-Duplessis* (1725–1802), Allegrain, the sculptor; *Pierre Subleyras* (1699-1749), The Abbé Cesare Benvenuti; *Hubert Robert* (1733–1808), The Pont du Gard; *Élisabeth Vigée-Lebrun* (1755–1842), Portrait of Hubert Robert; and examples of the work of *François Boucher* (1703–70), *Nicolas Lancret* (1690–1743), and *Jean-Baptiste Greuze* (1725–1805), including his Broken pitcher. *Claude-Joseph Vernet* (1714–89), The Ponte Rotto; *Jean-Baptiste Perroneau* (1715–83), Mme de Sorquainville; *Jacques-Louis David* (1748–1825), M. Sériziat, his wife and son, Mme Trudaine, The Marquise d'Orvilliers, Alexandre Lenoir, Mme Récamier in a familiar pose, Pope Pius VII, and Coronation of Napoleon I (by Pope Pius VII in Notre-Dame, 2 Dec. 1804).

19C: *Baron Antoine-Jean Gros* (1771–1835), Portrait of Madeleine Pasteur, Bonaparte at the bridge of Arcole (1796), Christine Boyer, first wife of Lucien Bonaparte, Bonaparte visiting the plague-striken at Jaffa, and at Eylau (with portraits of Berthier, Murat, Soult, and Davoust); *Baron François Gérard* (1770–1837), Portraits of his wife, of Comtesse Regnauld de Saint-Jean d'Angély, and of J.-B. Isabey; *Jean-Auguste-Dominique Ingres* (1780–1867), Portraits of the Rivière family, and of L.-F. Bertin, senior, of C.-J.-L. Cordier, The Turkish bath, 'La grande odalisque', 'La baigneuse', and the composer Cherubini; *Pierre-Paul Prud'hon* (1758–1823), The Empress Joséphine at Malmaison; *Théodore Géricault* (1791–1824), Officer of the Chasseurs de la Garde, The raft of the 'Medusa', The Vendéen, Equestrian portraits, including horses at Epsom; *Eugène Delacroix* (1789–1863), Self-portrait, Hamlet and Horatio, The orphan at the cemetery, Portrait of Chopin, Liberty leading the people (or 'Les Barricades'), Scenes of the massacre of Chois, Algerian women at home; *Alexandre Decamps* (1803–60), Defeat of the Cimbri; *Gustave Courbet* (1819–77), The artist's studio, The wave, Portrait of Pierre-Joseph Proudhon; *Joseph Berger* (1798–1870), Portrait of a man; *Marie-Guillemine Benoist* (1768–1826), A black woman; *Henri-François Risesener* (1767–1828), Portrait of Maurice Quay; *Martin Drölling* (1752–1817), Kitchen interior; *A.-L.-C. Pagnest* (1790–1819), Portrait of Nanteuil-Lanorville; *Amuray-Duval* (1808–85), Mme de Loynes; *P.-H. Valenciennes* (1750–1819), Views of Rome and the Campagna; *Louis Boilly* (1761–1845), Genre scenes; *A.-E. Michallon*

(1796–1822), Landscapes; *Camille Corot* (1796–1875), Landscapes, and Portraits; *Eugène Isabey* (1803–86), The wooden bridge; *Eugène Fromentin* (1820–76), Hawking in Algeria; *Théodore Rousseau* (1812–67), Oak-trees; *Charles Daubigny* (1817–78), The sluicegate; *Jean-François Millet* (1814–75), Paintings of peasants, The gleaners, and Mme Lecourtois, his sister-in-law; *Honoré Daumier* (1808–79), Crispin and Scapin, Don Quixote and the dead mule; *Pierre Puvis de Chavannes* (1824–98), Poor fisherman, etc.

Flemish and Dutch Schools

Frans Hals, Portraits of Paulus van Berestyn, and of his third wife, Catherine Both van der Eem; The van Berestyn family, now attr. to *Pierre Soutman*; also by *Hals*, The charming gipsy girl; *Gérard Verspronck*, Portrait of Agathe van Schoonhoven; *Salomon van Ruysdael*, The landing-stage; *Jan van Goyen*, View of Dordrecht. *Rembrandt*: Self-portrait, bareheaded; another wearing a toque and with an architectural background; and a third with a toque and gold chain; a fourth self-portrait is of the artist in his old age (1660) at his easel; Christ at Emmaus, Portrait of Hendrikje Stoffels, Bathsheba bathing, St Matthew inspired by an angel, The meditating philosopher, and Carcase of an ox.

Albert *Cuyp*, Cavaliers; *Allart van Everdingen*, Landscape with hunters and fishermen; *Paul Potter*, Horses at a cottage door; *Jacob van Ruysdael*, The bush; *Philips Wouwerman*, Landscape with a cart; *Salomon van Ruysdael*, Still life with a turkey; *Karel Dujardin*, Italian charlatans; *Jan van der Heyden*, The Town Hall, Amsterdam; *Bol*, The mathematician; *Frans Post*, Tropical landscapes painted in Brazil; *Cornelis van Poelenburgh*, Orpheus charming the beasts, and Ruins of Rome with the Castel Sant'Angelo, etc.; *Willem Claesz Heda*, The dessert; *Willem Cornelisz. Duyster*, Robbers; *Pieter Codde*, Dancing-lesson; *Hendrik Pot*, Copy of Daniel Mytens's portrait of Charles I of England; *David Teniers*, The Seven Works of Mercy, 'Les joueurs de Hoquet', Winter scene, Tavern interior; *Frans Francken the Younger*, The Prodigal Son; *Adrien Brouwer*, The inn, Landscape at dusk; *Joos van Craesbeek*, The smoker (? self-portrait); *Denis van Alsloot*, Winter landscape; *Paul Bril*, Landscape with a pond, Fishing; *Gotthard de Wedig*, Still-life; *Roelant Savery*, Polish mercenaries in the forest; *Pietersz. van de Venne*, Celebrating the truce of 1609; *Jan Brueghel the Younger (Velours)*, The battle of Arbela, Virgin and Child with a garland of flowers, Air and Earth (part of a series of the four elements: Fire and Water are in the Ambrosiana Museum, Milan), and Landscapes.

Joos *van Cleve*, Triptych of the Descent from the Cross, Francis of Assisi receiving the stigmata, and The Last Supper; *Master of the St Bartholomew Altarpiece*, Descent from the Cross; *Master of the View of St Gudule*, Pastoral instruction; *Thierry Bouts*, Descent from the Cross, Virgin and Child; *Gérard de Saint-Jean*, Raising of Lazarus; *Jan van Eyck*, Chancellor Nicolas Rolin before the Virgin; *Rogier van der Weyden*, Salvator Mundi, triptych of the Braque family; *Petrus Christus*, Pietà; *Memling*, The Mystic Marriage of St Catherine, with the donor praying under the protection of St John the Baptist, Portrait of an old lady, The martyrdom of St Sebastian, Resurrection of Christ, Ascension, The Virgin of Jacques Floreins; *Gerard David*, Triptych of Mary, Marriage at Cana; *Cornelis van Dalem*, Farmyard in winter; *Brueghel the Elder*, Beggars; the *Brunswick Monogramist*, Sacrifice of Abraham; *Lucas van Leyden*, The card-dealer, Lot and his daughters; _Mabuse_, Diptych of Jean Carondelet (Chancellor of Flanders) and the Virgin; _Quentin Metsys_, Moneylender and his wife, The dead Christ; _van Orley_, Portrait of an old man; _van Cleve_, Monk offering his heart to the Virgin and Child; _Patinir_, St Jerome in the desert; _Hieronymus Bosch_, The Ship of Fools; _van Valckenborgh_, The Tower of Babel; _Brueghel the Elder_, contemporary copy of The blind men; _Antonio Moro_ (Anthonis Mor van Dashorst), Card. de Granvella's dwarf, A nobleman in the Cardinal's entourage; _anon._ Portrait of a lady of quality; _Nicolaes Berchem_, Landscape with animals; _Gerard Dou_, Woman with dropsy; _Gabriel Metsu_, The female toper, Soldier and young girl, and The grass-market at Amsterdam; _Nicolaes Maes_ (?), Bathing scéne; _Gerard Ter Borch_, The military gallant, Reading lesson; _Pieter de Hooch_, Card-players; _Ter Borch_, The concert, Portrait of a man; _Jan van der Heyden_, The Herengracht in Amsterdam; _Adriaen Coorte_, Shells; _Vermeer_, The lacemaker; _van Ostade_, The schoolmaster; _Michiel Sweerts_, Young man and matchmaker (?); Sketches by _Rubens_.

Van Dyck, Portraits of the Marchesa Spinola Doria; Francisco de Moncada, Conde de Osuna and Gov.-Gen. of the Spanish Netherlands; the Duke of Richmond; Charles-Louis, Elector Palatine, and his brother Prince Rupert, later Duke of Cumberland; Charles I of England; A gentleman with his sword; A lady of quality with her daughter; and A gentleman with his daughter.

Rubens, Kermesse (the village fair), Portraits of his wife Helen Fourment with two of her children, her sister Suzanne, Baron Henri de Vicq—a portrait of the ambassador who obtained for the artist the commission to paint the Medici canvases (see below)—and The Adoration of the Magi; _Jan Fyt_, Still life with game; _Victor Boucquet_, Standard-bearer; _Jordaens_, The king drinks; and _David Teniers the Younger_, Riverside tavern.

Also by _Rubens_, the 21 large allegorical paintings depicting the Life of Marie de Médicis, which he designed in 1622–25 to decorate the Luxembourg Palace, in the execution of which he was largely aided by his pupils. They follow a chronological sequence, from her birth in April 1575 to the reconciliation with her son, Louis XIII, in 1619.

Paintings from the _de Croy Bequest_ include _van Honthorst_, The dentist, and Portrait of Frederic-Henri of Nassau; _Samuel van Hoogstraten_ (?), The slippers; _Jan Verspronck_, Young woman from Haarlem; _Joos van Craesbeek_, Spring; _Barent Avercamp_ and _Jan van Goyen_, Skating scenes.

German School

Hans Baldung Grien, A knight, a young woman, and Death; _Master of the Legend of St Ursula_, Pagan ambassadors at the court of St̀ Ursula; _anon. painter from Cologne_, Pietà of St-Germain-des-Prés; _Ludger Tom Ring, the Elder_, Sibyl; also a fine _anon._ (L.C.Z.) Flagellation; _Hans Holbein the Younger_, Portraits of Sir Henry Wyatt, Anne of Cleves (painted for Sir Thomas More), Nicolas Kratzer (Henry VIII's astronomer), and William Warham, Abp of Canterbury; _Dürer_, Self-portrait (1493); _Wolf Huber_, The grieving Christ; _Lucas Cranach the Elder_, Venus in a landscape, A young girl (?Magdalena Luther); _Hans Maler_, Mathäus Schwartz.

Also Studies for the decoration of the Ducal Palace at Urbino, by _Justus of Ghent_ and _Pedro Berruguete_.

Spanish School

Jaime Huguet, The Flagellation, and Entombment; *Barnat Martorell*, Four episodes from the life of St George; Man with a glass of wine (?Portuguese School); *El Greco*, Crucifixion with two donors (signed in Greek characters), St Louis of France; *Ribera*, St Paul the hermit; The Entombment, Adoration of the shepherds, and Club-footed boy; *Zurbarán*, St Bonaventura at the Council of Lyon, and The saint's corpse exposed; *Murillo*, Legend of S. Diego, known as 'the angels' kitchen' (one of a series of 16 painted for the Franciscan convent at Seville, another of which has been recently acquired by the Louvre); *Carreño*, Foundation of the Trinitarian Order; *Zurbarán*, Sta Apollina; *Velázquez*, Mariana of Austria, her daughter The infanta Margarita, and The infanta María Teresa; *Collantes*, The Burning Bush; *Murillo*, Young beggar; *Meléndez*, Self-portrait, and Still-life; *Goya*, The unequal wedding, Woman with a fan, and portraits of Ferdinand Guillemardet, and of Evaristo Pérez de Castro.

Italian Schools

Primitives: *Cimabue*, Madonna with angels; *Giotto*, St Francis receiving the stigmata; an *anon.* 14C Florentine Calvary; *Bernardo Daddi*, Annunciation; *Bartolo di Maestro Fredi*, Presentation in the Temple; *Barnaba da Modena*, Madonna and Child; *Lorenzo Veneziano*, Madonna enthroned; twelve *anon.* Venetian scenes from the Life of the Virgin; *Simone Martini*, Christ bearing the Cross; *Guido da Siena*, Nativity, and Presentation in the Temple; *Pisanello*, A princess of the House of Este; *Gentile da Fabriano*, Presentation; *Jacopo Bellini*, Madonna and Child with donor; *Benozzo Gozzoli*, The triumph of St Thomas Aquinas; *Alessio Baldovinetti*, Madonna adoring the Child; *Paolo Uccello*, Battle of San Romano, in 1432; *Fra Angelico*, Coronation of the Virgin, and The martyrdom of St Cosmas and St Damian; *Sano di Pietro*, Five episodes from the dream of St Jerome; *The Master of the Observance*, St Anthony; *Sassetta*, Madonna and Child with angels, St Anthony of Padua and St John the Evangelist, and The miraculous deliverance of the poor incarcerated in the prisons of Florence; *School of Fra Filippo Lippi*, Nativity; *Botticelli*, Madonna and Child surrounded by angels, Portrait of a young man, 'The Madonna of the Guidi of Faenza', Madonna and Child with St John the Baptist; *Mantegna*, St Sebastian, and Calvary; *Antonello da Messina*, The condottiere; *Giovanni Bellini*, Portrait of a man; *Catena*, Portrait of Giulio Mellini; *Bernardo Parentino*, Adoration of the Magi; *School of Fra Angelico*, Herod's banquet; *Pesellino*, St Francis of Assisi receiving the stigmata, and St Cosmas and St Damian nursing the sick; *Signorelli*, Birth of St John the Baptist; *Bartolomeo di Giovanni*, Marriage of Thetis and Peleus, and Wedding procession; *Ghirlandaio*, The bottlenosed old man and his grandson, The Visitation; *Piero di Cosimo*, Madonna and Dove; *Perugino*, Madonna with saints and angels, and Tondo showing the Madonna and Child with St Catherine and St John the Baptist; *Giovanni Bellini*, Crucifixion, Resurrection, and Blessing, Portrait of two men; *Carpaccio*, St Stephen preaching; *School of Gentile Bellini*, Reception in Cairo of the Venetian Ambassador Dom. Trevisano; *Cima da Conegliano*, Madonna and Child with St John the Baptist and the Magdalen;

Jacopo de Barbieri, Madonna at the fountain; *Palmezzano*, Christ supported by two angels.

16C. *Veronese's* huge Marriage at Cana; others by Veronese are the so-called 'La belle Nani', a Calvary, and Supper at Emmaus; *Titian*, Lady at her toilet (called 'Alfonso da Ferrara and Laura de' Dianti'), St Jerome in the desert, Man with a glove, and another male portrait, Supper at Emmaus, The Entombment, Allegory representing the wife of Alfonso d'Avalos being entrusted to Chastity and Cupid, François I (painted from a medal of the king the artist never saw), Jupiter and Antiope, known as 'the Venus of the Pardo', and Pastoral concert (once attrib. to Giorgione); *Tintoretto*, Susanna and the elders, and Self-portrait (1590); *Palma Vecchio*, Adoration of the shepherds; *Giulio Romano*, Portrait of Joanna d'Aragón (the face by *Raphael*); *Andrea del Sarto*, Charity; *Correggio*, The Mystic Marriage of St Catherine of Alexandria, Jupiter and Antiope; *Lotto*, The woman taken in adultery; *Raphael*, St George, and St Michael, Portrait of Baldassare Castiglione (author of 'The Courtier'), 'La belle Jardinière', Self-portrait with a friend; *Leonardo da Vinci*, Annunciation, Madonna and Child with St Anne, The Virgin of the Rocks (1482; probably earlier than the similar composition in London), St John the Baptist (apparently painted from a female model or worked on later by another hand); *School of Leonardo*, Bacchus, and the so-called 'La belle ferronnière' (from the chain round her forehead.

A Portrait by *Leonardo da Vinci*, traditionally assumed to be of Monna Lisa Gherardini, third wife of Francesco di Zanobi del Giocondo, hence also 'la Gioconda', or in French, 'La Joconde'.

Leonardo worked intermittently on this portrait between 1503–06. In spite of drastic restoration at different periods, this remains one of the outstanding achievements of the Italian Renaissance. In Aug. 1911 it was stolen from the Salon Carré by a thief disguised as a workman, but was recovered in Florence in Dec. 1913. It has also been claimed that the sitter was Costanza d'Avalos, mistress of Giuliano de' Medici, and that another somewhat similar portrait in a private collection represents Monna Lisa.

17–18Cs. *Caravaggio*, Portrait of Alof de Wignacourt, and The fortune-teller; *Bart. Schedone*, Entombment; *Guido Reni*, St Sebastian, Ecce Homo; *Domenichino*, Herminia among the shepherds, St Cecilia; *Pietro da Cortona*, Venus as a huntress appearing to Aeneas; *Carlo Maratta*, Maria-Magdalena Rospigliosi, niece of Pope Clement IX; *Lionello Spada*, Return of the Prodigal Son; *Bernardo Strozzi*, Holy Family; *Salvator Rosa*, Landscape with hunters; *Paolo Porpora*, Still life; *Aniello Falcone*, Battle scene; *Giuseppe Angeli*, The little drummer; *G.-M. Crespi*, Woman with a flea; *Guardi*, 8 of 12 scenes depicting festivities organized for the coronation of the Doge Alvise IV Mocenigo; *Longhi*, The Presentation; *G.-P. Panini*, Concert in Rome (26 Nov. 1729) to celebrate the birth of the Dauphin Louis to Marie Leczinska and Louis XV, and Preparations for festivities in the Piazza Navona; *Michele Marieschi*, View of S. Maria della Salute, Venice; *Guardi*, View of the church of SS Giovanni e Paolo; *G.-B. Tiepolo*, The Last Supper; *Domenico Tiepolo*, Carnival scene, and The charlatan.

Among the larger 17–18C canvases may be mentioned *A. Carracci*, The Virgin appearing to St Luke and St Catherine, Hunting, and Fishing; *Caravaggio*, Death of the Virgin; and *Guercino*, The raising of Lazarus.

The undispersed *Beistégui Collection* (donated to the Louvre in 1953) contains an *anon. Franco-Flemish* Virgin and Child; *Master of Moulins*, Portrait of the Dauphin Charles Orlando (1494; son of Charles VIII and Anne of Brittany): among other portraits are *François-Hubert Drouais* (1727–75), Anne-Françoise Doré, his wife; *van Dyck*, A Genoese gentleman (*not* Livio Odescalchi); *Lawrence*, Mrs Cuthbert; *Zuloaga*, Carlos de Beistégui (donor of the Collection); *David*, Gén. Bonaparte, sketched near Rivoli (c. 1797), M. Mayer, envoy from the Batavian Republic; *Gérard*, Mme Lecerf, his cousin; *Ingres*, Mme Panckoucke; and *Goya*, The Condesa del Carpio, Marquesa de Solana.

English School

Ramsay, Lord Elcho (?); *Gainsborough*, Conversation in the park, Lady Gertrude Alston; *Reynolds*, Master Hare; *Romney*, Sir John Stanley; *Wright of Derby*, The Lake of Nemi; *Lawrence*, Charles William Bell, John Julius Angerstein and his wife; *Raeburn*, Capt. Robert Hay of Spott; *Bonington*, The Adriatic; and examples of the work of *John Hamilton Mortimer, Fuseli, Constable, Turner, Angelica Kauffmann*, and *Burne-Jones.*

One may perhaps add here the Portrait of the Artist's Mother, by *Whistler.*

On the SECOND FLOOR of the Pavillon de Flore are displayed a number of masterpieces of *pastel portraiture*, a very small part of the collections of the *Cabinet de Dessins*: also some miniatures.

The **Cabinet de Dessins** itself is not open to the general public, but researchers and connoisseurs (who on their first visit will require a letter of introduction) are courteously allowed to study its superb collections, which include some 1200 miniatures, 30,000 engravings, and 90,000 drawings.

Although drawings had already existed in the Bibliothèque du Roi, it was not until 1671, when Louis XIV acquired the 5542 drawings (in addition to important paintings) collected by *Everard Jabach* (d. 1695) that the main nucleus of the Royal Collection was formed. To this were added drawings by Le Brun, Mignard, and Coypel, and by 1730 an inventory included some 8593 works, to which were added some 1300 drawings collected by the great connoisseur *Pierre-Jean Mariette.* By 1792 some 11,000 drawings were listed, and in following decades the figure almost doubled (including the Saint Maurice collection; the collection of the Dukes of Modena, and of Filippo Baldinucci, etc.).

The Codex Vallardi (including a number of drawings by Pisanello) was acquired in 1856, and Jacopo Bellini's sketchbook in 1884, and the collection was further enriched by a number of important donations in succeeding years. Among more recent collections thus acquired by the Cabinet des Dessins have been those of Gustave Caillebotte, Isaac de Camondo, Étienne Moreau-Nélaton, Walter Gay, D. David-Weill, Carle Dreyfus, and Baroness Gourgaud, among others.

Approximately one hundred pastel portraits are exhibited, among them: *Leonardo da Vinci*, Isabella d'Este, Duchess of Mantua, and new acquisitions; *Charles Le Brun* (1619–90), Three portraits of Louis XIV; *Robert Nanteuil* (c. 1623–78), Jean Dorien, Dominique de Vigny, Bp of Meaux, Henri de la Tour d'Auvergne, vicomte de Turenne (attrib. doubtful); *Joseph Vivien* (1657–1734), The sculptor François Girardon, and The architect Robert de Cotte, among others; *Rosalba Carriera* (1675–1757; who did much to popularize the technique in France), Young girl with a monkey (the model may have been the daughter of the financier John Law); *Maurice-Quentin Delatour* (1704–88), Hermann-Maurice, Comte de Saxe, Philibert Orry, Jacques Dimont, and The Marquise de Pompadour; *Jean-Baptiste Perronneau*, Abraham van Robais, The engraver Laurent Cars; *Chardin*, His second wife, Self-portraits, with spectacles, with a green eye-shade, and at his easel.

Other portraits by *Gustav Lundberg*, *Adélaïde Labille-Guiard* (1749–1803), *Joseph Boze*, and *John Russell* (1745–1806) follow, together with a representative selection of 19C pastels.

B. Greek and Roman Antiquities

Among the outstanding objects in the extensive collection (in addition to the Nike of Samothrace: see p128) are the following (on the Ground Floor): the *Apollo 'of Piombino'*, a 5C bronze figure, with copper encrustations—lips and nipples—which was retrieved from the sea near Piombino, and perhaps a replica of a work by *Kanachos*; a Female torso similar in type to the Esquiline Venus at Rome; Frieze with Apollo and Hermes and nymphs and graces (early 5C) from Thasos, and the upper part of the stele 'Exaltation of the Flower', from Pharsalus.

The *Venus 'de Milo'*, one of the most beautiful and celebrated surviving examples of antique sculpture, found by a peasant in 1820 on the island of Melos in the Greek archipelago; it is now regarded as a copy by an unknown master of the 2C after a 4C original. When discovered, it was in five fragments, and was restored in the Louvre.

The so-called '*Dame d'Auxerre*', possibly of Cretan origin; the 6C '*Rampin*' head, with a plaster cast of the equestrian figure (in the Acropolis Museum at Athens) to which it belongs; *Hera of Samos*, one of the oldest and best authenticated works of island sculpture (c.520 B.C.); inscribed *Cheramues*; torso of *Apollo* (Miletus; 5C); Metopes from the Temple of Zeus at Olympia, with Hercules overcoming the Cretan bull, and presenting to Athene one of the Stymphalian birds; statue of *Persephone, after Pheidias*.

Fragments of the E. frieze of the Parthenon at Athens (5C B.C.; the greater part of the frieze, which represents the Panathenaic procession, is in the British Museum); a fine Head of a goddess; the '*Laborde Head*', from one of the pediments of the Parthenon; Centaur carrying off a Lapith woman; the so-called *Barberini Supplicant*.

The '*Borghese Warrior*', signed on the tree-trunk by *Agasias*, an otherwise unknown sculptor of the late Hellenistic period (found at Anzio in the 17C); replicas of works by Praxiteles and his school, including the *Venus of Arles*, altered by Giradon; the huntress *Artemis*, known as the 'Diana of Versailles' (c.A.D. 100), acquired from Rome by François I; *Hermes fastening his sandal*, and *Eros stringing his bow*, antique copies of originals by *Lysippus*: *Silenus and Dionysus*; *Apollo Sauroktonos* (killing a lizard); the *Aphrodite of Cnidos*; the so-called '*Kaufman Head*', all *after Praxiteles*; and *Aphrodite and Eros, after Scopas*.

The COUR DU SPHINX, with a façade by *Le Vau*, at present contains bas-reliefs from the architrave of the Temple of Assos (near Troy, in Asia Minor), representing Hercules battling against the Triton, a banquet, a procession of animals and centaurs, etc.; frieze from the temple of Artemis at Magnesia on the Maeander, depicting a battle between Greeks and Amazons (2C B.C.); the God of the Tiber, a colossal group found in the 16C; and a huge mosaic of the Seasons (4C) from near Antioch.

Among other sculptures, together with a number of powerfully sculpted heads, are: *Augustus*, with a head earlier than the body; *Octavius* representing Mercury, of Parian marble, found near Rome: it is signed 'Cleomenes of Athens, son of Cleomenes' on the tortoise at the foot; *Agrippa*; and *Livia* (in black basalt), are outstanding.

Other objects include mosaics, one of the Judgement of Paris; a number of decorative monumental vases and sculptures in porphyry, etc., of the late Roman period; fragments of Graeco-Roman frescoes; Roman cameos, and two ivory plaques (Etruscan; 6–5C B.C.). Among other **Etruscan** objects are five terracotta panels from Cerveteri (600 B.C.); an imposing terracotta Sarcophagus (also discovered at Cerveteri, by Campana, in 1850), where, as if on a funeral couch, recline the lifelike figures of a man and his wife represented as if still alive and conversing. The woman wears a cap (tutulus) and a small gorget; the man, bare-footed, is draped. There is also a collection of pottery, mostly in the Greek style, some black ('bucchero') ware; and a number of small bronzes.

The exhibits of the department are continued in a series of rooms on the First Floor, outstanding among which is the 'Treasure of Boscoreale' (near Pompeii), a collection of superbly decorated silver objects discovered in 1895 in a fine state of preservation on the site of a villa overwhelmed by the eruption of Vesuvius in A.D. 79; two silver masks from the Gallo-Roman 'Treasure of N.-D. d'Allençon', and the Silver 'Treasure of Graincourt lès-Havrincourt'.

Among exhibits of the pre-Hellenic civilisations: pithoi from Knossos (Crete; 1700–1600 B.C.), and from Thera and Rhodes (14C B.C.); marble idols from the Cyclades (2500–2000 B.C.); terracotta and bronze figurines and painted ceramics (Minoan) from Crete (14–12C B.C.), and funerary objects.

Other impressive collections of Greek and Roman bronzes, jewellery, arms, and utensils, etc., are arranged in chronological and geographical groups, outstanding among which are: ARCHAIC GREEK ART—a *Minotaur*; statuette of *Athene*; a Warrior; a Javelin-thrower; and *Silenus* dancing (all 6C B.C.).—*Pan* and his syrinx.—mirrors, including one in its box decorated with scenes in relief.—CLASSICAL GREEK statuettes (5C B.C.); Group of *Lycurgus and the Maenads*; a Stag; *Ephebus* (School of Polykleitos); *Hercules fighting*; and *Zeus*.—Athlete's head (Greek; 5C B.C.), found at Benevento, Italy.—HELLENISTIC ART—*Aphrodite fastening her sandal*; an Hermaphrodite figure; and 'Napoleon's cist' (a cylindrical box on which women kept jewels and toilet accessories).—ROMAN GAUL. Statuettes and busts: note eyes; Bull; and Boar; and a Cock found at Lyon.—A Winged helmet encircled by a gold crown; Gladiator's armour; and a magnificent collection of jewellery and goldsmiths' work from all the periods and regions covered by other exhibits.

Among the superlative collection of **Antique Pottery** from the 10C B.C. to the 4C B.C., are examples of the Geometric style; Boeotian figurines, etc.; Attic vases found in the Dipylon cemetery (c.800 B.C.); pottery from the Greek islands; and vessels in the 'orientalised' style; pottery from Corinth; Tyrrhenian amphorae, kraters, and other

vessels; and black-figure Attic ceramics; Oenochoai and vases in the
Attic style, signed by *Nikosthenes* and *Andokides* respectively,
including both black and red figures; coloured terracottas; Attic
red-figure pottery (c.500 B.C.), including works by *Euphronius* (a
large krater with the combat of Hercules and Antaeus), *Douris* (a
kylix with Eros and Memnon), and *Myson* (amphora with Croesus on
a pyre); terracotta figurines, and statuettes from Tanagra; figurines
of the Hellenistic period; and antique glassware.

C. Egyptian Antiquities

At present this department cannot be entered direct from the *Porte Champollion*, on the S. side of the *Cour Carrée*, named after the great Egyptologist
and first curator, J.-F. Champollion (1790–1832), who had in 1826 acquired the
collection of the British Consul-general Henry Salt (1780–1827), to which others
were added in subsequent decades.

One may enter from the *Porte St Germain l'Auxerrois*, or from the
Porte Denon, thence going through Greek and Roman Antiquities, to
reach the *Crypt*, and the stele of Antef, first herald in the service of
King Thothmes III (1504–1450 B.C.), and other steles of the 12th
Dynasty; the crypt itself contains a stele dedicated by Queen
Hatshepsout to her father Thothmes (1530–20 B.C.); a colossal sphinx
in pink granite, from Tanis (Lower Egypt; Old Kingdom).
    Among remarkable objects in the collection are a colossal statue of
Seti II (19th Dyn.) in red sandstone; the limestone cult chamber of the
'mastaba' or tomb of Akhouthotep, an Egyptian dignitary (c.2500 B.C.;
5th Dyn.), found at Sakkara: inscribed in the architrave above the
door are the occupant's name and titles. Within, the walls are
covered with vivid scenes in bas-relief of contemporary life in the
Old Kingdom, as well as depicting the funeral of the deceased, some
of them among the finest extant examples of the art. The offerings of
food and drink were placed on the adjacent table of pink granite.
    Among smaller objects from the Egyptian collection, are, from the
PREHISTORIC AND THINITE PERIODS (4000–2800 B.C.): schist palettes, for
grinding and mixing paints, one decorated with a bull—symbolising
the king—pinning an enemy to the ground, and another depicting
both imaginary and real animals (giraffes, etc.); a knife from
Gebel-el-Arak (c. 3400 B.C.), and small ivory nudes, known as
'concubines of the dead'.

THINITE EPOCH (c.3100–2700 B.C.). Stele of King Zet, known as the
Serpent King, his name being represented here as a serpent; the
falcon above symbolises Horus, the god of kingship: it was found
near the king's tomb at Abydos (c. 3000 B.C.).

OLD KINGDOM (c. 2700–2200 B.C.). stele of Nefertiabet, in painted stone
(4th Dyn.): she is seated before a table of offerings, dressed in a
leopard's skin; Three fine columns of pink granite with palm-leaf
capitals, one being marked with the name of King Uni (5th Dyn.); the
other two, which were taken by Rameses II, are of the same period.
Sarcophagus in the 'palace façade' style, found at Abu Roash (5th
Dyn.): note the charming low relief in limestone of a girl smelling a
flower; finds from the pyramid of Didoufri, son of Cheops, including a
red quartzite head of King Didoufri. Small limestone figure of a

scribe seated cross-legged, known as the 'Scribe accroupi', remarkable for its lifelike appearance, with eyes of white quartz, and rock crystal. Limestone group of the official Raherka, and his wife Merseankh (5th Dyn.); alabaster and hard-stone vessels dating from pre-dynastic times to the 6th Dyn. (c. 3400–2300 B.C.).

MIDDLE KINGDOM (2200–1750 B.C.). Limestone lintel of Sesostris III (1887–1850 B.C.): the king is shown making an offering of bread to the hawkheaded god Montou; sandstone statue of the scribe Mentuhotep; statuette of Sesostris III in green schist, and part of the head

Karohama, the divine votress of Amun; bronze inlaid with gold, silver, copper, and platinum, c. 850 B.C. (Photo Chuzeville)

of the same king in grey granite; statues in black granite of Sesostris III in his youth, and as an old man. Silver and lapis-lazuli treasure discovered in four bronze caskets, marked Amenemhat II (1938–1904 B.C.), in the foundations of the temple of Tod; a portico with papyrus-like columns (13th Dyn.).

ARCHITECTURAL and colossal stone pieces, including Black granite statue of the god Amon protecting King Tutankhamen (18th Dyn.); the head (the r. half eroded by sand and wind) and feet of a huge pink granite statue of Amenophis III (18th Dyn.), with a list of the peoples he subdued inscribed on the base; the sarcophagus of Rameses III (20th Dyn.), the lid of which is in the Fitzwilliam Museum at Cambridge; painted bas-relief of Seti I and the goddess Hathor, from the tomb of the former (19th Dyn.); a red granite fragment from the base of the Obelisk of Luxor (see Rte 8), with four cynocephali (dog-faced baboons) adoring the rising sun, and cartouches of Rameses II; also several statues of Sekhmet, the lion-headed goddess; Hathor capital of pink granite, from Bubastis, where Sekhmet was especially worshipped; limestone statue of a dog; a statue of a Nubian woman from Korosko; and mummy-shaped sarcophagi, including that of Tenthapi.

The **Crypt** contains a number of imposing funerary monuments of the late period, among them a wooden statue of Osiris; also smaller funerary objects and statues—many zoomorphic—of the Ptolemaic and Roman periods. On the ceiling, the large circular sandstone zodiac from the temple of Hathor at Dendera.

Coptic Antiquities: painted cloths used as shrouds, showing masks of the deceased, outstanding amongst which is the Fayoum portrait, and the mummy of a woman showing the form of its wrapping, and how the mask was mounted; plaster mask of a child; and colourful Coptic woven fabrics; fragments of mural-paintings from one of the first monasteries, and a collection of bronze statuettes, crosses, lamps, and candlesticks, etc.; reconstructed part of the nave of the monastery of Bawit (5–9C A.D.): note the Coptic icon, painted on wood, of Christ protecting Apa Mena, superior of the monastery.

On the staircase leading up to the First Floor are displayed objects discovered by Mariette in 1850–53 at the Serapeum at Memphis, including the limestone sphinxes which bordered its approach. The serapeum itself was the underground burial-chamber of the sacred bulls, and canopic jars held the entrails of two Apis bulls (18th Dyn.). Note also a limestone statue of the god Bes from the temple of Nectanebo, and a limestone statue of the bull of Apis, of the 30th Dyn. (378–341 B.C.).

FIRST FLOOR. Note the sphinx from Medamoud, and a huge bust of Amenophis IV (who adopted the name Akhnaton), from Karnak.

R 'A': MIDDLE KINGDOM (cont.): models of granaries; funerary furniture from the tomb of Chancellor Nakhti, and wooden statue of the same, one of the largest wooden funerary effigies known of this period; statue of stucco and painted wood known as the 'Porteuse d'Auge', a young girl, clothed in a tunic of netted pearls, carrying on her head a trough containing a joint of an ox, an essential of the funerary offering; statuette of a concubine (nude), the thumbs having been intentionally cut off; five wooden figures of girls carrying offerings; the inner case of the coffin of Chancellor Nakhti (note the two mystical eyes painted on the outside); models of funerary boats for transporting the dead down the Nile; examples of blue-glaze ware, including several hippopotami.

R 'B': BEGINNING OF THE 18TH DYN. (c. 1555–1365 B.C.): Prince Ahmosis, a seated statue of painted limestone; a wooden one of the priestess Toui (1200 B.C.); life-size statues of Seny Nefer and his wife Hatchepsout; two statuettes of the scribe Nebmertuf writing to the dictation of the cynocephalic god Thot.

R 'C': NEW KINGDOM: household objects; furniture; musical instruments; games; the toilet, etc.

R 'D': AMARNA PERIOD: limestone bust of Akhnaton, and statuette of the young king with his wife Nefertiti, also a bas-relief of the royal couple; painted limestone head of a princess of El-Amarna; quartzite female torso; objects from the time of Tutankhamun, and Horemheb, and reliefs from the tomb of the latter; a royal head in blue glass paste; and fragments of reliefs of this period.

R 'E': RAMESSIDE PERIOD: (1320–1086 B.C.): green enamelled schist statuette of the priestess Nacha. Note the wooden statues, among them that of Piay; statue of the scribe Sethi, kneeling, and holding a naos containing a figure of Osiris (19th Dyn.). Note, in the showcase containing jewellery, the gold shell of the Middle Kingdom; a bracelet of sphinxes of King Ahmosis (New Kingdom); a collar with gold pendant fishes; General Djchouty's gold and silver bowl; jewels from the tomb of Prince Khaemouaset, son of Ramses II; the triad of Osorkon II, in gold and lapis-lazuli, with the divinities Osiris, Isis, and their son Horus; necklace of Pinedjem I, of gold and lapis-lazuli; and Roman jewellery from Egypt.

R 'F': THIRD INTERMEDIATE PERIOD (1085–663 B.C.): large bronze statues: note that of Horus, the falcon-god, making a libation; bronze sistrum; bronze tablet-cover, decorated in silver, gold, and electrum; bronze figures of kings and priests; a damascened bronze statue of queen Keramana, wife of Takelot II (847–823 B.C.); bronze statuette of King Taharqa on a silver-plated wooden stand, kneeling before the falcon-god Hemen, of gold-plated schist; a showcase displays 'Shawabty' figures, placed in tombs to serve the dead; sarcophagi and other funerary objects of the 21st Dyn.

R 'G': SAÏTE PERIOD (663–525 B.C.), and the last native dynasties (525–333 B.C.): Portrait reliefs; bronzes representing Bastet, the cat-faced goddess of Bubastis; images of Bes, god of recreation, and other deities in the form of animals; protective steles, amulets, and other objects associated with magic and superstitious beliefs, and a black basalt 'healing statue' representing Horus on the crocodiles, covered with magical signs.

R 'H': PTOLEMAIC AND ROMAN PERIOD (332 B.C.–A.D. 337): Ptolemaic and Roman sculpture; highly decorated 'Mit-Rehineh' faïence objects; a section devoted to mummification; portrait masks, which covered the deceased; and papyrus 'Book of the Dead', etc.

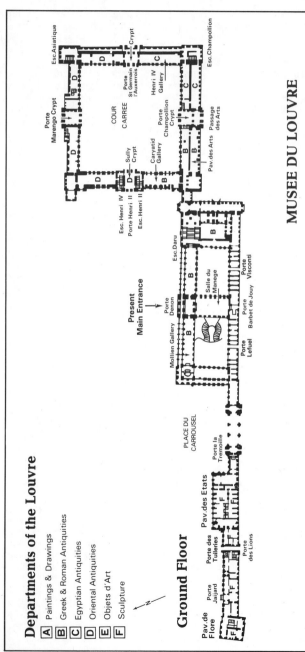

MUSEE DU LOUVRE

Departments of the Louvre

A Paintings & Drawings
B Greek & Roman Antiquities
C Egyptian Antiquities
D Oriental Antiquities
E Objets d'Art
F Sculpture

Ground Floor

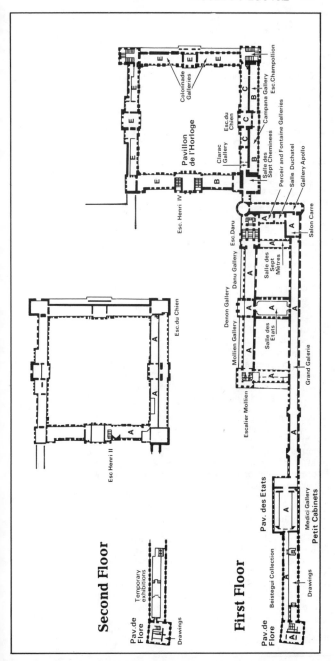

Second Floor

Pav. de Flore

Temporary exhibitions

Drawings

Esc. du Chien

Esc Henri II

A

First Floor

Pav. de Flore

Beistegui Collection

Drawings

Petit Cabinets

Medici Gallery

Pav. des Etats

A

B

A

Grand Galerie

Escalier Mollien

Mollien Gallery

Salle des Etats

Denon Gallery

Danu Gallery

Esc. Daru

Salle des Sept Mètres

Salon Carré

A

Gallery Apollo

Salle Duchatel

Perceir and Fontaine Galleries

Salle des Sept Cheminees

Esc. Champollion

Campana Gallery

Clarac Gallery

Esc. du Chien

Pavillon de l'Horloge

Colonnade Galleries

Esc. Henri IV

B

C

E

D. Oriental Antiquities

This department is concerned with objects from the *Middle East*, apart from Egypt: antiquities from the *Far East* may be seen in the *Musée Guimet* (Rte 17).

The *Crypte Sully* at present contains antiquies from Palestine, including an ossuary in the form of a house, from Azor (4th millennium), and one of the jars in which were preserved the 'Dead Sea Scrolls' (2C B.C. and 1C A.D.), found by Bedouin in 1947; jewellery, glass, and metal objects; the Moabite Stone, or stele of Mesha, king of Moab (842 B.C.), discovered in 1868 in a remote village E. of the Dead Sea.

The 34-line inscription, recording victories over the Israelites in the reigns of Omri, Ahab, and Ahaziah, is one of the most important, if not the earliest, examples of the alphabetic writing which has come down to us from the Phoenicians through Greek and Latin.

SUMERIAN ANTIQUITIES: objects from Lagash (Mesopotamia), and Semitic reliefs and sculptures of the Akkadian Dynasty (2340–2190 B.C.) from Susa; bas-reliefs of a 'plumed figure' from Girsu (Sumer; 3rd millenium) and of Ur-Nanshe, prince of Lagash, carrying a basket of bricks on his head, with his sons; bronze bull's head, etc.; stele of the Vultures, commemorating the victory of Eannadu, king of Lagash, over a rival city, Umma; silver vase of Entemena, with a frieze of incised animals and the Lagash 'crest', a lion-headed eagle; stele of the victorious Naram-Sin, king of Akkad.

NEO-SUMERIAN ANTIQUITIES, of c.2150 B.C.: eleven diorite statues of Gudea, ruler of Lagash; a large clay cylinder recording, in cuneiform, Gudea's achievements as a builder; 'turbaned' head (Gudea); goblet belonging to Gudea, decorated with serpents and winged dragons with scorpion tails; alabaster statuette of Ur-Ningirsu, son of Gudea; woman with a scarf, from Girsu; the dog of Sumu-ilu; terracotta figurines (one strangling a bird); late cuneiform documents (3–2C B.C.); seals and cylinders.

MARI AND LARSA: objects from the temple of the goddess Ishtar (c. 2500 B.C.) at Mari, including an alabaster statue of the intendant of Mari, Ebih-II, and head of Ishtar; mosaic panel showing a scene of war; two murals from the 2nd millennium palace, depicting Ishtar investing King Zimrilim with regal powers, and a sacrificial scene; two bronzes, one of Hammurabi on bended knee, his face and hands covered in gold leaf; the other of a group of three rampant ibex, with horns interlaced, from Larsa; ceremonial vase from Larsa, with Ishtar and figures of animals; relief of a goddess smelling a flower; statuette of Idi Ilum, prince of Mari; a bronze lion from the temple of Dagon.

BABYLON: alabaster statuettes, including reclining female figures, some with jewelled eyes and navels; bronze horned dragon (6C B.C.), symbol of Marduk; terracottas (c.2000–1700 B.C.); and the *Codex of Hammurabi*, a block of black basalt, covered with the closely written text of 282 laws embracing practically every aspect of Babylonian life of c.1800 B.C., at the top of which the god Shamash dictates the law to the king; 'Kudurrus' or boundary-stones, with inscriptions; statues of the princes of Ashnunnak, a rival state, captured by Shutruk-Nakhunté, an Elamite prince, who erased the original inscriptions and substituted his own (c.1100 B.C.).

SUSA: pottery and the first attempts at metallurgy from Susa (Mesopotamia; 4th millennium), northern Iran (3–2nd millennia), Tepe Giyan and Tepe Sialk; silverware and jewellery (12–5C B.C.): note the ornamental vase-handle in the form of a winged ibex (6C B.C.); brick reliefs from Achemenian times, of lions, winged bulls, and griffins.

Susa (3–2nd millennia): vase 'à la cachette', with treasure hidden inside it; headless bronze statue of Queen Napir Asu, and ritual scene celebrating the sunrise, known as the Sit Shamshi; vessels in bitumen and terracotta; votive offerings, and toys; monumental capital in grey marble from the palace of Darius I at Susa (521–486 B.C.); lion in enamelled terracotta (700 B.C.); reliefs in enamelled brick of a winged bull and a lion, and two warriors; two rhytons (silver and bronze); bronze fibula; alabaster vase; and a bronze cup decorated with an ostrich hunt, etc.; *Charter of Darius*, reporting how he had the raw materials required for building his palace brought from distant lands; friezes of enamelled brick with royal archers in relief; also lions, griffins, and winged sphinxes, from the palace of Darius; sculpted head in stone; bronze lamp with a monkey on the lid, etc.; Luristan bronzes; four large earthenware pots from Susa (3–2C B.C.); funerary lions; cast of a mural niche from the palace of Shapur (3–4C A.D.), and Parthian and Sassanid antiquities (3–9C A.D.).

The *Crypte Marengo* at present contains lead Phoenician sarcophagi, and the black sarcophagus of Eshmunazar, king of Sidon (5C B.C.), which although Egyptian in style, has an inscription in Phoenician (cursing the eventual violator of the tomb); also statues from the sanctuary of the god Mithra.

Busts and funerary reliefs from tombs found at Palmyra in Syria, and three divinities in military attire (2–3C A.D.); PHOENICIAN sculptures, and collections of objects from their great cities of Baalbek (Heliopolis), Sidon, Tyre, Byblos, and Rase-Shamra (Ugarit); bust of the pharaoh Osorkon (924–895 B.C.); the 'Lady of Byblos' stele (5–4C B.C.), and an unusual three-sided stele in relief; woman's head in marble (3C B.C.); statuettes of Jupiter of Heliopolis, flanked by bulls (3–2C); votive hand, and other examples of the same cult; head of a sphinx (Roman; Baalbek); terracotta figurines; gold plaquettes; Syrian glass, etc.; a headless Aphrodite from Dura-Europos; wall-painting of a wild-ass hunt (194 B.C.); gilded bronze figurines of the god Reshef, from Byblos; sphinx dedicated by princess Itar, daughter of pharaoh Amenemhat II, found at Qatna.

Antiquities from excavations at Ugarit; Cypriot, Mycenaean, and Canaanite pottery; ivory pyxis depicting a goddess of fertility in Minoan style; gold cup with hunting scene; bronze and gold figurines of the god Ba'al; alphabetic tables describing Canaanite epics.

Reliefs from the great ASSYRIAN palaces of Nimrud, Khorsabad, and Nineveh (9–7C B.C.); carved ivories from Arslan-Tash; a bronze lion, and winged bulls from Khorsabad (7C B.C.), each with an extra leg, for the sake of symmetry: note the reliefs of Kings Assurnasirpal, Tiglathpileser III, and Sargon with his ministers; reliefs from the palace of Assurbanipal at Nineveh; two bulls from the temple of Arslan-Tash (8C B.C.).

CYPRUS: 'Vase of Amathus', a huge monolithic cistern (5C B.C.); statues of the 'King of Cyprus' (5C B.C.); sculptured heads in the Greek style; a bronze charioteer with silver inlay; gold jewellery and repoussé work from Enkomi; Bronze Age ceramics; Mycenaean kraters, terracotta and painted stone figurines, etc.

The HITTITE, CAPPADOCIAN, and ISLAMIC antiquities are not at present on display.

E. Objets d'Art

The collections of this department may—for the time being—be conveniently divided into the art of the Gold and Silversmith, some examples of which may be displayed in other sections; Medieval and Renaissance Objets d'Art; and French Furniture and Objets d'Art or de Vertù, mostly 16–early 19C.

The display of MEDIEVAL AND RENAISSANCE GOLDSMITHS' WORK may also contain some furniture and furnishings, including a Florentine mosaic table from the Château de Richelieu, a coloured marble table-top dating from the reign of Louis XIV, and one of 13 Savonnerie carpets (1667; usually rolled).

A number of items were originally part of the collection of the French royal house, including semi-precious vessels of lapis-lazuli, jade, amethyst, amber, red and green jasper, agate, sardonyx, and basalt, etc. Individual objects include: the crown of Louis IX (St Louis; c.1255); crown of Louis XV (1722): after his coronation the gems were replaced by coloured stones, according to custom; crown of Napoleon I (after Charlemagne's), never placed on his head; the Crown Jewels which were retained when the rest were sold in 1887, including the Regent diamond (137 carats), discovered in India, and bought by the Regent in 1717; the 'Côte de Bretagne' ruby, once owned by Marguerite de Foix, Anne of Brittany, Claude de France, and François I, and later cut into the shape of a dragon as a decoration of the Order of the Golden Fleece; the 'Hortensia' diamond, acquired in 1691; reliquary brooch of the Empress Eugénie (1855); and plaque of the Order of St-Esprit.

Ecclesiastical ornaments from the Abbey of St-Denis, presented by Abbot Suger; antique porphyry vase mounted in silver gilt as an eagle; rock-crystal vase given by Eleanor of Aquitaine to Louis VII, who gave it to Suger; rock-crystal vase with decorations illustrating Noah in his vineyard, and other vessels; antique sardonyx ewer, mounted c. 1150; crystal ewer of the 10C (Islamic); serpentine paten inlaid with gold dolphins (5-6C) in an 8-9C border; lapis-lazuli plaque with figures of Christ and the Virgin (Byzantine; 11-12C); two Byzantine reliquary plaques from the Sainte Chapelle and the so-called 'Ring of St Louis' (14-15C) from St-Denis; silver-gilt statuette of the Virgin (14C), presented in 1339 to St-Denis by Jeanne d'Évreux; gold sceptre of Charles V; coronation gold spurs, set with garnets and fleurs-de-lys (12C; restored); coronation sword 'of Charlemagne' (? 11C); enamelled gold shield and morion of Charles IX; sword of Charles X; candlestick and rock-crystal mirror presented to Marie de Médicis on her marriage to Henri IV (1600); sword and dagger of the Grand Master of the Knights of Malta (Augsburg; 16C), given to Napoleon in 1797; reliquaries and church plate from the chapel of the St-Esprit, founded by Henri III in 1578.

MEDIEVAL AND RENAISSANCE OBJETS D'ART: four ceremonial mantles of the

Order of St-Esprit; tapestry of the Battle of Jarnac, from the workshop of *Claude de Lapierre*; a chest belonging to Marie de Médici, with her monogram; a richly decorated late 17C altarpiece; a Mortlake tapestry (1630–35), and 17C wall-hangings in silver thread; the shrine of St Potentin, in copper gilt, from Steinfeld, near Trèves (13C); other tapestries include an Adoration of the Magi (15C Flemish); St Luke painting the Virgin (Brussels; 16C), the Virgin in Glory (Flanders; 1485); three hangings illustrating the life of St Anatole de Salins (Bruges; early 16C); an embroidered cross from a chasuble (Bohemia; early 15C); two porphyry columns from the 4C basilica of St Peter at Rome.

A beautiful and extensive collection of **ivories**, including the Harbaville triptych (Byzantine; 10C); triptych of the Nativity (Byzantine; 11C); caskets with scenes from the Life of Christ (Metz; 10C), and with mythological scenes (Byzantine; 10C); plaques, including Christ and St Peter (5–6C), Miracle of the Loaves (Ottoman; 10C), and the Rout of Silenus (Alexandria; 3C); two 6C pyxes; Virgin (English?; 11C); liturgical comb depicting Samson and the lion (Metz; 10–11C); 12C chessmen; a huge ivory altarpiece by the *Embriachi* (c.1400), presented to the abbey of Poissy by Jean, duc de Berri; 13–14C ivories from Paris workshops, some with distinctive decoration (c.1320–40); and of Spanish and Italian origin.

Among **enamels**: the reliquary of the arm of Charlemagne (Mosan; c.1170) from Aix-la-Chapelle; cross-reliquary given to the abbey of St-Vincent at Laon (1174–1205); champlevé work from Cologne and the Moselle (12–13C); chalice and paten (Spanish; c.1200); Limoges and other enamels of the 12–13C, including a small shrine, a Crucifixion, and a Eucharistic dove; the casket of St Louis, a wooden box with enamel and metal decoration (Limoges; late 13C); enamelled ciborium, signed 'G. Alpais of Limoges' (mid 13C); Limoges enamels with repoussé and champlevé work; and Spanish and Italian enamels, notably a Spanish 14C communion cup.

Reliquaries, including that of the arm of St Louis of Toulouse (Italian; 1337), of St Martin (14C), and of Jaucourt (Byzantine 11–12C work with French 14C supporters); a ring containing a portrait of Jean sans Peur, and a ring of the Black Prince; a bronze equestrian statue of Charlemagne (9C); 12–15C metalwork and 'dinanderie'; and fragments of 13C stained-glass from Reims.

Renaissance **bronzes** of the Florentine and Paduan Schools (15–16C), including a Flagellation attrib. to *Donatello*, Gnome with a snail (Paduan; 15C), and eight bronze reliefs from the tomb of Marcantonio della Torre, in San Fermo, Verona, by *Andrea Riccio* (1470–1532), and examples by *Bellano*; a collection of French and Italian **medals** by *Pisanello, Matteo de'Pasti, Germain Pilon*, and *G. Dupré*; 16C engraved Italian crystals, including work by *Valerio Belli*; twelve small busts of Caesars (16C); the 'Spinario', a Renaissance cast of the antique original (c.1541); 16C Florentine table, with a bronze fountain (Spanish).

Later Italian and Limoges enamels (15–16C), including superb examples from the workshops of *Poillevé, Jean* and *Pierre Pénicaud, Jacques* and *Pierre Nouailher, Jean* and *Suzanne de Court, Pierre Courteys, J., Pierre*, and *Martial Reymond, Jacques I* and *Jacques II Laudin*, and *Jean* and *Léonard Limousin*, including a Portrait of the Constable Anne de Montmorency by the latter (1556); also a medallion with a self-portrait by *Jean Fouquet*.

An impressive collection of Hispano-Moresque, French, and Italian

ceramics of the 15–17C, with fine examples of the art of *Bernard Palissy* (c.1510–89), and from the St-Porchaire workshop. Notable are three intarsia panels attrib. to *Fra Vicenzo dà Verona* (c.1500), and four ceramic medallions attrib. to *Girolamo della Robbia*, from the Château of St-Germain-en-Laye (16C). Also a series of twelve tapestries of the months, 'Les Chasses de Maximilien', *after van Orley* (Brussels; c.1530).

FRENCH FURNITURE AND OBJETS D'ART: among tapestries, etc., the Martyrdom of St-Mammès, by *Jean Cousin the Elder*, and another of an Elephant Hunt (mid 16C); pre-Gobelins tapestries *after Simon Vouet*, including Moses in the bulrushes; a Gobelins tapestry of the Life of Scipio, from designs by *Jules Romain* (1689); Gobelins tapestry of Sheepshearing (1735); Gobelins tapestries, and bed-hangings from the Chambre Rose, woven for the Condé family at the workshop of *Neilson*, c.1775; Gobelins tapestries representing the story of Don Quixote, *after Tessier* and *Coypel* (c.1785); and 'Chinese' hangings *after Blain de Fontenay* and *Vernansal* (Beauvais; early 18C); also a screen woven in the Savonnerie after a design by *Desportes*.

Notable examples of furniture include a walnut coffer from the Château of Azay-le-Rideau, in the Italian manner; an inlaid desk belonging to Marie de Médicis; the 'nécessaire' of Marie Leczinska (1729); examples of the ornate style of *André-Charles Boulle* (1642–1732), and other furniture of the period, including a pair of ebony cupboards once owned by William Beckford; French Regency furniture, by *Charles Cressent* (1685–1768); a bureau by *Mignon* and *Dubois*; four armchairs by *Nicolas Heurtaut* (c.1755–75); works by the ébéniste *Jean-François Oeben* (c.1720–63); roll-top desk 'of the King of Sardinia' (c.1770), by *Mathieu-Guillaume Cramer* (d.1794); a flat-topped bureau by *Hauré* and *G. Beneman* (1787) made for Louis XVI's library at Fontainebleau; roll-topped secrétaire in mottled mahogany (1784) by *Jean-Henri Riesener* (1734–1806); a large commode by *Beneman*, from Compiègne; armchairs by *J.-B. Sené* (1748–1803); lacquered corner-pieces and commodes by *Martin Carlin* (c.1730–85), in the Chinese taste; Marie-Antoinette's travelling-case, made in Paris c.1787; chairs by *Rode*, and *Georges Jacob* (1739–1814).

The latter, who usually signed his work 'G. Jacob', had two sons, and their furniture was often marked 'Jacob Frères' until 1804, after which François-Honoré-Georges Jacob—'Jacob Desmalter'—worked on his own for another decade. The latter's son—Alphonse Jacob—signing his work 'Jacob', flourished in the 1840s.

Napoleon's throne from St-Cloud, by *Jacob Desmalter*, and a cradle for his son, by the same ébéniste and *Pierre-Philippe Thomire* (1751–1843) after a design by Proudhon (1811); the 'Grand Écrin' jewellery-case by *Jacob Desmalter* and *Thomire* after a design by *Percier* (1809); a commode decorated with Wedgwood plaques (1790); and a nécessaire by *M.-G. Biennais* (1764–1843) and *Lorillon*, offered by Napoleon to Tsar Alexander I in 1808; bed belonging to Louis XVIII at the Tuileries, by *Jacob Desmalter*.

Also preserved are panels of Chinese papers of the late 18C, and gilt and white panelling from the Hôtel de Luynes. Sections are devoted to the display of a magnificent collection of **silverware** (16–18C), including work by *Thomas Germain* (1674–1745); a silver-gilt tea-service by *Biennais* ordered by Napoleon for his marriage with Marie-Louise, and a Sèvres porcelain coffee-service decorated with views of Egypt, made for the wedding, and which the emperor took with him to St Helena. Also notable are bronzes from the workshops of *Jean Bologne* and *F. Tacca*; and a superb collection of snuffboxes and watches of the 17–18C, with examples dating from 1746–59, by *Moynat, Noël Hardivilliers* (1752–79), *J.-J. Barrière* (1765–76), the *Drais* family (1769–82), and *P.-J. Menière* (1773–82), as well as representative works from other countries, notably Switzerland, together with more silverware, jewellery, clocks, 15–16C ivories, a Delft tulipière (17C), etc.

Individual Donations have so far been displayed in separate rooms, among them that of ADOLPHE DE ROTHSCHILD, containing a 15C Flemish tapestry of the Miracle of the Loaves; a bas-relief of the Madonna and Child by *Agostino di Duccio*, and a remarkable late 13C polyptych-reliquary from the abbey of Floreffe, Flanders.—The COLLECTION CAMONDO contains four armchairs by *S. Brizard* (c.1775); a chaise-longue by *Delanois* (c.1765); a bed, signed *G. Jacob*, covered with Genoa velvet; six chairs by *Tilliard* (c.1755); a marble clock, 'the Three Graces', attrib. to *Falconet* (c.1770), and a collection of Meissen porcelain, etc.—The COLLECTION SCHLICHTING: a roll-top desk (c.1780) attrib. to *David Roentgen* (1743–1807), once the property of the Tsarina Catherine II; a child's armchair (? the Dauphin's) by *Gay* (1780); and a portrait of Louis-Élisabeth de Maillé by *Drouais*.—The COLLECTION THIERS preserves a number of Italian Renaissance bronzes, ivory carvings, etc., collected by the statesman, together with examples of Sèvres and Vincennes porcelain (18C), among others.

F. Sculpture

The collections of Medieval, Renaissance, and 17–19C Sculpture are at present displayed in two sections in the Pavillon de Flore, entered by the *Porte de la Trémoille* and *Porte Jaujard*.

MEDIEVAL PERIOD. 11–12C: fragments of the cloister of St-Genis-des-Fontaines; two capitals from Moutiers-St-Jean, one depicting the vintage, rare at this period; others of the Sacrifice of Abraham, and of David and Goliath, from Parthenay; a marble Merovingian capital recarved in the 11C of Daniel in the Lions' den, from the former abbey of Ste-Geneviève, Paris; a relief of St Michael and the Dragon, from Nevers; a Descent from the Cross (painted wood), probably Burgundian (early 12C); Doorway from the priory of Estagel (Gard).

Early French 'Gothic' Sculpture: fragments of a frieze from N.-D-en-Vaux (Châlons-sur-Marne); column-statues of Solomon and the Queen of Sheba from N.-D. de Corbeil (c.1180–90); two historiated spiral columns from the abbey of Coulombs (mid-12C); and a remarkable head of St Peter (1170–89), with eyes lined with lead, from Autun.

13–14C: the Virgin 'de la Celle' (Île de France; 14C); tomb statues of Charles IV (le Bel) and Jeanne d'Évreux, from the abbey of Maubuisson (1372), by *Jean de Liège*; a marble figure of Guillaume de Chanac (d.1348); painted wooden statue of a woman praying (early 14C).

15–early 16C: tomb of Philippe Pot, Grand Seneschal of Burgundy (d.1493), formerly in the abbey of Citeaux; marble high relief of St George and the Dragon, by *Michel Colombe* (c.1508); marble tomb (1515–24) of Renée d'Orléans-Longueville, from the Célestins church, Paris; tomb of Louis de Poncher and his wife, from St-Germain-l'Auxerrois.

FRENCH 'RENAISSANCE': The Three Graces, *Germain Pilon* (c. 1535–90), a funeral monument for the heart of Henri II; Diana leaning on a stag, an early garden figure, from the Château of Anet; tomb-statue of Adm. Philippe Chabot in armour, attrib. to *Pierre Bontemps* (1505–68); Deposition and the Evangelists (reliefs, c. 1545), *Jean Goujon*; effigies of the Constable Anne de Montmorency and his wife, *Barthélemy Prieur* (c. 1540–1611); and tomb of Valentine Balbiani, by *Pilon*.

ITALIAN SCULPTURE. A collection of enamelled earthenware from the Florentine *workshop of Della Robbia*; Madonna and Child surrounded by angels (marble bas-relief), by *Agostino di Duccio*; Dietisalvi Nerobi (marble), by *Mino da Fiesole* (1418–81); Madonna and Child, and a St John the Baptist as a youth, both by *Donatello* (1386–1468); Bust of a Woman, in painted and gilded wood, attrib. to the *workshop of Desiderio da Settignano*; Mercury, by *Jean Bologne* (1524–1608); Monumental portal of the Palazzo Straga at Cremona, attrib. to *Pietro da Rho*; the Nymph of Fontainebleau, a bronze bas-relief by *Benvenuto Cellini* (1500–72); the Two Slaves, by *Michelangelo Buonarotti* (1475–1564), intended for the tomb of Pope Julius II, but given to Henri II in 1550 by Robert Strozzi; and a bronze bust of Michelangelo by one of his pupils.

GERMAN SCULPTURE. Virgin of the Annunciation, kneeling, by *Tilman Riemenschneider* (1468–1531), of painted and gilded marble; a naked Magdalen, 'the beautiful German girl', by *Gregor Erhardt* (1470–1541), of painted wood.

FRENCH 17–19C SCULPTURE. Representative works by *Antoine Coysevox* (1640–1720), *Sébastien Slodtz* (1655–1726), *Nicolas* and *Guillaume Coustou* (1658–1733, and 1677–1746 respectively), *J.-L.* and *J.-B. Lemoyne* (1665–1755, and 1704–78), *René Fremin* (1672–1744), *Edme Bouchardon* (1698–1762), *Allegrain* (1710–95), *J.-B. Pigalle* (1714–85), and *E.-M. Falconet* (1716–91).

Pierre Julien (1731–1804), sculptures of Poussin, and La Fontaine; *Jean-Jacques Caffieri* (1725–92), Corneille; *Augustin Pajou* (1730–1809), Pascal, Mme du Barry, and Mme Vigée-Lebrun; a bronze bust of Lemoyne, his master, and a bust of Pajou by his pupil *Roland* (1746–1816). Among works by *Jean-Antoine Houdon* (1741–1828), a bronze Diana (1790), and busts of his contemporaries, including Voltaire, the singer Sophie Arnould, Rousseau, Houdon's smiling wife (original plaster), Diderot, Washington, Franklin, the Brongniart children, and Mme Adelaïde.

Among other notable sculptures are *F.-N. Delaistre* (1746–1832), Cupid and Psyche; *Claude Ramey* (1754–1838), Sappho; *Claude Michallon* (1751–99), Alexandre Lenoir; *Antonio Canova* (1757–1822), Psyche revived by the kiss of Cupid, and Cupid and

Psyche standing; *C.-L. Corbet* (1758–1808), La Tour d'Auvergne; *J.-E. Dumont* (1761–1844), Gén. Marceau; *Joseph Chinard* (1756–1813), bust of a young woman; *James Pradier* (1790–1852), Niobe wounded; *François Rude* (1784–1855), Mercury, and Louis Davia, showing the deformation of his mouth; Works by *A.-L. Barye* (1795–1875), and *J.-B. Carpeaux* (1827–75; whose 'La Danse', commissioned for the façade of the *Opéra*, will be displayed in the *Musée d'Orsay)*, and other 19C French sculptors of varying merit, notable among which are a bust of Mme Sabatier (1847), who inspired some of Baudelaire's poems, by *Auguste Clésinger* (1814–83); and that of Mme Renoir, and several nudes and ballet studies, by *Degas.*

10 Pl. Vendôme; Palais-Royal; Bibliothèque Nationale and Cabinet des Médailles

MÉTROS: *Concorde, Tuileries, Pyramides, Palais-Royal, Bourse.*

The **Rue de Rivoli** constructed in 1811–56, and named in honour of Bonaparte's victory over the Austrians in 1797, runs E. from the *Pl. de la Concorde* (Pl. 7;7). The S. side of the street, flanking the *Tuileries Gardens* and the *Louvre*, is, in its W. half, uniform in design and is built above arcades, but except for the inveterate window-shopper, it makes a tiring promenade. No.107 (r.), in the *Pavillon de Marsan* of the Palais du Louvre, is the entrance of the *Musée des Arts Décoratifs*; see pp120-3.

At the W. end, at the corner of the Rue St-Florentin, stands the 18C *Hôtel de la Vrillière,* or *de Talleyrand,* built to designs by *Chalgrin,* where Talleyrand (1754–1838) died, and where the Princesse de Lieven held her salon in 1846–57. The design of the *American Embassy* (see Rte 16A) was inspired by this building, and completes the symmetry of the N. side of the PL. DE LA CONCORDE. At No.228 Rue de Rivoli, the *Hôtel Meurice,* Gen. Von Choltitz, commander of the German forces in Paris, allowed himself to be captured (25 Aug. 1944), having refused orders to destroy the capital's principal buildings. No.374 was the home of Mme Geoffrin (1699–1777) from 1750, where she entertained many of the artists, writers, and intellectuals of the day, among them Marivaux, Helvétius, Saint-Lambert, Diderot, d'Alembert, Falconet, Boucher, Delatour, et al.

Turning l. into the Rue Cambon, where at No.5 (prev. No.3) Stendhal lived from 1810–14, and where Hubert Robert died in 1808 (at No.21), the birthplace likewise of Eugène Sue (1804–75), we cross the Rue du Mont-Thabor, where Alfred du Musset (1810–57) died at No.6 and where Washington Irving lodged at No.4 in 1821, to enter the Rue St-Honoré, leading E., parallel to the Rue de Rivoli.

At its junction with the Rue Cambon stands the church of the *Assumption,* built in 1670 as the chapel of the convent of the Haudriettes and now used by the Polish community. Funeral services for La Fayette, and Stendhal, were held here. At No.398 (opposite) stood the house where Robespierre lodged with the cabinet-maker Duplay from July 1791 to the day of his arrest.

Turning E., we shortly cross the Rue de Castiglione, leading N. into the octagonal *PLACE VENDÔME (Pl. 7;8),—in fact a rectangle of 213m by 124m with canted corners—a superb example of the Louis-XIV style, surrounded by houses with uniform façades, designed by *Hardouin-Mansart* (1645–1708). Many of the buildings here were erected after Mansart's death, but the façades of all conformed to the original design. Originally called *Pl. des Conquêtes*, it owes its present name to a mansion built here in 1603 by César, Duc de Vendôme, son of Henri IV and Gabrielle d'Estrées.

A number are now luxury hotels (the *Bristol* at No.3; the *Ritz* at No.15), or shops, etc. Nos 5, 22, and 28 were built for John Law (who also lived at No.23 as controller-general of finance); Chopin died at No.12 (1849); Nos 11–13 are the *Ministère de la Justice* (since 1815); No.16 was let to Dr Mesmer, the famous quack, in 1778; the composer Piccini lived at No.17 in 1787.

The centre of the Place is dominated by the *Vendôme Column*, constructed by *Denon, Gondouin,* and *Lepère* in 1806–10 in the style of Trajan's Column in Rome. It replaced an equestrian statue of Louis XIV by Girardon, which stood there previously.

Encircling the column (43·50m high) is a spiral band of bronze bas-reliefs, designed by *Bergeret* and made of the metal of some 250 Russian and Austrian cannon, in which the principal feats of arms in the campaigns of 1805–07 are glorified. The statue of Napoleon surmounting it is a copy (1863) of the original by *Chaudet* thrown down by the royalists in 1814 and replaced at the Restoration by a fleur-de-lys. In 1833 Louis-Philippe put up a statue of Napoleon, which is now at the Invalides. The present statue narrowly escaped destruction in 1871, when a group of Communards, led by the painter Courbet, brought the whole column crashing to the ground, an act that led to Courbet's exile in Switzerland and his ruin, since he had to pay for its re-erection in 1873–74.

The once fashionable Rue de la Paix (now lined with travel agencies and airline offices) leads N. to the *Pl. de l'Opéra* (see Rte 13), crossing the Rue Danielle-Casanova (named after a Resistance heroine; previously Rue des Petits-Champs), with 17–18C houses, where at No.22 Stendhal (1783–1842) died of apoplexy.

We may regain the Rue St-Honoré by turning down the Rue du Marché-St-Honoré, passing the site of a Dominican convent where the Jacobin Club met in 1789–94.

To the E., steps ascend to the Baroque church of **ST-ROCH** (Pl.7;8), begun by *J. Lemercier* in 1653. Work was abandoned in 1660, but a donation by John Law on his conversion to Rome in 1719 enabled the nave to be completed; *Robert de Cotte* was responsible for the façade (1735). The church was consecrated in 1740.

The unkempt INTERIOR (126m long) contains monuments of interest. To the l. of the entrance is a medallion of Corneille (1606–84), who died in the neighbouring Rue d'Argenteuil (plaque on No.6), and is buried in the church. In the 1st bay (r.) are a bust of François de Créquy (d. 1687) by *Coysevox,* and the tomb of the Comte d'Harcourt (d. 1666) by *Renard.* 2nd bay: statue of Card. Dubois (d. 1723) by *G. Coustou,* and a monument to the astronomer Maupertuis (1698–1759; the first Frenchman to be made a member of the Royal Society, London), by *Huez.* In the Lady Chapel, by *Hardouin-Mansart,* is a marble group of the Nativity by *Fr.* and *Michel Anguier,* from Val-de-Grâce.

W. AISLE. On the last pillar of the ambulatory (r.) is a bust of Le Nôtre (d.1707) by *Coysevox.* The 3rd chapel (beyond the transept) contains a mourning figure, by *J.-B. Le Moyne the Elder,* of Catherine, comtesse de Feuquières (c.1700) incorporated in a monument, the central feature of which is the bust of her father, Pierre Mignard (1610–95), by *Girardon*. Diderot, Holbach (1723–89, whose hospitable home from 1759 was No.8 in the Rue des Moulins, a few minutes walk to the N.), Mme Geoffrin, Le Nôtre, Cherubini, and the Abbé de l'Épée (see p81) are also buried in St-Roch.—The Organ-case dates from 1755.

The adjoining Rue St-Roch, where Vauban (1633–1707) died, rejoins the Rue de Rivoli just W. of the PL. DES PYRAMIDES, with a bronze-gilt statue of Joan of Arc, by *Frémiet*.

Continuing E. along the Rue St-Honoré, the scene both here and in neighbouring streets of Bonaparte's suppression of the royalist rising of 5 Oct. 1795 (some marks of his 'whiff of grape-shot' may be detected on the front of St-Roch), we shortly enter the newly-named PL. ANDRÉ MALRAUX (Pl. 8;7), with a view N. W. towards the *Opéra*. The two fountains are by *Davioud*. To the S. the short Rue de Rohan leads to the Rue de Rivoli opposite the arch leading to the *Pl. du Carrousel*.

On the E. of the Place stands the **Théâtre Français**, built in 1786–90 by *Victor Louis*, but largely remodelled after a fire in 1900, and recently restored again.

As an institution the *Théâtre-Français* (or *Comédie-Française*) dates from the amalgamation in 1680 of the Hôtel de Bourgogne actors with Molière's old company, which had already absorbed the Théâtre du Marais. In 1812 Napoleon signed a decree (at Moscow) reorganising the Comédie-Française, which is still a private company although controlled by a director nominated by the government and enjoying a state subsidy.

The vestibule contains, among other statues of actors, Talma, by *David d'Angers*; the staircase and foyer display busts of eminent dramatists including Dumas fils by *Carpeaux* and Mirabeau by *Rodin*, a statue of George Sand, by *Clésinger* (her son-in-law), and a *Seated statue of Voltaire, by *Houdon*. The chair in which Molière was sitting when acting in 'Le Malade Imaginaire' and taken fatally ill, is also preserved. The Library may also be consulted.

An inscription at the corner of the Rue de Valois (on the E. side of the *Palais-Royal*) marks the site of the 'Salle de Spectacle du Palais-Cardinal', occupied by Molière's company from 1661 to 1673, and by the 'Académie Royale de Musique' from 1673 until a fire in 1763.

Abutting the *Théâtre Français*, the ***PALAIS-ROYAL** and its surroundings constitute one of the most attractive and interesting areas of Paris. The name is now applied not only to the original palace, but also to the extensive range of buildings and galleries surrounding the gardens to the N. The latter, a pedestrian thoroughfare, entered from neighbouring streets by several passages, now a delightful backwater and haunt of the philatelist, played an important role in the Revolutionary period, and among the profligate society of the late 18th and early 19C, was the scene of unbridled licence and revelry, pullulating with '*tripots*' or gaming-houses, cafés, restaurants, and numerous haunts of lesser repute.

The Palais-Royal proper was originally known as the 'Palais-Cardinal', having been built by *J. Lemercier* in 1634–39 for Richelieu, who, as chief minister, wished to be near the Louvre. He died there in 1642. Bequeathed to Louis XIII, it was first called 'Palais-Royal' during the residence of Anne of Austria (d. 1666), then regent, and her sons Louis XIV and Philippe d'Orléans. Richelieu's apartments were then occupied by Card. Mazarin. During the Fronde they all

Galeries du Palais Royal, 1809, by Louis Boilly *(detail; Photographie Giraudon)*

had to escape to St-Germain-en-Laye; Louis therefore disliked the palace and it was Philippe and his wife Henriette d'Angleterre who returned to live there, as did the latter's mother, Queen Henrietta Maria, in 1652.

Louis housed the Royal Academy of painting and sculpture in the W. wing, and also his mistress Louise de la Vallière. This was the period of Mansart's alterations. In 1692 the palace was given by Louis to his brother and his heirs. It acquired an equivocal reputation from the dissolute 'petits soupers' given by the Regent (1715–23). Changes were made for the latter's son by *Constant d'Ivry* and *Cartaud*. In 1763 a fire destroyed the E. wing. The houses and galleries around the gardens were built as a speculation by Philippe-Égalité, the Regent's great-grandson, in 1781–86, under pressure of debt, and let out as shops and cafés, etc. He also built the *Théâtre-Français*; and the *Théâtre du Palais-Royal*, in the N. W. corner, dates from the same period.

The cafés became a rendezvous for malcontents, since the police were excluded from entry, and on 13 July 1789 Camille Desmoulins delivered in the gardens the fiery harangue which precipitated the fall of the Bastille the following day. Its name was changed to the 'Palais-Égalité', and it was used as government offices. In 1814 it was returned to the Orléans family, and reverted to its earlier name; and Louis-Philippe lived there until 1832. In 1848 it was plundered by the revolutionaries, and occupied for a time by the 'Rights of Man' club. During the Second Empire it was the residence of Jérôme Bonaparte, and Taine, Flaubert, Sainte-Beuve, and the brothers Goncourt were often entertained there. The Palais was rebuilt by *Chabrol* in 1872–76 after damage during the Commune. It is now occupied by the *Conseil d'État* and the *Ministère des Affaires Culturelles*.

The *Hôtel de Rambouillet*, built on part of the site of the Palais-Royal, and the town house of Catherine de Vivonne, Marquise de Rambouillet (1588–1665; known in her circle as 'Arthénice'), was, during c. 1618–50, a famous intellectual centre, Saint-Évremond, Malherbe, La Rochefoucauld, the Scudérys, Bossuet, and the Duchesse de Longueville being among its habitués.

The buildings in the *Cour de l'Horloge*, facing the PL. DU PALAIS-ROYAL, were erected by *Constant d'Ivry* (1763–70), with sculptures by *Pajou* (l. wing) and *Franceschi* (r.; 1875). The façade on the N. side, overlooking the *Cour d'Honneur*, was begun by *d'Ivry*, continued by *Louis*, and completed by *Fontaine*, who also restored the E. and W. wings. The so-called '*Galerie des Proues*', on the E. side of the court, is the only relic of *Lemercier*'s 17C building. To the N., the *Cour d'Honneur* is separated from the gardens by the *Galerie d'Orléans*, a double Doric colonnade by *Fontaine* (1829–31), which was restored and cleared of its shops in 1935.

The **Gardens** of the *Palais-Royal* are surrounded on three sides by arcades and buildings (by *Louis*; 1781–86), still occupied by shops and dwellings.

(Gabrielle) Colette (1873–1954) lived from 1938 until her death at No.9 Rue de Beaujolais, beyond the *Galerie Beaujolais* to the N. On the W. side is the *Galerie de Montpensier*, and opposite is the *Galerie de Valois*, altogether a charming and harmonious ensemble. Other residents in recent times were Jean Cocteau and Jean Marais, while at Nos 79–82 Gal. de Beaujolais, the *Grand Vefour* was the fashionable rendezvous of writers in the Second Empire. Earlier, in the same house, Mlle de Montansier entertained the leaders of the Revolution in 1789. This disappeared in 1847, to be replaced in 1882 by the *Musée Grevin*: see p197. Charlotte Corday bought her knife at No.177 Gal. de Valois: No.17 Gal. de Montpensier was in 1785 a museum of waxworks, having been founded by Curtius, the uncle of Mme Tussaud. Here (Nos 83–86) Fragonard died in 1806. The *Café du Caveau* (Nos 89–92) was the rendezvous of the partisans of Gluck and his rival Piccini; other habitués were Méhul and Boïeldieu.

Immediately E. of the *Palais-Royal* lies the Rue de Valois, with (Nos 1–3) the *Pavillon du Palais-Royal* (1766, by *d'Ivry* and *Moreau*); at Nos 6–8, once the *Hôtel Melusine*, took place the first meetings of the French Academy in 1638–43, and the ox sculptured above the door recalls its period as the restaurant 'Boeuf à la Mode' from 1792 to 1936.

In the parallel street to the E., the Rue Croix-des-Petits-Champs, is the entrance to the **Banque de France** (Pl. 8;7), founded in 1800 and accommodated here in 1811.

The buildings incorporate the former *Hôtel de la Vrillière*, built by *Mansart* in 1635–38 and restored by *Robert de Cotte* in 1719. Later known as the *Hôtel de Toulouse* from its occupancy by the Comte de Toulouse, son of Louis XIV and Mme de Montespan, it became the residence of the Princess de Lamballe, murdered in the prison of *La Force* in 1792.

The profusely decorated *Galerie Dorée*, within the Bank, may be visited by those providing suitable bona fides.

The *Hôtel Portalis* (by *Ledais*; 1750) stands at the corner of the Rue de la Vrillière and the Rue Croix-des-Petits-Champs, No.13 in which is the site of a house occupied by Malherbe from 1606–27. Vincent de Paul lived in the street in 1613–16, and Bossüet in 1699–1702, at No.52. Another resident was Mme de Pompadour (1721–64), from 1725 to 1745, before her departure for Versailles; she was born (as Antoinette Poisson) in the Rue de Cléry, a short distance to the N. E. Richelieu is believed to have been born (in 1585) in a house on the corner of the Rue du Bouloi, just to the E. Corneille lived in this latter street from 1665–81; La Rochefoucauld also resided here in his youth.

No.33 in the Rue Radziwill, on the N. side of the *Banque de France*, has an unusual double staircase; while Mansart's projecting angle here, supported by a bracket, is admired as a masterpiece of stonework.

To the N. E. of the Bank lies the circular *Pl. des Victoires*, laid out by *J. Hardouin-Mansart* in 1685; the surrounding houses were designed by *Pradot*. The equestrian statue of Louis XIV by *Bosio* (1822) replaces the original, destroyed in 1792; the bas-reliefs on the pedestal depict the Passage of the Rhine, and Louis XIV distributing decorations.

Thackeray lived in the Rue Hérold, to the S. E., after his marriage in 1836. The street is named after the composer Louis-Joseph-Ferdinand Hérold (1791–1833), born at No.10.

Immediately N. W. is the PL. DES PETITS-PÈRES, with a surprisingly provincial aspect, off which the Rue du Mail leads N. E., where Colbert lived (at No.5, richly decorated), and Mme Recamier reclined (No.12), while Liszt was a frequent visitor at No.13 between 1823 and 1878. Spontini also lived in this street in 1803.

On the N. side of the Place stands **N.-D.-des-Victoires,** or the church of the *Petits-Pères*, dedicated in 1629 by Louis XIII in memory of the ·capture of La Rochelle from the Huguenots. Replacing a chapel, it was not actually commenced until 1666, and only finished in 1740. Every interior wall is plastered with ex-voto tablets. In the 2nd chapel on the l. is the tomb of the composer Jean-Baptiste Lully (1633–87) by *Pierre Cotton*, with a bust by *Gaspard Collignon*; in the choir are elaborately carved stalls, and seven paintings by *C. Van Loo*.

The adjoining street leads N. to the **Bourse des Valeurs** or *Stock Exchange*, built by *Brongniart* and *Labarre* in 1808–27, and resembling the Temple of Vespasian in Rome. The N. and S. wings were added in 1903.

The Rue Feydeau, to the N., built on Louis-XIII fortifications, and the Rue des Colonnes, to the W., retain some interesting houses in an old district through which the Rue du Quatre-Septembre was driven in 1864, before being renamed on the proclamation of the Third Republic.

The Rue Vivienne leads S. from the Bourse along the E. side (r.) of the *Bibliothèque Nationale* (see below), and retains several 17–18C houses; Simón Bolívar lived at No.2bis in 1804.

Of more interest is the parallel Rue de Richelieu, to the W., laid out by the cardinal, running S. to the Pl. André Malraux. Rossini and Meyerbeer lived in its N. half; Grétry resided at No.52, further S., in 1780. No.101, with decorative masks in the courtyard, was the home of the Abbé Barthélemy (1716–95), author of the 'Voyage du jeune Anacharsis', and antiquary, who had charge of the royal collection of medals, then housed in the *Hôtel de Nevers* (see below). Anthelme Brillat-Savarin (1755–1826), author of the 'Physiologie du goût', died at No.66; Ninon de Lenclos (1620–1705) had lived there in 1653–59.

On the l., at the corner of the Rue Colbert, stands part of the *Hôtel de Nevers*, built by Mazarin in 1649 to house his library (see below). As the home of the Marquise de Lambert (1647–1733) it was a famous literary salon from 1710, where Montesquieu and Marivaux met.

Further on is a fountain of 1708, and beyond (r.) in the SQ. LOUVOIS (Pl. 8;5–6), the *Fontaine Louvois*, by the younger *Visconti* (1844).

The *Square* was laid out in 1839 on the site of a theatre (the *Salle Louvois*) built in 1794, which housed the Opéra until 1820. On 13 Feb. 1820 the Abp of Paris was called here to administer the last sacraments to the Duc de Berry (assassinated here—by Louvel—while on his way to watch the dancing of his mistress, Virginie Oreiller), consenting to do so on such unholy ground on condition that the theatre was afterwards pulled down (see Rue le Peletier).—Donizetti lived at No.5 Rue de Louvois in 1840.

Bossuet (1627–1704) died at No.46 Rue Ste-Anne, the street to the W.

On the E. side of the Square (with its entrance at No.58 Rue de Richelieu) rises the W. façade of the **BIBLIOTHÈQUE NATIONALE**.

Adm. Most departments of the *Bibliothèque Nationale* are open daily from 9.00 or 10.00–18.00, except public holidays. Foreigners wishing to use the Library should apply to the Reception Desk with some form of identity, two identity photographs, a letter of recommendation (in the case of students, from their director of studies), etc. Information regarding the completion of requisition forms, photocopying services, etc., is freely available. Catalogues may be bought at No.71 Rue de Richelieu, opposite. Frequent temporary exhibitions are also held in the building.

The Library is divided into the following departments: *Maps and Plans*; *Prints*; *Printed Books, Manuscripts*; *Oriental Manuscripts*; *Music* (at No.2 Rue de Louvois); *Periodicals*; and *Medals* (see below). The *Bibliothèque de l'Arsenal*, a subsidiary collection, is at No.1 Rue de Sully (see Rte 11.).

The *Bibliothèque Nationale* ranks with the British Library as one of the two largest libraries in W. Europe. The extensive buildings were erected at various times on the site of the 17C *Hôtel Mazarin*, and include the *Hôtel Tubeuf*, whose brick and stone façade, set back in the Rue des Petits-Champs, was built by *Le Muet* in 1635.

Formerly known as the *Bibliothèque Royale* and the *Bibliothèque Impériale*, it originated in the private collections of the French kings. Largely dispersed at the end of the Hundred Years War, the Library was refounded by Louis XII, and moved to Blois. During the next two centuries it was removed to Fontainebleau, and then Paris, before finding its present home in the Rue de Richelieu in 1721. Guillaume Budé (c. 1468–1540) had earlier been appointed the first Royal Librarian. It was enriched by purchase or by gift of many famous private libraries and smaller collections (including that of Colbert), and at the Revolution its range was further increased with the confiscation of books from numerous convents and châteaux. In 1793 it was enacted that a copy of every book, newspaper, etc., printed in France, should be deposited by the publishers in the Bibliothèque Nationale.

The main entrance vestibule is on the r. of the *Cour d'Honneur*. The *Reading Room* (seen through glass doors opposite), roofed by nine faience domes, seats 360 readers who have access to over 10,000 works of reference. The *Galerie Mansart*, used for exhibitions, lying to the r. at the foot of the stairs, was formerly Mazarin's sculpture gallery; note his arms above the door, and the carved foliage and paintings by Grimaldi. The *Cabinet des Estampes*, beyond, contains over 5 million prints. The collections of musical scores, books on music, and MSS. (including Mozart's 'Don Giovanni') previously in the Library of the *Conservatoire de Musique* (see Rte 14) have been transferred to the Bibliothèque Nationale, the Department of Music in which contains over 300,000 works.

The ***Musée du Cabinet des Médailles et Antiques**, beyond the iron gates on the first floor landing l. of the main entrance, entirely reformed in 1981, will be of considerable interest to the connoisseur. The collection, founded in the 16C, but containing objects known to be in royal hands some time prior to that date, preserves c.250,000 coins and medals, in addition to antiquities of outstanding quality, only a small proportion of which are on display.

To the r. of the entrance is a Parian marble torso of Aphrodite (Hellenistic period), while in a series of showcases on this and on the mezzanine floor are selected examples of French and foreign coins and medals, engraved cameos, and jewels, etc. Notable is the 'Grand Camée', from the Sainte Chapelle, representing the Apotheosis of Germanicus, with Tiberius and Livia—the largest antique cameo known; the aquamarine intaglio of Julia, daughter of Titus, one of the best glyptic portraits extant; an engraved Chaldaean stone (1100 B.C.), found near Baghdad; the agate nef from St-Denis; the Dish of Chosroes II, king of Persia (c.600 A.D.); the sardonyx Cup of Ptolemy; the 'Patère de Rennes' (a Roman gold dish found in 1774); a Merovingian chalice and oblong paten (6C), from Gourdon, in the Charollais; a bust of Constantine the Great, once the head of the cantor's wand at the Sainte Chapelle; and a series of ivory chessmen (11–12C), which were once reputed to have belonged to Charlemagne (d.814).

Other cases contain Renaissance medals and bronzes; Egyptian terracottas, and painted limestone statuettes; Roman bronze statuettes; ancient arms and armour, and domestic utensils; Greek and Etruscan vases, etc., including a red-figured amphora, signed Amasis; cyclix of Arcesilaus, king of Cyrene; vase of Berenice (239–227 B.C.), from Bengazi, and other ceramics; gold objects from the tomb of Childeric I, at Tournai; ivory consular diptychs, and Byzantine diptychs; gold bullae of Charles II of Anjou, king of Naples (1285–1309), of Baldwin I, Emperor of Constantinople in 1204–06, and of Edmund, Earl of Lancaster, titular king of Sicily, 1255–63; gold coins found at Chécy (Loiret); a Celtic bracelet (Aurillac; 5–6C); a silver hoard from the temple of Mercurius Canetonensis (Berthouville, Eure), including silver figurines and vessels of the 2C B.C. and others of the best Greek period.

Also displayed is the so-called Throne of Dagobert, on which the kings of France were crowned: a Roman curule chair of bronze, with arms and back added in the 12C by Suger.

The Salon Louis-XV, decorated by *Van Loo* and *Natoire*, with dessus de portes by *Boucher*, and retaining its original coin cabinets, is under restoration.

Stairs ascend to the floor above, with (r.) the *Manuscript Room* (with more than 130,000 MSS., of which some 10,000 are illuminated); and l., the *Galerie Mazarine*, by *Mansart* (1645), with a ceiling by *Romanelli*. Beyond is the *Department of Maps and Plans*.

Immediately S. of the *Bibliothèque Nationale* we cross the Rue des Petits-Champs, in which No.45 was the residence of Lully until 1683, built by him with financial help from Molière; the garret of No.57 was the home of Rousseau and Thérèse Levasseur c.1754; Mme Récamier (1777–1849) died (of cholera) at No.8.

Chamfort (1741–94) attempted suicide in 1793 at No.10 Rue Chabanais, immediately to the W. No.12 in this street had an equivocal reputation in the late 19C; while No.6 Rue des Moulins, leading S. further W., was the scene in 1894 of Toulouse-Lautrec's painting 'Au Salon'. Holbach entertained Diderot, Marmontel, Grimm, Helvétius, and Saint-Lambert at No.6 in the Rue des Moulins during the years 1759–89.

Continuing S., at the corner of the Rue Molière (where at No.37 lived Voltaire and Mme du Châtelet) is the *Fontaine Molière*, by *Visconti* (1844; the dramatist is by *Seurre*, and the figures of Comedy by *Pradier*).

.Molière (1622–73) died in a house on the site of No.40 Rue de Richelieu. Denis Diderot (1713–84) died at No.39; and Pierre Mignard (1610–95) at No.23. No.21, formerly the *Hôtel Dodun*, by *Bullet* (1715), preserves some of its 18C grandeur; the composer Sacchini (1734–86) died at No.14.

The street ends at the PL. ANDRÉ-MALRAUX (previously the Pl. du Théâtre-Français).

11 From the Pl. du Palais-Royal to the Pl. de la Bastille

METROS: *Palais-Royal; Louvre; Les Halles; Étienne-Marcel; Châtelet; Rambuteau; St-Paul; Sully-Morland; Bastille* and *Châtelet-les Halles* (RER).

Proceeding E. from the Pl. du Palais-Royal, with the façade of the *Palais-Royal* on our l. (see Rte 10), we follow the Rue St-Honoré, skirting the N. side of the **Louvre des Antiquaires**.

The building, of 1852, formerly the department store of the *Grands Magasins du Louvre*, was acquired in 1975 by the British Post Office Staff Superannuation Fund as an investment, and gutted. Since 1978 it has tastefully accommodated, on three floors, some 250 professional antique-dealers' stalls, open to the public daily from 11.00–19.00, except Mon. (also closed on Sun. from mid July–mid Sept.). They also provide facilities for transport, settling customs formalities, and can provide certificates of authenticity, etc. Lectures and exhibitions are also frequently held there.

A short distance to the E. is (r.) the **Temple de l'Oratoire**, designed by *Clément Métezeau the younger* and *Jacques Lemercier*, and built in 1621–30 for Card. Bérulle, as the mother church in France for his Congregation of the Oratory. In 1811, Napoleon assigned it to the Calvinists. The portal was added in 1845.

Against the apse is a monument to Adm. Coligny (1519–72), the chief victim of the massacre of St Bartholomew, who was murdered in a house now replaced by No.144 Rue de Rivoli. Here stood the *Hôtel de Ponthieu*, where the actress and singer Sophie Arnould (1764–1804) was born.

Further E. in the Rue-St-Honoré, Molière was born on the site of No.96 in 1622; opposite is the *Fontaine du Trahoir* (rebuilt by *Soufflot* in 1778, replacing an earlier fountain by *Goujon*), with its stalactites and shells. The chemist Lavoisier (1743–94) owned No.47; and Riesener (1734–1806), the cabinet-maker, died at No.2.

Gallows stood at the point where the street is intersected by the Rue de l'Arbre-Sec, and nearby Card. de Retz was attacked during the Fronde (1648). Well-preserved 17C houses can be seen at Nos 33–45.

For the continuation E. of the Rue de Rivoli, see p168.

A short distance past the *Oratoire*, at No.11 Rue du Louvre leading N. to the small PL. DES DEUX-ÉCUS, are slight remains of Philippe Auguste's fortifications. Off the Rue J.-J. Rousseau (leading S.W. from this point) is the once fashionable *Véro-Dodat arcade* (1822), named in fact after two characters—M. Véro and M. Dodat—and beyond, the Rue du Pélican, which long lived up to its original name of 'Poilcon'.

To the E. of the Pl. des Deux-Écus stands the **Bourse du Commerce** (Pl. 8;8), formerly the *Corn Exchange*, a circular mid 18C building, which Arthur Young considered 'by far the finest thing' he had seen in Paris—'so well planned and so admirably executed'. It was remodelled in 1888.

A fluted Doric column abutting its S.E. side is the only relic of the *Hôtel de la Reine* (later *Hôtel de Soissons*, in the garden of which stock-jobbing took place from 1720), built for Catherine de Médicis in 1572 on the site of the earlier Hôtel d'Orléans which had belonged to Blanche of Castile. The column may have been used as an astrologer's tower.

This building, recently cleaned, was the westernmost and is now the only remaining relic in Paris of the *Halles Centrales*, which by mid 1969 had been moved to extensive modern markets at *Rungis*, a short distance N. of *Orly* airport (see Rte 31). Markets had stood here since the early 12C, but the huge pavilions constructed by *Victor Baltard* (1805–74) in the 1850s were torn down and demolished by 1974 with the exception of No.8, which was re-erected at *Nogent-sur-Marne* (see Rte 28A).

What Zola called 'Le ventre de Paris' is no more, although the excavated site some distance further E. was for a decade jocularly known as the '*trou*' or hole; and more recently it has been gratuitously endowed with the epithet '*cul*' de Paris.

Work is still in progress with the radical redevelopment of the whole **Area of Les Halles**, and until this is completed one cannot pass judgement on the overall design, which has already been subject to numerous changes and compromises, too involved to detail here. A number of architects have taken part in the project, among the foremost being *Ricardo Bofill*, who later left the scene.

The technical problems posed and resolved have been prodigious. These included the siting of the important underground railway-station at the intersection of the N.–S. and E.–W. lines of the RER system at the bottom of the 'trou'; the provision of underground road tunnels, and parking facilities; air-conditioning plants, skilfully disguised behind the façades of houses; the erection of new blocks of buildings, which to a large extent harmonise with the old, etc.

Certainly the church of *St-Eustache* (see below) comes into its own (as does the *Bourse du Commerce*), while the restored *Fontaine des Innocents* (see below) is also now seen to advantage. Large areas have been designated a pedestrian precinct—indeed the Pl. Ste-Opportune has already been styled Ste-Importune—both in streets to the E. and W. of the transverse BLVD SÉBASTOPOL, and there has been a notable revival of *trade* in the district, which has, with the improvements in communication, become a hub of activity of all kinds, some of it distasteful.

The much-vaunted **Forum des Halles**, its ribbed and glazed courtyard forming the sunken lid to the 'trou', and embellished by curious pink marble statuary entitled 'Pyègemalion' (sic), by *Julio Silva*, has been the object of considerable critical comment since it was inaugurated in Sept. 1979. Most of the building is on three subterranean floors, and although partially lit from the central square, and supplied with numerous escalators and lifts, the feeling experienced by many visitors is of claustrophobia combined with

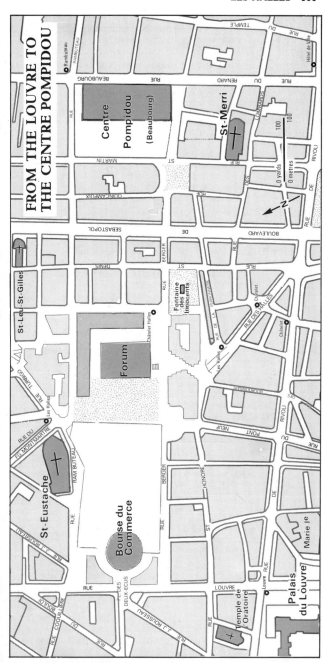

FROM THE LOUVRE TO
THE CENTRE POMPIDOU

·agoraphobia. There is little in it which is imaginative. Certain walls, ceilings, and pillars in passages are decorated with examples of pop art; the various levels contain eight cinemas, and some 200 shops.

A variety of colourful projects have been promised for the area in the immediate vicinity of the Forum, and between it and the Bourse du Commerce, terraces N. and E. of the former having already been covered by mirrored mushroom-shaped pavilions: that to its S. being occupied by new buildings. Further W. *Gardens* are to be laid out, and near St Eustache, an open-air auditorium is planned, with a covered swimming-pool below; aquariums and dolphin-pools; conservatories and hanging-gardens, etc., etc., all of which must be seen to be believed.

The reader is meanwhile requested to turn back to the *Bourse du Commerce*, from the W. side of which the Rue du Louvre continues N., on the r. of which is the **Hôtel des Postes** (1880–84), the main *Post Office* of Paris: opposite, in the *Hôtel d'Ollone* (built in 1639 and altered in 1730), the *Caisse d'Épargne* (or Savings Bank) is installed.

From the 13th to the 18C, the *University of Paris* was responsible for the postal service for private citizens, while from 1461 the royal mail was carried by relays of post riders. In 1719 the University lost its privilege and all mail was controlled by the royal service. In 1757 the postal headquarters was in the *Hôtel d'Hervart*.

On the E. façade of the *Hôtel des Postes*, facing the N. extension of the Rue J.-J. Rousseau (where, at No.52, Rousseau lived in 1776), is an inscription marking the site of the Hôtel which had been occupied by La Fontaine (1621–95) at the time of his death.

Richard Twiss visited Rousseau in 1776, to ask him to copy out some music for him, and remarked that Rousseau—who at that time was thus supporting himself (refusing to draw his British pension)—had apparently only two books with him: 'Robinson Crusoe', and Tasso's 'Jerusalem Liberata'.

Nos 64 and 68 in the street are worth noting.

Just N. of the *Bourse du Commerce*, the Rue Coquillière (with a remarkable shop selling kitchen utensils) leads E.

*ST-EUSTACHE (Pl. 8;8), just beyond, in detail and decoration a Renaissance building, but in plan and in its general lay-out of medieval design, dominates the area.

Begun in 1532, perhaps by *Pierre Lemercier*, it was consecrated in 1637. The main W. doorway was rebuilt in 1754–88 in a completely inharmonious classical style. Both transepts have handsome round-headed doorways (c. 1638–40). The N. transept is approached by a passage from the Rue Montmartre. The open-work bell-tower ('Plomb de St-Eustache') above the crossing, has lost its spire. Above the Lady Chapel in the apse is a small tower built in 1640 and restored in 1875.

The church was the scene of the riotous Festival of Reason in 1793, and in 1795 it became the 'Temple of Agriculture'. Molière was baptized here in 1622, and Antoinette Poisson (Mme de Pompadour) in 1721; Lully was married here in 1662. In 1791 the body of Mirabeau lay in state here before its removal to the Panthéon. Among those buried here are Colbert (1619–83), Adm. de Tourville (d. 1701), and Rameau (1683–1764). *St-Eustache* has always been noted for its music. Berlioz here conducted the first performance of his 'Te Deum' (1855), and Liszt his 'Messe Solenelle' (1866). Its organ recitals are worth attending.

The INTERIOR is unusual in its striking combination of classical forms with a Gothic plan. The double aisles and chapels of the nave are continued round a choir. The square piers are flanked by three storeys of columns in Renaissance variants of the classical orders. The chapels are decorated with paintings from the time of Louis XIII, but restored. The eleven lofty windows of the apse were executed by *Soulignac* (1631), possibly from cartoons of *Philippe de Champaigne*. The churchwardens' pew by *Pierre Le Pautre* dates from c. 1720. The stalls came from the convent of Picpus.

S. Aisle. The 2nd chapel commemorates Rameau; by the transept doorway is a 15C statue of St John the Evangelist; the 2nd choir chapel has a Pietà by *Luca Giordano* (?). In the Lady Chapel, on the altar, is a Virgin by *Pigalle*; the murals are by *Thos. Couture*.

N. Aisle. In the 1st choir chapel as we return is the tomb of Colbert, designed by *Le Brun*, with statues of Colbert and Fidelity by *Coysevox*, and of Abundance by *Tuby*. Above the W. door is the Martyrdom of St-Eustache, by *Simon Vouet*.

The Rue de Turbigo leads N.E. from *St-Eustache* towards the *Pl. de la République*, soon reaching the Rue Étienne-Marcel, in which, to the l. (at No.20), rises the *Tour de Jean-sans-Peur*, a graceful defensive tower of c. 1400 once incorporated in the *Hôtel de Bourgogne*. Part of this mansion (see No.29) was used in the 16–18C as a theatre, where Corneille's 'Le Cid', and Racine's 'Andromaque' and 'Phèdre' were performed.

The next street to the E. is the old Rue St-Denis.

At No.135, in its N. section, an inscription indicates the former position of the *Porte St-Denis* or *Porte aux Peintres*, a gateway in the *Walls* of Philippe Auguste. At the corner of the Rue Tiquetonne (then the Rue du Petit-Lion), stood the old shop bearing the sign of the 'Cat and Racket', celebrated in Balzac's story 'La Maison du Chat qui Pelote'. On No.142 is the *Fontaine de la Reine* (1730).

Passing S. down the street, where at No.133 are some statues from the medieval *Hospital of St-Jacques* (on this site), we reach (l.) **St-Leu-St-Gilles** built in 1235, and first rebuilt after 1319. The nave is of this date; the aisles were added in the 16C; the choir, still partly Gothic, in 1611, the last having been reconstructed in 1858–61 to make way for the adjacent boulevard. The façade and windows were remodelled in 1727, and a crypt excavated in 1780. The church contains three Nottingham alabaster reliefs (in the sacristy entrance) and a sculptured group of St Anne and the Virgin, perhaps from Écouen, by *Jean Bullant* (2nd S. chapel). The organ gallery is by *Nicolas Raimbert* (1659).

Marivaux (1688–1763) was born on the site of No.106 Rue Rambuteau, two streets further S.

Continuing S. in the Rue St-Denis, we reach the small SQ. DES INNOCENTS, on the site of the medieval *Cimetière des Innocents*, the main burial ground of Paris until 1785, when the remains were transferred to the *Catacombs* (see Rte 4). Those of La Fontaine were probably among them. According to Pantagruel, 'the grave-digging rogues of *St Innocent* used in frostie nights to warme their bums with dead mens bones'. Traces of the arches of the cemetery galleries are still to be seen on Nos 11 and 13 in the Rue des Innocents.

The charming Renaissance ***Fontaine des Innocents** (1548; recently restored) was originally erected in the neighbouring Rue St-Denis by *Pierre Lescot*, with bas-reliefs by *Jean Goujon* (now in the Louvre). It was remodelled and set up here by *Payet* c. 1788, the

The Fontaine des Innocents

S. side (for it had earlier abutted a building) being decorated by *Pajou*.

To the S. is the Rue de la Ferronnerie, where, in front of No. 11, Henri IV was assassinated by Ravaillac in 1610.

No. 33 Rue St-Denis has an 18C sign, Au Mortier d'Argent'; the playwright Eugène Scribe (1791–1861) was born at No. 32.

Crossing the ugly BLVD DE SÉBASTOPOL (l.) we may enter the narrow Rue Quincampoix (parallel to the E.), one of the oldest streets in Paris (and still, apparently, partly devoted to the oldest profession), although most of the houses date from the 17–18C. At No. 43 John Law (1671–1729, in Venice), the celebrated Scottish financier, established in 1716 his Mississippi bank which, after frenzied speculation, óbstructed by jealous rivals, ended in a bankruptcy (1720) even more catastrophic than the 'South Sea Bubble'. No.54 (demolished) was the Cabaret de l'Épee de Bois, where the *Royal Academy of the Dance* had its origins in 1658. After the creation of Law's bank the wealthy 'Mississipiens' made it their club, when it was frequented by Louis Racine and Marivaux. Nos 10, 12, and 14 (further S.) have rococo façades: No.36 is also worth noting.

To the E. opens the PL. EDMOND-MICHELET (or *Sq. de la Reynie*), diagonally across which we get a view of the *Centre Beaubourg*, as we approach the *Piazza Beaubourg*, flanked to the W. by the Rue St-Martin.

At No.168 in this street (then No.96) was born Gérard de Nerval (1808–55). At the junction of the Rue Bernard-de-Clairvaux, leading E. into this recently re-developed *Quartier de l'Horloge*, and the Rue Brantôme, is an imaginative modern *Clock*, with automata, by *Jacques Monestier* (1979).

The **CENTRE BEAUBOURG** is officially called the *Centre National d'Art et de Culture Georges-Pompidou* (which will thus long enshrine the name of the well-meaning late Président, who in 1969 conceived the idea of a form of cultural centre—but perhaps not quite as it turned out), which is likewise known by the initials CNAC, or merely the **Centre Pompidou** (Pl. 14;2).

The building—selected from 681 projects received—designed by the Anglo-Italian team, *Richard Rogers* and *Renzo Piano*, in association with *G. Franchini*, and the *Ove Arup* group, was inaugurated early in 1977, but already looks the worse for wear, which is not surprising. The superstructure is 166m long from N. to S., 60m wide, and 42m in height. Its superficial area is 103,300m^2, with a floor area on eight open-plan levels comprising 60,000m^2, of which 19,000m^2 is available for exhibitions, semi-permanent and temporary. The glazed surface is 11,000m^2; the *'ossature métallique'* weighs 15,000 tonnes.

On its W. side the animated 'Piazza Beaubourg', on which a variety of 'manifestations' and exhibitions—both extemporised and organised—take place (beware of pick-pockets), slopes down from the Rue St-Martin to the main entrance on the ground floor of the Centre.

To the N. is a reconstruction of a studio, once at No.11 Impasse Ronsin, which belonged to *Constantin Brancusi* (1876–1904).

Stairs and escalators (l.) rise to a mezzanine floor on a level with the Rue Beaubourg to the E. Turning l. again we reach an 'external' escalator traversing a glazed intestine-like tube, which writhes up to connect a series of platforms, each of which provides access to the upper five floors. On the first three are sections of the *Library* (Bibliothéque Publique d'Information; B.P.I.), containing upward of 350,000 volumes (less quantities already missing);250,000 diapositives; 12,000 records; reference material; films; video-cassettes, etc.

These levels are also partly occupied by the *Centre de Création Industrielle* (C.C.I.), and the sonorous-sounding *Institut de Recherche et de Coordination Acoustique/Musique* (I.R.C.A/M.), director Pierre Boulez, happily muffled in sound-proof bunkers (below ground between the Centre and St-Merri).

On the THIRD LEVEL is the entrance to the ***MUSÉE NATIONAL D'ART MODERNE** (previously accommodated in the *Palais d'Art moderne*: Rte 17)—see below. It also extends to the floor above, reached by an interior escalator. On the top floor, devoted to temporary exhibitions (and occasional 'animations') is a *Cinémathèque*; a restaurant, and a terrace (in addition to others on a lower level), the last providing some unusual views over Paris.

If the success of a museum or monument is to be gauged by the number of people whose curiosity has provoked them to enter it, then the *Centre Georges-Pompidou* has been a spectacular success, with over 7,775,000 visitors in 1980 alone, even if many fewer visited the permanent exhibition of modern art. Some have asserted that it is 'a remarkable achievement': others have been less kind. Various indeed have been the reactions to the ungainly and incongruous physical appearance of what has been well-described as a 'culture factory' in the midst of the staid *Marais*, with its dignified 17–18C architecture. The more critical have made uncomplimentary comparisons between Zola's *Ventre* de Paris, and Pompidou's *Centre*—claiming that these Gargantuan entrails had been neatly wrested from the adjacent 'trou' of Les Halles, and then unceremoniously flung over the tubular scaffolding. And no doubt the discriminating visitor will add his own comments.

For those many travellers with an interest in modern art and who will want at least to visit the collections on the third and fourth floors, what is perhaps far more disturbing is to contemplate the likely *condition* of the paintings within a very few years unless something is done soon to protect them from the dust and general contamination stirred up by the many thousands who press past them daily, in spite of air-conditioning.

The fact that neither the canvases nor the dividing screens are adequately labelled, is another matter. One is left to wander at will through the various sections, but by following a vaguely clockwise direction after turning half-r. on entering the museum, one can *see* everything.

Visitors are warned that the position of canvases may be changed without notice; some may be relegated to *réserves*, (or away on exhibition), and others added. It is planned to improve the quality of display.

We are met by the Snake-charmer, by *Henri Rousseau*; *Bonnard*, 'en barque'; *Picasso*, Lying nude (1901), Seated nude (1905), and Tête de femme rouge (1906); and examples of the art of *Vlaminck*, *Matisse*, *Derain*, *Marquet*, and *Dufy*.

R1 *Matisse*; *Robert Delaunay*, Portrait of Henri Carlier; *Manguin*, Portrait of Ravel.—**R2** *Albert Marquet*, Bassin du Havre; Portrait of Marquet, by *Camoin*; *Utrillo*, L'Impasse Cottin, Jardin de Montmagny.—**R3** *Kupka*.—**R4** *Vlaminck*; *Dufy*; *Roger de la Fresnaye*, La Ferté-sous-Jouarre, The cuirassier.

R5 *Picasso*.—**R6** *Picabia*, Young girl (1912).—**R7** Sculpture by *Gaudier-Brzeska*. Returning through R5 we see examples opposite from the Cubist period of *Picasso*, *Braque*, *Chagall*, and *Léger*, backing onto which is *Braque*, Girl playing mandolin.

We later reach a section devoted to *Robert Delaunay*, including his La Ville de Paris, Eiffel Tower, Towers of Laon, Self-portrait, and La verseuse; *Sonia Delaunay*, Prismes électriques, Marché au Minho (together with others in **R13**).—**R14** *Kandinsky*.—**R15** *Kupka*; *Dufy*, Three bathers. The following section contains *Chagall*, Double-portrait with a glass of wine; *Robert Delaunay*, Le manège de cochons, works by *Gris*, and sculpture by *Lipchitz*.

Below the 'Escalier mécanique', which we now ascend, is *Marie Laurencin*, Apollinaire and his friends.

At the head of this escalator is *Lipchitz*, Head of Gertrude Stein (1920), and *Matisse*, Plaques of female bottoms, turning discretely from which we may enter **R16**—containing *Picasso*, La Liseuse (1920), and **R17** devoted to *Braque*.—**R18** *Jacques Villon*; *Gargallo*, Statue of the Prophet.—To the W. are displayed *Picasso*, Minotaure (1927), Confidences (1934), and Nature morte à la tête antique.

The housing of the external escalator of the Centre Pompidou

Continuing in an anti-clockwise direction, we pass works by *Schwitters*; and *George Grosz*, Remember uncle August, the unhappy inventor.—**R20** *Klee*, and *Ernst*.—**R23** *Kandinsky*; Sculpture by *Antoine Pevsner*.—**R24** *Matisse*, L'Odalesque à la culotte rouge, and La blouse roumaine. Close by are rooms devoted to *Peyronnet*, and *Dubuffet*.

Continuing N. we pass *Chagall*, The acrobat, and **R25** *Derain*, Nude against green curtain; *Marquet*, Seated nude; *Bonnard*, The toilette, and Landscapes.—**R26** *Suzanne Valadon*. The blue room; *Soutine*, The groom, and Portrait of Miestchaninoff; *Kisling*, Woman with Polish shawl; *Modigliani*, Portrait of Dédié; *Felix Vallatton*, Romanian woman in a red dress.

Outside **R26**, *Chagall*, Guerre (1943), and *Rouault*, The wounded clown; and close by, works by *Miró*. We pass through another section (r.) devoted to *Dalí; Man Ray*; and *Magritte*, Le modèle rouge.—**R29** *Andrè Masson*. The next section displays *Matisse*, Le Ciel; *Picasso*, Portrait of Mme Paul Eluard, and in **R30** *Picasso*, Portrait of Dora Maar, Two women on a beach.—**R31** Sculpture by *Julio González*.

Near the adjacent terrace are works by *Balthus*, and in adjoining rooms, examples of sculpture by *Giacometti* and *Kemeny*; and Three people in a room, by *Bacon*.

The collection is continued in the N. part of the building devoted to aspects of modern art with which the Editor has little sympathy and would prefer not to commit his opinions to print. But to quote from a recent brochure, sections are concerned with 'abstraction lyrique', 'nouveau réalisme', 'abstraction géométrique', 'art cinétique', 'Pop art', 'Hyperréalisme et la nouvelle figuration', etc., etc.

Immediately S. of the *Centre*, suitably sited above the studios of I.R.C.A/M. is the PL. IGOR-STRAVINSKY, flanked by relics of the Rue Brisemiche, in which Pascal's family once lived.

Here rises **St-Merri**, built in the Flamboyant style (1515–52) on the site of at least two older churches, which covered the grave of St Médéric of Autun (d.700). In 1796–1801 it was called the 'Temple of Commerce' (much of which in this area, from the 14C at least, being of the carnal kind). The W. front is notable for its rich decoration, but the statues are mostly poor replacements of 1842. The N.W. turret contains the oldest bell in Paris (1331); the S.W. tower lost its top storey in a fire. The nave has a double aisle on the r.; a single, on the l. The pulpit was designed by *M.-A. Slodtz* (1753); who also altered the choir. The organ dates from 1567; Saint-Saëns was organist here. The remaining stained-glass windows, contemporary with the church, are good.

In the *r. aisle*, the 1st outer chapel has remains of the 13C church; further on is a large chapel by *Boffrand* (1743–44), with decorations by *P.-A. Slodtz*. In the *l. aisle*, the 1st chapel contains a 15C tabernacle; the 3rd a Pietà attr. to *Nic. Legendre* (c.1670); the 4th, a painting by *Coypel* (1661). From the 5th, a staircase descends to the crypt (1515), which has grotesque corbels, and the tombstone of Guillaume le Sueur (d. 1530). In the *N. Transept* is St Merri delivering prisoners, by *Simon Vouet*, Among other paintings are a late-16C work of the Fontainebleau School (S. of the *Lady Chapel*) of St Geneviève guarding her flocks, with Paris in the background.

The old quarter round *St-Merri*, with its narrow and picturesque alleys, retains a number of interesting houses, which it is hoped will survive the present rage for demolition in the Halles-Beaubourg redevelopment scheme.

Traditionally Boccaccio (1313–75), whose mother was French, was born near the junction of the adjacent Rue des Lombards and the Rue St-Martin (in which note the 17C bas-relief of the Annunciation on No.89). No.14 in the Rue des Lombards (now a restaurant) preserves in its basement the vaulted chapel of the former women's prison of St-Merri. This ancient street is continued to the E. by the Rue de la Verrerie, in which both Boucher and Bossuet were born (on the sites of Nos 60 and 83 respectively).

We regain the Rue de Rivoli just S. of St-Merri, this E. section of the street constructed by Napoleon III to allow a rapid access for troops to the *Hôtel de Ville* in case of emergency.

In the centre of the SQ. ST-JACQUES rises the only relic of the church of *St Jacques-la-Boucherie* (demolished 1797), the Flamboyant Gothic **Tour St-Jacques**, dating from 1508–22, and now serving as a meteorological station. It was used as a shot-tower after 1836 until 'restored' in 1858 by *Ballu*.

Among the 19C statues is one of Pascal, who in 1642 verified here (or on the tower of St-Jacques-du-Haut-Pas) the barometric experiments he had caused to be made on the Puy de Dôme.

Adjoining, to the S.W., is the PL. DU CHÂTELET (Pl.14;2), bounded by the Seine, here crossed by the *Pont au Change*: see Rte 1.

The square is named after the vanished *Grand Châtelet*, a fortress gateway leading to the Cité, once the headquarters of the Provost of Paris and the Guild of Notaries. It was commenced in 1130, and demolished between 1802–10. Both François Villon and Clément Marot—in 1448 and 1526 respectively—were mewed up here. A plan of the fort may be seen on the front of the *Chambres des Notaires* on the N. side of the square.
On the E. side is the *Théâtre de la Ville*, restored after a fashion and reopened in 1980, only to be severely damaged by fire in 1982. To the W. is the *Théâtre du Châtelet* (1862), in which the Communards were court-martialled in 1871. The painter David (1748–1825) was born in a house which stood on the S. side of this site. In the centre of the Square is the *Fontaine du Châtelet* (or de la Victoire, or du Palmier) dating from 1808 and 1858. An inscription indicates the position of the 'Parloir aux Bourgeois', the seat of the municipality of Paris from the 13C until 1357 (see below).

From the N. side of the Square, the Av. Victoria (named in honour of Queen Victoria's visit to Paris in 1855) leads E. to the PL. DE L'HÔTEL-DE-VILLE (Pl. 14;2), known until the Revolution of 1830 as the PL. DE GRÈVE, for here, since the 11C, ships had moored on the strand, or *grève*.

This Square was the usual site for public executions: among the more famous of which (many incredibly barbarous) were those of the Comte de St-Pol (1475), constable of France, on the orders of Louis XI; Briquemont and Cavagnes, the Huguenot leaders (1572; among many other Protestants); the Comte de Montgomery (1574), captured at the siege of Domfront and formerly captain in the Scottish Guard; François Ravaillac, the assassin of Henri IV (1610); Eléonore Galigaï (the favourite of Marie de Médicis), executed for sorcery in 1617; the Marquise de Brinvilliers (1676), poisoner; the highwayman Cartouche (1721); and Damiens (1757), for attempting to murder Louis XV. In 1789, Foullon (controller-general of finance) and his son-in-law Bertier were hanged here by the Revolutionary mob. In 1795 Fouquier-Tinville suffered the same fate as his countless victims. Louvel, who assassinated the Duc de Berry, was executed here in 1820.
It was often a rendezvous for the unemployed or dissatisfied workers, who were said to 'faire grève', which came to mean 'to go on strike'.

The present **Hôtel de Ville**, on the E. side of the Square, is of more interest for its history than its architecture. Its famous predecessor, begun c.1532, was burnt down by the Communards in 1871, and this caricature replica, in the style of the French Renaissance, was erected (on a larger scale) in 1874–84 from the plans of *Ballu* and *Deperthes*.
Its over-decorated façades are embellished with statues of eminent Frenchmen: its interior is likewise lavishly adorned in the degraded official taste in architecture of the period, with sculpture, elaborate carvings, mural paintings, etc., including *Puvis de Chavannes'* The Seasons.
At No.29 Rue de Rivoli, on the N. side of the edifice, is the Municipal Tourist Office.

In 1264 Louis IX created the first municipal authority in Paris by allowing the merchants to elect magistrates ('échevins'), led by the 'prévôt des marchands', who was also head of the 'Hanse des marchands de l'eau'. This merchant guild, which had the monopoly of the traffic on the Seine, Marne, Oise, and Yonne, took as their emblem a ship, a device which still graces the arms of the city. Their first meeting-place was known simply as the 'Parlouer aux Bourgeois'; later they met at the *Grand-Châtelet* itself; and finally, in 1357, the Provost Étienne Marcel bought the 'Maison aux Piliers' or 'Maison du Dauphin', a mansion in the *Pl. de Grève*, for their assemblies. In 1532 plans for an imposing new building were adopted, but work was stopped at the second floor, and the new designs approved by Henri II in 1549 were not completed until 1628.

In 1789, the 300 electors nominated by the districts of Paris met there. On 17 July, Louis XVI received the tricolour cockade from the hands of Bailly, the Mayor. On 10 Aug. 1792, the 172 commissaries elected by Paris gave the signal for a general insurrection. In 1794 Robespierre took refuge here, but was arrested on 27 July, and dragged hence, his jaw smashed by a bullet, to the Conciergerie. In 1805 it became the seat of the Préfet de la Seine and his council, and was the scene of numerous official celebrations (on Napoleon's marriage to Marie-Louise, etc.)

The Swiss Guards put up a stout defence of the building during the stormy days of 1830. In 1848 it became the seat of Louis Blanc's provisional government, and witnessed the arrest of the revolutionary agitators Barbès and Blanqui. Verlaine was employed here in the mid-1860s. The Third Republic was proclaimed here in 1870 (4 Sept.), and in the following March, the Commune. On 24 May 1871 the building was evacuated before being set ablaze by its defenders.

In 1944 the *Hôtel de Ville* was a focus of opposition to the occupying forces by the Resistance movement, who by 19 Aug. had established themselves in the building, repelling German counter-attacks until relieved by the arrival of Gen. Leclerc's division five days later.

From behind the *Hôtel de Ville*, we may cross the Rue de Rivoli to visit the **Temple des Billettes**, at No.22 Rue des Archives, which although properly in the *Marais* (see below) is more conveniently approached from here. It was built in 1756 for the Carmelites, but since 1812 has been used as a Lutheran church. Abutting it to the N., the *cloister*, the only medieval example in Paris, is a relic of an older convent (1427).

The Rue de Rivoli, and its E. extension, the Rue St-Antoine, split the ancient **Marais** district into two unequal sections; the smaller, to the S., is that part described in our route; for the area to the N., see Rte 12.

To the E. of the *Hôtel de Ville*, between two of its annexes, lies the PL. ST-GERVAIS, with its elm tree, a reminder of the famous elm of St-Gervais, beneath which justice used to be administered. The proverbial expression for waiting for Doomsday is ironically, 'Attendre sous l'orme' (the elm). This was one of the first inhabited areas on the Right Bank, and the Rue François-Miron follows the course of a Roman road which led from Lutetia to Senlis.

To the E. it is dominated by the church of ***ST-GERVAIS-ST-PROTAIS** (Pl. 15;1–3), which, founded in the 6C, dates its present form from the rebuildings of 1494–1578 (choir and transepts) and 1600–57 (nave, chapels, and tower).

The original plans are attributed to *Martin Chambiges*, whose work was continued by his son *Pierre*. The lower stages of the tower are an early-15C survival. The façade (1616–21), by *Clément Métezeau* and (probably) *Salomon de Brosse*, is the earliest example in France of the superimposition of the three classic orders—Doric, Ionic, and Corinthian. In 1795 the church was converted into a 'Temple of Youth'. Bossuet preached here; Mme de Sévigné was married here; and here are buried Philippe de Champaigne (1602–74), Scarron (1610–60), and Crébillon the elder (1674–1762).

François Couperin (1668–1733) and seven members of his family served as organist here from 1653 to 1830, and their organ, restored, still survives. Couperin 'le Grand' himself was born in a house on the site of No.4 Rue François-Miron.

The INTERIOR, impressive from its loftiness and unity of style, is remarkably rich in works of art. The high windows of both nave and choir contain much stained-glass of c.1610–20 by *Robert Pinaigrier* and *Nic. Chaumet*. The nave was completed in Flamboyant Gothic at a time when Renaissance influence was strongest.

S. Aisle. The 2nd chapel has an altar commemorating some 50 victims of the bombardment of Good Friday, 1918, when a German shell struck the church. In the 3rd, seven low 17C painted panels of the Life of Christ; 5th and 6th, stained-glass of 1531. In the 8th chapel, the tomb of Michel Le Tellier (d. 1685), by *Mazeline* and *Hurtrelle*; the bearded heads supporting the Chancellor's sarcophagus are from the tomb of Jacques de Souvré (d. 1670), by *François Anguier*, the rest of which are in the Louvre. The *Lady Chapel*, an overdecorated example of Flamboyant Gothic (1517), has fine contemporary glass.

The Sacristy, in the N. choir aisle, retains a good iron grille of 1741. In the N. transept is a painting of the Passion (Flemish; mid-16C, at present under restoration). From the next chapel we may enter the well-restored *Chapelle Dorée* (1628); in the adjacent chapel are a 13C high relief of the Dormition of the Virgin (below the altar), and a portrait by *Pajou* (1782) of Mme Palerme de Savy.

In the *Choir*, the stalls are of the 17C (W. end) and mid-16C, the latter with curious misericords. Against the N. entry-pillar is a 14C Virgin, known as N.-D. de Bonne-Délivrance; and on either side of the altar, wooden statues of the patron saints, by *Michel Bourdin* (1625). The 18C bronze-gilt candelabra are by *Soufflot*.

The S. façade of the church can now be seen since the area has been the subject of clearance and restoration: note also the façades of some houses in the Rue des Barres, behind the building.

The stepped Rue François-Miron, leading N.E. from *St-Gervais*, is one of the more imposing streets in the district, Nos 2–14, built c. 1735, adorned with wrought-iron work displaying the famous elm (see above); Nos 30, 36, and 42 all have good features.

No.26 in the Rue Geoffroy-l'Asnier (r.) is the *Hôtel de Chalons-Luxembourg* (1608), with a magnificent doorway (1659) and an attractive Louis XIII pavilion in the courtyard. No.22 also retains a handsome 17C façade. No.17 is a *Jewish Study Centre*, with a memorial.

Further E. in the Rue François-Miron (off which diverges the Rue de Jouy; see below) is the mutilated **Hôtel de Beauvais** (No.68; by *Le Pautre)*, with an interior courtyard, ornate circular vestibule, and carved staircase. Anne of Austria and Card. Mazarin watched the entry of Louis XIV and Marie-Thérèse into Paris in 1660 from its balcony.

It had been built in 1655 for Pierre Beauvais, on the proceeds of having turned a blind eye to the fact that his 40-year-old wife Catherine-Henriette Bellier, a 'lady-in-waiting' to the queen-mother, and better-known as 'Cateau-la-Borgnesse' (for *she* had indeed only one eye), had taught the 14-year-old king certain essential facts of life.

Christina of Sweden was a later tenant, and here in 1763 Mozart (aged 7) was the guest of the Bavarian ambassador.

The balcony of the *Hôtel du Président Hénault* (No.82) should be noted.

To the r. in the Rue de Jouy, No.7, the *Hôtel d'Aumont*, by *Le Vau*

(1648) and *Fr. Mansart* (1656), retains some of its original decoration, including work by *Le Brun*.

Beyond, the Rue du Figuier diverges r. to the **Hôtel de Sens** (Pl. 15;3), built c. 1474–1519 for the archbishops of Sens, at a time when the bishopric of Paris was suffragan to the metropolitan see of Sens (before 1623; see Rte 30); it is older than the *Hôtel de Cluny* (see Rte 2), the only other example of 15C domestic architecture in Paris. Unfortunately it has suffered a long period of neglect, and has been poorly restored.

It now houses the *Bibliothèque Forney*, a reference library devoted to the fine arts.

Marguerite de Valois (1553–1615), whose memoirs may well have assisted Brantôme in the composition of his 'Dames illustres', passed peccant years here with her younger lovers, one of whom, in 1605, she had executed for the jealous murder of another on her very doorstep.

To the W. are the modern buildings of the *Cité Internationale des Arts*, providing accommodation and facilities for foreign art students, on the pattern of the *Cité Universitaire*.

To the E., the QUAI DES CÉLESTINS, commanding attractive views of the *Île Saint-Louis*, passes (l., at No.32) the site of the *Tour Barbeau*, completing, on the river bank, the N. perimeter of Philippe Auguste's defensive *Wall*, a section of which may be seen from the Rue des Jardins-St-Paul, adjoining.

Here also stood the tennis-court of the Croix-Noire, where Molière performed in 1645 until his arrest for debt. Rabelais (1494?–1553) died in the Rue des Jardins-St-Paul, and was buried in the vanished church of *St-Paul-des-Champs* (see below), as were the Mansarts (1666, and 1708), and the 'Man in the Iron Mask', who had died in the Bastille (1703).

The neighbouring Rue St-Paul had acquired its name before 1350; at No.32, part of the church belfry survives.—See below for the eastern end of the Quai des Célestins. Turning r. at the N. end of this street, and then l. brings us to the Rue St-Antoine, an ancient thoroughfare retaining many elegant façades.

A few paces to the W. is the church of **St-Paul-St-Louis** (Pl. 15;3), or the *Grands-Jésuites*, built for that Society by Louis XIII in 1627–41 to replace a chapel of 1582. St-Paul was added to the original name in 1796 to commemorate the demolished church of *St-Paul-des-Champs*.

Designed by *Père Fr. Derrand*, its florid style, founded on 16C Italian churches, is the earliest example of the Jesuit school of architecture in France. Richelieu said the first mass here. The handsome Baroque portal is by *Père Martellange*. The interior is over-decorated but imposing, and contains, in the l. transept, a Christ in the Garden by *Delacroix*; and in the r., Louis XIII offering a model of the church to St Louis, by *Simon Vouet*. Bp Huet (d. 1721), the original editor of the Delphin classics, is buried here, and Louis Bourdaloue, who here made most of his famous orations: 'he preached like an angel', commented Mme de Sévigné, herself a worshipper here.

Gérard de Nerval, who was educated at the adjacent *Lycée Charlemagne*, occupying a 17C Jesuit house, was found hanged in the old Rue de la Vieille Lanterne, near the *Sq. St-Jacques* (see above) in 1855.

Turning E. along the Rue-St-Antoine, we shortly pass (l.; No.62) the *Hôtel de Sully* (CN) (or de Béthune-Sully), now occupied by offices of the *Monuments Historiques*, who can give information about any Guided Tours to the sites and monuments of Paris that may be joined, etc.; they also publish a review devoted to the restoration of architecturally important buildings: 'Les Monuments Historiques de

The courtyard of the Hôtel de Sully

la France', and have a bookstall, not only selling their own publications. These are also available at Porte F of the *Grand Palais*, facing the Cours-la-Reine.

The mansion, by *Jean du Cerceau* (1624–30), was acquired by Sully, the minister of Henri IV, in 1634. The courtyard, a particularly fine example of the Louis-XIII style, the entrance pavilions, and the interior, retaining 17C ceilings and panelling, have been the subject of extensive restoration. The *Hôtel de la Mouffle* had previously stood on this site, from 1407.

Parts of the interior may be visited on a lecture tour taking place at 15.00 every Wed., Sat., and Sun.

The extensive *Photographic Archives* of the Caisse Nationale, invaluable to the student of French art and architecture, are at 4 Rue de Turenne, adjacent to the W.

From just E. of the Hôtel de Sully, the Rue de Birague approaches the S. entrance of the *Pl. des Vosges* (see Rte 12); Nos 12 and 14 have elegant features.

Opposite this point, from the S. side of the Rue St-Antoine, we may follow the Rue Beautreillis. Beneath the carriage-entrance of No.22, the *Grand Hôtel de Charny* (where Baudelaire lodged in 1858–59), are some woodcarvings in the purest Louis-XIII style. No.16, the *Petit Hôtel de Charny*, was the birthplace of the dramatist Sardou (1831–1908).—To the r. in the Rue Charles V, is the imposing *Hôtel d'Aubray* (Nos.12; 1620), residence of the notorious Marquise de Brinvilliers (1630–76), the poisoner. No.10, the *Hôtel de Maillé*, retains its Louis-XIII façade, and No.15, opposite, dates from 1642.

No.10 Rue Beautreillis was the *Hôtel des Princes de Monaco*, built c. 1650, but altered in the 18th and 19Cs; No.7, with a wooden staircase and wrought-iron balcony, is one of the finest bourgeois houses of its period in Paris (late 16C).

On reaching the Rue des Lions, with a number of 17–18C mansions, including No.10 (the passage in the modern façade leads to a courtyard of 1642) and No.11, in which Mme de Sévigné lived in 1645–50, turn l. and then r. to regain the Quai des Célestins.

At No.4 QUAI DES CÉLESTINS is the stately *Hôtel de Fieubet*, with an interesting courtyard, built by *J. H.-Mansart* (1676–81) for Gaspard de Fieubet, chancellor to Anne of Austria; unfortunately it was badly disfigured in 1857, and now accommodates the *École Massillon*. The *Hôtel de Nicolai*, No.4, is also of the late 17C.

At No.1 Rue de Sully, on the far side of the BLVD HENRI-IV, in the Quartier de l'Arsenal (named after the arsenal established here by Henri IV), stands the **Bibliothèque de l'Arsenal** (Pl. 15;4).

The library was founded in 1757 by Antoine-René d'Argenson, Marquis de Paulmy (1722–87), and partly installed in the former residence of the Grand Master of Artillery, built in 1594 for Sully. The façade in the parallel BLVD MORLAND (facing the starkly functional *Préfecture de Paris*) is by *Boffrand* (c.1723).

The library possesses some 15,000 MSS., one million printed volumes, and 120,000 engravings. It is known particularly for its incomparable series of illuminated MSS., and its almost complete collection of French dramatic works. The Gordon Craig collection was acquired in 1957. Among its archives are the papers of the Bastille; documents relative to the 'Man in the Iron Mask', and the 'Affair of the Diamond Necklace'; letters of Henri IV to the Marquise de Verneuil, etc.; also St Louis's Book of Hours, and Charles V's Bible, among others. Nodier, Hérédia, Mérimée, and Anatole France were librarians here.

Noteworthy are the *Salon de Musique*, by *Boffrand*, with superb Louis-XV woodwork, and the *Apartment of the Duchesse de La Meilleraie*, with a ceiling by *Simon Vouet*.

Turning N.E. (r.) past the *Caserne des Célestins* (barracks of the Gendarmerie Mobile, built on part of the site of the famous Celestine monastery founded in 1362, but suppressed in 1779), we shortly diverge l. off the BLVD HENRI-IV, to regain the Rue St-Antoine (viâ the Rue Castex). On the corner is the circular *Temple de Ste-Marie*, originally the chapel of the convent of the Visitation, and now a Protestant church. It was built by *Fr. Mansart* in 1632–34.

The unscrupulous Surintendant des finances Nícolas Fouquet (1615–80) and Henri de Sévigné (killed in a duel in 1651) were buried here. Vincent de Paul was almoner of the convent for 28 years.

A few paces to the W., at No. 21, is the *Hôtel de Mayenne* (or d'Ormesson), retaining a turret and charming staircase. Now the *École des Francs-Bourgeois*, it was built by *Jean du Cerceau* in 1613–17. It is flanked by the Rue du Petit-Musc, a corruption of the names it went by in the 14C, which were either 'La pute y Muse' or 'La Pute qui muse'.

Turning E. we pass (r.) the Rue de Lesdiguières, where at No.9 was Balzac's first Paris lodging, in a garret at three sous a day. A tablet on No.5 Rue St-Antoine marks the position of the court of the *Bastille* (see below), by which the Revolutionary mob gained access to the fortress. Near the junction of this street and the PL. DE LA BASTILLE was the site of the great barricade of 1848, and also the last stronghold of the Communards in 1871.

12 The Marais

MÉTROS: *Bastille; St-Paul; Hôtel-de-Ville; Rambuteau; Temple; Arts-et-Métiers; Réamur-Sébastopol.*

The ***Marais**, one of the most interesting districts of old Paris, is bounded by the *Grands Boulevards* on the N. and E., by the *Blvd de Sébastopol* to the W., and by the Seine to the S. It includes the greater part of the 3rd and 4th Arrondissements. In spite of past neglect, demolition, and some rebuilding, it remains substantially as developed in the 17C, and contains many scores of buildings of outstanding architectural interest, affording a fascinating and unique reminder of the elegance of this period.

The *Centre Beaubourg* and the S. sector of the *Marais* are described in Rte 11.

So called from the marshy land ('marais', marsh or morass), the *Marais* only became habitable with the arrival of the Knights Templar and other religious houses, who settled here in the 13C, and converted the marshes into arable land. Royal patronage began with Charles V, who, anxious to forget the associations of the *Palais de la Cité* with the rebellion of Étienne Marcel in 1358, built the *Hôtel Saint-Paul* here. In the 16C, the *Hôtel de Lamoignon* and *Hôtel Carnavalet* were built, but the seal of royal approval came with the building of the PL. ROYALE (1605; later known as the *Pl. des Vosges;* see below).

Courtiers unable to find room here began to build themselves houses as near to the Place as possible, and the Marais remained the most fashionable residential area of Paris until the creation of the Faubourg St-Germain in the early 18C. It was the Revolution which ended its long reign of splendour. The nobles had to flee; the State confiscated their property and sold it to the growing number of craftsmen, mechanics, and merchants who flooded into the area, who appeared to take a brutish pleasure in disfiguring as much as possible. Much of the Marais continues to be a commercial district, even if its architectural merits are more appreciated as the value of its properties has increased.

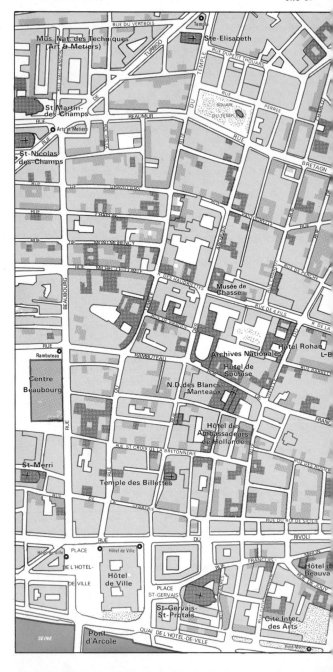

RUE DU VERTBOIS

Temple

Mus. Nat. des Techniques
(Art & Metiers)

Ste-Elisabeth

TURBIGO

RUE DUPETIT THOUARS

DE

RUE

PERREE

DE

REAUMUR

SQUARE
DU TEMPLE

St-Martin-
des-Champs

RUE

Arts et Metiers

RUE

St-Nicolas
des-Champs

BRETAGN

TEMPLE

DU

GRAVILLIERS

DE

RUE

CHAPLIN

BEAUBOURG

RUE

DE MONTMORENCY

RUE

MICHEL-LE-COMTE

RUE DE PERCHE

R DES HALIORETTES

RUE DE BRAQUE

Musée de
Chasse

RUE DE 4 FILS

R DE LA

TEMPLE

DES

Hôtel Rohan

L-B

Rambuteau

RAMBUTEAU

Archives Nationales

RUE BARBET

Hôtel de
Soubise

Centre
Beaubourg

RUE

N.D des Blancs-
Manteaux

FRANC

RUE

Hôtel des
Ambassadeurs
de Hollande

RUE ST-CROIX DE LA BRETONNERIE

RUE DES ROSIER

St-Merri

DE

Temple des Billettes

VERRERIE

RUE DU ROI DE SICILE

RIVOLI

RUE

DU

FRANCOIS-

MIRION

Hôtel de Ville

PLACE
DE L'HOTEL-

DE VILLE

Hôtel
de Ville

RUE

Hôtel d
Beauva

RUE DE JOUY

PLACE
ST-GERVAIS

St-Gervais-
St-Protais

Cite Inter.
des Arts

SEINE

Pont
d'Arcole

QUAI DE L'HOTEL-DE-VILLE

Pont-Mar

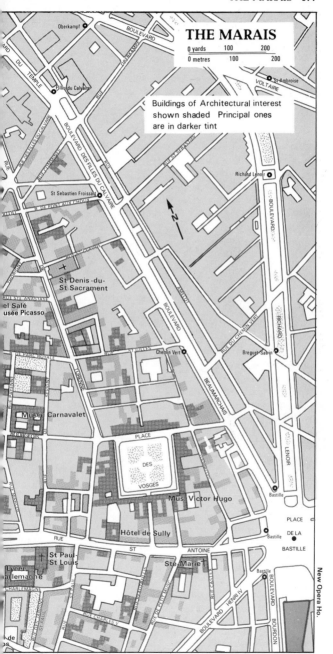

THE MARAIS

| 0 yards | 100 | 200 |
| 0 metres | 100 | 200 |

Buildings of Architectural interest shown shaded Principal ones are in darker tint

A popular print showing the Bastille in the process of demolition, after its capture by revolutionaries on 14 July 1789.

Immediately E. of the *Marais* lies the **Pl. de la Bastille** (Pl. 15;4), laid out in 1803.

The ground plan of the famous fortress prison is marked out by a line of paving-stones in the Place, beneath which some cellars are said to survive.

Its keep (a model of which may be seen in the *Musée Carnavalet*) stood on the W. side, across the end of the Rue St-Antoine, and the main drawbridge was slightly N. of the junction of the *Blvd Henri-IV* with the Place. The *July Column* (see below) stands approximately in the centre of what was the E. bastion. The *Canal St-Martin* now runs

beneath the Place, appearing to the S. in the *Gare d'eau de l'Arsenal*, which shortly enters the Seine.

The **Bastille** (more correctly the *Bastille St-Antoine*) originated as a bastion-tower defending the E. entrance to Paris. It was developed under Charles V into a fortress with eight massive towers, immensely thick walls, and a wide moat. By the reign of Louis XIII, the Bastille had become almost exclusively a state prison for political offenders, among whom were the mysterious 'Man in the Iron Mask' (1698–1703) and Voltaire (twice). The arbitrary arrest by 'lettre de cachet' of persons obnoxious to the Court, and their protracted imprisonment without trial, made the Bastille a popular synonym for oppression. Bassompierre was imprisoned in 1629 for twelve years by Richelieu, 'not that he had done wrong, but for fear he might be led into mischief'. Bernard Palissy was incarcerated here in 1588, at the age of 78; and among other notable temporary residents were Cagliostro, Marmontel, the Duchesse du Maine, and Mme de Tencin. Vanbrugh enjoyed Louis XIV's hospitality (for obscure reasons) for most of 1692. Linguet's 'Memoires' (1783, published in London) describe his

own experiences when incarcerated there in 1780–82. Another inmate was the notorious Marquis de Sade, who here wrote 'Justine' and other lubricious works. Mirabeau the Younger was also imprisoned here, another victim of the practice of arrest by 'lettre de cachet', albeit at his father's instigation.

In 1789, the Revolutionary mob, aided by a few troops, attacked and overwhelmed its defenders, and murdered the governor, the Marquis de Launay, and freed a handful of prisoners. In the same year the building was razed to the ground, and its key, presented by La Fayette to Washington, is now at Mount Vernon. The anniversary of the fall of the Bastille (14 July) is celebrated by the French as a Fête Nationale.

The **July Column** (*Colonne de Juillet*) is in no way connected with the above event, but was erected by Louis-Philippe in 1840–41 to commemorate the 504 victims of the three days' street-fighting of July 1830, who are buried in vaults beneath the circular base of the column. The victims of the Revolution of February 1848 were subsequently interred there, and their names added to the inscription. The bronze-faced column, 51·50m high, is surmounted by a bronze-gilt figure of Liberty; its ascent is provisionally suspended.

The new **Opéra de la Bastille**, designed by Carlos Ott, a Uruguayan-born Canadian (chosen from 744 projects: that of the Centre Pompidou was one of a mere 680!) is to be raised on a site immediately S.E. of the Pl. de la Bastille, but it is unlikely that it will be completed by the end of this decade.

Nos 2–20 in the BLVD BEAUMARCHAIS, leading N. from the *Pl. de la Bastille*, are built on the site of a luxurious mansion and garden belonging to the dramatist Caron de Beaumarchais (1732–99). The Hôtel de Mansart-Sagonne (see below) is well seen from Nos 21–23

In the Place des Vosges

in the boulevard, which with its continuation, the BLVD DES FILLES-DU-CALVAIRE (recalling the site of a former convent; 1633–1790) and BLVD DU TEMPLE (see Rte 13), leads to the *Pl. de la République*.

The Rue de la Bastille leads N.W. from the *Pl. de la Bastille* to the Rue des Tournelles, No.28 in which is the *Hôtel de Mansart-Sagonne*, built for himself in 1674–85 by *Jules Hardouin-Mansart* (1646–1708), and decorated by *Le Brun* and *Mignard*. No.50 has a splendid façade. The cultured courtesan Ninon de Lenclos (1620–1705) lived here from 1644, and died at No.56.—Before reaching these two houses, the Rue du Pas-de-la-Mule leads l. to the *Pl. des Vosges*.

The ***PLACE DES VOSGES**** (Pl. 15;2–4), the heart of the *Marais*, a large quadrangle surrounded by 39 houses in red brick with stone facings, was built on a uniform plan with arcaded ground floors (1606–11), and is one of the most attractive squares in Paris. Trees were not planted in the central gardens until 1783, and although they provide welcome shade, they spoil the effect of harmonious symmetry. The main approach to the *Pl. des Vosges*, from the Rue St-Antoine, is by the Rue de Biragues (see p 174), passing through the *Pavillon du Roi* (see below). The whole Place is at present the subject of slow but thorough restoration.

The square occupies the site of the royal *Palais des Tournelles*, the residence of

MUSEE CARNAVALET

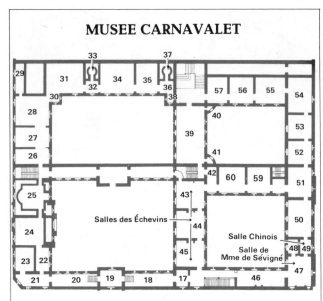

Salles des Échevins

Salle Chinois

Salle de Mme de Sévigné

First Floor

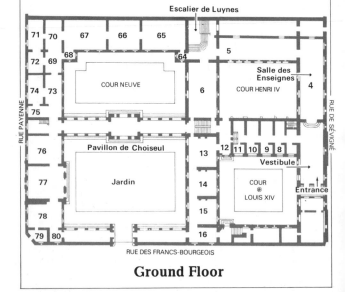

Escalier de Luynes

COUR NEUVE

Salle des Enseignes

COUR HENRI IV

RUE PAYENNE

RUE DE SÉVIGNÉ

Pavillon de Choiseul

Jardin

Vestibule

COUR LOUIS XIV

Entrance

RUE DES FRANCS-BOURGEOIS

Ground Floor

the Duke of Bedford, regent of France after the death of Henry V; in 1559 this was the scene of the fatal tournament when Henri II was accidentally killed by Montgomery, and it was in consequence abandoned by his widow, Catherine de Médicis. The square in its present form was laid out for Henri IV, probably by *Baptiste du Cerceau*, as the PLACE ROYALE, and opened in 1605; the king's pavilion was above the gateway in the centre of the S. side, while the queen's was the corresponding building on the N. (No.28). In the earlier part of the reign of Louis XIV this was one of the most fashionable addresses in Paris, and the centre of the 'Nouvelles Précieuses' satirized by Molière. It only acquired its present name in 1799, the department of the Vosges having been the first to discharge its liabilities for the Revolutionary Wars.

At the corners of the square are fountains (1816), and in the centre a poor equestrian statue of Louis XIII (1825) set up to replace one destroyed in 1792. Mme de Sévigné (1626–96) was born in the *Hôtel de Coulanges* (No.1bis; 1606), next to the *Pavillon du Roi*; No.3 is the *Hôtel d'Estrades*. No.6 (see below) was built in 1610 for the Maréchal de Lavardin (d.1614). No.7, the *Petit-Hôtel de Sully*, was built by *Jean Androuet du Cerceau*. Both Gautier and Daudet lived for a while in No.8, the *Hôtel de Fourcy* (1605). No.9, the *Hôtel de Chaulnes*, was the residence of Rachel (d.1858), the tragedienne. No.11 was occupied by Marion Delorme, the courtesan, in 1639–48. No.21 was the mansion of Card. de Richelieu (1615), in front of which, on the very day after the cardinal's edict against duelling, took place the famous duel between François de Montmorency and Des Chapelles against Bussy and Beuvron (1627). No.12 occupies part of the *Hôtel Dangeau*, the home of Philippe, Marquis de Dangeau (1638–1720), the memorialist.

No.6 in the *Pl. des Vosges*, in which Hugo lived in 1832–48 (2nd floor), is now the **Musée Victor-Hugo** (adm. daily, except Mon.), perhaps of more interest for the numerous pen and wash *Drawings (c.350) by *Hugo* (1802–85) displayed there than for the family souvenirs.

Note the bust of Hugo by *Rodin*; portrait of Juliette Drouet by *Bastien-Lepage*; The Première of Hernani, by *Besnard*; portrait of Adèle Foucher, the poet's wife, by *Louis Boulanger*; Hugo on his death-bed, by *Bonnat*; and works by *Célestin Nanteuil* and *Delacroix*, etc. Note also the furniture and woodwork, designed or carved by Hugo.

From the N.W. corner of the *Pl. des Vosges* we cross the Rue de Turenne (where l., in the court of No.23, is the *Hôtel de Villacerf*, of c. 1660, with a fountain), and enter the Rue des Francs-Bourgeois, taking its name from the citizens who, being vassals to a feudal lord, were exempt from municipal taxes. For the N. section of the Rue de Turenne, see p.189

The ***MUSÉE CARNAVALET**, or *Musée Historique de la Ville de Paris* (Pl. 15;1; MÉTRO: *St-Paul*), at the corner of the Rue des Francs-Bourgeois and the Rue de Sévigné, is a highly important collection illustrating the history of Paris from the 16C to the middle of the 19C.

The museum is housed in the ***Hôtel Carnavalet**, an imposing mansion begun in 1544 for Jacques de Ligneris, President of the Parlement, and adorned with sculptures by *Jean Goujon*. It was altered in 1660 by *Mansart*, who built the present façade, but retained the 16C gateway with its *Goujon* sculptures (on the keystone, a winged figure of Abundance standing on a globe which was later carved into a carnival mask, in punning allusion to Carnavalet). Further alterations and enlargements were made earlier this century.

There is a project to extend the museum into the adjacent *Hôtel Le Pelletier de St-Fargeau* (see below).

The name Carnavalet was derived from the Breton family of Kernevenoy, the second owners of the building. Mme de Sévigné lived here from 1677 until her death in 1696; her apartments, which were shared by her daughter, Mme de Grignan, and her uncle, the Abbé de Coulanges, were in the S.E. corner of the First Floor. The building was acquired by the municipality in 1866, and the museum was inaugurated in 1880.

The bronze statue of Louis XIV in the centre of the courtyard is by *Coysevox*. Of the sculptures in the courtyard, the best are those by *Jean Goujon* on the entrance arch and above the door on the l. The reliefs of the Seasons, on the side opposite the entrance, were probably done under his direction. On the r., the relief above the door is a 19C copy of the one opposite; those on the first storey are by *van Obstal* (1660).

Some rooms are in the process of rearrangement, but the following itinerary will take the visitor round the building in an approximate chronological progression, with one or two slight breaks in continuity. **RR7–11** (once stables), to the l. of the entrance vestibule, are reserved for temporary exhibitions.

From the vestibule we enter the *Salle des Enseignes* (**R4**), with a wrought-iron grille, containing material relative to trades and guilds, including a collection of shop and tavern signs of the 15–19C. In the central cases are weights and measures, and models of glassworks and locksmiths' works, merchants' tokens etc.—In **R5**, continuing the display, is the front of an apothecary's shop of the First Empire.

R6 (l.) conserves some magnificent gilt panelling from the *Hôtel d'Uzès*, Rue Montmartre, from designs by *Ledoux*, while the adjoining room, also by *Ledoux* (1752), was saved from the 'café Militaire' in the Rue Saint-Honoré. Behind the latter is a large 19C maquette of the *Palais-Royal.*

RR12–16 contain engravings of Paris from the 16th to early 17C.—From R16 we ascend to the FIRST FLOOR.

RR17–25 illustrate the topography of Paris from the 17C to the beginning of the 18C. Note also the *anon.* 16C Flemish painting of the Prodigal Son in the company of courtesans, and a portrait of Mary Stuart in a white mourning veil (1561) in **R19**, and the views of Paris by *P.-D. Martin* in **RR20, 22**, and **24** (the Inauguration of the church of Les Invalides). **R23** contains the richly painted and gilded woodwork (c.1656) from the *Hôtel Colbert de Villacerf* at 23 Rue de Turenne; **R24** is the 'grand cabinet doré', by *Le Vau*, from 14 Pl. des Vosges; the ceiling painting is by *Le Brun*, as is that in **R25**, of 1651, with decorations from the same hôtel.

Returning through these rooms, we may visit **R46**, devoted to Mme de Sévigné, with a pastel of the marquise by *Nanteuil*, and of her daughter Mme de Grignan, by *Mignard*, and other souvenirs.—**R47** contains paintings of St-Germain and Vincennes, by *van de Meulen.*—**RR45-43**, nearby, the *Salles Des Echevins*, contain portraits of aldermen by *Largillière, de Troy*, and *Duplessis*, and the Allegory of the Peace of Aix-la-Chapelle (1749) by *Dumont le Romain*. In **R45** is a monumental chimneypiece of the Louis-XIII period.

Hence we may visit **R39**, the first of a series of rooms (**RR39-42, 60, 59, 58, 51-53**) accommodating the important collection of furniture donated by Henriette Bouvier in 1965.—To the r. of **R51, R50** contains an early painting by *Chardin* of a game of billiards. **R49**, adjoining, contains examples of 18C furniture, in the Chinese taste.

RR54-57, well-panelled, concentrate on furniture of the period of Louis XV. **R56** is devoted to the theatre; **R57** to Rousseau and Voltaire, with a portrait of the latter, aged 24, *after Largillière.*— Crossing the landing of the Escalier des Luynes (a reconstruction of a stairway from the *Hôtel de Luynes*, decorated with wall-paintings of the family, by *Brunetti*, of 1748), we reach **R36**, with a portrait of Benjamin Franklin, by *Duplessis*, and **R37**, conserving the rotunda from the ground floor of the *Hôtel de Fersen*. The following suite of rooms is devoted to furniture from the Bouvier collection, of the Louis-XV–XVI period; **R31**, painted by *Boucher* and *Fragonard* (1750–65), is from the house of the engraver Gilles Demarteau in the Rue de la Pelleterie.

R26 contains views by *A.-J. Noël*, and *J.-B. Lallemand*, among others.—The adjoining stairs ascend to the *Library*, with an extensive reference section devoted to the history of Paris, etc.—After passing along the gallery opposite (**RR61–63**), displaying topographical views of 18C Paris by *Nicolas* and *J.-B. Raguenet*, and others, we may turn l. through R39 and descend the *Escalier de Luynes*, and then traverse **RR64–68**, containing archaeological collections, to reach the wing comprising **RR69** on, devoted to the period from the Revolution to the present. Sections cover the Pillage of the Invalides, containing a portrait by *Vestier* of Dr John Moore (1729–1802), the author of descriptions of Paris during this disturbed time; a model of the Bastille cut from one of its stones under the direction of *Palloy*, the demolition contractor; a painting of the Storming of the Bastille, by *Henry Singleton*, and of its Destruction, by *Hubert Robert*; 'Lettres de Cachet' signed by Louis XV, etc.; busts, documents, and portraits (Marat, Danton, Robespierre, etc.) of the period; and souvenirs of Louis XVI and his family during their imprisonment in the Temple. Other sections are devoted to Napoleon and his family, with personal souvenirs, etc. Note the portraits of Napoleon by *Lefèvre*; of Mme Récamier, by *Gérard*; and of Talleyrand in 1809, by *Prud'hon*.

Aspects of Paris (literary, theatrical, etc.) are also covered.—From the hall beyond **R75** we may traverse the central colonnade of the *Pavillion de Choiseul* to regain the entrance.

No.29 Rue de Sévigné was formerly the *Hôtel Le Pelletier de St-Fargeau* (by *Bullet*; 1687). No.48, opposite, the *Hôtel de Jonquières*, retains the relief (1810) from an old fountain; No.52, built by *Pierre Delisle-Mansart* for himself, has been much altered.

In the Rue Payenne, immediately W. of the *Hôtel Carnavalet*, No.11, the *Hôtel de Polastron-Polignac*, now houses the *Swedish Cultural Centre* and *Musée Tessim*, containing paintings by Alexander Roslin (1718–93), among others. No.13, the *Hôtel de Lude*, is another good example of an early 18C mansion. There is a small lapidary collection in the SQ. GEORGES-CAIN opposite.

S. of the *Hôtel Carnavalet*, on the corner of the Rue Pavée (No.24), is the *Hôtel Lamoignon*, built in 1584 for Diane de France, the legitimized daughter of Henri II, but named after Lamoignon, President of the Parlement of Paris (1658), a later occupant, and enlarged in the 17C. Daudet set up house here on his marriage in 1867.

It now houses the *Bibliothèque Historique de la Ville de Paris*, containing over

400,000 vols and 100,000 MSS relative to the history of the city, and of the Revolution.—Adjacent are traces of the notorious prison of *La Force* (demolished 1850), where some 170 victims of the Revolution were massacred in Sept. 1792.

On the S. side of the Rue des Francs-Bourgeois, No.31 is the *Hôtel d'Albret*, built c. 1640 by *Fr. Mansart*, with an 18C street façade. At the end of the courtyard of No.33 is a fragment of the *Walls* of Philippe Auguste. The *Hôtel de Guillaume Barbès* (No.35) was built in the second half of the 17C.

In 1642 Ninon de Lenclos lived at No.16 in the Rue Elzévir (leading off the N. side of the Rue des Francs-Bourgeois); No.8 has a good façade.

No.26, the *Hôtel de Sandreville* (late 16–18C); and No.30, the *Hôtel d'Alméras*, a red-brick mansion of the Henri-IV period, are noteworthy. The Allée des Arbalétriers (No.38) was one of the entrances to the *Hôtel Barbette* (see p188), and led to the field alongside the walls, once a practice ground for crossbowmen.

We now reach the transverse Rue Vieille-du-Temple, on the corner of which (r.; No.54) survives the pretty turret (c.1510; restored) of the *Hôtel Hérouët*.

A short distance S. is the **Hôtel des Ambassadeurs de Hollande** (No.47), built by *Cottard* in 1657–60 on the site of the house of the Maréchal de Rieux in front of which, returning from Isabeau de Bavière's residence (see below), the Duc d'Orléans was assassinated in 1407 by the hired bravos of Jean sans Peur (Duke of Burgundy).

The building was never in fact the property of the Dutch ambassadors, but in 1720–27 belonged to the chaplain of their Embassy, and its chapel was several times used for Protestant ceremonies. Mlle Necker (later Mme de Staël) was baptized there in 1766, and Franklin's daughter was married there. Beaumarchais also lived here, where he wrote his 'Mariage de Figaro'; in 1788 turning the house into a provident institution for poor nursing mothers.

Nos 36,24, and 15 (the *Hôtel de Vibraye*) further S., are of some interest.

For the N. half of this street, see below.

We next reach (l.) the church of **N.-D. des Blancs-Manteaux** (deriving its name from the white habits of an earlier order of mendicant monks established here in 1285 by Louis IX), the 18C door of which comes from the church of *St-Barthélemy* in the Île de la Cité, demolished in 1863. The church contains a rococo pulpit in the Flemish style (1749) and a good organ (restored).

At No.55 Rue des Francs-Bourgeois are the offices of the *Crédit Municipal*, formerly the Mont-de-Piété (a government pawnbroking establishment), founded by Louis XVI in 1777.

Among other striking houses in the Rue des Francs-Bourgeois are Nos 54, the *Hôtel de Camus*; 56, the *Hôtel de Fontenoy* (early 18C); 58, which belonged to Louis Le Tonnelier, baron de Breteuil, minister of Louis XVI; and 58bis, the *Hôtel d'Assy* (early 17C).

We now reach the imposing portal of the ***Hôtel de Soubise** (No.60; Pl.15;1), the greater part of which was built by *Delamair* in 1706–12 on the site of the mansion of the Duc de Guise. The **Archives Nationales** have been housed here since 1808, the presence of which has ensured the survival of the interior decoration (1712–45) by *Natoire, Boucher, Van Loo, Restout, Lemoyne*, etc. The splendid *Cour d'Honneur*, with its colonnade, has copies of the Four Seasons by *Robert Le Lorrain* on the façade.

The earlier entrance, the turreted Gothic gateway of 1380 (at No.58 Rue des Archives), was part of the *Hôtel de Clisson*, built in 1372–75 by the Constable Olivier de Clisson, a supporter of Charles V against the English. Bolingbroke (later Henry IV) gave a farewell banquet there in 1399 before setting out for England. During the English occupation of Paris (1420–35) Thomas, Duke of Clarence and later the Duke of Bedford lived here. With its purchase in 1553 by Anna d'Este, wife of François de Lorraine, Duc de Guise, it became the *Hôtel de Guise*, remaining in the family until 1696, when Anne de Soubise bought it. Another occupant during this period was Henri II de Lorraine, who killed the last of the Colignys in a duel in the *Pl. des Vosges* in 1643: his grandfather had instigated the murder of Adm. Coligny in the massacre of St Bartholomew. Here he entertained lavishly, and gave hospitality to Corneille.

The *Chapel* bears traces of the *Chapelle de Clisson* of 1375 transformed in 1533 for the Guise by *Primaticcio*. The *Oval Room* is a masterpiece of the style of transition from Louis XIV to Louis XV. Here and elsewhere are exhibited some of the outstanding documents arranged to show the development of French institutions, etc.

Among the earliest is a will of 627; others concern Clovis and Charlemagne. Letters from foreign potentates and statesmen include some from the Emperor Charles V, Christina of Sweden, Tamerlane, Franklin, and Washington, etc.; among treaties displayed are those of Brétigny, Westphalia, and the Pyrenees; the Edict of Nantes (with the signature of Henri IV) and its Revocation; the Oath of the Jeu de Paume; Marie-Antoinette's last letter, and Louis XVI's will; also his diary with 'rien' written against the date 14 July 1789, etc. The Orléans archives were donated to the Archives Nationales in 1969.

From the Rue des Archives, skirting the W. side of the Hôtel de Soubise leads the Rue de Braque, in which Nos 4–6, the *Hôtel Le Lièvre de la Grange*, is a fine late-17C mansion; No.7 belonged to Vergennes, foreign minister to Louis XVI and supporter of American Independence.

At the corner of the Rue des Archives and the Rue des Haudriettes, further N., is a fountain, with a naiad by *Mignot* (1765).

Diagonally opposite is the *Hôtel de Guénégaud* (No.60 Rue des Archives) by *Fr. Mansart* (c.1650), containing a **Musée de la Chasse**, and an exclusive Hunting Club (with an annexe at Chambord).

The first room displays a portrait, in falconer's costume, of Philip the Fair (father of Charles V), and 'La Chasse de Diane' by *Brueghel le Velours* and *van Balen*. Stairs ascend to rooms containing hunting weapons, powder flasks, daggers, crossbows, etc., and to the second floor. Here are collections of stuffed big game, swords, porcelain decorated with hunting scenes, and paintings by *François Desportes* (1661–1743), *Chardin, Oudry*, and *Carle Vernet*, among others.

No.62, adjacent, the *Hôtel de Montgelas* (1709), is noteworthy.

No.22 Rue des Quatre-Fils, leading S. E., was the home of the Marquise du Deffand (1697–1780). Her salon was frequented by Voltaire, Montesquieu, d'Alembert, Condorcet, Turgot, and Hénault. She later became blind, and Mlle de Lespinasse, her companion in 1756–64, set up a separate salon; see p100. No.20, retaining a fine doorway, was the residence, after 1800, of the Comte de Sèze (1748–1828), Louis XVI's lawyer.

In the Rue Charlot, leading N. E. from the Rue des Quatre-Fils, is *St-Jean-St-François*, built as a Capuchin chapel on the site of a tennis-court, and completed in 1715. No.7, opposite, the *Hôtel de Brévannes*, is partly 17C.

Continuing along the Rue des Quatre-Fils we shortly regain the Rue Vieille-du-Temple, at No.87 in which, a few paces to the r., stands the **Hôtel de Rohan,** known also as the *Hôtel de Strasbourg,* begun in 1704 by *Delamair.*

It was successively occupied by four cardinals of the Rohan family, all of whom were bishops of Strasbourg. From 1808 to 1925 the mansion was occupied by the *Imprimerie Nationale* (see Rte 7), after which it was thoroughly restored to house certain departments of the *Archives Nationales* not accommodated in the neighbouring *Hôtel de Soubise* (see above). In the second courtyard is a fine relief of the Horses of Apollo by *Robert Le Lorrain;* the *'Cabinet des Singes'* contains paintings by *Chr. Huet* (1745–50). It was here that the Card. Edouard de Rohan was arrested during the 'Affaire du Collier' (1783–84; see p255).

Slightly to the S., No.17 in the Rue Barbette, recalling the name of the *Hôtel Barbette,* the favourite residence of Isabeau de Bavière, which stood on this site, retains a mutilated door with two medallions.

From the intersection of the Rues Vieille-du-Temple and des Quatre-Fils we may make a detour towards the N. E. section of the Marais viâ the *Hôtel Salé* (see below), the garden façade of which may be approached by turning r. off the former street along the Rue des Coutures-St-Gervais, lined with a number of 17C houses.— Alternatively, we may follow the Rue de la Perle S. E. to the tastefully redeveloped PL. DE THORIGNY, just before reaching which we pass (r.; No.1) the restored ***Hôtel Libéral-Bruant,** built in 1685 for his personal use by the architect of Les Invalides. The pedimented façade, decorated with four busts in niches, is notable. The building now houses the **Musée de la Serrure* (or *Musée Bricard,* after Eugène Bricard, the 19C collector of this splendid decorative door-furniture, including locks, keys, handles, and plaques, etc. of all periods). A few minutes' walk to the S. E. will bring us back via the Rue Payenne, to the *Hôtel Carnavalet.*

We turn N. E. up the Rue de Thorigny, where at No.5 (l.) is the entrance to the ***Hôtel Salé,** (Pl.15;1) an impressive mansion also known as the *Hôtel Aubert de Fontenay,* after the financier for whom it was built in 1656–60 by *Jean Boullier de Bourges.* It was once called the *Hôtel de Juigné,* but became known as the *Hôtel Salé* on account of the huge profits its owner had made out of the salt tax. Its staircase is notable. The whole fabric has undergone a thorough and well-deserved restoration, and now houses a museum devoted to the work of *Pablo Ruiz Picasso* (1881–1973).

The ***Musée Picasso** comprises several thousand works of art by that prolific artist, given to the State in lieu of death duties, together with a number of canvases by other artists once owned by Picasso; see below. The collection includes among works *by* Picasso, some 230 paintings, 140 sculptures, 45 ceramics, almost 1,500 drawings and over 1,650 prints (displayed in rotation), apart from several 'constructions', etc. They are displayed in approx. chronological order, and are representative of most of his 'periods', although weak in youthful works.

Notable are his Self-portrait (with a blue background; 1901); Self-portrait unshaven; The two brothers; Les demoiselles d'Avignon (1907); Sculpted female head (Fernande); Still-life with a cane chair (1912); Portrait of Olga Khoklova seated (1917); Bathers (Biarritz, 1918); Jug and apples; Women running along a beach (1922); Paul 'en arlequin' and 'en pierrot'; Female bust (1932); Corrida (1933); Portrait of Marie-Thérèse Walter (1937); Portraits of Dora Maar (1937); Maya and her doll (1938); Massacre in Korea (1951); The picnic (after Manet; 1960, etc.); The young artist (1972); sculpted

Nanny-goats; and among drawings, etc., The frugal meal (1904), Young girl wearing a hat (c. 1920), and Minotaur (1936).

Also *Balthus*, The children; *Cézanne*, The Château Noir; *Corot*, Little Jeannette; *Miro*, Self-portrait; *Modigliani*, Seated girl; *Henri Rousseau*, Self-portrait with lamp, The artist's wife, likewise, and The sovereigns; *Renoir*, Seated bather; and works by *Braque*, *Matisse*, and *René-Hilaire de Gas* (1770–1858; grandfather of Edgar Degas).

It is likely that Marion Delorme died in a house on the site of No.2 in 1650. Nos 6, 8, and 10 were built together as the *Hôtel de Percey*; No.8 belonged to Mme de Sévigné in 1669–72.

The Rue Ste-Anastase leads r. off the Rue de Thorigny into the Rue de Turenne, where (r.) Nos 52–54 form the 17C *Hôtel de Montrésor*. No.56 was once the home of Scarron (1610–60; who died there) and his wife Françoise d'Aubigné (1635–1719; granddaughter of the poet Agrippa d'Aubigné), later Mme de Maintenon. Crebillon the elder died here in 1762; and Le Sage was a later occupier. No.60 is the *Hôtel du Grand-Veneur*, with a boar's head on the façade, while No.66 retains traces of the *Hôtel de Turenne*, built for the great marshal's father. On the site of the chapel of the convent later installed here, the church of *St-Denis-du-St-Sacrement* was built in 1835 in the Grecian style, by *Godde*. No.80, a short distance N., belonged to the Marquis de Launay, the last governor of the Bastille.

The nearby Rue Debelleyme, leading N. W., crosses the Rue Vieille-du-Temple, at the junction of which (No.110) is the *Hôtel d'Espinay* (which belonged to a favourite of Henri III), with a magnificent staircase. Nos 106–100 (to the l.) all preserve features of the early 17C, when they were built.—Just to the N., the Rue de Poitou leads back across the Rue de Saintonge, retaining some attractive façades, to the Rue Charlot (in which No.28, a short distance to the r., is the *Hôtel de Béramcourt*; 1690), across which we continue N. E. by the Rue Pastourelle, off which (r.) in the Rue de Beauce, Mlle de Scudéry (1607–1701) lived from 1670, and died.

To the l. in the Rue des Archives (the next main street), at No.70, died Lamennais (1782–1854), the subversive religious writer. No.78, to the r., was built by *Bullet* (c. 1660), with a beautiful staircase by *Le Muet*, and was the residence of Marshal Tallard (1712). Further N. at No.90 are traces of the *Hôpital des Enfants-Rouges*, founded by François I and his sister Marguerite in 1534, so-called because the children wore a red uniform.

Just beyond is the SQ. DU TEMPLE (Pl. 9;7), the centre of the densely populated Quartier du Temple, laid out in 1857 on the site of the late-12C stronghold of the Knights Templar, and the headquarters of their order in Europe until 1313, when it was occupied by the Order of St John.

The area owned by the Templars lay for the most part between this point and the *Pl. de la République*, to the N.E. (see Rte 13). Before the Revolution it was occupied by wealthy noble families, artisans who did not belong to the corporations and therefore were free from many restrictions, and debtors who were protected here from action for debt.

The palace of the Grand Prior of the Knights of St John was renowned for luxurious living, but with the Revolution the Tour du Temple, of 1265, was transformed into a prison, and in Aug. 1792 Louis XVI and the royal family were incarcerated here. On 21 Jan. 1793, the king was taken hence to the guillotine; Marie Antoinette was transferred to the *Conciergerie* on 2 Aug.; and on 9 May 1794, Mme Elisabeth was carried off to execution. The Dauphin (Louis XVII) is believed to have died here on 9 June 1795, and the sole survivor, Mme Royale (Marie Thérèse de France; 1778–1851), was released on 19 Dec. of the same year. Adm. Sir Sidney Smith escaped hence in 1798, after two years' imprisonment. The tower was demolished by Napoleon I, and its last vestiges were removed under Napoleon III.

A short distance to the N. (195 Rue du Temple) is the church of **Ste-Élisabeth**, founded in 1630 by Marie de Médicis. The façade is a copy of *Sta Maria Novella* at Florence. The main feature is the woodwork, including, in the ambulatory, 16C carvings of scriptural scenes from the abbey of *St-Vlaast* at Arras.

The Rue Réaumur leads W. from the Sq. du Temple, passing (l.) the Rue Volta, in which No.3, of c. 1300, is possibly the oldest surviving house in Paris. The Rue Réaumur crosses the Rue de Turbigo to meet the Rue St-Martin (the original Roman road from Lutetia to the N.) between the former priory of *St-Martin-des-Champs* (r.) and (l.) *St-Nicolas-des-Champs*.

The **Musée National des Techniques**, or *Conservatoire National des Arts et Métiers*, the Science Museum of Paris, with its entrance at No.292 Rue St-Martin (Pl.9;7), occupies the site of the ancient priory of *St-Martin-des-Champs*, the exterior of the *Church* of which is best seen from the Rue Réaumur, to the S.

During the Revolution, these were taken over by the Société des Jeunes Français, an educational institution, and later were used as a small-arms factory. In 1798 they were assigned to the Conservatoire des Arts et Métiers; which had been founded by a decree of the Convention in 1794, and here were assembled the collections of Vaucanson and other scientists. Its administrator was Joseph-Michel Montgolfier (1740–1810), who with his brother Jacques-Étienne (1745–99; a paper-manufacturer) were the inventors of the air-balloon (1783).

Two important buildings remain of the earlier priory, founded in 1060 by Henri I and presented to the Abbey of Cluny by Philippe I in 1079, which until the early 14C stood without the city walls.

To the r. of the entrance courtyard (its gateway is of 1850) is the ***Refectory**, a 13C masterpiece, built by *Pierre de Montreuil* (architect of the *Sainte Chapelle*). This remarkable hall (42·80 by 11·70m), its vaulting sustained by a central row of columns (recalling those of the *Église des Jacobins* at Toulouse), now accommodates the Library. Note the 13C reader's pulpit at the E. end. The external side of the S. doorway is a good example of decorated Gothic, and the sole relic of the original cloîsters. Further S. one may see the restored 13C portal of the church (not entered from here, but see below). The turret is a comparatively recent addition.

On the GROUND FLOOR are models of locomotives and rolling-stock; rooms on the l., and in the wing beyond, display an extensive collection of astronomical and surveying instruments; clocks (by Berthoud, Lepaute, Bréguet, Janvier, and other famous 18C clockmakers); and a collection of elaborate automata, including Marie-Antoinette's 'Joueuse de Tympanon'.

On the FIRST FLOOR, are rooms (l.) displaying examples of machinery employed in the processes of printing; apparatus used by Daguerre, Niepce, and Lumière, etc., in the pioneering days of photography and cinematography; and historical equipment illustrating the development of recording, television, radio-astronomy, etc.

To the r. on the First Floor, are rooms devoted to domestic lighting and heating; models of machines, including the 'Machine de Marly' (see Rte 22).

From the far end of this wing, steps descend to the former Abbey Church of **St-Martin-des-Champs**, now sheltering a curious congregation of cars and planes. Although 'restored' in 1854–80, the fabric of the Choir, with its 'chevet'

The apse of St-Martin-des-Champs

of chapels, is perhaps the earliest Gothic vault in Paris (1130–40), while the aisleless nave dates from the 13C.

Among the prototypes of the motor-car are Cugnot's steam-carriage of 1770, and one by Serpollet (1888); petrol-driven vehicles include a Panhard (1896), Peugeots of 1893 and 1909, a Berliet phaeton (1898), a De Dion-Bouton (1899), a Renault of 1900, etc. Among the aeroplanes are those of Ader (1897), Esnault-Pelterie (1906), the plane in which Blériot made the first flight across the Channel (1909), a Bréguet of 1911, etc.

Most other sections of the museum, including that devoted to agriculture, are at present closed or are being reformed.

At the N.W. corner of the building is the *Fontaine du Vertbois* (1712), which, with the adjoining tower, has been restored.

Adjacent is **St-Nicolas-des-Champs**, with a square tower, built in 1420 but enlarged in 1541–87, when the choir was rebuilt and the outer nave aisles added. At the Revolution, it served as the 'Temple of Hymen'. The original W. doors have survived, and the fine S. portal (c.1576), *after Philibert Delorme*, likewise retains its contemporary doors. There is good woodwork in the nave vestibule. Paintings include a Baptism of Christ by *Gaudenzio Ferrari*, and Madonna and Saints by *Amico Aspertini* (both c.1500). The ambulatory chapels have 17C wall-paintings; also (1st S. chapel), Our Lady of Victories (c.1610–20); and (6th chapel) a 14C Italian altarpiece. The Apostles at the tomb of the Virgin, with the Assumption (on the 17C high-altar), is by *Simon Vouet*.

Guillaume Budé (or Budaeus; 1468–1540), Théophile de Viau (1590–1626), Gassendi (1592–1655), the astronomer, and Mlle de Scudéry (1607–1701), are buried here.

We may regain the Rue du Temple by turning E. along the Rue des Gravilliers (just S. of *St-Nicolas-des-Champs*). Balzac lived at No.122 Rue du Temple in 1814–19; at No.13 Rue Chapon (the first turning r., going S.), with an interesting court, was the house of the archbishops of Reims. No.115 Rue du Temple marks the probable site of a residence of Jean Bart (1650–1702), a privateer created Admiral of the Fleet by Louis XIV. Nos 101–103, the *Hôtel de Montmorency*, the residence of Fouquet in 1652, has its entrance at No.5 Rue de Montmorency. No.51 in this street, the *Maison du Grand-Pignon*, restored in 1900, was built in 1407 by Nicolas Flamel.

The Rue Michel-Le-Comte, parallel to the S., retains a number of early 17C houses, including the *Hôtel Le Tellier* (No.16), with a fine courtyard; No.21, the home of Verniquet, architect to Louis XVI; and No.28, the *Hôtel d'Hallwyll*, by *C. Ledoux* (18C), and the birthplace of Mme de Staël (1766).

Nos 67–87, on the W. side of the Rue du Temple, provide a charming ensemble of 17C houses, of which Nos 71, 73, and 75 form the *Hôtel de St-Aignan*, built by *Le Muet* in 1640–50; the courtyards and gate are particularly elegant. No.79, dating from c.1620, but altered after 1751, is the *Hôtel de Montmor*, also with a good gateway and attractive pediment in the courtyard.

No.62 was the site of a house in which Anne de Montmorency, constable of France, died in 1567; No.41, the *Auberge de l'Aigle d'Or* (17C), is the last remaining example in Paris of a coaching inn of the period. The square turret on No.24 dates from 1610; and an inscription on No.17 indicates the site of the house of Du Guesclin (1372–80).

We regain the Rue de Rivoli at the *Hôtel de Ville* (see Rte 11).

13   The Grands Boulevards: From the Madeleine to the Pl. de la République

MÉTROS: *Concorde, Madeleine, Opéra, Richelieu-Drouot, Rue Montmartre, Bonne-Nouvelle, Strasbourg-St-Denis, République.*

The Grands Boulevards, a succession of wide thoroughfares extending in a curve from the Pl. de la Concorde to the Bastille, were laid out in 1670–85 on the site of the inner ramparts, demolished in previous decades. These had comprised the E. part of the 'enceinte de Charles V', erected after 1370, and the new fortifications to the W. built by Louis XIII in 1633–37.

Young visited them in 1787 after attending a theatre, and remarked: 'Coffee-houses ... music, noise and *filles* without end; everything but scavengers and lamps. The mud is a foot deep; and there are parts of the boulevards without a single light'. They have since changed in some respects.

Although the Western Boulevards are no longer the centre of

fashion they once were, they are still busy shopping and commercial areas.

The Rue Royale forms a convenient approach to the Boulevards from the PL. DE LA CONCORDE. As far as the Rue St-Honoré it is lined with uniform 18C houses, with shops below, including that of *Lalique*. No.3, *Maxim's*, was a haunt of 'high society' in the 1890s; the *Café Weber*, celebrated earlier in the century as a literary forum, stood at No.21. Mme de Staël lived briefly in 1816 at No.6; No.8 was the home of the architect Gabriel.

The street is dominated by the church of *St Mary Magdalen*, better known as the **Madeleine** (Pl.7;6), built in the style of a Roman temple, and surrounded by a majestic Corinthian colonnade.

Two earlier churches had been demolished unfinished in 1777 and 1789, before *P. Vignon* commenced work in 1806 on Napoleon's orders, who, before he had thought of the *Arc de Triomphe*, intended it as a 'Temple of Glory' for the 'Grande Armée'. It was finished by *Huvé* in 1842. In the pediment is a relief of the Last Judgement (restored), by *Lemaire*; the bronze doors are adorned with bas-reliefs from the Decalogue by *Triqueti* (1838). Some 300 insurgents were massacred here by M. Thiers's troops during the last days of the Commune.

The statue of St Luke at the back of the building was decapitated by a shell in May 1918 from 'Bertha', the German long-range gun.

The INTERIOR consists of a domed cella, meretriciously decorated and inadequately lighted. In chapels on either side of the entrance are the Marriage of the Virgin, by *Pradier*, and the Baptism of Christ, by *Rude*; the affected group of the Ascension of the Magdalen, on the high-altar, is by *Marochetti*.

The church stands in the centre of the PL. DE LA MADELEINE, on the E. side of which is a small flower market. At No.2 (now Thomas Cook's agency) stood the *Café Durand*, which played a dominant role in the 1848 Revolution, and where Zola wrote 'J'Accuse', an open letter denouncing the army, and in defence of Dreyfus, published in 'L'Aurore', 13 Jan. 1898.

Marcel Proust spent much of his youth at No.9 in the BLVD MALESHERBES, leading N.W. from the *Madeleine*, its S. section dominated by *St-Augustin*, an early example of the use of iron in church-construction (1860–71), by *Baltard*, architect of *Les Halles* (see Rte 11).

The BLVD DE LA MADELEINE, the westernmost of the Grands Boulevards, leads N.E. Marie Duplessis (1824–47), the prototype of 'La Dame aux Camélias', died at No.15 (formerly 11).—The *Crédit Foncier* occupies an 18C mansion in the neighbouring Rue des Capucines, leading S.E. towards the *Pl. Vendôme* (see Rte 10). The boulevard is continued by the BLVD DES CAPUCINES, crossing the *Pl. de l'Opéra* (see below). Offenbach (1819–80), who had lived in Paris since 1833, died at No.8 Blvd des Capucines.

Opposite the *Théâtre des Capucines*, the Rue Édouard-VII leads N. to a small Place containing an equestrian statue of Edward VII (by *Landowski*), who as Prince of Wales and King was a frequent visitor to Paris, and a promoter of the 'Entente Cordiale'.

At No.14 in the boulevard a tablet records the first exhibition of a cinema film (in the 'Salon Indien' of the *Grand Café*) given by the brothers Louis and Auguste Lumière (28 Dec. 1895). The first demonstration of X-rays, a discovery of Dr Roentgen, took place in the same room a few days later.

The ***MUSÉE COGNAC-JAY**, a small elegant collection of French 18C furniture and works of art, occupies three floors at No.25 Blvd des Capucins. It was originated by Ernest Cognac, founder of the 'Magasins de la Samaritaine', advised by Camille Gronkowski, then conservateur of the Musée du Petit Palais, and was inaugurated in 1929.

Its paintings and drawings, including a number by English artists, have recently been re-catalogued, and questionable attributions corrected, and some of the finer works are listed below.

One room on the third floor preserves panelling from the Château of Eu, in Normandy; and among furniture, much of it marquetry, is a good desk; also a Louis XVI bed, 'à la polonaise'; and a set of chairs covered with Beauvais tapestry. Among objets d'art three colourful 'Kien-Lung' porcelain birds are notable; also terracotta busts by *J.-B. Lemoyne* of the Maréchal de Saxe, and the Maréchal de Lowendal. Likewise a collection of Meissen porcelain and French terracotta figures, including *Clodion*, Project for the tomb of Mme Dubarry's Dog; and another collection of enamelled and jewelled boxes, etc.

Outstanding among the portraits are: *Boucher*, Mme Baudouin, his daughter; *Francis Cotes*, Charles Colmore; *Drouais*, Alexandrine Lenormant d'Étioles (daughter of Mme de Pompadour); *Daniel Gardner*, Lady Auckland and her daughter, and Albinia Hobart; *Baron Gérard*, Mme Bauquin du Boulay and her niece; *Marguerite Gérard*, Claude-Nicolas Ledoux, the architect; *Hugh Douglas Hamilton*, Lady Carhampton (?); *Adélaïde Labille-Guiard*, Comtesse de Maussion; *Largillière*, The Duchess of Beaufort (?); *Maurice Quentin Delatour*, Mme La Présidente de Rieux, Self-portrait, Man in a blue waistcoat, and The Marquis de Bérenger; *Lawrence*, Princess Clémentine de Metternich, and a copy of The Calmady children; *Lépicié*, La Coiffe blanche; *Nattier*, Madame Henriette, Marie Leczinska; *Perronneau*, Charles Lenormant du Coudrey; *Reynolds*, Lord Northington (once in an oval frame); attrib. to *Romney*, Female portrait; *John Russell*, Miss Power; *Mme Vigée-Lebrun*, The Vicomtesse de Mirabeau playing a guitar, and A Dancer; and an *anon.* Portrait of the Marquise de Sassenage.

Other works include *Boucher*, La belle cuisinière, and attrib. to him, The Music Lesson; *Canaletto*, two Venetian scenes; *Chardin*, Still life with a copper cauldron; *Morland*, The first steps; *Rembrandt*, Balaam's ass, an early work (1626); *Ruisdael*, The old oak; *G.-B. Tiepolo*, Cleopatra's banquet; *Watteau*, Assembly in the park; and a number of *galante* scenes by *Baudouin*, *Boilly*, *Jollain*, *Lavreince*, and *Mallet*, apart from representative works by *Boucher*, *Fragonard*, *Greuze*, *Guardi*, *Hubert Robert*, *Watteau*, et al.

At No.35 in the Blvd des Capucines, once the studio of Nadar (Félix Tournachon; 1820–1910), the portrait-photographer (and aeronaut), took place the exhibition of paintings (1874) by Renoir, Manet, Pissarro, and Monet, which included the latter's 'Impression—Soleil levant', which gave the group its name.

The PL. DE L'OPÉRA (Pl. 7;6), a busy focus of traffic, is dominated to the N. by the opera-house, while to the N.W. is the *Café de la Paix*, once a fashionable meeting-place for visitors to Paris.

The grandiose ***OPÉRA**, an appropriate monument to the most extravagant and brilliant period of the Second Empire, was built in 1861–75 from the designs of *Charles Garnier* (1825–98), the successful entrant of 171 competitors. Although covering a huge area, it contains only 2158 seats, few in comparison with some other large theatres.

*The ostentatious S. façade of Garniers's Opéra,
representative of the taste of the Second Empire,
embellished with numerous busts, statues, and medallions of
composers, some of whom are now totally ignored.*

The first opera-house in Paris was established in 1669 by Perrin, Cambert, and the Marquis de Sourdéac on the Left Bank, between the Rue de Seine and the Rue Mazarine, and the first director was Lully, under whom it acquired its secondary title of *Académie Royale de Musique.*

The façade, flanked by a flight of steps, is lavishly decorated with coloured marbles and sculpture. On either side of the arcade opening into the vestibule are allegorical groups, including (r.) The Dance, by *Carpeaux* (a copy of the original, which will grace the new *Musée d'Orsay*). Above are medallions of composers; and bronze-gilt statues of other composers and librettists are seen between the monolithic columns of the loggia. Behind the low dome of the auditorium is a triangular pediment crowned by a statue of Apollo of the Golden Lyre.

The E. pavilion in the Rue Halévy is the subscribers' entrance; to the W., in the Rue Auber, is the 'Pavillon d'Honneur', and the entrance to the *Museum* and *Library*, containing a complete collection of the scores of all operas and ballets performed here since its foundation and over 100,000 drawings of costumes, and scenery, and photographs of artistes, etc.

This latter entrance, originally known as the 'Pavillon de l'Empereur', was designed so that his coach could be driven up to the level of the dress circle—a precaution welcomed since Orsini's attempt on the life of Napoleon III on his way to the old Opera-house in 1858, and a device which won Garnier the competition, so it was rumoured: see Rue le Peletier, below.

Passing through two vestibules, the second containing the box-office (open 11.00–18.30), we reach the *Grand Staircase,* with its white marble steps 10m wide, and with a balustrade of onyx.and rosso and verde antico. On the first floor, where it divides, is the entrance to the stalls and the amphitheatre, flanked by caryatids, and on each floor are arcades of monolithic marble columns. The *Avant-Foyer* leads to the *Grand Foyer;* glass doors communicate with the Loggia overlooking the *Pl. de l'Opéra,* and by the middle door is a bust of Garnier by *Carpeaux.*

The *Auditorium,* resplendent in red plush and gilt, and with five tiers of boxes, is—except during performances—not normally on view, but visitors may, on making application, be allowed to join an escorted group. The dome, resting on eight pillars of scagliola, was redecorated in 1964, many would say inappropriately, by *Chagall*. The huge stage is 60m high, 52m wide, and 37m deep, behind which is the *Foyer de la Dance* (the scene of many paintings by Degas), with a mirror measuring 7 by 10m.

The AV. DE L'OPÉRA leads S.E. to the *Pl. André-Malraux* (see Rte 10), its southern reaches now more oriental than occidental in character! It is crossed by the Rue Louis-le-Grand, in which (at No.3) Mme de Montespan and the painter Hyacinthe Rigaud (1659–1743), who died at No.1, had houses; while Napoleon and Joséphine Beauharnais were married in 1796 at No.3 Rue d'Antin (the next cross-street), which was then the Mairie of the 2nd Arrondissement. The *Fontaine Gaillon* (1828), just to the E. in the Rue St-Augustin, is by *Visconti* and *Jacquot*.

Immediately behind the *Opéra*, facing the PL. DIAGHILEV, are the department stores of *Galeries Lafayette* (1898) and, to the W., *Du Printemps*, whose huge central halls should be seen to be believed.
   Just E. of the former is the Rue de la Chaussée-d'Antin, leading N. to *La Trinité* (see p201). In its S. section, at No.2, Rossini lived from 1857. No.5 (rebuilt) sheltered Mozart after the death of his mother, and was the residence of Chopin in 1833–36. No.7 (also demolished) was the home of the Neckers, who entertained Gibbon here; in 1798 it was bought by Jules Récamier, the banker, whose wife here presided over the most distinguished salon of the Directory, frequented also by Lord and Lady Holland, and many other English *en passage*.

The BLVD DES ITALIENS (the continuation N.E. of the *Blvd des Capucines*), whose many cafés have been largely replaced by cinemas .and commercial buildings, derived its name from the *Théâtre des Italiens* (1783), where Donizetti's 'Don Pasquale' was first performed in 1843. Grétry lived at No.7 from 1795 to 1813.
   In 1784–85, Jefferson had lodgings in the Impasse Taitbout (now Rue du Helder), leading left. No.5 Rue Taitbout, further E., was the house of Sir Richard Wallace, where Lord Hertford accumulated the works of art now in the Wallace Collection, London (see also p225). Wagner lived at No.25 in 1840–41.
   At the corner of the next street, the Rue Laffitte (named after Jacques Laffitte, 1767–1844, the financier), stood the house of Mme Tallien (1773–1835), daughter of the Spanish financier Cabarrus, and wife of the revolutionary, and later Princesse de Chimay. Part of the building (No.20) became the *Café Hardy*, rival of the *Café Riche* at No.16 ('Il faut être bien riche pour dîner chez Hardy, et bien hardi pour dîner chez Riche').

At the far end of Rue Laffitte is seen *N.-D.-de-Lorette* (Rte 14), with *Sacré-Coeur* in the background. No.17 was the residence of Queen Hortense of Holland, and here Napoleon III was born in 1808. From No.27, then Laffitte's residence, was issued the manifesto of Thiers proposing the coronation of Louis-Philippe. At Nos 39 and 41 stood Ambroise Vollard's art gallery, where many paintings by Gauguin and Cezanne were first displayed. Vollard was also responsible for the first exhibitions in Paris of works by Picasso and Matisse (in 1901 and 1904, respectively).
   It was in the parallel Rue Le Peletier (to the E.) that the 'Carbonaro' Orsini flung a bomb at the carriage conveying Napoleon III to the opera, killing or injuring 156 people, but leaving the emperor unharmed (1858). No.3 was the *Café du Divan*, frequented by Balzac, Gautier, de Nerval, and Baudelaire. On the site of No.6 stood the *Salle Le Peletier*, from 1821 until 1873, when it was burned out, the Opera-house. Here were first performed the works of Meyerbeer, and Wagner's 'Tannhäuser', among many others.

In the Rue de Marivaux (opposite) stands a building until recently the *Opéra-Comique*, but now housing an experimental *Opéra-Studio*.

The Opéra-Comique originated in a company which produced pieces during local fairs, and in 1715 purchased from the Opéra the right of playing vaudevilles interspersed with ariettas. Discord between the two theatres continued until in 1757 Charles Favart (1710–92) finally established the rights of the Opéra-Comique, which moved to the 'Salle Favart' on this somewhat confined site in 1783, since rebuilt.

At the junction of the boulevard with that of the BLVD MONTMARTRE and BLVD HAUSSMANN (the latter only extended to this point in 1927), the Rue Drouot leads N. past (No.6) the *Mairie of the 9th Arrondissement* in a mansion of 1746–48, and No.9 (l.), the *Hôtel des Ventes de Paris*, or **Nouveau Drouot**, the main auction-rooms of Paris, where important sales are held from Feb. to June, and which since 1801 has occupied the same place in Parisian life as Christie's or Sotheby's in London. It has been rebuilt recently in an ugly 'modern' style.

To the S., the Rue de Richelieu leads to the *Bibliothèque Nationale* (see Rte 10). Thomas Paine wrote 'The Age of Reason' at No.95 in this street (1793).

The short BLVD MONTMARTRE, in spite of its name, is some distance from Montmartre. At No.10 (l.) is the *Musée Grévin*, a waxwork collection equivalent to Mme Tussaud's.—On the r. is the Rue Vivienne, leading to the *Bourse*; the *Passage des Panoramas* (named after an entertainment displaying views of cities, introduced to Paris by the American Robert Fulton, who had also tested his first steamboat on the Seine in 1803); and the *Théâtre des Variétés*, scene of several Offenbach successes.

The Rue Montmartre leads S.E. towards *St-Eustache* (Rte 11), and was already so named in 1200.—Émile Zola (1840–1902) was born at No.10 Rue St-Joseph, a short distance S.

The Rue du Faubourg-Montmartre, diverging N.W. towards the 'suburb' of Montmartre, recalls the time when the boulevard formed the city boundary. Lautréamont (1846–70) died at No.7, where he had written 'Les Chants de Maldoror'.—The Rue Geoffroy-Marie, a turning off to the r. (commemorating a saddler and his wife who in 1260 presented to the *Hôtel-Dieu* a little farm which sold for over 3 million francs in 1840), leads to the titillating cabaret known as the *Folies Bergère* (originally the *Café Sommier élastique*, founded in 1869 to produce vaudevilles), situated in a mainly Jewish enclave, and a centre of the diamond trade.

Continuing E. along the BLVD POISSONNIÈRE (in which No.27 was Chopin's first Paris home, in 1831–32), we pass (r.) the Rue du Sentier, where, opposite the end of the Rue du Croissant, Mozart and his mother lodged in 1778. In the same year she was buried in the vanished *Cimitière St-Joseph* nearby, the original burial-place of Molière also.

Necker lived in 1766–89 at the junction of the adjacent Rue de Mulhouse and the Rue de Cléry (in a house replaced by No.29) and here every Friday Mme Necker (Suzanne Churchod; 1739–94) held her salon, frequented by Voltaire, Diderot, d'Alembert, Marmontel, Buffon, et al.

To the N., at No.2 Rue du Conservatoire (beyond the Rue Rougemont), is the *Conservatoire National d'Art Dramatique*, a small theatre of 1802, reputed for its excellent acoustics.

The boulevard is now crossed by the Rue Poissonnière (r.) and its N. extension, the Rue du Faubourg-Poissonnière, both named after the fishmongers who used to pass by on their way to the *Halles*. Beyond this junction, the line of boulevards is continued by the BLVD DE BONNE-NOUVELLE, on the N. side of which is the façade (1887) of the *Théâtre du Gymnase*, where Rachel made her début in 1837.

At the far end of the next street running N. we see the church of *St-Vincent-de-Paul* (see Rte 14).
    To the S. steps lead up to *N.-D. de Bonne-Nouvelle*, rebuilt in 1824. André Chénier (1762–94) lived in 1793 at 97 Rue de Cléry, close by; the same street was Corneille's home in 1665–81.

The short BLVD ST-DENIS (Pl. 9;5) lies between the *Porte St-Denis* and the *Porte St-Martin*, beyond which the *Blvd St-Martin* continues as far as the *Pl. de la République*. The **Porte St-Denis**, a triumphal arch 23m high, designed by *Blondel*, was erected in 1672 to commemorate the victories of Louis XIV in Germany and Holland.

The bas-reliefs were designed by *Girardon* and executed by the brothers *Anguier*. It faces the Rue St-Denis, or 'Voie Royale', once the processional route of entry into Paris, and last so used on the occasion of Queen Victoria's visit in 1855.

On the far side of the BLVD DE SÉBASTOPOL, which with its N. extension, the BLVD DE STRASBOURG, stretches from the *Pl. du Châtelet* to the *Gare de l'Est*, we pass the **Porte St-Martin**, another supererogatory triumphal arch in honour of Louis XIV, c.18m high, built in 1674 by *Bullet*, and decorated with bas-reliefs of contemporary campaigns, by *Desjardins* and *Marsy* (S. side), and *Le Hongre* and the elder *Legros* (N.).

At No.6 in the *Blvd St-Denis* stood the 'Cinéma Saint-Denis', opened in 1896 by the brothers Lumière, which claimed to be the first cinema.

The Rue St-Martin (the original Roman road leading N. from Lutetia) leads S. to the *Conservatoire National des Arts et Métiers*, and *St-Nicolas-des-Champs* (see Rte 12), off which the Rue N.-D. de Nazareth diverges l. The façades of Nos 41–49 are of interest; Rudolf Diesel (1858–1913), the inventor of the engine which bears his name, was born at No.38.

We pass two famous theatres in the BLVD ST-MARTIN, just E. of the Arch, the *Théâtre de la Renaissance* and *Théâtre de la Porte-St-Martin*, both rebuilt after being burnt down during the Commune.

The 'Renaissance' was managed by Sarah Bernhardt in 1893–99. The 'Porte-St-Martin', in its original form a foundation of Marie-Antoinette (who had it built in seventy-five days in 1781 to house the opera), is remembered as being the theatre of Frédérick Lemaître (1800–76), and here Coquelin aîné (who created the name-part in Rostand's 'Cyrano de Bergerac') was seized by a mortal illness during a rehearsal of 'Chantecler' in 1909.
    Paul de Kock (1794–1871), the novelist, died at No.8.

The **Pl. de la République** (Pl. 9;8), on the site of the Porte du Temple, and the junction of seven important thoroughfares, was laid out in 1856–65 by Haussmann for strategic reasons, but it has maintained a political role as the scene of radical manifestations. The pedestal of the *Monument de la République* (1883; 25m high), has bronze bas-reliefs by *Dalou*.
    At the corner of the Rue Leon-Jouhaux (previously Rue de la Douane) leading N.E. from the Place, was Daguerre's workshop (1822–35). Gounod's 'Faust' was first performed in 1859 in the *Théâtre Lyrique*, one of many (including 'Des Funambules', 1816–62)

which stood on a section of the BLVD DU TEMPLE demolished by Haussmann, known earlier in the 19C from the melodramas enacted here as the 'Boulevard du Crime', and immortalized by Carné in the film 'Les Enfants du Paradis' (1945).

Beyond the *Pl. de la République* the boulevards are of little interest, and change their character. The BLVD DU TEMPLE, with its continuations, leads S.E. to the *Pl. de la Bastille* (see Rte 12). Flaubert lived at No.42 in this boulevard in 1856–69; and a little to the N. is the site of the house from which Fieschi discharged his 'infernal machine' at Louis-Philippe in 1835, killing Marshal Mortier and several others, but not the king.—Just to the W., at No.5 in the parallel street named after him, died Béranger (1780–1857).

14   Gare de l'Est to Gare St-Lazare (Faubourg St-Martin and Faubourg St-Denis)

MÉTROS. *République, Gare de l'Est, Gare du Nord, Poissonnière, N.-D.-de-Lorette, Trinité, St-Lazare, St-Augustin, Madeleine.*

The BLVD DE MAGENTA leads N.W. from the *Pl. de la République* to meet the outer boulevards beyond the *Gare du Nord*.

Just E. of its intersection with the BLVD DE STRASBOURG is **St-Laurent**, one of the oldest foundations in Paris. Gregory of Tours mentions that a church existed here near the Roman road as early as 583.

The present building, begun before 1429, retaining an older N. tower, was continued in the 16–17C, the nave having been vaulted in 1655–59, and the choir remodelled at the same time, with a high-altar by *Ant. Le Pautre*. The *Lady Chapel* dates from 1712. The 17C façade was demolished in 1862–65, when the Flamboyant W. front was built and the St-Laurent spire erected. The roof has elegantly carved pendentives. Mme du Barry (Jeanne Bécu; 1746–93) was married here in 1764.

The courtyard of the **Gare de l'Est** (Pl. 9;3; the terminus of the line to Strasbourg, etc.) just to the N., occupies the site of the medieval St Lawrence fair.

To the W. of the boulevard at this point stood the *Prison de St-Lazare* (since 1935 partly demolished and rebuilt as a hospital), from 1632 the headquarters of the Lazarists or Priests of the Mission, founded in 1625 by St Vincent de Paul (1576–1660). Among its inmates were André Chénier and Hubert Robert.

The boulevard next crosses the Rue La Fayette before passing (r.) the **Gare du Nord**, by *Hittorf* (1863), the terminus of the line from Calais, Boulogne, etc. (Pl.9;3), and also of a rapid shuttle service to the *Charles de Gaulle airport*.

There is little of interest in the thickly populated cosmopolitan Quartier de la Chapelle to the N. Adjacent to the ugly modern basilica stands the 13C *St-Denis-de-la-Chapelle*, much restored, where Joan of Arc received communion in Nov. 1429 before besieging the walls of Paris.

Turning S.W. along the Rue La Fayette, we pass (r.) *St-Vincent-de-Paul* (1824–44), by *Lepère* and *Hittorf*, with two square towers dominating a pedimented portico of twelve Ionic columns, and approached by a monumental flight of steps.

At No.58 Rue d'Hauteville, leading S., is the *Hôtel de Bourrienne*

(1787), finely decorated in First Empire style by Napoleon's secretary.

This street is crossed by the Rue de Paradis, where at No.30bis is the shop of the glass-maker Baccarat, replacing one existing since 1764, with a *Museum* adjoining. At No.18 in this street is the **Musée de la Publicité** (posters; adm. 12.00–18.00, except Tues.), opened in 1978 as a department of the Union Centrale des Arts Decoratifs, containing the Pochet, Buquet, and Roger Braun collections, among others. Its computerised catalogue is of assistance in searching for subjects, etc. among over 70,000 examples. The colourful entrance cannot be overlooked.

Corot (1796–1875) died at No.56 in the Rue du Faubourg-Poisson-nière, further W.; No.9 Rue de Montholon (leading E. from the SQ. DE MONTHOLON) was the residence of Liszt in 1831.

We shortly diverge due W. along the Rue de Châteaudun, passing (r.) **N.-D.-de-Lorette**, another of the drearily magnificent basilican churches of the early 19C, built in 1823–36, with a portico of four Corinthian columns, by *Hippolyte Lebas*.

Bizet (1838–75), born at No.26 Rue de la Tour-d'Auvergne (leading off the Rue des Martyrs, ascending behind the church), was christened here.—The Rue des Martyrs, the ancient approach to Montmartre, was already well known for its 'cabarets' in the 18C; Géricault (1791–1824) died at No.49, later occupied by Béranger.

The Rue N.-D.-de-Lorette ascends N.W. from the church through a quarter whose name was synonymous with the *demi-mondaine* or *femmes entretenues* of the mid-19C who congregated here, and to whom newly-built dwellings in the neighbourhood were let off cheaply until the plaster dried! These 'Lorettes', a favourite subject of the caricaturist Gavarni (1801–66), are represented on his monument in the small PL. ST-GEORGES, which the street crosses. Delacroix lived from 1844 to 1857 at No.58 (then 54) in the Rue N.-D.-de-Lorette; Gauguin was born at No.56 in 1848; while at No.27 in the Place is the *Hôtel Thiers*.

This latter building, burned down by the Communards, was the residence of President Thiers (1797–1877), and reconstructed, it now contains the *Bibliothè-que Thiers* (80,000 vols on the history of France since the Revolution; and the Napoleonic collection of Frédéric Masson, of 30,000 vols; drawings by *David*; bust of Joséphine by *Houdon*, etc.). Permission to visit should be requested of the Librarian, Institut de France, 23 Quai de Conti.

At No.28, opposite, Thérèse Lachman, later Marquise de Païva, held her salons in 1851–66, at which the brothers Goncourt, Gautier, Sainte-Beuve, Taine, and Wagner, were frequent visitors: see also Rte 16A. Mallarmé (1842–98) was born in the nearby Rue Laferrière (No.12).

The, Rue St-Georges runs downhill, and crosses the Rue de Châteaudun. The Goncourt brothers lived at No.43 from 1849 to 1868. Auber (1782–1871) lived for thirty years and died at No.22; Henry Murger (1822–61), author of 'Scènes de la Vie de Bohème', was born the son of a concierge at No.19.

In the Rue Taitbout (parallel to the W.) lodged Rossini (at No.28), when musical director of the *Théâtre des Italiens* (1824–25); and Mirabeau (1749–91) died at No. 42.

In 1842–47 Chopin and George Sand lived at Nos 5 and 9 respectively in the SQ. D'ORLÉANS, off the E. side of the N. end of this street.—At No.14 Rue de la Rochefoucauld, to the W. at this level, is the *Musée Gustave-Moreau* (adm. 10:00–13.00, 14.00–17.00 except

Mon. and Tues.), containing an extensive collection of paintings and drawings left by Moreau (1826–98) to the State.

To the W. stands *La Trinité*, a conspicuously ugly church built in 1863–67 by *Ballu* in a hybrid style, with a tower 63m high. It was erected on the site of the disreputable Cabaret de la Grande Pinte, later Les Porcherons.

From a point N.E. of the church, the Rue Pigalle and Rue Blanche ascend N.E. and N. towards Montmartre. To the W. of the church the Rue Clichy (in which, at No.21, Hugo lived in 1880) ascends N. to the *Pl. de Clichy*. No.16 is the *Casino de Paris*, a famous music-hall.—To the S., the Rue de Mogador leads to the *Opéra*.

The Rue St-Lazare leads W. from the sq. de la trinité. Mme Vigée-Lebrun died at No.29 in 1842. Just E. of the **Gare St-Lazare** (Pl. 7; 4), the Rue d'Amsterdam leads N., in which lived Manet (at No.77; in 1879–83) and Alexandre Dumas, père (No.97; from 1854).

The station itself is the terminus of the western region of the S.N.C.F. The *Hôtel Terminus* was the home of Georges Feydeau in 1909–19, who, intending to stay a week while his family moved house, remained a decade.

To the W. of the station, the Rue de Rome leads N.W., in which No.89 was the home of Mallarmé from 1885, and here his friends would congregate on Tuesday evenings.

At No.14 Rue de Madrid, diverging W. off this street, is the **Conservatoire National Supérieur de Musique** (Pl. 7;3), founded in 1765 as the *Académie Royale de Chant*, amalgamated with the École de Déclamation Dramatique in 1786, and refounded in 1795. It moved to these buildings, formerly a Jesuit college, in 1911. There is a plan to move both the Conservatoire and its museum of musical instruments to a site at La Villette.

Among past directors have been Cherubini (1796–1842), Auber (1842–71), Ambroise Thomas (1871–96), the academic Théodore Dubois (1896–1905; during whose period the institution four times rejected Ravel's attempts to win the Prix de Rome), Gabriel Fauré (1905–20), Henri Rabaud (1920–40), and Marcel Dupré (1954–56). Among pupils were Florent Schmitt, Charles Koechlin, Georges Enesco, and Paul Dukas.

The ***MUSÉE INSTRUMENTAL** (adm. 14.00–16.00 Wed.–Sat.) originated in the Clapisson collection, and now contains over 4000 instruments, unfortunately displayed in a somewhat cramped space. Of particular importance and interest are the collections of medieval, Renaissance, and 17C instruments, which have again come into their own, together with the *vielle à roue* or hurdy-gurdy. Among earlier items is a Bible-regal (16C German); a clavecin (Venice; 1543); a variety of lutes, viols, theorbos, basset-horns, spinets, harpsichords (outstanding amongst which is one of 1646 by *Andreas II Ruckers*), clavichords, virginals (including a fine example by Ruckers), square pianos, harps, finely decorated guitars, a curious one-stringed marine-trumpet, and a unique octobasse (c.1850), constructed by *J.-B. Vuillaume*. Also representative brass, woodwind, and percussion instruments of all periods. The collections of stringed instruments (some owned by Lully, Kreutzer, and Sarasate), including 5 violins by *Antonio Stradivari* of Cremona, and others by *Amati*, and *Guarneri*, are notable. Among pianos are examples manufactured by *Erard, Pleyel* (including Chopin's, and Bizet's), *Longman and Broderip*, etc. Other instruments of historic or artistic interest are Beethoven's clavichord (1786), Marie-Antoinette's harp, and Adolphe Sax's saxophone.

Since 1967 a department for the restoration of old instruments has flourished; and constructional plans of early examples can be bought. The *Library* contains an extensive collection of photographs of instruments, but the valuable series of scores, books on music, and MSS. (including Mozart's 'Don Giovanni'), are now preserved in the *Bibliothèque Nationale*.

Jules Renard (1864–1910), author of 'Poil de Carotte', died at No.44 Rue du Rocher, to the W., where he had lived since 1888.

The Rue du Havre leads S. from the *Gare St-Lazare*, where No.8, the *Lycée Condorcet*, founded in 1804, occupies the former buildings (with a Doric cloister court) of a Capuchin convent; on the site of its chapel (in the parallel street to the E.) is *St-Louis d'Antin*, by *Brongniart* (1782). Proust was but one of the school's many famous pupils.

The street is continued S. of the *Blvd Haussmann* by the Rue Tronchet (in which Chopin lived, at No.5, in 1839–42) to the *Madeleine* (see Rte 13).

The BLVD HAUSSMANN, one of the main streets in the area, commemorates Eugène-Georges, Baron Haussmann (1809–91) who, as Préfet de la Seine, initiated extensive urban development in central Paris. Work began here in 1857 as part of a scheme to construct an unbroken thoroughfare from the *Blvd Montmartre* to the *Arc de Triomphe*, and was only completed in 1926.

A short distance to the W., on the S. side of the *Blvd Haussmann*, is the SQ. LOUIS XVI (Pl. 7;5), formerly the *Cimetière de la Madeleine*, where rest the bodies of the victims of the panic of 1770 in the *Pl. de la Concorde* (see Rte 8), the Swiss guards massacred on 10 Aug. 1792, and all those guillotined between 26 Aug. 1792 and 24 March 1794 (among them Charlotte Corday and Philippe-Égalité).

The **Chapelle Expiatoire** (CN) (adm. 10.00–17.00 or 18.00), erected in 1815–26 from the plans of *Percier* and *Fontaine*, stands in the S.W. corner of the Square. The chapel, in the style of a classical funeral temenos, was built by order of Louis XVIII and dedicated to the memory of Louis XVI and Marie-Antoinette, whose remains, first interred in the graveyard on this site, were removed to St-Denis in 1815.

In the interior are two marble groups: Louis XVI and his confessor Abbé Henry Essex Edgeworth (1745–1807), by *Bosio* (below which is inscribed the king's will, dated 25 Dec. 1792); and Marie-Antoinette supported by Religion, by *Cortot*, the latter figure bearing the features of Mme Élisabeth. (Below is inscribed a letter said to have been written by the queen to her sister-in-law from the Conciergerie on 16 Oct. 1793.) The bas-relief by *Gérard* above the doorway represents the removal of the remains to St-Denis.

15 Montmartre

Best approached from the MÉTRO stations of *Clichy, Lamarck-Caulaincourt*, or *Anvers*.

The PL. DE CLICHY (Pl. 7;2) was the site of the 'Barrière de Clichy', which on 30 March 1814 was defended against the Russians by pupils from the École Polytechnique and the Garde Nationale under

Moncey, an action commemorated by a bronze group by *Doublemard* (1869).

To the E. lies the wide BLVD DE CLICHY, forming, with its continuation, the BLVD DE ROCHECHOUART, the S. boundary of Montmartre proper.

The first turning r. off the Blvd. de Clichy, the Rue de Douai (where at No.30, the house of Turgenev and Mme Viardot, the singer, Dickens met George Sand in 1856), whom he found 'just the kind of woman in appearance whom you might suppose to be the Queen's monthly nurse'. The street shortly crosses the PL. ADOLPHE-MAX, in which Vuillard had a studio. Zola (1840–1902) died at No.21bis Rue de Bruxelles, crossing this square; and Berlioz (1803–69) died at No.4 Rue de Calais, leading S.E.

The *Blvds de Clichy* and *de Rochechouart* are now the focus of the seedy night life of an increasingly sordid area, where *colour*-ful and motley crowds congregate in the cafés and around the so-called 'cabarets artistiques' of the PL. BLANCHE, on the N. side of which stood the *Moulin Rouge*, built 1889, where one of its star performers was Joseph Pujol, (1857–1945, 'Le Pétomane'), and PL. PIGALLE, etc.

A century has passed since *Montmartre* was rendered easier of access by the construction of new streets ascending through the N. slums, and poorer artists, migrating there because it was both picturesque and cheap, made it for about thirty years an artistic centre, vividly depicted by Toulouse-Lautrec (1864–1901), among others, whose studio was at No.5 Av. Frochot, near the *Pl. Pigalle*.—No.16 in the adjacent Rue Frochot was the home of Mme Sabatier ('La Présidente'), often the rendezvous of de Musset, Flaubert, Sainte-Beuve, Gautier, and Baudelaire.

About 1881 the famous 'Le Chat Noir' (No.84 Blvd de Rochechouart; closed in 1897) was opened, and the advertisement thus given to the attractions of the district invited a tide of pseudo-bohemians, tourists, and less desirable hangers-on, before which the serious artists retired, and have now all but vanished. There remain, however, a few old-fashioned streets and backwaters, made familiar in the paintings of Utrillo, among others, and an hour or two may be pleasantly spent wandering around the 'Butte' (see below), preferably during daylight.

Seurat and Signac had adjoining studios at No.128bis BLVD DE CLICHY in 1886; Seurat (1859–91) died at No.39 Rue André-Antoine (leading N. from the Pl. Pigalle). Picasso lived at No.130 in 1909; and Degas died at No.6 in 1917.

The short Av. Rachel, the first turning on the l. off the *Blvd. de Clichy*, as we walk E., leads to the main entrance of the **Cimetière de Montmartre**, on the W. slope of the Butte (Pl. 7;2).

Although less important than that of *Père-Lachaise*, it contains the graves of many famous 18–20C figures, among whom may be listed Gautier, de Vigny, the Goncourt brothers, Alex. Dumas (fils), Stendhal, Heine, Murger, Zola, Feydeau, Maxime du Camp, Renan, and Giraudoux; among composers, Berlioz, Delibes, Offenbach, Halévy, Adam, and Ambroise Thomas; also Adolphe Sax; among artists, Fragonard, Greuze, Delaroche, Horace Vernet, and Degas; the actors Frederic Lemaître and Louis Jouvet; the dancers Vestris, Taglioni, and Nijinsky; Mme Récamier, Pauline Viardot, and Marie Duplessis ('La Dame aux Camélias'); Ampère, and Dr Charcot.

From the *Pl. de Clichy*, the Rue Caulaincourt is carried over the cemetery by a viaduct, the latter being the most convenient approach to Montmartre by car.—Continuing along the BLVD DE CLICHY, we pass (l.) the once-famous *Moulin Rouge* (now a cinema; see above), facing the PL. BLANCHE, and turn l. up the steep Rue Lepic (at No.54 lived van Gogh in 1886) towards the rebuilt *Moulin de la Galette*. Turning E. along the Rue Norvins, we shortly reach the central PL. DU TERTRE (Pl.

8;1–2), with the former Mairie (No.3), now much commercialised, and surrounded by cafés, etc.

To the E. of the *Pl. du Tertre* stands the old church of **St-Pierre-de-Montmartre**, the successor of an earlier church erected to commemorate the martyrdom of St Denis, a relic of a Benedictine nunnery founded in 1134 by Adélaïde de Savoie (d. 1154). It was consecrated in the presence of her son Louis VII by Pope Eugenius III in 1147. In 1794 it served as the 'Temple of Reason'. The façade dates from the time of Louis XIV. Inside, against the W. wall, are two ancient columns with 7C capitals, the date also of two other capitals, one at the apse entrance and another in the N. aisle. The nave has 15C vaulting; the aisle vaulting was added in a restoration of 1900–05. The apse also has been almost entirely rebuilt, but the choir retains perhaps the earliest example of an ogee arch in Paris (1147). The foundress's tomb lies behind the altar.

In the *Jardin du Calvaire*, S. of the church, are stations of the Cross executed for Richélieu; to the N. of the building S foundations of a Roman temple have been discovered, while in the derelict graveyard is the tomb of the navigator Bougainville (1729–1811); also buried here is the sculptor Pigalle (1714–85), and members of the Fitz-James family.

The Rue Azaïs, to the S., leads past a water-tower to the terrace below the *Basilique du Sacré-Coeur*, with extensive views S. over the entire city with its changing denticulated horizon. Commanding Paris in this way, the history of the Butte Montmartre is one long series of sieges and battles.

The **Butte Montmartre** rises 130m above sea-level and 104m above the level of the Seine (traditionally the highest point in Paris; comp. *Belleville*), and the name has been variously derived from Mons Mercurii, Mons Martis, and Mons Martyrum. Of these, the two first presuppose the existence of a Roman temple on the hill; the last the probability that St Denis and his companions, SS Rusticus and Eleutherius, were beheaded at the foot of the hill, St Denis afterwards walking to the site of the Basilica of St-Denis (see Rte 23), 'with his head in his hands'. The *Chapelle du Martyre* (in the convent at 9 Rue Yvonne-le-Tac, just E. of the Métro Abbesses) occupies the probable position of a chapel erected on the site of the martyrdom. It was in the crypt beneath this that Ignatius of Loyola and his six companions, including Francis Xavier, took the first Jesuit vows, in 1534, thus founding the Society of Jesus. It was occupied by Henri of Navarre in 1589, and here in 1814 took place the final struggle between the French and the Allies.

Here on 18 March 1871 Génerals Thomas and Lecomte were murdered by insurgents when attempting to seize cannon entrusted to the National Guards, an insensate action which precipitated the Communard rebellion.

In 1873 the National Assembly decreed the building of a basilica here as an expiatory offering after the Franco-Prussian War of 1870–71. **SACRÉ-COEUR**, the resulting erection, only too visible from almost every part of Paris, is a conspicuous oriental-looking white stone edifice in a neo-Romanesque-Byzantine style derived from *St-Front* at Périgueux. Its ugliness does not seem to deter a constant press of visitors; see Pl. 8;2.

Work was begun in 1876 from the plans of *Abadie* (who had restored *St-Front*), and although used for services in 1891, it was not consecrated as a basilica until 1919. 100m long, and 75m across the ambulatory, it is surmounted by a dome 83m high, and abutted by a square bell-tower. The undaunted tourist may survey its meretriciously decorated interior, and, for a fee, visit both the crypt and dome (for the panoramic view).

Hence flights of steps descend the steep slope of the Butte to the SQ. WILLETTE (a funicular railway on its W. side will assist those making the ascent here), whence the Rue de Steinkerque leads downhill to the Pl. d'Anvers and Blvd. de Rochechouart.

Not much remains of 'Old Montmartre', with its cottages and little gardens, although in the Rue des Saules, leading N. from the Rue Norvins, one may see the last surviving vineyard of Paris. No.4 in this street is 'Au Lapin Agile', made famous by its artistic clientele. Harriet Smithson (Mme Berlioz; d. 1854), Honegger (1892–1955), and Utrillo (1883–1956) are buried in the nearby *Cimetière St-Vincent*.

At No.42 Rue des Saules is the *Musée d'art Juif*.

At No.17 in the Rue St-Vincent, to the r. beyond the vineyard, steps climb to the *Musée de Vieux-Montmartre*, installed in a 17C house once belonging to Roze de Rosimond, a member of Molière's 'Illustre Théâtre'. It contains, apart from ephemera and material of very local interest, a small collection of Clignancourt (or Montmartre) porcelain, made in 1767–99 in a pottery at the junction of the Rues du Mont-Cenis and Marcadet. This house was occupied by Renoir in 1875, and later by Utrillo, and Dufy, among others.

At the corner of the Rue St-Vincent, at No.24 Rue du Mont-Cenis (house rebuilt) lived Berlioz and Harriet Smithson in 1834–37.

Not far S. of the Rue Norvins, the PL. ÉMILE-GOUDEAU was a favourite 'artistic' residence c. 1910, where (at No.13, the 'Bateau-Lavoir'; rebuilt since burnt out in 1970) lived Modigliani, Picasso, and Max Jacob, and where a banquet was given in honour of Douanier Rousseau.

16 From the Pl. de la Concorde to the Arc de Triomphe

A. Viâ the Champs-Élysées

MÉTROS: Concorde, Champs-Élysées-Clemenceau, Franklin D. Roosevelt, George-V, Charles de Gaulle-Étoile.

To the W. of the *Pl. de la Concorde* (see Rte 8) extend the *Champs-Élysées*, through which the wide *Av. des Champs-Élysées* gently ascends to the *Arc de Triomphe*. The lower-lying area, drained and planted in 1670 according to Le Nôtre's designs, was rearranged in 1770 by the Marquis de Marigny (brother of Mme de Pompadour), who extended the avenue to the Pont de Neuilly in 1774. Cossacks encamped there in 1814, as did English troops in the following year. It must be admitted that however fashionable a promenade it may have been under the Second Empire, time has treated it harshly, and although still crowded, few of its attractions are of an aesthetic nature, however superb may be the vistas.

The **Champs-Élysées** consist of two parts; the first, forming a park, extends to the ROND-POINT DES CHAMPS-ÉLYSÉES; hence the increasingly commercialized avenue, largely flanked by the offices of airline companies, car showrooms, cinemas, banks, and a few expensive cafés, continues N.W. towards the commanding bulk of the *Arc de Triomphe*, a striking silhouette against the setting sun.

Skirting the N. side of the *Champs-Élysées* is the Av. Gabriel, with the *American Embassy* (1931–33) at the corner of the Rue Boissy-d'Anglas, built on the site of a mansion of 1769 belonging to Laurent Grimod de la Reynière, a noted gourmand, and later by his more famous son, Alexandre-Balthazar (1758–1838), author of the 'Almanach des Gourmands', etc.

Further on (r.) are the gardens of the British Embassy, and then those of the *Palais de l'Élysée* (see Rte 16B).

From the PL. CLEMENCEAU, the Av. de Marigny leads N., off which (l.) is the *Théâtre Marigny*, and an open-air stamp market (Thurs. and Sun.); to the S. the Av. Winston Churchill, with a fine view of *Les Invalides* (see Rte 7), leads between the *Petit-Palais* (l.) and *Grand Palais*, both built for the Exhibition of 1900, to the wide *Pont Alexandre-III* (1896–1900, a single steel arch 107·50m in length).

The **PETIT-PALAIS**, or *Musée des Beaux-Arts de la Ville de Paris* (Pl. 7;7), in itself a building of no great merit (1900, by *Girault*), contains various **Collections of paintings,*, etc., donated to the city by private collectors, which are often unjustifiably ignored by the visitor. Unfortunately the quality of display leaves something to be desired. It is often the site of temporary exhibitions.

MÉTRO: *Champs-Élysées-Clemenceau*. The entrance, with a domed vestibule, is in the Av. Winston-Churchill, on its W. side.

The collections may be roughly divided into four sections. First the 19–early 20C **French** paintings, including representative canvases by *Édouard Vuillard*, *Pierre Bonnard*, and *Gustave Courbet*, with the latter's Portrait of M. Corbinaud, of his Father, a Self-portrait with his dog, and Pierre-Joseph Proudhon and his children. Among other important works may be mentioned: *Cézanne*, Portrait of Ambroise Vollard, and wall-panels of the Seasons (signed 'Ingres' in derision); *Gauguin*, Old man with a stick; *Toulouse-Lautrec*, the Nice mail-coach, Portrait of André Rivoire; *Renoir*, Portrait of A. Vollard, Woman with a rose; *Mary Cassatt*, Head of a girl (pastel), Portraits of Lydia Cassatt and of 'M.D.'; Landscapes by *Sisley* and *Pissarro*; *Monet*, Sunset at Lavacourt; *Manet*, Portrait of M. Duret; *Marie Bashkirtseff*, Self-portrait; *Berthe Morisot*, A young girl, In the park; *Baudry*, Mme Singer; *Sargent*, Mme Allouard-Jouan; *Bonnat*, Mme Ehrler.

Paintings of the **Dutch** school include: *W. van de Velde*, Marine views; *Hobbema*, Mills, Forest scene; *van Goyen*, Landscapes; *Guil. de Heusch*, Landscape; *Ter Borch*, The fiancée; *A. van Ostade*, The gazette, Woman with a letter, The analyst; *Pot*, Portrait of a man; *Metsu*, The toilet, Woman playing the virginal; *Rembrandt*, Self-portrait in oriental costume; *Neefs*, Church interior; *Palamedes*, Palace interior, 'Réunion galante'; *I. van Ostade*, Farmyard; *Teniers the Younger*, Tavern scenes; *Jan Steen*, Idiot begging alms; *W.K. Heda*, Still life; *Wouwerman*, Gypsies, The cavaliers' halt; *Jordaens*, Diana's repose; *Brakenburgh*, Tavern interior; *A. van de Velde*, Landscape; *van der Meulen*, Cavalry combat; *Both*, Landscape; *Berghem*, The watering-place; *Hackert* and *van de Velde*, Ash-trees; *Jouvet*, Portrait of Corneille.

The **Edward Tuck Collection**: Chinese porcelain of the Kang-Hi period (1662–1722; famille noire); Battersea enamels; Meissen figures; 18C Beauvais tapestries, *after Boucher* and *Huet*; *Greuze*, Portrait of Benjamin Franklin; terracotta bust of Franklin by *Houdon*; and a representative collection of Louis-XV furniture.

The **Dutuit Collection**: among the paintings, *Cranach*, The burgomaster's daughter; *Brueghel (de Velours)*, Wedding; and *Cima de Conegliano*, Madonna and Child. Also an impressive collection of Grolier bindings, among others; Gubbio and Urbino ware; Limoges enamels; ivories; German and Burgundian wood carvings; Gallo-

Roman bronzes; Egyptian statuettes; and an extensive collection of Greek ceramics, etc.

Two recent acquisitions are *Fragonard*, Portrait of the astronomer Lalande; and *Jongkind*, View of Notre-Dame from the Quai de la Tournelle.

The **Grand Palais**, facing the *Petit*, with a classical façade, surmounted by a lofty portico, at present accommodates various exhibition-halls; its W. half contains a *Planetarium* and the *Palais de la Découverte*, devoted to the popularisation of scientific knowledge (adm. 10.00–18.00, except Mon.). It is planned to move the scientific sections and planetarium to *La Villette* in due course: see Rte 19.

Publications of the *Caisse Nationale des Monuments Historiques* are available from Porte F, facing the *Cours-la-Reine*; those of the *Inventaire général des Monuments et des Richesses artistiques de la France*, from Porte D.

Six avenues radiate from the ROND-POINT DES CHAMPS-ÉLYSÉES, with its six fountains. At No.3 Av. Matignon, leading N.E., died Heinrich Heine (1799–1856); to the S.W. extends the wide Av. Montaigne.

On the r. at the beginning of the built-up area of the Av. des Champs-Elysées are the offices of the newspaper *Le Figaro*.

Two streets beyond, at No.107 Rue La Boétie, are showrooms of the *Institut Géographique Nationale*, where a large range of French maps may be bought: see p27.—At the corner of the Rue de Berri, parallel to the W., a plaque marks the site of a mansion in which Thomas Jefferson lived in 1785–89, as American minister.

No.25 in the avenue, since 1904 the *Travellers' Club*, was built in 1855–66 by *Pierre Maugin* in an ostentatious Renaissance style for the Marquise de Païva, who here continued to hold the artistic and political salon, which advanced her career of adventuress and spy (see also p200). Dickens lived at No.49 in 1855–56.—Byron stayed in the street named after him, N. of and parallel to this section of the avenue.

At No.127 (l.) beyond the upper end of the Av. George-V, is the **Office de Tourisme de Paris**, whose long-suffering and helpful hostesses can often advise the tourist with problems or in need of information: see p43.

Twelve avenues radiate starwise from the PL. CHARLES-DE-GAULLE (formerly **Pl. de l'Étoile**, and still commonly known as such: Pl. 6;5). The uniform façades facing it between each avenue were designed by *Hittorf* in 1854–57.

In the centre stands the grandiose *****Arc de Triomphe**, the largest triumphal arch in the world (almost 50m high, and 45m wide).

Designed by *Chalgrin*, and begun in 1806, it was not completed until 1836. The main façades of the arch are adorned with colossal groups in high relief. Facing the *Champs-Élysées* are (r.) the Departure of the Army in 1792 (otherwise known as 'La Marseillaise') by *Rude*, and (l.) the Triumph of Napoleon in 1810, by *Cortot*; facing the Av. de la Grande-Armée are (r.) the Resistance of the French in 1814, and (l.) the Peace of 1815, both by *Étex*.

The four spandrels of the main archway contain figures of Fame by *Pradier*, and those of the smaller archways have sculptures by *Vallois* (S. side) and *Bra*. Above the groups are panels in relief of incidents in the campaigns of 1792–1805. On the row of shields in the attic storey are inscribed the names of 172 (victorious) battles of the Republic and the Empire, including some claimed to be French victories, but in fact not so! Below the side arches are the names of some hundreds of generals who took part in these campaigns, those who fell in action being underlined, considerately. A discreet silence is maintained with regard to the other hundreds of thousands of Frenchmen and foreigners who fought for and against the Emperor, both in his victories and defeats, and who also died: but culpability for carnage is an inevitable if disagreeable ingredient of 'La Gloire' and any monument to that abstraction, however imposing.

Beneath the arch is the *Tomb of the Unknown Soldier*, the equivalent to the Cenotaph in Whitehall, and symbolic of the dead of both World Wars. Its constantly burning flame has been revived every evening since 11 Nov. 1923. At its foot is a bronze plaque representing the 'Shaef' shoulder-flash, and dated 25 Aug. 1944, the day of the liberation of Paris after the German occupation. On the summit is a platform commanding panoramic views of Paris: adm. 10.00–17.00 or 18.00 daily; fee.

Since 1840, when the route was followed by a cortège bearing Napoleon's ashes, watched, despite the intense cold, by 100,000 people, the Champs-Élysées has been used for state processions on a number of occasions, funereal, triumphal, and in celebration of liberation, etc.

Richard and Minna Wagner lived in the Rue Newton, a short distance to the S., in 1859–60.

A short distance W. in the Rue Rude, is the *Irish Embassy*. In The Av. de la Grande Armée lived Maud Gonne (Mme Gonne MacBride) in the 1890s, who founded the French society of Friends of Irish Freedom.

B. Viâ the Rue du Faubourg-St-Honoré

MÉTROS: *Concorde, Madeleine, St-Philippe-du-Roule, Pl.-des-Ternes, Villiers, Monceau, Charles de Gaulle-Étoile.*

The RUE DU FAUBOURG-ST-HONORÉ, the N.W. continuation of the Rue St-Honoré, extends from the Rue Royale (leading from the *Pl. de la Concorde* to the *Pl. de la Madeleine*, see Rte 13) to the *Pl. des Ternes* (N.E. of the *Arc de Triomphe*), following the course of the medieval road from Paris to the village of Roule.

It became fashionable at the end of Louis XIV's reign, and in the 18C its splendid mansions made it a rival to the Faubourg St-Germain as an aristocratic quarter. Its pretensions are now sustained by a succession of luxurious and expensive boutiques, jewellers, etc., and houses devoted to the exploitation of male, female (and 'unisex') vanity, both cosmetic and sartorial, but, like Bond Street, its standards are sophisticated, and the tyranny of fashion is fragile.

At No.8 Rue d'Anjou, leading N., died La Fayette in 1834; Benjamin Constant (1767–1830) died at No.29.

We shortly pass (l.) the exclusive *Cercle Interallié* (No.33; of 1714), it was the Russian Embassy during the Second Empire; and adjacent (No.35), the *Hôtel de Charost*, since 1825 the **British Embassy** (Pl. 7;5).

The 4th Duc de Charost commissioned *Antoine Mazin* to build the mansion in 1722. In 1785 it was let to the Comte de La Marck, during whose tenancy much of its interior decoration was completed, and the 'jardin à l'Anglaise' laid out. It was bought in 1803 by Pauline Bonaparte (later Princess Borghese; much of whose furniture remains), and was sold by her to Wellington in 1814 for £32,000, the figure including numerous clocks, chandeliers, candelabras, and chimney-pieces, etc.

Sydney Smith preached an eloquent sermon in the dining-room (then serving as a chapel), and here were married Berlioz and Harriet Smithson (with Liszt as their best man) in 1833; and Thackeray to Isabella Shawe in 1836. Sir Edward

Blount, attaché here in 1829, later promoted French railways, constructing lines from Paris to Rouen and from Amiens to Boulogne, in 1843 and 1845 respectively, thus making his contribution to the improvement in communications between the two countries. Somerset Maugham (1874–1965), whose father was solicitor to the Embassy, was born at the residence, at No.39 in the street. Some few diplomatic representatives have distinguished themselves—like Duff Cooper (who held the post of Ambassador immediately after the last war), ably assisted by his indulgent wife—by throwing lavish parties, which some older men and women might prefer to forget, but protocol is perhaps now less lax; the scene more sober. Among ambassadors of consequence during the last 150 years were Granville, Cowley, Lyons, Lytton, Bertie, Derby, and Tyrrell.

The old *Embassy Church* (St Michael's), in the Rue d'Aguesseau, opposite, demolished in 1971, has been replaced by a functional modern basement hall.

No. 41 is the *Hôtel Pontalba*, built by *Visconti* and restored by E. de Rothschild; No.45 was the residence of Thiers at the end of his term as President, in 1873.

The **Palais de l'Élysée** (no adm.), stands at the corner of the Av. de Marigny. This heavily guarded mansion (since greatly altered and enlarged) was built by *Molet* as the *Hôtel d'Évreux* in 1718.

It was occupied later by Mme de Pompadour, Murat, Napoleon I (who signed his second abdication here in 1815), Wellington, and Napoleon III, who lived here as Président from 1848 until he moved, as Emperor, to the Tuileries in 1852. It then reverted to its use as a residence for visiting heads of state (including Queen Victoria in 1855, and Elizabeth II in 1957), but since 1873 it has been the official residence of the Président of the Republic. Here, in 1899, gallantly died Felix Faure, in the arms of Mme Steinheil.

To the r., the Rue des Saussaies (No. 11 in which was the Gestapo H.Q. in Paris during 1940–44) leads to the PL. DES SAUSSAIES and the *Hôtel du Maréchal Suchet* (No.16 Rue de la Ville-l'Évêque), built by *Boullée* c. 1750. Alexis de Tocqueville (1805–59), author of 'Democracy in America', was born at No.12 in the same street.

Passing (r.) the *Ministère de l'Interieur* (Home Office), built in 1769—in which the poet-Marquis de Saint-Lambert (1716–1803) died—flanking the PL. BEAUVAU, we continue past No.100 Rue du Faubourg-St-Honoré, Fanny Burney's residence in 1806–12. —Beyond the Av. Matignon is the Rue de Penthièvre (r.), in which No.26 may occupy the site of Benjamin Franklin's city office. Meyerbeer (1791–1864) died in the Rue Jean-Mermoz, to the l.

Further on, to the r., stands *St-Philippe-du-Roule*, built in 1769–84 by *Chalgrin* on the site of the parish church of Roule and later enlarged.

At No.45 Rue La Boétie (to the r.) is the *Salle Gaveau*, one of the more important concert-halls in Paris.

The Rue du Faubourg-St-Honoré soon meets the wide Av. de Friedland, which leads W. to the *Arc de Triomphe* (see Rte 16A), off which, to the l., at No.12 Rue Balzac (then No.22 Rue Fortunée, demolished), is the site of the house where Honoré Balzac (1799–1850) died.

Alfred de Vigny (1797–1863) died at No.6 Rue d'Artois, parallel to and S. of the Rue du Faubourg-St-Honoré.

At No.208 in the Rue du Faubourg-St-Honoré, beyond the Av. Friedland, are the buildings of the old *Hôpital Beaujon* (1784); opposite, at No.11 Rue Berryer, is the former *Hôtel Salomon de Rothschild*, where Président Doumer was assassinated in 1932.

Just beyond the intersection with the Av. Hoche is the *Salle Pleyel*

(1927), the largest concert hall in Paris, radically revamped in 1981.—Mme de Caillavet held her salon at No.12 Av. Hoche, which was frequented by Anatole France, Maupassant, and Proust.

In the Rue Daru, parallel to the N., is the neo-Byzantine Russian Orthodox church of *St-Alexandre-Nevsky* (1859–61).

Gustave Flaubert (1821–80) lived from 1875 until his death at No.240 **Rue** du Faubourg-St-Honoré; from 1869 to 1875 he had lived at No.4 **Rue** Murillo, just S. of the Parc Monceau.

From behind the church of St-Philippe-du-Roule (see above) the Rue de Courcelles crosses the *Blvd Haussmann*. At No.38 in the Rue de Courcelles (then No.48) Dickens lodged in 1846; Proust lived at No.45 in 1901–05 (before moving to No.102 Blvd Haussmann where he remained until 1919), containing his cork-lined 'sound-proof' room. Saint-Saëns lived at No.83bis. Henri Barbusse (1873–1935) died at No.105.

The ***MUSÉE JACQUEMART-ANDRÉ** (Pl. 6;4), at No.158 BLVD HAUSSMANN (MÉTRO: *St-Philippe-du-Roule)*, contains an important collection of French art of the 18C (on the Ground Floor), and Renaissance and Italian art on the First Floor.

The house was built c.1870 by Édouard André (d.1894), who in 1881 married the painter Nélie Jacquemart, who survived her husband until 1912, bequeathing their collection to the Institut de France.

From the Vestibule, we turn l. into **R2**, with four Gobelins tapestries, and a Savonnerie carpet (1663), and displaying *Nattier*, Portrait of the Marquis d'Antin; *Prud'hon*, Cadet de Gassicourt; and busts of Caumartin by *Houdon*, the architect Gabriel by *Coysevox*, the painter Nicholas Vleugels by *Slodtz*, and the Marquis de Marigny by *Le Moyne*.—**R3**, with Beauvais tapestries of Russian games after *Le Prince*.—**R4** *Rubens*, Hercules strangling the lion, and (from his studio) Portrait of a Flemish couple; *van Dyck*, Count Henry of Peña; *Rembrandt*, Amalia von Solms, Pilgrims at Emmaus, Dr Arnold Tholinx; *Hals*, Portrait of a man; *Ph. de Champaigne*, Portrait of a man; *Ruysdael*, Landscape; *Jan de Bray*, Portrait; *School of Bruges*, Virgin and Child illuminating a book; and in a case, the *Boucicaut Book of Hours, which belonged to Diane de Poitiers.

R5 *Canaletto*, St Mark's Square and The Rialto, Venice; *Chardin*, Still life, and drawings by *Lancret, Pater, Watteau*, and *Boucher*.—**R6** *Tocqué*, Portrait of a man; *Vigée-Lebrun*, Countess Skravonska; *-Greuze*, Girl in confusion; *Perroneau*, Woman in a bonnet, Portrait of the painter Gillequin, and *Chinard*, A woman's head; in a case, book-bindings. We return to **R7**, with *Mantegna*, Madonna and Child between two saints, and Mocking of Christ; *Quinten Massys*, Posthumous portrait of an old man; *Luini*, Virgin with SS Margaret and Augustine; a bronze plaquette of the Martyrdom of St Sebastian, by *Donatello*; a horse in gilt bronze, attr. to *Leonardo da Vinci*; ivories, and an enamelled plaque by *Jean Pénicaud I*.

From the Winter Garden (**R8**) we turn l. into **R9**, dominated by *Uccello*, *St George killing the dragon; *di Conti*, Head of a man; *Pontormo*, An old woman; book-bindings.—On the *Staircase*, frescoes by *J.-B. Tiepolo*, including Henri III welcomed by Fed. Contarini to the Villa de Mira. Passing through the gallery, we reach **R10**, devoted to the arts of the Italian Renaissance, against the walls of which have been re-erected a number of 15C marble doorways, one with a frame sculptured by *Bened. da Rovezzano* (attr.). Among the terracottas from the della Robbia workshops, a Madonna and Child by *Luca della Robbia*; the Legend of St Emilian, a marble bas-relief in the form of a triptych (*Venetian School*); *Donatello*, two bronze winged torch-bearers, and bust of Lodovico Gonzaga, Marquis of Mantua; and *Ricciarelli*, posthumous bust of Michelangelo (bronze).

R11, with Brussels tapestries, *after van Orley*; *Botticini*, The dead Christ with the Virgin, saints, and others; Portrait of a young man (*Venetian School*), and marquetry choir-stalls, c.1505 (N. Italian) **R12**, adjoining, retains 25 ceiling panels in grisaille attr. to *Girol. Mocetto*, (15C).

Descending to the Ground Floor, we turn l. into **R13**, with a bust of Richelieu by *Warin*, and a fine collection of Sèvres, Meissen, Vincennes, and Vienna porcelain, and Chinese porcelain and stoneware.

A short distance E., the Rue de Téhéran leads N. across the Av. de Messine to meet the Rue de Monceau.

At No.8 Théodore Herzl, proselyte of Zionism, lived in 1891–95 in the latter street; No.28 belonged to Prince Murat; and No.32 was the birthplace of Oscar I of Sweden (1799–1859), son of Bernadotte and Désirée Clary.

The ***MUSÉE NISSIM DE CAMONDO**, at 63 Rue de Monceau (Pl. 7;3; MÉTRO: *Villiers*), housed in a tastefully furnished mansion, containing a large number of Savonnerie and Aubusson carpets, and now an annexe to the *Musée des Arts Décoratifs*, was bequeathed by Count Moise de Camondo as a memorial to his son Nissim, killed in 1917. A high proportion of the individual pieces of furniture are of outstanding quality.

From the entrance *Vestibule*, with a red marble fountain (1765) from the Château de St-Prix, Montmorency, and a writing-desk by *Riesener*, stairs lead up past two lacquered Louis-XV corner cupboards in the Chinese style, and a pair of Regency armchairs upholstered in Savonnerie tapestry.

FIRST FLOOR. *Grand Bureau*: white marble chimneypiece of c.1775, inlaid with bronze, etc.; a pair of low cabinets by *Leleu*; cylinder-top desk and secretaire by *Saunier*, the latter from the château de Tanly; desk-armchair of 1778; a white marble-topped table by *Carlin* from the château de Bellevue; pair of low chairs by *Séné*; eight chairs by *N.-Q. Foliot* covered in Aubusson tapestry (scenes from La Fontaine); Aubusson tapestries with six fables from La Fontaine after *Oudry*, and a Beauvais screen with the fable of the Cock on the Dunghill; bronze bust of Mme le Comte by *G. Coustou* (1716–77); *Vigée-Lebrun*, Bacchante.

Grand Salon: White and gold panelling from No.11 Rue Royale of c.1775–80; marquetry cabinet and tables by *Riesener*; round table and bureau de dame (with Sèvres procelain plaques) by *Carlin*; a pair of low tables by *Weisweiler*; oval table attr. to *Roentgen*, and one by *Lacroix*; suite of furniture (which belonged to Sir Richard Wallace), including two sofas and an armchair by *Georges Jacob*; four chairs by *Henri Jacob*; a six-leaved Savonnerie screen; 'L'Été' (Hubert Robert's daughter), a marble bust by *Houdon*: *Vigée-Lebrun*. Mme Le Coulteux du Molay; 'La Pécheuse', a Beauvais tapestry *after Boucher*; and among Savonnerie carpets, one ('L'Air') woven for the Grande Galerie of the Louvre (1678) and one made in 1660.

Salon Huet: Seven panels and three dessus de portes of 'Scènes pastorales' painted by *J.-B. Huet*, dated 1776; cylinder-top desk by *Oeben*; pairs of small cabinets by *Garnier* and *Carlin*, the latter once belonging to Adm. de Penthièvre; sofa, two bergères, and eight chairs by *Sené*; table with chased bronze given by Louis XVI to Vergennes; silver-gilt candlesticks by *F.-T. Germain* (1762) embossed with the arms of Mme de Pompadour.—*Salle à Manger*: console and a pair of ebony and chased bronze tables by *Weisweiler*; pair of small cabinets by *Leleu*; silver, including two tureens by *Auguste* and *Roettiers* (the latter's work was ordered by Catherine II of Russia for Orloff).—*Cabinet des Porcelaines*. (with a view of the *Parc Monceau*), with services of Sèvres, Chantilly, and Meissen porcelain; silver-gilt service by *Dehanne* and *Cardeilhac*, etc.— *Galerie*: sofa and chairs by *Pierre Gillier*; Aubusson tapestries after *Boucher* ('La Danse Chinoise', etc.).

Petit Bureau: furniture by *Topino*, *Riesener*, and *Lacroix*, among others; snuffboxes, clocks, Chinese porcelain (Kien-Loung; 1736–95); terracotta medallions by *J. B. Nini*; marble bust of Mme Le Comte by *Coustou*; four views of Venice by *Guardi*; portrait of Necker by *Duplessis; Oudry*, eight sketches for Gobelins tapestries of 'Les Chasses de Louis XV'; three paintings by *Hubert Robert*.—On the *Stairs* leading to the Second Floor, two Aubusson tapestries in the Chinese style, after *Boucher*.

SECOND FLOOR. *Galerie*: sofa and chairs by *Nogaret*; a series of engravings after *Chardin*; 18C Chinese porcelain. Turning r. we enter the *Salon Bleu*: pair of tables attr. to *Riesener*; bookcase attr. to *Carlin*; red morocco casket embossed with the arms of Marie-Antoinette; views of Paris by *Bouhot* (1813), *Canella* (1830),*Demachy* (1774), and *Raguenet* (1754); a family portrait by *Gautier-Dagoty* (1740–86); watercolour of the Quai Malaquais by *Thomas S. Boys*; Chinese porcelain of the period 1662–1795.

Bibliothèque (oak-panelled): secretaire by *Leleu*; two bronze and Sèvres biscuit candelabras by *Blondeau* after Boucher; two paintings by *Hubert Robert*; Aubusson tapestry screen (1775).—*Chambre à Coucher*: furniture by *Cramer*, *Topino*, and *Jacob Frères*; six-leaved screen by *Falconet* (1743). Among paintings: *Danloux*, Rosalie Duthé; *Lavreince*, The singing lesson; *Lancret*, Les Rémois; *Houdon*, Sabine Houdin (?), a plaster bust; *Drouais*, Alexandre de Beauharnais as a child; Savonnerie carpet (1760) for the chapel at Versailles.—*Deuxième Chambre*: secretaire attr. to *Riesener*; screen by *Canabas*; 'Scènes de chasse' by *de Dreux, Shayer, Fontaine, H. Vernet*, etc.

At No.7 Av. Vélasquez, a parallel street to the N. (MÉTROS: *Villiers or Monceau*), is the **Musée Cernuschi**, bequeathed to the city in 1895, in many ways a pendant to the more comprehensive collections of Oriental art in the *Musée Guimet* (see Rte 17). Of particular interest are the funerary figurines of the T'ang and Wei dynasties, neolithic terracottas, and bronze vases, etc., of the Chang dynasty (14–11C B.C.), while outstanding are the paintings on silk of horses and grooms of the T'ang period (8C). Note also the collections of clasps, mirrors, jade amulets, etc. On the FIRST FLOOR is an extensive collection of bronze objects from Louristan and Iran (8–7C B.C.), a bronze basin of 5–3C B.C., and porcelain of various periods.

The neighbouring *Parc Monceau (Pl. 6;4; 88 hectares) derives its name from a vanished village, and is a remnant of a private park laid out by *Carmontel* in 1778 for Philippe-Égalité d'Orléans, Duc de Chartres, and father of Louis-Philippe. Its gardener was Thomas Blaikie (1750–1838), a Scot. It was then known as the 'Folie de Chartres', and certain 'picturesque' details remain. Near the N.E. corner is the *Naumachie*, with a Corinthian colonnade which may have come from either the Château du Raincy or from the projected mausoleum at St-Denis for Henri II and Catherine de Médicis. To the E. of the lake is a Renaissance arcade from the *old Hôtel de Ville*; to the W., the round *Pavillon de Chartres*, a toll-house of the 18C city wall erected by the Farmers-General, is now used as a keeper's lodge.

There are a number of imposing mansions in the streets to the N., including those in the Rue de Prony, leading N.W., off which the Rue Fortuny (where at No.2 Edmond Rostand lived in 1891–97, and wrote 'Cyrano de Bergerac') turns N.E. to the re-named PL. DU GÉN. CATROUX (but still Métro *Malesherbes*). Slightly to the N. of the latter is the *Salle Cortot*, a concert-hall (78, Rue Cardinet).

Further N.E., in the **Batignolles**, some quaint areas still survive the pressures of modernization, and deserve exploration. The Quartier gave its name to a school of impressionist painters under the leadership of Manet.

In the *Cimetière des Batignolles* (best approached by the Av. de Clichy, and some distance N.W. of the Cimetière de Montmartre) lie Verlaine, André Breton, Léon Bakst, and Féodor Chaliapine.
    The Av. de Villiers leads N.W. from the Pl. Malesherbes, in which No.43 is the *Musée Henner*, devoted to the work of Jean-Jacques Henner (1829–1905).—Some distance further W., near the *Porte de Champerret*, stands *Ste-Odile* (1938–46), with a flattened dome and rocket-like tower.

17 Chaillot, Passy, and Auteuil

MÉTROS: *Concorde, Alma-Marceau, Iéna, Trocadéro, Passy, Muette, Porte-d'Auteuil.*

From the *Pl. de la Concorde* (see Rte 8), the COURS-LA-REINE, with its extension, the COURS ALBERT-IER (in which No.40 preserves glass doors by *Lalique*), leads W. to the *Pl. de l'Alma*. It was laid out in 1616, and followed the old road to the villages of Chaillot, St-Cloud, and Versailles, and the Roman canal which brought water from Chaillot.

The sculptures embellishing the so-called 'Maison de François-Ier', which stood from 1826 to 1957 in the Cours-la-Reine, have been returned to Moret-sur-Loing.
    The parallel PORT DE LA CONFÉRENCE, flanking the Seine, takes its name from the *Porte de la Conférence* (demolished in 1730), through which the Spanish ambassadors entered Paris in 1660 to discuss with Mazarin the projected marriage between Louis XIV and María Teresa.

The *Pont des Invalides*, beyond the *Pont Alexandre-III* (see Rte 16), of

1827–29, was rebuilt in 1879–80 and enlarged in 1956.—The wide new *Pont de l'Alma* (1970) retains the figure of a Zouave, which was long used as a gauge in estimating the height of the Seine in flood.

Immediately E. of the S. end of the Pont de l'Alma is the public entrance to the **Sewers** (*Égouts*) of Paris, a formidable system laid out by the engineer *Eugène Belgrand* (1810–78). Part of it may be visited between 14.00–17.00 on Mon. and Wed., and the last Sat. in each month: closed when raining. The tour is not so hazardous as that experienced by Jean Valjean in 'Les Misérables'. The total combined length of the sewers of Paris which may be entered has been estimated at 2100km.

Several handsome streets radiate N. from the PL. DE L'ALMA (Pl. 11;6), many of the mansions being the showrooms of 'haut-couturiers', who have replaced the once ubiquitous Parisian 'midinette' in the folklore of fashion.—At No.13 Av. Montaigne, leading N.E., is the *Théâtre des Champs-Élysées*, by *A.* and *G. Perret* (1911–13), with bas-reliefs by *Bourdelle*.—On the W. side of the Av. George-V, leading N., is the American church of the *Holy Trinity* (1885–88), built in a Gothic style by *G. S. Street*.

The Av. de New York, with its continuations, skirts the N. bank of the Seine for some distance before bearing W. to the *Porte de St-Cloud*. When parallel to the long narrow *Allée des Cygnes* (or 'Isle of Swans') lying in mid-stream S. of the *Pont de Bir-Hakeim*, the thoroughfare passes (r.) the cylindrical **Maison de la Radio** (or de l'O.R.T.F.), designed in 1960 by *H. Bernard*, impressive in size even if its tower is out of proportion to the rest of the building, the only one of note in the area (Pl. 10;8). A *Museum* devoted to Radio as a means of communication has been installed here (adm. 10.00–12.00; 14.00–17.00 except Mon.).

On the S. extremity of the *Allée des Cygnes*, crossed here by the *Pont de Grenelle* (rebuilt 1875), and facing downstream, is a reduced bronze replica of *Bartholdi's* statue of Liberty, presented to France by the United States, where the original stands at the entrance to New York harbour.

The Av. du Président-Wilson leads W. from the PL. DE L'ALMA, from which the Av. Marceau immediately diverges r. uphill towards the *Arc de Triomphe*, passing (l.) *St-Pierre-de-Chaillot* (1937), built in a bogus Byzantine/Romanesque style by *Émile Bois*, and replacing the parish church of 1750.

To the r. in the Av. du Président-Wilson is the main façade, behind gardens, of the *Hôtel Galliéra* (1888), built to house the collections of the Duchesse de Galliéra (d.1889), who had subsequently changed her mind and bequeathed the majority of them to the city of Genoa. At present it accommodates the **Musée de la Mode et du Costume**, with its entrance at No.10 Av. Pierre-1er de Serbie. Parts of the extensive collections, enriched by numerous donations, are usually shown in rotation in a series of temporary exhibitions covering specific themes or periods.

Normally there is a display of dresses, designs, costume and fashion-plates, and photographs, and an astonishing variety of accessories: belts, buttons, and ribbons; scarves, feathers, and gloves; handbags and hats; fans, and parasols; stays, and stockings; and numerous other forms of clothing, from costume jewellery to shoes, apart from dolls, wigs, and what not.

On the S. side of the Av. du Président-Wilson stands the **Palais d'Art Moderne**, constructed for the Exhibition of 1937 (by *Aubert, Dondel, Viard*, and *Dastugue*) on the site of a military bakery, itself replacing the old *Savonnerie* (see p79). The wall of the terrace is decorated with bas-reliefs by *Janniot*; and here, with other statues by *Bourdelle*, is 'La France', in memory of French patriots who fell in the Second World War.

It consists of two wings, that to the E. housing the **Musée d'Art Moderne de la Ville de Paris**, often showing temporary exhibitions. The permanent collection is arranged on two floors, but contains few canvases of great interest. Near the entrance are two series of engravings: *Picasso*'s Vollard Suite, and *Derain*'s suite 'Le Satyricon'. Notable is *Modigliani*, Woman with a fan; also on view are representative works by *Jules Pascin, André Lhote, Chaim Soutine, Othon Friez, Marie Blanchard, Marcel Gromaire,* and *Jean Lurçat*. Among other works on the floor below are: *Francis Gruber*, Nude in a red waistcoat (sic); *Buffet*, three Nudes, and Self-portrait; *Foujita*, The bistro; and *Pierre Soulages*, Composition.

The W. wing, now styled the **Palais de Tokyo**, was, until the translation of its contents to the *Centre Beaubourg*, known as the *Musée National d'Art Moderne*. Its present contents are temporarily here while awaiting the inauguration of the *Musée d'Orsay*; see Rte 6.

Adm. 9.45–17.15, except Tues.: at variance to the E. wing (see above).

Both long-term and temporary exhibitions are also held here. That entitled *'Préfiguration du Musée d'Orsay'* contains a number of interesting works, a selected few of which are listed, many of which have slumbered in the réserves of the Louvre for some decades, which are displayed in seven rooms: **R1** *Émile Bernard*, Madeleine au Bois d'Amour; *Pierre Bonnard*, Man and woman, Woman reclining on a bed; *Maurice Denis*, The Muses, Portrait of Felix Vallotan, The Mellerio family; *Felix Vallottan*, Poker-party, Dinner under a lamp, Moonlight, The ball; *Gauguin*, Breton landscape, La Belle Angèle; *Van Gogh*, Salle-de-danse à Arles; *Henri Cross*, Portrait of his wife; *Seurat*, The circus; *Armand Seguin*, Portrait of Mlle Vien; *Vuillard*, Au lit, The sleeper, Public garden; *Maillol*, Woman in pink with a parasol; and representative works by *Eugène Carrière, Pissarro, Signac,* and *Paul Sérusier*, among others.—**R2** *Odilon Redon*, Portrait of his wife, and of Gauguin; *Albert Besnard*, The eclipse; *Homer Winslow*, Summer night; *Joseph Granie*, Portraits of Marguerite Moreno, and of Yvette Guilbert in 1895; *Alphonse Mucha*, Le gouffre.—**R3** *Alma Tadema*, Roman potter; *Eugène Burnard*, Peter and John running to the Sepulchre; *George Hitchcock*, The vanquished; *Giovanni Boldini*, Portrait of the Comte de Montesquiou (1897); *Edmond Aman-Jean*, Portrait of a young woman; *André Devambez*, The charge; also examples of glass, pottery, and sculpture of the period.—**R4** *Bonnard*, The yacht, Toilet-table; *Vallottan*, Portrait of Martha Mellot; *Vuillard*, Vase of flowers, Children in a garden, and Portraits of Claude Bernheim de Villers, Mme Benard, and The Comtesse Jean de Polignac; also Carved panelling for a dining-room of c.1900, by *Alexandre Chapentier* (1856–1909).—**R5** *Max Liebermann*, La brasserie à Brannenburg.—**R6** *Maillol*, House in Roussillon, and examples of sculpture.—**R7** *Burne-Jones*, The Wheel of Fortune; *Léonide Pasternak* (father of Boris), Portrait of Tolstoy in 1901; *Valentin Serov*, Portrait of Mme Lwoff; *Gustav Klimt*, Roses under trees.—In lower rooms are a number of donated works by *Braque, Rouault,* and *Dunoyer de Segonzac*.

Among additional paintings being assembled are: *Alexis Axilette*,

Self-portrait, and of Maurice Barrès; *Bonnat*, Portrait of Joseph Dreyfus; *Cézanne*, Portrait of his wife; *Degas*, unfinished Portrait of his grandfather, René-Hilaire de Gas; *Édouard Dubufe*, Portrait of the Duchesse d'Uzès; *Ingres*, Venus at Paphos; *Monet*, The Rue Montorgueil, and The garden at Giverny; *Berthe Morisot*, A bench in the Bois de Boulogne.—Among sculptures, *Camille Claudel*, L'Age mûr; *Daumier*, 36 caricature busts; *George Lacombe*, Isis; and *Paul Troubetzkoy*, Robert de Montesquiou.

Among collections of decorative art and furniture are examples of the work of *Emile Gallé, Hector Guimard, Josef Hoffmann, Adolf Loos*, and *Kolo Moser*; among drawings are several from the *Gustave Eiffel* archive.—Examples of early photography include studies by *Eugène Atget, Edouard Baldus, L.-A. Humbert de Molard, Felix Nadar, Charles Nègre, Pierre Petit, George Charles Beresford, Julia Margaret Cameron, Lewis Carroll, Roger Fenton, George Shaw*, et al.

To the W. is the PL. D'IÉNA (Pl. 11;5), from which seven streets diverge. No.2 Av. d'Iéna is the residence of the U.S. ambassador. To the N. of the Place stands the *Musée Guimet* (see below).

At No.24 Rue Boissière, to the N.W., the poet Henri de Régnier (1864–1936) died; at No.44 Rue Hamelin (forking off the latter) died Marcel Proust (1871–1922).

In the Rue Paul-Valéry (the continuation N.W. of the Rue Hamelin), No.40 was the home of Paul Valéry (1871-1945) from 1902, and from 1883 had been the studio of his aunt by marriage, Berthe Morisot, and a favourite literary and artistic rendezvous.

The ****MUSÉE GUIMET**, installed at No.6 Pl. d'Iéna (MÉTROS: *Iéna* and *Trocadéro*), was founded at Lyon in 1879 by Émile Guimet, presented by him to the State, and transferred to Paris in 1888. In 1945 it officially became the *Département des Arts Asiatiques des Musées Nationaux*, the original collection having been considerably augmented, and now including those of the Asiatic department of the *Louvre*, illustrating the arts of India and the Far East. The building also houses a *Library* and photographic section.

GROUND FLOOR. From the entrance vestibule we pass into **R'N'**, which together with **RR'L'**, **'O'**, and **'H'**, are devoted to Khmer sculpture from *Cambodia*, including a statue of Hari-Hara (pre-Angkorian style; late 6C), uniting in one person the two gods Siva and Vishnu; lintel of 7–12C; sculpture of 9–10C; Vishnu in the Kulen style; Brahma in the Koh Ker style; pediment from the temple of Banteai Srei (967); seated Buddha in the style of Angkor Wat (early 12C); carvings of a lion, an elephant, and of the magic serpent, Naga (12C). Also sculptures in the Bayon style (12–13C); each meditative statue wears the enigmatic 'Angkorian smile'; portrait of King Jayavarman VII; frieze of dancing *apsaras*.

R'M': *Champa Art of Assam* (central Vietnam). Note the head of Buddha (9C) and a dancer with two young elephants (10C).

R'K' (l.): *Java*: Heads of Buddha (8–9C); lintel decorated in the Prambanan style (9C); bronzes (7–9C), and statuettes of Avalokitesvara and Kubera, gods of riches—note the seven treasure-pots at his feet; leather marionettes for a shadow-theatre, and a painted fabric calendar from Bali.

(Centre): *Siam* (Thailand): stuccoes from P'ra Pathom (c.8C); Buddhas of the Schools of Sukhodava and U-Thong (14–15C); head of Buddha (16C); on the walls, painted and worked leather hangings.—*Laos*: Buddha with a begging-bowl.—*Burma*: lacquered wooden Buddha, and illuminated MSS.

Tibetan Art (continued in **R'J'**): Statue in gilded bronze of Dakini; and statuettes decorated with coloured stones; religious objects, jewellery, silverwork, etc. On the walls, paintings illustrating the life of Buddha, gods and saints.—**R'I'**: *Nepal*: Buddhist paintings and statues of wood and gilded bronze.

FIRST FLOOR. **RR'K'** and **'J'**: *Indian Art*. Funerary furniture and stone sculpture from near Pondicherry; clay sarcophagus, pottery, and jewellery. Mathurâ and Amarâvatî sculpture (2–4C); serpent-king (sandstone); marble bas-reliefs; Buddhas. Among objects of the 'classical' period (4–8C), a Buddha in the Gupta style; steles of *Pâla Art* (8–12C); S. Indian stone sculpture; bronzes of Siva; *gouaches and watercolours of the Mogul, Rajput, and Pahâri period (16–18C), including one of Louis XIV when young.

RR'M' and **'P'**: *Pakistan, and Afghanistan*, including examples of Græco-Buddhist Gandara sculpture (1–c.5C); decorative bas-relief (schist); figurines from the Buddhist monastery of Hadda, including a Genie carrying a floral offering, and a demon in a fur; fragments of frescoes from the monastery of Kakrak (c.5C); and the Treasure of Begram (1–2C): Græco-Roman and Syrian objects, Indian ivories, and Chinese lacquer-work discovered together by the French archaeological mission to Afghanistan in 1937 and 1939–40.

RR'N', **'F'**, **'G'**, and **'H'**: the *Arts of China*. Carved bone objects of the Chang Dynasty (16–11C B.C.), and important collections of archaic bronze implements, ritual vases, and arms, etc., from Ngan-Tang, capital city of the dynasty; ritual vase in the shape of an elephant; a 'p'an' bowl of the Chou Dynasty (11–5C B.C.); the Treasure of Li-Yu, a remarkable find from the 'Fighting Kingdoms' Dynasty (5–3C B.C.), notably a jade, turquoise, and gold-ornamented sword.—Jades: the earlier ones in the form of symbols (Pi, the sky; Tsong, the earth; Kwei, the mountain, etc.), and bronzes—Han Dynasty tombstone (206 B.C.—A.D. 220); Buddha from Yun-Kang (5C); heads of Bodhisattva and Kasyapa, from Long-men (early 6C); Ananda and Kasyapa, disciples of Buddha (Suei Dynasty; 561–618), marble with traces of polychrome; Dvarapàla, guardian of the temple, and funerary statuettes of the T'ang Dynasty (618–906); gilded bronzes of the Wei, Suei, and T'ang dynasties (5–10C), including a small stele representing Sakyamuni and Pradhutaratna, dated 518; lacquer-work; polychrome bowls of the Han Dynasty and Sung Dynasty (960–1279); black lacquer cabinet decorated in gold (17C).

SECOND FLOOR. **R'K'**: the *Arts of Japan*. Jômon and Yayoi pottery (2000–1000 B.C., and 1C B.C.–3C A.D. respectively); figurines (Haniwa) of the era of the Great Tombs (5–6C); wooden Buddhas (8–9C); carved masks of the Nara Dynasty (8C); portraits of bonzes (14–15C); pottery for the Tea Ceremony ('Cha-no-yu'); Imari Kakiemon, and Satsuma porcelain; sword-furniture (kozukas); screens, one illustrating the arrival of the Portuguese in Japan (16C).

R'K: *Korea*. Gilded bronze crown, and silverware, from the kingdom of Silla (5–6C); and ceramics.

RR'D', **'L'**, **'P'**, and **'I'** contain an important collection of *Chinese* porcelain, formed principally from the Calmann Collection—'three colour' ware (T'ang Dynasty), celadon, black and white wares (Sung Dynasty)—and from the Grandidier Collection: Ming (1368–1643) and Ch'ing (1644–1912) dynasties.

R'M': *Central Asia*. Buddhist paintings from Touen-houang; votive banners, one representing Kasyapa in old age, dated 729.

Among recent acquisitions are the Torso of a finely sculpted sandstone Buddha (India; mid 5C), and of a Female divinity (Khmer sculpture, from Cambodia; early 9C).

The *Annexe*, at No.19 Av. d'Iéna, is devoted to Oriental *Religious* Art.

To the S.W. is the *Palais du Conseil Économique et Social*, by *A. Perret* (1937–38), originally designed for a Musée des Travaux Publics. The N. wing was added in 1960–62, to house the *Western European Union*. No.34 in the Av. du Président-Wilson was the home of Laure Haymann, the model for Proust's Odette de Crécy.

The Av. du Président-Wilson ends at the PL. DU TROCADÉRO (Pl. 10;6), semi-circular in shape, from which six thoroughfares fan out. In the centre stands a good equestrian statue of Maréchal Foch (1851–1929). It is flanked to the S.E. by the *Palais de Chaillot* (see below). The Place is situated on the 'Colline du Trocadéro', named after a fort near Cádiz occupied by the French in 1823.

Catherine de Médicis built a country house on this eminence; later embellished by Anne of Austria, it was sold to Maréchal de Bassompierre, and in 1651 Henrietta Maria bought it from his heirs and established the *Convent of the Visitation of St Mary* here. This was destroyed during the Revolution, and Napoleon wanted to use the site for a palace for his son which would be more magnificent than the Kremlin, but the disasters of 1812 intervened.

To the W., steps ascend to the small *Cimètière de Passy*, where Debussy, Gabriel Fauré, Manet, Berthe Morisot, Marie Bashkirtseff, and Las Cases lie buried.

The **PALAIS DE CHAILLOT** (MÉTRO: *Trocadéro*), on the S.E. side of the *Pl. du Trocadéro*, was erected for the Paris Exhibition of 1937, and replaced the earlier Palais du Trocadéro designed for the 1878 Exhibition. The new building (by *Carlu, Boileau*, and *Azéma*) encases in its two curved wings the two wings of the original structure. Between them is a square, its terrace affording a striking perspective towards the *Eiffel Tower* and across the *Champ-de-Mars* to the *École Militaire*, and the *Unesco* buildings beyond: see Rte 7.

Below the square, adorned with gilded bronze statues, is an *Aquarium*, and the *Théâtre de Chaillot*, seating over 2000, the home of the Théâtre National Populaire (decorated by *Bonnard, Dufy*, and *Vuillard*, among others). Here took place the third General Assembly of the United Nations (1948).

To the r. and l. of the Colline du Trocadéro, gardens flank fountains which include a battery of 20 jets shooting almost horizontally towards the Seine, crossed here by the *Pont d'Iéna* (1806–13, and since twice widened).—The next bridge downstream is the *Pont de Bir-Hakeim* (formerly the *Pont de Passy*, 1903–06), a double bridge; the upper part being used by the Métro. It is named after a French exploit in N. Africa in 1942.

The *Palais de Chaillot* at present accommodates four museums; in the E. wing, the *Musée des Monuments Français* and *Musée du Cinéma*; in the W. wing, the *Musée de la Marine* and the *Musée de l'Homme*.

The **Musée des Monuments Français** was founded by Viollet-le-Duc in 1879 as the *Musée de Sculpture Comparée*, and the unprejudiced must admit that although it only contains *copies* of masterpieces of French sculpture, mural paintings, and stained-glass, they are faithfully copied, and the collections are exhibited with ingenuity and taste. It provides for the layman both an interesting introduction to the range of early French sculpture and architecture, displaying examples from all over France, and valuable reproductions of early wall-paintings, many of which have since deteriorated or are fast disappearing. The items shown are well lit and well labelled. The *Sculpture* is arranged in a series of rooms to the l. of the entrance.

The *Wall-paintings* occupy rooms to the r., and on the three floors above, outstanding among which are:

FIRST FLOOR: mural and ceiling paintings from St-Gilles (Montoire); Berzé-la-Ville (nr Cluny); St-Martin at Vicq (nr Nohant); St Michael from Le Puy cathedral; St-Aignan-sur-Cher; St-Chef (Isère); Rocamadour (Lot); St-Savin-sur-Gartemp.

SECOND FLOOR: Asnières-sur-Vègre; St-Julien at Le Petit-Quevilly (nr Rouen), St-Jean at Vic-le-Comte (Puy-de-Dôme); dome of Cahors cathedral; Frétigny (Eure-et-Loir); Étigny (Yonne); La Clayette (Saône-et-Loire); Chapelle du Chalard, St-Geniès (Dordogne); the Tour Ferrande, Pernes (Vaucluse); Chartreuse at Villeneuve-lès-Avignon; crypt of Auxerre cathedral; walls of the château of Ravel (Puy-de-Dôme); Les Brignes (Alpes-Maritime); Transfiguration from Le Puy cathedral.

THIRD FLOOR: Kernascléden (Morbihan); Abondance (Haute-Savoie); La Chaise-Dieu; château de Dissay (Vienne); château du Pimpéan (nr Angers); Ennezat (nr Riom); château de Rochechouart (Haute-Vienne); and Albi cathedral.

The devotee of the art of the film will find much to interest him in the **Musée du Cinéma** located in the basement of this wing, established by the late Henri Langlois (1914–77). Over 3000 items are displayed in 60 sections, vividly presenting diverse aspects of the history of the film during its earlier decades. At present it may only be visited by a guided group at 10.00, 11.00, 14.00, 15.00, and 16.00, except Mon.

On the GROUND FLOOR of the W. wing of the *Palais de Chaillot* is installed the ***MUSÉE DE LA MARINE**, with a remarkable collection of material illustrating French naval history, including an outstanding series of ship models, and paintings of maritime subjects, among which are Vernet's *Ports of France*.

From the entrance, we turn r. into the main gallery, dominated by the richly carved poop of the 'Reale' (1690–1715), some of the sculpture of which is attributed to *Puget*. Note the paintings (Nos 61 and 62) of the Embarkation of Henry VIII for the Field of Cloth of Gold, by *Bouterwerke* (a copy of the original by *Vincent Volpi*) and a View of Amsterdam by *Bakhuysen* (1664). Four *anon.* views of Malta (Nos 138–9) are also of interest; likewise two views of Port Mahon (nos 147 and 416, the latter by *Joseph Chiesa*), and a number of marine paintings by *Jean-François Hue* (1751–1823).

In the centre of the gallery are displayed 13 (of the 15 completed of the original 24 commissioned) views of the *'Ports of France' by *Claude-Joseph Vernet* (1714–1789), depicting Dieppe, Antibes, tunny-fishing near Bandol, Rochefort, La Rochelle, Cette, two views of Toulon, two of Bordeaux, two of Bayonne, and Marseille, and all painted between the years 1754 and 1765.

We pass the Emperor's Barge (1811) before entering a section devoted to early steamships. **R15**, at the far end of the wing, contains recent models and paintings, and a section concentrating on the fleet air arm, etc.

Returning along a parallel gallery, we pass further sections displaying marine instruments, diving and underwater exploration equipment, a model of a nuclear submarine, models of the careening of a ship and of the raising and transportation of the obelisk of Luxor (now in the *Pl. de la Concorde*: see Rte 8), of ship construction, etc., while among individual items are a sectional view of the transatlantic liner 'Normandie', and Dr Bombard's raft.

The **Musée de l'Homme** is housed on the First and Second Floors of this wing, and was formed by the amalgamation of the *Galerie d'Anthropologie* and the *Musée d'Ethnographie du Trocadéro*. A comprehensive Library, Photographic Library, Cinema, and various technical services are also accommodated in the building.

In comparison with some more recently installed museums (such as the *Musée National des Arts et Traditions Populaires*; see Rte 18), its quality of display leaves something to be desired, but the items exhibited are more or less self-explanatory.

The sections devoted to Anthropology, Paleoanthropology and Prehistory, Africa, the Near East, and Europe, are found on the FIRST FLOOR. On the SECOND are rooms displaying exhibits from the Arctic, Asia, Indonesia and Oceania, and America.

The Rue Franklin leads S.W. from the *Pl. du Trocadéro*, and is continued by the Rue Raynouard.—From their junction, the PL. DE COSTA RICA, the Rue de Passy, high street of the old village of **Passy**, runs W. to the *Jardin du Ranelagh* (see below). Steps descend to the l. in the Rue Raynouard to the *Sq. Charles Dickens*, in which the vaulted medieval cellars of a *Musée du Vin* may be visited. No.47 Rue Raynouard is **Balzac's House** (adm. daily except Mon. 10.00–17.40), containing souvenirs of the novelist, who lived here in 1841–47. Here he wrote 'La Cousine Bette', and 'Le Cousin Pons', among other novels. It is worthwhile entering the unexpected ivy-covered Rue Berton, behind the house, one of the most charming lanes remaining in Passy.

Earlier inhabitants of the Rue Raynouard include the architect Robert de Cotte, and the Abbé Prévost, and Benjamin Franklin (in 1777–85), who erected on his house (the *Hôtel de Valentinois*, which stood on the corner of the Rue Singer) the first lightning conductor seen in France.

In the Rue d'Ankara, between Rue Berton and the Seine, No.17, now the *Turkish Embassy*, was once the residence of the Princesse de Lamballe, and later the private clinic of Dr Émile Blanche, where Maupassant died in 1893; Gérard de Nerval and Gounod had also sought treatment there.

Not far S.W. of Balzac's House (before reaching the *Maison de l'O.R.T.F.*; see p214, the Rue des Vignes leads·N.W., where at No.32 Gabriel Fauré (1845–1924) died; James Joyce lived at No.34 during the latter period of his stay in Paris.

Other distinguished residents of Passy include 'Fanny' Burney (Mme d'Arblay; 1752–1840), in 1802–06; Béranger, in 1833–35; and Maeterlinck, in 1897–1910. Others were Rossini, from 1857–68; Gossec, from 1822–29; and Joseph Proudhon, from 1861–65: the last three died there.

The Rue des Vignes also leads to the Chaussée de la Muette and the E. end of the **Jardin du Ranelagh** (Pl. 10;7), part of the ancient royal park of *La Muette*. It was designed to emulate its fashionable namesake in London, and just before the Revolution was a favourite resort. The first balloon ascent in France was made nearby in 1783 by Pilâtre de Rozier and the Marquis d'Arlandes.

The royal *Château de la Muette*, originally a hunting-lodge, improved by the Regent Orléans, and restored by Louis XV for Mme de Pompadour, has completely disappeared. It is also associated with Marie-Antoinette, who was welcomed here by Louis XVI on her arrival in Paris on the eve of her wedding in 1770. Twelve years later she set forth hence for *Notre-Dame* and *Ste-Geneviève* on on the occasion of the thanksgiving for the birth of the Dauphin. The Château was later occupied by Philippe-Égalité, who stood on the terrace watching the mob bringing Louis XVI from Versailles to the Tuileries in 1789. From 1820 to 1920 it belonged to the Erard family, piano manufacturers. The present mansion, just N. of the *Jardin du Ranelagh* and E. of the *Porte de la Muette*, was built by Baron Henri de Rothschild, and is now the property of the *European Council for Economic Co-operation*.

At No.2 Rue Louis-Boilly, leading off the W. side of the gardens, is the **MUSÉE MARMOTTAN** (MÉTRO: *La Muette*. Regrettably (like some other buildings whose collections are under the aegis of the *Institut de France)* it is—despite the attempts of some conservateurs—still pervaded by a fin-de-siècle atmosphere; nevertheless, it contains, apart from the *Monet donation* (see below), a number of interesting paintings, among which are works attr. to *van der Weyden*, and *Schongauer,*.

Also displayed are portraits of Talma by *Riesener* and of A young woman by *Lawrence*; of Désiree Clary, by *Gérard*; and of the Duchesse de Feltre and her children, by *F.-X. Fabre*; also works by *L. de France* (1735–1805), *J.-B. Mallet* (1759–1835), *Carmontel* (1717–1806), *A.-I. Melling* (1763–1831), *Louis Boilly* (1761–1845), and *P.-L. Debucourt* (1755–1832), together with drawings by *Fragonard* and *Hubert Robert*. There are also some pleasant views of Schönbrunn, etc., by *B.* and *C. Vernet*, and of Rowing at Fontainebleau by *J. Bidault* and *L. Boilly*.

In a gallery to the l. of the entrance are works by *Claude Monet* (1840–1926) and his friends, including *Berthe Morisot*, Young girl at a ball; *Carolus Duran*, Portrait of Monet; of Monet and his wife by *Renoir*, and by *Monet* himself, of Poly, the fisherman from Belle-Isle, Argenteuil in the snow, Vertheuil in the mist, A train in the snow, and The beach at Trouville, together with sketches for his later canvases and several caricatures; also displayed are characteristic works by *Caillebotte, Guillaumin, Jongkind, Berthe Morisot, Pissarro, Renoir,* and *Sisley*. The collection also contains drawings by *Constantin Guys, Boudin,* and *Signac,* among others.

The Museum also houses the notable ***Wildenstein Collection** of medieval illuminated miniatures, some 230 in all, assembled in one room as they were when in private hands. They deserve a better display, and some examples are also in need of restoration. Among those of the Italian schools are several by *Lucchino Giovanni Belbello da Pavia* (fl. 1430–62); and among the French, some by *Jean Colombe* (fl. 1467–1529), *Jean Perreal* (1455–1530), *Jean Bourdichon* (c. 1475–1521), and *Jean Fouquet* (c. 1420–77/81), together with a charming depiction of a boar-hunt (late 15C); also some Flemish works of the period.

Stairs descend to an underground gallery recently built to house the spectacular collection of *Monet's* colourful paintings of water-

L'Averse, by Louis Boilly; *Musée Marmottan*

lilies, wisteria, and other flower-pieces, the majority of them donated
to the museum in 1971 by the artist's son Michel Monet, and which
form a complementary collection to those displayed in the *Orangerie*
(see Rte 8).

In the residential district of **Auteuil**, to the S., Henri Bergson
(1859–1941) lived and died at No.47 Blvd de Beauséjour, skirting the
Jardin du Ranelagh, and the Goncourt brothers (Edmond, 1822–96;
and Jules, 1830–70) lived and died at No.67 Blvd de Montmorency
('le Grenier'), its continuation S., where they entertained Huysmans,
Zola, Daudet, and Maupassant. In parallel streets to the E. of the
latter lived Dr Émile Blanche and his son, the painter J.-E. Blanche
(at 19 Rue Docteur-Blanche). At No.10 Sq. Dr-Blanche is the *Le
Corbusier Foundation*, in a villa he built in 1923. André Gide lived in

the nearby Av. des Sycomores.—Paul Dukas (1865–1935) died at No.82 Rue du Ranelagh, leading E. from the Blvd de Beauséjour.

At the S. end of the Blvd de Montmorency is the *Porte d'Auteuil*, the S.E. entrance to the *Bois de Boulogne*, and an approach to the A13 autoroute and Blvd Périphérique; hence the BLVD EXELMANS swings S.E. across the Seine by the *Pont du Garigliano* and the Rue d'Auteuil leads E. to *N.-D. d'Auteuil*, built in the Romanesque-Byzantine style (1877–88) on the site of the 12C parish church; in front is the tomb of the chancellor D'Aguesseau (d.1751) and his wife. Sir Benjamin Thompson, Count von Rumford (1753–1814), lived at No.59 Rue d'Auteuil from 1808 until his death. Previously it had been the home of Maurice Quentin Delatour (1770–72), and then of Mme Helvétius until her death in 1800.—Proust (1871–1922) was born at a house on the site of No.96 Rue La Fontaine, a short distance to the N. Boileau, and probably Molière (in 1667) were also residents of Auteuil.

In the small *Cimetière d'Auteuil*, in the Rue Claude-Lorrain (S. of and parallel to the Blvd Exelmans), lie Rumford (see above; whose original tombstone was shattered by a shell from Mont-Valérien in 1871), Hubert Robert, Mme Helvétius, Carpeaux, and Gounod.

18 The Bois de Boulogne and Neuilly

MÉTROS: *Porte-d'Auteuil, Muette, Porte-Dauphine, Porte-Maillot, Les Sablons.*

The **Bois de Boulogne** (Pl. 10;1–3), familiarly known as the 'Bois', lies immediately to the W. of the 16th Arrondissement of Paris (*Chaillot, Passy*, and *Auteuil*: see Rte 17), and was originally bounded on the E. by part of the peripheral fortifications of the city. Now the BLVD PÉRIPHÉRIQUE tunnels below the E. and S. edges of the Bois, which is bounded on the N. by *Neuilly*; the suburb of *Boulogne-Billancourt* to the S., and by the Seine to the W., on the far side of which rise the hills of Mont Valérien, St-Cloud, Bellevue, and Meudon.

Although the châteaux of La Muette, Madrid, and Bagatelle, and the abbey of Longchamp were erected on its borders, until the middle of the last century the Bois was utterly neglected. Much timber was cut down for firewood during the Revolution, and a large part of the Allied army of occupation bivouacked there after Waterloo. It was the haunt of footpads and often the scene of suicides and duels. In 1852 it was handed over by the State to the City, was transformed into an extensive park (863 hectares), and became a favourite promenade of the Parisians. The model was Hyde Park, which had so impressed Napoleon III. More trees were felled in 1870 to prevent them affording cover to the enemy. The equestrian scenes which were such a favourite subject of Constantin Guys (1805–92) often had the Bois in the background.

Carlyle condemned it as 'a dirty scrubby place', and in many respects it has little changed since.

Note. Visitors of either sex are *strongly* advised not to stray into the Bois at dusk or after dark, in view of the present prevalence—one is assured—of Brazilian transvestites, among other equally undesirable denizens of bosky beats; and drivers are also liable to be attacked.

There are four main entrances to the Bois from Paris, namely the *Porte Maillot* (at its N.E. corner); the *Porte Dauphine* (at the W. end of the Av. Foch); the *Porte de la Muette* (at the S. end of the Av. Victor-Hugo); and the *Port d'Auteuil* (at its S.E. corner). Between the last two is the subsidiary *Porte de Passy*.

The usual approach to the Bois is by the imposingly wide, garden-flanked AV. FOCH (opened in 1855 as the Av. de l'Impératrice), leading W. from the *Étoile* to the *Porte Dauphine*. Note one of the original art-nouveau entrances to the *Métro* on the N. side of the avenue here.

Not far from the Étoile is a monument to Adolphe Alphand (1817–91), who laid out the Bois and many other parks in Paris in their present form.

At No.59 Av. Foch, on the l., is the **Musée d'Ennery**, with a collection of oriental art formed by the dramatist Adolphe d'Ennery (Eugène Philippe; 1811–99); the building also houses a small museum of Armenian art.—Anatole France (1844–1924) died at No.5 Villa Said, leading N.W. off the avenue. No.80 Av. Foch was the home of Claude Debussy (1862–1918), who died at No.24 Square de l'Av. Foch (off the N.W. end of the avenue). Nos 82–6 Av. Foch were the German counter-espionage H.Q. in Paris during 1940–44.

There is a curious *Museum of Forgeries* (Musée de la Contrefaçon) at No.16 Rue de la Faisanderie, leading S. near the Porte Dauphine.—S.W. of the park entrance is a huge building (1955–59) constructed for N.A.T.O. but now accommodating *Paris Université IX.*—Claudel (1868–1955) died at No.11 Blvd Lannes, skirting the Bois to the S.; Supervielle lived from 1918 to 1943 at No.**47.**

The direct approach to the *Porte de la Muette* from the *Étoile* may be made by following the Av. Victor-Hugo, in which Victor Hugo (1802–85) died in a house on the site of No.124. Lamartine (1790–1869) died near the square named after him off the S. section of this avenue (house demolished), beyond the PL. VICTOR-HUGO.

At No.24 Rue Copernic, just E. of the Place, took place a deplorable bombing incident outside a Synagogue in 1980.

The '**Bois**' is divided diagonally by the long ALLÉE DE LONGCHAMP, leading S.W. from the Porte Maillot towards the CARREFOUR DE LONG-CHAMP, and a popular equestrian rendezvous. It is intersected by the ROUTE DE LA REINE MARGUERITE (from the CARREFOUR DE LA PORTE DE MADRID to the PORTE DE BOULOGNE, on the S. side of the Bois).

Of particular interest in this N. section of the Bois is the *****MUSÉE NATIONAL DES ARTS ET DES TRADITIONS POPULAIRES** (Pl. 10;2), approached with ease from either *Porte Maillot* or *Porte Dauphine*, or, more directly, from the MÉTRO: *Les Sablons*. The Museum is housed in a not unattractive functional building by *Jean Dubuisson*, completed in 1966, standing just W. of the CARREFOUR DES SABLONS.

Those sections of this fascinating museum open to the public, in addition to rooms devoted to temporary exhibitions, are exceptionally well displayed on two floors.

The GROUND FLOOR contains the 'Galerie Culturelle', laid out in a series of convoluted sections covering aspects of rural life in the pre-industrial period, in which some 5000 objects are seen in context or 'ecological groups', among which are those concerned with sheep and shepherding; baking; the smithy; stone-splitting; forms of rural transport; wood-turning; and furniture carving; viticulture; the fabrication of objects of horn and wood; the embellishment of metalwork; ceramic production; together with sections devoted to peasant costumes, coiffes, etc., with a charming painting of an Arlesienne (1858).

In the BASEMENT is the 'Galerie d'Etude', where similar objects are more systematically displayed in a series of nine parallel passages or 'rues'. By the entrance is a bell-forge.

Rue 1. Farming equipment: yokes, harnesses, traps, etc.—2. Harrows, hoes, rakes, flails, scythes and sickles, and viticultural implements.—3. Cowbells, branding-irons, protective collars, crooks; bee-keeping equipment; sheepsh-earing, and dairy implements.— 4. Spinning, carding, rope-making, and basket-weaving; brick and tile manufacture; surveying equipment and carpenters' tools.—5. Lamps and candlesticks; andirons, jacks, and bedwar-mers; kitchen utensils— jars, waffle-irons, butter-moulds, etc.; furniture and lacework. —6. Ritual costumes; rural medicine; cradles and early toys; regional and traditional costumes: capes and sabots, etc—7. Games and pastimes: archery, tennis, skittles and *boules*, marbles and croquet. Musical instruments: rattles, hurdy-gurdies, flutes, and whistles; bagpipes, etc.—8. Fairs and circuses: puppets, marionettes, and silhouettes.—9. Graphic arts: metal and wood blocks; engraving and lithographic equipment: stencils, etc.

There are audio-visual cabins adjacent. The *Library* contains upward of 60,000 volumes and 2000 periodicals; the *Archives* over 80,000 old post-cards, 40,000 designs, almost 200,000 photographs, among numerous other specialised collections of ethnographical studies, etc.; the *Record collection*, some 50,000 recordings; an additional 70,000 objects may be seen on request, together with c.90,000 drawings, paintings, prints, and other illustrative material. The building also contains an auditorium, and laboratories, the whole comprising an important centre for the study of French ethnography.

N.W. of the museum is the *Jardin d'Acclimatation*, with a small-scale zoo and children's playground. To the W., near the *Porte de Madrid*, stood the *Château de Madrid*, built in 1528 by François I (who is said to have named it in memory of his captivity in Spain, after Pavia). It was gradually demolished between 1793 and 1847.

Further W., skirted by the ROUTE DE SÈVRES À NEUILLY, are the walls of the park of **Bagatelle** (24 hectares), famous for its rose-garden, at its best in mid-June. This elegant little domed Château, replacing an earlier residence, was built for a wager within 64 days by *Bélanger* for the Comte d'Artois, later Charles X, in 1779. It was acquired by the Ville de Paris in 1904.

Henry Swinburne observed that during the Revolution it had been turned into a tavern. It was later the residence of Sir Richard Wallace (1818–90), supposed natural son of the Marchioness of Hertford. Wallace had a town house at No.25 Rue Taitbout where he accumulated art treasures in addition to those he had inherited from the eccentric 4th Marquis of Hertford, who had bought the mansion in 1835 and died there in 1870. These are now in the *Wallace Collection* in London. He was also a great benefactor of Paris, which he provided with drinking fountains, and helped to equip ambulances during the 1870–71 war. He founded the *Hertford British Hospital* in Paris (opened 1879), and built the Anglican church of *St George* (1887–88; Rue Auguste-Vacquerie, off the Av. d'Iéna).

The attractive **Bagatelle Gardens* are open to the public until dusk (fee); the restaurant is expensive.

To the W. are various sports grounds (including polo; *tiercé*, etc.); to the S.W. is the *Hippodrome de Longchamp*, opened in 1857, seen at its gayest on the day of the 'Grand Prix' in June. On the N. side is a windmill (restored), practically the only relic of the *Abbey of Longchamp*, founded in 1256 by St Isabel of France, sister of Louis IX.

From the CARREFOUR DE LONGCHAMP (just E. of the windmill), a road leads due E. past the *Grande Cascade* (an artificial waterfall) to skirt the enclosure of the *Pré-Catelan* (named after the troubadour Arnaud Catelan, murdered here c.1300), with a huge copper beech, and a 'Jardin Shakespeare' (containing all the plants and trees mentioned in his plays).

Further E. are buildings of the *Racing Club de France*, flanking the W. bank of the *Lac Inférieur*, with two linked islands. Boats may be hired on the E. bank. Further S. is the *Lac Supérieur*, beyond the CARREFOUR DES CASCADES; in the S.E. corner of the Bois, is the *Hippodrome d'Auteuil* (steeplechasing).

Just S. of the Bois is the *Jardin Fleuriste* (municipal nursery gardens), with occasional flower-shows, just W. of which is *Stade Roland Garros*, one of several in the vicinity.

N.-D.-des-Menus, in the Av. J.-B. Clément, leading S.W. from the *Porte de Boulogne*, although frequently restored (by Viollet-le-Duc among others), preserves a 14C nave. Beyond (r.) are the *Jardins Albert Kahn* (including one laid out in the Japanese style), open daily Apr.–Nov.

From the *Arc de Triomphe* (see Rte 16A), the Av. de la Grande Armée slopes N.W. to the **Porte Maillot** (Pl. 10;2), the site of extensive works in recent years, and commanded on the N. side by a complex of buildings comprising the *Palais des Congrès*, a hotel, shopping-centre, and one of the *Aérogares* (or air terminals) of Paris.

A short distance to the N.W., near the PL. DU GÉN. KOENIG, or DE LA PORTE DES TERNES, stands *N.-D. de la Compassion*, a mausoleum in the Byzantine style (1843) moved here from its original neighbouring site, where stood an inn at which Ferdinand, Duc d'Orléans, son of Louis-Philippe, died as the result of a carriage accident. As a travesty of taste it equals the other Orléans mausoleum at *Dreux*, see Rte 34.

Beyond the *Porte Maillot*, we continue to approach, viâ the wide Av. Charles-de-Gaulle (which bisects *Neuilly-sur-Seine*: see below), the concrete jungle known as **La Défense** (named after a monument commemorating the defence of Paris in 1871), an aggressive example of high-rise building housing miscellaneous international companies (among others), against which there appears to be no defence. Few will appreciate its attractions, and those who may wish to do so at close hand will have to cross the *Pont de Neuilly* (or take the RER from *Étoile*). The stone bridge, by *Perronet* (1768–72, almost entirely rebuilt in 1935–39), replaced an earlier bridge erected in 1606 after Henri IV and Marie de Médicis were almost drowned here.

On the l. beyond the bridge is the *Tour Nobel*, built on the site of the house in which Bellini died in 1835, while to the N.W. of this area is a large triangular-shaped domed edifice built to accommodate exhibitions, etc., and known as the CNIT building. Nearby is the *Fiat Tower*, and adjacent, the last 'stabile' by Calder. Also to the N. of the main axis are the *Manhattan Tower* and *GAN Tower*, among others.

W. of La Défense lies *Nanterre*, the préfecture of the department of Hauts-de-Seine.

To the N. of the *Île de Puteaux*, crossed by the *Pont de Neuilly*, is the *Île de la Grande Jatte*, painted by Seurat in 1884.

Neuilly itself, once the most fashionable suburb of Paris, was partially laid out in what was formerly the park of Louis-Philippe's château (built in 1740 and burnt down in 1848), and later developed as a colony of elegant villas, but the construction of blocks of flats has overwhelmed the distinctive character of the neighbourhood.

Its S. half, has the attraction of being adjacent to the *Bois de Boulogne*. At a house on the site of No.33 Rue de Longchamp (leading S. from near the bridge), Théophile Gautier died in 1872. Ossip Zadkine (1890–1967), the sculptor, also died at Neuilly. Further to the E., in the old cemetery, lie Anatole France and André Maurois.

In the *Cimetière de Lavallois-Perret*, the suburb abutting Neuilly to the N., lie Louise Michel (1830–1905), the revolutionary, and Maurice Ravel (1875–1937).

19 The Eastern Districts: From the Buttes-Chaumont to the Fauborg St-Antoine

MÉTROS: *République, Buttes-Chaumont, Jourdain, Télégraphe, Philippe-Auguste, Nation, Bastille, Faidherbe-Chaligny, Gare-de-Lyon.*

The Rue de Lancry, the first main turning r. off the BLVD DE MAGENTA (leading N. from the *Pl. de la République*), shortly crosses the *Canal St-Martin*, beyond which the Rue Bichat leads r. to the entrance of the *Hôpital St-Louis (Pl. 9;6; for skin diseases), founded by Henri IV and built by *Claude Vellefaux* in 1607–12. It is an excellent and now rare example of the Louis-XIII style, and its Courtyards and *Chapel* may be visited on application at the porter's lodge; the latter is not normally open except on Sundays. Extensive works are in progress to modernize the hospital internally.

Turning r. on making our exit, we follow the Rue de la Grange-aux-Belles, where to the N. of the next crossroad stood a small Protestant cemetery, now built over, where in 1792 Paul Jones was buried (and subsequently exhumed; and now at Annapolis). Nearby stood the *Gibet de Montfaucon*, the 'Tyburn' of Paris, set up in the 13C and finally removed in 1790.

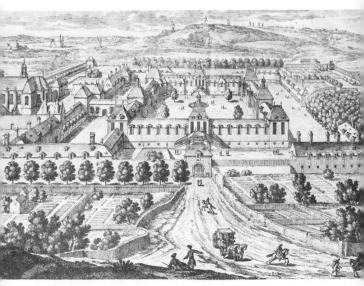

Late 17C view of the Hôpital St-Louis

The Rotonde de la Villette

It proved fatal to three 'surintendants des finances': Enguerrand de Marigny, who erected it; Jean de Montaigu, who repaired it; nor did Semblançay, who tried to avoid it, fare better. Olivier le Daim, confidential barber to Louis XI (1484; comp. 'Quentin Durward'), was hanged here, and Coligny's body exposed after the massacre of St Bartholomew.

Further to the N. is the PL. DU COLONEL-FABIEN, from which the BLVD DE LA VILLETTE leads to the PL. DU STALINGRAD. Here, in the shadow of the overhead Métro line, on a small island site, stands the **Rotunda,** built as a toll-house by *Ledoux* in 1789, and now a repository for archaeological finds in the Paris area.

At No.44 Rue de Flandre, leading N.E. from the N. side of the Place, is a relic of the old *Portuguese Jewish Cemetery*, in use between 1780 and 1810.

The Av. Jean Jaurès leads E.N.E. towards the *Porte de Pantin* and the *Blvd Périphérique*, a short distance before reaching which is the S. entrance to the *Parc de La Villette*.

There is an ambitious project to convert an extensive area (165,000m^2) to the N., until recently covered by the demolished *Abbatoirs de La Villette*, and a cattle-market, into a park of over 30 hectares lying on both sides of the transverse *Canal de l'Ourcq*, on the far bank of which will be the new **Musée National des Sciences et de l'Industrie**, at present under construction (architect, *Adrien Fainsilber*). It will be served by Métros *Porte de Pantin*, and at its N. entrance, by *Porte de La Villette*.

Three older buildings in the S. sector will be retained, comprising two pavilions between which is the *Halles aux Boeufs*, erected by

Baltard. Parallel to and E. of the latter a canal arm will be excavated, fed by the *Canal de l'Ourcq*. On the far bank (to the E. of the *Canal St-Denis*) will rise the *moated Museum*, a rectangular structure of twelve sections, lit by glazed domes and large conservatory-like windows. The museum itself is expected to provide some 40,000m² of exhibition space, apart from all the usual amenities now expected of such establishments.

It will incorporate a *Planetarium*, and other manifestations of the popularization of scientific knowledge, which have been unsuitably housed in the *Grand Palais* (see Rte 16A). Among themes it will cover are: The Universe (astronomy; space; atmosphere; and the structure of our planet, earth); Man and his Environment (heredity; the brain; and bodily functions, etc.); Man-made works, and the Use of materials; Forms of energy, and forms of communication; Sound, Light, the Structure of matter, Mathematics, etc., etc.

We are told that part of the site was once used as an iron-foundry by the English engineers Davidson and Richardson, 'well-known for the beauty and precision of the machines which left their workshops': we have no doubt that, when completed—in 1986, or thereabouts—the new *Science Museum* will be similarly praised.

It is also planned to transfer the *Conservatoire National Superieur de Musique*, with its collection of instruments, to a site at the S.W. corner of the park.

From the PL. DU COLONEL-FABIEN we may follow the Av. Mathurin-Moreau to the W. entrance of the **Parc des Buttes-Chaumont**, one of the more picturesque, and least known, of Parisian parks (23 hectares) lying in the midst of the district of *Belleville* (which belies its name).

It was laid out under Haussmann's régime in 1866–67 by *Alphand* and *Barillet* on the bare hills ('*monts chauves*') which had long been used as a general rubbish-dump and slaughterhouse for horses, etc., its extensive gypsum ('plaster of Paris') quarries being ingeniously transformed into rock-scenery. These heights had been the scene of the 'Battle of Paris' in 1814, and in 1871 were held by the Communards until dislodged by bombardment from Montmartre to the W.

From near the S.E. end of the park, the Rue Fessart leads E., crossing the Rue de la Villette, where at No.51 the painter Georges Rouault (1871–1958) was born, to the Gothic-revival church of *St-Jean-Baptiste* (by *Lassus*, 1854–59).—From the S. side of the church, the Rue de Belleville continues E., passing a developing area to the N., to the *Cimetière de Belleville*, the second highest point in Paris (128m).

An inscription to the r. of the entrance in the Rue du Télégraphe records that Claude Chappe here experimented with the aerial telegraph that was to announce the victories of the French Revolutionary Wars. Originally called 'Tachygraphe', it was set up in 1792 on this site, and was the base of lines to Lille and Strasbourg.

In the Rue Haxo, parallel to the E., at No.79 (r.), is the *Chapelle des Otages*, built in 1936–39 on the site of the Villa des Otages, behind which (at the end of the passage just N. of the chapel) 52 hostages held by the Communards were shot on 26 May 1871.

The return to the centre may be made from the *Métro Télégraphe*, viâ *République*.

From the PL. DE LA RÉPUBLIQUE, the Av. de la République leads E.S.E. across the BLVD RICHARD-LENOIR, built over the *Canal St-Martin* in 1860 by Haussmann, to the N.W. corner of *Père-Lachaise*, the main entrance of which is in the BLVD DE MÉNILMONTANT.

The quarter of *Ménilmontant*, N. of the cemetery, was the home of the philosophical fraternity of the Saint-Simoniens in the 1830s.

The *Cimetière de l'Est*, better known as *PÈRE-LACHAISE, is the largest (47 hectares) and long the most 'fashionable' cemetery in Paris, and its tombs display the work of many 19C French sculptors, funerary and otherwise.

Père François de La Chaise (1624–1709) was the confessor of Louis XIV, and lived in the Jesuit house rebuilt in 1682 on the site of a chapel. The property, situated on the side of a hill from which the king, during the Fronde, watched skirmishing between Condé and Turenne, was bought by the city in 1804 and laid out by *Brongniart*, and since extended.

The first interments were those of La Fontaine and Molière, whose remains were transferred there in 1804. The monument to Abélard and Héloïse, set up in 1779 at the abbey of the Paraclete, was moved here in 1817, its canopy composed of fragments collected by Lenoir from the abbey of Nogent-sur-Seine. In the E. corner of the cemetery is the *Mur des Fédérés*, against which 147 Communards were shot in 1871 (28 May); and here also is a monument to the many thousand Frenchmen who died either in German concentration camps or during the Resistance of 1941–44.

Some thousands of Parisians still converge on the cemetery on 1 and 2 Nov. ('Jour de la Toussaint'—All Saints' Day—and 'Jour des Morts'). A guide-plan may be obtained for a nominal sum from the keeper's lodge at the main entrance, which will indicate the position of the tombs of the illustrious dead interred here, which indeed make an impressive list.

Among *writers*: Beaumarchais, Hugo, Béranger, Proust, Balzac, Constant, Mme de Genlis, Gérard de Nerval, de Musset, Daudet, Rémy de Gourmont, Apollinaire, de Régnier, Barbusse, Bernardin de Saint-Pierre, Villiers de L'Isle-Adam, Colette, Éluard, and Sartre.

Among *musicians*: Méhul, Gossec, Grétry, Boieldieu, Hérold, Pleyel, Leseur, Rossini (later removed to Florence), Cherubini, Bellini (removed to Catania), Bizet, Reynaldo Hahn, Chausson, Kreutzer, Chopin, Lalo, Gustave Charpentier, Auber, Poulenc, Dukas, and Georges Enesco; the librettist Scribe; and the singer Adelina Patti.

Among *artists*: David, Corot, Doré, Ingres, Gros, Daumier, Daubigny, Delacroix, Géricault, Seurat, and Modigliani.

Among Napoleon's *marshals*: Davout, Kellermann, Lefèbvre, Masséna, Ney, Murat, Victor, Macdonald, Suchet, Gouvion-Saint-Cyr, and Augereau; and generals Foy, Junot, and Marbot.

Other famous names in their respective fields are: Mlle Mars, Rachel, Talma, Isadora Duncan, Sarah Bernhardt, and Yvette Guilbert; Manuel Godoy; De Sèze; Brillat-Savarin; Champollion; Parmentier; Blanqui; Baron Haussmann; the philosophers Saint-Simon, and Comte; Lammennais; Michelet; Arago; Cuvier; Monge; Barras; and Thiers (see below).

Also interred here are Oscar Wilde (1856–1900; but not moved here until nine years after his death; with a monument by *Epstein*); Sir William Keppel (1702–54), second Earl of Albemarle; Adm. Sir Sidney Smith (1764–1840); and Sir Richard Hertford-Wallace (1818–90), the connoisseur and benefactor of Paris (see p225).

N. of the Rue de la Roquette, opposite the main entrance of the cemetery, stood the *Prison de la Grande-Roquette*, itself on the site of the convent of the *Hospitalières de la Roquette*, founded in 1639, replaced in 1899 by the *Petit-Roquette* (for women). From 1853 to 1899 condemned prisoners were held at *La Roquette* while awaiting execution. Here in 1871 some 50-odd Commune hostages were shot, although c.130 were also released. Thiers's victorious government forces 'of law and order' then proceeded to round up thousands of Communards—both repentant and unrepentant—and in two days shot out-of-hand a mere 1900 in retaliation, or 'in expiation'!

To the S.E. of the cemetery, approached by the BLVD DE CHARONNE (forking off the Blvd de Ménilmontant) and Rue de Bagnolet, stands **St-Germain-de Charonne**, a rustic church of the 13–14C, restored in the 19th, retaining its village cemetery (the only other in Paris being *St-Pierre-de-Montmartre*).—*St-Jean-Bosco* (1937), of concrete, and with a lofty tower, stands a short distance S.E. of the junction of the Blvd de Charonne and the Rue de Bagnolet.

The Faubourg St-Antoine

The BLVD DE MÉNILMONTANT, with its continuation S., the Av. Philippe-Auguste, leads S.E. to the *Pl. de la Nation*, also approached direct from the *Pl. de la Bastille* by Métro. The RUE DU FAUBOURG-ST-ANTOINE leads E.S.E. from the Bastille to the *Pl. de la Nation*, through an area memorable in the history of the Revolutions of 1789 and 1848. It was also the scene of skirmishing during the Fronde (1652), when Turenne defeated Condé.

Since the late 13C it has been a centre of cabinet-making, and many courtyards and passages still accommodate busy workshops behind 18C façades.

At No.1 Rue du Faubourg-St-Antoine, leading away from the Pl. de la Bastille (see Rte 12) and the projected opera-house, Fieschi hatched the plot against Louis-Philippe. At No.61 (l.), at the corner of the Rue de Charonne, is the *Fontaine Trogneux* (1710). Further on (r.) the SQ. TROUSSEAU occupies the site of the *Hospice des Enfants-Trouvés*, in the graveyard of which the Princesse de Lamballe was buried after her corpse had been paraded through the streets.—In front of No.151, Baudin, representative of the people for the department of the Ain, was killed on a barricade while inciting the Parisians to protest against the coup d'état of Napoleon III (1851).

To the l., the Rue St-Bernard leads to the church of *Ste-Marguerite*, built in 1634 but many times altered since. Behind the high-altar is a Pietà by *Girardon*. It is believed that the 10-year-old Louis XVII, who in all probability died at the *Temple*, was buried in the graveyard here, with other victims of the Revolution.

S. of the Rue du Faubourg-St-Antoine at this point lies the *Hôpital St-Antoine*, rebuilt in 1905 but retaining part of *Lenoir's* 18C building for the former *Abbaye de St-Antoine-des-Champs*.

A number of thoroughfares converge on the spacious **Pl. de la Nation**, at the hub of which is a colossal bronze group representing the 'Triumph of the Republic', by *Dalou* (1899). It was known formerly as the *Pl. du Trône* (named after the throne erected for Louis XIV's triumphal entry in 1660 with Maria Teresa); in 1794 no less than 1,306 victims of the Terror were guillotined here. Between 1793 and 1880 it was known as the *Pl. du Trône-renversé*. To the E. of the 'circus' are two pavilions, built as toll-houses by *Ledoux* in 1788, each surmounted by a Doric column 30.50m high; one with a statue of Philippe Auguste (by *Dumont*), the other, of Louis IX, by *Étex*. The COURS DE VINCENNES (where took place in Easter Week the Foire aux Pains d'épice, a festival dating back to the 10C, when bread made with honey and aniseed was distributed by the monks of the Abbey of St-Antoine) leads directly E. from the *Pl. de la Nation* to the *Porte de Vincennes*, and beyond to the *Château de Vincennes* (see Rte 20), also reached direct by the Métro.

The Rue Fabre-d'Églantine leads S. to the Rue de Picpus, where, at the end of the garden at No.35, a convent of Augustinian nuns, is the little ***Cimetière de Picpus** (open, 14.00–16.00 or 18.00, except Mon.), a private burial-ground for 'emigrés' and descendants of victims of the Revolution.

Among individuals interred there is La Fayette; among famous families, those of Chateaubriand, Crillon, Gontaut-Biron, Tascher de la Pagerie, Choiseul, La Rochefoucauld, Du Plessis, Montmorency, Talleyrand-Périgord, Rohan-Rochefort, Noailles, Quélen, Salignac-Fénelon, etc., as well as sixteen Carmelites of Compiègne martyred in 1794. In a second section are buried members of the house of Salm-Kyrbourg, and those guillotined in the *Pl. du Trône-renverse*, including André Chénier.

A short distance S.E. of the PL. DE LA BASTILLE, in the Rue de Charenton, is the rebuilt *Hospice des Quinze-Vingts*, founded as a asylum for 300 blind persons by Louis IX in 1260. The previous building was later—until 1775—the *Caserne des Mousquetaires-Noirs*.
Nos 40–60 in the street occupy the site of the *Couvent des Filles-Anglais de la Conception*, which from 1635–55 accepted only daughters of English parents.

The Rue de Lyon leads S. from the PL. DE LA BASTILLE to the **Gare de Lyon** (Pl. 5;6), terminus of lines to Dijon, Grenoble, Lyon, Provence, Côte d'Azur, and Italy, etc.; it preserves a fin-de-siècle buffet. The boarding-point for auto-couchettes hence is at No.48 Blvd de Bercy, further S.E.

Opposite the station once stood the *Mazas Prison*, where 400 Communards were rounded up and massacred by Thiers's troops in 1871.
On its S. side the station is now overlooked by developments, including the *Tour Gamma A*, 195 Rue de Bercy, containing offices of the *Observatoire économique de Paris* (Institut National de la Statistique et des Études Économiques), a mine of information.
Just E. of the *Pont de Bercy* (1864) rears the hexagonal *Palais Omnisports*, a stunted pyramid topped by a tubular platform sustained by four cylindrical towers. It was inaugurated in 1984, and accommodates 17,000 spectators. The site of the new *Min. of Finance* will be immediately to the N.
The area to the S.E. is to be laid out as a park. Here stood the once extensive *Entrepôt des Vins*, with bonded warehouses and cellars. This spiritous district has been the subject of a number of calamities in the past, among them the diluting inundations of 1817, 1833, 1836, and 1850; and being *flambé* by ravaging fires in 1820, 1823, 1853, 1859, and 1860!

The BLVD DIDEROT leads W. from the *Gare de Lyon* to the *Pont d'Austerlitz* (also approached direct from the *Pl. de la Bastille* by the BLVD DE LA BASTILLE), built in 1802–07, rebuilt in stone in 1855, and widened in 1884–86.
To the N.W., the QUAI HENRI-IV occupies what was until c. 1840 the *Île Louviers*, now joined to the Right Bank.—To the S.E., at No. 12 QUAI DE LA RAPÉE, is the *Institut Médico-Légal* (no adm.), which replaced the old Morgue, which stood at the S. end of the *Île de la Cité*. Just beyond it the Métro crosses the Seine on a single span of 140m. Other bridges seen in this direction beyond the *Pont de Bercy* are the *Pont de Tolbiac* (1879–84), *Pont National* (1852, enlarged in 1939–42), and the new bridge carrying the Périphérique. The *Porte de Bercy*, on the N. Bank here, is the commencement of the A4 autoroute to the E.

The *Pont d'Austerlitz* crosses the Seine to the *Gare d'Austerlitz*, see Rte 3.

A photograph by Atget *in the former Entrepôt des Vins, Bercy*

20 Vincennes: The Château and Park

Approx. 2km E. of the *Porte de Vincennes*, and reached directly from the centre by the MÉTRO (*Château de Vincennes*), stands the impressive bulk of the historic ***CHÂTEAU DE VINCENNES** (CN) , rectangular in plan, and flanked by nine square towers. All except the entrance tower, the finest and largest, which lost only its statues, were reduced to the level of the walls in the 19C. Michelet called it 'the Windsor of the Valois'.

The present castle, succeeding an earlier hunting-lodge fortified by Louis IX, was begun by Philippe VI in 1337, and its fortification was completed by his grandson Charles V (1364–73), who also commenced work on the Chapel, which was not finished until 1552. Some idea of how it once looked may be gained from the illustration of December in the 'Très Riches Heures of the Duc de Berri', or *Fouquet*'s panel of Étienne Chevalier. The foundations of the *Pavillons du Roi* and *de la Reine* (to the S.) were laid in the 16C, but these buildings were not completed for nearly a century, when the château, then in Mazarin's possession, was altered and decorated by *Le Vau*.

With the completion of the palace at Versailles (c. 1680), Vincennes was deserted by the court, and the château was occupied in turn by a porcelain factory (1745; transferred to Sèvres in 1756), a cadet school, and in 1757, a small-arms factory. Offered for sale in 1788, it found no purchaser, and in 1791 La Fayette rescued it from destruction by the Revolutionary mob. In 1808 Napoleon converted it into an arsenal, when the surviving 13C buildings were demolished. In 1840 it was made into a fortress, and much of Le Vau's decoration was destroyed or masked by casements.

During the Second World War, German occupying forces had a supply depot here, and the *Pavillon de la Reine* was partially destroyed by an explosion in 1944 during their evacuation of the building. Restoration continues to be undertaken sporadically, but much work is still to be done.

The historical associations of Vincennes are numerous. Here died Jeanne de Navarre in 1305, Louis X in 1316, Charles IV in 1328, Charles IX in 1574, and Mazarin in 1661; and Charles V was born here in 1337. In 1326 the 'Auld Alliance' or treaty between France and Scotland was signed here. Henry V of England died here in 1422, seven weeks before the death of Charles VI, whom he was to succeed as king of France. During the reign of Louis XIII, the keep was used as a state prison; and among its inmates were the Grand Condé, Card. de Retz, Fouquet, Diderot (visited there by Rousseau in 1749), and Mirabeau (who here wrote his 'Essai sur les lettres de cachet' in 1784). Prince Charles Edward Stuart was imprisoned here briefly after Culloden. A later prisoner was J.-H. Latude (1725–1805), who, for a fraudulent attempt to extract money from Mme de Pompadour, was incarcerated here (and elsewhere), untried, for thirty-five years.

In 1804 the Duc d'Enghien, son of the Prince de Condé, arrested five days before on Napoleon's orders, was tried by court-martial and shot here the same night. Gén. Daumesnil was governor of the château from 1809 to 1814, during the Hundred Days, and from 1830 until his death in 1832. When summoned to surrender to the Allies in 1814, his answer was 'First give me back my leg' (which he had lost at Wagram). In 1830, when the mob broke into the building in search of some former ministers of Charles X, he dispersed them by threatening to blow up the powder-magazine. Mata Hari was shot here in 1917. In 1944, three days before evacuating it, the Germans shot some thirty hostages against the interior of the ramparts.

Crossing the moat, we enter the fortress beneath the imposing *Tour du Village*, 48m high, and pass between a range of tawdry buildings in military occupation to reach the central courtyard. The **Keep*, 50m in height, a square tower flanked with round turrets, is enclosed in a separate turreted enceinte, and is the finest of its type in France (since the *Château de Coucy* was blown up by the Germans in 1917), and as such deserves further restoration. The two doors on the ground floor facing the postern came from the prison of Louis XVI in the Temple. A wide spiral stair ascends to the first and second floors (third floor closed), supported by vaults springing from a central column; the corbels at each corner of the room symbolize the four Evangelists. Note the oak beams between the ribs.

The SECOND FLOOR was a favourite residence of Charles V, and contains a fine chimneypiece, and an oratory in the N.W. turret. Henry V (of England) and Charles IX died on this floor. 17C prisoners of state were lodged above. The energetic may climb to the roof, commanding a wide view of the area, with the main landmarks of central Paris easily discerned to the W. The kitchen, with its internal well, is shown on the ground floor as we make our exit.

The **Chapel* opposite was founded by Charles V in 1379, and, retaining the Gothic style, was only completed in 1552. The Flamboyant *Façade* has a magnificent rose-window surmounted by an ornamental gable filled with tracery. The interior, bare of furniture, contains graceful vaulting, and at the E. end, seven stained-glass windows by *Beaurain* (16C), restored after an explosion in 1870. A monument to the Duc d'Enghien (see above; by *Deseine*, 1816) may be seen in the oratory.

To the S., approached through a portico, lies the immense *Cour d'Honneur*, and beyond, the monumental *Tour du Bois*. To the r. stands the *Pavillon du Roi* (now containing military archives), and opposite, the *Pavillon de la Reine*, where Mazarin died in 1661. Both were completed by *Le Vau* in 1654–60. The latter houses the *Musée de la Guerre de 1914–1918.*

Some 3·5km N.E.—as the crow flies—in the *Parc de Montreau* (to the E. of *Montreuil*), is the *Musée de l'Histoire Vivante*, largely devoted to the Socialist ethic and the history of the revolutions of 1830, and 1848, the Paris Commune, and other proletarian movements, etc. which will be of interest to some.

The **Bois de Vincennes**, first enclosed in the 12C, was replanted in 1731 by Louis XV and converted into a park for the citizens of Paris. It was further enlarged in 1860. To the S.E. of the château are extensive *Floral Gardens*, and beyond are stadiums and sports grounds. Further E. is the *Lac des Minimes*, a *Jardin Tropical*, and an *Indo-Chinese pagoda*.

Towards the S.W. end of the Bois, approached directly from the château by the Av. Daumesnil (S. of which are University buildings), is the *Parc Zoölogique de Vincennes* (open 9.00–17.30 or 19.00 daily), the main zoo of Paris. Beyond it is the *Lac Daumesnil*, S. of which is a *Buddhist Temple*.

As the Avenue leaves the Bois near an underground section of the Blvd Périphérique, the Av. Ste-Marie leads r., at No.60 in which stands the *Musée des Transports Urbains*.

Slightly further to the W. is the reformed *****Musée National des Arts Africains et Océaniens**, housed in a building erected in 1931 for a Colonial Exhibition, with an ornately sculpted façade. It also contains an *Aquarium*.

As its name implies, it concentrates on the *arts* of the ci-devant French colonies rather than their ethnography, for which see *Musée de l'Homme* Rte 17. Adm. 9.45–12.00; 13.30–17.15: daily, except Tues.

GROUND FLOOR: l., the Oceanian Collection: masks, wooden drums, and statues from the New Hebrides: to the r., naïf bark paintings from Australia. FIRST FLOOR: l., arts of the W. African coast, including gold figurines, etc., from Akan; brass and gold powder figures from Ghana and the Ivory Coast; note also the carved wood woman and child from Kran (Liberia). To the r., work from the Niger and Congo basins, Yoruba (Nigeria), and the Cameroons; Benin bronzes; nail-studded magic statues from the Congo; Bembe figurines, masks, jewellery, and pottery.

SECOND FLOOR: l., Moroccan jewellery, including a fine necklace from Fez (16–17C); arms; and a section devoted to fabrics, brocades, embroidery, caftans, etc. To the r., the arts of Tunisia and Algeria, including bonnets, pendants, fibulas, etc.

The return to the centre may be made from the MÉTRO *Porte Dorée*, adjacent.

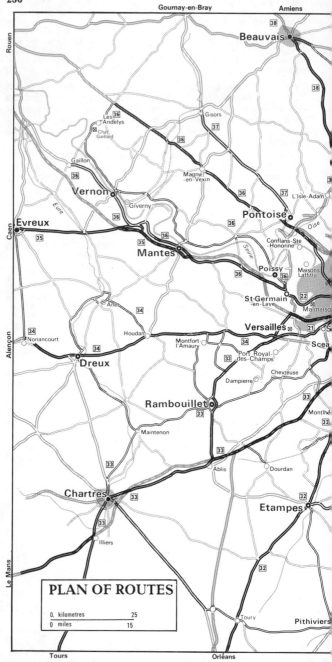

PLAN OF ROUTES

0	kilometres	25
0	miles	15

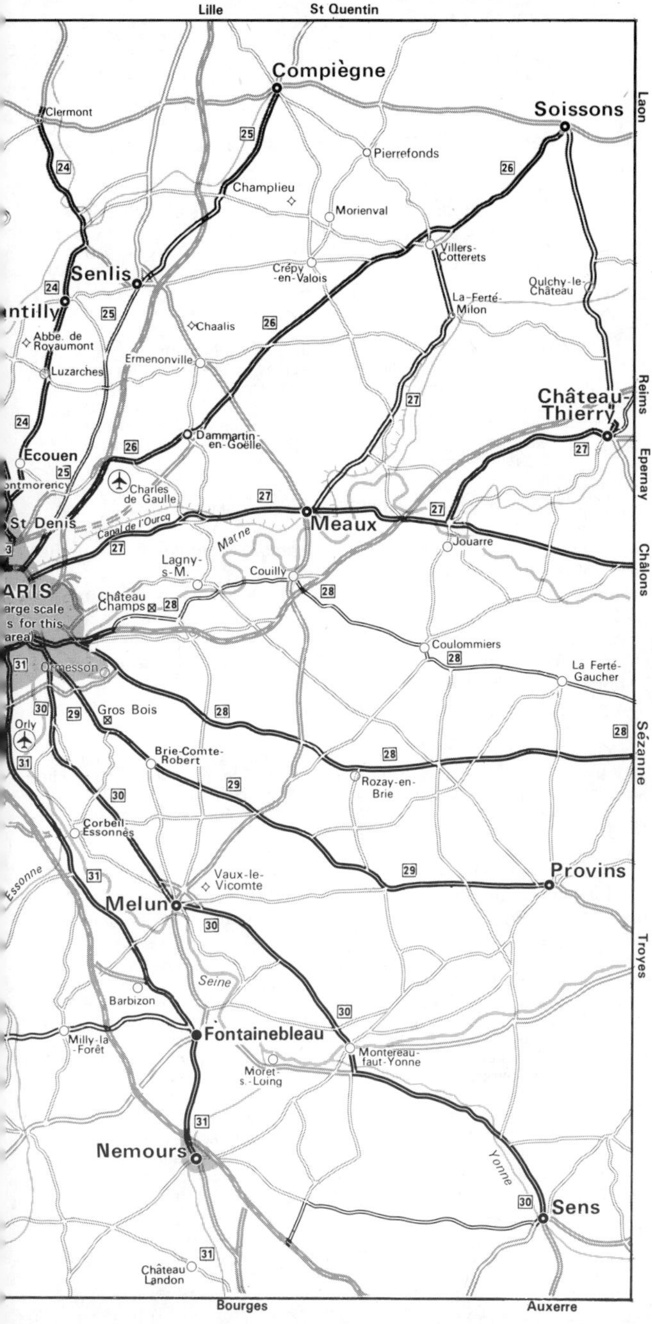
Lille
St Quentin
Compiègne
Soissons
Laon
Clermont
25
24
Pierrefonds
26
Champlieu
Morienval
Villers-Cotterets
Senlis
Crépy-en-Valois
Oulchy-le-Château
24
ntilly
25
La-Ferté-Milon
Chaalis
26
Abbe. de Royaumont
Ermenonville
Luzarches
27
Reims
Château-Thierry
24
Dammartin-en-Goële
26
27
Ecouen
25
Epernay
ontmorency
Charles de Gaulle
27
St Denis
Canal de l'Ourcq
Meaux
27
Marne
27
Jouarre
Châlons
Lagny-s-M.
Couilly
ARIS
arge scale
s for this
area
Château Champs
28
28
Coulommiers
28
31
Ormesson
La Ferté-Gaucher
30
29
Gros Bois
28
Orly
28
Sézanne
Brie-Comte-Robert
28
31
Rozay-en-Brie
29
30
Corbeil-Essonnes
Essonne
31
29
Provins
Vaux-le-Vicomte
Melun
30
Troyes
Seine
Barbizon
30
Fontainebleau
Milly-la-Forêt
Montereau-faut-Yonne
Moret-s.-Loing
31
Nemours
Yonne
30
Sens
31
Château Landon
Bourges
Auxerre

THE ENVIRONS OF PARIS

21 Paris to Versailles

BY ROAD. Versailles is best approached by taking the A13 motorway and turning l. at the first exit after passing through the tunnel at St-Cloud. Hence a road leads S.W. towards the palace of Versailles (parking in the *Pl. d'Armes*). An alternative is the N10, bearing S.W. from the Porte de S-Cloud over the Pont de Sèvres, which our route follows.

BY RAIL. A convenient approach is the new RER line running along the S. bank of the Seine, where the train may be boarded at, for example, *St-Michel, Gare d'Orsay, Invalides, Champ-de-Mars*, or *Javel*, etc., a branch of which has its terminus at *Versailles-Rive Gauche* (the station nearest the palace). There are also lines from the *Gare St-Lazare* to *Versailles-Rive Droit*, and from the *Gare Montparnasse* to *Versailles-Chantiers*.

BUS 171 from the *Pont de Sèvres*, served by MÉTRO.

Note that the *Palace* of Versailles is closed on *Mondays*, although the Gardens are open every day until dusk.

The N10, on leaving the *Porte de St-Cloud* (with fountains by *Landowski*), traverses the suburb of *Boulogne-Billancourt* before crossing the *Pont de Sèvres* (rebuilt 1963). The most interesting object in **Sèvres** itself is the ***Musée National de Céramique**, which, it should be emphasised, also displays china and porcelain other than that produced in the famous Porcelain Factory founded in 1738.

The *Museum*, which lies immediately r. of the main road (4, Grande Rue), may be visited daily 9.30–12.00; 13.30–17.15, except Tues.; guided tours of the adjacent *workshops* (no children under 16) take place from 14.00–15.30 on the first and third Thurs. of each month; the *Sale-room* is open 9.00–12.00; 13.30–18.00 from Mon. to Fri. MÉTRO *Pont-de-Sèvres*.

The factory was moved here from Vincennes in 1756 at the instance of Mme de Pompadour, and since 1760 has been State-controlled. Amongst designers of Sèvres ware may be mentioned *E.-M. Falconet* (1716–91), and *J.-B. Pigalle* (1714–85).

On the FIRST FLOOR are Islamic ceramics (8–15Cs), and from Anatolia (16–18Cs); and historical collections, mostly from France; Italian majolica; Hispano-Moresque ware, etc., from the Middle Ages to the 18C.—SECOND FLOOR; *N. Gallery*: Delft ware; faïence from Nevers; from Moustiers, Rouen, Strasbourg, Marseille, and Sceaux; and copies of Oriental pieces manufactured at St-Cloud, Mennecy, Meissen, and Chantilly. *S. Gallery*: Porcelain from Vincennes and Sèvres, and Saxe, etc.

Lully once resided in a nearby pavilion, named after him. Some distance to the W., in the suburb of *Ville d'Avray*, the 'Villa des Jardies' was the country retreat of Balzac in 1837–41, where he was visited by Hugo and Gautier. It was later the home of Léon Gambetta (1838–82), who died there. The 18C church contains frescoes by *Corot*, who often painted the lakes in the *Bois de Fausses Reposes*, further S.W.

Immediately S.E. of Sèvres lies **Meudon**, the benefice of which was enjoyed by Rabelais in 1551–52. Wagner composed 'The Flying Dutchman' here in 1841, at 27 Av. du Château; here too is the 'Villa des Brillants', once the home of Rodin, with his grave; and a *Museum* of local history at 11 Rue des Pierres.

Further S. is the *Observatoire d'Astronomie Physique*. The building, formerly the *Château Neuf*, was built for the Grand Dauphin ('Monseigneur', the son of Louis XIV), by *Mansart*, but a fire in 1870 reduced it to the single-storeyed building which it is today. The Terrasse commands an extensive view. The *Forêt de Meudon* extends to the S. and W.

2km N. of Sévres lies **St-Cloud**, birthplace of Hilaire Belloc (1870–1953). The royal castle—in which Henri III was assassinated in 1589; Philippe d'Orléans born (1674); where Napoleon's second marriage, to Marie-Louise, was celebrated in 1810; and where Charles X signed his infamous 'Ordonnances' in 1830—was burned down during the German occupation in 1870, but the **Park** (392 hectares), with its cascades, fountains, and views over Paris—which Queen Victoria thought splendid—is open to the public. At *Montretout*, the upper part of St-Cloud, is the H.Q. of *Interpol*.

On a height some 3km N. is seen the fort of *Mont Valérian*, where Col Henry, implicated in the Dreyfus Affair, committed suicide; and where during the years 1941–44 some 4500 members of the Resistance, among others, were murdered. Off the Blvd Washington is an *American Military Cemetery*.

From Sèvres, the N10 continues S.W. (through *Chaville* and *Viroflay*) to (c.8km) *Versailles*.

VERSAILLES (95,000 inhab.), préfecture of the department of Yvelines, lies in a low sandy plain between two lines of wooded hills. With its regular streets and its imposing avenues converging on the palace, it seeks to retain its royal cachet, although the palace, with which the history of the town is inextricably—some would say parasitically—entwined, quite overshadows it in interest. Nevertheless, it does contain a certain number of buildings of importance, which are described below.

Versailles emerged from obscurity in 1624, when Louis XIII built a hunting lodge here, which subsequently developed into a small château. But the real creator of Versailles was Louis XIV, who in 1661 conceived the idea of building a lasting monument to his reign—a trophy of self-glorification. *Louis Le Vau* was entrusted with the renovation and embellishment of the old building round the Cour de Marbre, while *Le Nôtre* laid out the park. After Le Vau's death in 1670 the work was continued by his pupil *François d'Orbay*, while the interior decoration was superintended by *Charles Le Brun*. In 1682 Louis XIV transferred here from St-Germain, the court and seat of government. *Jules Hardouin-Mansart*, appointed chief architect in 1676, remodelled the main body of the palace and built the two great N. and S. wings, giving the immense façade (with its 375 windows) a total length of 580m. The chapel, begun by him, was finished by his brother-in-law *Robert de Cotte* in 1710.

More than 30,000 workmen were employed at one time on the building of the palace and in laying out and draining the grounds; the cost, impoverishing France, amounting to over 60 million livres. In 1687 *Mansart* built the *Grand Trianon*. Under Louis XV a series of royal apartments, decorated in the current style, were incorporated; and one of the colonnaded pavilions in the entrance court, the interior of the opera-house, and the *Petit Trianon* were built by *J.-A.*

A bird's eye view of the Palais de Versailles in 1668, painted by Pierre Patel, as it was just prior to Le Vau's and Mansart's later extension and rebuilding.

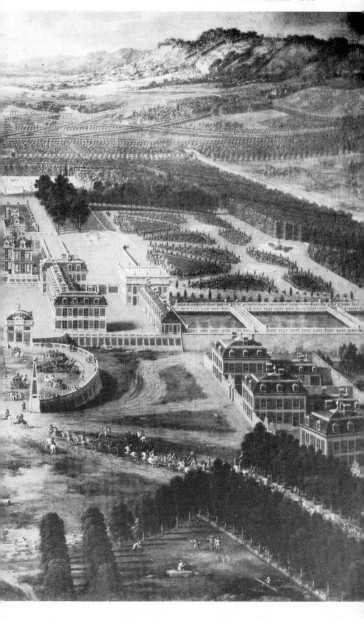

Gabriel. Louis XVI redecorated a suite of apartments for Marie-Antoinette and built the 'rustic village' or *Hameau.*

Not all visitors from England were impressed by Versailles. The poet Gray, in 1739, wrote of it as 'a huge heap of littleness'; Dr Johnson was more interested by the menagerie than the palace; Smollett described it as a 'most fantastic composition of magnificence and littleness, taste and foppery'.

The independence of the United States was formally recognized by England, France, and Spain, at the Treaty of Versailles, signed in 1783. The meeting of the Assembly of the States-General was held in Versailles in 1789, where on 20 June the deputies of the Third Estate constituted themselves into the National Assembly. On 6 Oct. the Paris mob, led by the women of the Halles, marched to Versailles, massacred the bodyguard, and conveyed the king and the royal family to the Tuileries.

In 1792, when Richard Twiss visited Versailles, he found it almost bare: glasses, tapestries, and pictures removed. It had been uninhabited for over two years, and the Grand Canal was quite dry. In 1814 the palace was occupied by Tsar Alexander I and Frederick William III of Prussia. Under the Restoration, the second colonnaded pavilion was completed by *Dufour,* but the building later fell into disrepair. Louis-Philippe did irreparable damage to the palace in housing a pretentious museum there, containing few canvases of any importance, and reflecting his prodigious lack of taste.

In the Franco-Prussian War Versailles became the H.Q. of the German armies operating against Paris, and Moltke occupying No.38 Blvd de la Reine. On 18 Jan. 1871, William I of Prussia was crowned German Emperor in the *Galerie des Glaces;* and on 26 Jan. the peace preliminaries were signed at Bismarck's quarters at 20 Rue de Provence. In 1871–75 the National Assembly sat in the opera-house, and here the Third Republic was confirmed on 25 Feb. 1875. Its restoration began after the appointment of Pierre de Nolhac as curator in 1887.

During the First World War Versailles was the seat of the Allied War Council, and the Peace Treaty with Germany was signed in the *Galerie des Glaces* on 28 June 1919. Extensive restorations were made in 1928–32, and have continued since the Second World War. During that war, the Allied G.H.Q. was at Versailles from Sept. 1944 until the following May, and many buildings were requisitioned by the military, which hardly improved them.

Versailles was the birthplace of Louis XV (1710–74), Houdon (1741–1828), the sculptor, Marshal Berthier (1753–1815), Louis XVI (1754–93), Louis XVIII (1755–1824), Charles X (1757–1836), Kreutzer (1766–1831), the violinist, Gén. Hoche (1768–97), and de Lesseps (1805–94; at 18 Rue des Réservoirs). Mme de Pompadour died in the palace in 1764; the painter Georges Rouault (1871–1958) is buried in the St-Louis cemetery. Sir Jonah Barrington (1760–1834), author of diverting 'Personal Sketches', and the art dealer Ambroise Vollard (1865–1939) died at Versailles.

At 7 Rue des Réservoirs, N. of the palace, is the *Hôtel des Réservoirs,* built by *Lassurance* for Mme de Pompadour (but much altered), still bearing the marquise's arms. The *Théâtre Montansier* (No.13), founded by the actress Mlle Montansier, was built by *Heurtier* and *Boulet* in 1777, and since restored. La Bruyère (1645–96) lived and died at No.22, the *Hôtel du Prince de Condé*

A few minutes' walk to the N.E. brings one to the *Musée Lambinet,* in an 18C mansion (at 54 *Blvd de la Reine*) containing sculptures by *Houdon,* sketches by *Dunoyer de Segonzac,* and a painting of Lalande and Couperin sharing a ham, by *Robert Tournières.*—To the S. stands *Nôtre-Dame,* by *Jules Hardouin-Mansart* (1684), with a pulpit of the period.

By the same architect is the *Grand-Commun,* immediately S. of the Palace, built to accommodate a swarm of court functionaries, which retains several fine bas-reliefs. Adjacent is the former *Hôtel de la Guerre* (1759), and *Hôtel de la Marine et des Affaires Étrangères* (1761), now the municipal library, with Louis-XV decoration. The Marquis de Louvois (1641–91) died at No.6 in the street, once the *Hôtel de la Surintendance.*

Hence the Rue du Vieux-Versailles (l.) brings us shortly to the **Jeu de Paume**, the royal-tennis court, built in 1686, but of little interest in itself (adm. on application to the Conservateur, Château de Versailles).

In 1789, the deputies of the Tiers-État, finding themselves locked out of the States-General, adjourned here, and with the astronomer Bailly as their president, swore not to separate until they had given France a proper constitution. It was later used as a studio by Gros and Horace Vernet.

To the S. stands a rare but frigid example of a Louis XV church, **St-Louis** (1742–54; by *Jacques Mansart de Sagonne*), designated a cathedral in 1802.

To the W. is the former royal kitchen-garden, now a horticultural college (entrance No.4 Rue du Potager).—To the S.E. is the Pl. du Marché-St-Louis, with quaint 18C houses. Further on, at No.4 Rue St-Médéric, was the *Parc-aux-Cerfs*, purchased in 1755 by Louis XV—when in rut—for the indulgence of his amours.

In the Av. de Paris, leading directly E. from the palace, No.3 occupies the *Hôtel de Mme du Barry* (1751; adm. on application), preserving contemporary woodwork. Robert de Montesquiou (1855–1921) lived at No.53, where he entertained many writers and dilettantes. Further on at Nos 57–61, are the *Laiterie de Madame* and *Pavillon de Musique,* built by *Chalgrin* in 1781 in emulation of the 'hameau' at ·the Petit Trianon, for Joséphine-Louise de Savoie, Comtesse de Provence, wife of the future Louis XVIII.

**The Palace of Versailles

Admission. The Palace is open every day from 9.45–17.30, except Mondays, but only the *Grands Appartements*, the *Galerie des Glaces*, and the *Appartements de la Reine* may be visited entirely without restriction. Regulations with regard to visiting the Chapel, the Trianons, and certain other galleries are liable to variation. Normally the *Opèra, Appartements du Roi, de Mme de Maintenon, Mme du Barry*, and the *Petits Appartements de la Reine* may only be visited with a guided group, and information with regard to the times of departure of such groups (some with an English-speaking guide) should be requested at the entrance vestibule, to the r. (N.) of the Cour Royale. Those groups perambulating the Appartements du Roi normally leave the *Salle des Gardes* (R120 on Pl.) every ten minutes between 10.30–16.15.

An enquiry in advance to the *Service éducatif* (Tel. 950 58 32) may avoid delays and inconveniences attendant on those attempting to cover the ground unaided, particularly when wishing to explore those parts of the palace not so frequently visited by the masses.

Certain sections, such as the *Appartements de Mme de Pompadour*, the *Salles du 18C*, and *du Consulat et l'Empire*, apart from the *Musée des Voitures*, may still be closed for restoration.

Note that the *Petit Trianon* is only open from 14.00–17.30 (except Sat. and Sun).

By the main entrance are cloakrooms, bookstalls, and an Information bureau. Refreshments may be obtained adjacent.

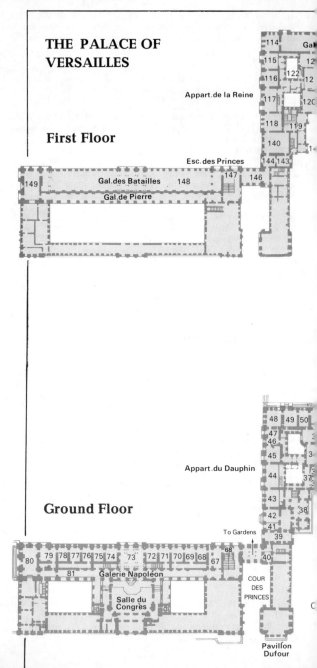

THE PALACE OF VERSAILLES

Appart. de la Reine

First Floor

Esc. des Princes

Gal. des Batailles   148
Gal. de Pierre

149
147   146
144 143

114 Gal
115 12
116 122 12
117 120
118 119
140

Ground Floor

Appart. du Dauphin

To Gardens

80 79 78 77 76 75 74 73 72 71 70 69 68 67 68
81 Galerie Napoléon
Salle du Congrès

48 49 50
47
46
45
44
43
42
41
39
40
38
37

COUR DES PRINCES

Pavillon Dufour

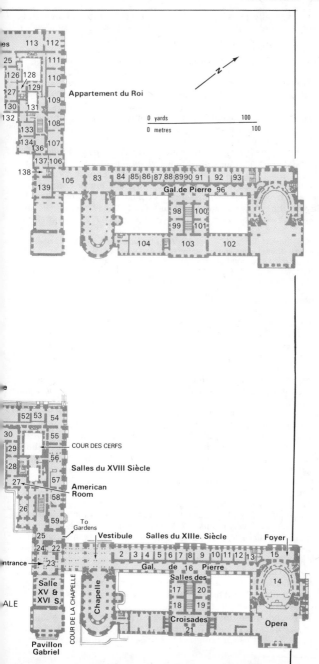

113 112
25 111
126 128
127 129
130 131
132
133
134 136 107
137 106
138
139 105 83 84 85 86 87 88 89 90 91 92 93

Appartement du Roi

Gal. de Pierre 96

98 100
99 101

104 103 102

0 yards 100
0 metres 100

52 53 54
30 55
29
28 56
27 57
26 58
59

COUR DES CERFS

Salles du XVIII Siècle

American Room

To Gardens

Vestibule   Salles du XIIIe. Siècle

Foyer

25
24 22
23   2 3 4 5 6 7 8 9 10 11 12 13   15

ntrance

Gal. de 16 Pierre

Salle XV & XVI S.

Salles des

17 20

18 19

14

ALE

Chapelle

COUR DE LA CHAPELLE

Croisades

21

Opera

Pavillon Gabriel

It is virtually physically impossible to visit *all* the galleries, the park, and the Trianons, in one day, although many attempt to do so. The *Gardens* are described on pp252-4.

The wide avenues de St-Cloud, de Paris, and de Sceaux, converge on the *Pl. d'Armes*, E. of the palace, bounded to the E. by the **Grandes Écuries** and the **Petites Écuries**, the royal stables, built by *Mansart* in 1679-85, which once accommodated 2000 carriages and 2500 horses; and in which Communards were incarcerated in 1871.

Their façades have been restored recently, and there is a project to convert the latter into studios for the restoration of paintings in the national collections.

Flanking the gateway to the palace, with *Mansart's* original grille, are groups of sculpture: (r.) France victorious over the Empire, by *Marsy*, and over Spain, by *Girardon*; and l., Peace, by *Tuby*, and Abundance, by *Coysevox*. The *Avant-Cour* or *Cour des Ministres* is flanked by detached wings once assigned to secretaries of state. Beyond the equestrian statue of Louis XIV (1837) is the *Cour Royale*, between two colonnaded pavilions dating from 1772 (r.) and 1829.

In the time of Louis XIV, only those who possessed the honours of the Louvres—those called 'cousin' by the king, and who had the right to bring their coach or chair or liveried servants into the great Courtyard of the Louvre—could enter this court in a similar fashion.

The visitors' entrance to the palace is in the r.-hand pavilion. Before entering, walk over to the *Cour de Marbre*, a deep, marble-paved recess at the end of the *Cour Royale*; this was the courtyard of Louis XIII's château and the nucleus of the whole palace, before being transformed by *Le Vau* and *Mansart*.

The ticket-office, cloakroom (obligatory for umbrellas, parcels, etc.), and bookstalls are accommodated in the *Vestibule Gabriel* (**R23**).

Beyond this is the *Vestibule de la Chapelle*, which has handsome carved and gilded doors and contains a bas-relief by *Nicolas* and *Guillaume Coustou* of Louis XIV crossing the Rhine. To the r. we get a view of the **Chapel** (adm. only for mass on Sun. at 11.30), with its colonnade of Corinthian columns, begun by *Mansart* in 1699 and completed in 1710 by *Robert de Cotte*. The high-altar is of marble and bronze, with sculptures by *Van Cleve* and *G. Coustou*, above which is the organ. François Couperin was but one of the great organists who played here. The central ceiling-painting is by *Antoine Coypel*, and above the royal pew is a Descent of the Holy Ghost, by *Jouvenet*.

From the vestibule we may enter the **17C Gallery** (*Salles du Dixseptième Siècle*), with an impressive collection of portraits displayed in eleven rooms. **R2** *Rubens*, Marie de Médicis and her parents. **R3** Richelieu, by *Ph. de Champaigne*. **R4** is devoted to the Jansenists of Port-Royal, with perspectives and portraits, including *Ph. de Champaigne*, Angélique Arnauld, and the architect Lemercier. **R8** portraits of Racine, Molière, La Fontaine, etc. **R9** views of Versailles by *P.-D. Martin*, and others; and of sieges, by *Van der Meulen*, and a portrait of Mansart by *De Troy*. **R11** portraits by *Beaubrun* of the royal family.

At the far end of this gallery is the *Foyer de l'Opéra*, retaining its 18C decoration by *Pajou*. Off the parallel *Galerie de pierre*, to the r., are the *Salles des Croisades*, etc. (**RR17–21**), of very slight interest.

The **Opéra**, or *Salle de Spectacles*, was built for Louis XV by *Gabriel* in 1753–70, and first used on the occasion of the marriage of the Dauphin (Louis XVI) and Marie-Antoinette.

It was later repainted in the poor taste of the period of Louis-Philippe, and in 1855 was the scene of a banquet given in honour of Queen Victoria.

Modelled on the King of Sardinia's theatre in Turin, it is a perfect example of Louis-XV decoration, having been skilfully restored (1955–57) by *Japy*, even the upholstery being copied from the original specifications. Seating 700 spectators and with a stage second in size only to the Paris Opéra, it is now reserved for rare gala performances.

Stairs ascend to **RR 93–84**, continuing the series of 17C portraits and busts, etc. **R92** four battle scenes by *van der Meulen*, and equestrian portrait of Louis XIV by *Houasse*. **R91** views of palaces: St-Germain and Vincennes by *J.-B. Martin*, Marly and Trianon by *P.-D. Martin*, and St-Cloud by *Allegrain*. **R88** Mme de Maintenon by *Mignard*, and Fénelon by *Vivien*. **R87** *Rigaud*, Marquis de Dangeau. **R86** Princesses, including the Duchesse de Bourgogne in a red dress, by *Gobert*. **R85** *Benoist*, wax portrait of Louis XIV aged 68, with his own (?) wig. **R84** *Rigaud*, the Duchesse d'Orléans.

From the *Upper Vestibule* (**R83**), with figures of the Virtues by various sculptors, a striking view may be had of the *Chapel* and *Royal Gallery*, the door of which has a chased lock by *Desjardins*.

We now enter the *Salon d'Hercule* (**R105**), fitted up by Louis XV in the Louis-XIV style. The elaborate decorations were sculptured by *Vassé* (1729–34). On the ceiling is the Apotheosis of Hercules by *François Lemoyne*, who, after three years' work (1733–36), committed suicide on its completion. Swiss Guards used to be posted here to prevent the intrusion into the State Apartments of 'those freshly marked with smallpox, the shabbily dressed, petitioners, begging friars, and dogs'.

The *Salon de l'Abondance* (**R106**) is the first of the **King's State Apartments**, which, although they have lost their original furniture, have preserved their decorations of marble inlay, sculptured and gilded bronzes, carved doors, and painted ceilings, executed under the supervision of *Charles Le Brun*. The ceiling-painting here—used as a refreshment room at royal receptions—is by *Houasse* (freely restored).

The *Salon de Vénus* (**R107**), named after its ceiling-painting (also by *Houasse*), is noteworthy for its marble decorations in the early Louis-XIV style. The carved doors are by *Caffieri*; above are bronze bas-reliefs. The mural decorations of this salon (and the succeeding one) are original. In the central alcove is a statue of Louis XIV in Roman costume *and wig*, by *Warin*: and on either side of the room are trompe-l'oeil paintings by *Jacques Rousseau*.

The *Salon de Diane* (**R108**), the former billiard room, has a ceiling by *Blanchard*, and contains a bust of Louis XIV by *Bernini* (1665).

The *Salon de Mars* (**R109**), once the *Salle des Gardes*, later a gaming-room and subsequently a ballroom and concert-room, has a ceiling by *Audran*, *Jouvenet*, and *Houasse*. The dessus de portes are by *Simon Vouet*, and the portrait of Marie-Antoinette and her children by *Mme Vigée-Lebrun* (1787). The tapestries are the first of a series by *Le Brun*, illustrating 'The Life of the King', and are among the earliest works from the Gobelins manufactory (1668–72).

The *Salon de Mercure* (**R110**), a card-room under Louis XIV, where that monarch lay in state for eight days, has a ceiling by *J.-B. de*

Champaigne. The Savonnerie carpet and the clock (by *Morand*) should be noticed.

The *Salon d'Apollon* (**R111**), the former throne-room, is the last of the King's State Apartments. On the ceiling, by *Lafosse*, is Louis XIV (the 'Roi Soleil') as Apollo in a chariot escorted by the Seasons.

The three following rooms—the *Galerie des Glaces*, with its antechambers, the *Salons de la Guerre* and *de la Paix*—together form a grandiose decorative ensemble. The *Salon de la Guerre* (**R112**), completed in 1678, has preserved its original decoration of coloured marble and bronze, and contains six busts of Roman emperors, bequeathed by Mazarin. Over the mantlepiece is a stucco relief of Louis XIV on horseback, by *Coysevox.*

The ceiling-painting, the first of a series designed by *Charles Le Brun,* represents France victorious, with a thunderbolt in one hand and a laurel-wreathed portrait of Louis XIV in the other; in the semicircles appear Bellona in anger, and figures of defeated Germany, Holland, and Spain.

The ***Galerie des Glaces**, or *Grande Galerie* (**R113**), 73m long, 10·50m wide, and 12·30m high, is a masterpiece of the Louis-Quatorze style. It was begun by *Mansart* in 1678, and its decoration, designed by *Le Brun*, was completed in 1686. Among the artists employed were *Caffieri, Coysevox, Le Comte,* and *Tuby*, for the sculptures; *Cucci,* for the mirror frames; and *Ladoiseau*, for the trophies on the walls.

The gallery is lighted by seventeen windows looking on to the park, and facing these are as many bevelled mirrors of equal size. The red marble pilasters have bronze capitals decorated with cocks' heads, fleurs-de-lys, and suns. The cornice of gilded stucco is adorned with crowns and the collars of the Orders of the Saint-Esprit and St Michael. The marble statues of Venus, Paris, Mercury, and Minerva in the niches are copies from the antique; some other statues are also copies of originals. Twenty silvered bronze and Bohemian glass chandeliers illuminate it.

The central ceiling-painting represents Louis XIV omnipotent, while the numerous other paintings depict the subjection of Holland, Germany, and Spain, the Peace imposed by Louis on his enemies, his embassies abroad, the Protection of the Arts, and of the People, and the great Foundations established during his reign.

We now enter the *Salon de la Paix* (**R114**), the queen's card-room. The ceiling completes *Le Brun's* scheme (see above), depicting France as bringing the benefits of peace to Europe, etc. Over the chimneypiece (left unfinished by *Le Brun*) is a painting by *Lemoyne* (1729), showing Louis XV following his great-grandfather's example as the bringer of peace.

The *Chambre de la Reine* (**R115**), the first of the **Queen's State Apartments**, has been restored to its pre-Revolution appearance, the chimneypiece having been brought back from the Trianon and the silk hangings copied (at Lyon) from pieces of the original material. Here died Marie-Thérèse (1683) and Marie Leczinska (1768), and here took place the confinements of the queens of France. The jewel cabinet of Marie-Antoinette (by *Evalde*; 1770) was brought from the Château of St-Cloud. Above the doors are allegorical paintings of the children of Louis XV by *Natoire* and *De Troy*. The grisaille panels of the ceiling are by *Boucher*, and the portrait of Marie-Antoinette is by *Mme Vigée-Lebrun*; the unfinished pastel of the queen is by *Kucharski* (1792).

R116, the *Salon des Nobles* (or *Salon de la Reine*), was the queen's presence chamber. The ceiling is by *Michel Corneille* (d.1708); the busts are of Louis XVI by *Pajou*, and Marie-Antoinette by *Le Comte*.

In the *Antichambre* (**R117**), where the queen dined in public, are Gobelins tapestries, and busts of Louis XIV by *Coysevox* (1681), Louis XV by *Gois*, and Louis XVI by *Houdon*. The *Salle des Gardes de la Reine* (**R118**), with marble decoration of the period of Louis XIV, retains its ceiling by *Noël Coypel, the Elder*. It was here, on 6 Oct. 1789, that the revolutionary mob burst in, and three of the Swiss Guards died in the queen's defence.

From the *Chambre de la Reine* we may visit the ***Petits Appartements de la Reine (R122)**, the small and cramped private suite of Marie-Antoinette, preserving its superb decoration. The *Boudoir* or *Petite Méridienne*, with its gilded woodwork and mirror-frames, and the *Library*, with imitation bookshelves, were designed by *Mique* (c.1781). In the *Small Library*, used by the ladies-in-waiting, is a marriage-chest of Marie-Antoinette. In the *Salon de la Reine*, with elaborate decoration by the brothers *Rousseau*, she received her intimate friends, and her musicians, Gluck and Grétry, and sat to Mme Vigée-Lebrun for her portraits. The last two rooms are the *Bath Room*, and the *Chambre de repos* or *Salon Jaune*.

To the l. of R118 is the landing of the *Escalier de Marbre*, or *de la Reine*, built by *Le Vau* and *Mansart*, with an interesting perspective painting in the Italian style. Across the landing is a *Loggia* (**R119**) overlooking the *Cour de Marbre*, in which a door on the r. admits to the *Apartments of Mme de Maintenon* (see below), while on the l. is an entrance to the *Salle des Gardes du Roi* (see below).

It may be convenient to visit from this point **R140**, the *Salle du Sacre* (previously the *Grande Salle des Gardes*), restored since its mutilation by Louis-Philippe. The ceiling-painting is by *Callet*; the dessus de portes by *Gérard*; and the walls are adorned by huge paintings depicting Napoleon presenting eagles in the Champ-de-Mars (1804), and his coronation at Notre-Dame, both by *David*; and *Gros*, Murat at the battle of Aboukir (1799).

In the adjoining *Grand Cabinet* (**R143**), Racine's 'Esther' was played before the king, and in 1702 his 'Athalie' was presented by the princes and princesses.—**R144** leads to the *Salle de* 1792 (**R146**), containing military portraits, and originally the 'Salon des Marchands', to which vendors of goods were admitted for the convenience of the inmates of the palace.—The *Escalier des Princes* (**R147**), by *Mansart*, gave access to the S. wing, once reserved for the princes of the blood.

The series of rooms beyond this point are of little interest. The *Galerie des Batailles*, nearly 120m long, constructed under Louis-Philippe by throwing into one most of the rooms on the first floor, displays a sad selection of huge canvases representing French military achievements—perhaps the only one of note being The Battle of Taillebourg, by *Delacroix*—indeed Thackeray considered them among 'the worst pictures that eye ever looked on'.

Returning to **R119**, we may visit (r.) the **Apartments of Mme de Maintenon** (**RR141–142**; shown on request), furnished by Louis XIV in 1682 for Mme de Maintenon, who became his second wife probably the following year. The *Antichambre*, and *Bedchamber* (where most of the business of State was transacted), now accommodate a fine collection of 16C portraits by *Corneille de Lyon* and other artists of the School of Clouet.

The adjoining *Escalier de Stuc* (built under Louis-Philippe) ascends to the SECOND FLOOR. Here, in the **Attique de Chimay** (r.) and **Attique** du Midi, are displayed an outstanding *Collection of Historical Paintings* illustrating the early Napoleonic period. Unfortunately, the galleries are not always open, and it is as well to check beforehand.

We first enter **R174**, with battle scenes by *Bacler d'Albe*, Arcole, and Lodi, by *Lejeune*; and other views by war-artists of the period including *Lecomte*, *Morel*, *Taunay*, *Mulard*, *Berthon*, and *Boguet*. Note also *Gros*, Napoleon at Arcole, and the impressive collection of scenes by *Bagetti* (in display cases). In the small room to the r. are sketches by *Vernet* and others.—To the l. is **R176**, dominated by *Lejeune*, Battle of the Pyramides (among other scenes of the Egyptian Campaign).—**R177** *Lejeune*, Battle of Marengo; *Mongin*, Passage of the army through the defile of Albaredo; and *David*, Napoleon crossing the Alps.

R178 *Hue*, Napoleon visiting the camp at Boulogne.—**R179** *Desoria*, Portrait of Letourneur, member of the Directoire; *Gérard*, Joachim Murat; and miniatures by *Gauffier*.—**R180** *Gilbert*, Combat between 'La Canonnière' and 'The Tremendous' (1806); *Hoppner*, copied by *Healy*, Lord Nelson, and Lord St Vincent; *Lawrence*, copied by *Healy*, William Pitt.—**R181**, the first of a series devoted to *Small portraits by François Gérard*.

We cross to **R171**, dominated by *Gérard*, Napoleon as Emperor of the French, and 'Madame Mère'; *Lethière*, Joséphine; *Vigée-Lebrun*, Marie-Annunciade-Caroline Bonaparte, among other members of the Imperial family.—**R170** *Kinson*, Bernadotte; *Meynier*, Ney; and *Lejeune*, Napoleon visiting the bivouacs before Austerlitz.—**R169** *Lefèvre*, Napoleon I, and Augereau.

R168 (Life in Paris): *Lefèvre*, Baron Denon; *Girodet*, Chateaubriand; *David*, Pope Pius VII.—**R167** *Roehn*, Napoleon at Wagram (night scene).—**R166** *van Bree*, Launching of 'Le Friedland'; *Franque*, Marie-Louise and the King of Rome.

R165 (Peninsular War): *Lejeune*, Passing the Somosierra; Assault on the monastery of S. Engracia, Zaragoza; and The Battle of Chiclana (Barrosa); *Taunay*, Crossing the Guadarrama; *Heim*, Defence of the castle at Burgos. The second half of this gallery is devoted to the Russian Campaign.

From the *Salle du Gardes du Roi* (**R120**) we enter the **Appartements du Roi**, commencing with **R121**, the *Antichambre du Roi*, in which Louis XIV dined in private on the rare occasions when he could do so.—**R123**, known as the *Oeil-de-boeuf* after its small 'bull's eye window', where scandalmongering courtiers used to wait for admission to the king's 'lever'. The decorations are original, including the stucco frieze showing children's games on a gold background, by *van Cleve*, *Hurtrelle*, and *Flamen*. A curious picture by *Nocret* represents the royal family in mythological costume.

The lavishly restored **Chambre du Roi (R124)**, Louis XIV's bedchamber (in which he died in 1715), overlooks the *Cour de Marbre*. Here took place the ceremonious 'lever' and 'coucher' of the king, who used to lunch daily at a little table placed before the middle window. It was from the balcony of this room that Marie-Antoinette and Louis XVI, at La Fayette's suggestion, showed themselves to the mob on 6 Oct. 1789. The decorations of carved wood and the balustrade separating the reconstructed bed from the rest of the room are regilded, and are in part original: most of the rich brocades and other fabrics are of recent manufacture, woven at Lyon, scrupulously copying the original materials. The sculpture of gilded stucco above is by *N. Coustou*. The chimneypieces date from 1761, with bronzes by *Caffieri*; on one is a bust of Louis XIV, on the other, the Duchesse de Bourgogne, mother of Louis XV, both by *Coysevox*. Note the self-portrait by *Van Dyck*.

Hence we pass into the adjacent *Cabinet du Conseil* (**R125**), which dates in its present form from 1753. The *boiseries* are by *Antoine Rousseau*. Note the two Sèvres vases, and the table on which the Treaty of Versailles was signed.

We now enter a series of rooms constructed by Louis XV in 1738 to provide a retreat from the tedious etiquette of his court, known as the *Cabinets du Roi* or *Petits Appartements du Roi* (**RR126–130**). These comprise (**R126**) the *Chambre de Louis XV*, his bedroom, in which he died of smallpox in 1774; with *broiseries* by *Verberckt*; **R127**, the *Cabinet de la Pendule*, deriving its name from *Passemant's* clock (1749), executed by *Dauthiau*, with chased designs by *Caffieri*, surmounted by a crystal globe marking the phases of the sun, moon, and planets: note also the barometer. Hence we visit the *Cabinet des Chiens* (**R128**), with a frieze of hunting scenes, and decorated with flower-paintings, which was occupied by lackeys and the king's favourite hounds. On the staircase descending hence, Damiens attempted to assassinate Louis XV in 1757. Adjacent is a *Salle à Manger*, overlooking the much-altered Cour des Cerfs.

Returning through R127 (in which also note the meridian line marked on the floor) we enter **R130**, the *Cabinet de Travail*, with *boiseries* by *Verberckt* (1753), and a Savonnerie carpet; the ornate desk, the Bureau du Roi, ordered by the king in 1760 for this room, was designed by *Oeben* and *Riesener* (1769), with bronzes by *Duplessis, Winant*, and *Hervieux*.

Adjoining is the *Cabinet de Mme Adélaïde* (**R132**), with woodwork by *Verberckt*, where, in 1763, Mozart played before Mme Adélaïde (1732–1800), 4th daughter of Louis XV.—The *Bibliothèque de Louis XVI* (**R133**, with Louis-XV furniture) is decorated by *Antoine Rousseau*, with a chimneypiece by *Boizot* and *Gouthière*, and a candelabrum attr. to *Thomire*.

The *Salon des Porcelaines* (**R134**), with a desk by *Leleu*, was so called because of the annual sale of Sèvres ware arranged for the Court, which occupied also the two following rooms. These, the *Salle de Billiard* and *Salon des Jeux* (**RR136–137**), where Louis XIV's collections of paintings and gems were housed, later became part of Mme Adélaïde's suite.

The adjoining staircase ascends to the **Apartments of Mme du Barry** on the second floor. The beautiful boiseries here have been restored and repainted in their original colours.—The attic floor contains the diminutive **Apartments of Mme de Pompadour**.

An uninspired staircase descends to the ground floor adjacent to a passage leading to the gardens: see below.

On the GROUND FLOOR we may turn through **R26** into **R27**, that of American Independence', with portraits of Washington, *after C. W. Peale; van Blarenberghe*, Capture and siege of Yorktown; *G. P. A. Healy*, Portraits of Americans painted for Louis-Philippe.—**R28** *Vigée-Lebrun*, Marie-Antoinette; *Duplessis*, Louis XVI.—**R29** *Vigée-Lebrun*, The Dauphin Louis-Joseph and Madame Royale as children.—**R30** *Duplessis*, Portraits of M. and Mme Necker; *Houdon*, bust of La Fayette.—We pass through **R32** into **R33**, with scenes from the Revolution, including *David*, Death of Marat; two cartoons; and a bust of the Dauphin (Louis XVII) as a child, by *Deseine*

(1790).—**RR34–35** are devoted to the Convention and the Directory.

The rooms on the ground floor of the S. wing (**RR67–80**) are of only slight interest. They contain some paintings by *Gros*, and *H.* and *C. Vernet*, among others, and furnishings, made in the 1950s, reproducing original Napoleonic designs.

We may now turn r. to visit the **Salles du Dix-huitième Siècle**, which, looking out onto the gardens, were occupied at various times by the Regent Orléans, and the sons and daughters of Louis XV, and are also known as the Appartements du Dauphin et de la Dauphine, et de Mesdames. They have been repeatedly altered, and most of the original decorations were swept away by Louis-Philippe. They contain an admirable collection of 18C portraits, but some rooms may be closed for restoration.

R42 *Rigaud*, Louis XV; *Santerre*, The Regent Orléans.—**R43** *J.-B. Van Loo* and *Parrocel*, Louis XV on horseback.—Note the organ in **R44**.—**R45** Louis XVI, Louis XVIII, and Charles X were born in this room, which was also the bedroom of Marie-Antoinette on her arrival in France from Vienna; *Nattier*, Mme de Pompadour; the Marquis de Marigny, her brother, by *De Troy*; and Lenormant de Tourneheim (her mother's protector, and Marigny's predecessor as director of the royal buildings), by *Tocqué*.—**R46** *Nattier*, Marie-Josèphe de Saxe (mother of Louis XVI).—**R47** has retained some of its Louis-XV decoration.—**R48** (*Grand Cabinet du Dauphin*): *Nattier*, Portraits of the daughters of Louis XV; the balcony of wrought and gilded iron commands a splendid view of the gardens.

R49 was the Regent's study, where he died in 1723, and was later the bedroom of the Dauphin Louis, son of Louis XV. It preserves decorative details, including woodwork by *Verberckt*, and a red marble chimneypiece with figures by *Caffieri*; also *Nattier*, Infanta Luisa Isabel (1759), and *N. Coustou*, bust of Marie Leczinska.—**R50** retains traces of Louis-XIV decorations.

The *Galerie Basse* (**R51**), below the *Galerie des Glaces*, has been completely altered since the reign of Louis XIV, when Molière gave several of his plays in it, including the first performance of 'Tartuffe' (1664). It contains a series of paintings, by *Martin* and *Lenfant*, of battles; *Van Loo*, Louis XV; *Nattier*, Mme Anne-Henriette, 2nd daughter of Louis XV, playing the viola da gamba.

R52, once part of a suite of bathrooms, and later occupied by Mme de Montespan, Mme de Pompadour, and the daughters of Louis XV, contains *Nattier*, Mme Adélaïde as Diana, and Mme Henriette as Flora; and gouache drawings by *van Blarenberghe* of the campaigns of 1744–48 in Flanders.—**R53** *Nattier*, the Duc de Bourgogne as an infant, Marie Leczinska (1748), and Isabel, daughter of the Infanta Luisa Isabel (Louise-Élisabeth, eldest daughter of Louis XV).—**R54** *Roslin*, The Dauphin, son of Louis XV.—**R55** *L.-M. Van Loo*, Choiseul; *Rigaud*, Chancellor Maupeou, Comte d'Argenson; *Carle Van Loo*, Soufflot; *Drouais*, Louis XV.—In **RR56–59** a portrait of Louis XVI standing, by *Duplessis*, and two views of Versailles by *Hubert Robert*, are noteworthy. The 'perspective' decoration of **R59** has been restored; note also the clock.

The ***GARDENS OF VERSAILLES** are best approached by a passage just W. of the main visitors' entrance.

André Le Nôtre (1613–1708), the celebrated landscape-gardener (to whom London owes Greenwich Park, and Rome the Quirinal and

Vatican gardens), designed the gardens for Louis XIV, although the fountains and hydraulic machinery were the work of *J.H.-Mansart* and the engineer *François Francini*, while the sculptural decoration was executed under the supervision of *Le Brun* and *Mignard*.

The gardens were first laid out in 1661–68. The preliminary work of levelling and draining the site was prodigious, and thousands of trees were brought here from all parts. Inspired by Italian originals which were interpreted with an amplitude and harmony hitherto unknown, Versailles is the masterpiece of French gardening. In their general lines and their sculptural decoration, with the characteristic stressing of the 'classical' note, the gardens remain as they were laid out, but it was not until the 18C that the planting of trees was developed to its present extent, so that what we now see is basically the gardens of Louis XV and Louis XVI.

They are essentially formal, with their carefully planned vistas and straight tree-lined walks, their artificial lakes and ponds, arranged with geometrical precision, their groves and clumps of trees; lawns, and terraces, all interspersed with innumerable statues and vases of marble and bronze, and embellished with a variety of fountains.

Admission. The gardens and park are normally open free all day to pedestrians (no picnics); cars are admitted to the park on payment.

The *Fountains* play on certain Sundays of the months May-Sept. inclusive between 16.00–17.30; the *Fêtes de Nuit*, at the Bassin de Neptune, take place at dates—usually in July and Sept.—varying annually, which should be checked in advance.

The most direct approach to the **Grand Trianon** for the pedestrian is to follow the *Allée d'Eau* (see below), leading N. from the terrace behind the central block of the palace to the *Grille de Neptune*, thence bearing N.W. along the Av. de Trianon, approx. 20 minutes' brisk walk. But by taking this route, one sees little of the Gardens of Versailles, which themselves merit exploration.

The central axis of the main *Terrace* commands splendid *•Views*, and the terrace itself is adorned with bronze statues after the antique, and with marble vases of War, by *Coysevox*, and Peace, by *Tuby*. Beyond the *Parterres d'Eau*, two large ornamental pools decorated with bronzes (1690), are the *Marches de Latone*, monumental flights of steps, from which one may obtain an impressive view of the palace, and, in the opposite direction, a famous vista of the gardens. Flanking these steps are the *Fontaines de Diane* (r.) and *du Point-du-Jour* (Dawn). By the former are statues of Air, by *Le Hongre*, and Diana the Huntress, by *Desjardins*.

On the r. of the Terrace extend the *Parterres du Nord*, where the original design of Le Nôtre has been largely respected. Just beyond is the *Fontaine de la Pyramide* (in lead), by *Girardon*, and among the sculptures in the cross-walk (l.) is Winter, also by *Girardon*.—The *Allée d'Eau*, designed by *Perrault* and *Le Brun* (1676–88), with its groups of children, leads directly to the **Bassin de Neptune** (1740), the largest fountain-basin in the gardens, whence we may return by the *Allée des Trois Fontaines* (parallel to the *Allée d'Eau*), to reach the *Bains d'Apollon* (r.), by a grove laid out by *Hubert Robert* under Louis XVI, in a 'romantic' spirit very different from the formal symmetry of Le Nôtre.

To the W., the *Allée de l'Été* leads to the so-called *Tapis Vert* (or *Allée Royale*), a lawn 330m long and 36m wide, lined with marble vases and statues, many of them copies from the antique. Note (on the l.) Venus, by *Le Gros*, and Achilles at Scyros, by *Vigier*. Towards its far end (r.) is the entrance to the *Bosquet des Dômes*, with several statues, including Acis and Galatea, by *Tuby*.—Almost opposite, on the far side of the *Tapis Vert*, in the *Bosquet de la Colonnade*, is a *Circle* of marble arches by *Mansart* (1685–88), in the centre of which

View of the West front of the palace

is the Rape of Prosérpine, by *Girardon*.

At the end of the *Tapis Vert* lies the *Bassin d'Apollon*, in the centre of which is the impressive group of Apollo's Chariot, by *Tuby*. To the r. is the *Petite Venise*, where Louis XIV's Venetian gondoliers were housed. Beyond the *Bassin d'Apollon*, and separated from the gardens by railings, is the *Petit Parc*, divided by the *Grand Canal*, 1650m long, and 62m wide, the scene of Louis XIV's boating parties. Almost at its centre point it is crossed by a transverse arm (c. 1070m), extending from the *Grand Trianon*, to the N. to the few remaining buildings of the former royal *Menagerie*.

To regain the palace, we may traverse the '*Salle des Marronniers*' (so-called), a chestnut grove behind the *Colonnade*, and passing the *Bassin de Saturne* and *Bassin de Bacchus*, with sculptures by *Girardon* and *Marsy*, reach the *Bosquet de la Reine*.

This glade was notorious as the scene of the court scandal known as the 'Affaire du collier' (1784–85), in which the Card. de Rohan (seeking the favour of Marie-Antoinette by means of a costly gift) was duped by the Comtesse de la Motte.

The *Parterres du Midi* lead hence to the palace. To the r. two flights of steps, known as the *Cent Marches*, descend alongside the *Orangerie*, by *Mansart*.—To the S., beyond the St-Cyr road, is the *Pièce d'Eau des Suisses* (682m long, by 134m wide), excavated in 1678–82 by the Swiss Guards, many of whom are said to have died of malaria during the operation.

The ***GRAND TRIANON**, a miniature palace designed by *J. H.-Mansart* and *Robert de Cotte*, was built for Louis XIV in 1687 as a retreat from the formality of court life, yet retaining sumptuous marble decorations comparable with those of Versailles itself. It replaced a flimsy earlier building or Summer-house for picnics, tiled within with blue and white Delftware, and known as the 'Porcelain Trianon', which had been erected on the site of the village of *Trianon*.

The palace was occupied for a time by Mme de Maintenon. It was redecorated for Napoleon, who frequently stayed there, and the Empire furniture which he installed still remains. In 1818 the Duke of Wellington dined here with Louis XVIII. Louis-Philippe did his best to spoil the interior decoration in 1837. A restoration of both *Trianons* was carried out in 1925–27; the *Grand Trianon* (again) in 1963–66, and the *Petit Trianon* more recently.

While a special note of admiration must be recorded for the accurate work of reproduction of fabrics of the period, undertaken during the 1960s, it must be admitted that the sheets of plastic protecting them detract from the splendid effect intended. Somehow it is all too new, and however historically irreproachable the decoration may be, a little 'faded glory' would perhaps have been more becoming.

On reaching the courtyard, with the open colonnade or Péristyle ahead, we turn l. to the visitors' entrance. From the entrance Vestibules (**RR1–2**) we reach **R3**, with views of Versailles and Chambord by *Allegrain* and *P.-D. Martin* respectively, and a console table by *Jacob-Desmalter*.—A corridor leads to a small *Boudoir* (**R8**), containing a gondola-shaped sofa, to the r. of which we enter the splendidly mirrored *Salon des Glaces* (**R7**), furnished with a handsome set of white and gilt chairs covered with Beauvais tapestry.—**R6**, the *Salon des Colonnes*, with Napoleon's bed (1809) from the Tuileries, later broadened and mutilated by Louis-Philippe.—Passing through **RR5** and **4**, we cross the open Péristyle of Languedoc marble pillars to the RIGHT WING, first entering the circular *Drawing-Room* (**R9**), with paintings of American flowers and fruit, by *Desportes*.—**R10** (*Salon de Musique*): note the bronze table with Vosges granite top, two consoles by *Jacob-Desmalter*, and the Beauvais tapestry-covered set of chairs.—We are next conducted through the *Grand Salon* and *Malachite Room* (**R12**), the latter with a malachite bowl given to Alexander I of Russia after the Treaty of Tilsit, in 1807.—From the adjoining *Salon Frais*, with a painting of the view E. from Versailles by *J.-B. Martin*, we turn l. into the *Grande Galerie*, decorated by *Mansart*, with good views S. over the terrace. It contains 24 allegorical views, almost all similarly framed, of the Gardens of Versailles and Trianon, twenty-one by *Jean Cotelle* (1645–1708), two by *Allegrain*, and one by *J.-B. Martin*. The suite of rooms beyond, known as the *Trianon-sous-Bois*, is not open to the public.

Returning through the *Salon Frais*, we reach the *Salon des Sources*, with views of Versailles by *P.-D. Martin* (1663–1742) and *Charles Chastelain* (1672–1740) and turn r. through a further series of tastefully furnished rooms, the *Apartments of Mme de Maintenon*, subsequently occupied by Stanislas Leczinski, former king of Poland (1741), Mme de Pompadour, and Napoleon and Marie-Louise.—The remaining rooms (**RR23–24**) were installed on the site of a theatre which stood here until 1703, and from 1845 they formed a suite of rooms for Louis-Philippe's daughter, Louise-Marie, and her husband, Leopold I of Belgium.

The gardens were laid out by *Mansart* and *Le Nôtre*. To the W. is the *Buffet* (the main fountain), also designed by *Mansart*, with bas-reliefs and figures of Neptune and Amphitrite. A bridge leads from the *Jardin du Roi*, behind the palace, to the gardens of the *Petit Trianon*.

Between the *Grand* and *Petit Trianons* is the **Musée des Voitures**, containing among others the carriage used at the marriage of Napoleon and Marie-Louise (1810), the state coach used at the coronation of Charles X (1824), and the marriage of Napoleon III with the Empress Eugénie (1853); also *berlines* and *calèches* of the 18C.

To the E. is the ***PETIT TRIANON** (1751–68) on two floors, unlike the Grand Trianon, built by *Gabriel* for Louis XV as a country retreat for himself and Mme de Pompadour, who did not survive its completion. Mme du Barry then occupied it; and it was a favourite residence of Marie-Antoinette. The palace was subsequently occupied by Pauline Borghese, Napoleon's sister.

To the l. of the courtyard is a derelict *Chapel* (not shown). The interior of the palace, recently restored, contains an elegant suite of rooms on the first floor, many of them retaining their original decoration, including chimneypieces by *Guibert* in the *Dining Room* and *Grand Salon*, etc. In the former, traces of the trap-door, through which, in Louis XV's reign, the tables used to appear ready-laid, are still visible in the floor.

The GARDENS of the *Petit Trianon* were originally a menagerie and botanical garden laid out by *Jussieu* for Louis XV, but were altered for Marie-Antoinette in the English style (1774–86). Here, so Thicknesse was told, the king 'had a little garden...where he often picks his own salad, makes his own soup, and enjoys the conversation of a few select friends, without the plague, impertinence, and above all, the parade that generally attends royalty'.

To the W. of the main building is the *Pavillon Français*, built in 1751 by *Gabriel*, with a good view hence of the façade of the palace. To the N. is the *Theatre* (1780), where Marie-Antoinette made her début in court theatricals, beyond which is the octagonal *Belvedere* (by *Mique*), with charming interior decoration, overlooking a small lake. The queen was resting in a grotto here, when on 5 Oct. 1789, she was told the news that a revolting mob had broken into Versailles.

Some few minutes' walk to the N.E., on the far side of a larger lake, is the **Hameau**, a sort of theatrical village built for Marie-Antoinette to gratify her taste for 'nature', as popularized by Rousseau, although, apart from churning butter, the queen left the work of the farm to real, not royal, peasants. It comprises a mill, the *Maison de la Reine* (with a dining-room, billiard-room, and card-room, etc., with a kitchen or 'Réchauffoir' behind), and the 'Boudoir' on the

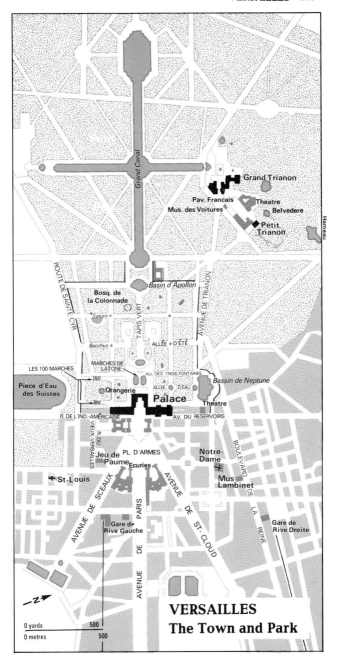

Grand Trianon

Pav. Francais
Mus. des Voitures

Theatre
Belvedere

Petit
Trianon

Hameau

Grand Canal

ROUTE DE SAINTE CYR

Basin d'Apollon

Bosq. de
la Colonnade

Saturn

TAPIS VERT

AVENUE DE TRIANON

ALLÉE · D'ÉTÉ

Bacchus

MARCHES DE
LATONE

ALL. DES · TROIS FONTAINES

LES 100 MARCHES

Basin de Neptune

Piece d'Eau
des Suisses

Orangerie

ALLÉE · D'EAU

Palace

Theatre

R. DE L'IND.-AMÉRICAINE

AV. DU RESERVOIRS

R. DU VIEUX-VERSAILLES

Jeu de
Paume

PL. D'ARMES

Ecuries

Notre-
Dame

BOULEVARD DE

+ St-Louis

AVENUE DE SCEAUX

AVENUE DE PARIS

AVENUE DE ST-CLOUD

Mus
Lambinet

LA REINE

Gare de
Rive Gauche

Gare de
Rive Droite

VERSAILLES
The Town and Park

0 yards   500

0 metres   500

r.; a *Colombier*, with pigeon-cote and chicken-run; the *Dairy*; the 'Tour de Marlborough'; and farm-buildings.

Hence we may return past the *Temple d'Amour*, with its Corinthian colonnade and *Mouchy*'s copy (1780) of *Bouchardon*'s statue of Love, to the courtyard of the *Petit Trianon*, and make our exit.

22   Malmaison and St-Germain-en-Laye

Malmaison may be approached either by road (N13; 7·5km) from the *Pont de Neuilly*, or on the RER from *Auber* viâ *Étoile* to *La Défense*, there taking the 158A bus to within a few minutes' walk of the château.

The *CHÂTEAU OF MALMAISON**, built in 1622 on the site of a leper colony dependent on the Abbey of Saint-Denis, was the home of Joséphine Bonaparte after 1798, and was enlarged in 1800. It now contains collections of considerable historical interest, as does its annexe, the *Musée du Château de Bois-Préau*.

At the height of her power, the empress held a literary and artistic salon at Malmaison, and after her divorce in 1809 she retired here and devoted herself to gardening, dying only five years later of a chill caught while doing the honours of the grounds to the allied sovereigns. Joséphine Tascher de la Pagerie (1763–1814), born in Martinique, had married Napoleon in 1796, two years after her first husband, the Vicomte de Beauharnais, had been guillotined. Napoleon spent five days here in 1815, between Waterloo and his departure for St Helena.

Malmaison was later bought by María Cristina of Spain, and by Napoleon III in 1861. Despoiled of most of its contents, it was sold in 1896 to the philanthropist Daniel Osiris (1828–1907), who refurnished it and presented the château to the State as a Napoleonic Museum. Further appropriate acquisitions have been made since, and the rooms redecorated.

GROUND FLOOR. From the entrance vestibule in Antique style, displaying busts of the Imperial family, we turn r. into the *Billiard Room*, containing Napoleon's throne from Fontainebleau, his portrait in Gobelins tapestry, and a Savonnerie carpet with his insignia. The *Salon Doré*, with a chimneypiece given to Napoleon by Pope Pius VII (its decoration torn off by the Germans occupying Malmaison in 1871), contains *Girodet*'s painting of Ossian welcoming the dead to Valhalla, a portrait of Joséphine by *Gérard*, and her embroidery frame, etc. The adjacent *Music Room*, restored to its original appearance, displays instruments which may have belonged to Joséphine, and her marble bust by *Chinard*.

Returning through these rooms, we enter the *Dining Room*, with its original frescoes of Pompeian dancers by *Lafitte*, restored, and the silver-gilt 'surtout' of table decorations presented by the city of Paris to the emperor on the occasion of his coronation. The *Council Chamber*, shaped like a tent, contains a yew-wood desk (gift of the city of Bordeaux), and a clock from the Tuileries. The adjoining *Library*, retaining its original decoration by *Percier* and *Fontaine*, accommodates a number of books from Napoleon's personal collection, which, previously widely dispersed, have been purchased and reassembled on their original shelves. Here also are Napoleon's bureau and armchair, and a clock made in 1791 for Louis XVI by *Janvier*, and purchased by Napoleon.

Stairs ascend to the FIRST FLOOR, with, on the landing, a Gobelins tapestry, after *Gérard*, of Joséphine at Malmaison.—*Salon de l'Empereur*, a reconstruction of Napoleon's bedroom at the Tuileries, with the original furniture and hangings, and a drawing by *Isabey* of Napoleon as First Consul at Malmaison. The three following rooms contain sumptuous services of Sèvres ware; the 'Table d'Austerlitz' decorated with portraits of Napoleon and his marshals; the silver-gilt ewer and basin used at his coronation, etc.—*Joséphine's Apartments*: Antechamber, with water-colours of Malmaison by *Garnerey*, of topographical interest; portraits of the empress, and personal souvenirs. In her *Bedroom* is the bed, designed by *Jacob-Desmalter*, in which she died; other contemporary furniture, and a fine Sèvres clock. The silk-lined *Salle des Atours* contains a work-table (from *St-Cloud*), etc.; the *Boudoir* is likewise hung with silk; and in the *Bathroom* are Joséphine's dressing-table and dressing-case by *Rémond*.

On the SECOND FLOOR is the *Salle de Ste-Hélène*, hung with the brocade that covered the catafalque in which the emperor's remains were transported to his tomb. It contains the camp bed on which Napoleon died in 1821, his death-mask moulded by Antommarchi (his Corsican doctor), clothing, MSS., and paintings. Other rooms are devoted to souvenirs of Queen Hortense (mother of Napoleon III) and Eugène de Beauharnais, Joséphine's children by her first marriage, etc.

The PARK, of which but 6 hectares remain of 200, contains a rose garden planted with the varieties of rose that were grown by Joséphine. The *Coach House*, to the r. of the entrance lodge, contains the 'Opal', the state carriage in which Joséphine drove to Malmaison after her divorce, a gala coach (temp. Louis XIV) used by Napoleon; his *'dormeuse'* used at Waterloo, and Blücher's *landau en berline*. Behind is the *Pavillon Osiris*, with collections of caricatures, medallions, and snuffboxes propagating the Napoleonic legend, and a portrait of Tsar Alexander I, by *Gérard*. Beyond the other side of the entrance drive is a *Summer-House* used as a study by Napoleon when First Consul.

A few minutes' walk to the E. will take one to the **Musée du Château de Bois-Préau**, in the Av. de l'Impératrice Joséphine, admirably displayed in a building bought by Joséphine in 1810, and in 1926 bequeathed to the State by Edward Tuck, its American owner (see also Petit-Palais, Rte 16A).

To the r. of the entrance is a room containing portraits by *Gérard* of 'Madame Mère'; Joséphine in her coronation robes; Joseph Bonaparte as King of Spain, and his wife; and Napoleon's sister, Elisa.—To the l. of the entrance we pass through a series of rooms containing such souvenirs as a *surtout* or *epergne* given to the emperor by Carlos IV of Spain; a portrait of the King of Rome by *Georges Rouget*; the King of Rome's cradle by *Jacob-Desmalter*, and other mementoes; and Marie-Louise, by *Gérard*.—On ascending the stairs, turn r. past a collection of sabres, Napoleon's grey coat and hat, flask, and nécessaire, his mantle (note bees); and Hortense's court dress. Other rooms display Murat's splendidly ornate bed, and sabre-legged *tabourets* or stools, and *Gérard's* portrait of Murat; Napoleon's hat and coat (and chairs) from St Helena; *Marchand's* sketch of the dead emperor; and a book given to Napoleon by Lord Holland.

In the nearby church of *Rueil*, (1584, with a W. façade by *Lemercier*, of 1635), is the tomb of the Empress Joséphine, erected in 1825 by her children, Eugène and Hortense de Beauharnais. The tomb of Queen Hortense, in the chapel opposite, was erected by her son, Napoleon III, in 1858, who also donated the 15C Florentine organ-case, by *Baccio d'Agnolo*.

The N13 skirts the S. bank of the Seine, passing at *Bougival*, with a Romanesque church tower, the house where Bizet died (1875), to **ST-GERMAIN-EN-LAYE** (40,800 inhab.), which may be reached with ease from central Paris by the RER from Auber or Étoile (replacing the first railway constructed in France, in 1837). By road, it may be approached from the *Pont de Neuilly* by the N13 (taking in en route the *Château of Malmaison*, see above), or by the N190 branching r. off the latter, which passes through the suburb of *Le Vésinet*. The *Terrasse*, to the N.E. of the Castle, commands a splendid *View of Paris (and particularly of *La Défense*): *Notre-Dame* itself is approx. 21km to the E. James II once compared the view to that from the Terrace at Richmond.

Claude Debussy (1862–1918) was born at St-Germain. Thicknesse rented a house here in 1766; Henry Swinburne lived 5km N. at *Les Mesnils* in 1786, and again in 1796. Maurice Denis (d. 1943) also lived here, and at No. 2bis in the street named after him is a museum devoted to the Symbolists and Nabis.
'The Juggler', by Bosch, was robbed from the *Municipal Museum* in 1978.

Its strategically placed royal château, overlooking a bend of the Seine, was built first in the 12C by Louis VI, and in 1539–48 completely rebuilt by François I, except for the keep. The so-called *Château-Neuf*, below the original castle, constructed for Henri II and Henri IV, was demolished in 1776, except for the *Pavillon-Henri-IV* and the *Pavillon Sully*, at the foot of the steep slope E. of the town, in the suburb of *Le Pecq*.

It was in this 'new' castle that Louis XIV was born in 1638, five years before the death of his father in the same building; and it remained one of the principal seats of the French Court until the completion of Versailles in 1682. Meanwhile, the older château afforded refuge to the widowed Queen Henrietta Maria of England; after 1688 it was also the residence—and Court—of James II in exile, who died there in 1701, as did his wife, Mary of Modena, in 1718. His tomb, erected by George IV in the church opposite the castle, contains only his heart.

In 1962, a century after the setting-up of an earlier museum in the château, the *MUSÉE DES ANTIQUITÉS NATIONALES was installed here, and has more recently been tastefully reorganized to display its impressive collections in chronological order, which are well labelled and described.

Crossing the courtyard, we ascend stairs and turn r. to reach **R1**, devoted to *Neolithic* finds.—**R2** *Bronze Age*, including (*Case 3*) swords and sword moulds, and (*Case 13*) torques, bracelets, and other gold objects.—**R3** *Hallstatt* period (1st Iron Age; 800–450 B.C.).—**R4** (across landing) *La Tène* culture (450–52 B.C.), with a good collection of bronze vessels and vases—note that in *Case 18*—and jewellery.—**R6** reconstituted chariot-burial from La Gorge-Meillet.—**R9**, with a model of the important fortified site of Alesia.

The series of rooms on the floor above concentrate on *Roman and Merovingian Gaul*. **R10** contains Celtic divinities; **R11**, divinities of the Graeco-Roman world, including some fine figures of Mercury; ex-votos and their moulds; note the Venus in *Case 5*. Here is also an exemplary display of silver utensils, etc., also glassware, bronze lamps, scales, handles, keys, etc., and sigillate pottery.—Across the landing are rooms displaying small sculptured objects—birds, boars, horses, and human figures: note the charming couple in bed, with a dog at their feet, from Bordeaux (*Case 6*); a collection of jewellery, buckles, and fibulas; games, etc.—**R16** contains a large mosaic pavement (3C A.D.) from St-Romain-en-Gal (Rhône), showing a rustic calendar of the seasons, while various agricultural implements, etc., are also shown here.—Articles of jewellery, plaques, glassware, and buckles, etc., of the *Merovingian* period are displayed in the adjoining room. Another section has been opened recently, devoted to the *Palaeolithic* period.

The adjacent *Chapel* of 1230–38, just predating the *Sainte Chapelle* in Paris, also by *Pierre de Montreuil*, has been sadly disfigured over the years. It contains copies of tombs from the Aliscamp at Arles. Here were baptized François I, Claude de France (1499–1524), daughter of Louis XII and first wife of François I, and Louis XIV.

To the N. of the castle is the *Parterre*, originally a park laid out by *Le Nôtre*, beyond which is a *Jardin Anglais*. At its S.E. corner is the *Pavillon Henri-IV* (see above), since 1836 a much-frequented hotel: Dumas wrote 'The Three Musketeers' and 'Monte Cristo' here; and Thiers died here in 1877.

To the N.E. extends the *Terrace of St-Germain* (see above). At the far end is the *Grille Royale*, the entrance to the *Forêt de St-Germain*, the former royal hunting preserve, once over 4000 hectares in extent, and still retaining a number of pleasant drives and walks (see IGN 419).

Some 4km further N. is **Maisons-Laffitte** (23,900 inhab.), birthplace of Jean Cocteau (1889–1963). It possesses training-stables and a racecourse.

Its celebrated ***Château** (CN) was built for Renè de Longueil, first Marquis de Maisons, a Surintendant des Finances prior to Fouquet; the masterpiece of François Mansart (1642–51), it is also notable for its interior decoration.

The château was bought in 1818, its stables demolished, and the park cut up into building lots by Jacques Laffitte (1767–1844), a banker and speculator who had already profited in the Napoleonic wars, as if that wasn't enough. Its shell was preserved from further destruction when acquired by the State at the turn of this century. Voltaire wrote 'Marianne' when a guest there in 1723, and it is claimed that he was dosed with 200 pints of lemonade to avoid death by smallpox; he is also said to have set light to his bed. Later visitors were La Fayette, and Benjamin Constant.

The N308 leads E. towards *La Dèfense*, and central *Paris*.

At *Chambourcy*, 4km W. of *St-Germain*, famous for its cheese since the 17C, are the tombs of the Chevalier d'Orsay and Marguerite Power, Countess of Blessington (1789–1849), author of 'The Idler in Italy', etc.

Some 4km S. of *St-Germain*, to the W. of the N386, stood the royal château of *Marly* (its name preserved in the town of **Marly-le-Roi**), built in 1679–86 by *Jules Hardouin-Mansart* for Louis XIV, and a favourite retreat from the formality of Versailles: indeed, regular visits to Marly (and vice versa) were essential, to allow the palaces to be cleaned and aired.

The château was destroyed at the Revolution, although vestiges remain of the park, where stood the famous hydraulic *Machine de Marly*, originally constructed in 1681 to raise water from the Seine to the Marly aqueduct, which in turn carried it to Versailles. New machinery had been installed in 1855–59, taking its water from an underground source, but the whole was dismantled in 1967.

The church of *Marly-le-Roi* was also built by *J.H.-Mansart* (1689), and contains some works originally in Versailles.

23   St-Denis

St-Denis (91,300 inhab.) is best approached by car, by turning off the Al autoroute c. 3km N. of the *Porte de la Chapelle*; or alternatively, by taking the MÉTRO recently extended to its terminus at *St-Denis-Basilique*.

Écouen can be approached hence by public transport (Métro to *St-Denis-Porte-de-Paris*, and thence 268C bus, direction *Ezanville*. Those with a car will continue N. on the N1, after 3.5km forking r. onto the N16.

The Gothic **CATHEDRAL OF ST-DENIS** (CN) stands in the centre of one of the most unattractive and communistic of the northern suburbs of Paris, beyond the site of the celebrated 'Foire du Lendit' which was held here from Dagobert's time until 1552. It was founded on the probable site of *Catolacus*, where the missionary apostle of Lutetia was almost certainly buried.

The W. front, although disfigured at the Revolution, retains one good 12C tower with a low modern steeple. The transeptal portals, each with a rose-window, are mid-13C work.

It is overshadowed in interest by the *Tombs it contains. Unfortunately, these may not be studied in detail in the normal course of the rapid conducted visit (commencing every 30 minutes from 10.00–17.30, except Sun. morning and during services), for chains obstruct their closer inspection, and the tedious monologue of the attendant guide is additionally disconcerting. Little has changed in this respect since Augustus Hare complained that parties were 'hurried full gallop round the church under the guardianship of a jabbering custode'!

The abbey of St-Denis was founded c. 475, perhaps at the instance of St Geneviève, and rebuilt in 630–38 by Dagobert, who also founded a monastery for Benedictines. The first substantial church on the site was built by Abbot Fulrad in 750–75, and here in 754 Pope Stephen III consecrated Pepin le Bref and his wife and sons, thus establishing them securely on the throne. This church was itself replaced by another built by Abbot Suger, of which the narthex (W. porch) and apse (c. 1136–44) survive, ranking among the most important examples of the earliest Gothic architecture. Recent excavations in the crypt, also of this period, and retaining the Romanesque arch, have brought to light Gallo-Roman Christian tombs, and remains of the earlier churches. The rest of the building dates from 1231–81, following the designs of *Pierre de Montreuil* (d. 1267), while c. 1375 the chapels on the N. side of the nave were added.

Most of the effigies of earlier kings were made during the reign of Louis IX (St Louis; d.1270), when St-Denis became recognized as a royal mausoleum; others were brought here during the Revolution. With the exception of Philippe I, Louis XI, Louis-Philippe, and Charles X, all the French kings since Hugues Capet are buried here. In 1422 the body of Henry V lay in state here on its way from Vincennes to Westminster, and seven years later Joan of Arc dedicated her armour here. In 1567 Condé's Huguenots captured the place, but he prevented them from despoiling the basilica: later in the year he was defeated in the plain to the S. by Anne de Montmorency, who was himself mortally wounded. Henri IV abjured Protestantism here in 1593.

After injudicious alterations in the 18C, the abbey was suppressed at the

Detail of a tomb in St-Denis

Revolution, the church unroofed, its tombs rifled and their contents dispersed, but the best of the monuments were saved from destruction by Alexandre Lenoir, who preserved them in his *Musée des Petits-Augustins* (École des Beaux-Arts), whence they were later returned, and drastically restored. Restoration of the fabric of the basilica was taken in hand in 1813, but it was so incompetently carried out that the stability of the N. tower was endangered, and in 1847 it had to be taken down. A subsequent 'restoration' by Viollet-le-Duc and Darcy went some way to repair the harm; but the explosion of a nearby bomb-dump in 1915 caused further damage.

INTERIOR. Only the more important tombs are listed. Smollett, who visited the abbey in Oct. 1763, condemned the 'attitudes' of the sculptures as 'affected, unnatural, and desultory; and their draperies fantastic; or, as one of our English artists expressed himself, *they are all of a flutter'*. The conducted visit begins in the *S. Aisle*, with, among others, the tomb of *Louis d'Orléans* (d.1407; see p186) and *Valentine de Milan* (d.1408), a fine Italian work of 1502–15, commissioned by their grandson, Louis XII. Opposite, against the S.W. pillar of the crossing, is the heart-tomb of *François II* (d.1560), by *Germain Pilon* and *Ponce Jacquiau*. Also in the S. Aisle, the Urn (1549–55) by *Bontemps*, containing the heart of *François I*.

In the *S. Transept*: the *Tomb of *François I* (d.1547) and *Claude de France* (d.1524), a masterpiece by *Philibert Delorme, Pierre Bontemps, Primaticcio*, and others, begun in 1548. The royal pair appear both recumbent and (above) kneeling with their children: reliefs depict the king's military exploits. On the E. side of this transept are the tombs of *Charles V* (d.1380), by *André Beauneveu*, and *Charles VI* (d.1422) with their queens; and of *Bertrand Du Guesclin* (d.1380), one of the few commoners buried here (his heart is at Dinan; his entrails at Le Puy).

At the W. end of the *Choir* are the tombs of *Philippe III*, le Hardi (d.1285), by *Pierre de Chelles* and *Jean d'Arras*, remarkable as being one of the earliest known French portrait-statues. The effigy of his queen, *Isabel of Aragón* (d.1271), is particularly fine. Also *Philippe IV*, le Bel (d.1314). Following the *Ambulatory*, we pass (to the l. of the steps) the tomb of *Dagobert* (d.638), showing reliefs of the torment and redemption of the king's soul, and with a beautiful *Statue (13C) of *Queen Nanthilde*: the figures of Dagobert and his son are 19C restorations. We next pass the tomb of *Léon de Lusignan* (d.1393). Note the 12–13C glass in the *Lady Chapel*, and adjacent chapels, including a Tree of Jesse. Turning W. along the N. side of the Ambulatory we pass (l.) *Blanche* and *Jean* (both d.1243), children of St Louis (from Royaumont), with fine enamelled plaques; *Frédégonde* (d.597), queen of Chilperic I, a remarkable slab in cloisonné mosaic (11C, from St-Germain-des-Prés); and also from St-Germain, *Childebert I* (d.558), a 12C statue. In the chapel at the top of the steps, draped statues of *Henri II* (d.1559) and *Catherine de Médicis* (d.1589) by *Germain Pilon* (1583). In the *Sanctuary* is the *Altar of the Relics* (by *Viollet-le-Duc*), on which are placed the reliquaries, given by Louis XVIII, of St Denis and his fellow-martyrs.

In the *N. Transept* is the splendid tomb of *Henri II* and *Catherine de Médicis*, designed by *Primaticcio* in 1560–73, with recumbent and kneeling effigies of the king and queen, and supporters and reliefs by *Germain Pilon* and other contemporary sculptors. The king and queen were kneeling at a bronze prie-dieu melted down at the Revolution. Here also are the tombs of *Philippe V* (d.1322), *Charles IV* (d.1328), *Philippe VI* (d.1350), and *Jean II* (d.1364, prisoner at the Savoy, London), the last two by *André Beauneveu*. Opposite (l., in the choir) are tombs of *Louis X* (d.1316) and his son *Jean I* (d.1316).

In the *N. Aisle*, the *Tomb of *Louis XII* (d.1515) and *Anne of Brittany* (d.1514), made by *Jean Juste* (Giov. di Giusto) in 1516–32. The royal pair are depicted naked and recumbent on the tombstone, and kneeling on the canopy above (the conventional design for Renaissance tombs); bas-reliefs illustrate episodes in the king's career. Lastly, among other 13–14C tombs, that of *Louis de France* (d.1260), the eldest son of St Louis, with Henry III of England as one of the bearers.—Note, before entering the Crypt, the *High Stalls* of the Ritual Choir (1501–07) from the chapel of the château de Gaillon; the *Low Stalls* are 15C work from St-Lucien, near Beauvais.

The *Crypt*, entered on either side of the Choir, was constructed by Suger round the original Carolingian 'martyrium', the site of the grave of St Denis and his companions, and retains some 12C capitals. Here are seen the sarcophagi of Louis XVI, Marie-Antoinette, and Louis XVIII, among other 18–19C royal personages. The ossuary on the N. side contains the bones that were thrown into a pit when the tombs were rifled in 1793. In a side chapel is a charming 12C Virgin, originally at the abbey of Longchamp.

To the S. of the basilica are the monastic buildings, in the process of restoration, rebuilt in the 18C by *Robert de Cotte* and *Jacques Gabriel*, and occupied after 1809 as a *Maison d'Éducation de la Légion d'Honneur.*—;Some five minutes' walk further S., at 22bis Rue Gabriel Péri, the **Musée d'Art et d'Histoire** is being installed in a Carmelite monastery founded in 1625. The compartmented cupola of its Chapel (1784), by *Mique*, built while Louise de France was in residence (1770–87), is notable. It preserves the reconstituted *Pharmacy* of the Hôtel-Dieu (demolished 1907), and the *Study* of the poet Paul Éluard (Eugène Grindel; 1895–1952), born in St-Denis; an archaeological section of interest; rooms devoted to the Commune de Paris (1870–71); some 4000 engravings and lithographs by *Daumier*; paintings and drawings by *Albert André, Cézanne, Léger*, and *Dufy*, etc.

24 Paris to Écouen, Chantilly, and Clermont

Total distance, 64km (40 miles). N16 for 20km **Écouen**.—21km **Chantilly**.—23km *Clermont*. Chantilly may also be approached by the N17 and D924A: see Rte 25; or even the D909, forking off the N1 8km N.W. of Écouen, later passing *Belloy-en-France* and *Royaumont*: see below.

From the *Porte de la Chapelle*, the N16 drives N. towards **St-Denis** (see Rte 23), which may be by-passed. The road now traverses a dreary dormitory area before by-passing (l.) *Sarcelles*, with relics of a 12C church with a Gothic nave and Renaissance façade, and (r.) *Villiers-le-Bel*, which belies its name, to reach (l.) **Écouen**, of slight interest in itself, although the church of *St-Acceul* retains some *Stained-glass* attrib. to *Jean Cousin* in its choir (1544).

The town is commanded by its magnificent Renaissance *CHÂTEAU D'ÉCOUEN*, now housing the *MUSÉE NATIONAL DE LA RENAISSANCE*, opened to the public in 1976, and displaying a number of outstanding objects from this epoch long stored at the *Musée de Cluny*. Some rooms may still be closed; the second floor is under restoration.

Its construction was commenced c.1535 for the Constable Anne de Montmorency, and among artists employed there were *Jean Goujon* and *Jean Bullant*, to the latter of whom is ascribed the interior portico of the S. Wing (in the niches of which once stood Michelangelo's 'Chained Captives'). It was put to a variety of uses during the Revolutionary period, and in 1805 became a school for the daughters of members of the Légion d'Honneur, with Mme Campan as *directrice*. It later reverted to the Duc d'Aumale, who chose to remove a number of its embellishments to Chantilly, including an altar by Goujon from the chapel.

From the entrance we turn l. into a vestibule, and then the *Chapel* (**R1**), with painted ribbed vaulting and delicately carved stonework, before traversing a series of rooms on the ground floor ranged around the central courtyard.—**R2**, with a painted chimney-piece (one of six similarly depicting biblical themes) in the style of the School of Fontainebleau, contains arms and armour. The chimney-piece of **R3** backs onto that of the adjoining room, displaying examples of Renaissance woodcarving; **R5** preserves a number of leather panels.

This is followed by a series of smaller rooms devoted to collections of (**R6**) carved wood plaques, (**R7**) larger panels, including some remarkable examples in ebony.—**R8** pear-wood statuettes, mainly German or Flemish; other examples in box-wood; coffers; a fine ivory flagon; bronze figurines, including fornicating fauns, by *Riccio*.—**R9** is devoted to metalwork, some damascened; cutlery; and a collection of Renaissance door-furniture. **RR10–11** contain mathematical instruments, and watches, and work in precious metals.—**R12**, known as

that of Catherine de Médicis, is traversed before reaching one
reserved for concerts, etc., and another with collections of sculpture.

FIRST FLOOR. **R1** Furniture, some ebony; and tapestries of the 'Labours of
Hercules'.—**R2** Chairs and *'caquetoires'*.—**R3**, with notable carved doors. In
RR4–7 are hung a remarkable series of tapestries entitled 'The story of David
and Bathsheba' (Brussels; 16C). Note also the finely carved stone fireplaces in
R5 from Chalons-sur-Marne (1562), with reliefs of Christ and the Samaritan,
and Actaeon surprising Diana in her bath.—**R6** contains a collection of
enamelled plaques by *Pierre Courteys* (Limoges; 1559), and tile-pictures.—
Passing a carved wooden staircase, we enter **R8**, with a made-up marble
chimney-piece, and a tiled pavement by *Masséot Abaquesne* (mid 16C),
beyond which are rooms displaying glass panels of 1544–52, majolicas,
including work by *Lucca della Robbia*, furniture, and embroideries, etc.

N. of *Écouen* we pass (l.) *Le Mesnil-Aubry*, with a Renaissance
church of 1531–82, and (8km, l.) the 18C château of *Epinay-Cham-
plâtreux*, built by *Jean-Michel Chevotet* for the Molé family.
    After 2km bear l. for **Luzarches**, with an old market-place, once
famous for the relics of the physicians Cosmas and Damian, martyred
in 303. The interesting *Church* dedicated to them bears, within its
porch, sculptured medallions relating to their lives. The building,
although preserving important 12C remains, dates principally from
the mid-16C, and, like *Le Mesnil*, is the work of *Nicolas de
St-Michel*. Robert de Luzarches, architect of Amiens cathedral, was
born here. The gateway to the castle, to the W. of the town, leads to
the ruins of the collegiate church of *St-Côme*, largely destroyed at the
Revolution.

About 3km E. lies the château *d'Hérivaux*, ruins of an abbey founded in 1160,
also demolished at the Revolution, and once the property of Benjamin Constant,
who entertained Mme de Staël there. He sold it in 1802 and moved to a smaller
house, 'Les Herbages', at *St-Martin-du-Tertre*, S.W. of Viarmes.

Chantilly (see below) lies 10km N. of Luzarches.

A DETOUR may be made to *Royaumont*, by driving W. from
Luzarches to (4km) *Viarmes*, with a church preserving a 12–13C
nave.—*Asnières*, 1km beyond, has a 12–13C church.—For *Belloy-en-
France*, 5km S. of Viarmes, see Rte 38.
    2·5km N. of *Viarmes*, to the r. of the D909, lies **Royaumont**,
retaining the considerable remains of the great Cistercian abbey
founded in 1228 by St Louis, who in 1234 was married in the church.
With the exception of a tall stair-turret, the huge church was
dismantled in 1791. The beautiful *Refectory* (used as a cotton-mill in
the 19C; and which would be better stripped of its furnishing), has
vaulting sustained by five monolithic columns, and retains the tomb
of Henri of Lorraine, by *Coysevox*; the *Kitchen*, and *Cloister*, with its
simple clustered columns, may be visited.

Closed Tues.; time is wasted waiting for a group to accumulate. During the
1914–18 War it accommodated a hospital for French troops run entirely by
Scotswomen; it now houses a cultural foundation (Gouin-Lang).—The nearby
Château, by *Le Masson*, dates from 1785–89.

At 2km N. we turn r. through *Gouvieux* for (6·5km) *Chantilly*.

Boran-sur-Oise, a riverside resort 2·5km S.W. of this junction, has a 13–15C
church with a Gothic belfry.

Chantilly (10,200 inhab.), the 'Newmarket' of France, where race-meetings have been held since 1836, is famous for its château, approached by turning r. along the Rue du Connétable in the town centre, which passes (r.) *Notre-Dame* (1686–92), built by the son of the Grand Condé, and the vast *Grandes-Écuries, built by *Jean Aubert* in 1719–40, with room for 240 horses. Passing through the *Porte St-Denis*, we see the château on our l.

A more direct approach from the Paris road may be made by turning r. after the railway bridge, and driving through the park along the Route de l'Aigle, passing behind the grandstands and the chapel of *Sainte-Croix* (one of seven erected by Madeleine of Savoy, wife of the Great Constable) to the *Carrefour des Lions*.

An alternative route from Paris is the N17 to (34·5km) *La Chapelle-en-Serval*; there branching l. onto the D924A through the forest to the Carrefour des Lions.

The *CHÂTEAU DE CHANTILLY, standing in a lake stocked with carp, consists of two connected buildings, the *Petit Château* or Capitainerie, on the S.W., and the *Grand Château* to the N.

Chantilly came into the possession of the Montmorency family in 1484, and after the execution of Henri II Montmorency passed to the Grand Condé (Louis II, prince de Condé, 1621–86; whose mother was a Montmorency) in 1632. The present *Petit Château* was erected about 1560 (probably by *Jean Bullant*) for the Constable Anne de Montmorency. The *Grand Château*, rebuilt by *Mansart* for the Grand Condé on the site of a mansion built by *Chambiges* for Constable Anne in 1528–31, was described by Lord Herbert of Cherbury as 'an incomparably fine residence, admired by the greatest princes of Europe'. Molière's 'Les Précieuses ridicules' was given for the first time at Chàntilly in 1659. During the visit of Louis XIV in 1671, François Vatel, the Grand Condé's *maître d'hôtel*, committed suicide because he thought the fish would be late for a Friday's repast (as described by Mme de Sévigné). The Duc d'Enghien (1772–1804), shot at Vincennes, was born here. In 1777 Philip Thicknesse saw the Prince de Condé at supper with some friends—8 people waited on by 25 servants. He also complained that the music played during the meal 'was all wind instruments'.

The *Grand Château* was destroyed at the Revolution, but after some repairs had been carried out by the last of the Condés (d.1830), it was entirely rebuilt in 1875–81 by his heir, the Duc d'Aumale (1822–97), fourth son of Louis-Philippe, from the designs of *Daumet*. Unfortunately, he also inherited his father's 'taste' in many respects.

After the confiscation of the property of the Orléans family in 1853, the Château was bought by the English banking firm of Coutts, but the property was returned to its rightful owner by a decree of the National Assembly in 1872. In spite of his banishment to Twickenham, the Duc d'Aumale bequeathed the whole domain, together with his art collections, to the *Institut de France* in 1886. Chantilly marks the farthest advance in this direction of German troops in Sept. 1914; it was later the headquarters of Joffre.

After passing the iron Grille d'Honneur, we leave on our r. the *Château d'Enghien* (1770), built by *Le Roy* for the unfortunate Duc d'Enghien, and now the curator's residence. We cross the *Terrasse du Connétable*, with a statue of the Constable Anne de Montmorency (1492–1567) by *P. Dubois*, pass between two bronze groups of hounds by *Cain*, cross the moat, and enter the *Cour d'Honneur* through a colonnade.

The **MUSÉE CONDÉ, one of the most interesting collections within easy reach of Paris (although a number of paintings reflect a certain lack of discrimination on the part of the Duc d'Aumale) is installed on the ground floor of the *Grand Château* and part of the first floor of the *Petit Château*. Containing a unique concentration of French paintings and illuminations of the 15–16C, it offers also a

A statue of Le Nôtre, by Tony Noël, which stands a short distance N. of the Terrasse du Connétable.

comprehensive range of Chantilly ware from the factory founded by the Duc de Bourbon in 1730, an important Library, and other works of art. Among the more valuable collections of drawings acquired by the Duc d'Aumale was that of Frédéric Reiset.

Grand Vestibule. On the l. is the *Grand Staircase*, but we ascend steps to the r. to enter the *Gal. des Cerfs*, on the ceiling of which are the arms of the successive owners of Chantilly. The walls are hung with 17C Gobelins tapestries of hunting scenes. Above the chimneypiece, the Vision of St Hubert; dessus de portes of Venus and Cupid, and Diana, all by *Baudry.*—Among the more important paintings displayed in the *Gal. de Peinture* are: *Fromentin*, Hawking; *Lancret*, 'Déjeuner au jambon'; *Ph. de Champaigne*, Mazarin, and Richelieu; *Lampi*, the Tsarina Marie Féodorowna; Views of Chantilly by *De Cort*; and *Nanteuil*; portrait of Colbert.

From the end of the gallery we enter the *Rotunda* (**Pl.1**) in the *Tour Senlis*, with a mosaic pavement from Herculaneum: *Clouet*, Odet de Châtillon; *anon.*, Gabrielle d'Estrées in her bath; *after Poussin*, Landscape; and portraits by *Andrea del Sarto*, and *Annibale Carracci*, and *Piero di Cosimo*, Simonetta Vespucci.

The *Gal. de Logis* (**Pl.3**) contains a magnificent collection of ***French Portrait drawings** of the 16–17C, including Anne de Montmorency; Charles IX; Henri II; *Marc Duval*, Gaspard de Coligny; *after Fouquet*, Charles VII; *anon.*, Double portrait; *after Jean Perréal*, Charles VIII; *after Clouet*, François de Scepeaux; Marguerite de Navarre; François II; *after Decourt*, Henri III; attrib. *Le Mannier*, Charles IX aged three playing with a cat; *Corneille de Lyon*, Old man; Anne, Duc de Joyeuse; Antoine de Bourbon; and Unknown women; Duc de Nemours; Mary Tudor; Laure de Noves;

Gabrielle d'Estrées; and Marguerite-Charlotte de Montmorency. Opposite is *anon.*, Fagon (?).

In the adjoining room are: Sully; attr. *Quesnel*, Martin Ruzé; opposite: *after Dumoustier*, Rogier de Saint-Lary; James I of England; *Wouwerman*, Cavalry combat.—**Pl.6** *Perrault* (after Horace Vernet), Louis-Philippe and his sons leaving Versailles, and *Bonnat*, the Duc d'Aumale.

Rotonde de la Minerve (**Pl.7**), in the *Constable's Tower*: Minerva, a Greek statuette of the best period; vase from Nola; Pourtalès Amphora, a red-figured vase of the time of Pheidias; Tanagra figures; bronze ewers from Herculaneum, etc.; *after Mignard*, Henriette d'Angleterre, Duchesse d'Orléans.

Cabinet des Antiques (**Pl.8**). On the l.: *Lawrence*, Franz I of Austria; Wall-cases: vases and bronze utensils, and coins minted within ten years of the eruption of Vesuvius in A.D. 79, found at Pompeii.

Cabinet du Giotto (**Pl.9**): *Enguerrand Quarton*, Virgin: *Iacopo del Sellaio*, Madonna; *School of Giotto*, Death of the Virgin; *Andrea del Sarto*, Young Man; *Ghirlandaio*, Louis de la Trémoille; *Frans Francken* (?), Ecce homo.

Salle Isabelle (**Pl.10**): *Rousseau*, Landscape; *W. van de Velde the Younger*, Calm sea; *J. van Ruisdael*, Coast at Scheveningen.

Salle d'Orléans (**Pl.11**): *Bonnat*, Duc d'Aumale (1880); *Jalabert*, Queen Marie-Amélie (1865); a collection of *Chantilly Porcelain*; and portfolios of drawings (not exhibited through lack of space) by *Primaticcio* (decorations for Fontainebleau), *Watteau*, the *Clouets*, and *Carmontelle* (18C portraits in water-colour), among others.

Salle Caroline (**Pl.12**): *Greuze*, Affection, Girl, a study for the 'Village Marriage Contract' in the Louvre, 'La Surprise'; *Duplessis*, Duchesse de Chartres watching her husband's departure for Ushant (1778); *Watteau*, 'L'Amante Inquiète', and 'La Sérénade'; *Mignard*, Comtesse de la Suze; *Nattier*, Duchesse d'Orléans as Hebe, and Duchesse de Nantes, daughter of Mme de Montespan; *Carle Vernet*, Duc d'Orléans and Duc de Chartres (1788); *Largillière*, Portrait; attrib. *Seb. Bourdon*, Portrait; attrib. *Rigaud*, Portrait; and of the Princesse des Ursins.

Pl. 13: attrib. *Clouet*, Jeanne d'Albret; and *after Clouet* or from his studio: two of Charles IX; Elisabeth of Austria; Odet de Châtillon; Catherine de Médicis; Marguerite de Valois as a child; Henri II as a child; attrib. to *Corneille de Lyon* or his studio: Gabrielle de Rochechouart (?); the Dauphin François, son of François I; *Jean Decourt*, Henri III (?); Albert de Gondi; *Marc Duval*, Jacques de Savoie; and anon. portraits of Marguerite d'Angoulême; Henri d'Albret, King of Navarre; Michel de l'Hôpital; François I; and *anon.* Portraits of Ferdinand of Austria; Claude de France (?); and Montaigne.

Returning through **Pl.5**, we pass portraits by *Mierevelt* of Grotius, and of Elizabeth of Bohemia, to regain the *Gal. de Peinture*, crossing which, we enter the *Gal. de Psyché*. 42 of the original 44 sepia *Stained-glass windows* representing the Loves of Cupid and Psyche (as related by Apuleius in 'The Golden Ass') were made about 1541 for the Constable de Montmorency's château at *Écouen*, and were probably designed by *Michel Coxie*. At the end is a wax portrait bust of Henri IV (1610) by *Guillaume Dubois*.

On the wall are important *Portrait drawings*, many ascribed to the *Clouets*, and others to *Jean Perréal*. They include: Diane de Poitiers;

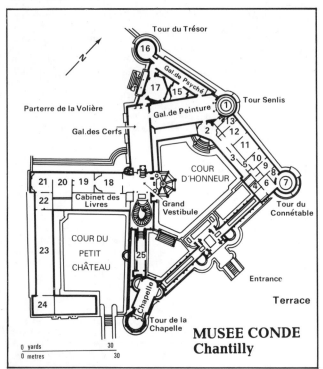

Marshal Strozzi; Hercule-François d'Alençon; Marguerite
d'Angoulême, Queen of Navarre, sister of François I; Jeanne
d'Albret, mother of Henri IV; Henri II; Henri, Duc de Guise; François,
Duc de Guise; Jeanne, Queen of Navarre; François II; Marguerite de
Valois (La Reine Margot), first wife of Henri IV; Charles IX as a child;
Anne de Montmorency; Admiral Coligny; Henri II as a boy; Marshal
Brissac.

The **Santuario (Pl.15)**, off the centre of the room, contains the main
treasures of the collection, including *Raphael*, Madonna of the House
of Orléans (painted about 1505), the Three Graces (or the Three Ages
of Woman), an earlier panel. Between these, Esther and Ahasuerus, a
long panel painted in tempera, which, although catalogued as by
Filippino Lippi, is probably by an unknown pupil of Botticelli ('*Amico
di Sandro*'). Reproductions are on view of forty (of 47) original
miniatures executed in 1453–60 for the Book of Hours ordered by
Étienne Chevalier (1410–74), Treasurer of France. They were
acquired by the Duc d'Aumale in 1891, and while plausibly ascribed
to *Jean Fouquet* (1415–81), they have not yet been proved to be the
work of that master. Two on the r. wall represent Étienne Chevalier
and his patron saint adoring the Virgin and Child.

Re-entering the *Gal. de Psyché*, we turn l. to reach the *Cabinet des
Gemmes* (**Pl.16**) in the *Tour du Trésor* (views). In the table-case near
the centre window are an enamel of Apollo guiding the Chariot of
the Sun, attrib. to *Cellini*, and the rose diamond known as the 'Grand

Condé'. In the wall-cases: a Cross from the treasury of Basle (15C); snuff boxes, with views and plans of Chantilly (by *Roussel*, 1775); a collection of fans, miniatures, and enamels, etc.

We return to the *Gal. de Psyché*, turn r., and pass through a small room in which is a bas-relief of the Departure of Phaethon, by *Jean Goujon*, to enter the **Tribune (Pl.17)**, a large octagonal room in the middle of which is a vase by *Clodion*. On the panels above the cornice are represented eight houses and châteaux connected with the Duc d'Aumale: Collège Henri-IV, Aumale, Palais-Royal, Palermo, Écouen, Guise, Villers-Cotterêts, and Twickenham.

On the walls hang: *Reynolds*, Countess Waldegrave and her daughter (1761); *A. Scheffer*, Prince Talleyrand; *Watteau*, 'Plaisir pastoral'; *van Dyck*, Gaston, Duc d'Orléans; *Memling* (?), Diptych of the Virgin appearing to Jeanne de Bourbon, daughter of Charles VII, and Christ on the Cross; *Perugino*, Madonna with SS Jerome and Peter; *Botticelli* (?), Autumn (once attrib. to Mantegna); *Fr. Clouet*, Card. Odet de Châtillon; *Flemish School*, Anthony, the 'Grand Bastard' of Burgundy; *Sassetta*, Mystic Marriage of St Francis (1444); *Pesellino*, Madonna with SS Peter and Anthony; *Mignard*, Molière; *Ingres*, Mme Devauçay, painted in Rome in 1807, and Self-portrait; *Ph. de Champaigne*. Angélique Arnauld; *Mignard*, Card. Mazarin; *H.-G. Pot*, portrait of Andres Hooftman; *after Rigaud*, Armand-Jean le Bouthillier de Rancé, Abbé de la Trappe; *anon.*, Marquise de Montespan; *Rigaud*, Louis XIV; *anon.*, the Duc du Maine, and Duc d'Anjou (later Philip V of Spain); and three portraits by *Mme Vigée-Lebrun*.—In the small room beyond is the Fall of Phaethon, by *Goujon*, a pendant to the bas-relief in the other vestibule.

We now return through the *Gal. des Cerfs* to the *Grand Vestibule* and turn r. to visit the apartments in the **Petit Château**, decorated from 1686 by *J.H.-Mansart* for the Grand Condé and furnished with Beauvais tapestry and contemporary clocks, ornaments, and woodwork.—*Antechamber* **(Pl.18)**: dessus de portes of dogs by *Oudry* and *Desportes*; enamel of Henri IV by *Claudius Popelin*; and Sèvres, Chinese, and Rouen porcelain.—*Salle des Gardes* **(Pl.19)**: *van Dyck*, Comte Henri de Bergues, and the Princesse Marie de Brabançon; four enamel portraits by *Léonard Limousin*; *Justus van Egmont*, the Grand Condé (1658); *after Nanteuil*, the Grand Condé in 1662; *anon.*, Abraham de Fabert, Maréchal de France; and François II de Montmorency, Duc de Luxembourg. The mosaic above the chimneypiece is from Herculaneum.

The richly decorated *Bedroom* **(Pl.20)**, with white and gilt wood, and painted panels by *J.-B. Huet*, contains a commode by *Riesener*, chairs by *J.-B. Sené*, and a fine chandelier.—*Cabinet* **(Pl.21)**. Equestrian statue of the Grand Condé by *Frémiet*.—The *Salon Des Singes **(Pl.22)** is named from the highly decorative chinoiserie panel-paintings of 'Singeries ou différentes actions de la vie humaine' by *Christophe Huet*.

The exquisite *Petite Singerie*, in a room below, *may* be shown to visitors, on making advance application.

***Gal. des Actions** de M. Le Prince **(Pl.23)**. The panels of this long room were painted in 1686–96 by *Sauveur Lecomte* with scenes from the battles fought by the Grand Condé, whose despatch-case lies on the bureau of the Duc de Choiseul. Over the fireplace is a *Trophy* formed of his swords and pistols; above is his portrait when twenty-two years of age, at Rocroi, by *J. Stella*; below, a medallion by *Coysevox* of 1686, the year of the Prince's death. The bust of the Grand Condé in biscuit de Sèvres on the mantlepiece is by *Roland* (1785); those in marble of Turenne and of the Grand Condé, are by *Derbais* (1695).—The next *Cabinet* (**Pl.24**) contains a portrait of the Duc d'Enghien by *Vallain*, and miniatures; and *Triophime Bigot*, the Supper at Emmaus.

Retracing our steps to the *Antichambre*, we turn r. to enter the **Cabinet des Livres**, containing some 12,500 volumes, many of great rarity or from a provenance of interest. The superb bindings are worthy of study. Some 1493 MSS. are also preserved here. Perhaps the greatest treasure is the *'Très Riches Heures du Duc de Berri'* (acquired in 1855), with magnificently illuminated pages of the Months, begun about 1415 by *Pol de Limbourg* and his brothers, painting direct from nature and not treated conventionally as had previously been the universal practice. They were completed by *Jean Colombe* some 70 years later. Only reproductions of the delicate originals are now on view.

We return to the *Grand Vestibule*. On the r. is the *Grand Escalier* (no adm.), with its superb balustrade of copper, brass, and galvanised iron, designed by *Daumet* and executed by the brothers *Moreau*, with caryatids by *Chapu*, and Gobelins tapestry after *Boucher* and *De Troy*.—Passing the staircase, we enter the *Gal. de la Chapelle* (**Pl.25**), with drawings by *Dürer*, Annunciation (1526); *Domenichino*, Flight into Egypt; *Seb. del Piombo*, Head of Christ; and *Raphael*, Madonna.

The *Chapel*, founded early in the 14C, but many times rebuilt, was virtually destroyed during the Revolution. It was restored in 1882 by *Daumet*. Behind the altar is the mausoleum of Henri II de Condé (d.1662), with bronze sculptures by *J. Sarazin*. The Altar itself, by *Jean Bullant* and *Jean Goujon*, the woodwork of 1548, and the stained-glass (1544; portraits of the Great Constable's children), were all brought here from Écouen. The flag was captured at Rocroi (1643).

The ***PARK**, with impressive parterres, was laid out for the most part by *Le Nôtre* for the Grand Condé, and is adorned with sculptures and ornamental water. Among the buildings which may be visited are the *Maison de Sylvie*, to the S.E. behind the Château d'Enghien, to reach which we pass the *Chapelle de St-Sébastien* (1552) and the *Cabotière* (Louis-XIII period). 'Sylvie' was the name given to Marie Félice Orsini, Duchesse de Montmorency, by the poet Théophile de Viau, who, when he was condemned to death in 1623 for his licentious verses, was hidden by the duchess in this building. Rebuilt by the Grand Condé in 1684, the Maison de Sylvie was in 1724 the scene of the romantic affair of Mlle de Clermont, sister of the Duc de Bourbon, and M. de Melun, who was killed in a hunting accident. It now contains Chinese curios, wood-carvings, tapestry, etc.

To the N.E. stand a group of cottages, the 'Hameau', built in 1776 by *Le Roy* for the penultimate Condé, and once the scene of many 'fêtes champêtres' of the period.—To the W., near the stables, is the *Jeu de Paume*, of 1757, containing carriages, two leaden dogs from Twickenham, Abd-el-Kader's tent, etc.

The ***Forest of Chantilly** (2100 hectares in extent; see IGN 404), composed of oaks, limes, birches, and clumps of Scots pines, is intersected by numerous roads or sandy tracks (in the interest of the training-stables), the latter being closed to cars.

The N324 leads 10km E. to *Senlis* (see Rte 25) viâ *Courteuil*, where the Abbé Prévost (1697–1763) died.

FROM CHANTILLY TO BEAUVAIS (47km). **St-Leu-d'Esserent**, 5·5km N.W. of *Chantilly* by the D44, has a particularly fine 12C *Church, with later additions, and recent restorations. To the N., the cloisters of the priory may be visited. The local quarries supplied stone for the cathedrals of Chartres, Sens, and later, the Palace of Versailles; in 1944 they were used for the assembly of V1 and V2 rockets.—From *St-Leu* we turn N.W. through *Cramoisy*, with a 12–13C church, to (9·5km) *Mello*, with an 11–13C church altered in the 16C, and an ancient château largely rebuilt in 1770.—5km. *Bury* has an interesting 11–13C priory-church containing a carved wood altarpiece of the Passion (16C).—3km. *Mouy*, with a 12–13th, and 16C, church, 6km W. of which is the restored Renaissance château of *Mouchy-le-Châtel*, with a 12C tower.—4km. At *Fillerval* (2km N.E.) is a château built by the geographer Cassini (see below), with a remarkable pediment displaying astronomical instruments.—7km. *Villers-St-Sépulcre*, named from a sculptured Entombment in its church, and incorporating a slab from the Holy Sepulchre in Jerusalem.—13km. *Beauvais*, see Rte 38.

The N16 leads N. from Chantilly to (8km) **Creil** (36,100 inhab.), an industrial town and important railway junction, which made it a military target in both World Wars. It retains a small museum (18–19C furniture, and a collection of Creil pottery and stoneware for which this expanding town is famous) housed in the remains of the royal castle. The church of *St-Médard* (13–16C) may also be visited.

Montataire, immediately to the W. of *Creil*, has a 12–15C church and a château of the 14–16C.—*Nogent-sur-Oise*, N. of *Creil*, has a 12–13C church, as has *Villers-St-Paul* (to the E. of *Nogent*), the latter with a geometrically decorated porch.

9km **Liancourt** (2km E.) retains a 15–17C church with curious bell-turrets, and a marble monument with good effigies of Charles du Plessis and his wife, but the site of the 17C château of the Dukes of la Rochefoucauld-Liancourt has been built over.

It was Duc Frédéric-Alexandre (1747–1837) who made the celebrated retort when Louis XVI remarked (on the evening of 14 July 1789) on hearing of the disturbance in Paris, 'Mais c'est une révolte': 'Non, Sire, c'est une révolution!'
    Cambronne-lès-Clermont, 4km to the W. of the N16, has a good 12–13C church with a Romanesque belfry, capitals, and remains of murals.

7km **Clermont** (8700 inhab.), built on a hillside above the Brèche, was in the Middle Ages the seat of a powerful countship; the House of Bourbon descended from Robert de Clermont, 6th son of Louis IX. It retains its *Hôtel de Ville* of 1328 (restored), preserving a portrait of Berwick, Duc de Fitz-James (natural son of James II), by *Van Loo*. Berwick acquired the village of *Fitz-James* (formerly *Warty*), N.E. of *Clermont*, in 1704. A statue commemorates C.-F. Cassini de Thury (1714–84), the geographer, who first employed the method of triangulation in making maps of France, and one of the celebrated local family (of Italian origin) of astronomers and cartographers. The church of *St-Samson*, later substantially altered after a fire, contains some good 16C stained glass. To the l. of the church are the ruins of a 13C *Gateway*. Crowning the hill are the walls and keep of the *Castle* (views), which was twice captured by the English, in 1359 and 1434, and was the birthplace of Charles IV, le Bel, in 1294.

The N31 leads W. to (26km) *Beauvais*, see Rte 38, passing near (2km, l.) *Agnetz*, with a 13–16C church, and through part of the FORÊT DE HEZ (see IGN 407).—31km E. lies *Compiègne*, see Rte 25. The D916 leads N. to (66km) *Amiens*: see Blue Guide France.

25 Paris to Senlis and Compiègne

Total distance, 75km (46 miles). N17 to (44km) *Senlis* and D932A to (31km) *Compiègne*.
While the Al motorway is the most rapid approach to *Senlis*, the N17 is the route described, leaving Paris by the *Porte de la Villette*.

At 16km, just beyond the old airport of **Le Bourget** (where the *Musée de l'Air*, with a notable collection of 140 aircraft, largely from 1919, but including earlier flying machines, has been installed: adm. 10.00–17.00, except Tues.), passing extensive tulip fields (at their best in April-May), *Gonesse* lies to the l., the birthplace of Philippe Auguste (1165), with a 12–13C church, behind which is the *Hôtel-Dieu*, built on the site of one founded in 1208.—*Goussainville* (4km N.) has a Renaissance church built by *Jean Bullant*, and 4km beyond, to the N.W., at *Fontenay-en-Parisis*, is an interesting 12–13C church.

7·5km, l. (after passing, r., the W. end of the **Charles de Gaulle Airport**) is *Louvres*, where *St-Justin* preserves an 11C W. portal; the rest of the church is 13–16C. The tower of the church of *St-Rieul* has a pointed vault said to date from c. 1110, and claimed to be the oldest existing example of the kind.—2·5km N.E., towards *Villeron*, is an impressive 13C tithe-barn.

7·5km *Survilliers*, with an interesting 16C church.—6·5km E. lies *Mortefontaine*, with an old château, once the property of Joseph Bonaparte, where a commercial treaty between the First Consul and the United States (represented by Franklin) was concluded in 1803. In the nearby *Parc de la Vallière* is a pretentious château built in the Renaissance style in 1897 by the Duc de Grammont.—Hence the N17 may be regained by following the D607 viâ *Thiers* to *Pontarmé*.

At 3·5km the D924A diverges l. through the forest to the *Château of Chantilly* (8km beyond; see Rte 24).

At 3km *Pontarmé*, we enter the FORÊT DE CHANTILLY (see above).

6·5km **SENLIS** (15,300 inhab.), while not quite the peaceful old town it once was, still retains many attractive alleys, particularly those within the Gallo-Roman ramparts of the Silvanectes.

The *gâteau senlisien*, game, and venison pâtés, and *cèpes* from the adjacent forests should be sampled.

Senlis, probably built on a site of *Ratomagnus*, was a royal residence from the time of Clovis to Henri IV; Hugues Capet was elected 'Duc des Francs' here in 987; in 1358 it was the scene of a massacre of nobles by the Jacquerie. The bishopric founded in the 3C lapsed in 1790. It was briefly in German hands in Sept. 1914, who set fire to some streets and plundered the town. It was also damaged in 1940.

From the S., the Rue de la République crosses the S.E. section of the town, the site of its outer medieval ramparts forming a concentric ring of tree-lined boulevards, except to the S.E., where some fortifications are preserved, including the *Porte de Paris*. In this quarter, reached by the Rue de Meaux, leading E. off the Rue de la République, lies the ancient *Abbaye St-Vincent*, founded in 1062, and retaining a 12C belfry and cloister of 1680. It was rebuilt in the 17C, and is now a theological college. Also in the Rue de Meaux is the former hospital-chapel of *La Charité* (1704).

In the Rue Ste-Geneviève, on the W. side of the Rue de la République, is the *Logis de Haubergier* (16C), with a hexagonal turret-stair, housing a good regional *Museum*. A few paces W. is the *Hôtel de Ville*, rebuilt in 1495. Beyond, in the Rue de Beauvais, is the former church of St-Aignan (now a cinema), and several 14–15C houses. The Rue du Châtel leads N. from the Hôtel de Ville into the Gallo-Roman enceinte, with 16 towers remaining, and among the most complete in existence, but most of them are hidden by abutting houses. We pass (No.20) the old *Hôtel-Dieu*. At the far end of the street is the *Hôtel des Trois-Pots*, first mentioned in 1292, and now with a 16C façade. Here is the entrance to the ruins of the royal castle (4th, 11th, and 16C), the *Priory of St-Maurice* (14C), and *Musée de la Vénerie* (Hunting), with canvases by *Oudry, Desportes*, and *Snyders*, etc. To the N. of the cathedral is the *Hôtel de Vermandois* (13–16C).

The ***Cathedral** was built in 1155–84 (almost coeval with St-Denis and Notre-Dame). Its S. Tower is surmounted by a fine 13C spire 78m high. The central door of the W. façade is embellished with statues and reliefs relative to the Life of the Virgin; the eight statue-columns were badly restored in the 19C. The transepts were rebuilt by *Pierre Chambiges* in 1530–56 after a fire, in a rich Gothic style, but displaying Renaissance tendencies. From the same period date the side portals and the five shallow E. chapels, of which that in the centre was remodelled in 1840.

The INTERIOR is notable for the beauty of its triforium gallery. The E. chapel of the S. transept has a splendid 16C vault. From the S.W. chapel in the nave a staircase leads to the beautiful *Chapter-house* (late 14C), with a remarkable central pillar; the glass is 14C. The *Sacristy*, octagonal in plan, in part a relic of the original early 11C church, should also be visited.

To the E. of the cathedral is the *Palais de Justice* (previously the Bishop's), to the S. of which is the disused church of *St-Frambourg* (1177–85), now a garage. Behind the Bishop's Palace is the former church of **St-Pierre** (now a market), a handsome building with a façade in the Flamboyant style (1516); one of the towers has a dome and is of Renaissance date; while the other, partly Romanesque, has a spire of 1432.

A short distance S.E., at No.12 Rue Bellon, is the *Hôtel Saint-Simon* (18C), belonging to the family of the industrious author of the famous 'Mémoires', who was himself a governor of the town.

A few minutes' walk S.W. of the PL. DE CREIL (at the far end of the Rue de Beauvais) are the remains of a Gallo-Roman *Amphitheatre*, discovered in 1863, and probably earlier than that of Nîmes.

The D924 leads 10km W. to *Chantilly*, see Rte 24.

2·5km S.E. of Senlis lie the picturesque ruins of the *Abbaye de la Victoire*, founded by Philippe Auguste to commemorate the Battle of Bouvines (1214), rebuilt in the 15–16C, and suppressed at the Revolution.

5km E. of Senlis, to the r. of the N324 leading to (21km) *Crépy-en-Valois* (see Rte 26), are the ruins of the château of *Montépilloy* (12C), partly rebuilt c.1400, and dismantled at the end of the 16C.—3km N.E., at *Rully*, is a 12–13C church with a fine belfry.—Hence the D932A (from Senlis to Compiègne) may be gained by driving N. through **Raray**, with a 17C château built on the site of an earlier one, with a remarkable decorated **Courtyard*, which served as the location for Cocteau's film 'La Belle et le Bête' (1946); the church is 15–16C.

10km N. of Senlis, on the N17, lies **Pont-Ste-Maxence**, taking its name from a bridge over the Oise built here by *Perronet* in 1774–85, damaged in 1914; and rebuilt since its destruction in 1940. A good view may be obtained from the *Moulin de Calipet* (1694) to the S.E. The church of *Ste-Maxence* dates from the

15–16C. Of more interest is the ***Abbaye de Moncel**, E. of the town (off the D123), partly 14C, and with the exception of the church, almost entirely preserved.

Hence the D932A for Compiègne may be gained 10km to the E., passing *Pontpoint*, where the 12C church preserves its Romanesque belfry, and *Rhuis*, with an interesting 11C church.

Shortly after leaving Senlis by the D932A, we pass (r.) the 12–15C church of *Chamant*.—11·5km *Villeneuve-sur-Verberie*, with an 11-12C church, with a nave altered in 1510.—*Raray* (see above) lies 2km S.E.

5·5km **Verberie**, an ancient town once residence of Merovingian and Carolingian kings, has a 13–15C church.—*St-Vlaast-de-Longmont*, 1km S.E., has a 12C church preserving good Romanesque decoration and a square tower surmounted by a stone spire, also 12C.

A number of early churches may be seen in the *Vallée de L'Automne*, through which the D123 leads to Villers-Cotterêts; among them those at *Saintines, Béthisy-St-Pierre, Béthisy-St-Martin*, and (9·5km from Verberie) *Orrouy. Morienval* (see Rte 26) lies c. 5km further E.

2km N. of Orrouy, on the ancient track (the 'Chaussée Brunehaut') from Senlis to Soissons, lies **Champlieu**, an important centre for Gallo-Roman remains (2-3C). The ruins, on the supposed site of *Castra Stativa*, comprise a theatre, baths, and temple. Adjacent are remains of a little Romanesque church on earlier foundations, a cemetery, and early Christian catacombs.—Continuing N. from this point we shortly meet the D932A some 10km S.E. of Compiègne.

Beyond Verberie we skirt the W. side of the FORÊT DE COMPIÈGNE, and at 14km, after passing *Royallieu*, the sad site of a concentration camp for some 48,000 deportees during the years 1941–44, enter **COMPIÈGNE** (43,300 inhab.), the *Compendium* of Latin chronicles, so called from its position on the 'short cut' between Beauvais and Soissons, later a country seat of the Frankish kings, and the site of the Benedictine monastery of St-Corneille.

Joan of Arc, leading a sortie from Compiègne in 1430, was captured by the Burgundians, who sold her to the English. The Treaty of Compiègne (in 1624 between Richelieu and the Dutch), and other treaties, were signed in the château which was a favourite residence of royalty, perhaps because of the facilities for hunting in the adjacent forest. Many of the hunting-paths and avenues therein were cut by Louis XIV and Louis XV. Here Marie-Antoinette was received by Louis XVI in 1770, and Marie-Louise by Napoleon in 1809.

It was also frequently visited by Napoleon III in preference to his other palaces, and the fatuities of court junketings here reached their zenith. It was occupied by the Germans 1-12 Sept. 1914, and was bombarded by them in June 1918. On 11 Nov. the Armistice was signed 6km. N.E. of *Compiègne* (see below). A large section of the town was destroyed by German bombs in June 1940. Its chocolates are famous.

The **Palace of Compiègne**, extensive in area, designed by *Gabriel* under Louis XV and restored by Napoleon I, is an example of French neo-classic decadence, imposing in its mass-effect, but unattractive in its extreme bareness and sobriety. The façade facing the Pl. du Palais is only relieved by a graceful portico and columns of the main courtyard; the façade giving upon the terrace and park is 104m in length. The interior contains a number of handsomely decorated apartments, many retaining the Empire furniture installed here by Napoleon.

The entrance lies to the r. of the courtyard, whence groups are escorted round the building.

On ascending the *Escalier d'Honneur* to the *Salle des Gardes*, impressive in size and decorated with trophies in grisaille by *Crosnier*, we enter the *Salon du Roi de Rome*, with furniture by *Jacob-Desmalter*, and chairs covered with Beauvais tapestries of the fables of La Fontaine after designs by *Oudry*. Note also the Gobelins tapestry after *Coypel*. To the r. is the *Queen's Salon des Jeux*, with silk hangings made at Lyon after original patterns, and two commodes by *Stockel*. Retracing our steps, we pass through the *Salle à manger*, with tromp-l'oeil dessus de porte by *Sauvage*, and furniture by *Jacob-Desmalter* .—The adjoining *Salon des Cartes* contains three huge wall-maps, two by *Pierre-Denis Martin* (1738–39) of Compiègne and the forest. The chairs are covered with Beauvais tapestries after cartoons by *Casanova*.—Note the chairs made by *Jeanselme* in 1859 in the Louis-XV style in the adjacent *Salon de Famille*, commanding a good view of the gardens and forest beyond.

The *Cabinet du Conseil*, next visited, contains an impressive silk hanging of the Crossing of the Rhine by *François Bonnemer* (1682–84) after *van der Meulen*. The woodwork in this room and the next has been restored after a fire in 1919.—The *Library* and its furniture were designed by *Jacob-Desmalter*. The emperor's bureau has been returned from Malmaison. Note the biscuit figures of Molière and Corneille by the mirror.—The adjacent *Music Room* is hung with two Beauvais tapestries (c. 1685) in the Chinese taste, and two from the Gobelins factory, after *Amédée Van Loo*, from the 1780s.

Passing through the *Chambre*, and *Boudoir*, of the empress, we enter the *Salon des Fleurs*, with panels painted by *Dubois* after Redouté.— Leaving the main wing, we are escorted through the *Empress's Dining-Room*, with mahogany furniture by *Jacob-Desmalter*, to Louis XV's *Gal. des Chasses*, with Gobelins tapestries of hunting scenes *after Oudry*.— Paintings of dogs by *Oudry* and *Desportes* are seen in the adjoining *Gal. des Cerfs*.

We now enter the heavily gilt *Gal. de Bal*, lit by fifteen chandeliers, and resplendent in its ugliness.—In the *Gal. Natoire* (r.) *Coypel's* 'Histoire de Don Quixotte' (at present under restoration) may be placed.—The *Vestibule to the Chapel* (l.) displays Gobelins tapestries *after Raphael*; the *Chapel* itself is particularly tasteless.— Hence we may pass through a series of rooms designated **Musée du Second Empire**, with contemporary furniture and decoration, including a Gobelins copy of *Winterhalter's* painting of the Empress Eugénie and Napoleon III, and descending stairs at the far end of the wing, make our exit.

Also accommodated in the palace is the **Musée National de la Voiture et du Tourisme** (opened here in 1927 under the auspices of the Touring-Club de France) with an interesting collection of coaches and carriages, Berlines, 'Désobligeantes', chaises, etc. Other sections are devoted to sledges, Velocipèdes, early bicycles, and cars, including examples by Amédée Bollée fils (1895), a Renault of 1900, a Panhard-Levassor phaeton of 1891, a de Dion limousine of 1907, etc.

The long S.E. façade lies on the perimeter of the old defensive walls of Compiègne, the best preserved section of which leads from the palace to the river. Another segment of the semicircle is hidden by abutting houses just S. of the Rue F.-Sarlovèze; the Rue Martel approximately marking the site of their position to the W.

From the N.W. corner of the PL. DU PALAIS, the Rue des Minimes (whose ancient church serves as a gymnasium) leads shortly to the PL. DE L'HÔTEL DE VILLE. The Flamboyant **Hôtel de Ville** (1499–1509; by Pierre Navier), which R.L. Stevenson condemned as 'a monument of Gothic insecurity', is decorated with late 19C statues; the tall belfry contains a bell cast in 1303 and a 16C clock, which every 15 minutes sets in motion three wooden figures known as 'Picantines'.

The building also accommodates sections of the *Musée Vivenel* (see below), and another devoted to the art of 'Figurines historiques', a collection of c. 100,000 items, the majority being tin soldiers. Among the various dioramas displayed is one of the Battle of Waterloo.

Off the Rue St-Corneille, and leading W. from the opposite side of the square, is (l.) the 14C *Cloister of St-Corneille* (damaged in 1940), sole relic of the ancient abbey. To the r., the Rue Jeanne d'Arc descends to the old *Hôtel-Dieu*, founded by St Louis, with a 13C façade, and preserving good woodwork.

To the W. is the cylindrical *Tour Beauregard* (or *Tour Jeanne d'Arc*; 12C), beyond which is the **Musée Vivenel**, housed in the *Hôtel de Songeons* (late 18C), built on the ruins of a church of the Jacobins, fragments of which are visible in the adjoining park.

The collections of Antoine Vivenel (1799–1868) form the basis of this museum, those of *'Greek Vases* taking second place only to those in the Louvre. Apart from Antiquities, representative examples of 12–13C ivories, Mennecy and Chantilly porcelain, etc., are displayed, besides paintings and drawings and collections of more local interest.

A short distance to the S.E. stands *St-Antoine*, a plain Gothic building (13–16C) with a florid portal, raised choir, and good gargoyles. The Rue St-Antoine is continued E. by the Rue des Lombard, No. 10 in which is a gabled house of the 16C. Beyond is the 13–15C church of *St-Jacques*, with its flying buttresses, and a lofty bell-tower with a Renaissance lantern. Continuing E., we shortly regain the *Pl. du Palais*.

To the W. of the château, the Rue d'Ulm leads to the *Porte Chapelle*, built in 1552 by *Philibert Delorme*.

Hence the N31 leads 28km W. to *Clermont*, see Rte 24.—*Noyon* lies 24km N.E. on the N32; *Amiens* 71km N.W. on the D935: see *Blue Guide France*.

A circuit of the **Forêt de Compiègne**, with an area of 14,450 hectares, may be made to include a visit to the '*Clairière de l'Armistice*', *Pierrefonds*, and *St-Jean-aux-Bois* (see IGN 403).

The former is approached by following the N31 driving E. from the *Porte Chapelle*, and is reached after 6km. German plenipotentiaries had presented themselves at the railway siding at *Rethondes*, 3km to the E., on 8 Nov., to sue for an armistice, which was signed at 5.00 on the morning of 11 Nov. 1918 in this forest clearing, and hostilities were ordered to cease on the whole front at 11.00.

Marshal Foch's railway-coach, in which the armistice was signed, was later preserved in a building erected for the purpose adjacent to the site. In June 1940 Hitler vindictively forced the French to sign an armistice in the same carriage. This was later destroyed by the Germans and replaced by an identical one, which may be entered on payment of a fee: thus is the memory of such occasions hallowed and turned to profit.

On regaining the N31, at a point just N. of *Les Beaux Monts* (views), we turn r. onto the D547, passing through *Vieux-Moulin*, and skirting the *Étangs de St-Pierre* (to the S. of which is *Mont St-Pierre* with a Roman camp), soon entering (c. 20km) *Pierrefonds*, a village on the S.E. border of the forest. Its restored 11–14C church has a crypt of 1060, and tower of 1552.

The huge and commanding bulk of the **Château de Pierrefonds** (CN) was long considered one of the outstanding examples of medieval military architecture; but a critical reaction to Viollet-le-Duc's criteria of restoration has since taken effect.

Built in 1392–1407 by Louis I d'Orléans, the ambitious brother of Charles VI, it passed to Charles d'Orléans, the poet. In 1422 it was occupied by the English; in 1617 it was dismantled, and remained in a state of picturesque ruin until the mid-19C. In 1813 Napoleon I had acquired the pile, which in 1857 was entrusted by Napoleon III to *Viollet-le-Duc*, whose scholarly excesses were regarded by some as his crowning achievement. Be that as it may, the powerfully constructed fortress impresses in spite of his questionable 'restorations'.

Constructed in the form of an irregular quadrilateral enclosing a central court, the castle is strengthened by massive towers at the angles and in the middle of each side, while two rampart walks, one above the other, are carried round the walls. To the l. of the entrance is the *Salle des Gardes*, with the *Salles des Preuses* above it; to the r. the *Keep*, and beyond, the Gothic *Chapel*, among other parts of the castle which may be visited.

Hence the D85 leads W. to *St-Jean-aux-Bois*, with à 13C church, and remains of a Benedictine abbey founded in 1152, shortly beyond which we bear N.W. to regain *Compiègne*.

26 Paris to Villers-Cotterêts and Soissons

Total distance, 104km (64 miles). A1 to 14km from the *Porte de la Chapelle*, then bearing r. to join the N2 to (20km) *Dammartin-en-Goële*—39km *Villers-Cotterêts*—25km *Soissons*.

The N2 bears N.E. not far S. of the *Aéroport Charles-de-Gaulle* at *Roissy*, just beyond which, 4km to the N.W., lies *Le Mesnil-Amelot*, preserving a 15–16C Gothic church, with a robust belfry and Flamboyant façade.

7km **Dammartin-en-Goële**, a hilltop town, was once defended by a castle, demolished in the 17C. Rebuilt *St-Jean* preserves a porch (1482) and other features of the original 13C building; *Notre-Dame*, dating from 1480, contains the *Tomb* of the founder, Antoine de Chabannes (d. 1488). It was the birthplace of the early 13C poet Jean Renart.

A DETOUR can be made hence to Ermenonville. The D13 leads N. viâ (2km) *Othis*, with a 16C church (Renaissance façade), shortly passing near *Eve* to the E., with a 12–16C church surmounted by a 14C spire.

9km **Ermenonville**, bounded to the N. and N.W. by the extensive FORÊT D'ERMENONVILLE, parts of it now spoilt by over-exploitation, is famous for its association with Jean-Jacques Rousseau (1712–78), who died in a pavilion (no longer existing) of the elegant 18C château of the Marquis de Girardin, and was buried on the *Île des Peupliers*, near the S. end of the lake in the *Parc d'Ermenonville* (entrance opposite the château). Rousseau's remains were removed from his tomb in 1794 and placed in the *Panthéon*, Paris. The sandy nature of the soil in the vicinity has earned it the soubriquet 'Desert'.

Some 2·5km N., to the r., stands the domain of **Chaalis**, once a famous and wealthy Cistercian abbey, founded in 1136, suppressed in 1785, and sold at the

Revolution. Tasso paid a visit here in 1570. In 1912 it was bequeathed by its last proprietor (Mme Jacquemart-André; see p2/15) to the Institut de France. Of the ruined 13C church, the only relic is the N. transept. To the E. is the Prior's chapel (late 13C; restored in the 19C).

Visitors are taken on a guided tour, but few individual items merit attention among the miscellaneous collections of medieval, Egyptian, and Italian furniture, and antiques. The first room entered contains a work ascribed to *van Orley*, and two by *Giotto*, but the majority of other paintings in the building are of doubtful attribution and little interest, with the exception perhaps of four battle-pieces by *J.-B. Martin* (in the billiard room) and, at the foot of the stairs, a portrait of Henrietta of England; and a view of the Tour de Nesle, Paris. Other rooms contain a watercolour of Rousseau's tomb by *S.-F. Meyer*, and a portrait of the Duc de Bourgogne, by *Nattier*.

4km E. of Ermenonville lies *Montagny-Ste-Félicité*, its church remarkable for its slender belfry. *Baron*, 5km N. of Montagny, has a 12–13C church with a 15C spire, and woodwork by the brothers *Slodtz*.—We may regain the N2 at *Nanteuil-le-Haudouin*, 6km E. of Montagny.

14km N.E. of Dammartin lies *Nanteuil-le-Haudouin*, its church retaining a fortified portal, whence another DETOUR may be made to **Crépy-en-Valois** (12,300 inhab.) 12km N.E. by the D136.

The old quarter of the town, to the N.W., was in medieval times the capital of Valois, an appanage of a branch of the royal family. Parts of the old *Walls* survive on the valley side. Crépy suffered severely during the Hundred Years War; in 1431 it was sacked by the English; in 1814 it withstood a Prussian attack; it was also occupied briefly by the Germans in 1914, and damaged by them in 1940.

Towards the centre, approaching from the S., is the *Porte de Paris* (18C). *St-Thomas*, to the E., begun in 1180 and dedicated to Thomas Becket, retains only a 13C façade, and a tower with a 15C spire. To the N. in the old town stands *St-Denis*, with a Romanesque nave, and graceful 15C choir (and 19C steeple). Opposite survives the undercroft of the abbey of *St-Arnould*. The scanty remains of the old *Château*, in which are preserved a chapel and an imposingly timbered Grande Salle, now contain an *Archery museum*. Note also the *Hôtel de la Rose* (1537) in the Pl. Gambetta.

9km N.E. of Crépy, on the N335, lies **Morienval**, its *Church*, with three Romanesque towers, preserving fine Gothic vaulting of the early 12C.—*Pierrefonds* (see Rte 25) lies 9km further N.

From Morienval we may turn E. up the valley viâ *Vez* (see below) to (15km) *Villers-Cotterêts*. Alternatively we may regain the N2 some 7km E. of Crépy.

10km *Lévignen*.—*Betz*, 5km S.E., has a church with a Romanesque portal.

7km **Vez** (pronounced Vé), 3km N., is dominated by a 13–14C *Château* (restored by Viollet-le-Duc), with a pentagonal keep. Its chapel contains various antiquities, some from *Champlieu*. The church is of the 12–13C, with a nave covered by 16C timbers.—2km S.W. lie the imposing ruins of the 12C abbey of **Lieu-Restauré**, restored in 1540 (and again since 1964), with a Flamboyant *Rose-window* on one façade.—At *Largny-sur-Automne*, between Vez and Villers-Cotterêts, is a 12C church.

1km. Both *Vauciennes* (r.) and adjacent *Coyolles* retain 13C churches, the former unaltered.

At 7km, bypassed to the N., lies **Villers-Cotterêts** (8400 inhab.), almost surrounded by the extensive FORÊT DE RETZ (see IGN 405). The town suffered severely in June 1918, but on 18 July it saw the opening action of the great Allied offensive under Gén. Mangin (when 20,000 German prisoners and 400 guns were captured) which lasted until the Armistice.

Alexandre Dumas (*père*; 1802–70) is its most famous native, who was born at

The church of Morienval

No.50 in the street which bears his name, and is buried in the cemetery here. A small Museum devoted to the family is in the Rue Demoustiers. Dumas commended the local *andouillettes*.

The *Château* was built in 1522–45 by *Philibert Delorme* and *Jacques* and *Guillaume Le Breton* for François I, to replace an earlier castle razed by the English in 1429. The park was laid out by *Le Nôtre*. Although the building is now used as an old people's home, parts of the interior may be visited.

Some 5km due S., off the D936 to *La Ferté-Milon* (see Rte ·27), stand the picturesque relics, now farm buildings, of the manor of *Bourgfontaine* (14–17Cs).

A DETOUR may be made by following the D80 E. to (9km) *Corcy*, there turning N. to *Longpont, with the impressive ruins of a Cistercian abbey founded in 1131, parts of which have been converted into a château. The church (13C), of which some walls and buttresses remain, was as large as the cathedral at

Soissons.—By turning W. along the D2, we regain the N2 after 4·5km.

At *Montgobert*, 3km on the N. side of the main road at this junction, is the château of Pauline Bonaparte and the tomb of her first husband, Gén. Leclerc (1772–1802).

25km **SOISSONS** (32,200 inhab.), although one of the oldest towns in France, has few relics of its past remaining. Its oval-shaped cheese 'de clovis' should be sampled; also its pralines.

Soissons is believed to have been the *Noviodunum* of Caesar, known later as *Augusta Suessionum* or *Suessiona*, the second capital of Gallia Belgica. Here the Roman governor Syagrius was defeated by Clovis in 486, and in 511 Soissons became the capital of the kingdom of Neustria. Pepin le Bref was proclaimed king in the abbey of St-Médard in 752. Charles le Simpie was defeated outside its walls in 923, and the town was captured in 948 by Hugues le Grand. Its medieval history is one list of sieges, frequent during the Hundred Years War.

In 1814 and 1815 the fortress failed to prevent the passage of the Aisne by the Allies. In 1870 it fell after three days' bombardment. It was twice entered by the Germans in the 1914–18 War, and, on their final retirement in Aug. 1918, their gunners revenged themselves on its smoking ruins, when only 500 of its former 15,000 inhabitants remained. It was spared such barbarities in the Second World War.

The two most important monuments remaining are the ruins of *St-Jean-des-Vignes and the cathedral. The former, part of an abbey founded in 1076, in which Becket once resided, was suppressed at the Revolution, and dismantled in 1804, with the exception of the *Façade*, which bears a striking resemblance to Reims cathedral. The imposing towers, completed in 1506, and differing from each other in style, scarcely harmonize with the rest of the façade. The large 13C cloister and cellar, and 14C refectory, among other buildings, may be visited.

Some distance to the N. stands the **Cathedral**, very considerably restored, but retaining important sections of the original 12C Romanesque and 13C Gothic edifice. The N. side was mutilated, and the nave shattered, leaving the W. façade standing detached, and except for damage to the 14C tower, comparatively intact. The choir, completed in 1212, and the transepts, escaped serious injury in 1918.

The *S. Transept* is the oldest (1177) and most beautiful part of the building, with an apsidal ending, and above its graceful arcades are two triforium galleries beneath the loftily placed clerestory. The N. Transept has a straight façade of the 14C, and on its E. side, a portal of the same date, with pointed and decorated gables. Its 13C stained-glass in the apse and an Adoration *after Rubens* had been removed to safety before the bombardment.

To the N. of the apse, the *Pl. du Cloître* (note No.10) leads to the Rue du Collège, where, to the l., is a fine 17–18C gateway to the college.

To the E. of the cathedral is the central PL. F.-MARQUIGNY, on the far side of which are the 12C façade and two bays of the secularized church of *St-Pierre-au-Parvis*. Not far S. the Rue des Feuillants (l. off the main Rue St-Martin) leads to the *Pavillon des Arquebusiers* (1626) with an Ionic entrance-gate of 1638.

The Rue du Commerce leads N. from the main square to the rebuilt 18C *Hôtel de Ville*, on the site of the earlier castle of the Counts of Soissons. Just beyond is the church of *St-Léger*, relic of an abbey founded in 1152, retaining 13C transepts and choir, and an 11C crypt approached from the 13C cloister, and now housing a provincial *Museum*.

Some distance to the E., on the far bank of the Aisne, are the remains of the Abbey of **St-Médard**, with a 13C chapter-house and 9C *Crypt*, containing the tombs of Clotaire (d. 561) and Sigebert (d.575), son and grandson respectively, of Clovis.

From *Soissons* the N31 leads E. to (57km) *Reims*; the N2 leads N.E. to (30km) *Laon*; and the D1 N. viâ *Coucy-le-Château* to (61km) *St-Quentin*: see *Blue Guide France*.

The N31 leads due W. to (38km) *Compiègne*, see Rte 25.

27 Paris to Meaux and Château-Thierry

Total distance, 91km (56 miles). N3 to (45km) **Meaux**, (20km) *La Ferté-sous-Jouarre*, and (26km) *Château-Thierry*.

From the *Porte de Bagnollet* we may follow the A5 for 7km, before turning r. onto the N3; or alternatively follow the N3 direct from the *Porte de Pantin*, running parallel to the Canal de l'Ourcq, to the N. of which is *Bobigny*, the new préfecture of Seine-St-Denis. *Meaux* may also be approached by forking N. off the A4 autoroute.

At 19km (r.) stood the FORÊT DE BONDY, once the haunt of highwaymen; the remaining areas of forest to the E. and.S.E. of Paris may be seen on IGN 413.—At 12km the D404 leads N. to (7km) *Nantouillet*, with the interesting remains of a 16C château built by Card. Duprat, chancellor under François I, and a 13C church with a fine Renaissance portal.—7km beyond lies *Dammartin-en-Goële*, see Rte 26.

Just N.E. of Nantouillet is the *Collège de Juilly*, founded by the Oratorians in 1638, which numbers among its eminent pupils Marshal Villars, Montesquieu, the Duke of Berwick, D'Artagnan, Adm. Dupetit-Thouars, and Berryer.

At 9km (r.) we pass a Monument to Gén. Gallieni (1849–1916), military governor of Paris in 1914.

Some 4km to the N. is a Memorial to some of the first victims of that war, among them the Catholic poet Charles Péguy (1873–1914).

6km **MEAUX** (45,900 *Meldois*), whose main attraction is now the old quarter near the cathedral, was originally a stronghold of the Meldi, a Gallic tribe, commanding the abrupt river bend. Meaux was later the capital of the Haute-Brie.

During the revolt of the Jacquerie (1358) nine thousand peasants were massacred here and the town was sacked. It was twice besieged by the English in the 15C. Although its bridges were blown up by the retreating British army on 3 Sept. 1914, von Kluck's patrols entered Meaux two days later only to retire the same afternoon in the face of Gén. Manoury's advancing forces.

One of four types of Brie cheese comes from Meaux. Other varieties are those of Melun, Montereau, and Nangis. This form of cheese is recorded as early as 1217. Its andouillettes, and a confection known as 'croquettes d'or', have a local reputation. Meaux has long been famous for its mustard, which is now in fact made at Lagny-sur-Marne.

An early bishop of Meaux was the poet and musical theorist Philippe de Vitry (1291–1361); Jacques-Bénigne Bossuet (1627–1704), whom La Bruyère called 'last of the Fathers of the Church', famous for his sermons and funeral orations, was bishop from 1681.

The ***Cathedral of St-Étienne** is a beautiful but weather-worn structure of the 12–16C built over an earlier sanctuary. The Flamboyant W. front, although it lacks a S. tower (merely a slated stump), is imposing. The statues of its triple portal have been destroyed, but it retains some bas-reliefs in the tympana over the doors and some quaint gargoyles. The N. portal (13C) has a 12C statue of St Stephen and bas-reliefs illustrating his life. The S. portal (also 13C) resembles the S. portal of Notre-Dame, Paris. The *Porte Maugarni*, in the choir, dates from the 15C.

In spite of the short nave, the interior is elegant and airy. Bossuet is buried in the *Choir*, although his Monument (by *Dubois*, 1907) is in the N. nave aisle. Some panels of his pulpit have been incorporated into a reconstructed version. The organ (1627) rests on a 15C arcade.

To the N. of the cathedral is the **Bishop's Palace**, comprising various buildings of the 15–17C, and a 12C chapel. It now contains a *Museum*, which although largely devoted to Bossuet, contains paintings by *Largillière, Bouchardon, Millet*, and *Courbet*, etc. In the *Garden* is the Pavilion known as the '*Cabinet de Bossuet*', where many of his sermons and polemical works were composed.

To the E. of the palace is the **Old Chapter-House** (restored), a valuable example of 13C domestic architecture, with a covered exterior staircase (15C woodwork). Passing through an archway and turning l., we shortly reach a tree-lined boulevard, flanked by a section of the defensive *Town Wall* (with the episcopal gardens above), incorporating Roman work.

Ronsard lived during 1552–54 at *Mareuil-lès-Meaux*, 5km S.W.

FROM MEAUX TO VILLERS-COTTERÉTS (41km). The D405 shortly passes (r.) an American Monument—one of many in the area— to the Soldiers of the Marne, beyond which (7km) *Vareddes* experienced a sanguinary battle (6–10 Sept. 1914) centred on *Côte 139*, a good viewpoint to the W.—*Germigny-l'Evêque*, 2km S.E., retains slight remains of Bossuet's country retreat.—5km. *Lizy-sur-Ourcq*, 3km to the r., has a 15C church conserving some old glass, and a 17C market; *Ocquerre*, on the far bank of the river, preserves a Renaissance building with monumental chimneys.—4km. *May-en-Multien* has a curious church, partly 12C.—Hence a lane descends to (5km) *Crouy-sur-Ourcq*, with a ruined 14C château with an imposing keep, and a church retaining a Romanesque tower and Renaissance porch.—At *Acy-en-Multien* (7km N.W. of May) is another 12C church altered in the 15–16C, with a 19C spire; also a 13C *Hôtel-Dieu* and 15C manor.—14km. *Marolles* has a church with a good 12C belfry and curious Romanesque portal.

2km. **La Ferté-Milon** was the birthplace of Jean Racine (1639–99). The two churches retain good stained-glass (15–16C), while above the once-fortified town are the impressive ruins of the Castle (1382–1407), with a regular keep, to which the name Ferté (fermeté) refers. Note the monumental portal.—For *Villers-Cotterêts*, 9km N., in the centre of the FORÊT DE RETZ, see Rte 26.

At 8km E. of Meaux, a turning (r.) leads 2km to the imposing ruins of the château of *Montceaux* (1547–60), built by *Philibert Delorme* for Catherine de Médicis, and altered by Henri IV for Gabrielle d'Estrées; it was dismantled in 1798.

5km. The A4 autoroute for *Château-Thierry* and *Reims* may be joined here.

7km **La Ferté-sous-Jouarre** (7000 inhab.) derives its name from a 10C fortress, later held by the Bourbons, on a now vanished island.

Louis XVI and Marie-Antoinette, after the arrest of their flight at Varennes in June 1791, were brought here on their way back to Paris. The millstones in the vicinity are of repute. A pontoon bridge thrown across the river here by the British on 9 Sept. 1914 to replace the bridge destroyed by von Kluck, allowed the advance to be made which diverted the Germans from Paris.

Of more interest is **Jouarre**, 3km S., with the 13C tower remaining of its once-famous Benedictine abbey, and preserving (behind its 15C church) the important remains of a *Merovingian *Crypt* (634), with porphyry and jasper columns, surmounted by white marble capitals, and the *Sarcophagi* of sundry saints (one hypothetically an Irish princess). Note also the decoration of the walls, etc. For adm., enquire at the abbey, 9 Rue Montmorin.

FROM LA FERTÉ TO MONTMIRAIL (33km E. on the main road). Also reached by making the pleasant detour up the valley of the Petit Morin, S.E. of La Ferté, by the D204 and D31 (viâ *St-Ouen-sur-Morin*, with a 17C château by *de Brosse*) to (17·5km) *Sablonnières* (on the British front during the Battle of the Marne), with a church of the 12th and 16C, regaining the D407 at *Viels-Maisons* (11km N.E.), 21km E. of La Ferté.—6km S.W. of Sablonnières lies *Rebais*, see Rte 28.

15·5km *Montmirail*, the birthplace of Card. de Retz (1614–79), with a 14–16C church, and château commenced in 1553 by *Jean de Lilly* and finished by *Louvois*. On 11 Feb. 1814 Montmirail was the scene of Napoleon's victory over the combined forces of Russia and Prussia.—*Sézanne*, see Rte 28, lies 24km S.E. and *Épernay* lies 40km N.E.; see *Blue Guide France*.

Although the direct road (N3) between *La Ferté* and *Château-Thierry* (26km N.E.) is the most rapid, it is of little interest. To the r. of the road (3km) *Chamigny* has a partly 13C church, as does (6km) *Montreuil-aux-Lions*.

At 14km the D1390 leads 7km N.W. to BOIS BELLEAU, with a large American military cemetery (1918); to the r. at this junction a lane leads 1·5km S. to *Côte 204*, with another American Monument (commanding a good view of *Château-Thierry*, see below).

The ALTERNATIVE road (D402) leads N.E. from La Ferté, crossing the Marne, and threads its way through a number of riverside villages. At 17km the church of *Nogent-l'Artaud* (on the S. bank) has a 12C choir and nave, altered in the 16C.—*Chézy-sur-Marne* (4.5km N.E.) has a 15C church with a fine tower, and to the N.W. the ruins of a Benedictine abbey founded in the 9C.—Regaining the N. bank, we pass (6km N.) *Essômes*, with a 13–14C church (restored), before entering *Château-Thierry*.

Château-Thierry (14,900 inhab.), with the old town sheltering below the castle-crowned hill, and guarding the river-crossing, was the birthplace of Jean de la Fontaine (1621–95).

Said to be named from a castle built by Charles Martel for the Frankish king Thierry IV (d.737), Château-Thierry was later held by the counts of Champagne. It was captured in turn by the English (in 1421), by Charles V (1544), and by the Leaguers in 1591; pillaged in 1652 during the War of the Fronde; and bombarded in 1814, when Napoleon defeated the Russians and Prussians in the neighbourhood. It was held briefly by the Germans in 1914, and was re-entered by them on 31 May 1918; and until their withdrawal on 21 July, was the centre of bitter fighting both in containment and counter-attack. The town also suffered by bombardment in the invasion of 1940.

From the bridge, the Rue Gén.-de-Gaulle leads N., passing (r.) a 16C belfry, to the central PLACE, with the *Hôtel de Ville* ahead. Steps to the W. of the latter ascend to a footpath, which, followed to the r., leads to the *Porte St-Jean*, the entrance to the castle enceinte (views). Beyond is the *Porte St-Pierre*, a gateway in the town walls. This may also be approached by the Rue du Château, climbing N.E. from the S. side of the Place, passing a hospital (r.) preserving a late-17C chapel, and (at No.32), the old *Hôtel de Marnay d'Hangest*.

By turning l. at the top of the steps behind the Hôtel de Ville, we shortly reach the Rue de la Fontaine, where at No.12, dating from 1559, is the birthplace of the fabulist, the most eminent of the Casteltheódoriciens, and now a Museum. Lower down the hill, by turning r. across the Av. de Soissons, we reach *St-Crépin* (15–16C, restored), with a heavy square tower.

Montmirail (see above) lies 24km S.E., *Épernay* lies 48km E. on the N3 and *Reims*, 62km. N.E., may be reached by following the N3 and RD380, or alternatively the A4 autoroute, joined c.5km N.; see *Blue Guide France*.

FROM CHÂTEAU-THIERRY TO SOISSONS, VIÂ OULCHY-LE-CHÂTEAU (41km on the D1). At 14km *Coincy* (3km E.) is an interesting 12–15C church (restored) with a 12C crypt; at *Brécy*, 2km S., is another church of the 11–14C.—3km. *Armentières-sur-Ourcq*, to the E., retains picturesque ruins of a 14C castle.—4km. *Oulchy-le-Château*, one of many villages in the vicinity damaged in the fighting of July 1918, retains a Romanesque church within the enceinte of a castle of the counts of Champagne. There is a small British Cemetery behind the church.—Beyond, to the E., rises the *Butte de Chalmont*, with a Monument by *Landowski* to the Second Battle of the Marne.—2km N.W. of the N37 lies *Oulchy-la-Ville*, and *Rozet-St-Albin* (further S.W.), both with 12C churches.

12km At *Buzancy* (r.) is a Monument inscribed 'Ici fleurira toujours le glorieux Chardon d'Écosse parmi les Roses de France' after the Scots entry into the victorious attack of 22 July 1918.—2·5km *Berzy-le-Sec* and *Courmelles* to the l. of the road, contain interesting 12C churches, the latter with a remarkable aspe.—2.5km to the E. lies *Septmonts*, with a partly restored 14–15C castle of the former bishops of Soissons.—5·5km *Soissons*, see Rte 26.

FROM CHÂTEAU-THIERRY TO SOISSONS, VIÂ FÈRE-EN-TARDENOIS (48km on the D967 and D6). The D967 climbs N.E. from Château-Thierry at 17km passing near *Villeneuve-sur-Fère* (2km N.W.), birthplace of the Catholic poet Paul Claudel (1868–1955), and at 5km entering *Fère-en-Tardenois*, British G.H.Q. during the First Battle of the Aisne (Sept.-Oct. 1914), and the scene of fierce fighting in May-Aug. 1918. The 15–16C church has interesting painted woodwork and other carving. The robustly pillared market-hall (of 1552) has been re-roofed.—3km N.E. lie the ruins of the 13C *Castle of Fère*, approached by a Renaissance galleried viaduct of five arches, 20m high, built by *Jean Bullant*.—Continuing N. on the D6, we soon bear N.W. to (24km) *Soissons*, see Rte 26.

28   Paris to Sézanne

A. Viâ Champs and Coulommiers

Total distance, 111km (69 miles). N34 (21·5km **Champs**)—39·5km *Coulommiers*.—50km *Sézanne*.

The A4 autoroute, driving E. from the *Porte de Bercy*, towards *Reims* now facilitates the exit from Paris in this direction, and joins the N34 S. of *Couilly*, before bearing N.E. between *Meaux* and *La Ferté-sous-Jouarre*: see Rte 27.

The forest areas to the S.E. of Paris are covered in IGN 413.

From the *Porte de Vincennes*, after passing (r.) the *Château de Vincennes* (see Rte 20), we traverse the N.E. corner of the *Bois*.

Beyond the park, the N34 climbs N.E. through the suburb of **Nogent-sur-Marne**.

The sole surviving market pavilion from the *Halles* (see Rte 11), by *Victor Baltard*, of 1856, has been restored and re-erected on an esplanade overlooking the river, and converted into a theatre and exhibition hall.

The *Château de Bauté*, in which Charles V died in 1380, was given by Charles VII to his mistress Agnès Sorel, and was afterwards occupied by Diane de Poitiers; it was demolished in 1622 by Louis XIII. Watteau died at Nogent in 1721. Louis Daguerre (1787–1851), who gave his name to the daguerreotype, died at *Bry-sur-Marne*, further to the E., where Étienne de Silhouette (1709–67), controller-general of finances in 1759, is said to have decorated the walls of his château with outline portraits.

At 18·5km the D104 turns r. through *Gournay-sur-Marne*, to the E. of which (after 3km) is the *****Château de Champs** (CN) , built in 1703–07 by *J.-B. Bullet* on the site of an earlier edifice. It was later the residence of the Princesse de Conti (daughter of Louis XIV and Louise de la Vallière), and in 1757 of Mme de Pompadour. Pillaged during the Revolution, it was restored in the 1890s and since 1934 has been used occasionally by visiting heads of state.

From the entrance vestibule we ascend to the FIRST FLOOR and turn into the *Music Room*, with a frieze of instruments and dessus de portes by *Monnoyer*, and commanding an impressive view of the *****Gardens**, laid out by *Claude Desgots*, a nephew of Le Nôtre. To the l., the *Guest Room*, with dessus de portes by *Boucher*; to the r., *Mme de Pompadour's Bedroom*, with good painted woodwork, and dessus de portes by *Carle Van Loo*. The following room contains a portrait of Mme de Pompadour as 'La belle jardinière' by *Drouais*; the scenes of sheep and goats are by *Desportes*.

We descend to the GROUND FLOOR and to the *Grand Salon*, with a Coromandel screen, and furniture covered with Aubusson tapestry. To the l. is the *Dining Room*, with pink marble fountains and serving tables. *Desportes* and *Oudry* were responsible for the dessus de portes: A large canvas depicts a hunting-scene at Champs, by *J.-B. Martin* (?). To the r. is the sober *Smoking-Room*, with good panelling, 18C Beauvais tapestries, a *Boulle* bookcase, and a portrait of Louis XV by *Van Loo*, given by the king to Mme de Pompadour. We next enter the *****Salon Chinois**, decorated c. 1740 by *Christophe Huet*. Note the fine chandelier, Tabriz carpet, furniture covered with Beauvais tapestry depicting La Fontaine's fables, and console table in onyx. The next room displays *Mignard's* portrait of Louis XIV in his minority. The penultimate room which may be visited is the *Blue Boudoir*, also attractively decorated by *Huet*.

Hence we continue E. on the D217bis—skirting the new town of *Marne-la-Vallée*—at 7·5km passing (r.) the 17C château (with a long wing added by *Robert de Cotte*) of *Guermantes*, a name made familiar by Proust, but the building is in no way connected with the novel. Just beyond, we reach a road junction, 2km N. of which lies *Lagny*: see below.

Some 3·5km S., beyond the A4 autoroute, stands the château of *Ferrières*, rebuilt in the Renaissance style for the Rothschild family by *Joseph Paxton* in 1857.

Some 5km S.E. of Guermantes lies *Jossigny*, with an inexcusably dilapidated château of 1743, 6·5km further S.E. of which, at *Villeneuve-le-Comte*, a planned village of 1203, is a fine 13C church. The village stands on the edge of the FORÊT DE CRÉCY, where in Sept. 1914 the British army rested after its retreat from Mons, and before advancing on the Marne.

At (2km) *Chelles*, just N. of Champs, stood a Merovingian palace in the 6C, where Chilperic I was murdered at the instigation of his wife Fredegonde. Nothing remains of the famous abbey founded here in 660. The *Alfred-Bonno Museum* contains local prehistoric and medieval collections.

Passing (r.) the château of *Pomponne* (1682; restored in the 19C), we enter (8·5km) **Lagny** (18,300 inhab.), the ancient *Latiniacum*. *St-Pierre* (or *N.-D. des Ardents*), the choir of an unfinished abbey-church of the 13–14C, contains several fine tombs. Of the abbey (founded in 643 by a Scottish monk, St Furcy, or Fursa, and destroyed by the Normans), only a large 17C building remains, now used as the Hôtel de Ville. Other objects of interest are a 13C fountain, a 14C archway, and the ruined 15C church of *St-Furcy.*— The Romanesque church of *St-Thibault-des-Vignes* (12C), 3km S.W., retains historiated capitals.

3km (r.) *Montévrain* has a 12–13C church, with curious capitals.— 4·5km. Louis Braille (1809–52) was born at *Coupvray*, to the l. To the N. and E. of this point took place the Battle of the Ourcq (Sept. 1914). We cross the Grand-Morin at (5·5km) *Couilly*, with a Romanesque tower to its church.—*Meaux* (see Rte 27) lies 10km to the N.

Just to the S.E. of Couilly is *Pont-aux-Dames*, named after the Bernardine nunnery to which Mme du Barry retired after the death of Louis XV; it was destroyed at the Revolution.

5km **Crécy-la Chapelle**, retaining a number of mills, and remains of ancient fortifications.—*La Chapelle-sur-Crécy* (2km E.) has a fine 13–14C *Church*, with a beautiful triforium, and a series of curious masks in the choir. The road climbs up above the valley, descending again to (14km) *Coulommiers*, long famous for its cheeses.

Coulommiers (12,250 *Columériens*), the birthplace of the painter Jean de Boullogne (1591–1634), and a busy but dull market town, was the ancient *Columbariae*. The château built by *De Brosse* for the Duchesse de Longueville in the 17C, and described in Mme de la Fayette's 'La Princesse de Clèves', was demolished (with the exception of two pavilions of 1631 by *François Mansart*) by the Duc de Chevreuse in 1737. Adjacent to the moated site is the church of the Capuchins (17C) with a small museum. Of more interest, situated on the hill to the N.E. of the town, is the chapel (13C; with contemporary murals) and buildings (15–16C) of a *Commandery of the Templars*, now part of the Hospital farm.

Mauperthuïs (6km S.W.) is described in Gautier's 'Mademoiselle de Maupin'.
Rebais (12km N.E. on the D222) retains a 12C Romanesque church, part of an abbey founded c.615 by St Ouen, with a good 13C tomb.
Jouarre (see Rte 27) lies 14km N. of Coulommiers.

The N34 ascends the plateau at (4·5km) *Chailly-en-Brie*, and continues due E. to (14·5km) *La Ferté-Gaucher*. This is also approached by the more picturesque road (D66) following the river valley, viâ (18km) *Jouy-sur-Morin*, with a 13–16C church.—*La Ferté-Gaucher* also has a church of the same period.

19km *Esternay*, just beyond which (l.) lies its 16–17C château.— 13km **Sézanne** (6200 inhab.), lying amidst vineyards, retains a 15–16Ç church with a Renaissance S. portal and upper windows, and a good stone reredos. Its andouillettes are worth tasting.

To the N. and N.E. of the chalk plateau of Sézanne is a 'pocket' of clay forming the *Marshes of St-Gond*, in the neighbourhood of which was the scene of Foch's victory over von Bülow in the Battle of the Marne (9 Sept. 1914).

St-Dizier lies 92km further E. on the N4, off which after 17km the D5 leads 38km N.E. to *Châlons-sur-Marne*, see *Blue Guide France.*

B. Viâ Rozay-en-Brie

This faster but duller road (N4) drives E. from the *Porte de Picpus*, passing at (13·5km) *Champigny* a 13–14C church of some interest. At 3·5km it also passes near (r.) the château of *Ormesson* (see Rte 29).—The road bypasses (17·5km) *Tournan-en-Brie*, with a restored 13C church and 15C town gate used as the Hôtel de Ville.

3km to the r. lies the château *des Boulayes* (1785).—At 6·5km we bypass *Fontenay-Trésigny*, with a church typical of the region.

4km N., at *La Houssaye*, is the château where Marshal Augereau received Napoleon in 1807, and died in 1816; his tomb is in the 13–14C church.

7km (r.) **Rozay-en-Brie,** an attractive village with traces of fortifications, and a 13C church restored in the 16C, with a 12C belfry.—2km S. stands the Château of *La Grange-Bléneau* (16–17C), which belonged to La Fayette from 1799 until his death in 1834, and retains his library. He received Pitt here in 1802.

From the crossroads at 11km, the D231 leads 21km S.E. to *Provins* (see Rte 29), passing, at 2·5km, *Jouy-le-Châtel*, with remains of a 13C keep and other fortifications, a restored château, and a 12C church with 15–16C alterations.

12km *Béton-Bazoches* retains a 12C church, as does (15km) *Montceaux-lès-Provins*, the latter with 17C additions.—9km. *Esternay*, and (13km) *Sézanne*, see Rte 28A.

29 Paris to Provins

Total distance, 84km (52 miles). N19 to (29·5km) *Brie-Comte-Robert.* —34km *Nangis.*—20·5km **Provins.**

The forest areas to the S.E. of Paris are covered on IGN 413.

From the *Porte Picpus* we follow the N19 S.E. through *Créteil*, préfecture of the department of *Val-de-Marne.*

12km Here the N186 leads l. past the church of *St-Christophe* (13C, with a remarkable tower-porch of the 12C), and across the Marne to *St-Maur des-Fossés*, once famous for its Benedictine abbey, where the entrails of Henry V were buried. The magnificent château, a disfigured entrance of which may be seen at No.36 Rue du Four, bought by Catherine de Médicis in 1563; visited by Budé, Ronsard, Rabelais, Desportes, etc.; and where Mme de La Fayette wrote her 'Princesse de Clèves', was destroyed during the Revolution.

At 3km the D60 (continued by the D185) leads 5·5km E. (and S. of the *Porte de Bonneuil*) to the château of **Ormesson* (16–17C; for authorisation to visit, apply to the owner), built by *Androuet du Cerceau*, passing to the S. *Sucy-en-Brie*, with the lamentably deteriorated château of *Sucy*, built by *Lambert de Thorigny* in 1640; also that of *Montaleau* (now the Mairie), where Mme de Sévigné, when a girl, frequently visited her uncle.

6·5km to the l. stands the château of **Gros-Bois*, built by the Duc d'Angoulême at the beginning of the 17C, and sumptuously furnished during the First Empire by Marshal Berthier.

The churches at adjacent *Villecresnes* (with a Romanesque tower and 12C nave), at *Marolles-en-Brie* (2km E.), and at (5km) *Servon* (13C), retain features of interest.

3km **Brie-Comte-Robert** (10,550 inhab.), founded by Robert, Comte de Dreux in the 10C, is situated on the rich Plateau de la Brie, long famous for its cheese. The ruins of the castle (c.1170), opposite No.35 Rue du Gén.-Leclerc, and six 13C arches, the remains of the chapel of the old Hospital (1207) in the Rue des Halles, are of interest as is the exterior of *St-Étienne*; 13C but altered in the 15–16C, it contains 15C wood-carving, 16C glass and a fine 13C rose-window in the apse.

5km *Suisnes*, 1km E., retains a relic of a château once owned by Adm. de Bougainville, who initiated, with his gardener Cochet, the rose-culture of the region.—2km. *Coubert*, with a château built in the 18C by Samuel Bernard, the financier, just N. of which is that of *La Grange-du-Roy* (late 16C) partly demolished.—*Soignolles* (1·5km S.) has interesting stalls with misericords (1530–40) in its church.

4·5km *Ozouer-Courquetaine*, 1km E., has a late 16C church with a copper font-cover by *Robbe* (1731), and picturesque remains of a château.—6km beyond, at *Chaumes-en-Brie*, the 13–14C church contains a Christ by *Ph. de Champaigne*. The father and grandfather of Couperin 'le Grand' were organists here.—The ruined château of *Le Vivier*, 3km N., was once the rendezvous of royal hunts; and here the mad Charles VI was incarcerated, further distracted by Odette de Champdivers.

11·5km *Mormant*, 5km N. of which, at *Courtomer*, is a 13C church.—Beyond Mormant, we pass the extensive petrol refineries of Grandpuits, and at 11km enter *Nangis*, an old town with a 13–15C church with elegant flying buttresses, and remains of a 14–16C castle now partly occupied by the Hôtel de Ville, in which Arthur Young stayed briefly, in June/July 1789.

4·5km The *Church at **Rampillon**, 1 km S., with a remarkable sculptured portal, and flanked by a tower attributed to the Templars, whose quarters here were burnt by the English in 1432, is of considerable interest; of equal importance is ***St-Loup-de-Naud**, 4km S.E. at 11·5km., one of the earliest in the Île de France. Partly of the 11C, its sculptured portal is among the best-preserved examples of 12C work, but the interior of the church deserves a restoring hand.

4·5km **PROVINS** (12,700 *Provinois*), one of the most attractive towns within easy reach of Paris, is finely situated at the junction of the Voulzie and Durteint.

Once the capital of the Brie, with an important fair, and with a large and prosperous population, it was ruined by plague (1373), the English wars, and the Wars of Religion. Among its natives were the trouvères Guyot de Provins (12C) and Thibaut IV, Comte de Champagne (1201–53).

Provins has long been celebrated for its crimson roses (wrongly called Provence roses), which are said to have been originally brought by the Crusaders from the Holy Land. They were introduced into the coat-of-arms of Edmund of Lancaster (1245–96) when he married the widow of Henri le Gros, Comte de Champagne.

Provins consists of an upper and lower town, the former still partially surrounded by well-preserved ***Ramparts**, seen to advantage on approaching the town from the W. It is advisable to turn l. off the N19 and follow the tree-lined lane parallel to the walls, passing first the

Detail of the portal of St-Loup-de-Naud

Porte St-Jean, and the so-called 'Brèche des Anglais' (through which the English forced their way into the town in 1432), entering the Old Town by the *Porte de Jouy*. A short distance W. of the central PL. DU CHÂTEL is the *Grange-aux-Dîmes* (13C), the tithe-barn of the canons of St-Quiriace, consisting of two vaulted storeys resting on piers, in the pointed style. It now contains a small 'Musée lapidaire.'

To the S.E. rises the impressive ***Tour de Cèsar** or *Grosse Tour*, a massive early 12C keep on a motte now surrounded by a rampart ('Pâté-aux-Anglais'), added by Thomas Guerard, an Englishman, during their occupation of Provins. The tower is curiously constructed, and worth visiting.

Further downhill stands the conspicuous church of ***St-Quiriace**,

The Tour de Cèsar, and cupola of St-Quiriace, Provins

begun in 1160, and remarkable for its plain massive architecture. The large choir is early 12C; the unfinished nave, with a fine triforium, is 13C. The cupola over the crossing replacing a belfry destroyed by fire, dates from 1665. The crypt may be just seen. St Quiriace was a converted Jew (of whom there were once many in Provins), who assisted the Empress Helena in her search for the True Cross.

In the Rue du Palais, just to the N. stands a Romanesque house, partly 10C, in which an archaeological museum has been installed.

The Upper Town also commands a good view N. towards the **Hôpital Général** on the far side of the valley, beyond the umbrageous BLVD D'ALIGRE, built on the site of a monastery of the Cordeliers founded by Thibaut IV in 1237. Two sides of a beautiful 14–15C *Cloister and a chapter-house, survive; the heart of Thibaut V is enshrined in the wooden barrel-vaulted *Chapel*, containing some furniture of interest.

The Rue St-Thibault descends into the Lower Town, passing (r.) the *Hôtel-Dieu*, with a 13C portal. Further along this street (Rue des Capucines) are the *Hôtel de Vauluisant* and *Hôtel de la Croix d'Or*, both dating from the 13C.

To the N. of the PL. DU GÉN.-LECLERC stands *Ste-Croix*, with a nave and aisles of the 13C, and a choir of the 16C. Further E. is *St-Ayoul* (11–16C), with a 12C portal, and a reredos and other wood-carvings by *P. Blasset* (1612–63), buried in the church. Abelard sought refuge in the priory of which this church was a dependency, in 1122, the year before he founded the *Abbaye du Paraclet* (c. 25km. S.E., beyond *Nogent-sur-Seine*).

A few paces N. of St-Ayoul stands the *Tour Notre-Dame-du-Val* (1544), surviving from an earlier cloistered church. Some defensive walls may be seen along the BLVD CARNOT, and its extensions, skirting the river to the S. and E.

The church at *Voulton* (12–13C), 7km N.E., on the D71, is of interest for the elegant octopartite vaulting of its choir.

From PROVINS TO SENS, see Rte 30. *Troyes* lies 65km S.E. on the N19; see *Blue Guide France*.

30 Paris to Melun and Sens

Total distance, 112km (69 miles). N6 to (46km) *Melun.*— 30km *Montereau.*—36km **Sens**.

The forest areas to the S.E. of Paris are covered on IGN 413.

From the *Porte de Picpus*, we shortly bear S. through an industrial area to (18km) *Villeneuve-St-Georges*.

At adjacent *Crosne* (S.E.) was Boileau's country house, 'Les Préaux', from which he took his name. Further along the valley to the E., at *Yerres*, in the Pl. du Taillis near the church, is the entrance to a manor owned by Guillaume Budé.—*Brunoy*, 2km S., with its church curiously decorated in 1772, gave its name to a marquisate conferred on Wellington after Waterloo by Louis XVIII.—The picturesque *Moulin de Jarcy* lies some 4km S.E. We may regain the N5 from either Brunoy or Jarcy.

At 3km we enter the FORÊT DE SÉNART, once sacred to Druids, beyond which the New Town of *Melun-Sénart* is under construction. 25km **Melun** (36,200 *Melunais*), one of the capitals of the Brie, and now préfecture of Seine-et-Marne, is of Gallo-Roman foundation (*Melodunum*). The oldest part of the town lies on an island in the Seine, connected to either bank by bridges rebuilt since blown up during the heavy fighting here in 1944. Abélard founded a school of philosophy at Melun in 1101, when he was only twenty-two. Jacques Amyot (1513–93), the humanist, was born here. Its eel-pies are a local delicacy.

St-Aspais (15–16C), on the N. bank, was also damaged. *Notre-Dame*, on the island, was founded by King Robert, who died at Melun in 1031. It was much altered in the 15C.

6km N.E., off the D215, stands the château of ***Vaux-le-Vicomte**, built by *Le Vau* in 1656–61 for Nicolas Fouquet (1615–80), Louis XIV's superintendent of finance.

Molière's 'Les Fâcheux' was performed here on the occasion of the extravagant fête given on 17 Aug. 1661 in honour of the young king, which also caused Fouquet's downfall. La Fontaine described this splendid entertainment, and after Fouquet's arrest (only nineteen days later), wrote his 'Élégié aux nymphes de Vaux'. The tapestries were woven for the château in a manufactory specially set up locally, which was then transferred to the Gobelins at Paris. The building, which survived the Revolution, was bought in 1875 by an industrialist, Alfred Sommier (d.1908; whose family still live there), and thoroughly restored, as were the formal *Gardens*, one of *Le Notre's* first commissions.

The sumptuously furnished rooms on the Ground Floor, including the impressive domed *Grand Salon* contain *Rigaud's* portraits of the Duc

The South front of Vaux-le-Vicomte

de Villars (the second owner), the Duc de Villeroy, and the Duchesse d'Orléans, *Le Brun's* portrait of Fouquet, etc. The *Stables* are of less interest.

At *Champeaux*, 7km further E., birthplace of the scholastic philosopher Guillaume de Champeaux (d.1121), is a large 12–14C church (*St-Martin*), with quaint stalls and misericords by *Richard Falaise* (1522), 14C monuments, and good glass by *Nicolas Masson* and *Alain Courjon*.—At *Blandy* (3km S.W.) is a ruined castle of the 12–14C (views). The 17C château of *Bombon*, 4km E. of Champeaux, was Foch's H.Q. during the 2nd battle of the Marne.

3km S.W. of *Melun* (by the N372), in the park of the château, are the ruins of a Cistercian nunnery, the *Abbaye du Lys*, built in 1244 by Blanche of Castille.
    5·5 km S.E. of *Melun*, at *Chartrettes*, is a château built by Henri IV for Gabrielle d'Estrées.

The N6 drives S. from Melun through the forest, by-passing the resort of *Bois-le-Roi*, to (18km) *Fontainebleau*, see Rte 31.
    The N105 leads S.E. from Melun to (30km) **Montereau-faut-Yonne** (19,600 inhab.), at the confluence of the Yonne and Seine. It derives its name (*Monasteriolum*) from a monastery founded in the 6C. In the church hangs the sword of Jean sans Peur, Duke of Burgundy, assassinated on the bridge here in 1419 by partisans of the Dauphin, afterwards Charles VII. A statue of Napoleon (between the restored 18C bridges) commemorates his defeat of the Germans here in Feb. 1814.

Some 15km N.E., off the D18 to Provins, lie the impressive ruins of the Cistercian abbey of *Preuilly*, founded in 1118 by Stephen Harding, Abbot of Cîteaux (a native of Sherborne in Dorset).—3km beyond, at *Donnemarie*, are remains of ancient fortifications and a 12–13C *Church, the figures in its portal decapitated at the Revolution, and with two galleries of a 16C cloister.

3km S. of Montereau, we turn l. onto the N6, which ascends the valley of the Yonne past (21km) *Pont-sur-Yonne*, with an interesting 12–15C church.—The château of *Fleurigny* (13km E. on the D25), of c. 1526, retains a window by *Jean Cousin* in its chapel, and a fine carved chimneypiece in the Salle des Gardes.

12km **SENS** (27,500 *Sénonais*; pronounced *Sánss*), lying for the most part on the E. bank of the river, and on the borders of Burgundy, was described by Thicknesse as 'a large ragged ancient city, but adorned with a most noble cathedral well worthy of the notice of strangers'. It has been praised for its gastronomy, particularly its andouillettes.

Known in antiquity as *Agedincum* or *Agendincum*, Sens was the chief town of the Senones, a powerful Gallic tribe to which Brennus, who (according to tradition) captured Rome in 390 B.C., belonged. Christianized in the 3C, it became the seat of a widely-spread archbishopric, to which even Paris was suffragan until 1627. In 1140, the council at which St Bernard secured the condemnation of the doctrines of Abélard met here; in 1234 Louis IX was married to Margaret of Provence in the cathedral. During the Wars of Religion, its citizens were enthusiastic supporters of the League.

Thomas Becket spent part of his exile (from 1166) in the Abbaye de Ste-Colombe (see below); the architect William of Sens was born here, as was the poet Rutebeuf (d. 1285); Du Perron (1556–1618), the religious controversialist, was Abp of Sens. Marivaux lived some years in the town; as did Mallarmé in 1857–60.

We pass, to the r. on approaching Sens on the N5, the *Abbaye de Ste-Colombe*, founded in the 6C, rebuilt in the 13C, and restored since its destruction in 1793.

The old centre is surrounded by a pleasant oval of wide tree-lined boulevards, some sections of which are abutted by medieval walls, of which an isolated tower and a postern of 1260 survive.

From the PL. J.-JAURÈS (in the centre of the N. perimeter) this oval is bisected by the Rue de la République, in turn bisected at right-angles by the narrow Grande-Rue, leading W. to the river, and the church of *St-Maurice* (12–16C). To the N.E. of this intersection stands the earliest Gothic cathedral in France, coeval with the choir of Suger's basilica at St-Denis.

The *Cathedral of St-Étienne** was begun c. 1130 by Abp Sanglier and after alterations in the 13–14C, was completed in 1490–1520. Several of its features were reproduced at Canterbury by William of Sens, to whom the rebuilding of the E. end of the English cathedral was entrusted in 1175.

The W. FRONT, with three richly-sculptured portals, was ruthlessly mutilated in 1793; only the figure of St Stephen on the main pillar of the central portal escaped, being protected from the general destruction by the words 'La Loi' engraved on the book in his hand. The sculptures here are of the 12C, except the tympanum (Legend of St Stephen), which is 14C. The statues above the windows over the door are modern.

The N. PORTAL has two 12C reliefs, and the legend of St John the Baptist in the tympanum; the S. portal (14C) contains statuettes of prophets, and is devoted to the Death, Assumption, and Coronation of the Virgin.

The S. TOWER (73m) or 'Tour de Pierre' is mainly 14C (completed

1535); the N. Tower is known as the 'Tour de Plomb' from its former lead covering, destroyed in 1845. The richly-decorated transeptal portals, by *Martin Cambiges*, date from 1490–1513.

INTERIOR. The *Stained-glass* throughout the cathedral is worthy of note. The nave is supported by piers alternating with coupled columns. The altarpiece on the l. side dates from a tomb of 1515. The four marble columns of the 18C high-altar once formed part of the original monument of Louis XIV in the Pl. des Victoires, Paris.

The transepts contain early 16C glass. On the N. side of the Ambulatory are the oldest * *Windows*. In the *Chap. Ste-Colombe* (1st on l. of Choir) is the tomb of Dauphin Louis (1729–65), father of Louis XVI, by *G. Coustou*. Here are also reliefs from the destroyed tomb of Card. Duprat, Abp of Sens (1525–35), and the fine kneeling statues of two other archbishops (1636). In the *Chap. de St-Thomas-de-Cantorbéry* is a 12C statue; the saint's vestments and mitre may be seen in the *Treasury*, containing a 10C carved ivory coffer, among other objects.

Immediately to the S. of the cathedral is the *Palais Synodal* (13C), restored in 1860 by Viollet-le-Duc, impressed by its six fine windows. The Provincial Estates of Central France were assembled here by Charles V in 1367.

Further E., beyond a vaulted passage with a Renaissance doorway, stands the *Archbishops' Palace* (1510–65). The old *Seminary* nearby contains good 18C wood-carvings.

Opposite the cathedral, to the N. of the decrepit Market-Place, is the *Hôtel de la Pointe*, erected by the Card. de Bourbon in 1567.

To the S. of the cathedral, at the corner of the Rue de la République and Rue Jean-Cousin, is the *Maison d'Abraham*, with quaintly carved beams (but in urgent need of repair) and the *Maison du Pillier*. At No.8 (16C) in the latter street is the *Musée Jean-Cousin*, devoted to the artist (1501–89), born at *Soucy*, 7km N.E. of Sens.

Beyond is restored *St-Pierre-le-Rond* (13–16C); while in the adjacent *Hôtel Vésou* is the local *Museum* and *Library*, containing Gallo-Roman sculpture, etc., and early MSS.

To the E. of the main boulevard, in the grounds of a hospital, is *St-Jean* (13–17C), with a fine 13C apsidal chapel, a rare type of Burgundian Gothic.—Further E. is the ill-restored church of *St-Savinien* or *St-Pierre-le-Vief*, with an 11–13C belfry, and crypt of 1001.

Provins (Rte 29), 47km N., is reached by turning r. off the N6 12km N. at *Pont-sur-Yonne*, thence taking the D976 and D412.

The D81, continued by the D225, leads W. to (46km) *Nemours*: see Rte 31.

Troyes lies 65km E. on the N60; *Auxerre*, 51km S.E. on the N6; and *Montargis*, 51km S.W. on the N60; see *Blue Guide France*.

31 Paris to Fontainebleau, Nemours, and Château-Landon

Total distance, 94km (58 miles). A6 for 49km; N7 to (15km) **Fontainebleau**; N7 to (15km) *Nemours*.—15km *Château-Landon*.

The forest area is covered by IGN 401.

Although Fontainebleau may also be approached viâ *Melun* (see Rte 30), the most direct (and recommended) road is the A6 autoroute, leaving Paris by the *Porte de Gentilly* or *Porte d'Italie*. Just after leaving the Blvd Périphérique we pass a new hospital, replacing the *Hospice de Bicêtre*, a famous lunatic asylum founded by Richelieu in 1634 on the site of a 13C castle built by John, Bp of Winchester (whose name Bicêtre is thought to be a corruption).

At 11km the l.-hand fork leads past *Rungis-Halles*, the main market complex of Paris, built to replace the congested Halles Centrales (see Rte 11).—5km **Orly Airport**. The old village of *Orly*, N.E. of the airport, clusters round its church.

Shortly beyond this intersection the A10 (for *Orléans*), off which diverges the A11 (for *Chartres*; see Rte 33C), bears S.W.

The A6 bypasses (13km, l.) the New Town of *Évry* (29,600 inhab.), préfecture of the department of Essonne, and at 3km (l.) *Corbeil-Essonnes* (38,100 inhab.). Near the church of *St-Spire* (close to the Seine at *Corbeil*), with a 12C nave and earlier transept (the Romanesque part of the choir has been detached from its 15C addition), is the 14C gatehouse of a former abbey.

At 17km we bear S.E. off the A6 which continues across country towards *Nemours, Auxerre*, etc.; see pp 304-5 and *Blue Guide France*.

2km The N373 leads S.W. to (9·5km) *Milly-la-Forêt*, passing (5·5km) **Courances**, with a château in the Louis-XIII style, and gardens designed by *Le Nôtre*. It was briefly Gen. Montgomery's residence after the Liberation. The *Moulin de Grena* (1370) may be seen at adjacent *Moigny*. **Milly-la-Forêt**, on the W. outskirts of the FORÊT DE FONTAINEBLEAU has an 11–12C church, a ruined 12C castle, and market-hall of 1479. The 12C *Chapelle-St-Blaise* was restored and decorated by *Jean Cocteau* (1889–1963), who died at Milly, and is buried there. The *Botanical Garden* of medicinal plants is of interest. *Fontainebleau* lies 17km due E. For this forest area see IGN 401.

At 1km (r.) *Fleury-en-Bière*, is an imposing **Château* built by *Pierre Lescot* and enlarged by Richelieu, containing fine woodwork, furniture, and paintings (by *Natoire, Oudry*, and *Rigaud*, etc.).

5km Millet and Th. Rousseau are both buried at *Chailly-en-Bière*, 1km N.; Bazille, Monet, Renoir, Sisley, and Seurat also painted there.—1km S. at this junction lies the village of **Barbizon** (the terrines de gibier of which should be sampled), which is now more sophisticated than it was in its early days, when it gave its name to the Barbizon School of painters, who made it their headquarters, among them Millet, Corot, Th. Rousseau, Diaz de la Peña, and Daubigny (as described in the Goncourts' novel 'Manette Salomon', 1867).

On meeting the N7, we enter the FORÊT DE FONTAINEBLEAU and at 9km reach the *Carrefour de la Libération*, on the perimeter of the town itself.

Perhaps a more interesting, if longer, approach, is the *Route Ronde*, a turning r. 3km prior to reaching the Carrefour, from which we circle through the picturesque forest to (11·5km) the *Croix de St-Hérem*, on the N7, there turning l. to reach the CARREFOUR DE L'OBELISQUE from which the BLVD MAGENTA leads N.E. to the Palace: see also p304.

FONTAINEBLEAU (18,800 *Bellifontains*), from *Fons Blandi* or *Fontaine de Bland*, with its palace, and finely situated in the middle of its forest—or as Evelyn put it: 'encompassed with hideous rocks'—is one of the pleasan*t*est resorts in the neighbourhood of Paris.

The railway station (regular service from the *Gare de Lyon*) is c.2km N.E. of the palace; bus service between the two. S.I., 38 Rue Grande (for information regarding autocar circuits of the forest, etc.).

Fontainebleau is first mentioned as a royal hunting-seat in 1137, and was later fortified. In 1169 Thomas Becket, then in exile, consecrated the chapel of *St-Saturnin*. In 1259 St Louis founded, nearby, a monastery for the Trinitarians, who had a hospital here. Philippe IV was born at Fontainebleau, and died here; but its real creator was François I, who after 1527 here assembled a group of Italian artists, including Serlio, Rosso, Primaticcio, Vignola, and Nicolo dell'Abate.

The keeper of the Library was the poet Mellin de Saint-Gelais (1487–1558). The humanist Pierre Duchatel (1480–1552) was likewise employed there. The MSS of the cataloguer Ange Vergèce (d.1569) were imitated in type by his contemporary, the famous type-founder Claude Garamond, and cut in 1541 for Robert Estienne's Greek classics. François found the palace almost derelict, for Charles VII and his successors had deserted it for the Loire. His grandsons François II and Henri III were also born here. Henri IV spent vast sums on the building, where in 1601 his son Louis XIII was born. Queen Christina of Sweden retired here in 1657. In 1685 Louis XIV signed the revocation of the Edict of Nantes at Fontainebleau; and Louis XV received many distinguished visitors here, including (during his minority) Peter the Great (1717), and in 1768, Christian VII of Denmark.

Napoleon spent 12 million francs on the restoration of the palace, where in 1804 he received Pope Pius VII, who in 1811 was kept prisoner here, before renouncing temporal power the following year. Here in April 1814 Napoleon signed the act of abdication, and said farewell to his Old Guard; and on his return from Elba, he reviewed his grenadiers here before leading them to the Tuileries. The palace was again restored by Louis-Philippe, at enormous cost, but in his usual questionable taste. From 1941 it was the headquarters of Gen. von Brauchitsch, until liberated by Gen. Patton in Aug. 1944, and for some years after was the military H.Q. of the Allied powers in Europe. Dancourt (1661–1725), author of 'Chevalier à la mode', was born, and died, in Fontainebleau.

From the *Carrefour de la Libération*, the BLVD A. MAGINOT and the Rue Royale approach the PL. DU GÉN.-DE-GAULLE opposite the W. façade of the palace. Facing it is the *Hôtel du Card. de Ferrare*, its doorway the only authentic work of *Serlio* surviving. Relics of other old mansions remain in the BLVD MAGENTA, to the S., and in the Rue Royale, where at No.15, is a small museum of military costume.

Young, who visited the place in Sept. 1787, remarked that the landlord of the inn there 'thinks that royal palaces should not be seen for nothing; he made me pay 10 livres for a dinner which would have cost me not more than half the money at the Star and Garter at Richmond'.

The ****PALACE** is composed of many distinct buildings erected over the years, and for the most part two-storeyed. Because some of the stone used was unsuitable for sculpture, the exterior is comparatively plain when compared with the sumptuous interior decoration.

The main courtyards and gardens are open all day. Some apartments may be closed for restoration.

The COUR DU CHEVAL-BLANC (152m by 112m), which we first enter, is named after a vanished cast of the horse of an equestrian statue of Marcus Aurelius in Rome; it is also known as the *Cour des Adieux*, after Napoleon's farewell to his Guards (see above).

In front of the central pavilion is the *Escalier du Fer-à-Cheval*, a horseshoe-shaped staircase by *Jean du Cerceau* (1634) ascending to

The Escalier du Fer-à-Cheval, Fontainebleau

the FIRST FLOOR. To the l. of the *Vestibule d'Honneur* (**Pl.33**), with six massive oak doors, two of them original (Louis XIII period), is the gallery (**Pl.2**) of the *Chapelle de la Sainte-Trinité*, built by *Philibert Delorme* for Henri II and decorated during the reign of Henri IV. The chapel was the scene of the marriage of Louis XV and Marie Leczinska in 1725 and of the baptism of Napoleon III. In the centre of the ceiling are five religious paintings by *Fréminet* (1608–14), while the woodwork and elaborate reredos (by *Bordoni*) are of the time of Louis XIII.

To the r. of the entrance vestibule are the **Apartments of the Queen-Mothers** and of *Pius VII* (**Pl.34–43**), at present only visited in guided groups. They were occupied by Catherine de Médicis, Anne of Austria, and Marie-Thérèse, and by the Pope as both guest and prisoner. From the *Antechamber*, we enter the *Salon des Officiers* (**Pl.35**), with a splendid marquetry commode by *Riesener*, and the adjacent *Grand Salon de Réception*, with a ceiling designed by *Philibert Delorme*, and over the doors, portraits of Charles IX and Catherine de Médicis. The *Queen-Mothers' Bedroom* (**Pl.37**) has a fine old Gobelins tapestry (*after Raphael*) and a **Ceiling* decorated with paintings by *Cotelle de Meaux*; above the doors are portraits of Anne of Austria and Marie-Thérèse, by *Desève*; the furniture is upholstered in Beauvais tapestry, with subjects taken from La Fontaine's fables. The clock, with ten dials, was made for Napoleon.—The adjoining *Pope's Study* contains a replica of *David's* portrait of Pius VII, and the pope's calotte.

In the *Cabinet de Toilette* **(Pl.39)** are tapestry portraits of Henri IV and Louis XIII. The *Pope's Bedroom* contains a Louis-XVI bedstead, and another fine commode, by *Beneman*, and two cabinets de nuit. Note the furniture by *Jacob*, combining Joséphine's rose and Napoleon's bees. The Pope used to say mass during his captivity in the *Salon d'Angle*.—In a room beyond **(Pl.43)** are displayed two Venetian scenes, and a painting of Napoleon's meeting with the Pope, by *J.-L. Demarne*. The *Salle d'Attente* has an 18C 'Chinese' lacquered commode.

The *Gal. Des Fastes* (under restoration), which we next enter, has superb carved foliage (Louis-XV period) and three fine tapestries of the Victories of Louis XIV (*after Le Brun*). The *Gal. des Assiettes* is decorated with Sèvres plates (1837) painted with views of French royal palaces, etc. On the ceiling are frescoes by *Ambroise Dubois*.

Opposite the main entrance is the ***Galerie François 1er**, 64m long, built in 1528–44 in the Renaissance style; the initial and salamander device of the king are conspicuous. The paintings and stucco reliefs by *Rosso* were completed after his death by *Primaticcio*. The frescoes represent allegorical and mythological scenes, with references to the life of François I. It is one of the few extant rooms of the original palace of François, and here the Italian influence is seen at its strongest.

At the far end we turn r. into the *Salon des Aides-de-Camp* (or *Salle du Buffet*), containing two fine ebony cabinets of the Louis-XIII period, and three paintings removed from the Salon Louis-XIII (see below), and other works by *Dubois*.

The adjacent *Salle des Gardes* (r.), completed in 1564 by Charles IX, was redecorated in 1834. The ceiling and frieze, however, date from François I and Henri II. The magnificent marquetry floor reproduces the design of the ceiling. The chimneypiece, with figures of Strength and Peace, by *Jacquet*, was made up under Louis-Philippe, of sections of the great chimneypiece of Henri IV removed from the next room (not visited), when it was turned into a theatre by Louis XV.

The *Escalier du Roi* was built by *Gabriel* in 1749, the upper part having been the **Bedchamber* of the Duchesse d'Étampes in François I's time. The sculptures are ascribed to *Primaticcio*: the nude figures ('the nymphs of Fontainebleau') were veiled at the request of Marie Leczinska! The frescoes, in which François I is depicted as Alexander the Great in eight episodes from the life of the Macedonian hero, were painted by *Nicolo dell' Abate* from Primaticcio's designs, and restored by Pujol. The stucco figures are of the period of Jean Goujon.—Passing through a vestibule containing a statue of Mercury by *Francavilla*, we traverse a narrow corridor.

The ***Salle de Bal** or *Galerie Henri-II*, 30m long, the most splendid room in the palace, was built by François I and decorated under Henri II, *Philibert Delorme* being the designer. The windows command the best view of the *Cour Ovale*. The elaborate ceiling is of walnut, and the design of the parquet floor (made under Louis-

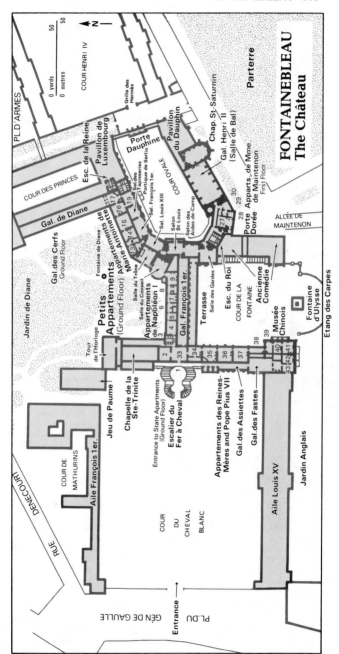

FONTAINEBLEAU
The Château

0 yards 50
0 metres 50

—N—

COUR HENRI IV

PL. D'ARMES

Grille des Hermès

COUR DES PRINCES

Esc. de la Reine

Pavillon de Luxembourg

Porte Dauphine

Salle des Tapisseries

Portique de Serlio

Gal. de Diane

Gal. des Cerfs
(Ground Floor)

Fontaine de Diane
(Ground Floor)

Petits Appartements
(Ground Floor)

Appartements de Marie-Antoinette

13 14 15 16 17 18 19

Sal. François 1er.

Sal. Louis XIII

Sal. St-Louis

Salon des Aides-de-Camp

Pavillon du Dauphin

Chap. St-Saturnin

Gal. Henri II (Salle de Bal)

Apparts. de Mme de Maintenon
First Floor

COUR OVALE

Parterre

ALLÉE DE MAINTENON

30

29

28

27

Porte Dorée

Ancienne Comédie

COUR DE LA FONTAINE

Esc. du Roi

Salle des Gardes

Terrasse

Salle du Trône

Salle du Conseil

Appartements de Napoléon I

5 6 8

7 P 9

10 11 12

4

3

Gal. François 1er.

Tour de l'Horloge

Jardin de Diane

Jeu de Paume

Chapelle de la Ste-Trinité

Entrance to State Apartments (Ground Floor)

Escalier du Fer à Cheval

Appartements des Reines-Mères and Pope Pius VII

Gal. des Assiettes

Gal. des Fastes

Aile Louis XV

Jardin Anglais

Musée Chinois

Fontaine d'Ulysse

Etang des Carpes

38

39

40

41

42

43

37

36

35

34

33

2

1

Aile François 1er.

COUR DE MATHURINS

RUE DENECOURT

COUR DU CHEVAL BLANC

PL. DU GÉN. DE GAULLE

Entrance

Philippe) corresponds with it. Everywhere are seen the interlaced monograms of Henri II and Diane de Poitiers and the emblems of Diana (bows and arrows, and crescents). The mythological paintings were designed by *Primaticcio*, executed by *Nicolo dell' Abate* (1552), and restored under Henri IV, and again in 1834. The satyrs flanking the fireplace are copies of the originals melted down at the Revolution.

Returning, we visit the *Apartments of Mme de Maintenon*, with *Boulle* furniture, and a fine clock. It is said that the Revocation of the Edict of Nantes (1685) was signed in her salon. Originally the royal suite of François I, they were converted by Louis XIV into salles de réception.

Passing through the Salle des Gardes, we enter the first of the *Appartements Royaux*, overlooking the Cour Ovale. The *Salon de St-Louis*, in the original keep of the castle, was the king's bedchamber until the 17C; it was redecorated by Louis-Philippe with paintings of episodes in the life of Henri IV. On the chimneypiece is an equestrian statue of the king by *Jacquet* (1599) from the 'great chimneypiece' (see above).

The *Salon Louis-XIII, known also as the *Grand Cabinet du Roi* or *Chambre Ovale*, one of the most interesting rooms in the palace, was decorated by *Paul Bril* under Henri IV, and restored in 1837. Marie de Médicis gave birth to Louis XIII here in 1601. *Ambroise Dubois* painted thirteen pictures (the Loves of Theagenes and Chariclea) for this room, but three were removed (see above) during the reign of Louis XV, when the doors were widened to admit the voluminous dresses of the period. The little Venetian mirror was one of the first to be seen in France.

The *Salon François-Ier*, adjoining, a dining-room under Napoleon, has an original chimneypiece with a medallion of Venus and Adonis by *Primaticcio*, and several Gobelins tapestries depicting hunting scenes.—The *Salon des Tapisseries*, once the anteroom of the queen, contains 17C Gobelins tapestries of the Story of Constantine. Three Gobelins tapestries of the Seasons are displayed in the adjoining Antechamber.

We now reach the vestibule of the *Gal. de Diane* (**Pl.17**), over 80m long, built by Henri IV and remodelled under the Restoration, and with ceiling-paintings of that period. Since 1859 it has served as a Library, and includes several early printed books (15–16C; no adm.).

The *Appartements de la Reine* (or *de Marie-Antoinette*, who chose the decorations) were built between 1545 and 1565. The first two rooms contain Louis-XIV woodwork, and Louis-XVI furniture by *Stockel* and *Beneman*. The *Music Room* (**Pl.15**) was Marie-Antoinette's card-room. The bust of the queen, in Sèvres biscuit-ware, is by *Pajou*. Note also the grisaille dessus de porte, and table of Sèvres ware (1806). The *Bedroom* (**Pl.14**), with its fine ceiling, was occupied successively by Marie de Médicis, Marie-Thérèse, Marie Leczinska, Marie-Antoinette, Joséphine, Marie-Louise, Marie-Amélie, and the Empress Eugénie, and is sometimes known as the 'Chamber of the six Maries'. The silk hangings of the bed, and on the walls, were given to Marie-Antoinette by the city of Lyon.—The adjoining *Boudoir*, beautifully proportioned, has a ceiling-painting of Aurora by *Barthélemy*, and stucco dessus de portes by *Beauvais*.

The *Salle du Trône* was first used as a throne-room by Napoleon; it served previously as the king's bedroom. The magnificent ceiling dates from the time of Louis XIII. The fine portrait of Louis XIII is after an original by *Philippe de Champaigne*, which was burned in 1793. The lustre-candelabrum is of rock-crystal; the carpet is from the Savonnerie. The woodwork is of the period of Louis XIV.—A small adjacent cabinet was the 'Brûle-Tout', where state papers were burned after council-meetings.

The magnificent ***Salle du Conseil** (so used by Charles IX) is decorated by *Boucher*, *C. Van Loo*, and *J.-B. Pierre*, c.1753; the bay, with a ceiling by *Lagrenée*, was added in 1773.

The *Apartments of Napoleon I*, in a wing built by Louis XVI abutting the Galerie François-Premier, are furnished partly in the Empire style, and contain a number of Napoleonic relics. In the *Bedroom* (**Pl.9**), with Louis-XVI decoration, is the emperor's bed; in the adjacent *Study*, his camp-bed, and a desk by *Jacob-Desmalter*.—The *Cabinet de l'Abdication* or *Salon Rouge* (**Pl.7**) contains the little table on which Napoleon signed his abdication in 1814 (although probably not in this room), and a facsimile of the document.—In the *Antichambre des Huissiers* (**Pl.4**), with the emperor's hat, worn on the return from Elba, and relics, the painting of the Duchesse de Bourgogne is a copy of the original, by *Godert*.

On the GROUND FLOOR are the **Petits Appartements de Napoléon et de Joséphine**, preserving their Louis-XV and Louis-XVI decoration, and Empire furniture and Napoleonic relics. Beyond, below the Galerie de Diane, is the *Gal. des Cerfs* (so called because of the stag-heads which form part of the decoration), where Christina of Sweden had Monaldeschi, her favourite, murdered (1657).

Also opened on request are the **Chinese Museum** (entered from the Cour de la Fontaine), displaying in three rooms, once part of the suite of the 'grand maréchal', a small collection of oriental art. The *Appartements des Chasses* (entered from the Escalier de la Reine), to the S. and S.E. of which are the *Desportes*, and others, illustrating the hunting achievements of Louis XV, are still under rearrangement.

The Conservateur, on receiving written application, may authorize a visit to the *Chapelle St-Saturnin*, in the S.E. wing, rebuilt for François I, the *Theatre*, and the *Musée de l'Histoire du Château* (on the Second Floor).

EXTERIOR. A pleasant walk may be taken round the outside of the château, starting at the N.E. corner of the *Cour du Cheval-Blanc*, passing the *Jeu de Paume* (Tennis Court; r.), and entering the *Jardin de Diane*, with a bronze fountain-figure of Diana (1684). Passing (r.) the *Galerie des Cerfs*, we bear round the N. wing, following the line of the old moat, to reach the *Grille des Hermès* (l.) adorned with heads of Hermes (Mercury) by *Gilles Guérin* (1640) facing the *Cour Henri-IV* (1609), the main entrance of which faces the *Pl. d'Armes*; and r., the *Porte du Dauphin*, by *Primaticcio*, one of the entrances to the *Cour Ovale*.

Beyond the *Pavillon du Dauphin*, we reach the *Parterre*, a formal garden with ornamental ponds, laid out by Henri IV and again by *Le Vau* for Louis XIV. To the r. is the apse of the *Chapelle St-Saturnin* (poorly restored), beyond which a passage admits to the *Cour de la Fontaine*, to the S. and S.E. of which are the *Étang des Carpes* and the *Jardin Anglais*, laid out for Napoleon. Somewhere in these gardens Thomas Coryate, passing through Fontainebleau in May 1608, was amazed to see ostriches running wild.

The *Park* (84 hectares) extends to the E. of the Parterre. On the S. side, beyond the canal dug by order of Henri IV, are the buildings of the former School of Artillery, now barracks.

Beyond the walls lies the suburb of **Avon** (15,300 inhab.), with a 13–16C *Church* entered below a curiously gabled porch. It contains the tombs of Monaldeschi, the painter Ambroise Dubois, and the naturalist Daubenton. In the cemetery lies Katherine Mansfield (1888–1923), who died at the _Prieuré des Basses-Loges_, while under the malign influence of Gurdjieff, the mystic. Avon had a thriving pottery in the early 17C. There are notable vineyards at _Thomery_, further to the E.

At _Valvins_, 1·5km N.E. of Fontainebleau station, lived Mallarmé (1842–98) from 1884 until his death; he is buried in the cemetery.

The ***Forest of Fontainebleau**, is approx. 17,000 hectares in extent, and although traversed by a number of good roads, is best explored on foot. The forest area is covered in detail on IGN 401. Its thick glades and picturesque groups of ancient oaks, which with beech, hornbeam, birch, and Scots pine, are the commonest trees; its sandy clearings, and wildernesses of rocks, make it a pleasant centre for excursions. The legend of the 'Grand Veneur' tells how Henri IV, shortly before his assassination, hearing the sound of a rapidly approaching hunt, was suddenly confronted by a Black Huntsman of huge and hideous appearance, who on uttering a warning cry, as abruptly vanished.

The best general view of the forest is commanded by the _Tour Denecourt_ (4·5km N.E. of the palace), erected in 1851 by C.-F. Denecourt (1788–1875), nicknamed 'Le Sylvain', who devoted his life and fortune to the study of the forest. Among the more picturesque sites are the _Gorges de Franchard_ (4km W. of the _Carrefour de la Libération_), a rocky wilderness lying not far S. of the D409; and the _Gorges d'Apremont_ (6km N.W., S. of the N7). Although skirted by roads, the exploration of these areas should be undertaken on foot.

FROM FONTAINEBLEAU TO SENS (53km). From the _Carrefour de l'Obélisque_, immediately S.E. of the palace, we follow the N6, after 6·5km turning l. for **Moret-sur-Loing**, an ancient town retaining two of its 14C _Gates_, besides a tower and part of its walls. _Notre-Dame_, consecrated to Thomas Becket, has a fine portal (15C), and contains some remarkable wood-carvings. In an old timbered house to the r. of the church, is sold the famous barley-sugar of the nuns of Moret. Behind the church, at No.9 Rue du Château, Sisley (1840–99) spent the last four years of his life. Behind the _Hotel de Ville_ (with a local museum) one may see sculptures once embellishing the courtyard of a mansion built in 1572, placed here in 1957, having been moved from the so-called Maison François-1er in the Cours la Reine, Paris. Pissarro painted here in 1901–02. Just beyond is the castle-keep (1128), in which Fouquet was imprisoned for some months in 1664. Good view from the bridge. Its quails are famous, prepared in the style of _St-Mammès_, an adjoining village.

Continuing on the N6, at 18km we may bear l. to _Montereau-faut-Yonne_. See Rte 30 for the road hence to _Sens_, 33km further S.E.

FROM FONTAINEBLEAU TO PITHIVIERS (46km). We follow the N152 S.W. through the forest, at 10km crossing the A6.—4km **Larchant** (5km S.) has a fine 12C church, with a richly decorated apsidal chapel of the 13C.—12km **Malesherbes**, in the 12–13C church of which is a bust of Guillaume de Lamoignon de Malesherbes (1721–94), Louis XVI's minister and defender, who owned the château to the S. of the town, rebuilt in the 15C, with a huge barn, and pigeon-house. To the N. of the town lies the Château _de Rouville_ (late 15C, but over-restored in the 19C).—At _Champmotteux_, 10km N.W. on the D949, the church contains the reconstructed tomb of Chancellor Michel de l'Hôpital (d. 1573), which was smashed in 1793.—19km _Pithiviers_, see Rte 32.

Following the N7 S. from _Fontainebleau_, we bypass (8km l.) _Grez-sur-Loing_, with an interesting 12–16C church, containing Romanesque capitals. Louise de Savoie (1476–1531), mother of François I, died in the castle, now ruined.

R.L. Stevenson moored his canoe here after his 'Inland Voyage' (1876), and the composer Frederick Delius (1862–1934) lived here from 1897 until his death. His remains were reburied in Limpsfield, Surrey, the following year.

15km. **Nemours** (11,700 inhab.) stood originally on an island in the Loing, and was once the capital of the Gâtinais. It now covers the adjacent island, and the E. bank of the river. *Nemoracum* was fortified at an early date, and between 1420 and 1437 was in English hands.

A local confection, known as *coquelicots*, is worth sampling, as are its hams and pâtés.

Eleuthère-Irénée, one of the family of Du Pont of Nemours, founded in the State of Delaware a factory which formed the basis of the chemical 'empire' which bears his name.

The fortified *Château* (15C, but parts of it dating from the 12C) defending the river crossing, has been restored to house a local museum. An interesting view of the outer walls and keep may also be obtained from the river side, preserving some old mills. A *Museum* devoted to the prehistory of the Île de France has recently been inaugurated further E. The *Grand Pont* commands a view of the apse of *St-Jean Baptiste* (16C), with a fan-vaulted nave and with pendant bosses. A few quaint old houses survive in its vicinity.

The D40 follows the W. bank of the river to (94km) **Château-Landon**, a well sited village on a bluff above the Fusain valley, and birthplace of ancestors of the Plantagenets. *Notre-Dame* (11–14C), with a 13C tower, is notable, and the view from the terrace adjoining the main square of the ancient fortifications, and the ruined Romanesque tower of *St-Tugal*, is impressive. The ruins of the abbey of *St-Séverin*, founded by Childebert in 545, at the E. end of the village, may be visited (enquire at the S.I.).

The churches of *Arville* and *Puiseaux* (12 and 19km N.W. of Château-Landon respectively), *Boësse* (7km S.W. of Puiseaux), and *Mondreville* (7km W. of Château-Landon) are of interest.

At *Ferrières*, 8km S.E., is an abbey church (11–15C) remarkable for a rotunda formed of eight columns at the crossing, and for its 16C stained glass; also a pilgrimage chapel of 1620.

FROM CHÂTEAU-LANDON TO SENS (46km). The D43 crosses the N7 at *Dordives*, beyond which the road skirts the impressive ruins of the 13C fortress of *Mez-le-Maréchal*.—15km. **Égreville**, with a 13–15C church and 15C beamed market-hall. The Duchesse d'Étampes—Anne de Pisseleu—mistress of François I, lived in the 16C château, where Jules Massenet (1842–1912) passed his last years; he is buried in the cemetery.—There are remains of 13C ramparts, and a fortified church at *Lorrez-le-Bocage*, 7km N.—Veering S.E. we regain the so-called 'Chemin de César', a Roman road leading due E. to (31km) *Sens*, see Rte 30.

Montargis lies 18km S. of Château-Landon on the D40; *Gien* is 39km further S. (N7 and D940), and *Bourges* lies 76km S.W. of Gien; *Nevers* lies 125km S. of Montargis: see *Blue Guide France*.

32 Paris to Sceaux and Étampes (for Orléans)

N20 to (10km) *Sceaux*—40km. *Étampes*. Orléans lies 66km further S. Those wishing to approach the latter direct may take the A10 autoroute, bearing off the Blvd Périphérique just E. of the Porte d'Orléans, which may be also joined 5km S. of Sceaux.

Sceaux may also be approached by the RER, stopping at *Sceaux* or *Bourg-la-Reine*.

We drive S. from the *Porte d'Orléans* parallel to the A6; the roads converge some 15km S. of Paris.

At 7km (l.; 2km S. of the Blvd Périphérique) we pass the double *Aqueduct* crossing the valley of the Bièvre, the lower part of which was built in 1613–24 by Marie de Médicis to supply the Luxembourg fountains; it was preceded by a Roman one, built in the 4C to bring water to the Palais des Thermes (see Rte 2).

4·5km (r.) **Sceaux**. A broad avenue (the Allée d'Honneur) ascends W. from the N20 to the entrance of the **Château**, a 19C building replacing the sumptuous 17C château built by *Claude Perrault* for Colbert, which, during the first half of the 18C, was the scene of the literary and artistic court of the ambitious Duchesse du Maine (1676–1753) as described by Mme de Launay, among others. Here Voltaire wrote three of his tragedies, and works by Racine, Molière, and Lully were performed in the adjacent *Orangerie* (l.), constructed by *J. Hardouin-Mansart* (1684; restored).—To the r. is the *Pavillon de l'Aurore*, also by *Perrault*.

Since 1937 the *MUSÉE DE l'ÎLE DE FRANCE has been installed in the château, illustrating the history and topography of the area now covered by the departments of Hauts-de-Seine, Seine-St-Denis, Val-de-Marne, Essone, Yvelines, and Val-d'Oise. It is well worth visiting, not only for its site, but for the wealth of interesting material depicting the appearance of, and life in, the environs of the capital in past centuries. The building also contains a Reference Library, etc.

Adm. Mon. and Fri. 14.00–18.00; Wed., Thur., Sat. and Sun. 10.00–12.00; 14.00–18.00/19.00; closed Tues. The library is open daily from 9.00–12.00; 14.00–18.00, except Sun.

The majority of the rooms are devoted to specific regions. **R2** contains a model of the château, and **R3** portraits of Colbert attrib. to *Lefebvre*, and of the Duchesse du Maine by *De Troy*.—**R4** (commanding a good vista): Sceaux ceramics (1754–95).—**R5** Sèvres and St-Cloud ware.—**R7** Views of St-Cloud by *Dunouy, Fleury*, etc.—**R8** is devoted to Meudon. Stairs ascend to the SECOND FLOOR, where a series of rooms display views of the Machine de Marly, of St-Germain by *James Basire* (1730–1802); of Mousseau, by *J.-M. Morel*, drawings, watercolours, and engravings by *Dunoyer de Segonzac* (1874–1946); two of Etry occupied by Cossacks in 1814, by *J. Randon*, and a number of attractive views by *Paul Huet* (1803–69), among others of great topographical value, including also the Tower of Vincennes, by *Bonington*.

The extensive *Park, laid out by *Le Nôtre*, forms one of the most attractive open spaces near Paris, and contains, S. of the château, a series of cascades leading to the *Octagon*, to the W. of which is the

Grand Canal. Hence we have a view of the *Pavillon de Hanovre*, removed here in 1832 from the Blvd des Capucines, 9e. It was built in 1760 with money extorted from the Hanoverians in the Seven Years War.

A short distance N.W. of the château, approached across the park, is the old churchyard of *Sceaux*, where the fabulist Florian (1755–94) lies buried. The simple tombs of Pierre (1859–1906) and Marie Curie (née Sklodowska; 1867–1934), the discoverers of radium, may be found in the local cemetery.

13·5km **Longpont-sur-Orge**, 2km l., has a *Church* of considerable archaeological interest, begun c.1060 and formerly attached to a Cluniac priory.

The choir, transepts, and spire were unhappily demolished in 1822 to save the cost of upkeep, but the two former were rebuilt in 1878. The W. front is original, with a 13C portal surmounted by a 15C rose-window. In the doorway are headless statues (13C); that of the Virgin has been restored (badly). In the archivolts are 13C statues of the Wise and Foolish Virgins. The nave, remodelled in the 12C, has good Romanesque arches and foliate capitals, with a blind triforium above. Behind the high-altar is the statue of N.-D. de Bonne-Garde, with ex-votos. Among the tombs are those of the foundress, the Comtesse de Montlhéry, and Louis of France (d.1318).—S. of the church is the château of *Lormoy* (rebuilt 1837), with a chestnut avenue.

1km **Montlhéry**. Near the church is the *Hôtel-Dieu*, founded by Louis VII in 1146, with a mutilated 13C carving on the door. Spanning the Grande Rue is the massive *Porte Baudry*, with an inscription recording its history. The town is dominated by the *Tour de Montlhéry* (CN) , a cylindrical keep (13–15C), a relic of a famous medieval fortress dating from 991, and demolished in 1591. By the entrance are some tombstones from a Gallo-Roman cemetery.

There is an interesting 15–16C church at *Marcousis*, 3km to the W. Also noteworthy is the *Collégial St-Merry* at *Linas* just S. of Montlhéry, altered in the 16C, but retaining a 13C choir and belfry. At 1km (r.) is the 'Autodrome' of Montlhéry, a popular motor-racing track.

4km **Arpajon** (8000 inhab.), called *Châtres* until 1720, takes its name from a marquisate in Auvergne. The church dates from the 13C, and there is a 17C *Market-house*.

FROM ARPAJON TO ABLIS (34km). The D19 leads S.W. viâ (2km) *Égly*, with 15–17C paintings in its church, to (9km) *St-Chéron*, just N. of which is the château of *Baville*. 3·5km N.W. of St-Chéron stands the château of *Le Marais*, c. 1770, by *Barré*, in an extensive park, and the residence of Boni de Castellane from 1897. The mid 17C château of *Courson* lies 4km N.E. of the latter. The château of *Villeconin* (8km S. of St-Chéron) retains a gatehouse of the 13C.—9km. **Dourdan** (8100 inhab.), the Gallo-Roman *Dordincum*, and later capital of the Hurepoix, has a curious church of 12C foundation, but provided with two steeples and an elaborate vault in the 15C. The comic dramatist Jean-François Regnard (1655–1709), who owned a property nearby, is buried here. The royal *Castle*, preserving its square turreted rampart and its keep (under restoration), was rebuilt by Philippe Auguste in 1220 on the site of an earlier fortress, where Hugues Capet was born c.941, and where his father Hugues le Grand died in 956. It was besieged and taken many times: by Salisbury in 1428; by Montgomery in 1567; and by Biron in 1591, in the name of Henri IV.—The village of *St-Cyr-sous-Dourdan*, 5km N., retains a 16C church and fortified priory.—*Ablis* (see Rte 32A) lies 14km W. of Dourdan.

FROM ARPAJON TO MILLY-LA-FORÊT (31km). The D449 leads S. E. to (16km) *La Ferté-Alais* (the fortress of Adélaide, wife of Guy Trousseau, lord of Montlhéry in the 11C), whose castle no longer exists; boulevards have replaced the former ramparts. The church dates from the 11–12C.—The D105 leads S. along the E. bank of the Essonne before bearing S.E. to *Milly* (see Rte 31.)

At 8km, a lane leads 2·5km r. to **St-Sulpice-de-Favières**, with an unexpected elegant *Church*, built in 1260–1320 to accommodate pilgrims to the shrine of St Sulpicius. It has an exceptionally fine tower and choir, and contains two good contemporary stained-glass windows, and a 17C altarpiece in painted wood. The chapel with the saint's relics, adjoining the N. aisle, is a survival from an earlier 12C church.

The N20 ascends the once notorious hill known as the 'Côte de Torfou', just to the E. of which is *Chamarande*, with a 17C château built by *Fr. Mansart* on the site of a 9C castle.—The road now passes (r.) *Étréchy*, with a graceful Gothic church, at 7km passing (l.) the château of *Jeurre*, in the park of which are many 18C follies, including some taken from *Méréville* (see below).

2km. *Morigny* (1km E.) has a church occupying the 13–15C choir of a late 11C Benedictine abbey. The château (adm. on application) contains an interesting prehistoric collection, and three Gallo-Roman mosaics.

2km. **ÉTAMPES** (19,500 inhab.), with a bypass, is an ancient town (known as *Stampae* in the 6C) strung out along the old Orléans road, and dominated by the *Tour Guinette*, a huge 12C keep where Philippe Auguste confined his queen, Ingeborg of Denmark, for 12 years (1201–13). Geoffroy St-Hilaire (1772–1844), the naturalist, was a native of Étampes. Its pâtés d'alouettes are famous.

Near the town centre stands *St-Basile* (15–16C), retaining an elaborate Romanesque W. door and a 12C tower, and within, ten 16C reliefs of the Passion, three of them mutilated. The Rue de la République leads S.E. to **N.-D. du Fort**, an interesting church preserving much 11C work in its nave; the steeple (62m) is a fine 12C composition. The W. and S. doorways are somewhat later, while the transepts and choir (with 16C glass) are of the 14C. In the N.E. chapel are some 12C figures, and beneath is a crypt, possibly Merovingian.

A short distance S. in the Rue de la Tannerie is the early 16C *Hôtel St-Yon*. Further S., seen from the *Pont Doré*, spanning a branch of the Juine, is the *Tour de Jean-le-Bâtard*, a relic of the ancient ramparts. Turning N. along the Rue Ste-Croix, we pass (l.) the *Hôtel de Ville*, with two turrets of 1614, and the Renaissance *Hôtel d'Anne de Pisseleu*.—The *Palais de Justice*, to the S.W., contains a curious 14C mural painting. Further N., behind St-Basile, is the so-called *Maison de Diane de Poitiers* (1544), with a good courtyard.

Some distance S.W. along the main street lies *St-Gilles*, a 16C church (damaged in 1940), with a 12C doorway and grotesque carvings in the N. aisle.—1km beyond is *St-Martin* (12–13C), with a beautiful apse, and a dangerously leaning tower displaying Renaissance decoration.

From this end of the town, the D21 leads W. to (8km) *Châlo-St-Mars*, with a restored 12C church, 6km S.W. of which, in the valley of the Chalouette, at *Chalou-Moulineux*, are two late-12C churches, one (ruined) dedicated to Becket.

The most rapid road from ÉTAMPES TO CHARTRES is the N191 to (30km W.) *Ablis*, there turning l. onto the N10 to (28km) *Chartres*, see Rte 33A.

FROM ÉTAMPES TO FONTAINEBLEAU (44km). The D837 leads E. passing at 10km (l.) the château of **Farcheville**, with well-preserved fortifications built in 1291.—25km. *Milly-la-Forêt.*—19km. *Fontainebleau*; for both see Rte 31.

FROM ÉTAMPES TO PITHIVIERS (32km). The direct road (D921) runs S. across the plateau viâ *Sermaises*, with an interesting church, to **Pithiviers** (9800 inhab.), noted for its almond cakes, a rather dull old town (whose original site was probably at *Pithiviers-le-Vieil*, 3km W.), which sprang up after 874 around the shrine of the sainted king Solomon II of Brittany, whose body was brought here to save it from desecration at the hands of the Normans. It was the birthplace of the artist Lubin Baugin (1612–66).

In the medieval centre, surrounded by tree-lined boulevards on the site of earlier ramparts, stands the *Church*, dedicated to St Salomon and St Gregory (a 10C hermit of Armenia, who died nearby), dating mainly from the 16–17C, but the mid-12C crossing of an older church (now at the E. end of the S. aisle) supports a tower of 1180, with a spire of 1855. The 17–18C furniture is handsome.

The *Hôtel de Ville* adjoins the 13C tower of the former church of *St-Georges*, while a *Museum* occupies the chapel and other rooms of the former *Hôtel-Dieu* (18C). Among the paintings are works by *Coypel, Carle Van Loo, Natoire, Leprince, David, Fragonard, J.-B. Huet*, and *Corot*, among others; and some of the Italian Schools. A *Transport Museum* may also be visited in Pithiviers.

The village of **Yèvre-le-Châtel** (6km E. on the D123) lies adjacent to the ruins of a *Castle* built c. 1236 by Amaury de Montfort. Only a gate remains of the outer ward, but the square inner ward, with four drum towers and immense supporting arches, is still to be seen. The 11–13C chapel serves as a parish church.

For the route from PITHIVIERS TO CHARTRES, see Rte 33A; to *Fontainebleau*, Rte 31. The D26, continued by the D7, leads 38km E. to *Château-Landon*, see Rte 31.

The N20 continues S.W. from *Étampes* across the monotonous but fertile Beauce plateau.

At 13km *Méréville* (5km S.E.), with a 16C market-house, is a château on which, from 1784, the banker Laborde spent a fortune. The park was designed by the painter Hubert Robert in the 'English' style (comp. *Jeurre*; see p308).

5km *Angerville*, bypassed, has a 15C church with a 12C tower.— 13km *Toury* retains a 13C church with a curious porch. A monument on the Orléans road commemorates Blériot's first monoplane flight (31 Oct. 1908) to *Artenay*, some 12km S.

Orléans lies 34km S. of Toury; see *Blue Guide France*.

33 Paris to Chartres

A. Viâ the N10 (Rambouillet and Ablis)

Total distance, 83km (51 miles).

The A12 and N10 converge a short distance S.W. of Versailles (approx. 18km from the *Porte d'Auteuil*).

At 32km we pass near (r.) *Elancourt*, where the church retains a 12C choir and Romanesque tower.—To the l. the New Town of *St-Quentin-en-Yvelines* is under construction.

16·5km. *Rambouillet* (see Rte 33B). The N10 circles round the E. side of the town before continuing S. crossing the A11 autoroute, to (11·5km) *Ablis*, whose church has a Romanesque nave, and a late Gothic choir, with 16C stained-glass.

7·5km S.W., at *Auneau*, is a fine 11-14C castle, 4·5km S.E. of which, at *Aunoy-sous-Auneau*, is a notable Gothic church (13-15C).

At *Ablis*, the N10 turns abruptly W. across the Beauce plateau, parallel to the A11.—5·5km. *St-Symphorien*, to the N., where stands the first of the 'Bornes de la Liberté (1946), stones set up to mark the advance of the army of liberation through France in 1944.—1km N.E. is the imposing but over-restored 16C château of *Esclimont*.

3·5km. *Gallardon* (4km N.W.) retains a ruined cylindrical keep (11C), the 'Épaule de Gallardon', below which is a notable 12–13C church, with a large choir; also a number of 16C houses.

The N10 drives directly towards the spires of (14km) Chartres cathedral, which are seen from some distance away, Crossing the A11, we enter the town through an unattractive industrial zone, and ascend the BLVD DE LA COURTILLE towards the centre.

CHARTRES (39,200 Chartrains), the old capital of the province of Beauce, and now préfectúre of the department of Eure-et-Loir, is chiefly famous for its magnificent cathedral, one of the noblest creations of medieval architecture, its tall but unequal spires still dominating the town, itself retaining an attractive quarter of ancient houses. Chartres has a reputation for its gastronomy, its pâtes and its *pain d'épices*.

Chartres, the chief place of the Carnutes, called by the Romans *Antricum*, was one of the main strongholds of Gallic Druidism. Edward III's siege of Chartres in 1360 was his last military operation before the Treaty of Brétigny (see p316); and in 1417–32 the town was held by allies of the English until retaken by Dunois. It was besieged again in 1568 by the Huguenots, and in 1591 by Henri IV, who, after his renunciation of Protestantism, returned here to be anointed in 1594. During the Franco-Prussian War, Chartres was for almost five months the centre of German operations against the second army of the Loire. It suffered some damage in 1944, before being liberated by the Americans on 16 Aug.

John of Salisbury (1120–80) was Bp. of Chartres from 1176 until his death. Philippe Desportes (1546–1606) and Mathurin Régnier (1573–1613) the poets, Philippe Dangeau (1638–1720), author of the famous 'Journal', Jean-Pierre Brissot (1754–92), the Girondist, and François Marceau (1769–96; a soldier at 16 and a general at 23), were natives of Chartres; Jean Moulin (1899–1944), founder of the Conseil National de la Résistance, who was deported and murdered by the Germans, was prefect of the department.'J.-K. Huysmans's 'La Cathédrale' (1898) is largely concerned with Chartres. 'Mont-St-Michel and Chartres', by Henry Adams, is also of interest.

The PL. DES ÉPARS. the modern centre of the city, where the *Hôtel Grand Monarque* has an 18C façade, lies on the perimèter of the old ramparts, to the N. of which is the BLVD DE LA RÉSISTANCE, with a monument to Jean Moulin. The line of boulevards continues downhill, with a view of the N.E. ramparts, to the river.

From the Pl. des Épars, the Rue Colin-d'Harleville leads directly N.E. to the cathedral, passing (r.) the *Chapelle Ste-Foy* (16C, with an 11C portal), and l., the *Préfecture*, with the 16C *Hôtel de Champrond* opposite.

An alternative route is that viâ the Rue Noël-Ballay, in which No.8 is the 16C *Maison de Claude-Huvé*, the Rue Serpente, and Rue des Changes, in which the last house on the r. is 13C.

The **Cathedral of Notre-Dame**, is, as it stands, almost entirely a work of the 13C, only the W. front, with its twin towers, and the crypt, having survived from its predecessors, while later additions have been relatively unimportant. Among its most striking features, apart from its sheer size, are the rich lateral portals, the wealth of its stained-glass, scarcely equalled in France, and the three rose-windows.

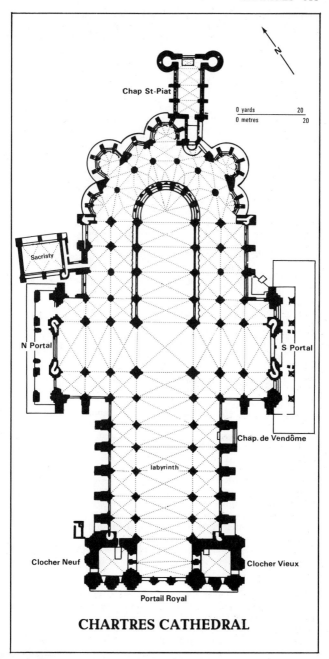

Chap St-Piat

0 yards 20
0 metres 20

Sacristy

N Portal

S Portal

Chap. de Vendôme

labyrinth

Clocher Neuf

Clocher Vieux

Portail Royal

CHARTRES CATHEDRAL

A cathedral, with St Aventinus as the first bishop, was founded here in the 4C, on the site of a Druidic sanctuary and a temple of the Dea Mater; and this, the earliest church in France dedicated to the Virgin Mary, became an important goal of pilgrimage. This building and its successors were repeatedly destroyed or burned, and the first great church erected on the site was begun by St Fulbert (960–1028), bishop after 1020. The oldest parts of the existing building, above ground, are the W. tower and the lower part of the façade of this Romanesque cathedral, which survived the fire of 1194.

It was rebuilt in the first quarter of the 13C, and was consecrated in its present form in 1260, although additions were made in the 14-16C. Almost miraculously, it escaped the ravages of the Religious Wars, the Revolution, and the Second World War; but a fire in 1836 destroyed the ancient wooden roof, which was replaced in metal. Regrettably, the choir did not escape the attention of the Chapter, who in the 18C destroyed much of the earlier work (including a 13C rood screen) in an attempt to 'modernise' it: but such has been the fate of too many buildings left to such vandals.

EXTERIOR. The splendid *W. Façade* is pierced by the triple *Portail Royal* (1150–75), decorated with statues and statuettes, mainly illustrating the Life of Christ. The doorways are flanked by statues of biblical kings and queens, attenuated figures with formal pleated drapery, characteristic of 12C sculpture. In the central tympanum is Christ Blessing, with the symbols of the Evangelists, and the Apostles below; the side arches represent the Ascension (N.) and Nativity (S.). The western rose-window, and the gallery with 16 statues of the kings of Judah, were added in the 13C.

The greater part of both *Towers* dates from 1134–44. The elegant crocketed N. spire (115m), and the 'Clocher Neuf' were raised in 1507–13, partly at the expense of Louis XII, by *Jean Texier* (Jehan de Beauce). The S. tower (105·6m without the cross), or 'Clocher Vieux', is the tallest Romanesque steeple in existence. At the corner a 12C angel bears a sundial of 1528. The Renaissance clock beside the N. tower was made in 1520 by *Jehan de Beauce.*

The two portals on the N. and S. sides are triple projecting Gothic porticoes resting on piers or clustered pillars with side openings between them. The stately sculptures are of a later date (1225 et seq.) than those of the W. front, but equally impressive. The *N. Portal* alone is embellished with more than 700 figures symbolic of the Coming of Christ; the *S. Portal* is dedicated to the Glorification of the Saints, and the Last Judgment. Above each portal is a fine rose-window. The tall windows of the nave and choir are separated by huge flying buttresses unique of their kind, particularly impressive at the E. end.

INTERIOR. The cathedral is 130·2m in length, and its height to the spring of the vaulting is 32·3m. The nave is the widest in France (16·4m between the piers). The style throughout the nave and choir is the most vigorous early Gothic, and the grandeur of proportion is enhanced by an extreme sobriety of sculpture. It too often remains unlit in dull weather.

More than 160 windows are filled with superb *Stained-glass*, dating for the most part from the 13C, although that of the three fine W. lancets, one of which contains a Tree of Jesse, survived the fire of 1194. The rose-windows of the nave and transepts are remarkable for their size (9-12m in diameter) and graceful tracery. The windows in general illustrate legends of saints; the represent-ations of various trades in the lower compartments of many indicate that they were presented by the trade guilds or corporations.

The St Fulbert window (E. side of S. Transept) was donated in 1954 by the Inst. of American Architects.

In the middle of the *Nave* (too often covered with chairs) a circular maze or labyrinth, called 'La Lieue' from its supposed length, is marked on the pavement in coloured stone; to follow its windings on one's knees, saying prayers at various points, was probably at

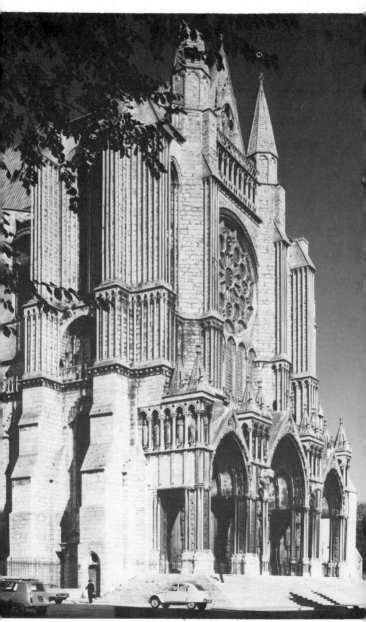

The South portal of Notre-Dame, Chartres

one time a penitential exercise. The *Chap. de Vendôme*, off the S. side-aisle, was added by Louis, Comte de Vendôme, in 1417.

The **Choir** is enclosed by a magnificent stone *Screen begun in 1514 from designs of *Jehan de Beauce*, and completed under Louis XIV, and of interest as being one of the last examples of Gothic art. Its 40 remarkable sculptures of events in the Life of Christ and of the Virgin (by *Jehan de Beauce*, *François Marchand*, *Jean Soulas*, and others) are surrounded by elaborate tracery and tabernacle-work. The inappropriate marble retable of the Assumption is the work of *C.-A. Bridan* (1767–73), who also carved the marble bas-reliefs around the sanctuary (1788). In the N.W. chapel of the ambulatory is the 'Vierge du Pilier', an early 16C image that was crowned with the Cap of Liberty at the Revolution. The window of the S.W. chapel enshrines 'N.-D. de la Belle Verrière', a 12C survival in a setting of 13C glass.

In the *Treasury*, behind the altar, a reliquary purports to preserve a garment of the Virgin sent to Charlemagne by the Empress Irene, and presented to Chartres by Charles le Chauve (c.876).

From the apse a staircase and corridor lead to the *Chap. St-Piat* (1349), flanked on the outside by round towers; its lower storey (1323–35), originally the chapter house, is now the bishop's funerary chapel.

The **Crypt**, dating partly from the 11C, the largest in France, is dedicated to 'N.-D. sous Terre', the earliest of the Christian Virgins, venerated on the supposed site of the Druidic sanctuary. We descend into the S. gallery, on the l. of which is a Gallo-Roman bas-relief. In the *Chap. St-Martin* are fragments of the 13C rood-loft of the cathedral and the cenotaph of St Calétric, Bp of Chartres (557). Near the *Chap. St-Nicolas* is a piscina surmounted by a 13C fresco, and further on, a 12C font. Returning past the entrance, we pass the seven apsidal chapels, four of them added in the 13C; a 9C inner crypt (no adm.), opposite the *Chap. Ste-Veronique*, is dedicated to St Lubin or Leobinus, a shepherd, afterwards Bp of Chartres (6C). Passing the well in which the earliest martyrs of Chartres are believed to have been drowned, we reach, in the N. gallery, the sanctuary of *N.-D. sous Terre*, but with a 19C image; to the r. of it is the *Chap. des Saints-Forts*, with a 13C triptych.

The *Maison Henri-III*, opposite the N. portal, retains six windows of the 13C.—To the r., installed in the former *Bishop's Palace* (17–18C), is the **Musée des Beaux-Arts**.

Among paintings displayed here are: *Hubert Robert*, L'Aqueduc de Maintenon; *Rigaud*, portrait of the Duc de Saint-Simon, and Molière, by *Mignard*; Fontenelle, by *Largillière*; Turenne, by *Ph. de Champaigne*; a pastel of Molière by *Nanteuil*; and St Lucy, by *Zurbarán*. In the **Chapel** (1764–74), decorated by *Bridan*, are 12 *Enamels of the apostles, executed in 1545–47 by *Léonard Limousin* for the castle chapel of Diane de Poitiers at Anet, moved here from the church of *St-Pierre* (see below). Also from the same church is the statue of St Paul, by *François Marchand* (d.1553).
Other paintings of merit include *Bol*, La kermesse d'Hoboken; *Teniers the elder*, Les joueurs de boules; *Teniers the younger*, Tabagie des singes, and Le Concert; two works by *Verdussen*; Catherine of Russia on horseback, by *Erichsen*. Note also the anon. 15C Flemish pietà, and a collection of alabasters. On the upper floor is a small collection of armour, and a section devoted to the architectural history of the cathedral.

The terraced gardens below form an approach to the lower town.

By turning r. on making our exit from the Museum and then l. we reach the **Cellier de Loens**, the 13C storehouse of the chapter, a fine vaulted crypt, to be reopened shortly as a *Museum of Stained-Glass*, with a section describing the techniques of its manufacture.

Further S., in the Rue du Cheval-Blanc, are the *Maison de l'Homme-Sauvage*, and other old houses.—Turning N. we shortly enter the Rue Chantault, with, at No.29, a 12C house. Just beyond, passing (r.) the gabled *Cloître St-André*, is the Rue de la Brèche, with (r.) the disused and mutilated church of *St-André*, a 12C building with a Romanesque façade and nave, and a 15C N. chapel with the grave of Jehan de Beauce.

Thence we may return to the *Musée* by stairs ascending from the PL. ST-ANDRÉ; or turning l., cross the Eure beside the chapel of *N.-D. de la Brèche*, erected in thanksgiving for the successful outcome of the siege of 1568, when the Protestants abandoned the breach made in the walls here (note the stone cannon-balls).

From the bridge we follow the quaint Rue du Massacre, Rue de la Tannerie, and Rue de la Foulerie to the *Pont St-Hilaire*. The ramparts on the W. side of this island are best seen from the BLVD MARÉCHAL-FOCH, on the far bank (where the *Porte Guillaume*, a 14C town gate, survived until its deliberate destruction by the Germans in 1944).

Recrossing the stream, we reach *St-Pierre, once the church of the powerful Benedictine abbey of St-Père-en-Vallée. It preserves a massive low tower of c. 1150, a 13C nave, and a 14C choir with a 12C apse. The flying buttresses and the stained-glass (late-13th and 14C) are notable.

The Rue St-Pierre (No.16 in which is the Renaissance *Maison des Trois-Pigeons*) passes below the church of *St-Aignan*, a 16–17C building with a wooden roof of 1625, and is continued by the Rue des Écuyers, where at No.35 a turret encloses the 16C *Escalier de la Reine-Berthe*, a spiral staircase of carved oak. The Rue St-Eman leads W. to the PL. DE LA POISSONNERIE, in which are the 15C wooden houses called the *Maison du Saumon* and *Maison de la Truite-qui-File*. Hence the Rue de la Petite-Cordonnerie and narrow Rue aux Herbes lead back to the S. front of the Cathedral.

Many ancient buildings in this quarter S.E. of the Cathedral are undergoing restoration; others of interest may be seen in the Rue des Grenets (No.12), the continuation of the Rue des Changes (leading S. from the Cathedral), and beyond St-Aignan, at Nos 8 and 10 PL. DE L'ÉTAPE-AU-VIN. Not far W. of this point is the *Hôtel Montescot* (1614), restored since the Hôtel de Ville, with its valuable library, was destroyed in 1944. A new town hall flanks the PL. DES HALLES, from the N.W. corner of which we may regain the *Pl. des Épars*.

A short distance to the S., approached by the Rue St-Brice, stands *St-Martin-au-Val* (now a hospital chapel; admission may be granted on request), a 12C abbey church on the l. of which, although much restored, are preserved some remains of a basilica dating from before the 10C. The vaulted crypt has Gallo-Roman capitals and contains sarcophagi of early bishops.

For the route from CHARTRES TO DREUX, see Rte 34; *Verneuil* lies 56km N.W. on the D939; *Le Mans* (119km S.W.; N23 or A11); *Tours* (129km S.W.; N10); *Blois* (92km S.); and *Orléans* (72km S.E.; N154 and N20). For all these routes, see *Blue Guide France*.

A short EXCURSION may be made to **Illiers** 25km S.W. of Chartres on the N921, a little town on the Loir (which here divides the Beauce from the Perche-Gouët) famous as the 'Combray' of Marcel Proust's 'À la recherche du temps perdu'.

The 14C church has a fine roof. Proust spent his childhood holidays with his uncle and aunt, M. et Mme Amiot (tante Léonie), whose house, No.4 Rue du Docteur-Proust, is preserved as a literary shrine (and 'centre de documentation proustienne'); for details of the many associations, refer to *George D. Painter's* 'Marcel Proust; a Biography', vol. 1 (1959).

FROM CHARTRES TO PITHIVIERS (73km). We follow the N154 S.E. across the monotonous Beauce plateau. Shortly after passing beneath the motorway, a turning (l.) leads to the hamlet of *Brétigny* where the famous treaty was signed in 1360, in accordance with which Jean II, le Bon, paying a ransom of 3 million crowns to regain his liberty lost at the battle of Poitiers, surrendered the whole of S.W. France to Edward III, who, in return, renounced all claim to the French crown. At 21km a crossroads leads 10km N.E. to *Santeuil*, with an important Romanesque church, once fortified, with a 13C apse.—*Voves*, 7km S.W. of the crossroad, has a 12–15C church.

17km *Allaines-Mervilliers*, 2km to the S. of which, a disused church preserves a remarkable 12C sculptured tympanum, said to represent St-Fiacre refusing the Scottish crown. We bear l. onto the D927, crossing the A10, past (3km) *Le Puiset*, with a beautiful 12C church and the ruins of a castle, which defied Philippe I but was destroyed by Louis VI. Most famous of its robber-barons was Hugh du Puiset (d.1195), nephew of King Stephen, and Bp of Durham.—6km *Toury.*—26km. Pithiviers: for both, see Rte 32. *Orléans* lies 34km S. of Allaines, and is also approached by the A10 autoroute, which may be entered 2km E; see *Blue Guide France*.

B. Viâ the Valley of the Chevreuse, Port-Royal, Rambouillet, and Maintenon

Total distance, 103km (64 miles). N306 to (40km) *St-Rémy-lès-Chevreuse*; (*Port-Royal-des-Champs*); (*Dampierre*). —21km *Rambouillet.*—23km *Maintenon.*—19km **Chartres**.

The N306 and the N118 bearing S. off the N10 at *Sèvres* towards the A10 converge at *Porte Clamart* (8km S.W. of the *Porte de Châtillon*, and 13km from the centre of Paris).

At 8·5km we cross the valley of the Bièvre, where, 4km to the W., at *Jouy-en-Josas*, with a 13–16C church, Christophe-Philippe Oberkampf (1738–1815) founded the famous manufacture of printed calico, called 'toiles de Jouy', c. 1780; a *Museum* may be visited.—At **Bièvres** itself, just N. of this junction, an interesting *Musée de la Photographie* has been installed at 78 Rue de Paris (10.00–12.00; 14.00–18.00 daily).

3km E. of the next main junction at (13·5km) *Saclay*, lies *Vauhallan*, where the church, originally 6C, was rebuilt in the 13C, and altered in the 18C.—We diverge r. onto the N306, passing, W. of Saclay, the research laboratories of the Centre d'Études Nucléaires, and climb down into the VALLÉE DE CHEVREUSE, in which lay the family estate of the duellist and author Savinien Cyrano de Bergerac (1619–55).

9km. *St-Rémy-lès-Chevreuse.*

At 1km a DETOUR may be made to **Port-Royal-des-Champs**, 6km N.W. by the D46 (r.), passing at 5km the church at *St-Lambert*, where in the cemetery a granite pyramid marks the common fosse where the remains of the nuns of Port-Royal were reinterred.—On reaching the D91, a footpath leads N. to the entrance of the enclosure.

The celebrated abbey of *Port-Royal-des-Champs*, founded in 1204, played an important part in the religious history of France, being the headquarters of the Jansenists. Mère Angélique, abbess 1602–61, removed the community to Paris in 1625 (see p82). In 1638 the abbey-buildings were taken possession of by the 'solitaires', among whom were Mère Angélique's nephews, and later, her father.

Their 'Petites Écoles' (1648–55) attracted much attention by their 'natural' methods of education; James Duke of Monmouth is said to have finished his education at one of them. The nuns, who returned here in 1645, devoted themselves to the education of girls. Racine spent three years (1655–58) at the abbey, as a pupil of Pierre Nicole. Pascal, whose sister Jacqueline was a nun there, championed the Jansenists in their protracted quarrel with the Jesuits (comp. 'Lettres Provinciales', 1656–57).

In 1709, as a result of these religious wranglings, a Papal bull authorized the demolition of the abbey and dispersal of its inmates. On the night of 28 Oct. the abbey was quietly surrounded by detachments of French and Swiss guards, and next morning, after being given a quarter of an hour to pack, the old nuns were led to waiting coaches, and driven to distant destinations. Most of the extensive buildings were then razed to the ground, the materials sold, and the site ploughed over: such was the inexorable and predatory power of the Jesuits.

Little remains to be seen: merely the foundations of the 13C church, the cloister wall, a dovecote, one of the towers built to defend the abbey during the Fronde, Mère Angélique's fountain, and the 'Solitude' (reconstructed).

The tombstones of thirty members of the community are now in the church of *Magny-les-Hameaux*, an attractive village 4·5km to the E.

Regaining the road (D91), we may drive N. to the top of the hill to visit (l., along an avenue) the ***Musée National des Granges de Port-Royal** installed in a building of 1651–52, and devoted to the history of the Jansenists and, more particularly, of *Port-Royal*, and including some portraits by *Ph. de Champaigne*. Adm. 10.00–11.30; 14.00–17.30 except Mon. and Tues.

5·5km S. of Port-Royal-des-Champs lies *Dampierre*, see below.

1km **Chevreuse**, with a church dating from the 12th to the 17C, is dominated by the imposing ruins of the château *de la Madeleine* (12th and 15C), once the home of the intriguing Marie de Rohan, Duchesse de Chevreuse (1600–79), the enemy of Richelieu.

The D58 diverges r. to (4km) **Dampierre**, with a splendid **Château* rebuilt for the Duc de Luynes by *Jules Hardouin-Mansart* in 1675–83, and restored in 1840. The park was laid out by *Le Nôtre*.

5km N.W. along the D58 is the church of *N.-D. de la Roche*, containing (after those in Poitiers cathedral) the oldest choirstalls in France, c.1275.—A short distance beyond, at *Le Mesnil-St-Denis*, is an attractive 16–18C château.

From Dampierre, the D91 leads S., passing (l.) the château of *Cour-Senlisse* (15–16C) to regain the N306 just beyond *Cernay-la-Ville*.

2·5km W. of this junction (by the D24) are the ruins of the abbey of **Les Vaux-de-Cernay**, founded in 1118, and shortly after taken over by the Cistercians, and suppressed at the Revolution. These comprise the church (c. 1170), the monks' parlour and dormitory adjoining the N. transept, a superb example of the Romanesque style, a chapel, and a well. The prior's lodging is now a modern residence. Regrettably, admission is at present rarely granted.

Shortly after quitting Chevreuse we pass (l.) the approach to the 17–19C château of *Breteuil*, and (7km) traverse *Cernay-la-Ville*.

4km. The brick château of *La Celle-les-Bordes*, dating from 1610, lies 4km to the S.E.

8km. **RAMBOUILLET** (22,500 inhab.), where since 1897 the **Château** (CN) has been the official country residence of the Président of the Republic. It may be visited when he is not in residence, except on Tues. and Wed. Only the machicolated tower of the original 14C castle survives; the remainder is a somewhat sombre pile of red brick, with five flanking towers of stone. It contains some good oak panelling, Gobelins tapestries, etc.

In 1547 François I died in the château, which then belonged to Jacques d'Angennes, one of his officers. Charles IX and Catherine de Médicis took refuge there during the Religious Wars; and here Charles X signed his abdication in 1830. The Marquise de Rambouillet (1588–1665), who held her famous salon in the *Hôtel de Rambouillet* in Paris in the early 17C, was a member of the Angennes family, who owned the castle from the 14C until 1700.

After that date the Comte de Toulouse, son of Louis XIV and Mme de Montespan, greatly enlarged the building; his son, the charitable Duc de Penthièvre, was left undisturbed by the Revolution. Florian lived here in 1768–83. Louis XVI was a frequent visitor, but Marie-Antoinette found the place unbearably dull. After 1830 the estate was used as a pleasure-resort, until restored by Napoleon III.

The *Gardens* (open daily until dusk) are mainly due to Penthièvre. Beyond the Parterre is the *Jardin d'Eau*, a lake with formally designed islands; the central 'Grand Canal' being extended by a Tapis Vert. To the E. is an avenue of Louisiana cypresses, while to the W. is the 'Jardin Anglais', with a shell grotto. To the N.W. is the *Laiterie de la Reine* (adm. at the same hours as the château), built to amuse Marie-Antoinette, and decorated with sculptures and grisailles. Beyond is a sheep-farm, endowed by Louis XVI, and populated by the descendants of Merinos imported from Spain, whence they walked, with their shepherds, in 119 days.

The FORÊT DE RAMBOUILLET, a presidential chase of some 13,100 hectares (see IGN 402), extends to the S.E. and to the N.W., but is perhaps best explored from *Montfort-l'Amaury* (see Rte 34), 18km to the N. viâ the D936 and D138. Near *Poigny-la-Forêt*, 4.5km N. and to the W. of this road, are the ruins of a 12C priory church on the bank of the picturesque ÉTANG D'ANGENNES.

We now follow the D906 to (14km) *Épernon*, an old town on a hillside, with a 13C vaulted cellar ('the winepress of Épernon'), and a large late Gothic church, whose game-pies should be sampled.

9km **Maintenon**. The *Château* was given by Louis XIV in 1674 to Françoise d'Aubigné (1635–1719), later Marquise de Maintenon who in 1683 became his second wife, and remains the property of her heirs, the Noailles family. Damaged in 1940, and since restored, it preserves a 13C keep and two 14C towers, but is mainly a 16C building, with additions due to Mme de Maintenon, personal souvenirs of whom may be seen together with family portraits, etc.

We turn S. onto the D6, leaving (r.) the direct road to *Chartres*, 19km S.W., shortly passing the ruins of an *Aqueduct* designed by Louis XIV to bring water from the Eure to Versailles, but the project was never completed.—5km. *St-Piat* preserves an ancient (5C) sculptured sarcophagus of the patron saint in its church.—At (5km) *Jouy*, the church has a charming 13C W. front.—Beyond *St-Prest*, with an 11–13C church, and before joining the main road, we pass the buildings of the *Hospice d'Aligre*, incorporating parts of the Benedictine abbey of Josaphet (founded 1117), including the tomb of John of Salisbury (see p 310); also tombs of the Aligre family, and a 16C cloister brought from Coulombs (see Rte 34).—11km. **Chartres**, see Rte 33A.

C. Viâ the A10 and A11

Total distance, 88km (54 miles).

This is the most rapid but least interesting road. Making our exit from
Paris by either the *Porte d'Italie* or the *Porte de Gentilly*, after approx.
12km (6km from the Portes), we veer S.W., at 6km turning W. again
near *Palaiseau* (with a 12–15C church), taking its name from the
Merovingian palace which once stood there.

5km (l.) *Orsay*, with the late-18C château of Gén. Moreau, victor of Hohen-
linden, built on the site of a castle taken by the English in 1424, and later the
home of the Chevalier d'Orsay, the 19C dandy. The grounds now accommodate
an annexe of the Faculté des Sciences, with spacious laboratories, etc.
    Hence the D988 leads S.W. to (11km) *Limours*, with a church built by François
I in the Flamboyant style, containing 16C stained-glass (restored).—5·5km S.E.,
at *Briis-sous-Forges*, is a square tower, which is supposed to be a remnant of a
convent where Anne Boleyn was educated.—The D988 continues S.W. to
(10km) **Rochefort-en-Yvelines**, on the S. limit of the FORÊT DE RAMBOUILLET,
retaining a number of 15–16C houses, the mairie occupying a 17C bailliage,
and with a partly Romanesque church dominated by a ruined castle. Hence we
may rejoin the A10.—*St-Arnault*, 4km W., has a church of some interest,
showing a strange mingling of Romanesque and late Gothic work, and
containing a crypt perhaps dating from the 6C. No.9 Rue de Paris has a façade
of 1523, restored in 1770.

25km *Rochefort-en-Yvelines* (see above) lies 2km N.—At 5·5km the
A10 bears S. towards *Orléans*.

6·5km (l.) *Ablis* (see Rte 33A).—At 23km we diverge r. to (5km)
Chartres, the A11 bypassing the town to rejoin the N10 to the S. For
the roads hence to *Le Mans*; see *Blue Guide France*.

34 Paris to Houdan and Dreux

Total distance, 84km (52 miles). N12. (46km; *Montfort-
l'Amaury*).—17km *Houdan*.—21km *Dreux*.

The A12 and N10 converge a short distance S.W. of Versailles
(approx. 18km from the *Porte d'Auteuil*), where we diverge onto the
N12.

2km N.E. of this intersection stood the famous Military Academy of **St-Cyr**,
founded by Napoleon in 1808, but destroyed in 1944; the academy has since
been transferred to *Coëtquidan* in Brittany. It occupied the buildings of the
school of St-Louis, established in 1680 for the daughters of poor but noble
families by Mme de Maintenon, who was buried there in 1719. Racine's 'Esther'
(1689) and 'Athalie' (1691) were written specially for, and played by, the
schoolgirls.
    16km. The D30 leads N. c.10km to the château of *Wideville (off the N307),
built in 1630 for Claude de Bullion (1580–1640), able minister and friend of
Richelieu, containing interesting paintings, and a fine fresco by *Simon Vouet*.

5km. **Pontchartrain**, with a château built by *Fr. Mansart* for the
Phelypeaux family, the last member of which, better known as the
Comte de Maurepàs (1701–81), was a minister under both Louis XV
and XVI. A later resident was the Marquise de Païva (see
p207).—Just to the S., at *Jouars*, is a church with a 13C choir and 18C
nave.

At 2km the N191 leads N. to (13km) *Maule,* with a late 11–12C church with a Renaissance tower. There is a curious *Musée du Velocipède* 1km N., with c.200 examples dating from the 17C to 1925.

At 1km the N191 leads 3·5km S. to crossroads.—At *Bazoches-sur-Guyonne* (1km E.) the church has a Romanesque portal and 12C tower.—There is a 17C château at *La Tremblaye-sur-Mauldre,* just beyond.—S. of these crossroads lies *Les Mesnuls,* with a fine château built in 1530. and altered by Marshal Villars (adm. by appointment).—3km N.W. (and also approached direct from the N12 at 4km) lies **Montfort-l'Amaury,** the ancient seat of the medieval counts of Montfort, notable among whom were Simon IV (d.1218), leader of the Albigensian Crusade, and Simon V (?1208–65), Earl of Leicester. It is now a fashionable week-end retreat.

The church of *St-Pierre,* with an attractive S. doorway, and containing some remarkable 16C *Stained-glass,* and elaborate roof-bosses, was rebuilt by Anne of Brittany (Countess of Montfort) at the end of the 15C, but was not completed until the 17C. A fragment of its Romanesque predecessor survives on the N. side of the nave.

A short distance N.W. is the *Old Cemetery,* preserving a 15C gateway and three galleries (16–17C). The Rue St-Laurent leads uphill to the *Porte Bardoul,* the most conspicuous section of the town walls, overlooked by ruins of the castle (10th and 15C). Nearby is the *Villa de Belvédère,* home of Maurice Ravel (1875–1937) from 1921, and containing mementoes of the composer. There are a number of old houses in the lower town.

From Montfort-l'Amaury, the D138 leads through part of the FORÊT DE RAMBOUILLET to (17km.) *Rambouillet,* see Rte 33B, viâ (7km) *St-Léger-en-Yvelines,* with a 12C church, passing (l., after 5km) the *Étangs de Hollande,* a series of artificial lakes created by order of Louis XIV.
The forest area is covered on IGN 402.

17km Houdan preserves a 12C keep flanked by four turrets, all that remains of the castle of the Montforts, a handsome 15–16C church with an impressive apse, and a number of old houses in the Rue Ernest-Chapelier. Houdan is also known for its breed of poultry and its pâtés.—*Dreux,* see below, lies 21km W.

At *Richebourg,* 5km N.E., is a 15C church retaining 16C glass; 8·5km beyond lies *Montchauvet,* an attractively situated fortified village.

An interesting DETOUR VIÂ ANET AND IVRY may be made by driving N.W. on the D933.—17km **Anet,** a village famous for its *Château* built by Henri II for his mistress Diane de Poitiers in 1548–55. *Philibert Delorme* was the architect, and the decoration was entrusted to *Jean Goujon, Germain Pilon,* and *Benvenuto Cellini.*

The building later passed to the Duchesse du Maine, visited there by Mme du Deffand, Mme du Châtelet, Fontenelle, and Voltaire, but was sold at the Revolution, and the greater part was demolished in 1804–11. The entrance gate, W. wing, and chapel survive. The original central façade has been re-erected in the courtyard of the École des Beaux-Arts in Paris, see Rte 5. The first performance of Lully's last work, 'Acis et Galatée' (1686), took place here.

The main entrance in the form of a triumphal arch, is adorned with a replica of *Cellini's* Nymph of Fontainebleau (the original of which is in the Louvre), above which is a clock surmounted by a sculptured stag-hunt. Beyond it is what is left of the château, with a vestibule and staircase added by the Duc de Vendôme in the 17C, and panelled rooms containing tapestries, portraits, old furniture, and mementoes of Diane.

The *Chapel*, on the plan of a Greek cross, with a central cupola, contains sculptured reliefs by *Goujon*. The tomb of Diane was rifled in 1795, but her body was rescued and buried outside the E. end of the parish church (which dates from the 13th and 16C).

Just E. of the château, a lane skirts the river Eure, which we shortly cross to **Ivry-la-Bataille**, where a 12C doorway is the sole remnant of an abbey of which the architect Philibert Delorme (1515–70) was titular abbot. A doorway of the 14–16C parish church is ascribed to him. Ivry owes its name to the decisive victory which Henri IV won over the forces of the Ligue led by the Duc de Mayenne in 1590.

Hence the D836 leads N. to (17km) *Pacy-sur-Eure*, see Rte 35.

The direct road FROM IVRY TO DREUX (D928; 18·5km) is reached by recrossing the river to *Ézy-sur-Eure*, thence driving S. through the FORÊT DE DREUX. An alternative route is that running parallel to the river through (11km from *Anet*) *Marcilly-sur-Eure*, shortly beyond which, in the grounds of a château near the river, stands the nave of the abbey church of *Le Breuil-Benoît* (1137).—5km *St-Georges-Motel*, where the 12C church contains fragments of a Tree of Jesse in 16C stained-glass.

Passing (l.) *Montreuil*; with an 11–15C church, we shortly enter **DREUX** (33,800 *Drouais*), once an attractive old town, but retaining few vestiges of its historic past.

Capital of the Gallic tribe of the Durocasses, it was in the Middle Ages the headquarters of a powerful line of counts, and although the county passed to Charles V in 1378, it was not formally united to the French crown until 1556. Henry V occupied the town in 1421. The 'Journée de Dreux' (1562), one of the bloodiest battles in the Religious Wars, was fought in the plain between the Blaise and the Eure, when Montmorency and Guise defeated the Huguenots under Louis de Condé. The fortifications were dismantled by Henri IV in 1593, after a stubborn siege. The place passed by marriage in the 18C into the hands of the Orléans branch of the Bourbons, who built there their mausoleum.

Among natives were the Métezeau family of architects: Clément (1479–1535), Thibault (1533–1600), Louis (1559–1615), and Clément (1581–1652); Antoine Godeau (1605–72), Bp of Vence, and one of the original members of the Académie Française; Jean Rotrou (1609–50), the poet; and Danican Philidor (1726–95), the composer and chess-player.

On the N. side of the PL. MÉTEZEAU, in the centre of old Dreux, in a loop of the river Blaise, stands **St-Pierre** (13–17C), much of which is the work of the Métezeau family. It was considerably damaged in the Revolution. The earliest part of the church is the N. transept, with the piers in the choir and in the aisles of the nave. The fine but mutilated W. doorway (1524) is flanked by two 16C towers, that on the r. remaining unfinished. The 15C nave contains contemporary glass in the first window on the l., and a carved Romanesque capital serving as a stoup by the first pier (r.). There is noteworthy glass in the *Lady Chapel* (15C) and in several of the aisle-chapels (16C). The fine organ-case (1614) in the 17C S. transept was carved by *Toussaint Fortier* of Dreux.

There is a small *Museum* of local antiquities housed in a chapel a short distance S. of the main square.

On the W. side of the square, facing down the Grande Rue, stands the sturdy Renaissance *****Beffroi** (1512–37), with two elegant turrets and windows with stone mullions.

Beyond the far end of the Grande Rue rises a hill surmounted by remains of a keep and other fortifications, and the Orléans mausoleum. This may be approached by car by circling to the W. of the hill, and immediately climbing to the r.; on foot, it may be reached by turning r. into the Rue Parisis (towards the far end of the Grande Rue) and taking the first lane on the l. A steep flight of steps ascends to the summit (views).

The **Chapelle Royale St-Louis** was begun in 1816 by the Dowager Duchess of Orléans and enlarged and completed by her son, Louis-Philippe, in his usual decadent taste. It is a pseudo-Gothic domed apsidal building, and is lavishly adorned with sculptures and stained-glass (those in the nave, dome, and lower crypt being executed at Sèvres after designs by *Larivière*). Those depicting saints, round the choir, are from cartoons by *Ingres*, and include portraits of Louis-Philippe as St Louis, Queen Marie-Amélie as St Amelia, and the Duc d'Orléans as St Ferdinand, etc.

In the *Upper Crypt* lies the tomb of Louis-Philippe (1773–1850) and his wife, whose remains were transferred here in 1876 from Weybridge, their home in exile in England.

Beyond the adjacent tomb of Ferdinand d'Orléans is that of his wife, Hélène of Mecklenburg-Schwerin (1814–58), placed in a separate chapel, because she was a Protestant. Among the funerary sculpture on the ostentatious tombs of this illustrious family are examples of the work of *Chapu, Walhain, Pradier* (of Mlle de Montpensier), and Princess *Marie d'Orléans* (d.1839).

Argentan lies 112km W. of Dreux viâ the N12 and N26; *Alençon* 100km S.W. on the N12; and *Nogent-le-Rotrou* (for *Le Mans*) 56km S.W. on the D928; see *Blue Guide France*.

FROM DREUX TO ÉVREUX (42km). We follow the N12 W. towards (13km) *Nonancourt* (bypassed), where we diverge r. onto the N154, after passing (10km, l.) *St-Remy-sur-Avre*, with a 12th and 16C church. The road beyond crosses a flat plain before descending into the valley of the Iton at *Évreux*, see Rte 35.

Nonancourt grew up around a castle built in 1113 by Henry I of England, where in 1189 was signed a treaty between Philippe Auguste and Richard Coeur-de-Lion determining their share in the Third Crusade. Henri IV slept at Nonancourt the night before the Battle of Ivry (see above). Here, in Nov. 1715, the local postmistress saved the life of James Francis Edward, the 'Old Pretender', who would otherwise have been assassinated by hirelings of the Earl of Mar, as described by Saint-Simon (whose home at *La Ferté-Vidame* lay 31km S.W.).

The church (1511) contains some good stained-glass, and an organ-loft, both of the 16C, and a 14C stone Virgin.

The direct road (N154) leads 32km S. from DREUX TO CHARTRES, see Rte 33A, in reverse; a more attractive road (D929) follows the valley of the Eure viâ (11·5km) *Villemeux-sur-Eure*, w:th a Romanesque church altered in the 16C, with a rose-window.—17km. **Nogent-le-Roi**, an old fortified town retaining some 16C houses, with a Gothic and Renaissance church with an elegant apse. On the opposite bank of the river are remains of the 12C abbey of *Coulombs*.—At 8km we enter *Maintenon*, see Rte 33B, and follow the road thence to *Chartres*.

35   Paris to Évreux

Total distance, 96km (59 miles). A13 to (56km) *Mantes*; at 5km bear l. onto N13.—9km *Pacy-sur-Eure*.—16km *Évreux*.

For the road to Mantes, see Rte 36A, 15km beyond which we leave the A13, and drive due W. to (24km) *Pacy-sur-Eure*, with an interesting church dating from the 12C.

Hence the D836 leads N.W. along the charming valley of the Eure, through (6·5km) *Cocherel*, scene of Du Guesclin's victory over the troops of England and Navarre in 1364, when Jean de Grailly, the 'Captal de Buch', was taken prisoner.—6·5km *Autheuil-Authouillet*. The church in the latter village contains remarkable 18C woodwork, including an elaborately carved priest's chair.—3km beyond, at *La Croix-St-Leufroy*, the moated castle of 1620 is the abbot's lodge of a former abbey, some sculptures and paintings from which are preserved in the church.

16km **ÉVREUX** (48,700 *Ébroïciens*), préfecture of the department of the Eure, stands on three branches of the Iton, the well-rebuilt town centre preserving a cathedral of considerable interest. It is reputed also for its *rillettes, quenelles,* poultry, and cider, etc.

Gallo-Roman *Mediolanum* seems to have occupied a site on the plateau some 5km S.E., but a town existed on the present site in the time of Augustus. A bishopric was founded by St Taurinus in the 4C, and the town walls were built 100 years later. Évreux was burned in 1119 by Henry I, who received permission to do so from the bishop on condition that he rebuilt the cathedral. In 1193 the principal citizens were treacherously massacred by Prince John of England, and in 1365 the town was burned by the Norman governor before its surrender to the king's troops. It was finally united to France in 1404, but in 1418–27 was again in English occupation, having been captured by Thomas, Duke of Exeter. Meanwhile (1427) Charles VII had bestowed the countship of Évreux on Sir Charles Stuart of Darnley, Sieur d'Aubigny (d.1429), commander of his Scottish bodyguard.

Évreux experienced another devastating fire in June 1940, on being bombed by the Germans, which caused extensive damage; Allied air attacks in June 1944 were confined to an area near the station.

Ambroise d'Évreux was a late 12C jongleur, who compiled a metrical history of the third Crusade, in which he had taken part.

The ***Cathedral of Notre-Dame**, many times ruined, rebuilt, and restored between the 12th and 17C (and again since 1940), atones for its lack of unity by presenting in juxtaposition successive phases of medieval and Renaissance architecture.

The main façade is Renaissance (1575–91), with a large portal flanked by towers (one of which was crowned by a cupola and stone lantern until 1940). The rose-window is an unusually late example, dating from c.1591. The N. façade exhibits the richest style of Flamboyant Gothic. The central tower, dating from 1467, had its elegant spire destroyed in 1940.

In the *Nave*, the Romanesque main arcades date from the rebuilding of Henry I, while the upper part is due to a later reconstruction following a fire in 1194. The E. parts of the church are noticeably sumptuous in contrast. The aisles were added in the 14C, but the window-tracery was altered in the 15th and 16C. Some of the aisle chapels preserve fragments of 13C glass. The pulpit (1675), by *Guillaume de la Tremblaye*, was brought from the abbey of Bec.

In the *Transepts* are an open triforium with Flamboyant arches, and good 16C rose-windows. The choir screen is iron-work of the 18C; the stalls date from the 14C, as do the *Stained-glass windows* (well restored), which are among the finest of their period in France. Delicate wooden Renaissance screens separate the transepts from the Ambulatory, where most of the chapels have screens of the same period. The 15C glass in the *Lady Chapel* is remarkable for its fine execution and perfect preservation, and much of the other glass in the ambulatory chapels is equally noteworthy. In the apse is a 15C Virgin and Child. The restored Gothic *Cloister* is entered from the S. transept.

To the S. is the former *Bishop's Palace*, a Flamboyant building of 1481 (considerably restored), now containing the **Museum**.

The collections include prehistoric and Gallo-Roman antiquities, including a bronze statue of Jupiter Stator, and a 4C glass goblet, from *Mediolanum;* two tombstones, one (1317) from the abbey of *Bonport,* and another (1290) from *Chanteloup;* Rouen faïence, etc.; the mitre of Jean de Marigny, Abp of Rouen (1317–57), 13C Limoges enamel crosses, and 14–15C English alabasters. The paintings include portraits by *Ph. de Champaigne* of Angélique Arnauld (Abbess of Port-Royal), and more modern works.

Parts of the old *Town Moat* can be seen from the Gardens behind the cathedral, from the N.W. of which one may follow a pleasant riverside walk, skirted by *Ramparts,* to the graceful Flamboyant *Tour de l'Horloge,* containing a bell of 1406.

The Rue de Verdun leads E. from the cathedral, passing (l.) the *Palais de Justice,* to meet the Rue Joséphine. A short distance further W., to the r., stands **St-Taurin**, the church of a vanished abbey founded in 1026, on the site of the saint's grave. The W. front dates from the mid-18C. Built over a crypt, the interior preserves some Romanesque arches and capitals (N. side), but the general effect is that of a 14C building although parts of the triforium (S. side) are Renaissance work. The beautiful 14C *Choir* contains 16C glass. To the N. of the choir is preserved the magnificent 13C *Shrine of St-Taurinus.*

The château (1676–89) of the Duc de Bouillon, built on the site of a castle of Charles the Bad of Navarre, which stood 2km to the W., was demolished in 1834.

Les Andelys (see Rte 36B) lies 36km N.E. on the N154 and D316 viâ *Gaillon.*

For the route from ÉVREUX TO DREUX, see Rte 34. The N154 leads N. to (51km) *Rouen,* and the N13 to (72km) *Lisieux,* 49km further W. of which lies *Caen;* see *Blue Guide France.*

36 Paris to Les Andelys

A. Viâ Mantes and Vernon

Total distance, 106km (66miles). A13 to (56km) *Mantes.*—N15 24km. *Vernon.*—26km. *Les Andelys.*

From the *Porte d'Auteuil* the A13 drives W., shortly spanning the Seine, and entering the tunnel below St-Cloud.—At 18km the N10 bears l. for *Chartres* and *Dreux,* see Rtes 33A and 34 respectively.

38km **MANTES** (43,600 inhab.), an industrial town, which hardly deserves its sobriquet 'la Jolie'.

It was burned in 1087 by William the Conqueror, whose horse is said to have trodden on a cinder, causing the fall from which the corpulent king died at Rouen. Philippe Auguste died here in 1223, and his heart is buried in the church. Sacked by Edward III in 1346, recaptured by Du Guesclin in 1364, but soon after retaken by the English, Mantes finally passed to France in 1440. Gabrielle d'Estrées, who had a house here (destroyed), was frequently visited by Henri IV. Mme Campan (1752–1822), lady of the Bedchamber to Marie-Antoinette, died at Mantes. The R.A.F. destroyed the main bridge over the Seine here in 1944, but it says much for the accuracy of the bombing that the beautiful collegiate church was left untouched.

Notre-Dame, dating mainly from the 12–13C, resembles Notre-Dame in Paris in style. The 12C façade, with a rose-window, has three fine doorways, that on the S. having an elaborate 14C gable: in the lintel of the N. door is a charmingly naïve Resurrection. The upper part of the N. tower and the gallery between the towers is an addition of 1844, while the apse-chapels and the *Chap. de Navarre* (S.) are of the 14C. The interior is notable for its lightness, for the absence of a transept, and for the remarkable ·CHAP. DE NAVARRE (restored), vaulted from a central pier, and containing four 14C statuettes of queens.

A short distance to the W. is the *Tour St-Maclou* (14–15C), relic of an earlier church.
    E. of Notre-Dame, opposite the ancient bridge (see *Limay*, Rte 36B), survives the 14C *Porte aux Prêtres*, part of the old fortifications.
    Some 1·5km N.W. of the central Pl. A.-Briand, lies the interesting church of *Gassicourt* (restored after damage in 1944), with a late 12C nave and 13C choir and transepts.

We now follow the N13, skirting the Seine, to (6km) **Rosny-sur-Seine**, with the château built by Maximilien de Béthune, Duc de Sully (1559–1641), Henri IV's favourite minister, who was born at Rosny. Henri IV retired here after the Battle of Ivry (see Rte 34), in which Sully was wounded. A later owner was the Duchesse de Berry, who made additions in 1818–26.
    We shortly climb the Corniche de Rolleboise, before descending through *Bonnières-sur-Seine*, where a Neolithic multiple grave has been exposed, near the church.
    Évreux (see Rte 35) lies 32km W., on the N13, off which we bear r. onto the N15 for (24km) **Vernon** (23,500 inhab.), an old town visited by both Bonington and Turner, but much damaged in 1940. It was the first meeting-place of the Estates of Normandy, in 1452. In Aug. 1944 the Allies threw bridges across the Seine here.
    The church of *Notre-Dame*, mainly of the 14–15C, has an elaborate W. front with a good doorway, and a striking rose-window between low balustrades; at the E. end of the lofty nave is an unfinished 13C tower. Within are 16C stained-glass; some Flemish tapestries; a fine 17C tomb; and a 16C sculptured organ-loft. The Choir preserves a Romanesque arcade.
    Adjacent is a half-timbered 15C house; others may be seen in the Rue Potard and Rue Carnot. Beyond the Rue d'Albuféra, leading from the rebuilt bridge, is the bold *Tour des Archives* (1123), attr. to Henry I.
    Giverny, a short distance S., on the far bank of the Seine, may be visited from here: see Rte 36B.

At **Bizy**, on the W. outskirts of the town, is a *Château* (c.1740, by Constant d'Ivry; since remodelled), with extensive stables, and mementoes of Marshal Suchet, where the Duc de Penthièvre died in 1793—Some 4km beyond, *Brécourt* gives its name to a skirmish between the Girondins and Sansculottes (July 1793), known also as the 'Battle without tears', because there were no casualties.

The N15 continues N.W. to (14km) **Gaillon** (5850 inhab.), where Card. Georges d'Amboise, the art-loving Bp of Rouen, erected a sumptuous château (1500–10), in the building and embellishment of which many Renaissance masters took part. This was destroyed in 1798, except for the entrance gateway and the lower part of the N. wall. Near the church, with 16–17C statues, is a fine 16C half-timbered house.

Évreux lies 24km S.W.; see Rte 35; *Les Andelys* (see Rte 36B), 12km N.E.; and *Rouen* 42km N.W.; see *Blue Guide France.*

B. Viâ Poissy, Meulan, La Roche-Guyon, and Château-Gaillard

Total distance, 106km (66 miles). N190 to (28km) *Poissy.*—14km. *Meulan.*—14km. *Limay (Mantes).*—15km. *La Roche-Guyon.*—13km. *Vernonnet.*—22km. *Les Andelys.*

From the *Porte Maillot,* we follow the N190 W. to (20·5km) *St-Germain-en-Laye,* see Rte 22.

Hence the N184 leads N. through the FORÊT DE ST-GERMAIN to (10·5km) **Conflans-Ste-Honorine** (29,000 inhab.) dominated by the ruins of a Romanesque keep, at the confluence of the Oise and the Seine, and a river-port since the 9C. The pseudo-Renaissance château houses a *Museum of the Inland Waterways,* with models of lighters, barges, etc. The church of *St-Maclou* is of the 12–16C.—*Pontoise* (see Rte 37) lies 8·5km to the N.—The church of *Andrésy* (2·5km S.W.) contains good 16C glass.

The N190 leads N.W. from St-Germain to (7·5km) **POISSY** (36,600 *Pinciaçais*), a favourite residence of St Louis and once the scene of an important cattle market. The modern bridge spanning the river replaces one of the 13C almost destroyed during the last war. A few arches remain of the *Dominican Abbey,* in the refectory of which, in 1561, took place the fruitless conference of Poissy between Protestants and Catholics, their respective protagonists being Théodore de Bèze and Card. Lorraine. At No.2 Enclos de l'Abbaye is a *Musée du Jouet,* devoted to toys, dolls, etc. from the 18C to the present.

Notre-Dame (1130–40, with later additions) retains two fine Romanesque towers, and three ambulatory chapels, two of which take the place of transepts. The Font of St Louis is somewhat worn, owing to the popular belief that its scrapings swallowed in a glass of water would cure a fever.

6km. *Triel-sur-Seine* has a 13–15C church, the choir of which is built above a street, containing good Renaissance glass.

There is a 12C church at *Vernouillet,* on the opposite bank of the Seine, with a Romanesque belfry; 2·5km S. of which, at *Médan,* was Zola's country house from 1877 until his death in 1902.

8km **Meulan** (8900 inhab.), an ancient town, with slight remains of a castle, and the church of *St-Nicolas,* with a 12C choir.—4km N.W., at *Gaillon-sur-Montcient,* is a 12–13C church with an octagonal stone spire.

Hence we follow the N. bank of the Seine through (5km) *Juziers,* with a fine late-12C apsed church, to (9km) **Limay,** also with an interesting 12–13C church with a graceful steeple, and rich in works of art. The composer Ernest Chausson (1855–99) was killed here in a bicycle accident, near his country villa.

Mantes, see Rte 36A, lies on the opposite bank of the Seine. The ancient bridge crossing to the *Île aux Dames* was partly destroyed by the French in 1940.

From *Limay,* the D147 leads N.W. to (6km) *St-Martin-la-Garenne,* with an interesting church with a 12C choir, a rebuilt tower, and fine

Renaissance façade.—**Vetheuil**, 3km beyond, was Monet's home in 1878–81. The church (12–16C) has a remarkable early Gothic choir, and an attractive Renaissance façade.—We pass troglodyte dwellings at *Haute-Isle*.

9km **La Roche-Guyon**, with the château of the La Rochefoucauld family, and where the author of the 'Maximes' (1665 and later editions) wrote a large part of his work. The keep, a remarkable example of military architecture, was built in the 10C by a baron named Guy. It was Rommel's H.Q. during part of the Battle of Normandy (1944). In the church is the tomb of François de Sillery, Duc de La Roche-Guyon (d.1627).

Beyond La Roche-Guyon, the D313 climbs steeply, off which (r.) runs the 'Route des Crêtes', with extensive views.—We descend to (3km) *Gasny*.—6·5km N.E. lies *Bray-et-Lû*, see Rte 36C.

6km S.W. lies **Giverny**, the residence, from 1883, of Claude Monet (1840–1926), who died there, and is buried near the Romanesque apse of the church. The *Gardens*, re-designed in the French style, with their lily-ponds, may be visited in the Spring and Summer. The house contains Monet's collection of Japanese prints, but none of his own paintings.

Hence we follow the D313 W. to (10km) *Vernonnet*, the N. suburb of *Vernon* (see Rte 36A), with the château *des Tourelles*, a 12C keep, and fragments of an ancient bridge.

11·5km N., off the D181, are the villages of *Tourny*, and beyond, *Fontenay*, the former with an interesting 13th and 16C church. The lane joining them passes near the famous avenue of the château of *Beauregard*.

The D313 continues to skirt the Seine, with the FORÊTS DE VERNON, and DES ANDELYS, to the r., to (22km) **Le Petit-Andely**.

The lesser of the twin towns of **Les Andelys** (8200 *Andelysiens*) came into existence as a bridgehead below the fortress of Château-Gaillard. *St-Sauveur* dates from 1197, while the domed *Hospice St-Jacques* was rebuilt by the Duc de Penthièvre in 1785.

Évreux (see Rte 35) lies 36km S.W., beyond *Gaillon*, and reached by the D316.

Le Grand-Andely was partially destroyed in the air attacks of 1940, but some half-timbered houses survive to the W. of the central PL. POUSSIN, near the *Tour de la Madeleine*.

To the N.E. stands 13C *Notre-Dame* (restored), with additions of the 15–16C. Within are good stained-glass (16C), an Entombment (16C), and a carved Renaissance organ; also, in the Renaissance N. transept, several paintings by *Quentin Varin*, Poussin's first master. Thomas Corneille (1625–1709), younger brother of Pierre, died here. Nicolas Poussin (1594–1665) was born in the hamlet of *Villers-sur-Andelys*, 1·5km S.

Opposite the church, a lane leads S. Turning l. across the bridge, we climb steeply, bearing r. at the next crossroad, and shortly reach a viewpoint overlooking the impressive ruins of *****Château-Gaillard**, and the Seine beyond.

This fortress was built on the chalk cliffs above the river by Richard Coeur-de-Lion in 1196, when the loss of Gisors left the frontier of Normandy undefended. Only eight years later this 'saucy' castle was starved into surrender by Philippe Auguste, after a six-month siege. In 1314 Marguerite of Burgundy and her sister Blanche, the frail wives of Louis X and Charles IV, were immured here, where the former was strangled on her husband's orders. In 1334 the castle afforded asylum to David II of Scotland, who had fled before

Edward III. In 1603 it was dismantled by order of Henri IV.

The ruins of this remarkable and picturesque example of military architecture, include two main enceintes, of which the outer has almost disappeared, the keep, and a southern outwork or châtelet.—The lane descends steeply to *Le Petit-Andely*.

C. Viâ Magny-en-Vexin

Total distance, 89km (55 miles). For the road to (33km) *Pontoise*, see Rte 37.—26km. *Magny-en-Vexin*.—30km. *Le Grand-Andely*.

At Pontoise we bear l., continuing on the N14 to (13km, l.) *Vigny*, with a Renaissance château built by Card. Georges d'Amboise, retaining pepper-pot towers.

6km *Guiry-en-Vexin* (1·5km, l.) has a 17C château attr. to *François Mansart*; a church containing good 14–16C sculpture; and a small archaelogical museum devoted to the Vexin.—2·5km. *Cléry-en-Vexin* has an early 13C church altered in the 16C, with a Flamboyant Gothic portal and nave.

4·5km **Magny-en-Vexin**. We pass, on entering, two 18C pillars on the site of medieval gates. To the N. of the centre, preserving a number of old houses, is *St-Martin*, rebuilt in the early 16C (its predecessor being burned by the English in 1436), containing notable monuments, a 14C stone Virgin, and a curious Font of 1534.

There is an interesting late-13C church with a double portal (16C) at *Genainville*, 4km S.—6km S.W. at *Villarceaux*, are two châteaux: one of 1737; the other, 15C, where Ninon de Lenclos lived with Louis de Mornay.

Ambleville, with a restored 16–18C château, and *Bray-et-Lû*, with the ruined château of *Beaudemont*, lie 7km and 10km respectively W. of Magny.—At *Ecos* (4km N.W. of Bray) there is a group in high-relief of c. 1400 in the church.—Hence the N14 may be regained viâ *Aveny* (4km E.), with a 15C bridge, *Berthenonville*, with a charmingly situated old church, and *Château-sur-Epte*, with remains of a keep of c. 1087.

2km N.W. of Magny, to the r. of the N14, the church of *St-Gervais* is of the 12–13C, with a Renaissance façade of 1550, 1·5km N. of which is the château of *Alincourt*, a cluster of buildings dating from the 14th to the 17C.—*Parnes*, beyond, retains a Romanesque church altered in the 15C, with a Flamboyant porch and preserving some of its original floor tiles.

At (10km) *St-Clair-sur-Epte* a treaty in 912 between Rollo and Charles le Simple established the river as the boundary of the Duchy of Normandy.—1·5km (r.). *Guerny* retains good sculpture in its church.

7km beyond St-Clair, after passing through *Les Thilliers-en-Vexin*, we turn off the N14 onto the D125, at 13km entering *Le Grand-Andely*, see Rte 36B.

Rouen lies 44km N.W. on the N14; see *Blue Guide France*.—To the r. of N14, 3km beyond the junction with D125, is *Hacqueville*, birthplace of Marc Isambard Brunel (1769–1849), the engineer, who received his early education at Gisors.

37 Paris to Pontoise and Gisors

Total distance, 79km (49 miles). N14 to (33km) *Pontoise*; D915 to
(46km) *Gisors*.

Both the N14 (from the *Porte de Clignancourt*) and the N309 (from
the *Porte d'Asnières*) converge c. 16km N.W. of central Paris. An
alternative route (apart from the uncompleted A15 autoroute), is the
N192, leading N.W. from *La Défense*, which meets the N14 some
5·5km further N.W.

A short distance E. of the former junction *Enghien-les-Bains* lies, on the bank of
a small lake, which as the nearest watering-place (sulphur-baths) to Paris, once
enjoyed a certain vogue, and preserves a casino.

5km N.E. of the second intersection, at *Taverny*, is a noteworthy
13–14C church, restored by Viollet-le-Duc, with a fine Renaissance
stone altarpiece.

Between the N309 and N192, on the N. bank of the Seine, lies **Argenteuil**
(96,050 inhab.), often painted by the Impressionists, and where Braque
(1882–1963) was born.—*Cormeilles-en-Parisis*, adjoining to the N.W., was the
birthplace of Louis Daguerre (1787–1851). The church here has a Romanesque
nave and Gothic and Renaissance choir. Adjacent *La Frette*, and *Herblay*, to the
W. have early churches, the latter with good 16C glass.

17km **PONTOISE** (29,400 *Pontoisiens*), also bypassed, now part of
the conurbation of *Cergy-Pontoise* and préfecture of the department
of Val-d'Oise, was the ancient capital of the VEXIN FRANÇAIS and
birthplace of Philippe le Hardi, Duke of Burgundy.

Of its fortifications, which guarded the river-crossing, nothing remains but the
shell of a castle, dismantled in 1742. In the snowy winter of 1437 these were
stormed by Talbot's English troops who, clad in white, approached the walls
unnoticed.
    Pontoise was the birthplace of Pierre Lemercier (d.1570), and his grandson
Jacques Lemercier (c. 1585–1645), and Fontaine (1762–1853), all architects;
Camille Pissarro spent the years 1872–84 at Pontoise, moving hence to *Eragny*
on the opposite bank of the river, where he lived until 1903; but see also
Eragny-sur-Epte, below.

In the older town, to the N.W. of the bridge, in the Pl. du Grand
Martroy, stands **St-Maclou**, with a 15–16C façade, a single tower
(1547), and three portals, two late Gothic, that on the S. of the
Renaissance. The choir and transepts date from 1140–65; the nave is
of the 16C, with two 15C W. bays. The N. arcade and N. aisle (1525),
with three windows of contemporary glass, have interesting capitals.
The N.W. chapel contains a fine Entombment (c.1550), with an 18C
group surmounting it, and two stained-glass windows of 1545. The
Renaissance work in the church is due to *Pierre Lemercier* and his
son *Nicolas* (1541–1637).
    A short distance to the E. is the *Hôtel de Ville*, accommodated in
what was part of a Franciscan convent, altered in the 19C. A Museum
of local interest is housed in a nearby mansion of 1477–83, while at
No.17 Rue du Château is a small museum mainly devoted to Camille
Pissarro.

To the S.W., in the lower town, is late-16C *Notre-Dame*, with an early 13C
Virgin, and the tomb of St Gautier, founder of the 11C abbey of St-Martin-de-
Pontoise.

St-Ouen, on the E. bank, is partly Romanesque, N. of which are the ruins of the Cistercian abbey of **Maubuisson** (cons. 1244), founded by Blanche of Castile, who died there in 1251, with the remains of a 13C chapter-house, refectory, and tithe-barn.

The abbey was notorious for the amorous exploits of Marguerite of Burgundy and her sister Blanche, and later for those of Angélique d'Estrées (sister of Gabrielle), who was appointed abbess by Henri IV, but whose conduct was such that she had to be forcibly removed by Louis XIII; her successor, Angélique Arnauld (1618–25), introduced the austere morals of Port-Royal.

Cergy itself, described as 'a pleasant village' in a previous edition of this Guide, but no longer so, retains a 13C church with a Renaissance doorway opening on the site of its vanished nave.—*Jouy-le-Moutier*, further S.W., has an interesting church; that at *Ennery*, 3·5km N. of Pontoise, of the 12–13C, has additions by the *Lemerciers*.

9·5km. *Cormeilles-en-Vexin* has a curious church with a Romanesque nave and Gothic and Renaissance choir.—4·5km *Marines* is an old town with a château that belonged to Sillery, chancellor of Henri IV, and an elegant Renaissance church porch.

4km. *Chars* has a church with a Romanesque nave, 12C rose-window, a striking late-12C choir, and Renaissance tower.—*Santeuil* (4·5km S.) has a Romanesque church with a 13C nave.

3·5km. The church at *Lavilletertre* (3km N.E.) preserves interesting Romanesque capitals.—At *Nucourt* (5km S.W.) the church (12C; altered in the 16C), with a fine stone altarpiece, stands a short distance N.W. of the village. Nucourt was a site for the assembly of VI rockets in 1944.—*Magny-en-Vexin*, see Rte 36C, lies 5·5km further W.—*Serans* (4km N. of Nucourt) has a Gothic church with a Flamboyant façade and Romanesque tower.

7·5km. *Montjavoult*, 3·5km W. (views), has a Renaissance church with a portal similar in style to St-Gervais at Gisors.

7km **GISORS** (8900 inhab.), the former capital of the VEXIN NORMAND, a territory long contested by English and French, suffered severely during the German invasion of 1940 (and again in 1944), when the Hôtel de Ville and museum were burnt out, and many of its timbered houses destroyed.

The Duc de la Rochefoucauld, cousin of the Duc de Liancourt, was brutally murdered at Gisors in 1792. The quality of its food has the flavour of Normandy, particularly the *pâtés de lapins truffés*.

The imposing church of *St-Gervais-St-Protais* (13–16C) presents a succession of styles. The 16C S.W. tower remains incomplete. The sculptured W. porch (1537–62) and its carved doorways were badly burnt. The Renaissance work is by *Robert* (fl. 1518–48) and *Jean Grappin* (fl. 1537–98). The side portals are Gothic; the N. doorway, the more elaborate, was also the worst damaged. The nave, seriously injured by fire, has been restored; the mural painting of the Bearing of the Cross (1561) in the N. aisle, and the large Tree of Jesse (16C) in the S. aisle, have been saved. In the ambulatory of the Gothic choir (1240) are a series of 16C painted panels depicting the legend of SS Gervase and Protase, and the Life of Christ; also two stained-glass windows of the 17C.

Slightly to the N., the *Passage du Monarque* is prolonged to the postern gate of the *Castle*, the extensive ruins of which dominate the town.

This famous fortress, begun in 1097 by William Rufus, being an outpost of Normandy towards the Île de France, was for a hundred years an object of strife between the two countries, until by the Treaty of Louviers (1196) Richard Coeur-de-Lion ceded it to Philippe Auguste. Richard then hastened to compensate his loss by erecting *Château-Gaillard*, see Rte 36B.

The 12C keep, with an octagonal staircase-turret added in the 15C, rises from a mound in the centre of the enceinte, which retains 12 towers overlooking the double fosse, and enclosing a public garden. The *Keep* and the cylindrical *Tour du Prisonnier* (29m high), built by Philippe Auguste, with three vaulted storeys and a dungeon, may be visited.

The D181 leads S.W. from Gisors towards (31km) *Les Andelys* (see Rte 36B) passing (3km, r.) *Neaufles-St-Martin*, with ruins of a keep built by Henry II (1182), (5km) *Dangu*, with good sculpture in its church, and (4km) *Vesly*, with 14th and 16C statues in its church, a feature of the district.

3km N. of Gisors, at *Bazincourt*, adjoining *Eragny-sur-Epte*, lived Camille Pissarro and his son Lucien; the latter village giving its name to the Eragny Press (London, 1894–1914).—The D915 continues N. to (22km) *Gournay-en-Bray*; see *Blue Guide France*.

FROM GISORS TO BEAUVAIS (32km). The D981 leads N.E., passing (4km) **Trie-Château**, its church with a restored Romanesque façade and early-13C choir. A round tower remains of the medieval castle (11C) on which site the 17C château was built. Here in 1767 Rousseau, when a guest of the Prince de Conti, finished writing his 'Confessions'. The tiny *Hôtel de Ville* preserves two Romanesque windows.—Just beyond, the D923 leads 4km S.E. to *Chaumont-en-Vexin*, with slight remains of the castle which once commanded the town, and with a Gothic church (1417–16C), with a fine Renaissance tower and N. doorway, by *Robert Grappin*, combining Gothic and Renaissance motives, and a charming choir.

For *Beauvais*, see Rte 38.

38 Paris to Beauvais

Total distance, 76km (47 miles). N1. (35·5km. *Beaumont-sur-Oise* lies 3km N.E.).—40·5km. *Beauvais*.

We follow the N1 N. from the *Porte de la Chapelle* through or by-passing *St-Denis* (see Rte 23).

At 17km, shortly after the N16 to Chantilly forks r. (see Rte 24), the D125 leads W. towards (2·5km) **Montmorency**, now a hilltop outer suburb of Paris which retains few relics of its fashionable past, with its elegant villas, its 'cherries, pears, and its donkey-rides'. We pass (l.) the site of the *Ermitage*, where in 1756 Rousseau began his 'Nouvelle Héloïse'; the composer Grétry died in the Ermitage in 1813.

After his rupture with Mme d'Épinay (1726–83), Rousseau moved to *Montluis* (a short distance S.W., approached viâ the Rue de Grétry and its continuation), where he wrote the 'Lettre à D'Alembert', 'Émile', and 'Du Contrat Social' (1762). A small museum here is devoted to Rousseau who, fearing arrest, took refuge in Switzerland in 1762.

Further S.W. stands the 16C church of *St-Martin*, situated on a terrace (views). The stained glass, representing members of the Montmorency and Coligny-Châtillon families, most famous of whom was Anne de Montmorency (1493–1567), for whom the dukedom was created, has been drastically restored. Note also the memorials to Polish refugees, who congregated in Montmorency in the 19C. The painter Le Brun had a château near here, demolished in 1814.—At *Deuil*, further S., at the foot of the hill, is an 11–12C church with an elegant choir, almost completely restored after war damage.

3·5km (l.). *Domont*, adjacent to the extensive FORÊT DE MONTMORENCY, stretching to the N.W., has an interesting church preserving a fine 12C apse. The

Van Gogh's painting of the apse of the church at Auvers

forest area, and that of the adjacent *Forêt de L'Isle-Adam*, are covered on IGN 418.

5km. At *Belloy-en-France* (6km N.E. off the D909) is a 14–16C church with an impressive Renaissance portal, and elegant vaulting. The road continues N. to (5km) *Royaumont*, see Rte 24.

2km (l.). *Maffliers* has a church with a choir rebuilt in 1643 by *Philibert Delorme*.
    At 4·5km we reach a crossroad.

6km S.W. (off the D9) are the ruins of the Cistercian *Abbaye du Val*, founded in 1136, but largely demolished after 1845.—The D64 leads 4·5km W. through the FÔRET DE L'ISLE-ADAM to **L'Isle-Adam** (9500 inhab.), where the Renaissance church of *St-Martin*, with a façade attrib. to *Jean Bullant* (damaged in 1940), contains a carved wood pulpit (German: 1560), stalls with quaint misericords (late-15C), and a tomb of the Prince of Conti (1717–76); the 15C carved retable was stolen in 1974.
    1·5km N.E. is a *Pavillon chinois* of 1778.
    4·5km S., on the far side of the Oise, lies **Auvers** (with a 12–16C church), a riverside village much painted by Corot, Daumier, Daubigny (who died there in 1878), Pissarro, Cézanne, etc. Dr Gachet (see p 115) lived here, and his most famous patient, Van Gogh, who died in the Café Ravoux (1890; now called 'Chez Van Gogh'), is buried in the cemetery.
    At *Méry*, on the opposite bank of the river, is a fine *Château*

The South transept of Beauvais Cathedral

(16–18C), built on the site of an earlier monastery, containing some interesting works of art.

Nesles-la-Vallée, 4km N.W. of L'Isle-Adam, has a 12C church, with a Romanesque belfry, curious vaulting, and three Virgins (13C and later).—*Champagne-sur-Oise* (3km N.E. on the W. bank of the river) retains a 13C church (restored by Viollet-le-Duc).

2km N. of the above mentioned crossroads (on the N1) lies *Presles*, where the church preserves some curious misericords.—3km beyond, passing (r.) *Nointel*, whose 17–18C château, once belonging to Prince Murat, had famous gardens, lies **Beaumont-sur-Oise** (8300 inhab.). Its ancient castle, guarding the river-crossing, was dismantled in 1422. The view from the ramparts is now largely of factories. The late-Transitional church of *St-Laurent*, with good capitals, and a Renaissance tower, is of interest.—The N1 may be regained 6km N.W., beyond *Chambly*, with a fine 13–14C church containing 16C paintings and a Flemish altarpiece. Immediately N. of Chambly, the D923 leads N.W. to (11km) *Méru*, with a 12–16C church; another interesting example of the 12–13C may be visited at *St-Crépin-Ibouvillers*, 5km beyond.

4km The N1 crosses the Oise and by-passes (r.) *Chambly* (see above).

17km *Noailles*, formerly *Longvilliers*, which assumed the name of the ducal family of Noailles in the 17C.—The villages of *Tillard* and *Silly*, not far W. preserve curious churches.—11km (l.). *Allonne* has an interesting 13–16C church.

4km **BEAUVAIS** (54,100 inhab.), préfecture of the department of the Oise, is very largely a new town, the centre having been almost totally burnt out by German incendiary bombardment in June 1940, which also destroyed the buildings of the famous tapestry factory; miraculously, the cathedral was virtually untouched. The town is also known for its *patisserie, quiches, fruits confits, saucissons chauds*, and *'côte de veau bellovaque'*.

The *Bratuspantium* mentioned by Caesar occupied a site in this neighbourhood, and after its destruction or abandonment, Beauvais became the capital of the Bellovaci, from whom it took its name. In the 9C it became a countship (Beauvaisis), and was later controlled by its worldly bishops, peers of France, who were frequently at odds with the townspeople. In 1358 it was a centre of the 'Jacquerie' or peasants' revolt.

In 1472 Beauvais withstood a siege by Charles the Bold, Jeanne Laisné ('Jeanne Hachette') leading the women to its defence. In 1664 Colbert founded the Tapestry Factory. The town was bombed in 1918, the damage being slight compared with the holocaust of 1940, when 2000 houses disappeared, 75 of which, mostly of the 15–16C, were classified as Historic Monuments. Pierre Cauchon (d. 1442), Joan of Arc's accuser and judge, was Bp of Beauvais.

Dominating the centre of the town by its great height, somewhat like a stranded whale, rises the ****Cathedral of St-Pierre**, which, had it been completed on the original scale, would have been the largest Gothic cathedral in the world; its choir and transepts alone form one of the most ambitious masterpieces of medieval architecture, although reflecting more the hauteur than the humility of the church. The bishop of Beauvais was condemned in 1789 as being a 'proud fool' by Arthur Young, for when attending a meeting of the society of agriculture, 'where common farmers were admitted to dine with people of the first rank', he 'made difficulties of sitting down in such company'.

The foundations were laid in 1227, and work continued until 1578. The inordinate boldness of the ground plan, with infrequent pillars and weak buttresses, made the building peculiarly vulnerable, and twice the roof caved in (1247 and 1284), and the tower erected above the crossing in 1550 by *Jean Vast*, together with its spire (153m high), collapsed in 1573. *Martin Cambiges* (1500–48) and then *Michel Lalye* (after 1532) worked on the transepts; the former built the N. portal at the expense of François I (whose salamander emblem and unfinished genealogical tree may be seen in the interior), while to the latter is due the S. portal.

EXTERIOR. The transepts end in superb Gothic façades; the S., framed by two highly decorative turrets, is approached by a flight of fourteen steps. Its portal, denuded of statues, is surmounted by a double open gallery, a rose-window, and pediment; the Renaissance doors of carved oak (mutilated) are by *Jean le Pot*. Those of the N. portal, in perfect preservation, are also by Le Pot. The W. end is somewhat abruptly and inelegantly finished by a covering of slate.

INTERIOR. The unfinished cathedral is 72·50m long and 48·20m high. The *Choir* itself is 36·60m in length, its vaulting supported by twelve double flying buttresses. Above the seven ambulatory chapels and the rectangular choir chapels are a blind triforium and a series of windows. The main triforium is glazed. The glass in the galleries of the S. transept is ascribed to *Nicolas Le Prince*. The rose-window dates from 1551. Note also the window depicting St Peter and St Paul

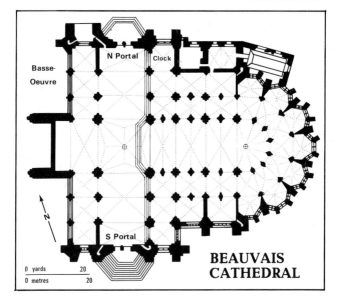

**BEAUVAIS
CATHEDRAL**

in the *Chap. des Morts*, and one devoted to St Hubert.

The gallery windows in the N. transept represent the sibyls, by *Jean Le Prince*. In the rose-window are figures of the sun and of a flame-coloured seraphim. In the *Chap. du Sacré-Coeur* (l.) are windows by *Eugrand Le Prince* (1522). To the r. of the N. portal is the famous *Astronomical Clock*, constructed in 1865–68 by a local horologist, with 52 dials, etc. Various figures perform evolutions at each hour; that of the Last Judgment working only at noon.

Ambulatory. The 4th, 6th, and 8th chapels retain some 13C glass (restored). The *Organ* (1530) is under restoration, and will be moved from its present position.

From the W. end of the cathedral (or *Haute-Oeuvre*) we may enter the so-called *Basse-Oeuvre*, in the place of the nave, and dating from 997 (one of the very few churches extant in France prior to the 11C), which served as the cathedral until the 13C. Here also is the restored *Cloister*.

The magnificent series of *Beauvais Tapestries** have been placed in the new *Galerie Nationale de La Tapisserie* (CN) , Rue St-Pierre (closed Mon.), immediately to the E., abutting the remains of the Gallo-Roman walls, where it is hoped they will be more secure than in the cathedral choir, from which five were mysteriously removed in 1974.

The finely woven *Beauvais Tapestry*, made of wool and silk, and often designed as panels or furniture coverings representing landscapes, flowers, or pastoral scenes, is made on a horizontal or 'low' warp (unlike *Gobelins*, which is made on a vertical or 'high' warp), and is woven from the reverse side. The looms from the manufactory, which stood S.E. of *St-Étienne*, were sensibly evacuated to *Aubusson* in 1939, and are now at the *Gobelins* in Paris.

Immediately to the W. of the cathedral are the two pepper-pot towers

(14C) of the entrance to the courtyard of the *Palais de Justice* (previously the Bishop's Palace; mostly 14th and early-16C), at the far end of which is the entrance (in a stair-turret) to the *Museum, an interesting collection saved from its previous site, destroyed in 1940. Outstanding among the sculpture is a St Barbara by *Jean le Pot*, a Decapitation of St Paul (16C); also, among the paintings, a portrait of Card. de Gesvres, by *Pompeo Batoni*. In an adjoining building are the prehistoric and Gallo-Roman collections, further examples of Gothic sculpture, Merovingian arms, etc.

On the W. side of the *Palais de Justice* is a restored Romanesque tower on a Gallo-Roman base.

A few minutes' walk S.E. from the cathedral will bring one to the modern PL. DE JEANNE-HACHETTE, flanked to the S. by the new *Hôtel de Ville*, behind which the Rue du Dr-Gérard leads W. to the Rue de la Banque, in which a few old houses remain.

S. of the town hall stands *St-Étienne, a notable building (12–16C) in two distinct styles, with a large W. tower of 1598. The nave and transepts illustrate externally the developments of later Romanesque, and internally, those of early Gothic architecture. The N. transept has a rose-window representing the Wheel of Fortune, and a reticulated gable. The contrast between the restored Romanesque nave and the late Gothic choir (1506) is striking. The stained-glass (1518–54) in the ambulatory chapels includes a remarkable window of the *Tree of Jesse. The animal painter J.-B. Oudry (1686–1755), also a director of the Tapestry Factory, is buried here.

1·5km E., off the Clermont road (N31), is the church of *Marissal*, painted by *Corot* in 1866, with a tower and apse of the 12C, choir of the 13C, and nave, portal, and spire of the 16C.

Also of interest in the immediate vicinity of Beauvais are the church at *Guignecourt*, 6·5km N.E., off the N1; *N.-D.-du-Thil*, 1km N.W., with the remains of the ancient *Abbaye de St-Lucien*; and the leper-house of *St-Lazare* and adjacent buildings in the suburb of *Voisinlieu*, 1·5km S.E.

The D981 leads S.W. to (32km) *Gisors*, see Rte 37, off which, after 13km, the D129 bears S. to (6·5km) *Jouy-sous-Thelle*, with a late Renaissance church.

The N31 leads 26km E. to *Clermont*, see Rte 24.

Amiens lies 60km N. on the N1; *Abbeville*, 86km N. on the D901. *Dieppe*, 104km N.W. on the N31 and D915; and *Rouen*, 80km W. on the N31; see *Blue Guide France*.

INDEX

Topographical names in Paris are in Roman type; those in the Environs (Rtes 20–38) are in **Bold**. The names of notable people are in *Italics*; those of artists and architects are followed by their dates in brackets. Subject entries are in CAPITALS.

The founding proclivities of kings, nobles, prelates, and saints are usually ignored; the names of those buried in the cemeteries of Paris are not included unless they are also referred to in the text. Similarly, while *Napoleon I* is of course indexed, not every member of his family mentioned in passing is listed.

Note that streets, etc. named after persons are known by and indexed under the full name: i.e. Rue Antoine-Bourdelle, not Rue Bourdelle, which can be confusing when the visitor is not aware of the Christian name in question. The names of Ministères are subject to change. These, together with Avenues, Bibliothèques, Boulevards, Cafés, Canals, Carrefours, Chapelles, Cimetières, Collèges, Ecoles, Fontaines, Forêts, Gares, Hôpitaûx, Hôtels (mansions), Instituts, Jardins, Musées, Palais, Places, Ponts, Portes, Prisons, Quais, Rues, Squares, Théâtres, and Tours, in Paris are indexed alphabetically in sub-groups under these headings, as are departments of the Musée du Louvre, etc.

Typeset by First Page Limited, Watford, England.
Printed in Great Britain by Hazell Watson & Viney Limited,
Member of the BPCC Group, Aylesbury, Bucks.

ATLAS CONTENTS

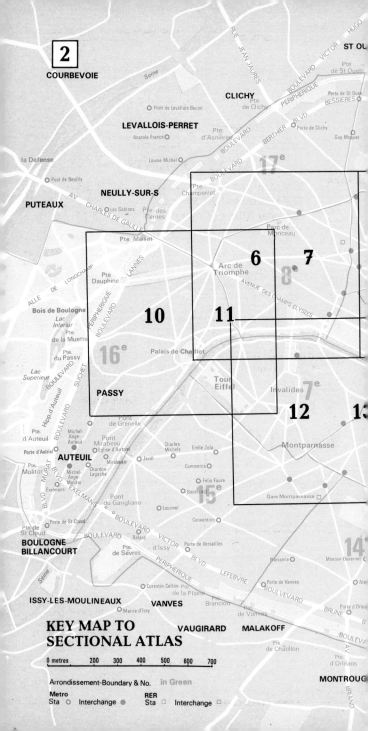

KEY MAP TO SECTIONAL ATLAS

2
COURBEVOIE

ST OU

Seine

CLICHY
Pte
de Clichy

Pont de Levallois Becon

LEVALLOIS-PERRET

Anatole France

la Defense

Pont de Neuilly

NEULLY-SUR-S

PUTEAUX

Louise Michel

Pte
d'Asnieres

Porte de St Ouen
BESSIÈRES

Porte de Clichy

Guy Moquet

17e

Pte
de Clichy

Pont de Neuilly

Les Sablons

Pte des
Ternes

Pte
Champerret

Parc de
Monceau

Pte Maillot

6

7

Arc de
Triomphe

8e

Pte
Dauphine

Bois de Boulogne

Lac
Inférieur

Pte
de la Muette

10

11

Palais de Chaillot

AVENUE DES CHAMPS-ELYSEES

16e

Lac
Supérieur

Tour
Eiffel

Invalides

7e

PASSY

12

13

Pont
de Grenelle

Pte
d'Auteuil

Michel-
Ange-
Auteuil

Pont
Mirabeau

Charles
Michels

Emile Zola

Montparnasse

Porte d'Autriel

AUTEUIL

Eglise d'Auteuil

Mirabeau

Javel

Commerce

Pte
Molitor

Michel-
Ange-
Molitor

Chardon-
Lagache

Felix Faure

Exelmans

Pont
du Gangliano

Boucicaut

15e

Gare Montparnasse

Lourmel

Pte de
St Cloud

Porte de St Cloud

Convention

BOULOGNE
BILLANCOURT

Balard

VICTOR

Porte de Versailles

14e

Pte
de Sèvres

d'Issy

BLVD

Monton-Duvernet

Plaisance

Porte de Vanves

Aléi

Corentin-Celton Pte
de la Plaine

ISSY-LES-MOULINEAUX

VANVES

Mairie d'Issy

Pte
Brancion

Porte d'Orléa

Pte
de Vanves

BRUNE

VAUGIRARD

MALAKOFF

Pte.
de Châtillon

Pte.
d'Orléans

MONTROUG

KEY MAP TO
SECTIONAL ATLAS

0 metres 200 300 400 500 600 700

Arrondissement-Boundary & No.   in Green

Metro		RER	
Sta ○	Interchange ●	Sta □	Interchange ▢

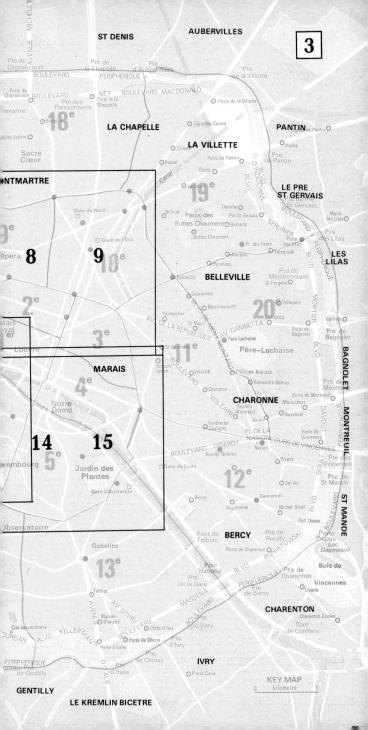

4

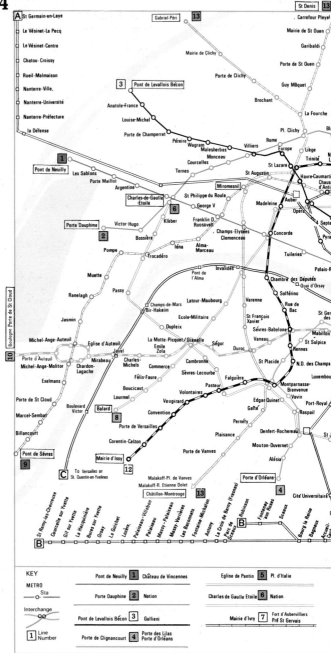

St Denis [13]

Gabriel-Péri [13]

A St Germain-en-Laye
Le Vésinet-Le Pecq
Le Vésinet-Centre
Chatou-Croissy
Rueil-Malmaison
Nanterre-Ville,
Nanterre-Université
Nanterre-Préfecture
la Défense

Carrefour Pleyel
Mairie de St Ouen
Garibaldi
Porte de St Ouen
Guy Môquet
Brochant
La Fourche

[3] Pont de Levallois Bécon
Anatole-France
Louise-Michel
Porte de Champerret

Mairie de Clichy
Porte de Clichy
Pl. Clichy
Rome
Europe
Bla

[1]
Pont de Neuilly
Les Sablons
Porte Maillot
Argentine
Charles-de-Gaulle-Étoile [6]

Péreire Wagram Malesherbes
Monceau
Courcelles
Ternes

Villiers
Liège
Trinité
N.D.
Lo

St Lazare
St Augustin
Havre-Caumartin
Chaussé
d'Antin

Porte Dauphine [2]

Victor-Hugo
Kléber
Bossière
Iéna

St Philippe du Roule
George V
Franklin D. Roosevelt
Champs-Élysées Clémenceau
Alma-Marceau

Miromesnil
Madeleine
Concorde

Auber
Opéra
Septer
Pyran

Pompe
Trocadéro
Muette
Passy
Ranelagh
Jasmin

Pont de l'Alma
Invalides
Latour-Maubourg
Varenne

Tuileries
Chambre des Députés
Quai d'Orsay
Solférino
Rue du Bac

Palais-Ro

Michel-Ange-Auteuil [10]
Porte d'Auteuil
Michel-Ange-Molitor
Exelmans
Porte de St Cloud
Marcel-Sembat
Billancourt
Pont de Sèvres [9]

Eglise d'Auteuil
Mirabeau
Chardon-Lagache
Javel

La Motte-Picquet / Grenelle
Champs-de-Mars/Bir-Hakeim
Ecole-Militaire
Dupleix

Ségur
Cambronne

St François Xavier
Sèvres-Babylone
Vaneau
Duroc
St Placide

St Gern des I
Mabillon
St Sulpice
Rennes
N.D. des Champs

Boulogne Porte de St Cloud

Charles-Michels
Boulevard Victor
Balard [8]

Félix-Faure
Boucicaut
Lourmel
Vaugirard
Convention
Porte de Versailles
Corentin-Celton
Mairie d'Issy [12]

Commerce
Sèvres-Lecourbe
Volontaires
Pasteur
Falguière
Montparnasse-Bienvenue
Vavin
Edgar Quinet
Gaîté
Pernéty
Plaisance
Porte de Vanves

Luxembourg
Port-Royal
Raspail
Denfert-Rochereau
Mouton-Duvernet
Alésia

St Je

C To Versailles or
St. Quentin-en-Yvelines

Malakoff-Pl. de Vanves
Malakoff-R. Etienne Dolet
Châtillon-Montrouge [13]

Porte d'Orléans
Cité Universitaire

Porte d'Orléans [4]

Ge

B
St Remy-lès-Chevreuse
Courcelle sur Yvette
Gif sur Yvette
La Hacquinière
Bures sur Yvette
Orsay
Le Guichet
Lozère
Palaiseau-Villebon
Palaiseau
Massy-Palaiseau
Massy-Verrières
Les Baconnets
Fontaine-Michalon
Antony
La Croix de Berny (Fresnes)
Parc de Sceaux
Robinson

B
Fontenay aux Roses
Sceaux
Bourg la Reine
Bagneux
Arcueil-Cachan

KEY

METRO
—o— Sta

Interchange
—oo—

[1] Line Number

Pont de Neuilly [1]	Château de Vincennes	Eglise de Pantin [5] Pl. d'Italie
Porte Dauphine [2]	Nation	Charles de Gaulle Etoile [6] Nation
Pont de Levallois Bécon [3]	Gallieni	Mairie d'Ivry [7] Fort d'Aubervilliers / Préf St Gervais
Porte de Clignancourt [4]	Porte des Lilas / Porte d'Orléans	

THE METRO and RER Systems

5

Roissy-Charles de Gaulle or Vitry Claye · B

7 Fort d'Aubervilliers

12 · Porte de la Chapelle

te de Clignancourt

4

Simplon

Aubervilliers

Porte de la Villette

Corentin-Cariou

5 · Eglise de Pantin

Joffrin

Marx Dormoy

Crimée

Marcadet-Poissonniers

Riquet

Hoche

Château Rouge

Barbès-Rochechouart

Stalingrad

Ourcq

Porte de Pantin

Lamarck-Caulaincourt

besses

Anvers

La Chapelle

Laumière

galle

Louis-Blanc

Jaurès

eorges

Gare du Nord

Bolivar

Danube

11 · Marie des Lilas

Poissonnière

Château Landon

Botzaris

Cadet

Gare de l'Est

Buttes Chaumont

7 · Pré St Gervais

etier

Colonel-Fabien

Pl. des Fêtes

Télégraphe

u-Drouot

Château d'Eau

Jourdain

Porte des Lilas

Rue/Montmartre

Jacques Bonsergent

Pyrénées

3

Bonne-Nouvelle

Belleville

St Fargeau

se

Strasbourg-St Denis

Goncourt

Couronnes

Pelleport

Sentier

Réaumur-Sébastopol

Temple

République

Parmentier

Ménilmontant

3 · Gallieni

Marcel

Arts et Métiers

Filles du Calvaire

Oberkampf

St Maur

Gambetta

Porte de Bagnolet

illes

Rambuteau

Père Lachaise

Mairie de Montreuil

11

Châtelet-Les Halle

St Sébastien-Froissart

Richard-Lenoir

St Ambroise

Philippe-Auguste

9 · Croix de Chavaux

Cité

Hôtel de Ville

Chemin-Vert

Voltaire

Alexandre-Dumas

Robespierre

St Michel

St Paul

Bréguet-Sabin

Charonne

Avron

Porte de Montreuil

on

Pont-Marie

Boulets-Montreuil

Maraîchers

Mutualité

Bastille

Ledru-Rollin

2

Faidherbe-Chaligny

Buzenval

rdinal-Lemoine

Sully-Morland

Nation

Porte de Vincennes

St Mandé-Tourelle

Vincennes

Jussieu

Quai de la Rapée

Reuilly Diderot

6

Picpus

Bérault

1 · Château de Vincennes

Monge

10 · Gare d'Orléans Austerlitz

Gare de Lyon

Montgallet

Fontenay sous Bois

ar-Daubenton

St Marcel

Bel-Air

Nogent sur Marne

Gobelins

Campo-Formio

Bercy

Daumesnil

Joinville le Pont

Quai de la Gare

Dugommier

Michel-Bizot

Saint Maur-Créteil

5

Chevaleret

Port Dorée

Le Parc de St Maur

Nationale

Porte de Charenton

Champigny

visart

Pl. d'Italie

Liberté

La Varenne-Chennevières

Tolbiac

Boulevard Masséna

Sucy-Bonneuil

Porte de Choisy

Porte d'Ivry

Charenton-Ecoles

Boissy St Leger · A

Maison-Blanche

Pierre-Curie

Porte d'Italie

Kremlin-Bicêtre

7 · Mairie d'Ivry

Alfort Ecole Vétérinaire

Maisons-Alfort Stade

Maisons-Alfort les Juilliottes

Maisons-l'Echat Hôpital H. Mondor

Créteil Université

8

To Massy- Palaiseau, Dourdan & St. Martin d'Etamps · C

Créteil Préfecture Hôtel de Ville

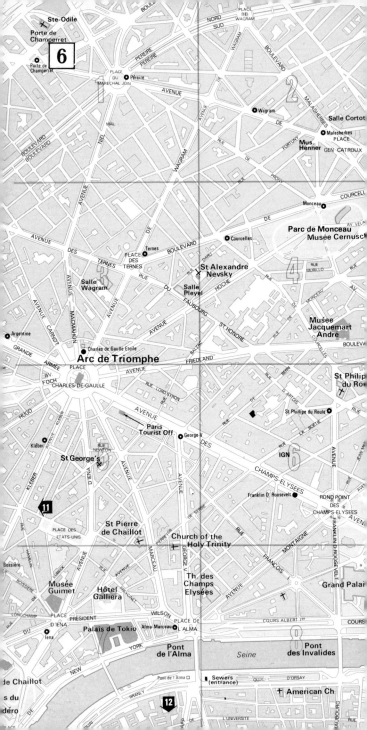

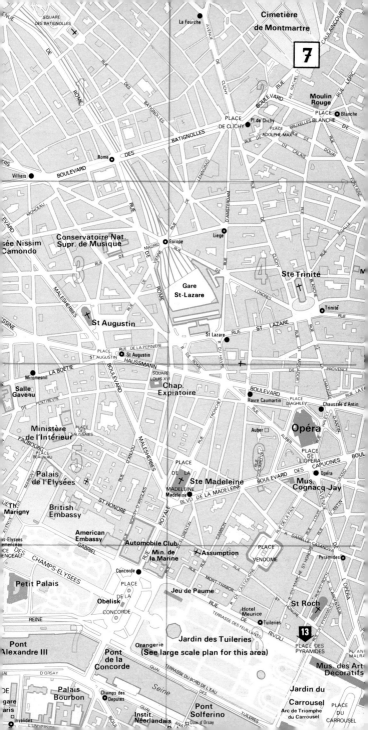

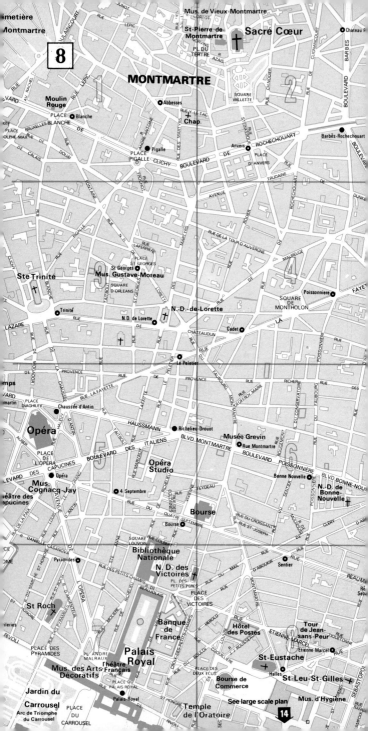

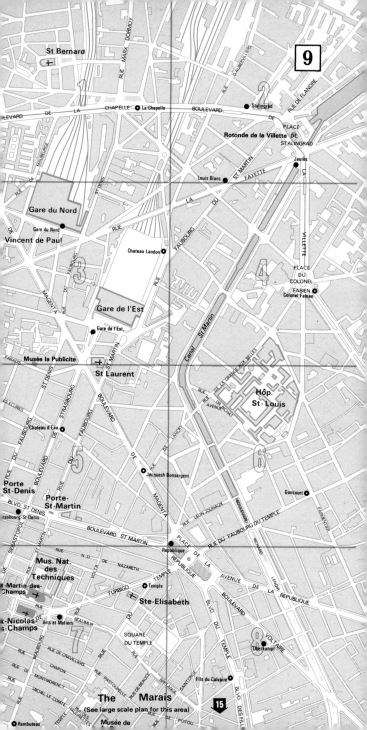

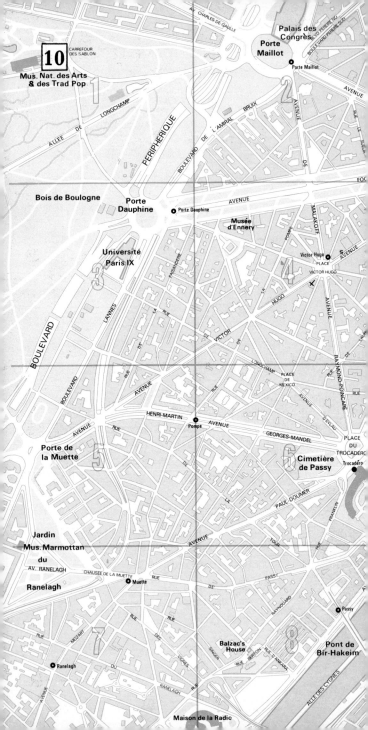

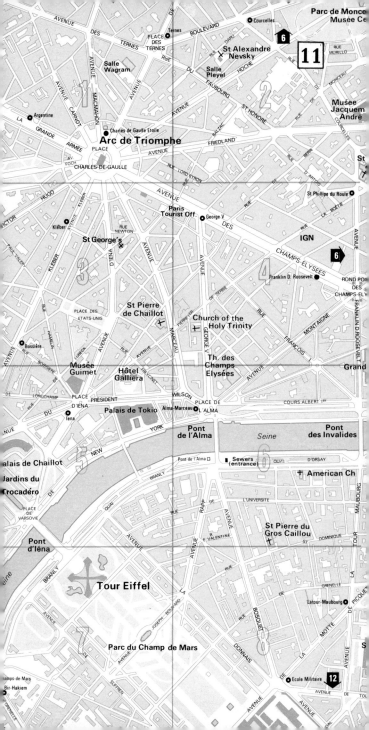

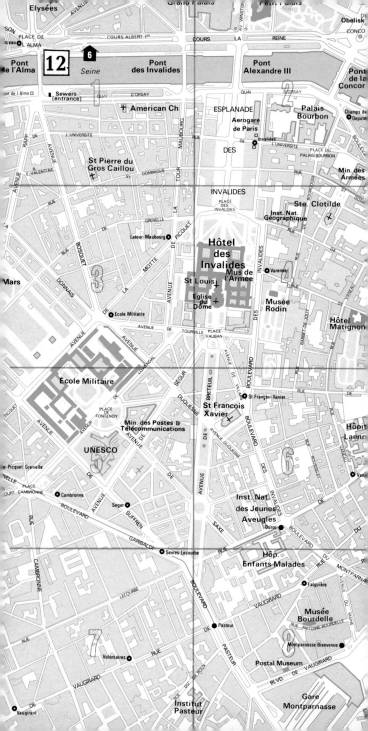

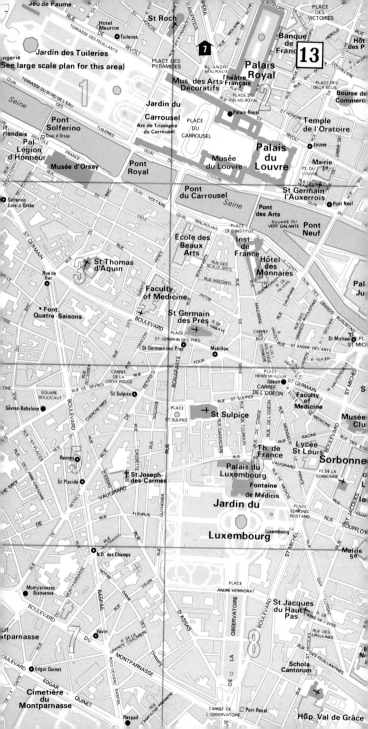

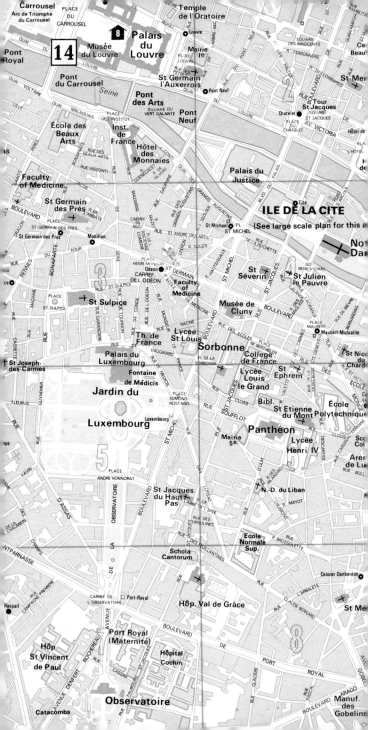

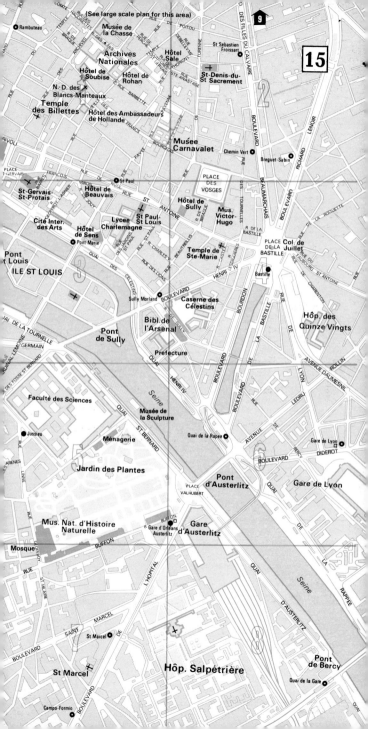